MACV
The Joint Command
in the
Years of Withdrawal, 1968–1973

United States Army in Vietnam

MACV
The Joint Command
in the
Years of Withdrawal, 1968–1973

by

Graham A. Cosmas

MILITARY INSTRVCTION

Center of Military History
United States Army
Washington, D.C., 2007

Library of Congress Cataloging-in-Publication Data

Cosmas, Graham A.
      MACV : the Joint Command in the years of withdrawal, 1968–1973 /
by Graham A. Cosmas.
          p. cm. — (United States Army in Vietnam)
          Includes bibliographical references and index.
      1.   Vietnam War, 1961–1975—United States. 2. United States. Military
Assistance Command, Vietnam—History. 3. Command of troops. 4. Vietnam
War, 1961–1975—Peace. I. Title. II. Series.

      DS558.C6823 2007
      959.704'340973–dc22

                                                                                   2007022084

                                    CMH Pub 91–7-1

                                    First Printing

For sale by the Superintendent of Documents, U.S. Government Printing Office
Internet: bookstore.gpo.gov Phone: toll free (866) 512-1800; DC area (202) 512-1800
Fax: (202) 512-2250 Mail: Stop SSOP, Washington, DC 20402-0001

ISBN 978-0-16-077118-7

United States Army in Vietnam

Richard W. Stewart, General Editor

Advisory Committee

Theodore A. Wilson
University of Kansas

William Allison
Weber State University

James J. Carafano
The Heritage Foundation

Brig. Gen. Patrick Finnegan
U.S. Military Academy

John F. Guilmartin, Jr.
Ohio State University

Brian M. Linn
Texas A&M University

Howard P. Lowell
National Archives and
Records Administration

Lt. Gen. Thomas F. Metz
U.S. Army Training and
Doctrine Command

Joyce E. Morrow
Administrative Assistant to the
Secretary of the Army

Brig. Gen. Mark E. O'Neill
U.S. Army Command and
General Staff College

Mark P. Parillo
Kansas State University

Reina Pennington
Norwich University

Ronald H. Spector
George Washington University

Col. Thomas G. Torrance
U.S. Army War College

U.S. Army Center of Military History

Jeffrey J. Clarke, Chief of Military History

Chief Historian
Chief, Histories Division
Editor in Chief

Richard W. Stewart
Joel D. Meyerson
Keith R. Tidman

. . . to Those Who Served

Foreword

MACV: The Joint Command in the Years of Withdrawal, 1968–1973, is the second of two volumes that examine the Vietnam conflict from the perspective of the theater commander and his headquarters. It traces the story of the Military Assistance Command, Vietnam (MACV), from the Communist Tet offensive of early 1968 through the disestablishment of MACV in March 1973. It deals with theater-level command relationships, strategy, and operations and supplements detailed studies in the Center of Military History's United States Army in Vietnam series covering combat operations, the advisory effort, and relations with the media.

MACV: The Joint Command recounts how the MACV commander and his staff viewed the war at various periods and how and why the commander arrived at his decisions. Central themes are the gradual withdrawal of U.S. forces from combat operations, the American effort to prepare South Vietnam's military establishment to take over defense of the country, and the implementation of the Paris peace agreement of 1973. The volume analyzes MACV's relationships with Pacific Command, the Joint Chiefs of Staff, and the secretary of defense, as well as the evolution of the command's dealings with its South Vietnamese and third-country allies. Perhaps most important, it traces the commander's role in developing and executing U.S. national policy in Vietnam, a role that extended beyond military operations to encompass diplomacy and pacification. As an experiment—not entirely successful—in nation building, the story of the Military Assistance Command contains many parallels to more recent Army engagements and so serves as a potential source of important lessons.

This is the tenth volume published in the United States Army in Vietnam series. Its appearance constitutes another step in the fulfillment of the Center of Military History's commitment to produce an authoritative history of Army participation in the Vietnam War.

Washington, D.C.   JEFFREY J. CLARKE
4 May 2007   Chief of Military History

The Author

Graham A. Cosmas was born in Weehawken, New Jersey, and received his education from the schools of Leonia, New Jersey, and from Columbia University, Oberlin College, and the University of Wisconsin. After teaching at the University of Texas (Austin) and the University of Guam, he joined the staff of the U.S. Marine Corps History and Museums Division in December 1973. Dr. Cosmas moved to the U.S. Army Center of Military History in 1979 and remained there until 2001, when he became deputy director of the Joint History Office of the Joint Chiefs of Staff. Dr. Cosmas is the author of *MACV: The Joint Command in the Years of Escalation, 1962–1967*, and *An Army for Empire: The U.S. Army in the Spanish-American War, 1898–1899*. He is also the coauthor of *U.S. Marines in Vietnam: Vietnamization and Redeployment, 1970–1971*, and *The Medical Department: Medical Service in the European Theater of Operations*, a volume in the United States Army in World War II series. He served in 1984–1985 as the Harold K. Johnson Visiting Professor of Military History at the U.S. Army Military History Institute, Carlisle Barracks, Pennsylvania. He has published numerous articles and book reviews.

Preface

*M*ACV: *The Joint Command in the Years of Withdrawal, 1968–1973,* describes the evolution of the command during the period of U.S. disengagement from Vietnam. By late 1967 the Military Assistance Command, Vietnam (MACV), had grown from a small, temporary advisory and assistance organization into a large, permanent headquarters that directed more than half a million American soldiers, sailors, airmen, and marines in a wide range of combat and pacification operations. By that same time, however, President Lyndon B. Johnson and his principal advisers had concluded that it was necessary to begin reducing the cost in lives and money of a seemingly stalemated war. The Communist Tet offensive of January–February 1968 confirmed the president in his decision and set the United States upon a path of disengagement that President Richard M. Nixon also followed. During the period covered by this volume, MACV gradually withdrew its American troops from South Vietnam and worked to prepare Saigon's forces to defend their country by their own efforts. The MACV headquarters itself drew down toward reversion to an assistance and advisory group.

This volume tells the story of MACV's evolution as an organization and of the command's role in making and implementing American national policy in Southeast Asia during the period of U.S. disengagement from the Vietnam War. It treats both national-level decisions and military operations from the perspective of the theater joint commander. In relation to the Army's Vietnam series, this volume and its predecessor, *MACV: The Joint Command in the Years of Escalation, 1962–1967,* which dealt with the earlier period of the conflict, will provide a general overview of aspects of the war that are covered in much greater detail in the other works. The inclusion of this study of a joint command in a series devoted principally to the activities of a single service results from two circumstances: that MACV throughout its existence was an Army-dominated headquarters and that upon the command's inactivation its records were placed in the custody of the Adjutant General of the Army.

The preparation of a work of this scope was possible only with the assistance and support of a great many other people. Throughout the years, my colleagues in the Southeast Asia Branch of Histories Division guided me through the sources, read and criticized drafts of chapters, and broadened and deepened my understanding of the war through many hours of conversation. Vincent H. Demma helped me get started through his encyclopedic knowledge of the Center of Military History's documents on the Vietnam War. Charles R. Anderson, Dale W. Andrade, Dr. John M. Carland, Dr. William M. Hammond, Dr. Richard A. Hunt, George L. MacGarrigle, Dr. Joel D. Meyerson, and Adrian G. Traas generously permitted me to draw upon their work and made an imprint upon mine.

Others at the Center of Military History contributed to this book. This project could not have been carried to completion without the assistance of the Publishing Division staff, including Hildegard J. Bachman, editor; S. L. Dowdy, cartographer; and Gene Snyder, visual information specialist. The Historical Resources and Organizational History Branches were always responsive to my requests for books, documents, and information.

As Chief of the Southeast Asia Branch, Dr. John Schlight guided my early steps on this volume and made sure that I gave due attention to the role of air power in MACV's war. I am grateful to a succession of division chiefs who supervised this project over its lengthy gestation—Lt. Col. Richard O. Perry; Cols. Robert H. Sholly, William T. Bowers, and Clyde L. Jonas; and Dr. Richard W. Stewart. Several Chiefs of Military History supervised and supported this work. Brig. Gen. Douglas Kinnard (U.S. Army, Ret.) initiated the project and set its direction. Brig. Gens. William A. Stofft, Harold W. Nelson, John W. Mountcastle, and John S. Brown all helped it on its way. I owe a special debt of thanks to my current supervisor, Brig. Gen. David A. Armstrong (U.S. Army, Ret.), Director, Joint History Office, Joint Chiefs of Staff, for allowing me duty time after leaving the Center's employ to finish this volume.

Very helpful were the comments and recommendations of the review panel convened by Dr. Jeffrey J. Clarke, the Center's Chief Historian, who chaired the panel. I am grateful to the members—General William A. Knowlton (U.S. Army, Ret.), Brig. Gen. Douglas Kinnard, Dr. Larry Berman, Dr. Robert Buzzanco, Dr. Paul Miles, Dr. William M. Hammond, John W. Elsberg, and R. Cody Phillips. My especial thanks go to General William B. Rosson (U.S. Army, Ret.), who provided detailed written comments on the manuscript.

As appropriate for a volume on a joint command, members of other service historical offices helped me with advice and access to sources. They include Dr. William Heimdahl and Dr. Wayne W. Thompson of the Office of Air Force History; Dr. Edward J. Marolda of the U.S. Naval Historical Center; and Dr. Jack Shulimson, formerly of the History and Museums Division, U.S. Marine Corps. Dr. Walter S. Poole of the Joint History Office, Joint Chiefs of Staff, read and criticized a draft of the manuscript. Dr. Poole also provided me with invaluable source material on the role of the Joint Chiefs of Staff in the period of the conflict covered by this book.

Like all historians, I could have accomplished little without the assistance of the archivists of records repositories. Dr. David C. Humphrey and Dr. Gary Gallagher, both of whom have since moved on to other positions, were of great help at the Lyndon Baines Johnson Library. The staff of the Richard Nixon Papers, then located in Alexandria, Virginia, facilitated my access to the unprocessed Nixon National Security Files for Southeast Asia. Their help allowed broader and deeper coverage of many aspects of the MACV story during the Nixon years than otherwise would have been possible. At the U.S. Army Military History Institute, Dr. Richard J. Sommers, David A. Keogh, Randy Rakers, and John J. Slonaker guided me through the Institute's extensive Vietnam collections. Richard L. Boylan and the staff of the National Archives and Records Administration were responsive to all my requests.

Lt. Gen. William E. Potts (U.S. Army, Ret.), former MACV director of intelligence, gave graciously of his time in discussing with me the work and achievements of the MACV J–2 during the later stages of the war. He also provided me with a useful briefing on the subject.

It remains only to note that the conclusions and interpretations in this book are mine alone and that I am solely responsible for any errors.

Washington, D.C.   GRAHAM A. COSMAS
4 May 2007

Contents

Table

Charts

Maps

Illustrations

Illustrations courtesy of the following sources: U.S. Army cover photograph and p. 77 (left to right) of Lt. Col. Hugh J. Bartley, commander, 3d Squadron, 5th Cavalry, 9th Infantry Division, and Lt. Gen. William B. Rosson, commanding general, Provisional Corps, Vietnam; pp. 13, 142, 312, 348, 382, U.S. Army Center of Military History, Washington, D.C.; pp. 19, 196, National Archives and Records Administration (NARA), Washington, D.C.; p. 26, China Pictorial; pp. 72, 79, 101, Lyndon Baines Johnson Library, Austin, Texas; p. 106, Tim Page/CORBIS; pp. 155, 156, 187, 189, 197, 221, 261, 352, 401, Bettmann/COBRIS; p. 191, Naval Historical Center; p. 233, 246, UPI/CORBIS; p. 247, Hulton-Deutsch Collection/CORBIS; p. 294, Francoise de Mulder/CORBIS; p. 303, 323, U.S. Military History Institute; pp. 50, 317, Getty Images; p. 406, U.S. Navy; p. 405, Nik Wheeler/CORBIS; p. 329, Col. Robert Leonard; p. 353, Defense Visual Information Center. All other illustrations from the files of Department of Defense or U.S. Army.

MACV
The Joint Command
in the
Years of Withdrawal, 1968–1973

1

The Command and the War, January 1968

In January 1968, the Military Assistance Command, Vietnam (MACV), looked forward to its seventh year of war. Established in 1962 as a small, temporary headquarters to advise and assist the South Vietnamese government in its struggle against the Communist-led Viet Cong insurgency, MACV had grown as the war did. As of early 1968, the command, in addition to continuing its advice and support efforts, directed the operations of almost half a million American military personnel engaging an enemy that comprised division-size light infantry formations as well as guerrillas. MACV also had assumed primary responsibility for the allies' pacification campaign to remove Viet Cong military and political influence from South Vietnam's rural villages and had played a substantial role in American efforts to develop a stable, constitutional Saigon government. MACV had a hand, too, in the U.S. bombing campaign against North Vietnam and in operations against the enemy bases and supply networks in Laos and Cambodia.[1]

Command, Forces, and Allies

As the year began, General William C. Westmoreland was serving as Commander, U.S. Military Assistance Command, Vietnam (COMUSMACV). In command since June 1964, Westmoreland had established the operational and organizational pattern of the expanding American military role in the war. As he began his fifth year in Saigon, he was nearing the end of his tour of duty in Vietnam. His designated successor, General Creighton W. Abrams, had arrived at MACV in May 1967 and was serving as Westmoreland's deputy pending his elevation to command at a date yet to be specified. That date was approaching. When Westmoreland visited Washington in November, General Earle G. Wheeler, chairman of the Joint Chiefs of Staff, privately told the MACV commander that he was the "obvious candidate" to replace the chief of staff of the Army, General Harold K. Johnson, who was expected to

[1] Unless otherwise noted, this chapter is based on Graham A. Cosmas, *MACV: The Joint Command in the Years of Escalation, 1962–1967*, U.S. Army in Vietnam (Washington, D.C.: U.S. Army Center of Military History, 2006) (hereafter cited as Cosmas, *Years of Escalation, 1962–1967*).

General Westmoreland greets Secretary of Defense Robert S. McNamara
(right) *and Ambassador Ellsworth Bunker on arrival in Saigon, July 1967.*

retire in mid-1968. Following up this conversation, Wheeler indicated to Westmoreland late in December in a private letter that the administration would make its decision on that and other command changes "shortly after the first of the year."[2]

From its establishment, MACV was a subordinate unified command under Pacific Command, the U.S. headquarters in Honolulu that directed American forces throughout the Pacific Ocean and the Far East. This meant that General Westmoreland reported to Washington through Admiral Ulysses S. Grant Sharp, Commander in Chief, Pacific. Sharp delegated the conduct of ground and air operations in South Vietnam and parts of Laos and North Vietnam to Westmoreland. However, under close supervision from Washington, the admiral exercised direct command of the ROLLING THUNDER air raids against North Vietnam. Through Sharp, Westmoreland's chain of command ran to

---

[2] William C. Westmoreland, *A Soldier Reports* (Garden City, N.Y.: Doubleday and Co., 1976), pp. 361–62. Msg, Gen Earle G. Wheeler, Joint Chiefs of Staff (JCS) 11081–62 to Westmoreland, 22 Dec 67, Westmoreland Message files, Dec 67; Ltr, Wheeler to Westmoreland, 22 Dec 67, tab A–13, Westmoreland History file 27 (19–26 Dec 67); William C. Westmoreland Papers, U.S. Army Center of Military History (CMH), Washington, D.C.

Secretary of Defense Robert S. McNamara and President Lyndon B. Johnson. Both men transmitted questions and directives to Westmoreland through the chairman of the Joint Chiefs, General Wheeler. To save time and ensure a united military front in dealing with the civilian principals, Wheeler usually sent communications simultaneously to Sharp and Westmoreland. The two theater commanders followed the same practice in their replies to Wheeler. Although complicated in appearance, this arrangement kept the major administration policymakers and military commanders in close and constant touch and allowed the military leaders to speak with one voice in their advice to the civilians.

Secretary of Defense McNamara briefs the press.

In Saigon, Westmoreland worked closely with the U.S. ambassador to South Vietnam, Ellsworth Bunker. Although Bunker was head of the American country team, Westmoreland was independent of the ambassador's authority. Under a principle established by President John F. Kennedy for organizing U.S. overseas activities, the ambassador did not command American military forces in his country. Instead, the ambassador and the general were to reach decisions by consultation and mutual agreement, referring unresolved issues to Washington through their respective chains of command. In practice, Westmoreland deferred to Bunker on political questions and the ambassador rarely interfered in military operations. Bunker, who had worked closely with soldiers in previous diplomatic assignments and had a strongly favorable view of the military, agreed with Westmoreland on most Vietnam policy issues. The two men constituted a smoothly running team. The same could not be said of the civilian agencies under Bunker's purview. To varying degrees, the State Department, the Central Intelligence Agency (CIA), and other civilian operatives in South Vietnam resented the growing preponderance of the military in what they still regarded as primarily a political conflict. Frequently, they criticized MACV's operations and challenged its assumptions in reports to their own agencies.

In August 1967, the MACV headquarters had moved from scattered leased buildings in downtown Saigon to a specially constructed complex at Tan Son Nhut Air Base on the outskirts of the South Vietnamese capital.

The sprawling two-story edifice, one-third the size in square feet of the Pentagon in Washington, housed the command group, the general staff directorates, most of the special staff sections, and other offices. Additional head-quarters elements, for example, the Combined Intelligence Center, were housed in buildings of their own at Tan Son Nhut or elsewhere in the city.

General Wheeler

Although the MACV head-quarters was a joint organization, some two-thirds of its approxi-mately 3,000 personnel were members of the U.S. Army. The commander, the deputy com-mander, the chief of staff, and the heads of five of the six gen-eral staff directorates were Army officers; and that service domi-nated the mid- and lower-level staff positions as well. In response to complaints from the other ser-vices, notably the Air Force, that they were underrepresented in MACV headquarters, General Westmoreland defended Army predominance as appropriate to what was essentially a ground war. He also pointed out that MACV's South Vietnamese counterpart, the Joint General Staff, was essentially an army organization, although it directed all of Saigon's armed forces. Secretary McNamara supported Westmoreland on this issue, to the continuing frustration of the other American services.

MACV headquarters contained the standard general staff director-ates for personnel (J–1), intelligence (J–2), operations (J–3), logistics (J–4), planning (J–5), and communications-electronics (J–6), as well as special staff offices of the inspector general, comptroller, chaplain, surgeon, judge advocate, provost marshal, and public information. The headquarters included additional organizations developed to meet the unique demands of the war in Vietnam. A Data Management Agency maintained the command's automated record-keeping and reporting systems; its computer—a state-of-the-art machine by the standards of the time although primitive compared to the computers of today—churned out the reams of statistics demanded by the authorities in Honolulu and Washington. Employing these statistics, a Systems Analysis Division applied the discipline of operations research to a range of military and pacification problems, supplementing the work of the MACV scientific adviser, who was another Vietnam War addi-tion to the headquarters. To unify advice and support to the South

Aerial view of MACV headquarters at Tan Son Nhut

Vietnamese, General Westmoreland during 1967 had added to the general staff an office of the Assistant Chief of Staff for Military Assistance, headed by an Army brigadier general. *(Chart 1)*

A unique element of the headquarters was the Office of Civil Operations and Revolutionary Development Support (CORDS). In May 1967, President Johnson established CORDS to resolve a long-standing interagency dispute over single management of U.S. support to the South Vietnamese pacification effort. The president combined into one organization under MACV the military personnel and the people from the State Department, the U.S. Agency for International Development, and other civilian agencies working on the problem in Saigon and the provinces. In MACV headquarters, Ambassador Robert W. Komer, as Westmoreland's civilian deputy COMUSMACV for CORDS, had under him a staff directorate with a civilian chief and a military deputy. In each of South Vietnam's four corps areas, a CORDS deputy to the U.S. military commander oversaw the military and civilian pacification advisers in the provinces and districts. While still completing its organization as 1968 began, CORDS promised to ensure that MACV gave high priority and unified direction to the struggle to recapture the countryside from the Viet Cong.

Westmoreland directed his American forces through Army, Air Force, and Navy component commands and through tactical headquarters in each of the four South Vietnamese corps areas. *(Map 1)* Of the component commands, the Seventh Air Force and U.S. Naval

CHART 1—ORGANIZATION OF MACV HEADQUARTERS, 1967

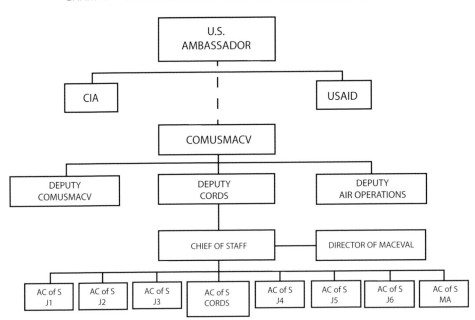

Forces, Vietnam, exercised both tactical and administrative control of their subordinate organizations and also provided advice and support to their counterpart Vietnamese services. The Army component, U.S. Army, Vietnam (USARV), had only administrative and logistical functions. General Westmoreland, who commanded U.S. Army, Vietnam, as an additional duty, directed the Army advisory effort through MACV headquarters and controlled his Army and Marine combat units through the area tactical commands. From north to south, those commands included the III Marine Amphibious Force (which also functioned as the Marine Corps component command) in I Corps, the I Field Force in II Corps, the II Field Force in III Corps, and an advisory group in IV Corps, where few American ground combat units were stationed. Each area commander was directly subordinate to Westmoreland for tactical operations, as well as for combat and pacification advisory functions, but dealt on administrative matters with his service component command.

Westmoreland's command relations with the two Army-dominated field force headquarters were harmonious, but his relationship with the III Marine Amphibious Force was contentious. In one of MACV's most persistent unresolved interservice disputes, the Seventh Air Force waged a constant feud with the Marine headquarters over control of the marines' fixed-wing jet aircraft. The Air Force commander insisted that he should conduct the allocation and mission tasking of all fixed-wing aircraft in the theater, including those of the marines. On their part, the

Map 1

marines jealously guarded the integrity of their air-ground team and claimed first call on their fighters and bombers. On the ground, Marine commanders considered that MACV was overemphasizing large-unit operations at the expense of territorial security and pacification, and they publicly advertised their own claims of success in the latter field. They also objected to General Westmoreland's plans for a fortified barrier just below the Demilitarized Zone. Lt. Gen. Victor H. Krulak, the commander of Fleet Marine Force Pacific, III Marine Amphibious Force's immediate senior service headquarters in Honolulu, jealously watched over his marines in Vietnam and carried their viewpoints and complaints directly to Admiral Sharp.

At the beginning of January 1968, the Military Assistance Command had an authorized strength of 525,000 American personnel. The command's actual strength stood at a little over 497,000, of which about 331,000 were Army troops. Rounding out MACV's force were 78,000 marines, 31,600 Navy personnel, and 56,000 Air Force personnel plus a small Coast Guard contingent. Seven Army and two Marine divisions constituted the core of MACV's ground fighting power, supported by some 1,700 Air Force and Marine fixed-wing combat and transport aircraft and thousands of helicopters. Westmoreland's naval element included task forces of coastal surveillance and riverine craft. Available for support, although not under MACV's command, were the aircraft carriers and other large warships of the Seventh Fleet and the Guam and Thailand based B–52 heavy bombers of the Strategic Air Command.[3]

The Republic of Vietnam Armed Forces (RVNAF) numbered about 650,000 officers and men in January 1968. About half of these troops were in the regular Army, Navy, Air Force, and Marine Corps; the other half were in two territorial security components, the Regional Forces and the Popular Forces. Still other armed men served the Saigon government in Civilian Irregular Defense Group units recruited from South Vietnam's ethnic minorities and in the National Police and various paramilitary organizations. In deference to Vietnamese nationalist sensitivities, the Americans had decided against placing the South Vietnamese military under General Westmoreland's command. Instead, the American and Vietnamese forces worked together on the basis of "cooperation and coordination." Westmoreland and his subordinates sought to influence and improve their allies' operations through the U.S. adviser network, which extended down to battalion level. They also cultivated working relationships with senior RVNAF commanders and attempted to exercise leverage by providing or threatening to withhold American combat and logistical support. Despite the persistent efforts by MACV, South Vietnamese forces still suffered from major deficiencies that had plagued them since the late 1950s—poor leader-

---

[3] Headquarters, United States Military Assistance Command, Vietnam (MACV), Command History, 1968 (Saigon, Vietnam: Military History Branch, Office of the Secretary, MACV, 1969), vol. 1, p. 225, CMH (hereafter these histories are cited as MACV History, year).

ship by a corrupt and politicized officer corps, a lack of aggressiveness in combat, neglect of troop training and welfare, and a crippling
drain of manpower through desertion. Widely differing in capabilities,
American and South Vietnamese troops usually operated separately,
the Americans conducting mobile offensives against the enemy's large
units and base areas and the South Vietnamese concentrating on static
territorial security and pacification missions.[4]

Besides the Americans and South Vietnamese, the Military Assistance
Command had under its purview an assortment of about 60,000 troops
from America's Far Eastern anti-Communist allies. Their presence was
the result of President Johnson's assiduous effort to add "more flags"
to the struggle in Vietnam. The largest contingent, from South Korea,
comprised two infantry divisions operating in coastal II Corps and a
marine brigade posted in I Corps. In III Corps, a brigade-size Australian
and New Zealand task force conducted counterguerrilla operations, as
did an infantry regiment (soon to be expanded to a small division)
from Thailand and a brigade-size Philippine paramilitary civic action
group. Each of these contingents had its own national commander.
In MACV headquarters, a Free World Military Assistance Office oversaw the allies' administrative affairs. MACV's command relationships with these allied forces were heavily influenced by diplomatic
considerations. The Australians, New Zealanders, Thais, and Filipinos
placed their units under General Westmoreland's operational control,
although with political strings on where they could be stationed and
on what missions they could perform. For their part, the South Koreans
rejected any semblance of U.S. command of their soldiers, although
their general promised to be responsive to requests from MACV and
I Field Force. In fact, the Koreans operated for the most part independently in their coastal enclaves and joined in American offensives only
when provided with lavish U.S. helicopter and artillery support.[5]

Outside South Vietnam, the Military Assistance Command conducted air and ground raids and reconnaissance against the enemy's
bases and supply lines in Laos, assisted in the officially unacknowledged
U.S. campaign to support the Royal Laotian government against the
Communist Pathet Lao, and provided forces for the bombing of North
Vietnam. In these operations, the command worked within highly
restrictive guidelines from Washington. Final authority over military
activities in Laos rested with the U.S. ambassador in Vientiane, who in
effect was in command of the war in that country, while Admiral Sharp
directed ROLLING THUNDER. Under MACV, the commander of the Seventh
Air Force handled the details of cross-border air operations, receiving

---

[4] MACV History, 1968, vol. 1, pp. 224, 250. Jeffrey J. Clarke, *Advice and Support: The Final
Years, 1965–1973*, U.S. Army in Vietnam (Washington, D.C.: U.S. Army Center of Military History,
1988), chs. 12–14, describes South Vietnamese military deficiencies and American reform efforts.

[5] MACV History, 1968, vol. 1, pp. 345–46. For command arrangements, see Cosmas, *Years of
Escalation, 1962–1967*, ch. 10.

missions variously from General Westmoreland, Admiral Sharp, and the embassy in Vientiane for the different campaigns. For ground raids in Laos, as well as for clandestine harassment and intelligence activities in North Vietnam, MACV employed its Studies and Observations Group (SOG). Commanded by an Army colonel, the Studies and Observations Group had its own staff within MACV headquarters, composed of officers from all the services and representatives of the Central Intelligence Agency. In the field, the Studies and Observations Group commanded some 2,500 American military personnel and 7,000 indigenous irregulars who conducted platoon and company-size attacks on the Ho Chi Minh Trail and performed espionage and propaganda missions—none very successful—in North Vietnam.

The Enemy and the War

As 1968 began, the Military Assistance Command confronted a formidable and tactically sophisticated enemy. MACV estimated that the North Vietnamese and Viet Cong military force numbered slightly more than 300,000 men. The Viet Cong regulars, formally known as the *People's Liberation Armed Forces (PLAF)*—light infantry divisions, regiments, and battalions recruited primarily from the South Vietnamese but with a growing proportion of northern cadres and fillers—were about 66,000 strong. About 53,000 North Vietnamese soldiers of the *People's Army of Vietnam (PAVN)*, similarly organized in divisions and regiments, fought alongside their southern comrades. These troops comprised what the Americans called the Communist "main force" and were employed usually for offensive operations directed by the enemy's military region and province headquarters. Supporting the main force were some 40,000 administrative service troops, perhaps 90,000 guerrillas, and a Communist party political-military administration of around 85,000 people.[6]

In addition, the enemy had available at least 150,000 part-time civilian irregulars—men, women, and children too old or too young for combat service who lived in the cities and villages. Usually unarmed or possessing only primitive weapons, these people collected intelligence for the armed components, moved supplies for them, and helped in constructing fortifications and planting mines and booby traps. During the fall of 1967, MACV and the CIA had engaged in a bitter dispute over the status of the irregulars. The military command declined to include them in the enemy order of battle because they were not armed, full-time soldiers and their participation in the war effort was at best sporadic. CIA analysts, on their part, considered the paramilitary elements to be a significant part of the Communist "revolutionary base" and noted that members of this group were among the

---

[6] Figures are from MACV and Joint General Staff (JGS) Combined Campaign Plan, 1968, AB 143, 11 Nov 67, an. A (Intelligence), p. 1, Historians files, CMH.

Viet Cong troops equip themselves with AK47 assault rifles and U.S.-type radios.

enemy casualties and defectors that MACV reported. The command and the agency finally compromised by mentioning the irregulars in intelligence estimates but not counting them as part of the enemy military strength.[7]

Not counted at all in MACV's enemy order of battle but very much involved in the war were large North Vietnamese forces outside the borders of South Vietnam. These included the soldiers and laborers who maintained and defended the enemy's increasingly elaborate supply route through eastern Laos, the so-called Ho Chi Minh Trail. In North Vietnam, many more thousands of troops and civilians manned antiaircraft defenses against the ROLLING THUNDER attacks and repaired bomb damage as well as trained and equipped the steady flow of replacements who traveled along the Ho Chi Minh Trail to the south.

Although they lacked the air and artillery firepower of the Americans, the North Vietnamese and Viet Cong by early 1968 possessed lethal weaponry appropriate to their operations and sustainable by their logistical system. Their main force units, as well as an increasing number of the guerrillas, were armed with the excellent Soviet- and Chinese-made AK47 assault rifle, with various types of modern Communist-bloc machine guns, and with an effective hand-held antitank rocket launcher. These weapons made Communist main force battalions approximately equal in organic firepower to

[7] This controversy is recounted in Cosmas, *Years of Escalation, 1962–1967*, ch. 13.

the American battalions and superior to many South Vietnamese battalions that still were fighting with U.S.-made World War II–era rifles. American artillery, strategic and tactical bombers, and helicopter gunships usually rectified this imbalance, but the enemy's arsenal also included some heavy weapons—most notably, rockets of up to 140-mm. and mortars of up to 160-mm. In northern I Corps, North Vietnamese troops had the support of heavy caliber guns and howitzers emplaced just across the Demilitarized Zone and in Laos. The Soviet Union, the People's Republic of China, and other Communist-bloc nations provided North Vietnam with a steady stream of arms and ammunition, as well as with aid to sustain Hanoi's war economy. In addition, although unknown to MACV at the time, as many as 150,000 Chinese air defense and engineer troops were reinforcing North Vietnam's resistance to Rolling Thunder.[8]

In their military operations, the Communists followed the general tenets of the people's revolutionary war as outlined by Mao Tse-tung in China and Ho Chi Minh in Vietnam, with its successive stages of guerrilla, mobile, and conventional combat. However, the Vietnamese opportunistically used different mixtures of these stages at different times and places depending on circumstances. In general, they used their main forces to attack American and South Vietnamese units in order to inflict casualties and to drive them out of areas targeted for subversion. They also maintained concentrations of troops along the Demilitarized Zone in I Corps, in the Central Highlands in II Corps, and around Saigon in III Corps in an effort to tie down American and South Vietnamese units. Meanwhile, the guerrillas, irregulars, and political cadre whittled away at Saigon's territorial forces and rural administration, seeking to expand Communist control in the villages and hamlets. To the surprise of many Americans, the North Vietnamese and Viet Cong had not reverted to the guerrilla phase in response to the arrival of U.S. forces. Instead, they kept up the large-unit war, even at the cost of heavy losses to themselves, in the belief that they could bleed the Americans and wear down Washington's will to continue the struggle. The enemy had as his ultimate goal the launching of the General Offensive–General Uprising, a large-scale military assault combined with mass popular revolts in the cities to overthrow the South Vietnamese government. Unbeknownst to the Americans, by late 1967, the Communist leaders believed that the time for this revolutionary climax was near at hand.[9]

The Military Assistance Command conducted its operations in support of the U.S. national policy objective—keeping South Vietnam out

---

[8] Combined Campaign Plan, 1968, an. A, p. 3, Historians files, CMH; Xiaoming Zhang, "The Vietnam War: A Chinese Perspective, 1964–1969," *Journal of Military History* 60 (October 1996): 731–62.

[9] MACV's analysis of enemy strategy can be found in Combined Campaign Plan, 1968, an. A, pp. 3–5.

of Communist hands. The United States had held consistently to this purpose since the early 1950s. Equally consistent was the method for achieving the goal: providing military and other assistance to an anti-Communist but nationalist South Vietnamese government. At the time of MACV's activation in February 1962, the United States had pinned its hopes to President Ngo Dinh Diem. After Diem's overthrow, as one successor regime after another proved ineffective and enemy pressure increased, President Johnson incrementally expanded the American commitment, ultimately to the point of large-scale, although still limited, war. Even as U.S. troops took over much of the fighting, however, President Johnson still insisted on maintaining the appearance and as much as possible the reality of Saigon's sovereignty. He also was determined to prevent any expansion of American military operations that might provoke direct intervention by China or Russia. To that end, he closely restricted the targets of the ROLLING THUNDER campaign and prohibited all but the smallest U.S. ground incursions into Laos and North Vietnam.

Within the restrictions, General Westmoreland conducted a campaign that consisted of two principal elements, often referred to in shorthand labels as attrition and pacification. On the attrition side, Westmoreland used his American divisions plus some of the Free World allies and elements of the South Vietnamese Army in mobile offensives against the enemy main forces and logistic bases. These attacks were intended to destroy the North Vietnamese and Viet Cong big units or, failing that, to wear them down, preempt their attacks, keep them away from populated areas, and uproot their supply systems. In addition, Westmoreland maneuvered his American troops on South Vietnam's borders to hold back enemy divisions that threatened to invade from north of the Demilitarized Zone or from Communist bases in Laos and Cambodia. Below the Demilitarized Zone, the III Marine Amphibious Force, at Westmoreland's direction, by late 1967 had constructed and manned a line of infantry and artillery strongpoints within South Vietnam. Along with a belt of electronic sensors across Laos, the marines' fortifications comprised a barrier that Secretary McNamara had ordered to be established in an attempt to reduce infiltration from North Vietnam. Some of the war's bloodiest fighting occurred along this line, under conditions that in places resembled the trench combat of World War I.[10]

While the Americans fought the main force, the bulk of the South Vietnamese Army and the Regional and Popular Forces, with their U.S. advisers, pursued the pacification campaign. They attempted to clear Viet Cong guerrillas out of selected populated areas and to protect the police and Revolutionary Development teams who moved in to eradicate the Communist shadow administration and reestablish government authority. Together, the two parts of the military effort, in

---

[10] This account is based on Cosmas, *Years of Escalation, 1962–1967*, ch. 12.

the words of the allies' Combined Campaign Plan for 1968, were "to provide territorial security at a level adequate to permit the destruction of the VC [Viet Cong] infrastructure and the uninterrupted and accelerated progress of political, economic, sociological and psychological programs" of the Saigon government. In fact, the military campaign was a slow process of trying to exhaust a foe able to draw supplies, replacements, and reinforcements from sources outside South Vietnam that the allies could damage but not shut down.[11]

Despite the frustrating aspects of the campaign, as 1967 came to a close, General Westmoreland, Ambassador Bunker, Ambassador Komer, and other senior American officials in Saigon believed that they were making progress in grinding down the enemy's interlocked military and political systems. The ROLLING THUNDER air raids were imposing strain on North Vietnam's economy and society and increasing the cost and difficulty of Hanoi's prosecution of the war in the south. Although the enemy's big units remained formidable in South Vietnam, American and allied troops were inflicting heavy casualties on them in every engagement, pushing them away from the population and agricultural centers, and invading and destroying their base areas. When the North Vietnamese and Viet Cong attacked in strength, their offensives seemed regularly to end in bloody failure. Evidence was mounting of declining enemy strength and morale, especially among the southern Viet Cong. Enemy forces were encountering difficulties in attracting recruits within South Vietnam, and the flow of reinforcements from North Vietnam appeared to be slowing down.

Rural pacification continued to progress slowly, if at all; but the future seemed to hold promise. With growing allied help, South Vietnamese regular and territorial forces were putting gradually increasing pressure on the Viet Cong guerrillas and political infrastructure. On the government side, a series of orderly, reasonably honest elections during 1967 had produced, for the first time since the fall of Ngo Dinh Diem four years before, a stable Saigon regime with a degree of constitutional legitimacy and popular support. With the CORDS organization in place to strengthen American backing for pacification, the elements finally seemed to be coming together for an effective allied paramilitary and political effort to reclaim the countryside.

To the end of the year, General Westmoreland continued to report progress in the military campaign, in pacification, in establishing a constitutional South Vietnamese government, and in improving the South Vietnamese armed forces. Enemy losses, the MACV commander asserted in December, were averaging 14,600 per month while their gains from recruitment and infiltration were no more than 9,700. The U.S.–South Vietnamese Combined Campaign Plan for 1968, issued on 11 November 1967, in General Westmoreland's words, was "based on a strategy of exploiting past successes." It called for continuing attacks

---

[11] Quotation is from Combined Campaign Plan, 1968, p. 6.

16

on the entire spectrum of enemy military forces, from guerrillas to the North Vietnamese divisions threatening the frontier, and for an aggressive and expanded pacification program.[12]

On 10 December, General Westmoreland told Admiral Sharp that the allies during 1968 would "defeat the VC/NVA [Viet Cong/North Vietnamese Army] main [force] units, destroy the enemy's base areas and resources, and drive him into sparsely populated areas where food is scarce." Intensified bombing of North Vietnam would "further reduce his war-making base and deny him the opportunity to bring his total resources to bear on the war in South Vietnam" even as the anti-infiltration barrier along the Demilitarized Zone and in Laos hindered movement of what men and materiel Hanoi did send. Within South Vietnam, the military offensive and the pacification effort would reduce enemy recruiting, erode the Viet Cong political infrastructure, and bring more of the population under government control. "In essence," Westmoreland concluded, "every effort for 1968 will be directed towards the defeat of the enemy and the establishment of a viable government" in South Vietnam. The MACV commander offered every reason to believe those efforts would succeed.[13]

General Westmoreland felt confident enough about the direction in which the war was moving that he could envision a gradual reduction in the American combat role. On 21 November, during a public relations trip to the United States, he delivered a generally optimistic assessment of the conflict to the National Press Club in Washington. During his speech, he declared that as the military situation continued to improve and the Saigon government became stronger, "it is conceivable to me that within two years or less, it will be possible for us to phase down our level of commitment and turn more of the burden of the war over to the Vietnamese armed forces, who are improving and who, I believe, will be prepared to assume this greater burden." Tempering his optimism with caution, as was his custom, the general elaborated in response to the newspeople's questions that American troop withdrawals would be "token" at first but that "we're preparing our plans to make it progressive."[14]

A Shifting Policy

In looking ahead to what later would be called "Vietnamization" of the war, Westmoreland expressed more than his own views. He also gave

---

[12] Quotation is from Msg, Westmoreland MAC 14624 to Sharp, 10 Dec 67, tab A–1, Westmoreland History file 26 (29 Nov–16 Dec 67), CMH. See also Msg, Westmoreland MAC 12397 to Wheeler, 20 Dec 67, Westmoreland Message files, Dec 67, CMH; Combined Campaign Plan, 1968, pp. 1–28.

[13] Msg, Westmoreland MAC 14624 to Sharp, 10 Dec 67, tab A–10, Westmoreland History file 26 (29 Nov–16 Dec 67), CMH.

[14] Gen William C. Westmoreland, Address to National Press Club, Washington, D.C., 21 Nov 67, Historians files, CMH.

voice, as was his wont, to a developing consensus within the Johnson administration in favor of topping off the American military effort and attempting to turn the fighting over to the South Vietnamese. By late 1967, President Johnson and his closest advisers were reaching the conclusion that American military escalation in Indochina had reached the limits of political, financial, and moral sustainability without any prospect of achieving an early decisive result. Prompted by this realization and beleaguered by an expanding domestic antiwar movement, Johnson was edging toward a change of policy.

Contributing to this change was a decline in official acceptance of the Military Assistance Command's reporting. Westmoreland's upbeat assessments were the latest in a steady flow of claims of success that had begun with MACV's establishment in 1962. The predicted successes, however, had regularly failed to materialize. By late 1967, a growing number of American officials in the United States and in Vietnam no longer accepted MACV's evaluations at face value. To the dissenters, who included key civilian assistants of Secretary of Defense McNamara in Washington, as well as many lower-ranking military officers and government civilians in Vietnam, the incremental advances regularly reported by the command and the embassy appeared more like stalemate, especially when weighed against the apparently limitless duration and steadily increasing human and economic cost of the conflict. CIA analysts, in particular, challenged MACV's optimistic view of war trends. The order of battle dispute, during which many CIA analysts, as well as a number of MACV's own junior intelligence officers, became convinced that Westmoreland and his command were deliberately underreporting enemy strength to sustain a false picture of military success, further undermined MACV's credibility with other agencies. In Saigon, dissenting officials found in the American press corps an outlet for their views. Although most newspeople in Vietnam at this time agreed with American objectives in the war, they freely publicized particular failures and mercilessly exposed instances of government misstatements or outright falsifications of the facts.[15]

In the United States, public questioning of and opposition to the war mounted even as combat intensified and American casualties increased. By the end of 1967, antiwar protest had spread beyond the university campuses and left-wing fringe groups and was drawing in major political, religious, labor, and civil rights leaders. Even more ominous, belief in victory was declining among politically moderate Americans. Members of Congress who initially had supported

---

[15] Harold P. Ford, *CIA and the Vietnam Policymakers: Three Episodes, 1962–1968* (Washington, D.C.: History Staff, Center for the Study of Intelligence, Central Intelligence Agency, 1998) recounts CIA controversies with MACV. See also Cosmas, *Years of Escalation, 1962–1967*, ch. 13. The evolution of news media disillusionment with government reporting is traced in William M. Hammond, *Public Affairs: The Military and the Media, 1962–1968*, U.S. Army in Vietnam (Washington, D.C.: U.S. Army Center of Military History, 1988).

President Johnson and his advisers at the White House

the administration's war policy began moving away from that position, mainly on the grounds that the war was costing too much and making too little progress. Important newspapers and their reporters and columnists were beginning to reflect official and popular doubts, although the bulk of news coverage of Vietnam was still neutral or favorable to the administration's position. In public opinion polls, President Johnson's performance ratings steadily declined, and an ever-growing percentage of respondents to the same polls agreed with the proposition that U.S. intervention in Vietnam had been a mistake.

On its public face, the Johnson administration responded to the growth of doubt and dissent with a full-throated campaign of optimism. The president pushed every government agency to produce good news about Vietnam that would give the lie to allegations that the war was stalemated. In every forum of discussion, members of the administration cited these reports in defense of their claims of progress. Supporting the campaign, Westmoreland and his public affairs officers kept up a barrage of news conferences and official reports detailing slow but steady improvement in every aspect of the war. At administration direction, they gave special emphasis to stories that would refute persistent press charges that the South Vietnamese armed forces were incompetent and ineffective. It had been under President Johnson's orders that Westmoreland returned to the United States in April and November 1967 to report on the state of the war, making the prediction of future U.S. disengagement during the second trip. Despite the effort devoted to it, the optimism campaign failed to dispel public doubts. By playing a prominent role in it, General Westmoreland, who previously had enjoyed much respect as a nonpolitical, professional military leader, became in the eyes of the press simply another pitchman for

19

the administration line. From then on, his command's assessments, no matter how valid they might be, would be received at best with skepticism.[16]

While they put on a positive face in public, in private administration officials expressed growing doubt about the rightness and sustainability of the course they were on in Vietnam. To an increasing extent, they shared Vice President Hubert H. Humphrey's conclusion after a visit to Vietnam in October 1967 that the nation was "throwing lives and money down a corrupt rat hole" and that "the American people would not stand for this involvement much longer."[17]

By late 1967, Secretary of Defense McNamara had become the administration's most prominent doubter. An early advocate and implementer of escalation, from mid-1966 on he grew increasingly convinced that heavier bombing of North Vietnam and the dispatch of still more U.S. troops to South Vietnam would only increase America's costs and casualties without causing the other side to give up. On 1 November, McNamara summed up his views in a memorandum to President Johnson. To bring the war's financial burden under control, reduce domestic unrest, and create a stable position that the United States could hold during a prolonged period of fighting and negotiation, McNamara urged Johnson to fix American troop strength in South Vietnam at its current level of 525,000 and to make no further expansion of the ROLLING THUNDER campaign. In the south, the United States should "endeavor to maintain our current rates of progress but with lesser U.S. casualties and lesser destruction" to the Vietnamese people and countryside while gradually shifting the "major burden of the fighting" to Saigon's forces. For the north, McNamara strongly advocated a complete cessation of the bombing in the hope that Hanoi in response would agree to negotiations and possibly halt or reduce its attacks across the Demilitarized Zone. Even if these results did not occur, he insisted, the United States at least would have established its good faith in the search for peace in the eyes of domestic and world opinion.[18]

President Johnson responded to McNamara's memorandum by arranging for the defense secretary to leave the administration for the presidency of the World Bank, although McNamara remained at Defense until February 1968. At the same time, however, Johnson's principal advisers were approaching a consensus in favor of leveling

---

[16] Hammond, *Military and the Media 1962–1968*, chs. 12–14; Cosmas, *Years of Escalation, 1962–1967*, ch. 13.

[17] Hubert H. Humphrey is quoted in U.S. Congress, Senate, Committee on Foreign Relations, *The U.S. Government and the Vietnam War: Executive and Legislative Roles and Relationships, Part IV: July 1965–January 1968* (Washington, D.C.: Government Printing Office, 2002), p. 895 (hereafter cited as U.S. Congress, Senate, *Government and the Vietnam War, 4*).

[18] U.S. Department of State, *Foreign Relations of the United States, 1964–1968*, vol. 5, *Vietnam 1967* (Washington, D.C.: Government Printing Office, 2002), pp. 943–50 (hereafter cited as *FRUS Vietnam, 1967*).

off the American effort along the lines McNamara had recommended. At the president's request, Secretary of State Dean Rusk, Ambassador Bunker, and other official and unofficial presidential counselors commented on McNamara's 1 November memorandum. All opposed an immediate halt to ROLLING THUNDER and any publicly announced stabilization or de-escalation of operations in South Vietnam. At the same time, however, all rejected further escalation—whether by heavier bombing or a naval blockade of the North, dispatch of additional U.S. troops to the South, or ground offensives against enemy bases in Laos and Cambodia—as unlikely to achieve decisive success and certain to raise the costs of the war beyond what was politically supportable. All favored keeping ROLLING THUNDER at about its current intensity, holding MACV's forces at 525,000, and gradually shifting the major share of combat and pacification to the South Vietnamese.[19]

Always inclined to tailor his recommendations to the Washington policy trends as he understood them, Westmoreland joined in this consensus. He had discussed leveling off MACV's troop strength with McNamara the previous year and realized that Johnson's refusal since 1965 to call up the reserves had effectively established a ceiling on the forces he could expect to receive. Commenting along with Bunker on McNamara's memorandum, Westmoreland rejected a halt in bombing of the North but declined to recommend more severe measures, such as a naval blockade. He expressed the hope that 525,000 men would be all the troops he would need in South Vietnam and declared to the president and in his speech at the National Press Club that a force of that size would be "well-balanced, hard-hitting," one that the country would be "capable of sustaining as long as required" and that could continue "indefinitely" to maintain and increase pressure on the enemy. Although concerned with reducing casualties and destruction in South Vietnam, the MACV commander insisted that those considerations should not be allowed to restrict his conduct of tactical operations. He favored keeping open the option of ground attacks into North Vietnam, Laos, and Cambodia but did not advocate launching them at that point. Finally, he declared that over the next two years he would have as his "central purpose" the transfer of military functions to the South Vietnamese, to the end that ultimately the United States could leave behind in Vietnam "a military establishment capable of looking after itself increasingly."[20]

Lyndon Johnson expressed his views in a "memorandum for the file" dated 18 December. He declared that he had studied McNamara's proposals of 1 November and consulted about them with his Washington advisers and with Ambassador Bunker and General Westmoreland. He had, he said, reached certain conclusions. With regard to ROLLING

---

[19] U.S. Congress, Senate, *Government and the Vietnam War, 4*, pp. 884–91.

[20] *FRUS Vietnam, 1967*, pp. 1040–42; see also p. 1058. Westmoreland, Address to National Press Club, Washington, D.C., 21 Nov 67.

THUNDER, he had decided to continue the bombing at about the existing level of intensity and range of targets while trying at the same time to reduce the "drama and public attention" that the air campaign received in the United States. "Under present circumstances," the president ruled out a unilateral bombing halt because it would be interpreted in both North Vietnam and the United States as "a sign of weakening will." Johnson would play his "bombing card" only when he saw "reason for confidence that it would move us toward peace." As yet, he saw no such reason.

As to South Vietnam, Johnson was determined to keep his options open but essentially accepted McNamara's viewpoint. The president declared that "at the moment" he saw no reason to increase MACV's forces above the 525,000 level. He was "inclined to be extremely reserved" in considering proposals for American ground offensives outside South Vietnam unless a "powerful case" could be made for them. Such operations, he said, entailed political risks and would divert forces from "pressure on the VC" and pacification. Nevertheless, he deemed it unwise publicly to renounce these options. Johnson endorsed McNamara's recommendations that the administration try to reduce the toll of death and destruction from American operations in South Vietnam and accelerate the turnover of combat to Saigon's forces.[21]

By the end of 1967, the Johnson administration was close to abandoning its hope, which had never been very strong, of winning anything like a battlefield victory in Vietnam. Instead, the administration was pointed toward fixing an upper limit to the American military effort. The administration would try to hold the line militarily in Southeast Asia and politically at home until diplomacy or improvements in the Saigon government and its armed forces opened an honorable way out of the war. This approach had not yet been embodied in formal operational plans and orders, but the direction seemed clear. For the Military Assistance Command, as for the rest of the U.S. government, the years of escalation in Vietnam were nearing an end.

---

[21] Full text of this memorandum is in *FRUS Vietnam, 1967*, pp. 1118–20.

2

Prelude to Tet: Warnings and Preparations

Throughout the debate over whether the war was stalemated, the administration's progress campaign, and President Johnson's movement toward leveling off the American effort, all the participants assumed that the other side's war strategy would remain the same. They expected the North Vietnamese and Viet Cong to continue their mixed large-unit and guerrilla campaign of attrition with the aim of exhausting American patience and South Vietnamese resources and forcing a negotiated settlement favorable to the revolution. Reflecting this view, an interagency intelligence estimate issued in November 1967 concluded:

The Communists apparently recognize that the chances of a complete military victory have disappeared, and they aim instead at a protracted war. Their objectives . . . are to immobilize and wear down the Allied military forces, to maintain base areas, expand their political agitation and control in contested and GVN [government of Vietnam] areas, and defeat the RD [pacification] program. In pursuit of these objectives, their tactics are to combine and coordinate closely their military operations and political activity.[1]

In fact, when the intelligence estimate was published, the enemy was well into his preparations for something quite different: a nation-wide offensive intended to achieve decisive political and military victory within a short time. The Military Assistance Command, the American mission in Saigon, and the U.S. intelligence community, as well as the South Vietnamese government and armed forces, gradually became aware that the enemy was preparing for more than his ordinary annual winter-spring offensive. However, they failed fully to

[1] Special National Intelligence Estimate (SNIE) 14.3–67, p. 2, in U.S. District Court, Southern District of New York, *William C. Westmoreland, Plaintiff, v. CBS, Inc., et al., Defendants. 82 Civ 7913 (PNL). Plaintiff General William C. Westmoreland's Memorandum of Law in Opposition to Defendant CBS's Motion to Dismiss and for Summary Judgment, app. B*, p. 248 (hereafter cited as *Westmoreland Memorandum of Law, app. B*). For a similar view, see Combined Campaign Plan, 1968, an. A, pp. 4–5, Historians files, CMH.

appreciate the planned nature and extent of the attack and hence were taken at least partially by surprise when it began.

The Enemy Plans an Offensive[2]

Even as President Johnson and his advisers tentatively decided to level off the American war effort in Vietnam, their adversaries in Hanoi were getting ready to do the opposite. Undeterred by the increasing American pressure, the northern and southern revolutionary leaders held unwaveringly to their maximum goal: a unified Communist Vietnam. Like many Americans, the Communist leaders believed that the conflict had reached a stalemate, but for them a stalemate represented a temporary equilibrium of forces, a stage on their march to inevitable victory. Instead of a way out of the conflict, they sought a means to shift the balance in their favor.

By the spring of 1967, the Vietnamese Communists believed that they had passed through the first two stages of the people's revolutionary war—those of organization and base building and of guerrilla warfare—and entered the third and final stage. In that stage, large combat-seasoned guerrilla and main forces backed by a strong political infrastructure and mass popular following were in position to launch what the Communists called the General Offensive–General Uprising. In this revolutionary climax, North Vietnamese and Viet Cong military units would launch attacks to destroy the South Vietnamese Army and pin down American forces. As these actions went on, urban and rural popular uprisings spearheaded by commando assaults on South Vietnamese military headquarters, administrative facilities, and communications centers would sweep away the puppet regime and install National Liberation Front governments at every level from the hamlets to Saigon. Since the early 1960s, the North Vietnamese Communist Party had identified the General Offensive–General Uprising as the culminating point of its politico-military campaign in the south. For the Saigon area, the *Central Office for South Vietnam (COSVN)*, the senior enemy headquarters for the southern half of South Vietnam, had prepared detailed plans for such an operation. Since 1965, *COSVN* had been compelled to divert its resources to the growing battle against the Americans, but its plans remained in the files ready to be brought up to date and executed.[3]

More than the diversion of resources may have held back the offensive. In response to the massive intervention of American combat

---

[2] Unless otherwise noted, this section is based on John M. Carland, "The Tet Offensive of 1968: Desperate Gamble or Calculated Risk?" (Unpublished paper, U.S. Army Center of Military History, 2001) and William M. Hammond, "Preparations Begin" (Unpublished paper, U.S. Army Center of Military History, 2002).

[3] The uprising concept is explained in "The Process of Revolution and the General Uprising," document captured by U.S. troops, 22 May 68, *Vietnam Documents and Research Notes*, no. 45, CMH.

forces, factions among the North Vietnamese leaders engaged in a two-year debate over war strategy. Masking their differences in Marxist-Leninist jargon, the contending groups promoted their views through polemics published in the official Communist press and broadcast on North Vietnam's state radio. They argued over the proper relationship between large-unit and guerrilla operations, the relative roles of political and military struggle and of fighting and diplomacy, and the merits of protracted conflict versus an all-out drive for victory in the shortest possible time. By mid-1967, they had reached a consensus that would blend most of the contending elements of their strategy in the context of the General Offensive–General Uprising.[4]

In a mirror image of General Westmoreland's view of the conflict, the Communist leaders believed that they were making slow but steady progress in their struggle. Lt. Gen. Tran Van Tra, the *COSVN* military commander, for example, acknowledged in retrospect that his forces had encountered "difficulties and weaknesses" in replacing casualties, building political strength, and "conducting mass movements in urban areas." Nevertheless, he argued, these problems existed "in the context of a favorable situation" in which the revolutionary army held the initiative and the Americans were "bewildered by the new battlefield" and by the Communists "new form of war."[5]

Although the North Vietnamese and Viet Cong were taking heavy losses and winning few victories on the battlefield and the U.S. bombing was placing severe pressure on the North Vietnamese society and economy, the political situation held much promise. The leaders in Hanoi knew that antiwar sentiment was mounting in the United States and among "progressive" forces around the world. Still better, during 1968, a presidential election year, the American administration would be under additional strain that likely would inhibit its response to new Communist initiatives. Even more promising, South Vietnam appeared to be extremely vulnerable. The majority of South Vietnamese soldiers and people, the Communists assumed, in their hearts hated the Saigon regime and its American "imperialist" sponsors. Viewed from Hanoi, the I Corps revolt of 1966, the periodic anti-government demonstrations by Buddhists and other groups, the relatively small proportion of the popular vote received by the winning ticket of Nguyen Van Thieu and Nguyen Cao Ky in the September 1967 presidential election, and the presence of tens of thousands of impoverished displaced peasants in city slums were harbingers of incipient revolution in the urban centers of Saigon's power. Only a spark, a catalytic event, was needed to set South Vietnam's cities aflame, inspire Saigon's troops to defect, and sweep away the puppet regime.[6]

---

[4] Thomas K. Latimer, "Hanoi's Leaders and Their South Vietnam Policies, 1954–1968" (Ph.D. diss., Georgetown University, 1972), chs. 8 and 9, summarizes the controversies.

[5] Quotations are from Carland, "Tet Offensive," pp. 4–5.

[6] This account of North Vietnamese/Viet Cong plans and assessments is drawn from William J.

25

*North Vietnamese Communist leaders and government
officials arrive for an official visit in Peking.*

Taking all these considerations into account, the collective leadership of the North Vietnamese Communist (Lao Dong) Party decided to "prepare to strike a decisive blow against the enemy, win a great victory, bring about a great-leap-forward transformation, and force the United States to accept military defeat." In May 1967, the Politburo, the party's inner executive directorate, initiated planning for the General Offensive–General Uprising. At that time, the Politburo instructed the Central Party Military Affairs Committee, in coordination with the major theater commands in the south, to prepare an overall plan for the assault. During June, the party's Central Committee unanimously endorsed the Politburo's strategic decision to "prepare a decisive victory in 1968." In July, the Politburo approved the Central Party Military Affairs Committee's plan and set a tentative date for the offensive. At the end of October, on the basis of reports from the south, the leaders in Hanoi pushed the date forward to 30–31 January 1968, the beginning of Vietnam's Tet lunar new year holiday. The change left local commanders in the south with a short time for preparation, but the Communist leaders believed that an offensive during the festivities would catch Saigon's forces off-guard and have maximum military and political impact. The Politburo then developed a policy resolution and

Duiker, *The Communist Road to Power in Vietnam* (Boulder, Colo.: Westview Press, 1981), pp. 261–65; Latimer, "Hanoi's Leaders and Their South Vietnam Policies," chs. 8 and 9; Col. Hoang Ngoc Lung, *The General Offensives of 1968–1969*, Indochina Monographs (Washington, D.C.: U.S. Army Center of Military History, 1981), pp. 14–24; Lt. Gen. Phillip B. Davidson, *Vietnam at War: The History, 1946–1975* (Novato, Calif.: Presidio Press, 1988), pp. 434–42; and James J. Wirtz, *The Tet Offensive: Intelligence Failure in War* (Ithaca, N.Y.: Cornell University Press, 1991), chs. 1 and 2.

a detailed operational plan based on the earlier work of the Central Party Military Affairs Committee.[7]

In December, the Politburo presented the resolution to the Fourteenth Plenum, or general meeting, of the Lao Dong Party Central Committee. Approved by the delegates and formally issued on 1 January 1968 as Central Resolution Fourteen, the document defined the enemy's "crucial mission" during the winter-spring 1967–68 campaigning season as "to mobilize the greatest efforts of the entire Party, the entire army, and the entire people in both regions [North and South] to carry our revolutionary war to the highest level of development and use the general offensive and general uprising to secure a decisive victory in a relatively short time."

As used in Resolution Fourteen, the term "decisive victory" denoted the achievement of three important strategic objectives: the collapse of the Saigon regime and its armed forces, the establishment of a neutralist coalition government in the south dominated by the National Liberation Front, and the beginning of negotiations for the withdrawal of U.S. troops from South Vietnam. Although not mentioned in the resolution, another objective would be to compel the United States to end or at least to significantly curtail the bombing of North Vietnam. After "decisive victory" was achieved, what the Communists called "total victory" would follow later when North Vietnam absorbed South Vietnam into a single socialist state.

Specifically, the proposed offensive was to begin with a series of main force operations along South Vietnam's western border and the Demilitarized Zone, designed to bleed and demoralize U.S. and South Vietnamese troops and to draw the allies' attention away from the attack preparations in the lowlands and urban centers. Once this campaign was well under way, Viet Cong sapper and local force units, previously infiltrated into Saigon, Da Nang, Hue, and scores of province and district capitals, were to attack South Vietnamese military and government headquarters, police stations, and radio and television facilities. These assaults would paralyze the government and military high command so that the party's political agents could establish a revolutionary regime and call the people into the streets. Additional main force units, concentrated on the outskirts of the cities, then would move in to finish off armed resistance and secure the victory. If all went as planned, the Americans, fighting for their lives along the borders, would find the country to their rear in the hands of a new Viet Cong–dominated coalition government to which much of the South Vietnamese had defected. The United States would have no recourse

---

[7] Quotations are from War Experiences Recapitulation Committee of the High-Level Military Institute, *Vietnam: The Anti-U.S. Resistance War for National Salvation, 1954–1975: Military Events* (Hanoi: People's Army Publishing House, 1980) (hereafter cited as *Resistance War*), trans. by Joint Publications Research Service, Doc. no. 80968, 1982, p. 100; see also p. 101.

but to negotiate for withdrawal on whatever terms the victorious revolution chose to grant.[8]

To maximize his chances of achieving surprise, the enemy planned to launch his crucial attack on the cities at Tet, the Vietnamese new year, which in 1968 would be celebrated at the end of January. This holiday was deeply sacred to the Vietnamese as a time for renewal of bonds with family and ancestors and preparation for the year ahead. Its week-long celebration included much feasting, gift-giving, shooting of fireworks, and reunion with family and friends. Throughout the long war, Tet, like Christmas and the western New Year's, had been the occasion of temporary truces, which both sides exploited for maneuver and resupply but rarely for major attacks. The South Vietnamese normally furloughed large numbers of their troops for the holiday, and the extensive movement of travelers for the occasion offered ideal cover for infiltration of Viet Cong soldiers and supplies into the cities. Above all, a full-scale attack during the holiday would achieve maximum shock and surprise, thereby enhancing the likelihood of government collapse.[9]

Although the planners in Hanoi made some allowance for a less-than-complete triumph, they appear to have considered decisive victory a real possibility. Their directives to lower-level political and military cadres spoke of the new offensive as the climactic moment of the revolution's long struggle. The instructions called for total dedication and total sacrifice for the sake of total victory.[10]

This ambitious plan was controversial at its inception and, as the Communists themselves acknowledged in retrospect, was based on an overestimation of the revolutionary forces' military and political strength and capabilities and an underestimation of those of the allies. According to later Vietnamese Communist histories, many southern Viet Cong commanders from the first considered their forces inadequate to achieve the plan's maximum goals; but they dared not voice

---

[8] The enemy plan is conveniently summarized in Wirtz, *Tet Offensive*, pp. 61–64; and Davidson, *Vietnam at War*, pp. 443–46. Msg, Abrams MAC 10931 to Westmoreland, 15 Nov 67, Westmoreland Message files, 1–30 Nov 67, CMH, analyzes a captured enemy order for the border battles. For overall strategy, see "The Process of Revolution and the General Uprising," document captured by U.S. forces on 22 May 68, *Vietnam Documents and Research Notes*, no. 45; and Department of Defense (DoD) Intelligence Information Report no. 6–026–1418–68, 18 Apr 68, sub: VC Plans. Both in CMH.

[9] The significance of Tet to the Vietnamese is conveniently summarized in Westmoreland, *Soldier Reports*, p. 310. Col. Hoang Ngoc Lung, *Intelligence*, Indochina Monographs (Washington, D.C.: U.S. Army Center of Military History, 1982), p. 35, claims that North Vietnamese authorities had less respect for Tet as a sacred tradition than did the South Vietnamese government and people.

[10] War Experiences Recapitulation Committee, *Resistance War*, p. 100, recounts the Hanoi Politburo's view of the possible outcomes, including the possibility of a less-than-total victory. Present-day Communist Vietnamese historiography claims that the North Vietnamese all along envisioned the General Offensive–General Uprising as a prolonged process and that the southern Viet Cong misconstrued the campaign as a "one-blow" effort. See Capt Ronnie E. Ford, "Tet 1968: Understanding the Surprise" (Master's thesis, Defense Intelligence College, 1993), pp. 111–12.

their objections because the plan was based in part on their own earlier optimistic reports of political and military success. A number of important North Vietnamese leaders, reportedly including Defense Minister Vo Nguyen Giap, the architect of victory at Dien Bien Phu, argued against the offensive. They urged instead a continuation of protracted attritional warfare. Looking backward, General Tran Van Tra declared:

During Tet of 1968 we did not correctly evaluate the specific balance of forces between ourselves and the enemy, did not fully realize that the enemy still had considerable capabilities and that our capabilities were limited, and set requirements that were beyond our actual strength. In other words, we did not base ourselves on scientific calculation or a careful weighing of all factors, but in part on an illusion based on our subjective desires. . . .[11]

Warnings and Preparations

By the time the Central Committee adopted Resolution Fourteen, preparations for the campaign were well under way. During the summer and fall, the North Vietnamese increased the flow of men and materiel down the Ho Chi Minh Trail. According to a later Communist account, some 31,700 personnel entered South Vietnam during 1967, more than twice the number that infiltrated during the previous year, along with over 6,500 tons of weapons and supplies. The weaponry included thousands of automatic rifles, machine guns, and hand-held antitank rocket launchers. Gradually and secretly, the Communists disseminated orders down their chain of command and initiated local attack planning. Viet Cong units, often as yet unaware of the purpose of their efforts, clandestinely stockpiled supplies near South Vietnam's cities and prepared for their urban attack missions. Party cadres assembled lists of government officials and supporters to be killed and kidnapped, as well as lists of members of the prospective revolutionary town and province administrations. During the fall, main force regiments engaged allied forces in a series of unusually prolonged battles at Con Thien on the Demilitarized Zone and Song Be, Loc Ninh, and Dak To on the western edges of II and III Corps. These battles, which cost the enemy thousands of men but also pushed up the weekly American casualty rate, apparently were designed to draw allied forces to the borders and distract their attention from the offensive preparations against the cities.

---

[11] Quotation is from Col. Gen. Tran Van Tra, *Vietnam: History of the Bulwark B2 Theater*, vol. 5, *Concluding the 30-Years War* (Ho Chi Minh City: Van Nghe Publishing House, 1982), trans. Foreign Broadcast Information Service, Joint Publications Research Service, Southeast Asia Report no. 1247, 2 Feb 83, p. 35. Davidson, *Vietnam at War*, pp. 449–50, comments on Vo Nguyen Giap's opposition to the offensive; see also pp. 446–48. A senior Communist leadership review of the offensive is described in CIA Intelligence Information Report, 13 Aug 70, CMH. Ford, "Tet 1968," pp. 112–15, 163–67, 274, summarizes recent Communist accounts.

The battle for Dak To peaked with a costly attack by the 4th Battalion, 173d Airborne Brigade, against well-entrenched North Vietnamese on Hill 875.

Hanoi also made political and diplomatic preparations. North Vietnam signed new military and economic aid agreements with the Soviet Union and China. To curb home-front dissent, the Hanoi regime arrested over 200 senior party members and officials who lacked sufficient zeal for the war effort and decreed harsh punishment for persons guilty of "counterrevolutionary" crimes. The National Liberation Front, the political arm of the Viet Cong, announced a new program aimed at broadening its appeal to the South Vietnamese people and instigated rumors that the National Liberation Front and the United States were secretly negotiating to replace the Thieu-Ky regime with a Viet Cong–dominated coalition government. Finally, on 31 December, the North Vietnamese foreign minister issued a public declaration that seemed to commit Hanoi to enter peace negotiations if the United States stopped ROLLING THUNDER. In the light of what followed, the purpose of this statement was less than clear. Probably, it was aimed both at laying the groundwork for negotiations and at diverting American attention from what by that time were visible indications of an imminent major Communist offensive.[12]

---

[12] These preparations are conveniently summarized in Hammond, "Preparations Begin"; Wirtz, *Tet Offensive*, pp. 66–77; Lung, *General Offensives*, pp. 25–31; and Don Oberdorfer, *Tet!* (New York: Da Capo Press, 1984), pp. 65–69. Also, Msgs, Abrams MAC 10931 and MAC 11239 to Wheeler, 15 Nov 67 and 22 Nov 67; Westmoreland MAC 01001 to Sharp and Wheeler info Gen Johnson, 21

The enemy took great pains to conceal his preparations and intentions. Until almost the eve of the attack, a U.S. intelligence study later concluded, "probably no Communist officer below the level of *COSVN*, front, or military region was aware of the full scope of the offensive." The assault units received their final orders 72 hours or less before the time of execution. Nevertheless, the Communists had to distribute orders and plans and indoctrinate their troops and political cadre concerning the transcendent significance of the coming effort. Inevitably, as a result, American and South Vietnamese intelligence organizations during the fall and winter steadily accumulated evidence, primarily from captured documents and prisoner interrogations, of the scale, objectives, and timing of the attack. On the basis of this evidence, analysts at the MACV J–2 Current Intelligence Branch, the Combined Intelligence Center, Vietnam,[13] and the CIA Saigon station issued studies that predicted a nationwide enemy offensive, including major attacks on the cities. The CIA study, finished in November, accurately forecast the successive phases of the coming campaign. Its drafters suggested that the border battles were part of the first phase and that a second phase, possibly including the city attacks, would begin in January.[14]

Higher-ranking intelligence officers and commanders at MACV and elsewhere received these studies at best with skepticism. The MACV chief of intelligence, Maj. Gen. Phillip B. Davidson, and his chief estimator, Col. Daniel Graham, for example, heard briefings on the J–2 and CIA attack predictions but rejected their conclusions, as did George Carver, who oversaw Vietnam activities at the CIA. Often before, enemy documents had called for major attacks, but the attacks never had occurred. An all-out nationwide offensive seemed clearly beyond the capabilities of the North Vietnamese and Viet Cong and seemed inconsistent with their presumed strategy of protracted attritional warfare. An attempt to capture the cities, where the enemy hitherto had confined his efforts to terrorism, espionage, and political

---

Jan 68. All in Westmoreland Message files, 1–30 Nov 67 and 1–31 Jan 68, CMH. Latter message discusses rising American casualty rates.

[13] The Combined Intelligence Center, Vietnam, established in 1966, included both American and South Vietnamese personnel and was intended to bring together American technical expertise with Vietnamese knowledge of their language, people, and culture. It drew upon the product of similar combined centers for the exploitation of captured enemy documents and materiel and prisoners of war. For its establishment, see Cosmas, *Years of Escalation, 1962–1967*, ch. 8.

[14] Quotation is from the President's Foreign Intelligence Advisory Board (PFIAB), "Intelligence Warning of the Tet Offensive in South Vietnam" (Interim Report), ca. early 1968, p. 3, JX 397, in *Vietnam: A Documentary Collection*, card 698. Wirtz, *Tet Offensive*, ch. 4; Lung, *General Offensives*, pp. 32–37; Interv, Lt Col James E. Smith and Lt Col Edward P. Smith with Gen William B. Rosson, 1981, pp. 377–80, Senior Officers Oral History Program, Military History Institute (MHI), Carlisle Barracks, Pa. (hereafter cited as Rosson Interv); Phillip B. Davidson, *Secrets of the Vietnam War* (Novato, Calif.: Presidio Press, 1990), p. 105; U.S. District Court, *Westmoreland Memorandum of Law, app. B*, pp. 217, 267, 374–75. Saigon station analyses are summarized in Ford, *CIA and the Vietnam Policymakers*, pp. 119–21.

agitation, appeared especially improbable. The Communists lacked the conventional military strength to seize and hold major towns. According to the allies' political assessment (which turned out to be accurate), the Communists could count on little help from urban citizens who, while often hostile or apathetic toward the Saigon regime, were far from ready to rise on behalf of the National Liberation Front. Hanoi's leaders, whom the allies credited with possessing excellent intelligence on South Vietnamese affairs, would not be so foolish as to throw away their forces in a hopeless endeavor. The city attack plans, therefore, could be dismissed as propaganda and the border battles understood as desperate enemy efforts to gain limited successes largely for psychological and political purposes—efforts that, in fact, had merely exposed enemy troops to slaughter by American firepower. Thus ironically, the miscalculations in the North Vietnamese plan worked in its favor by causing the allies to discount the evidence that reached them of the nature of the attack.[15]

Although the Military Assistance Command's evaluations and plans discounted the likelihood of a nationwide enemy offensive, General Westmoreland took steps that had the effect of strengthening his position. During September and October, he secured Defense Department agreement to a speed-up in deployment of the major Army combat elements in the recently approved reinforcement Program Five—the headquarters and two brigades of the 101st Airborne Division and the 11th and 198th Light Infantry Brigades—so that all would arrive in South Vietnam before the expected Christmas cease-fire. The MACV commander obtained these accelerated deployments not in anticipation of a major nationwide Communist offensive but rather to get more troops in hand to meet the perennial enemy threat in northern I Corps and to provide additional forces for projected allied operations. He also wanted to make certain that his reinforcements were not being blocked by any diplomatic maneuvering attendant upon the Christmas truce.[16]

---

[15] Wirtz, *Tet Offensive*, ch. 3, examines allied assumptions; see especially pp. 111–19, 124–28, 175–77. Ford, *CIA and the Vietnam Policymakers*, pp. 121–23; Lung, *Intelligence*, pp. 145–52; and *General Offensives*, pp. 37–42. Westmoreland, *Soldier Reports*, pp. 316, 320–23; Davidson, *Vietnam Secrets*, pp. 104–11; and Interv, Lyndon B. Johnson Library (LBJL) with Lt Gen Phillip B. Davidson, 30 Mar and 30 Jun 82, sess. 1, p. 45 (hereafter cited as Davidson Interv); and Interv, LBJL with Col Daniel Graham, 24 May 82, sess. 1, pp. 39–41, and 3 Nov 82, sess. 2, p. 7 (hereafter cited as Graham Interv). Westmoreland gives his view of purpose of the border battles in Msg, MAC 10547 to Wheeler, 6 Nov 67, Westmoreland Message files, Nov 67, CMH.

[16] U.S. Congress, House Committee on Armed Services, *United States–Vietnam Relations, 1945–1967: Study Prepared by the Department of Defense*, 12 vols. (Washington, D.C.: Government Printing Office, 1971), sec. 4.C.6(b), pp. 215–22 (hereafter cited as *United States–Vietnam Relations*). Msgs, Gen Johnson WDC 13028 to Westmoreland, 2 Oct 67; Gen Johnson JCS 8356–67 to Sharp and Westmoreland, 5 Oct 67; Gen Johnson WDC 13666 to Gen Dwight E. Beach, CG, USARPAC, and Westmoreland, 14 Oct 67; Beach HWA 2978 to Gen Johnson info Westmoreland, 14 Oct 67; Westmoreland MAC 9810 to Johnson, 19 Oct 67; Beach HWA 3067 to Gen Johnson, 24 Oct 67; Westmoreland Message files, Oct 67, CMH.

Westmoreland campaigned as well to eliminate the holiday cease-fires or, failing that, to minimize their durations and their restrictions on his forces' freedom of action. Temporary truces for Christmas, the western New Year's, and Tet had become an established practice in the war which General Westmoreland and other American commanders deplored as affording the enemy periods free from allied attack during which the enemy could reinforce and resupply his troops. Early in October, Westmoreland, on the basis of a MACV staff study, recommended to the Mission Council that the United States and South Vietnam announce no holiday cease-fires at all during the coming season. If political considerations required truces, they should be limited to 24 hours each at Christmas and New Year's and 48 hours at Tet. Westmoreland initially floated the idea of tying the cease-fires to a mutual freeze on troop movements and logistical operations by both sides, but at Admiral Sharp's urging, he backed away from this proposal as potentially unmanageable and dangerous to allied forces if a truce should be extended by diplomatic maneuvering.[17]

The Mission Council accepted Westmoreland's 24/24/48 formula, as eventually did the administration. At State Department insistence, the administration rejected the MACV commander's suggestion that each truce be made conditional on enemy behavior during the previous truce, although it gave his forces ample latitude in reacting to major Communist cease-fire violations. On 19 December, Westmoreland transmitted to his commanders the agreed U.S. and South Vietnamese plan for 24-hour cease-fires at Christmas and New Year's and a 48-hour stand-down at Tet. He enjoined his commanders to bring "maximum pressure" on the enemy in the days immediately before each pause in operations and to position their troops to obstruct enemy troop and supply movements during each truce. The other side at the same time announced its own longer cease-fires for each holiday. Significantly, throughout these discussions, Westmoreland based his case for limiting the cease-fires on past violations by the enemy and the need to deny him unmolested movement of troops and supplies, not on any imminent threat of a Communist offensive.[18]

---

[17] Westmoreland, *Soldier Reports*, p. 279. Westmoreland History Notes, 1–30 Oct 67, tab A; Memorandum for the Record (MFR), Hendry, 8 Oct 67, sub: CIIB [Criminal Investigation and Intelligence Bureau] Meeting, 7 Oct 67, tab A–11. Both in Westmoreland History file no. 23 (1–15 Oct 67), CMH. Msg, Commander, U.S. Military Assistance Command, Vietnam (COMUSMACV) MAC 34790 to Commander in Chief, Pacific (CINCPAC), 22 Oct 67, COMUSMACV Signature file, 1967, CMH. Msgs, Sharp BNK 2376 to Gen Johnson and Westmoreland, 10 Dec 67; Westmoreland MAC 12000 to Sharp, 11 Dec 67. Both in Westmoreland Message files, Dec 67, CMH.

[18] Msg, Eugene Locke Saigon 8008 to Bunker, 9 Oct 67, tab A–23, Westmoreland History file no. 23 (1–15 Oct 67); Memo, Westmoreland for Bunker, 8 Dec 67, sub: Holiday Cease-fire Announcement, COMUSMACV Signature file, Dec 67; Msg, Bunker Saigon 13232 to Sec State, 12 Dec 67, tab A–17, Westmoreland History file no. 26 (29 Nov–16 Dec 67). All in CMH. Msgs, Westmoreland MAC 11960 to Sharp, 10 Dec 67; and MAC 12363 to Field Force and Component Cdrs, 19 Dec 67. All in Westmoreland Message files, Dec 67, CMH. Quotations are from latter message. Wirtz, *Tet Offensive*, p. 211, comments on lack of mention of any enemy offensive threat.

Despite these indications of business as usual, by late December, the Military Assistance Command, the U.S. Embassy in Saigon, and senior officials in Washington had come to recognize that the enemy's next winter-spring offensive would be much larger than ordinary and have unusually ambitious objectives. The indications were impossible to ignore. The sheer volume of captured documents and prisoner interrogations pointing toward a nationwide offensive and attacks on the cities commanded attention. Enemy willingness to stand and fight at Dak To and other places, at great cost to themselves, and its launching of nearly simultaneous attacks in several corps areas at once, represented a break with past patterns. Westmoreland in response commissioned a joint study by his intelligence and operations staff directorates to discover the Communists' intentions in these operations and determine how the command should react to and exploit them. As the new year began, a growing amount of intercepted radio traffic provided additional evidence that the enemy planned widespread assaults on an unprecedented scale, including some directed against cities and the coastal lowlands. Yet skepticism remained. In mid-December, for example, General Westmoreland directed the MACV psychological warfare office to consider a post-Tet program to "capitalize on those VC pre-Tet promises that do not materialize," specifically the reports that enemy troops in some areas "allegedly are being directed to go all out now on the basis that peace will come immediately after Tet."[19]

The Military Assistance Command and its overseers in Honolulu and Washington paid special attention to accumulating evidence of a sudden dramatic increase in North Vietnamese infiltration. Throughout most of 1967, the command believed that the enemy was dispatching fewer men per month to South Vietnam than he had during the previous year, probably because he had completed his buildup of units and now was only sending down replacements. As late as 5 October, General Westmoreland reassured the State Department that he possessed no "hard intelligence" of a major expansion of enemy forces. However, during November and December, analysts in the Combined Intelligence Center, Vietnam, extrapolating mathematically from

---

[19] Wirtz, *Tet Offensive*, pp. 180–90, 202–03; PFIAB, "Intelligence Warning," p. 3. Quotation is from MFR, Brig. Gen. William E. Bryan Jr., USAF, 17 Dec 67, sub: CIIB Meeting, 16 Dec 67, tab A–8, Westmoreland History file no. 27 (19–26 Dec 67), CMH. J–2 and J–3 evaluation is directed in MFR, Bryan, 18 Nov 67, sub: CIIB Meeting, 18 Nov 67, tab A-44, Westmoreland History file no. 25 (13–28 Nov 67), CMH. U.S. District Court, *Westmoreland Memorandum of Law*, app. B, p. 157n; U.S. District Court, Southern District of New York, *William C. Westmoreland, Plaintiff, v. CBS Inc., et. al., Defendants. 82 Civ. 7913 (PNL). Memorandum in Support of Defendant CBS's Motion to Dismiss and for Summary Judgment*, pp. 121–22; and app. A, p. 344; Davidson Interv, 30 Mar and 30 Jun 82, sess. 1, pp. 36–38, 41–42; Bruce E. Jones, *War Without Windows: A True Account by a Young Army Officer Trapped in an Intelligence Cover-Up in Vietnam* (New York: Vanguard Press, 1987), p. 141. Brig. Gen. John R. Chaisson, the MACV Combat Operations Center (COC) chief, predicted hard fighting ahead in Presentation at Headquarters, Marine Corps (HQMC), 2 Jan 68, in Chaisson, Oral History, pp. 141–42, Marine Corps Historical Center (MCHC), Washington, D.C.; see also pp. 108–12. See also Ltr, Chaisson to Mrs Chaisson, 29 Nov 67, box 7, Chaisson Papers, Hoover Institution, Stanford, Calif.

meager information in collateral sources, began estimating much higher infiltration rates than they reported in the published order of battle with its stringent requirement for documentation of each unit and replacement group. In addition to these estimates, which were based on experimental methodology and rejected higher up in J–2, MACV received and accepted reports, based on special intelligence, of the advance of several North Vietnamese divisions, hitherto held in reserve in North Vietnam, to positions within striking distance of Khe Sanh, the westernmost Marine position in northern I Corps. Col. Charles Morris, General Davidson's chief of intelligence production, and a select group of senior analysts concentrated full time on this troop movement, which involved at least 20,000 men. They were "terribly concerned with this," Morris later recalled, "this reshaped the whole bloody war." Similar concern was felt in the White House, where President Johnson and his advisers, privy to the same special intelligence MACV was receiving, anxiously watched the enemy converge on Khe Sanh.[20]

By the end of December, the administration and MACV had concluded that the Communists were preparing for some sort of major military assault early in the new year and that the offensive might be part of a larger change in Communist war strategy. However, they remained uncertain what the direction of change would be, the more so after the North Vietnamese foreign minister's announcement on 31 December. If a consensus existed, it was that the enemy, realizing his position was deteriorating, would try a last-ditch offensive before moving to the conference table. Epitomizing this view and echoing the conclusions of an assessment earlier in the month by the CIA Saigon station, General Westmoreland, on 20 December, told General Wheeler:

The enemy has already made a crucial decision concerning the conduct of the war. . . . The enemy decided that prolongation of his past policies for conducting the war would lead to his defeat, and that he would have to make a major effort to reverse the downward trend. . . . His decision therefore was to undertake an intensified countrywide effort, perhaps a maximum effort, over a relatively short period. . . . If the enemy is successful in winning a significant military victory somewhere in SVN [South Vietnam], or gaining even an apparent position of strength, he may seek to initiate negotiations. If, on the other hand, he fails badly, we do not believe that he will negotiate from weakness, but will continue the war at a reduced intensity. In short, I believe that the enemy has already made a

---

[20] Msg, Locke, Westmoreland, and Komer Saigon 15107 to State Dept, 5 Jan 68, Cable Chronological State Dept (Chron-State) (Jan–May 68), Deputy COMUSMACV for Civil Operations and Revolutionary Development (DepCORDS) files, CMH; Memo, Davidson for Komer, 6 Aug 67, sub: Monthly Report of Infiltration into SVN; Draft Ltr, Komer to President, 20 Aug 67, Robert M. Montague Papers. All in CMH. Msg, Westmoreland MAC 9311 to Fred Greene, 5 Oct 67, Westmoreland Message files, Oct 67, CMH. Col. Charles Morris' quotation is from his Deposition no. 2, pp. 155–57; see also Morris, Deposition (no. 1), pp. 38–39, 73–74, and (no. 2), pp. 106–11, in *Vietnam: A Documentary Collection*, cards 345, 348–49.

crucial decision to make a maximum effort. The results of this effort will determine the next move.[21]

This assessment, however, was not unanimous. Admiral Sharp, for example, declared on 26 December that he saw no "criticality in the current enemy situation which portends a final push effort." He rejected the theory that Hanoi "has misread the evidence and believes conditions are ripe for a Communist victory," insisting that the Communists' excellent intelligence network in the south must be telling them otherwise. Sharp expected the enemy in the next few months to strike some sharp blows aimed at pressuring the United States to accept a Viet Cong–dominated coalition government and acknowledged that it might be "considering further changes concerning the future conduct of the war." Nevertheless, "the likelihood of a final effort . . . sometime after Tet cannot be discounted but remains remote."[22]

The Military Assistance Command, although it acknowledged the probability of nationwide enemy attacks, expected the heaviest blow to fall in northern I Corps. Cut off from the rest of South Vietnam by the Hai Van Mountains, a spur that ran down to the sea just north of Da Nang, the area's land communications were tenuous. Its proximity to North Vietnamese bases and troop concentrations, along with the presence of Hue, the former Vietnamese imperial capital, and other important objectives, made it the logical place for the enemy to seek significant territorial gains or a major battlefield victory. Persistent North Vietnamese infantry and artillery attacks on Con Thien and other Marine positions below the Demilitarized Zone, as well as the movement of additional North Vietnamese divisions toward the area, reinforced this view. A war game of a possible enemy offensive, played at Military Assistance Command headquarters in late December and early January, confirmed that the enemy's best course of action would be to launch secondary attacks in the Central Highlands, along the central coast, and around Saigon while striking the main blow with four or five divisions in Quang Tri and Thua Thien, the two provinces of northern I Corps. Tending to confirm MACV's assessment, subsequent North Vietnamese accounts indicate that the divisions assembling along the Demilitarized Zone were intended to break through the strongpoint obstacle system and seize Hue and possibly Da Nang in conjunction with local uprisings. Although unaware of these facts at the time, MACV was preoccupied during December and January with preparations for large-scale combat in the region between the

---

[21] Msg, Westmoreland MAC 12397 to Wheeler, 20 Dec 67; see also Msg, Wheeler JCS 10897–67 to Sharp and Westmoreland, 16 Dec 67. Both in Westmoreland Message files, Dec 67, CMH. Compare to the Saigon CIA station estimate of 8 Dec 67, quoted in Ford, *CIA and Vietnam*, pp. 120–21.

[22] Msg, Sharp to Wheeler, 26 Dec 67, Westmoreland Message files, Dec 67, CMH.

Demilitarized Zone and the Hai Van Pass, which constituted the dividing line between northern and southern I Corps.[23]

Long concerned with the Communist threat to northern I Corps, General Westmoreland, in the spring of 1967, had deployed the Army brigades of Task Force OREGON (later renamed the Americal Division) to the southern part of the corps area so that III Marine Amphibious Force could shift more of its marines toward the Demilitarized Zone. The MACV commander also opened additional air and seaborne lines of communication to the endangered region. By the end of the year, the MACV staff was planning an extensive series of offensives against the enemy bases in western I Corps. Code-named YORK I through IV, these operations were to begin in March of 1968 and progressively work from south to north, cleaning out the enemy strongholds. To conduct these operations, General Westmoreland planned to transfer the 1st Cavalry Division to I Corps from its normal operating area in II Corps. As the enemy offensive threat increased, the MACV commander used the YORK plans as the basis for preparations to send the air cavalry to I Corps to help the marines counter or preempt the expected North Vietnamese assault.[24]

By the beginning of January, MACV had concluded that the climactic battle would take place at Khe Sanh. The Marine combat base and airfield, located on a plateau in northern Quang Tri Province close to the Laotian border, was the farthest western outpost of the McNamara barrier line. It obstructed a major enemy infiltration route from Laos into coastal I Corps, served as a base for Studies and Observations Group teams operating against the Ho Chi Minh Trail, and was potentially important for supporting larger attacks into Laos along Highway 9 if such ever were authorized. Surrounded by mountains and able to be supplied and reinforced only by air, Khe Sanh bore a superficial resemblance to Dien Bien Phu, where the Viet Minh had won their climactic victory over the French in 1954. Early in the new year, special intelligence, supplemented by information from prisoners and defectors, indicated that at least two North Vietnamese divisions and possibly more were converging on the base. Officials in Saigon and Washington,

---

[23] The war game is described in Davidson, *Vietnam Secrets*, pp. 104–05. Westmoreland's concern with I Corps is evident in his History Notes, 29 Nov–16 Dec 67, tab A, Westmoreland History file no. 26 (29 Nov–16 Dec 67) and 28 Dec 67–31 Jan 68, tab A–1, Westmoreland History file no. 28 (27 Dec 67–31 Jan 68). Both in CMH. Ford, "Tet 1968," pp. 152–62, 168–77, summarizes Communist accounts.

[24] Westmoreland History Notes, 28 Dec 67–31 Jan 68, tab A–1; MFR, Bryan, 7 Jan 68, sub: CIIB Meeting, 6 Jan 68, tab A–16. Both in Westmoreland History file no. 28 (27 Dec 67–1/31/68), CMH. Msgs, Westmoreland MAC 9592 and MAC 11636 to Johnson, 12 Oct 67; Westmoreland MAC 9619 to Sharp, 13 Oct 67, 3 Dec 67; Wheeler JCS 00043–68 to Westmoreland info Sharp, 2 Jan 68; Westmoreland MAC 00204 and MAC 00636 to Sharp info Wheeler, 5 Jan 68 and 14 Jan 68. All in Westmoreland Message files, Oct and Dec 67, Jan 68, CMH. Logistics and reinforcement actions are summarized conveniently in Admiral U. S. G. Sharp and General William C. Westmoreland, *Report on the War in Vietnam (as of June 1968)* (Washington, D.C.: Government Printing Office, 1969), p. 172 (hereafter cited as Sharp and Westmoreland, *Report*).

Aerial view of the base at Khe Sanh

including President Johnson, who had a relief map of Khe Sanh set up in the White House, anxiously observed developments, anticipating a desperate and possibly disastrous battle.[25]

The Marine commanders of III Marine Amphibious Force were less than enthusiastic about defending Khe Sanh, and some senior civilians in Washington suggested abandoning it as untenable. However, General Westmoreland insisted on holding the position. Khe Sanh, unlike Dien Bien Phu, was within artillery range of other friendly bases and easily reachable by airplanes and helicopters. Hence, Westmoreland was confident that he could supply the garrison by air and destroy enemy attackers with a curtain of bombs and shells. As with the other border battles, Westmoreland argued that it was better to fight the enemy in a remote, relatively unpopulated area like Khe Sanh rather than in the heavily settled coastal districts, and that a Communist attack on the

---

[25] Development of the threat is summarized in Davidson, *Vietnam at War*, pp. 554–55; Capt. Moyers S. Shore, II, USMC, *The Battle for Khe Sanh* (Washington, D.C.: Historical Branch, G–3 Division, Headquarters, U.S. Marine Corps, 1969), pp. 26–31; Sharp and Westmoreland, *Report*, p. 182; Westmoreland, *Soldier Reports*, pp. 198, 316–17. A proposed corps-size attack into Laos along Highway 9 is described in Msg, Westmoreland MAC 01382 to Sharp, 30 Jan 68, Westmoreland Message files, Jan 68, CMH.

base would offer the allies a chance to employ their overwhelming firepower with maximum effect. While the MACV commander later declared that his decision to hold Khe Sanh was a "military" one, he told General Wheeler on 12 January that, while Khe Sanh was important as a base for SOG teams and "flank security" for the strongpoint obstacle system, "it is even more critical from a psychological viewpoint. To relinquish this area would be a major propaganda victory for the enemy. It[s] loss would seriously affect Vietnamese and US morale." Eleven days later, he maintained "unreservedly" that Khe Sanh was "of significance: strategic, tactical, and most importantly, psychological."[26]

During January, the Military Assistance Command mustered its forces for the expected decisive battle. At MACV's direction, III Marine Amphibious Force reinforced the two Marine battalions already at Khe Sanh with two additional ones. MACV temporarily placed the SOG teams operating from the base under III Marine Amphibious Force's control. The South Vietnamese, at Westmoreland's urging, added a South Vietnamese Ranger battalion to establish its presence in the expected climactic battle. Additional American and allied troops massed in northern I Corps. In mid-January, Westmoreland, implementing his earlier contingency plan, ordered the headquarters and two brigades of the 1st Cavalry Division to deploy to the Hue–Phu Bai area; later he rounded out the division with a brigade of the 101st Airborne Division transferred from II Field Force. At the same time, the South Korean Marine brigade shifted northward in I Corps, allowing III Marine Amphibious Force to place part of the 1st Marine Division north of the Hai Van Pass. The South Vietnamese Joint General Staff, pressed by Westmoreland, dispatched two South Vietnamese airborne battalions to Hue to augment a two-battalion task force already there. By the end of January, MACV had concentrated more than 50 percent of all its American combat battalions in I Corps.[27]

In the small hours of 21 January, the North Vietnamese opened their long-awaited attack on Khe Sanh with a fierce but unsuccessful ground assault on a Marine outpost on one of the nearby hilltops north of the base, followed by an artillery and mortar bombardment

---

[26] Quotations are from Msgs, Westmoreland MAC 00547 to Wheeler, 12 Jan 68, tab 23, Westmoreland History file no. 28 (27 Dec–31 Jan 68), and Westmoreland MAC 0160 to Sharp info Wheeler, 23 Jan 68, Westmoreland Message files, Jan 68. Both in CMH. In latter file, see also Msgs, Wheeler JCS 00343–68 to Westmoreland info Sharp, 11 Jan 68; and Sharp to Wheeler, 14 Jan 68. Typical retrospective rationalizations for holding Khe Sanh are in Sharp and Westmoreland, *Report*, pp. 162–63; Westmoreland, *Soldier Reports*, pp. 335–38; and Shore, *Khe Sanh*, pp. vi–viii. III Marine Amphibious Force reluctance to commit itself to holding the position is recalled in Chaisson, Oral History, pp. 370–73, MCHC.

[27] Reinforcement decisions can be followed in tab A–8, Westmoreland History file no. 27 (19–26 Dec 67), and tabs A–1, 23, 26, 28, 32, and 71, Westmoreland History file no, 28 (27 Dec 67–31 Jan 68), CMH; Chaisson, Oral History, pp. 215–16; Sharp and Westmoreland, *Report*, pp. 160, 163–64, 182. Studies and Observations Group control is mentioned in Chaisson Diary, 5 Dec 67–13 Feb 68, box 9, Chaisson Papers, Hoover Institution.

that blew up the marines' ammunition dump. In response, MACV ordered the Seventh Air Force to initiate Operation NIAGRA, a previously planned round-the-clock campaign of B–52 and tactical air strikes and artillery bombardment targeted by an intensive reconnaissance effort, which included the use of advanced sensors originally procured for the anti-infiltration barrier. A special ad hoc group in MACV headquarters selected targets for the B–52 missions. General Westmoreland closely supervised the conduct of the NIAGRA campaign, occasionally specifying particular targets for bombing and reconnaissance. MACV and III Marine Amphibious Force began an equally large-scale aerial resupply effort for the base, using both helicopters and fixed-wing aircraft. To handle casualties, MACV prepared to open an Army surgical hospital in northern I Corps while two Navy hospital ships took position offshore. General Westmoreland secured permission from Admiral Sharp to continue bombing targets in Laos during the Tet cease-fire. The MACV staff began planning an amphibious feint against the southern Democratic Republic of Vietnam to divert enemy reinforcements from Khe Sanh.[28]

Preoccupied, as was the rest of the U.S. government, with the analogy between Khe Sanh and Dien Bien Phu, the MACV commander put his staff historian to work on a study of the earlier battle aimed at demonstrating its differences from the impending one. When the historian delivered a rather pessimistic initial report, Westmoreland emphatically told his staff, "We are not, repeat not, going to be defeated at Khe Sanh" and "strode deliberately from the room."[29]

Such expressions of confidence notwithstanding, General Westmoreland attempted to prepare his superiors, and his own command, for the worst. On 23 January, he warned General Wheeler that there were "problem areas to be overcome or circumvented" in the coming battle and that many aspects of the engagement would require "an additional element of interpretation" to prevent the press and public from developing "erroneous and misleading assessments of our battlefield posture." He urged that the administration take precautions so that "a withdrawal from the Khe Sanh salient or an initial setback" would not precipitate "an erosion of our military and civilian determination" to achieve America's objectives in South Vietnam.[30]

---

[28] The opening battles are recounted in Shore, *Khe Sanh*, pp. 33–45; Davidson, *Vietnam at War*, pp. 558–59; John Schlight, *The War in South Vietnam: The Years of the Offensive, 1965–1968* (Washington, D.C.: Office of Air Force History, United States Air Force, 1988), pp. 277–85; Bernard C. Nalty, *Air Power and the Fight for Khe Sanh* (Washington, D.C.: Office of Air Force History, United States Air Force, 1973), passim. See also Westmoreland Message files, Jan 68; and Westmoreland History file no. 28 (Dec 27 67–Jan 31 68), especially tabs 32, 49, and 73. Both in CMH. Jones, *War Without Windows*, pp. 161–68, describes work of the Khe Sanh targeting group.

[29] Westmoreland, *Soldier Reports*, pp. 337–38, describes the historical report and his reaction to it. See also tab 49, Westmoreland History file no. 28 (Dec 27–Jan 31 68), CMH.

[30] Msg, Westmoreland MAC 0160 to Sharp info Wheeler, 23 Jan 68, Westmoreland Message files, Jan 68; MFR, Bryan, 20 Jan 68, sub: CIIB Meeting, 20 Jan 68, tab 32, Westmoreland History file no. 28 (27 Dec 67–31 Jan 68). Both in CMH.

Even more ominous, on the twenty-fourth, Westmoreland cabled to Admiral Sharp a recommendation that the Commander in Chief, Pacific (CINCPAC), and MACV begin contingency planning for the use of tactical nuclear weapons in northern Quang Tri if necessary to prevent a major defeat. He noted that in the uninhabited mountains around Khe Sanh, such weapons could be used with great effect and with "negligible" civilian casualties. Sharp on the thirtieth accepted Westmoreland's proposal and ordered planners from MACV and CINCPAC's component commands to meet on Okinawa on 1 February. Assigning the project the code-name FRACTURE JAW, Sharp enjoined all concerned to "bear in mind the very sensitive nature" of the planning and to restrict knowledge of it to as few people as possible on an "absolutely essential need to know basis." Even before Sharp's action, Westmoreland had put a small MACV staff group to work on a detailed concept for the operation.[31]

Command Problems in I Corps

The impending crisis in I Corps brought to a head festering disagreements between the Military Assistance Command and the III Marine Amphibious Force over command arrangements. It also sharpened the doubts of General Westmoreland and the Army-dominated MACV staff about the ability of the III Marine Amphibious Force headquarters to direct the increasingly large and complex multiservice campaign that was developing. General Westmoreland in response set in motion changes in both air and ground command in I Corps, which plunged MACV into a new round of political and doctrinal conflict with the marines.

During the planning for Operation NIAGRA, General William W. Momyer, the Seventh Air Force commander and Westmoreland's deputy COMUSMACV for air, seized the opportunity to renew his service's campaign for operational control of the marines' fixed-wing tactical aircraft. Momyer was a strong proponent of his service's doctrine that airpower in a theater of operations should be under the central direction of the theater deputy commander for air. Hence, he considered the arrangement that CINCPAC had established early in 1965, under which III Marine Amphibious Force retained command of its aircraft wing and had first call on use of its planes, to be wrong in principle and unsatisfactory in practice. The problem worsened as Army divisions entered I Corps and fighting intensified along the Demilitarized Zone. With MACV mediating, the Seventh Air Force and III Marine Amphibious Force improvised working arrangements to coordinate

---

[31] Msgs, Westmoreland to Sharp, MAC 01164, MAC 01369, MAC 01439, 24 Jan 68, 29 Jan 68, and 30 Jan 68; Sharp to Westmoreland, Ryan, Beach, Hyland, and Krulak, 30 Jan 68 (quotation is from this message); Sharp to Westmoreland, 30 Jan 68; Westmoreland Message files, Jan 68. All in CMH.

41

their operations; but Momyer considered these a poor substitute for central direction of all fixed-wing air activity by himself as deputy COMUSMACV for air. The air campaign in support of Khe Sanh would require the most precise coordination of B–52 and tactical air strikes, as well as helicopter missions and artillery fire, in a restricted area—coordination, Momyer insisted, that could be achieved only by placing the marines' jet fighters and bombers under the control of the Seventh Air Force. Articulate, forceful, and persistent, Momyer pressed his case upon Westmoreland.[32]

On 17 January, Westmoreland opened the doctrinal battle. He informed Lt. Gen. Robert E. Cushman, the III Marine Amphibious Force commander, that in view of "the increased deployment of Army forces into I Corps, impending battles and the need for having more operational flexibility of the air effort," he was "contemplating placing operational control of the I [sic] Marine Air Wing under my Deputy for Air." Westmoreland reassured Cushman that III Marine Amphibious Force would retain operational control of its helicopters. He also declared that the proposed new arrangement was a "temporary measure to meet the current situation." The MACV commander sent a similarly worded message to Admiral Sharp. Emphasizing that the "impending major battle" made necessary "an immediate change in the control of tactical air in I CTZ [Corps Tactical Zone]," he insisted that it was "no longer feasible nor prudent to restrict the employment of the total tactical air resources to given areas." "I feel the utmost need," he said, "for a more flexible posture to shift my air effort where it can best be used in the coming battles."[33]

The tentative wording of Westmoreland's message to Cushman suggests that it might have been a trial balloon, designed to test reaction of III Marine Amphibious Force and other interested commands. If so, the balloon quickly drew a volley of arrows. On the eighteenth, General Momyer discussed the plan with Cushman and his staff but failed to win their agreement to the change. General Cushman the same day denounced the plan as "doctrinally and functionally" unsuited to his requirements. He protested to Westmoreland that the proposal amounted to "replacing my aviation commander and control over his

[32] Earlier air command controversies are recounted in Cosmas, *Years of Escalation, 1962–1967*, chs. 3 and 8. Air command arrangements in effect through late 1967 are contained in MACV Directive no. 95–4, 13 Jul 65, copy in MCHC Archives. See also Chaisson, Oral History, pp. 229–30, 235–37, MCHC; Ltrs, Chaisson to Mrs Chaisson, 17 Oct 67 and 14 Nov 67, box 7, John R. Chaisson Papers, Hoover Institution; Nalty, *Fight for Khe Sanh*, pp. 68–80; Schlight, *Years of the Offensive*, pp. 108–09, 203–05, 262–64, 269–70; William W. Momyer, *Airpower in Three Wars* (Washington, D.C.: Department of the Air Force, 1978), pp. 284–87.

[33] Quotations are from Msgs, Westmoreland MAC 00791 to Cushman, 17 Jan 68; and Westmoreland MAC 00797 to Sharp info Wheeler, Gen John Paul McConnell, Air Force Chief of Staff, Gen Leonard F. Chapman Jr., Commandant of the Marine Corps, and Lt Gen Victor H. Krulak, 18 Jan 68; Westmoreland Message files, Jan 68, CMH; Westmoreland History Notes, 28 Dec 67–31 Jan 68, tab A–1, Westmoreland History file no. 28 (27 Dec 67–31 Jan 68), CMH; MACV History, 1968, vol. 1, p. 436.

assets with one who is not directly under my command; yet my overall responsibilities in I CTZ remain the same." "I am unalterably opposed to any change [in air command]," Cushman concluded, "and to any fractionalization of the Marine air/ground team."[34]

If General Cushman punctured the trial balloon, Admiral Sharp blew it out of the sky. Responding quickly to Westmoreland's overture, Sharp made evident his extreme reluctance to change the rules he had established in 1965. Those rules, he declared, "conform to doctrine and to the accepted principles of command." Any alteration of them "must be viewed in the broadest context if we are not to create more problems than we seek to remedy." In particular, any proposal to "divest CG, III Marine Amphibious Force of operational control of his own assets" would require "full consideration of all aspects of the problem"—consideration that would be done by Admiral Sharp, not General Westmoreland. "I will make any decision necessary," Sharp told his subordinate. The admiral explained later: "I sent that message to be sure that [Westmoreland] didn't take things in his own hands and do something which I considered mine to do exclusively."[35]

Heeding Sharp's warning, Westmoreland and Momyer settled for another compromise ad hoc command arrangement for Operation NIAGRA. On 21 January, after further discussions with Cushman and his staff, Westmoreland directed Momyer, as his deputy for air operations, to develop a plan "to concentrate all available air resources" in the Khe Sanh battle area and to "coordinate and direct" the actions of Air Force, Navy, and Marine tactical aircraft and B–52s in defense of the base. However, he also declared that "the direct support of Marine units by the 1st Marine Air Wing is not affected by this plan." Reestablishing existing arrangements, Westmoreland required III Marine Amphibious Force to place at Seventh Air Force disposal only those Marine sorties not required for support of the Marine divisions. He also made the Seventh Air Force responsible for battlefield support of the 1st Cavalry and American Divisions as well as the South Vietnamese army units in I Corps.[36]

This directive received immediate endorsement from Admiral Sharp, though only after searching review by the CINCPAC staff. Implementing it, the Air Force and marines divided the Khe Sanh area into zones. The Marine air control agency inside the base controlled all strikes (made mostly by Marine aircraft) in the zones closest to the position while the Seventh Air Force, through an airborne command and control center, directed operations in the outer zones. The 1st Marine Aircraft Wing

---

[34] Cushman message is quoted in MACV History, 1968, vol. 1, pp. 436–37.

[35] Msg, Sharp to Westmoreland info Wheeler, McConnell, Chapman, and Krulak, 18 Jan 68, Westmoreland Message files, Jan 68, CMH. Final quotation is from Adm U. S. Grant Sharp, "Reminiscences of Adm U. S. Grant Sharp, USN (Ret)," 2 vols., Program, Transcript of Interviews by Cdr Etta Belle Kitchen, USN (Ret), for Oral History Program, U.S. Naval Institute, 20 Sep 69–7 Jun 70, pp. 641–42 (hereafter cited as Sharp, "Reminiscences"); see also pp. 643–46.

[36] Msgs, Westmoreland MAC 00992 and MAC 00994 to Sharp info Wheeler, 21 Jan 68, Westmoreland Message files, Jan 68, CMH. Quotations are from latter message.

reinforced its command and control facilities in northern I Corps and established liaison with the Seventh Air Force's NIAGRA targeting element at Tan Son Nhut. Under this arrangement, Operation NIAGRA proceeded without major mishaps. The marines were thoroughly satisfied with the system. General Momyer, however, considered it cumbersome and at best marginally satisfactory. He continued his campaign for full operational control of the marines' aircraft.[37]

Even as the NIAGRA command arrangement went into effect, a misunderstanding between Generals Westmoreland and Cushman over support of the 1st Cavalry Division helped keep the air control issue alive. During a visit to III Marine Amphibious Force on 19 January, the MACV commander directed Cushman to make sure that the Army division, which was taking position near Hue between the two Marine divisions, received adequate support from the 1st Marine Aircraft Wing. This instruction was in conflict with existing practice, which Westmoreland reaffirmed in his 21 January NIAGRA directive, under which the Seventh Air Force had primary responsibility for supporting the Army units in I Corps. The Marine wing was slow to tie the 1st Cavalry Division into its strike request and control network, because the cavalry lacked the necessary communications equipment and III Marine Amphibious Force had to assemble an outfit for it from its own resources. In the interim, on the twenty-third, Westmoreland visited the 1st Cavalry Division command post and heard reports of difficulty in obtaining missions from the Marine wing. Westmoreland, as he later recalled, "raised hell about this situation" with III Marine Amphibious Force. The marines in response accelerated their effort to establish communications with the division, which soon was receiving adequate air support. This incident appears to have contributed to Westmoreland's growing dissatisfaction with the air control situation in I Corps, ensuring that the MACV commander would remain receptive to persistent Air Force arguments for change.[38]

By the time of the 1st Cavalry Division incident, General Westmoreland was preparing to alter much more than air command relations in I Corps. He had concluded that he could not rely on III Marine Amphibious Force headquarters to fight the big battle that he expected. This decision was the

[37] Msgs, Sharp to Westmoreland, 21 Jan 68; Cushman to Westmoreland, 21 Jan 68; Westmoreland Message files, Jan 68, CMH; Sharp, "Reminiscences," p. 645. Schlight, *Years of the Offensive*, pp. 276–86, reflects the Air Force view of the arrangement. For Marine views, see MFR, Maj Gen Norman J. Anderson, USMC, 29 Jan 68, Anderson Papers, MCHC; Ltrs, Gen Keith B. McCutcheon, Deputy CofS (Air), Headquarters, Marine Corps, to Anderson, 23 Jan 68, and Anderson to McCutcheon, 7 Feb 68; box 20, Keith B. McCutcheon Papers, MCHC.

[38] Westmoreland's story of the 1st Cavalry Division incident is in his History Notes, 28 Dec 67–31 Jan 68, tab A–1, Westmoreland History file no. 28 (27 Dec 67–31 Jan 68), CMH. The III Marine Amphibious Force (III MAF)/1st Marine Aircraft Wing version is in Ltr, Anderson to Brig Gen Edwin Simmons (Ret) Director, Marine Corps History and Museums, 8 Sep 83, Anderson Papers, MCHC; and Interv, MCHC with Maj Gen Norman J. Anderson, USMC, 17 Mar 81, pp. 192–95 (hereafter cited as Anderson Interv). Westmoreland indicates his continued commitment to single management in Msg MAC 01326 to Krulak, info Wheeler, McConnell, Chapman, and Sharp, 28 Jan 68, Westmoreland Message files, Jan 68, CMH.

product of a long accumulation of disputes and irritants between MACV and the Marine command. Besides perennial Army-Marine professional rivalry, disagreements over the proper balance between offensive warfare and pacification, arguments over the McNamara barrier (work on which continued until 20 January when Westmoreland and Cushman stopped it pending the outcome of the Khe Sanh battle), and III Marine Amphibious Force's lack of enthusiasm for fighting at Khe Sanh contributed to contentious relations between the two headquarters and between MACV and the Marine Corps. General Westmoreland's relations with General Cushman were less than ideal. The two men differed in temperament and command style; Westmoreland considered Cushman sluggish and lacking in initiative in his response to the crisis facing III Marine Amphibious Force, a view shared privately by some marines.[39]

Over and above these specifics, Westmoreland had concluded that the marines were deficient in the general quality of their leadership, staff work, and tactical performance. These doubts came to a head on 20 January, when General Davidson, the MACV J–2, returned from a liaison visit to Khe Sanh. Davidson reported that the marines had neglected to dig in vital facilities, including their ammunition dump, which was destroyed in the first bombardment, and that the base commander, in the face of voluminous intelligence from both MACV and III Marine Amphibious Force, still did not believe there were two North Vietnamese divisions outside his perimeter. Two days later, Westmoreland informed General Wheeler that "the military professionalism of the Marines falls far short of the standards that should be demanded by our armed forces. . . . Their standards, tactics, and lack of command supervision throughout their ranks requires improvement in the national interest." As would be expected, the marines then and later disputed Westmoreland's aspersions. They pointed out that they trained and fought under the same tactical manuals as the Army and that most major troop dispositions and operations in I Corps, including the building of the barrier and the defense of Khe Sanh, in fact, were directed by COMUSMACV. Whatever the rights and wrongs of the issue, General Westmoreland approached the prospective critical battle in the north with severely diminished confidence in III Marine Amphibious Force and a "somewhat insecure" feeling about "the situation in Quang Tri Province."[40]

---

[39] Disagreements between MACV and III Marine Amphibious Force are summarized in Jack Shulimson, Lt. Col. Leonard A. Blasiol, USMC, Charles R. Smith, and Capt. David A. Dawson, USMC, *Marines in Vietnam: The Defining Year, 1968* (Washington, D.C.: History and Museums Division, Headquarters, U.S. Marine Corps, 1997), pp. 12–31. For a Marine expression of dissatisfaction with Cushman, see Ltr, Chaisson to Mrs Chaisson, 8 Feb 68, box 7, Chaisson Papers, Hoover Institution. In same collection and box, see Ltr, Chaisson to Mrs Chaisson, 30 Nov 67.

[40] Davidson, *Vietnam at War*, pp. 554–56, describes his visit to Khe Sanh and Westmoreland's reaction to his report. Quotations are from Msg, Westmoreland MAC 01011 to Wheeler [no info to Sharp], 22 Jan 68, Westmoreland Message files, Jan 68, CMH. In same files, see Msg, Wheeler WDC 1065 to Westmoreland, 22 Jan 68. From its number, Wheeler sent the latter message through Army rather than JCS channels. Cushman defends his and the marines' performance in Interv, MCHC with General Robert E. Cushman, 13 Sep 73, pp. 33–34 (hereafter cited as Cushman Interv); Chaisson Diary, 26 Jan

Even without the tensions between MACV and III Marine Amphibious Force, command rearrangements for the U.S. forces in I Corps were overdue. The war in the five northern provinces had grown large and complex. During 1967, I Corps accounted for nearly half of all the allied and enemy killed in action in South Vietnam; by early 1968, MACV had committed half of its American ground combat power there. With two Army divisions under its operational control, III Marine Amphibious Force was evolving from a simple Marine air-ground team into what amounted to a field army, all the time retaining responsibility for advice and support of the South Vietnamese I Corps and for pacification. It had to direct two different campaigns at the same time: a conventional infantry and artillery battle from fixed positions in northern I Corps and an intensive mixed large-unit and guerrilla struggle in the southern part of the corps area. To cope with its enlarged tasks, the Marine headquarters made some organizational modifications early in 1968. It acquired from MACV an Army brigadier general to serve as assistant to General Cushman on matters affecting that service and secured a second assistant commander for each of its Marine divisions. The 1st Marine Aircraft Wing also added an assistant commander and enlarged its command and control facilities north of the Hai Van Pass. It was clear, however, that larger changes were needed, in particular the creation of an intermediate headquarters through which III Marine Amphibious Force could control its northern theater of battle.[41]

General Westmoreland had something even more drastic in mind. After Davidson's report of 20 January, the MACV commander decided to send his deputy, General Abrams, to oversee operations in northern I Corps and if necessary take overall tactical command away from General Cushman. Westmoreland explained this action as necessary to strengthen III Marine Amphibious Force's capacity to control its forces. However, his dispatch of the four-star Abrams, who outranked Cushman, instead of a lieutenant general junior to the marine, indicated COMUSMACV's loss of confidence in the III Marine Amphibious Force commander. Abrams at this time concurred in Westmoreland's dim view of Marine professionalism. He told General Wheeler early in January: "While the Marines are second to none in bravery, esprit and the intrinsic quality of their men, I consider them less . . . qualified in

68, box 9, Chaisson Papers, Hoover Institution, confirms Westmoreland's worries about the marines and their commanders.

[41] Davidson, *Vietnam at War*, pp. 556–57; Chaisson, Oral History, pp. 268–69; Westmoreland, *Soldier Reports*, p. 315. Westmoreland History Notes, 28 Dec 67–31 Jan 68, tab A–1, CMH; MFR, Bryan, 14 Jan 68, sub: CIIB Meeting, 13 Jan 68, tab 24; Westmoreland History file no. 28 (27 Dec 67–31 Jan 68). Both in CMH; Interv, Lt Col Douglas R. Burgess with Gen Bruce Palmer, Jr, 1975, pp. 264–65, Senior Officers Oral History Program, MHI (hereafter cited as Palmer Interv); Shulimson et al., *Marines in Vietnam, 1968*, pp. 235–37; Msgs, Westmoreland MAC 01166 to Chapman, 24 Jan 68; Cushman to Westmoreland, 25 Jan 68; Westmoreland MAC 01300 to Cushman, 27 Jan 68. All in Westmoreland Message files, Jan 68, CMH.

the techniques and tactics of fighting than the U.S. Army, the Korean Army, and the Australians."[42]

On 25 January, General Westmoreland informed Admiral Sharp that he was considering establishing a "provisional field army (tactical)" in the Hue–Phu Bai area under Abrams' command. Abrams was to exercise operational control over "all US ground elements in I CTZ (including those of III Marine Amphibious Force)" with "primary emphasis" on those north of the Hai Van Pass, as well as "maneuver authority" over the South Vietnamese units in the area. The following day, Westmoreland significantly amended this plan. He renamed the new headquarters MACV Forward, in order, he said, "to accommodate the sensitivities of the Vietnamese and hopefully to avoid possible press efforts to portray this action in an unfavorable light." After a conference with General Cao Van Vien, chief of the Joint General Staff, Westmoreland dropped mention of "maneuver authority" over the South Vietnamese Army and indicated merely that the I Corps commander, Lt. Gen. Hoang Xuan Lam, would work with Abrams as a counterpart and Vien's representative. Concerning Abrams' own authority, Westmoreland said nothing specific. He declared only that "this action will start the wheels moving toward attainment of a capability which will hopefully provide the essential control mechanism and give me flexibility to cope with the exigencies of the situation."[43]

Westmoreland's imprecision concerning Abrams' exact authority may have resulted from continuing arguments over that issue within MACV headquarters and between MACV and III Marine Amphibious Force. General Cushman and his subordinates, although they perforce acquiesced in the creation of MACV Forward, suspected and resented the motives behind it. Maj. Gen. Rathvon McC. Tompkins, whose 3d Marine Division was in overall command of the defense of Khe Sanh, later declared of the establishment of MACV Forward: "I thought it was the most unpardonable thing that Saigon did" in that it was "tantamount to . . . a relief of a commander." Within MACV headquarters, Brig. Gen. John R. Chaisson, the Marine chief of the Combat Operations Center and a trusted adviser to General Westmoreland, campaigned strenuously against any action that could be construed as superseding Cushman. "I fought like mad . . . for two days," Chaisson recalled. At one point, he warned that if Westmoreland took tactical command away from the marines at the outset of the war's biggest

---

[42] Westmoreland gives conventional explanations of this decision in *Soldier Reports*, p. 315; and History Notes, 28 Dec 67–31 Jan 68, tab A–1, Westmoreland History file no. 28 (27 Dec 67–Jan 31 68), CMH. Davidson, *Vietnam at War*, p. 557, believes Westmoreland intended to supersede Cushman. Abrams' view of the marines is quoted in Lewis Sorley, *Thunderbolt: General Creighton Abrams and the Army of His Times* (New York: Simon and Schuster, 1992), pp. 208–09.

[43] Msgs, Westmoreland MAC 01215 to Sharp info Wheeler, 25 Jan 68; and MAC 01233 to Sharp, 26 Jan 68. Both in Westmoreland Message files, Jan 68, CMH. Westmoreland History Notes, 28 Dec 67–31 Jan 68, tab A–1; MFR, Bryan, 27 Jan 68, sub: CIIB Meeting, 27 Jan 68, tab 49. Both in Westmoreland History file no. 28 (27 Dec 67–31 Jan 68), CMH.

battle, "he could never again . . . expect the real loyalty of any Marine field commanders in the country." Chaisson and other opponents of the field army concept secured Westmoreland's tentative agreement that, while Abrams would oversee the conduct of the battle, he would leave Cushman in immediate charge and transmit orders to the Marine and Army divisions through III Marine Amphibious Force. The issue, however, was not fully settled. Chaisson wrote on the twenty-eighth: "This isn't over yet and may hit the papers."[44]

Despite the uncertainty over its terms of reference, work on setting up MACV Forward began at once. General Abrams visited III Marine Amphibious Force on the twenty-sixth and secured the marines' less-than-enthusiastic agreement to creation of the new headquarters. Logistic preparations began for housing the staff, expected to include 366 officers from all services, at Phu Bai, an American base just south of Hue, and for installing communications and other facilities. The headquarters was to go into operation around 5 February.[45]

Final Preliminaries

While MACV's attention remained fixed on northern I Corps during January, the command also received additional indications of a wider enemy threat to cities and coastal areas elsewhere. U.S. and South Vietnamese troops uncovered caches of new Communist-bloc weapons in the Mekong Delta and the environs of Saigon. Captured documents spoke of infiltration of enemy personnel into the capital and referred to the need to prepare the people for an imminent general uprising. Another document described a reorganization of the enemy territorial commands around Saigon into a pie-slice configuration radiating outward from the city, as if to facilitate a converging assault. A pattern developed of small enemy attacks on South Vietnamese police stations, prisons, and *Chieu Hoi* centers,[46] as well as American air bases. Nevertheless, most evidence, including signal intelligence, continued to point to the main effort coming in the northern two corps areas; and most MACV officers remained skeptical of the indications of a major attack on the cities. The II Field Force staff, for example, doubted the timeliness and authenticity of the captured Saigon-area command reorganization order, which contained outdated information on the

---

[44] Tompkins is quoted in Shulimson et al., *Marines in Vietnam, 1968*, p. 238. First Chaisson quotation is from his Oral History, pp. 230–34; second is from Ltr, Chaisson to Mrs Chaisson, 28 Jan 68, box 7, Chaisson Papers, Hoover Institution. In same collection, box 9, see Chaisson Diary, 27–28 Jan 68.

[45] Msg, Westmoreland MAC 01264 to Sharp info Wheeler, 26 Jan 68, Westmoreland Message files, Jan 68, CMH. HQ 3d Marine Div Handwritten Memo, 27 Jan 68, sub: Meeting . . . concerning MACV (Fwd) . . . , encl 123, 3d Marine Div Msgs, Jan 68, MCHC.

[46] These were facilities that screened and housed defectors from the Viet Cong, known as *Hoi Chanhs*, under the Saigon government's *Chieu Hoi* ("Open Arms") amnesty program for people who voluntarily left the revolutionary movement.

local terrain. Still, the indications were sufficient to induce General Westmoreland to warn General Wheeler and Admiral Sharp on 20 January: "The enemy is presently developing a threatening posture in several areas in order to seek victories essential to achieving prestige and bargaining power. He may exercise his initiatives prior to, during or after Tet."[47]

As General Westmoreland indicated, the allies remained uncertain of the timing of the expected offensive. The intelligence community became increasingly convinced that the enemy's "D-day" was set for the Tet period, but few analysts picked the holiday itself as the time. Most doubted that the Communists would risk alienating the people by making war during the most sacred of Vietnamese festivals, noting that the enemy in the past had used the Tet cease-fires for redeployment and resupply, not for widespread attacks. Americans and South Vietnamese alike seemed unaware that the Vietnamese several times before in their history had launched surprise assaults on their enemies during Tet. General Westmoreland believed that the enemy most likely would strike before the holiday, and then try to exploit the cease-fire to regroup for a second effort. His intelligence chief, General Davidson, on the other hand, expected the enemy to maneuver during the truce and attack after Tet. "Neither of us," the MACV commander later acknowledged, "saw a high probability of an attack on the day of Tet, so harsh and disaffecting would be the psychological impact on the very people the enemy was trying to rally to his side."[48]

Impressed by indications that the enemy was moving toward Saigon, MACV and II Field Force repositioned American troops the better to protect the capital. The initiative came from Lt. Gen. Frederick Weyand, the field force commander. Weyand's force, at MACV's direction, had been preparing for an offensive against War Zone D and other North Vietnamese base areas near the Cambodian border. On 9 January, Weyand telephoned General Westmoreland and requested a meeting, which took place at MACV headquarters the next day. Weyand reviewed for Westmoreland recent intelligence, drawn mainly from II Field Force analysis of enemy radio traffic, which indicated that

[47] Quotation is from Msg, Westmoreland MAC 00943 to Wheeler and Sharp, 20 Jan 68; see also Westmoreland MAC 00275 to Wheeler and Sharp, 7 Jan 68; and Sharp to Wheeler info Westmoreland, 20 Jan 68. All in Westmoreland Message files, Jan 68, CMH. Wirtz, *Tet Offensive*, pp. 181, 183, 191–94, 201–03, 210; Jones, *War Without Windows*, pp. 134, 158–60; U.S. District Court, *Westmoreland Memorandum of Law, app. B*, p. 119; Sharp and Westmoreland, *Report*, pp. 157–58; CIA Paper, The Intelligence Background of the Current Communist Offensive, 15 Feb 68, copy in CMH. II Field Force doubts about the Saigon command reorganization are noted in MFR, Graham A. Cosmas, 6 May 92, sub: Telephone Interv of Col James R. Paschall, 6 May 92, CMH (hereafter cited as Paschall Interv).

[48] Wirtz, *Tet Offensive*, pp. 106–11; Westmoreland History Notes, 28 Dec 67–31 Jan 68, tab A–1, Westmoreland History file no. 28 (27 Dec 67–31 Jan 68), CMH. Oberdorfer, *Tet!* pp. 71–72, reviews Vietnamese historical precedents, noting that Westmoreland had a statue of the victorious commander of one such Tet attack in his living quarters. Quotation is from Westmoreland, *Soldier Reports*, p. 318; see also pp. 317, 319.

General Weyand

Communist main force units in III Corps were moving inward from their border sanctuaries toward Saigon. He requested permission to reposition American units to repel possible attacks on "province and district population centers." Westmoreland, who claimed later that he also had been studying the same information and considering a change in plans, decided to cancel the projected border-area offensive. Instead, he permitted II Field Force to pull its troops in closer to the capital, which the field force did gradually in the course of several operations.

While Weyand's action in retrospect seemed prescient, it may have reflected as much the field force commander's general preference for population protection over offensives in remote areas as any expectation of a major attack on Saigon. Weyand's staff, as noted, discounted heavily the document on the enemy's capital-area command reorganization; and the field force commander himself doubted that Saigon itself would be attacked. At any event, as a result of these decisions, by the end of January, 27 U.S. maneuver battalions were operating within 30 kilometers and easy helicopter lift of the capital, twice the number that would have been there if MACV had followed its original plan. The South Vietnamese also adjusted their deployments so that by the time of Tet, more than half the allied maneuver battalions in III Corps and most of the territorial forces were defending the approaches to Saigon or operating along the infiltration corridors that connected the capital to the enemy's war zones.[49]

As evidence accumulated of an imminent Communist offensive, General Westmoreland revived his effort to cancel the Tet cease-fire.

---

[49] II Field Force Vietnam (II FFV) Tet Offensive After Action Report (AAR), 31 Jan–18 Feb 68, pp. 1–5; II FFV Press Briefing on VC Tet Offensive, 20 Mar 68. Both in CMH. Westmoreland History Notes, 28 Dec 67–31 Jan 68, tab A–1, Westmoreland History file no. 28 (27 Dec 67–31 Jan 68), CMH. MACV History, 1968, vol. 2, pp. 893–94, and Ford, *CIA and Vietnam*, p. 115, detail the intelligence indications behind General Weyand's recommendation. Sharp and Westmoreland, *Report*, pp. 157–58. For questions as to how much foresight Weyand actually had, see Graham Interv, 24 May 82, sess. 1, and 3 Nov 82, sess. 2, pp. 7–9; and Davidson Interv, 30 Mar and 30 Jun 82, sess. 1, p. 48; Paschall Interv, 6 May 92.

The enemy had committed dozens of violations of the New Year's truce, which the allies had extended by 12 hours at the request of the pope. Citing this fact, as well as the need to deny the enemy any opportunity for unmolested attack preparations, Westmoreland in mid-January urged General Vien and President Nguyen Van Thieu to join him in recommending cancellation of the Tet cease-fire. The Vietnamese insisted that "tradition and morale considerations" compelled them to give their troops a "respite" at Tet, but did agree to shorten the cease-fire period from 48 to 36 hours. Westmoreland, with the concurrence of Ambassador Bunker and Admiral Sharp, transmitted this proposal to Washington. It met initial resistance from Secretaries Rusk and McNamara and other officials, who expressed concern that a change in the allies' Tet plans might disrupt diplomatic exploration of the new North Vietnamese statement on bombing and negotiations. However, after the opening North Vietnamese bombardment of Khe Sanh on the twenty-first, the administration accepted the 36-hour proposal.[50]

Further truncation of the cease-fire quickly followed. On the twenty-fourth, Westmoreland and Bunker jointly recommended to the State and Defense Departments cancellation of the truce in I Corps and the lower portion of North Vietnam, on grounds that a pause of even 36 hours would give the enemy "advantages which we can not afford." The administration promptly agreed, as did President Thieu when Bunker and Westmoreland presented the proposal to him. The allies decided, however, to delay announcement of the cancellation until noon on the twenty-ninth, the day their cease-fire was to go into effect, so as to deny the other side any opportunity to react. On the twenty-eighth, Westmoreland informed his field commanders that "normal military operations" in I Corps and the Demilitarized Zone, as well as air attacks on enemy troops and lines of communication in southern North Vietnam, were to continue throughout the truce, which would be in effect in the rest of South Vietnam from 1800 on the twenty-ninth through 0600 on the thirty-first. Earlier, MACV had initiated Operation HOBBY HORSE, its own effort to take advantage of the truce. Under this plan, all American commanders were to use their reconnaissance and intelligence resources to locate enemy units and base areas and be ready for immediate attacks as soon as the cease-fire expired.[51]

---

[50] Msgs, Westmoreland to Sharp, 29 Dec 67; MAC 00338 to Sharp info Wheeler, 9 Jan 68; MAC 00943 to Wheeler and Sharp, 20 Jan 68; Sharp to Westmoreland info Wheeler, 9 Jan 68; Wheeler JCS 00554–68 to Westmoreland info Sharp, 18 Jan 68; Sharp to Wheeler info Westmoreland, 20 Jan 68. All in Westmoreland Message files, Dec 67 and Jan 68, CMH. MFR, Westmoreland, 9 Jan 68, sub: Meeting with Gen Vien, 1730 hrs, 8 Jan 68, tab 18; MFR, Westmoreland, 16 Jan 68, sub: Meetings with Pres Thieu, 0900, and Gen Vien, 1500, 15 Jan 68, tab 26. Both in Westmoreland History file no. 28 (27 Dec 67–31 Jan 68), CMH.

[51] Msgs, Westmoreland MAC 01165, MAC 01219 to Sharp and Wheeler, 24, 25 Jan 68; MAC 01307 to Momyer, Cushman, and Veth, 28 Jan 68. All in Westmoreland Message files, Jan 68, CMH. Msgs, Embassy Saigon/MACV to Sec State and Sec Def, Saigon 16851, 24 Jan 68, tab 39; Sec State 104215

While the Military Assistance Command prepared for contingencies in I Corps and elsewhere, it also carried on much business as usual. General Westmoreland, General Wheeler, and Admiral Sharp exchanged views on the military implications, dangers, and possibilities of a cessation of the bombing of North Vietnam. They also reviewed, and found not particularly alarming, a seasonal increase in enemy activity in northern Laos. With the Army chief of staff, General Johnson, Westmoreland concerted arrangements for remedying a shortage of replacements for U.S. Army, Vietnam. On the twenty-third, MACV, like the rest of the American government, was startled by the sudden North Korean seizure of the American intelligence ship U.S.S. *Pueblo*. This event soon forced MACV to begin contingency planning for return of its two Republic of Korea divisions to South Korea should the crisis there escalate further. The public relations campaign continued. General Westmoreland entertained 43 visiting members of Congress during January and made plans for hosting, among others, retired General James A. Van Fleet and a delegation of Argentine officers in February. Continuing the optimism offensive, Ambassador Komer, at a Saigon news conference on the twenty-fourth, reported significant pacification advances during the past year; he predicted still greater strides in 1968.[52]

During the final days of January, General Westmoreland continued to expect the major enemy attack to come at Khe Sanh, probably before Tet. On the twenty-second, he told General Wheeler and Admiral Sharp that the enemy was likely to attempt a "country-wide show of strength just prior to Tet, with Khe Sanh being the main event," and with subsidiary attacks on Pleiku, Kontum, and several Special Forces camps in II Corps. In III and IV Corps, he envisioned attacks by fire on province capitals and increased terrorism in and around Saigon.[53]

Yet the great assault on Khe Sanh did not come. On 24 January, North Vietnamese troops overran a Laotian position near the South Vietnamese border, driving a Laotian army battalion and several thousand refugees eastward toward the Marine base. Khe Sanh and its hilltop outposts came under fire from artillery as heavy as 152-mm., to which the Americans responded with a daily average of more than 500 tactical air sorties. Westmoreland declared on the twenty-fifth that intelligence indicated a major enemy attack that day. However, the hours passed with only sporadic shelling. Westmoreland reported to Admiral Sharp on the twenty-sixth: "The enemy has not jumped off on his major attack. Why

---

to Am Emb Saigon, 25 Jan 68, tab 41. Both in Westmoreland History file no. 28 (27 Dec 67–31 Jan 68), CMH. Msg, COMUSMACV MAC 02698 to Component and Field Force Cdrs, 24 Jan 68, tab 40, ibid.

[52] These activities can be followed in Westmoreland Message files for Dec 67 and Jan 68. General Westmoreland's daily schedule, with note concerning the 43 members of Congress, is tab A–2, Westmoreland History file no. 28 (27 Dec 67–31 Jan 68), CMH. Sharp, "Reminiscences," pp. 566–67; Wirtz, *Tet Offensive*, pp. 212–13; Hammond, *Military and the Media, 1962–1968*, p. 340.

[53] Msg, Westmoreland MAC 01049 to Wheeler and Sharp, 22 Jan 68, quoted in Wirtz, *Tet Offensive*, p. 212.

we do not know. Hopefully, the air strikes have hurt him, but we have only tenuous intelligence suggesting this."[54]

Meanwhile, intelligence concerning a nationwide enemy threat to South Vietnam's cities and the possibility of an attempted general uprising became steadily less tenuous. Troops of the 199th Light Infantry Brigade, operating near Saigon, captured two Viet Cong who claimed that local force companies were preparing to guide main force units in an attack on the capital. On 27 January, at General Westmoreland's regular Weekly Intelligence Estimate Update meeting with the senior members of his staff, General Davidson declared that a major countrywide enemy offensive was coming, which would include thrusts at Kontum and Pleiku. However, he specified neither additional objectives nor a starting date. The following day, South Vietnamese military police at Qui Nhon in II Corps apprehended eleven Viet Cong who told interrogators the enemy intended to invade cities during Tet. The captives had with them two tapes, for broadcast over captured radio stations, which announced that revolutionary forces had occupied Saigon, Hue, and Da Nang and called on the people to rise against the government. On the twenty-eighth and twenty-ninth, the Central Intelligence Agency and the Defense Intelligence Agency both issued analyses that declared the enemy was preparing for widespread coordinated attacks. The agencies, however, hedged on whether the offensive would be truly countrywide and considered it most likely to begin after, rather than during, Tet. About a week before Tet, a South Vietnamese intelligence agency, the Military Security Service, captured a senior Viet Cong cadre in the Saigon area who confirmed under interrogation that the enemy was planning a general offensive. However, the Military Security Service, which like other Vietnamese intelligence agencies jealously hoarded its information, neglected to pass this report to the J–2 of the Joint General Staff; hence, it never reached MACV. Skepticism continued to prevail in the MACV J–2 and the other intelligence agencies that the enemy really would attempt a general uprising.[55]

The allies' Tet cease-fire began on schedule at 1800 on the twenty-ninth in II, III, and IV Corps but was short-lived. There was last-minute confusion when the South Vietnamese, who were supposed to make the first announcement of the cancellation in I Corps, failed to do so because their press office had closed for the holiday. The American mission finally issued the statement on its own late in the afternoon. They need hardly have bothered. Soon after midnight on 30 January, forces of the enemy's *Military Region 5* command, evidently acting prematurely due to a mix-up in orders, attacked key towns and allied installations

---

[54] Msgs, Westmoreland MAC 01165, MAC 01168, and MAC 01263 to Wheeler and Sharp, 24, 25, 26 Jan 68; Westmoreland Message files, Jan 68, CMH. Quotation is from latter message.

[55] Wirtz, *Tet Offensive*, pp. 214–18; Lung, *General Offensives*, pp 21–30, 35–36, 40; Interv, Charles B. MacDonald with Lt Gen Phillip B. Davidson, 7 Sep 73, copy in CMH; Davidson Interv, 30 Mar and 30 Jun 82, sess. 1, pp. 44–46; CIA Paper, sub: Warning of the Tet Offensive, pp. 7–8, CMH; CIA Paper, 15 Feb 68, CMH; Davidson, *Vietnam Secrets*, pp. 106–07.

in southern I Corps and parts of II Corps. General Davidson at once realized the implications of this event. He told General Westmoreland around 0700 that morning: "just as sure as you and I are sitting here, this is going to happen tonight and tomorrow morning all over the country." His commander agreed.[56]

The allies took what final steps they could to prepare their forces. At 1000 Saigon time, President Thieu formally cancelled the truce throughout South Vietnam. At 1125, Maj. Gen. Walter T. Kerwin, the MACV chief of staff, sent "flash priority" messages to all U.S. commanders instructing them to resume operations. He enjoined them to place all troops on maximum alert and take defensive precautions at headquarters, logistical installations, airfields, billets, and population centers. General Westmoreland reinforced this warning through telephone calls to every senior commander. However, since he made such calls frequently for a variety of reasons, it is uncertain whether these efforts fully convinced all his subordinates of the immediacy and gravity of the threat. On 11 January, the Joint General Staff had directed South Vietnamese commanders to limit Tet leaves to no more than 5 percent of their strength. Despite this order, outside of I Corps, up to 50 percent of the soldiers of most units were absent for the holiday with or without authorization. When the truce was cancelled, the Joint General Staff sent last-minute alert messages to its forces; but these warnings were too late to recall many men. In I Corps, because of the threat to Khe Sanh and the earlier abrogation of the truce, South Vietnamese units were at more nearly full strength and readiness, although even there the absence rate was over 20 percent.[57]

General Westmoreland sent a prompt, rather optimistic, summary of the action to Admiral Sharp and General Wheeler. He commented that the North Vietnamese had "displayed what appeared to be desperation tactics" in assaulting populated areas and had tried to achieve surprise by attacking during the truce. Reaction of allied forces to the offensive, Westmoreland asserted, "has been generally good." The enemy, by engaging in open battle, had suffered at least 700 casualties so far and "when the dust settles, there will probably be more." He

---

[56] Wirtz, *Tet Offensive*, pp. 210, 219; Westmoreland, *Soldier Reports*, p. 319; and History Notes, tab A–1, Westmoreland History file no. 28 (27 Dec 67–31 Jan 68), CMH, describe the confusion over the truce announcement; in *Soldier Reports*, see also pp. 322–23. Sharp and Westmoreland, *Report*, p. 183. Quotation is from Davidson Interv, 30 Mar and 30 Jun 82, sess. 1, pp. 53–54. Captured enemy documents subsequently confirmed the mix-up in starting times; see DOD Intelligence Information Report no. 6–026–1418–68, 18 Apr 68, sub: VC Plans, CMH. Ford, "Tet 1968," pp. 181–89, 278.

[57] Msg, Westmoreland MAC 01392 to Wheeler and Sharp info Bunker, 30 Jan 68, Westmoreland Message files, Jan 68, CMH; Wirtz, *Tet Offensive*, pp. 220–21; PFIAB, "Intelligence Warning," pp. 6–7. Msgs, Westmoreland MAC 5802 to Momyer, Cushman, Weyand, Peers, Maj Gen George S. Eckhardt, Senior Adviser, IV Corps, and Veth, 3 May 68; Cushman to Westmoreland, 5 May 68; Lt Gen William R. Peers, CG, IFFV NHT 599 to Westmoreland, 5 May 68; Weyand HOA 0595 to Westmoreland, 6 May 68; and Eckhardt CTO 111 to Westmoreland, 5 May 68, all in Westmoreland Message files, May 68, CMH, review varying states of alertness in the different corps areas.

concluded: "All my subordinate commanders report the situation well in hand."[58]

Around Saigon on the thirtieth, the allies took some extra precautions. The South Vietnamese Capital Military District, responsible for defense of the city, confined all its troops to barracks. It also, too late to have much effect, tightened control of the major routes into Saigon. The district obtained an airborne battalion to strengthen its defenses. Two of the airborne companies deployed to protect a major prison and the national radio station. The two other companies remained in reserve at district headquarters. At Tan Son Nhut, the Vietnamese Air Force security elements that normally guarded the base went on alert. Fortuitously, additional airborne troops also were present at the field waiting to be airlifted to Da Nang the next day. In downtown Saigon, field police assumed defense positions at important street intersections. At II Field Force, General Weyand had alerted his troops on the twenty-ninth to expect corpswide attacks on allied installations during the truce. His forces improved the defenses of Bien Hoa and rehearsed plans for countering an attack on Tan Son Nhut. Weyand met with his counterpart, Lt. Gen. Le Nguyen Khang, the III Corps commander, to review reports of impending attacks on Bien Hoa, the Saigon radio station, and other facilities. The two commanders, who had a close working relationship of long standing, informally agreed that if a general enemy offensive occurred, Khang would oversee operations within Saigon while Weyand took care of the rest of III Corps.[59]

During this final flurry of warnings and preparations, the Military Assistance Command still gave little indication that it expected anything more in Saigon than an upsurge of Viet Cong terrorism. Rumors that the headquarters might be "hit" circulated through corridors and offices. A staff officer who ventured out of the MACV complex for a late meal found the nearby streets ominously deserted, even as the rest of the city was filled with holiday crowds and loud with exploding firecrackers, legally available this Tet holiday after years of a government ban. Nevertheless, the command made no real attempt to augment the close-in defenses of its own headquarters building, which consisted of a chain-link fence and military police guard towers and checkpoints. Officers in high-level sensitive positions, including General Davidson, the intelligence chief, dispersed for the night to their lightly guarded villas in the city, although some foresightedly equipped themselves with pistols, M16 rifles, and in Davidson's case a M60 machine gun. A number of colonels, including several from MACV J–2, attended a pool

---

[58] Msg, Westmoreland MAC 01438 to Sharp and Wheeler, 30 Jan 68, tab 53, Westmoreland History file no. 28 (27 Dec 67–31 Jan 68), CMH. See also Msg, Westmoreland MAC 01433 to Wheeler, 30 Jan 68, Westmoreland Message files, Jan 68, CMH.

[59] Lung, *General Offensives*, pp. 42–45; Wirtz, *Tet Offensive*, pp. 218–19; Paschall Interv, 6 May 92; II FFV Press Briefing on VC Tet Offensive, 20 Mar 68, CMH; II FFV Tet Offensive AAR, 31 Jan–18 Feb 68, p. 9.

party in Bachelor Officer Quarters One in downtown Saigon, seemingly oblivious to any impending crisis.[60]

General Westmoreland's South Vietnamese security guards had been doubled, both at his villa and during his movements around Saigon, in response to an intelligence report at the turn of the year that he was targeted for assassination. Hence, he was well protected as Tet approached. The MACV commander spent a busy day on the thirtieth, meeting with principal staff officers and conferring frequently by telephone with Ambassador Bunker and his field commanders concerning the attacks in the north and the nationwide alert. He also found time to attend parts of a briefing by the Seventh Air Force and U.S. Army, Vietnam, on post-exchange losses, met with the new *Time-Life* Saigon bureau chief, and played a mid-day game of tennis. Late in the evening, Westmoreland returned to his rented villa and went to bed. Around 0300 on the thirty-first, his aide, Maj. Charles Sampson, U.S. Marine Corps, awakened him to receive a call from MACV headquarters. Over the telephone, Westmoreland heard that the North Vietnamese and Viet Cong were attacking cities throughout South Vietnam and that enemy sappers had struck the U.S. Embassy. By that time, all over Saigon, the sound of real gunfire had replaced the reports of firecrackers. Citizens in many neighborhoods awoke to see in their streets armed strangers clad in the black pajamas and rubber-soled sandals of Viet Cong fighters.[61]

How Much of a Surprise?

The Communists' General Offensive–General Uprising caught the Military Assistance Command, in common with the rest of the U.S. and South Vietnamese governments, at least partially by surprise. While aware for months that a major attack was coming, MACV had anticipated a full-scale conventional assault on Khe Sanh and possibly other places in northern I Corps, with lesser efforts elsewhere in the two northern corps areas and some increase of pressure in III Corps. The command did not expect the offensive to occur during Tet, to be of nationwide scope, and to include a serious effort to take control of the big cities. To the end, the President's Foreign Intelligence Advisory Board later concluded, commanders and intelligence officers "did not visualize the enemy as capable of accomplishing his stated goals as they appeared in propaganda and in captured documents" and so viewed

---

[60] Davidson Interv, 30 Mar and 30 Jun 82, sess. 1, pp. 54–56; Jones, *War Without Windows*, pp. 168–71; Wirtz, *Tet Offensive*, pp. 221–22; Lung, *General Offensives*, pp. 12–13.

[61] Westmoreland's activities can be followed through his History Notes, 28 Dec 67–31 Jan 68, tab A–1, and his personal schedule, tab A–2, in Westmoreland History file no. 28 (27 Dec 67–31 Jan 67). Both in CMH. See also *Soldier Reports*, pp. 323–25, 328. Msg, Westmoreland MAC 01449 to Wheeler and Sharp, 31 Jan 68, Westmoreland Message files, Jan 68, is his first summary of the attacks for his superiors. Lung, *General Offensives*, pp. 12–13, describes the atmosphere in Saigon as the offensive opened.

their calls for a "general uprising" as "merely exhortatory, and not as a blueprint for what was to follow." MACV, on the basis of its own view of what was militarily practical for the enemy, centered its attention on northern I Corps as the one region of South Vietnam where the North Vietnamese had a chance to achieve a preponderance of strength. The enemy's assessments and logic, however, were quite different.[62]

Nevertheless, the allies did receive, and heed, enough warning to prevent their forces from being caught completely off guard. In III Corps, they had redeployed to protect Saigon. Elsewhere, simply as a consequence of their normal dispositions, they had enough troops at most threatened points to deny the enemy significant tactical success.

Indeed, it may be questioned whether the allies, had they known from the beginning the true nature of the enemy plan, could have done much more than they did to disrupt it. The Viet Cong regularly infiltrated the cities to conduct terrorism and small-scale attacks. They could expand those efforts whenever they were willing to risk heavier casualties and exposure of their clandestine urban political and military organization. Their first-wave Tet attack force entered the cities in small groups mingled with normal civilian traffic, with their weapons hidden in innocent-seeming trucks, carts, and sampans. The allies could have stopped such movement only by a complete cutoff of traffic into and out of the cities, with its attendant severe economic and political consequences. MACV could have withheld reinforcements from I Corps to strengthen the defense of the cities, but only at the risk of a spectacular North Vietnamese battlefield victory in South Vietnam's militarily most vulnerable region.[63]

The allies routinely kept large numbers of troops and police in and around the cities to protect political and administrative centers, prevent terrorism, and carry out pacification; and every American and South Vietnamese base possessed its own permanent security force. When organized enemy units began moving toward their assault positions, the allies often detected them and, as in III Corps, redeployed their own troops in reaction. In sum, short of cancelling the Tet cease-fire earlier, curtailing furloughs in the South Vietnamese Army, and further reinforcing security at key installations, the allies could have done little more to prepare for the assault; and their usual disposition of forces made a major Viet Cong success unlikely. Paradoxically, allied commanders' certainty of the latter fact helped the Communists achieve the degree of surprise that they did.

---

[62] Quotation is from PFIAB, "Intelligence Warning," pp. 4–5, see also p. 3. For other similar evaluations, see Wirtz, *Tet Offensive*, pp. 222–23; U.S. District Court, *Westmoreland Memorandum of Law, app. B*, p. 122, and *app. A*, pp. 135–36, 217–18; CIA Paper, sub: Warning of the Tet Offensive, pp. 13–14, CMH; and Davidson, *Vietnam Secrets*, pp. 103–04.

[63] Allied troop dispositions are reviewed in Sharp and Westmoreland, *Report*, p. 174. The ease of infiltrating relatively small numbers of enemy troops into Saigon is emphasized in MACV History, 1968, vol. 2, p. 894.

Viet Cong attack Bachelor Officers Quarters in Saigon.

While the strictly military effects of the Tet surprise thus were likely to be containable, the same could not be said of the psychological and public relations impact in the United States. The president and his senior advisers in Washington knew of the intelligence indicating the attack was coming. However, a subsequent review concluded, the reports did not convey "the full sense of immediacy and intensity which was present in Saigon" by the end of January. As noted previously, General Westmoreland's initial backchannel account of the 30 January attacks declared that the situation was well in hand. The Johnson administration, as a result, did little to prepare either itself or the American people for the coming shock. Its few tentative public warnings were submerged in the continuing stream of reassurance that the war was going well. The Tet offensive thus would pose for the American government not only the military problem of repelling enemy forces but also the more difficult task of reconciling the earlier drumbeat of claims that the foes were on the decline with the sudden brutal fact of Communist troops fighting in the streets of Saigon, Hue, and scores of other supposedly secure cities and towns.[64]

[64] Quotation is from PFIAB, "Intelligence Warning," pp. 5–6. Ambiguity of information reaching Washington is also emphasized in paper, sub: What info did Washington have on coordinated attacks on cities?, folder 42, Thomas C. Thayer Papers, CMH. Westmoreland, *Soldier Reports*, pp. 315–16, 321–22, acknowledges that he continued to emphasize optimism during late 1967 and did too little to alert the American public to the coming offensive. Hammond, *Military and the Media 1962–1968*, p. 342, summarizes the Johnson administration's failure to prepare the American public for the offensive.

3

Tet and Its Aftermath

The offensive that erupted the length and breadth of South Vietnam on 30–31 January was unprecedented in the war in scope and intensity. At least 84,000 North Vietnamese and Viet Cong troops took direct part in the attacks; probably most of the enemy's other available forces had offensive missions, many of which were not carried out. During the first two days of the attack, the Communists struck five of South Vietnam's six autonomous cities, 36 provincial capitals, 64 district towns, and the major American air bases with varying combinations of ground assaults and attacks by fire. They temporarily occupied parts of many cities, including Saigon; and they took virtually complete control of Hue for the better part of a month, being driven out only after weeks of stubborn house-to-house fighting by U.S. Army, U.S. Marine, and South Vietnamese Army units. Casualties and destruction were extensive: more than 2,100 American and 4,000 South Vietnamese soldiers killed in a month's combat, tens of thousands of South Vietnamese civilians dead and injured, hundreds of thousands homeless, sections of Saigon and other cities in ruins, South Vietnam's economy temporarily paralyzed, and rural pacification seemingly destroyed.[1] *(Map 2)*

At the cost of nearly 50,000 men killed in the first month of fighting—many of them hard-to-replace Viet Cong local troops, guerrillas, and political cadre—the offensive fell far short of the politico-military goals Hanoi set for it. The attackers, who suffered from local deficiencies in communications and coordination, were repulsed at many points, were unable to hold for long the objectives they did seize, and failed to destroy any large allied or South Vietnamese units. Most important, the Saigon government and its armed forces did not collapse and the urban population did not rise in support of the offensive. The General Uprising never took place. Yet military failure paradoxically produced

---

[1] Convenient overviews of the Tet offensive are in Sharp and Westmoreland, *Report*, pp. 158–61, 183–84; and MACV History, 1968, vol. 1, pp. 38, 536 and vol. 2, an. A. The classic journalistic overview is in Oberdorfer, *Tet!*. For casualties, see MACV Fact Sheet, 8 Mar 68, sub: Losses for Period 29/1800 Hrs Jan 68 to 05/2400 Hrs Mar 68, tab 16, Westmoreland History file no. 30 (1–31 Mar 68), CMH; II FFV Tet Offensive AAR, 31 Jan–18 Feb 68, CMH, pp. 25–26. For the question of enemy numbers, see Davidson, *Vietnam Secrets*, pp. 82–84; and Morris Deposition, p. 36, *Vietnam: A Documentary Collection*, card 345.

NORTH VIETNAM
DEMARCATION LINE

Tchepone
Savannakhet
Quang Tri
Khe Sanh
Hue
SOUTH CHINA SEA
I CTZ
Da Nang
Cu Lao Cham

THAILAND
Saravane
LAOS
Paksé
Tam Ky
Chu Lai
Cu Lao Re
Quang Ngai

Attopeu
Dak To
Kontum

Pleiku
An Khe
Qui Nhon

Stung Treng
Hau Bon

CAMBODIA
II CTZ
Tuy Hoa

Kratie
Ban Me Thuot
Ninh Hoa
Nha Trang

Snuol
Da Lat
Cam Ranh

An Loc
Phan Rang

PHNOM PENH
Tay Ninh
III CTZ
Bien Hoa
Xuan Loc
Phu Cuong
Long Binh
SAIGON
Phan Thiet
Svay Rieng
Mekong R
Chau Phu
Moc Hoa
Tan An
Phuoc Le
Dao Phu Qui
Go Cong
Sa Dec
My Tho
Vinh Long
Ben Tre
Rach Gia
Can Tho
Phu Vinh
SOUTH CHINA SEA

Gulf of Thailand
Soc Trang
IV CTZ
Bac Lieu
Ca Mau
Con Son

TET OFFENSIVE
1968

Engagement

0   100 Miles
0   100 Kilometers

Map 2

political success, not in South Vietnam but in the United States. The fact that the offensive had occurred at all and the magnitude of its casualties and destruction shattered the faith of many American political leaders in the possibility of victory. A shaken President Johnson and his advisers continued with increased urgency the major reconsideration of U.S. strategy and war aims that they had begun late in the previous year.[2]

Regaining Control

The Communist assault on Saigon temporarily disrupted the routine of MACV headquarters and placed the "Saigon Warriors" of "Pentagon East" very nearly on the firing line. Tan Son Nhut Air Base, which bordered the MACV compound, came under intense infantry, mortar, and rocket attack during the small hours of 31 January. At the unfortified headquarters, the personnel on duty, alarmed by the reports pouring in of fighting nationwide and by the sound of nearby gunfire, hastily improvised a thin defense perimeter manned by frightened clerks and military police led by equally frightened junior staff officers. Inside the building, other officers and enlisted men pulled desks into the corridors as last-ditch barricades. Fortunately, these defenses were never tested. American and South Vietnamese security forces, reinforced by South Vietnamese airborne units fortuitously on the base and by armored cavalry dispatched by II Field Force, stopped the main Viet Cong infantry attack well short of Tan Son Nhut's vital areas and the MACV complex. Nevertheless, occasional sniper fire and mortar rounds during the next several days gave headquarters life an unaccustomed spice of danger.[3]

General Westmoreland lost no time in seeking to regain control of the situation. He spent most of the morning of the 31st at the U.S. Embassy, which had been attacked by Viet Cong sappers who had broken into the courtyard before being trapped and killed by American military police and paratroopers. The MACV commander oversaw the post-attack cleanup. He also reassured the State Department by long-distance telephone that, contrary to initial news reports, the enemy had not entered the U.S. Embassy building itself; and he held an impromptu press conference on the grounds. Westmoreland then moved on to MACV headquarters, where he received briefings on the situation and began telephoning the field force and III Marine Amphibious Force

---

[2] For typical American evaluations of the enemy defeat, see Sharp and Westmoreland, *Report*, pp. 159, 161–62; MACV History, 1968, vol. 1, pp. 73–74 and vol. 2, an. A, pp. 894–95; II FFV Tet Offensive AAR, 31 Jan–18 Feb 68, CMH, pp. 15, 21, 24, 34. For American domestic reaction, see Oberdorfer, *Tet!* ch. 5, and Hammond, *Military and the Media, 1962–1968*, chs. 15 and 16.

[3] The battle for Tan Son Nhut is described in MACV History, 1968, vol. 2, pp. 896–98. For details of the first days at MACV headquarters, see Jones, *War Without Windows*, pp. 175–90; Westmoreland History Notes, 1–31 Mar 68, tab 1, Westmoreland History file no. 30 (1–31 Mar 68), CMH; Davidson Interv, 30 Mar and 30 Jun 82, sess. 1, pp. 56–60; and Chaisson to Mrs Chaisson, 1, 2, and 18 Feb 68, box 7, Chaisson Papers, Hoover Institution.

*Westmoreland tours the embassy,
31 January 1968.*

commanders to obtain information and give operational guidance. He was joined at headquarters during that and the following day by General Abrams and other senior officers of the staff, many of whom had their own tales to tell of tense drives across a city that suddenly had become a battleground.[4]

Despite the presence of Westmoreland and his key subordinates, MACV headquarters was only partially operational for several days. Many staff personnel who were off-duty at the start of the attack could not reach their jobs because of the fighting elsewhere in Saigon. Some were trapped in their billets for days as troops shot it out with holed-up Viet Cong infiltrators. Short of staff at the outset, the headquarters also lacked timely information because of overloaded and in some cases battle-damaged communications networks. MACV was slow, for example, to appreciate the seriousness of the situation in Hue. Yet at the same time, the headquarters labored to meet a flurry of special information demands from anxious Washington officials. Until early March, Generals Wheeler and Johnson telephoned Westmoreland daily. These demands, Westmoreland declared in mid-February, were "rapidly overwhelming us and beginning to detract from the performance of our primary duties."[5]

---

[4] Westmoreland's movements are recounted in Westmoreland History Notes, 28 Dec 67–31 Jan 68, tab A–1, Westmoreland History file no. 28 (27 Dec 67–31 Jan 68) and Westmoreland Calendar of Activities, Feb 68, tab 2, Westmoreland History file no. 29 (1–29 Feb 68). Both in CMH. Oberdorfer, *Tet!* pp. 26–39, describes initial confusion in press accounts. Sorley, *Thunderbolt*, pp. 211–12; Ltr, Chaisson to Mrs Chaisson, 1 Feb 68, box 7, Chaisson Papers, Hoover Institution; and Davidson Interv, 30 Mar and 30 Jun 82, sess. 1, pp. 56–60, describe adventures of senior officers making their way to headquarters.

[5] Palmer Interv, 1975, pp. 277–78. Communications problems are described in Davidson Interv, 30 Mar and 30 Jun 82, sess. 1, pp. 59–60. Wirtz, *Tet Offensive*, pp. 230, 235–40, recounts early MACV efforts to obtain accurate information on the Tet battles. Msgs, Westmoreland MAC 01464 to Wheeler, Sharp, Bunker, 1 Feb 68; Wheeler JCS 01275 to Westmoreland info Sharp, 3 Feb 68; Wheeler JCS 02445 to Westmoreland, 1 Mar 68. All in Westmoreland Message files, Feb–Mar 68, CMH. Quotation is from Draft Msg, Westmoreland to Sharp and Wheeler, "relayed in essence by telephone to Gen Wheeler on 13 Feb 68," tab 53, Westmoreland History file no. 29 (1–29 Feb 68), CMH.

During this period, U.S. Army, Vietnam (USARV) headquarters, the commanders and staff of which were quartered within the well-protected Long Binh base a short distance north of Saigon, took on much of the task of collecting information about the fighting throughout the country, making reports to higher authority, and coordinating resupply and helicopter and medical support of American units. The USARV deputy commander, Lt. Gen. Bruce Palmer, later recalled: "We were able to keep MACV informed on things that they didn't know about, as well as [U.S. Army Pacific] and [Department of the Army], to get very quick action as needed." Although the field force and division commanders directed the battle, USARV, according to General Palmer, "got into some tactical shifting of our own" in response to urgent immediate requirements.[6]

As the fighting in Saigon died down and people began returning, MACV headquarters rapidly adjusted to round-the-clock operations under enemy threat. The headquarters commandant, Lt. Col. Jack O'Shaughnessy, organized and took command of a 530-man MACV defense force made up of headquarters officers and enlisted men organized in four provisional rifle companies. As a precaution against future mortar and rocket attacks, the director of construction oversaw installation of a casemate around the combat operations center and other vital parts of the building. General Westmoreland and his senior officers bivouacked in the headquarters for several weeks after Tet because of the press of work and because at first, as General Davidson put it, it was "just too goddamned dangerous to get out in the streets." They returned to their villas only briefly during the day, for showers (the headquarters lacked this amenity) and short naps. Gradually, a semblance of regular routine returned, including the holding of the regular Saturday morning staff conference; and General Westmoreland resumed his trips to the field and to meetings of agencies, such as the Coordinating Committee for U.S. Missions in Southeast Asia. By mid-March, the situation had settled down to the point where Westmoreland could afford time for a brief visit to his family at Clark Air Force Base in the Philippines.[7]

Even then, working at headquarters remained far more strenuous than during pre-Tet days. General Chaisson, director of the Combat Operations Center (COC), described his routine for his wife:

[6] Quotation and description of USARV activities is from Palmer Interv, 1975, pp. 278–79. See also Msg, Palmer ARV 344 to Gen Johnson, 12 Feb 68, Creighton W. Abrams Papers, CMH.

[7] MACV History, 1968, vol. 2, p. 864. Westmoreland History Notes, 1–29 Feb 68, tab 1, Westmoreland History file no. 29 (1–29 Feb 68); Westmoreland History Notes, 1–31 Mar 68, tab 1, Westmoreland History file no. 30 (1–31 Mar 68). All in CMH. Sharp and Westmoreland, *Report*, p. 163; Palmer Interv, 1975, p. 280; U.S. District Court, *Westmoreland Memorandum of Law, app. A*, p. 57; Msg, Westmoreland MAC 03705 to Sharp info Wheeler, 18 Mar 68, Westmoreland Message files, Mar 68, CMH. Quotation is from Davidson Interv, 30 Mar and 30 Jun 82, sess. 1, p. 58; see also pp. 56–60.

Get up at five; go down to COC; Westy shows at six; fifty-five minutes of briefing; then to breakfast in his mess with C/S and Westy; then back to my desk for a couple of hours; then to field or briefings; twice a week home for lunch & bath; afternoon pushing papers; 1945 a beer in Westy's office; then to dinner in his mess; back to desk till 2230; then late evening briefing and selection of Arc Light targets. 2300–2400 bedtime. Interruptions as required through the night. I've been home now two nights in 6 and 1/2 weeks. . . .[8]

   Literally from the first day of the offensive, General Westmoreland, his principal staff officers, and his field commanders assessed the enemy attack as a failure, one which had left the Viet Cong and North Vietnamese in an exposed, vulnerable position. General Davidson later declared: "It became apparent quite early, I'd say almost by sun-down of the first day, that while we were going to have some trouble, . . . now they were playing in our ball game. We knew where they were; we just had to go get them, and we were going to go get them." General Weyand, deploying his reserves to counter the enemy's attack on Saigon, reached the same conclusion early in the morning of the thirty-first.[9]

   In a typical evaluation, General Westmoreland on 4 February acknowl-edged that the enemy had "dealt the GVN a severe blow" by bringing the war to the cities. However, he had paid a "high price" in casualties, had failed to hold any towns, and had not triggered a general upris-ing or disrupted the South Vietnamese government and armed forces. Westmoreland noted that the major airfields and the allies' nationwide communications system had remained in operation throughout the first wave of attacks and that the South Vietnamese Army and territorial forces in the main were fighting well. The MACV commander viewed the assaults on the cities as the second part of a three-fold offensive, which had begun with the autumn border battles and probably would culminate in a drive to take Khe Sanh and overrun northern I Corps. He credited the enemy with the capacity for another round of city attacks as well as the northern offensive but expressed confidence that his forces "have the strength, dis-position, and are in the proper frame of mind to keep at the enemy and inflict even greater losses if he persists in the attack."[10]

   Early Communist assessments of the offensive's shortcomings closely paralleled those of MACV. A *COSVN* directive, copies of which were captured during February, claimed a great victory over U.S. forces

   [8] Ltr, Chaisson to Mrs Chaisson, 16 Mar 68, box 7, Chaisson Papers, Hoover Institution; see other letters in this box for additional color on MACV headquarters during the offensive.
   [9] Quotation is from Davidson Interv, 30 Mar and 30 Jun 82, sess. 1, pp. 63–64. For Weyand's assessment, see Oberdorfer, *Tet!* pp. 140–42; and II FFV Press Briefing on VC Tet Offensive, 20 Mar 68, CMH.
   [10] Westmoreland quotations are from Msg, MAC 01614 to Wheeler info Sharp and Bunker, 4 Feb 68, Westmoreland Message files, Feb 68, CMH. In same file, see Msgs, Westmoreland MAC 01464 to Wheeler, Sharp, Bunker, 1 Feb 68; MAC 01497, MAC 01539, MAC 01588 to Sharp and Wheeler, 1, 2, 3 Feb 68; MAC 01592 to Sharp info Wheeler and Bunker, 3 Feb 68. Msg, COMUSMACV to CG III MAF et al., 4 Feb 68, in MACV History, 1968, vol. 1, p. 26.

and the "puppet" army and government. However, the directive went on to list a number of "shortcomings and weaknesses," specifically failure to seize key objectives, destroy enemy units, hold occupied areas, and bring about mass popular uprisings. Preparing the revolutionary forces for hard days to come, this directive and subsequent ones redefined the General Offensive–General Uprising as "a prolonged strategic offensive that includes many military campaigns and local uprisings" and admitted that "we cannot yet . . . achieve total victory in a short period." General Davidson and his staff initially doubted the authenticity of this document because of its appearance so soon after the offensive began, but other captured documents repeated the same points. Davidson finally decided that *COSVN* had prepared the directive before the attack as a precaution against the possibility of less than total success.[11]

As the Viet Cong were driven or withdrew from the cities, MACV and mission assessments grew steadily more confident in tone. Apprehension remained, however, over the threat to northern I Corps, where the North Vietnamese divisions had yet to make their move. Westmoreland, his views shared by Ambassadors Bunker and Komer, emphasized that the enemy, by abandoning protracted rural insurgency for a "go-for-broke" effort directed at the urban centers, had exposed his forces to allied firepower and created a power vacuum in the countryside for the pacification program to fill. Far from being a disaster for the allies, the enemy offensive thus was an opportunity if the Americans and South Vietnamese could take advantage of it. Exemplifying this point of view, Ambassador Komer declared on 12 February: "If the GVN can recover quickly enough from the near pre-Tet disaster, and we can go on the counter-offensive in other areas while containing the NVA up north, we may well force Hanoi to the negotiating table or otherwise materially shorten the war."[12]

The allied military response to the Tet offensive required few modifications of General Westmoreland's established system of command. III Marine Amphibious Force, the field forces, and the South Vietnamese corps fought the battles under the guidance of Westmoreland and his

---

[11] Circular from *Central Office of South Vietnam (COSVN)* Current Affairs Committee and Military Affairs Committee of South Vietnam Liberation Army Headquarters Concerning a Preliminary Assessment of the Situation, 31 Jan 68, in Gareth Porter, ed., *Vietnam: The Definitive Documentation of Human Decisions*, 2 vols. (Stanfordville, N.Y.: E. M. Coleman Enterprises, 1979), 2:485–86; quotations are from this document. Davidson Interv, 30 Mar and 30 Jun 82, sess. 1, pp. 15–18. A parallel captured evaluation is reported in Msg, Westmoreland MAC 02063 to Wheeler, Sharp, Bunker, Abrams, 13 Feb 68, Abrams Papers, CMH.

[12] Quotation is from Memo, Komer for Westmoreland, 12 Feb 68, Westmoreland Memos, RWK [Robert W. Komer] (1967–68), DepCORDS files, CMH. See also Msgs, Westmoreland MAC 01858 to Wheeler and Sharp, 9 Feb 68; Westmoreland MAC 1901 to Sharp info Wheeler, 10 Feb 68; Westmoreland MAC 01975 to Sharp and Wheeler, 12 Feb 68; Abrams PHB 166 to Westmoreland, 25 Feb 68; Westmoreland MAC 02701 to Sharp info Wheeler, Johnson, Bunker, Abrams, 26 Feb 68. All in Westmoreland Message files, Feb 68, CMH. MFR, Chaisson, 5 Apr 68, sub: MACV Commanders' Conf, 31 Mar 68, tab 68, Westmoreland History file no. 30 (1–31 Mar 68), CMH.

counterpart, General Vien, with whom the MACV commander worked closely throughout the crisis. In immediate response to the attack on Saigon, MACV and II Field Force activated a temporary U.S. headquarters, Task Force WARE (later renamed HURRICANE FORWARD), under the II Field Force deputy commander, to control American units fighting in the capital. Westmoreland also launched a campaign, under consideration before Tet, to strengthen the South Vietnamese command structure in the Capital Military District and place a more capable officer in charge of it. However, South Vietnamese political machinations prevented immediate action on the American proposal. In the interim, General Vien assumed personal direction of the battle for Saigon.[13]

General Westmoreland directed a few force redeployments in response to the enemy offensive. He reluctantly dispatched American combat units to Saigon and other hard-pressed cities to assist South Vietnamese clearing and securing efforts. Continuing the shift of MACV's forces to counter the expected enemy offensive in northern I Corps, in mid-February he began moving the headquarters and two brigades of the 101st Airborne Division, which had arrived in III Corps just before Christmas, to Thua Thien Province. Aside from these movements, however, and some shifting of units within corps areas, allied dispositions did not change significantly as a result of the Tet attacks.[14]

In the aftermath of Tet, General Westmoreland saw no need to revise his basic strategy. Westmoreland insisted to General Vien that the "mission, objectives, and goals" set in the Combined Campaign Plan for 1968 "remain valid." The plan, he declared, was "sufficiently flexible to permit the corps commanders . . . to accomplish destruction of VC units in the vicinity of cities, open and secure LOCs, and support the Revolutionary Development effort as required by the situation in the corps zones."[15]

Westmoreland did acknowledge that the enemy offensive had caused the allies to "re-evaluate our priorities" by devoting more resources to protection of the cities. Yet the MACV commander, throughout the

[13] Westmoreland describes his method of command in Msg MAC 02740 to Wheeler, 27 Feb 68, Westmoreland Message files, Feb 68, CMH. Examples of his activities are in Westmoreland Message files and Historical files, Feb–Mar 68, CMH; MACV History, 1968, vol. 1, p. 219 and vol. 2, p. 899; Msgs, Eckhardt HOA 1741 to Abrams, 1 Dec 67, and Abrams MAC 11885 to Eckhardt, 8 Dec 67, both in Abrams Papers, CMH. Also Clarke, *The Final Years*, pp. 308–09; Sharp and Westmoreland, *Report*, pp. 170–71.

[14] Msg, Westmoreland MAC 01808 to Wheeler info Sharp and Bunker, 8 Feb 68, Westmoreland Message files, Feb 68, CMH; Sharp and Westmoreland, *Report*, p. 159; Chaisson, MFR, 18 Feb 68, sub: Unit Deployments, tab 65, Westmoreland History file no. 29 (1–29 Feb 68), CMH; Chaisson, Oral History, pp. 217–18, MCHC.

[15] First quotation is from Msg, Westmoreland MAC 0218 to Wheeler info Sharp, 12 Feb 68, Westmoreland Message files, Feb 68; see also Seventeen Questions Posed by AP [Associated Press] and Gen Westmoreland's Answers, 24 Feb 68, tab 77, Westmoreland History file no. 29 (1–29 Feb 68). Both in CMH. Second quotation is from Ltr, COMUSMACV to CJCS, 12 Mar 68, in MACV History, 1968, vol. 1, pp. 19–20.

weeks after Tet, struggled to prevent the allies from huddling around the cities and surrendering the military initiative, and the country-side, to the enemy. While acknowledging the need to clear and secure the urban areas as the first military priority, Westmoreland continu-ally emphasized pursuit and attack of enemy forces and the earliest possible return of U.S. and South Vietnamese regular troops to their customary rural areas of operation. Repeatedly, he hammered on the fact that the Tet attacks had left enemy units exposed in a way they had not been previously and urged his commanders and his allies to seek out and destroy them. He emphasized as well the urgency of restor-ing military support of pacification. With General Vien, Westmoreland traveled to all four corps areas to preach the gospel of the offensive and prod commanders and advisers to develop and execute plans for attacking Communist units, reopening roads, and reestablishing the government presence in the villages.[16]

Response to these exhortations varied in speed and effectiveness from region to region, but by early March the allies gradually were turning urban defense back to the police and territorial forces and resuming search-and-destroy and pacification operations. On 11 March, for example, II Field Force and III Corps initiated a combined campaign to destroy enemy forces in the five provinces surrounding Saigon. Elsewhere, more modest but significant operations were getting under way, even as the allies still awaited the expected major North Vietnamese attack in northern I Corps.[17]

As urgent as the need to resume the military offensive was the requirement to relieve civilian distress and repair the damage, much of it caused by allied firepower, resulting from the fight to expel the enemy from the cities and towns. General Westmoreland and Ambassadors Bunker and Komer realized that, for both humanitarian and practi-cal political reasons, the South Vietnamese government had to act at once to help its injured and homeless citizens and restore as much as possible of normal social and economic life. They also knew that the government, never a model of administrative efficiency, had been stunned by the shock of the enemy offensive. Many of its officials, totally preoccupied with their own survival and with military secu-rity, often neglected or obstructed efforts to restore economic activity

---

[16] Msgs, Westmoreland MAC 1901 and MAC 02018 to Wheeler info Sharp, 10 Feb 68 and 12 Feb 68; Westmoreland MAC 02740 to Wheeler, 27 Feb 68. All in Westmoreland Message files, Feb 68, CMH. Msg, CG II FFV to COMUSMACV, 10 Feb 68, tab 48; Memo, JGS RVNAF for Cdrs of CTZs, 16 Feb 68, sub: Activity Guidelines for Corps Tactical Zones, tab 59; MFR, Chaisson, 27 Feb 68, sub: Commander's Guidance, tab 86. All in Westmoreland History file no. 29 (1–29 Feb 68), CMH. Westmoreland History Notes, 1–31 Mar 68, tab 1, Westmoreland History file no. 30 (1–31 Mar 68), CMH; in same file, see tabs 6, 10, 23, and 26. MACV History, 1968, vol. 1, pp. 19–20, 25.

[17] Msgs, Westmoreland MAC 02960 and MAC 02984 to Wheeler info Sharp, 2, 3 Mar 68; Westmoreland MAC 03572 to Sharp and Wheeler, 15 Mar 68; Peers NHT 0305 to Westmoreland, 6 Mar 68; Weyand HOA 0367 to Westmoreland, 19 Mar 68. All in Westmoreland Message files, Mar 68, CMH. For overviews of operations, see Sharp and Westmoreland, *Report*, pp. 165–66; and MACV History, 1968, vol. 1, pp. 390–93.

Aftermath of Viet Cong attack on Saigon

and basic public services. Even so, local governments and individual Vietnamese in the provinces were beginning self-help recovery and relief efforts. After a visit to the Mekong Delta during the first days of February, General Abrams reported that officials in every province had appointed relief committees and begun providing food, clothing, and medical assistance to their homeless citizens. The challenge for the U.S. Embassy and MACV was to push the central government to support and expand upon these initiatives.[18]

To get President Thieu and his officials moving promptly and in the right directions, Westmoreland and Komer, with Ambassador Bunker's approval, on 2 February hastily drew up plans for a nationwide Operation RECOVERY, to be directed by a Central Recovery Committee, chaired by Vice President Nguyen Cao Ky. With its own combined American-Vietnamese staff, the Central Recovery Committee would mobilize the various ministries for the effort and coordinate their actions. On 3 February, President Thieu promptly accepted the plan when Bunker, Westmoreland, and Komer presented it to him. The Central Recovery Committee, quartered in the presidential palace, was

[18] The reconstruction problem is conveniently summarized in Westmoreland, *Soldier Reports*, pp. 332–33, and Sharp and Westmoreland, *Report*, pp. 170, 235. Official obstruction of recovery is noted in Memo, Komer for Bunker and Westmoreland, 7 Feb 68, Chronological File: Komer (1968), DepCORDS files, CMH. Early South Vietnamese self-help efforts are described in Msg, Westmoreland MAC 01628 to Wheeler info Sharp, Bunker, 4 Feb 68, Westmoreland Message files, Feb 68, CMH.

in operation within a few days. Headed by Ky, with Komer and his military deputy, Maj. Gen. George W. Forsythe, overseeing respectively policy and operations, and with a staff of representatives from the ministries, MACV, and U.S. Agency for International Development, the Central Recovery Committee directed the work of subordinate councils at province, district, and village levels. On the U.S. side, CORDS set up an operations center at MACV to monitor activities and relay requests for materiel and engineering support. Throughout the country, the CORDS staff acted as the nucleus of the recovery organization, spurring action at every level and collecting information on progress and requirements.[19]

During the next several months, Vietnamese officials, under the direction of the Central Recovery Committee and aided and urged on by American "bottleneck breakers and problem solvers," fed and sheltered refugees, restored public utilities and services, and reestablished the normal flow of commerce within and between the cities and towns. They also conducted an intensive psychological warfare campaign to capitalize on popular resentment of the Communists' violation of the sacred Tet festival and promote people's self-help and self-defense movements. The South Vietnamese side of the effort gradually lost momentum, especially after President Thieu, fearing that Ky was gaining political advantage by his leadership of the recovery campaign, supplanted the vice president as chairman of the Central Recovery Committee. Nevertheless, despite setbacks, including a new wave of displaced persons from a second round of Communist attacks in May, by mid-1968 urban life was returning to what had passed for normality before Tet and the worst physical and economic damage of the offensive had been repaired. Operation Recovery and its MACV and CORDS sponsors had contributed much to these achievements, as had the long-suffering, resilient people of South Vietnam.[20]

Even as they promoted urban recovery, MACV and CORDS also tried to revive the rural pacification program, which barely had begun in earnest before the enemy offensive. It became clear, as Komer's staff pieced together the results across South Vietnam, that the Communist attack in most places had bypassed the villages and hamlets. However, the government had withdrawn many of the Regional and Popular

[19] Msg, Bunker Saigon 17920 to President, 4 Feb 68, tab 26, Westmoreland History file no. 29 (1–29 Feb 68), CMH; in same file, Westmoreland History Notes, 1–29 Feb 68, tab 1; Fact Sheet, 2 Feb 68, sub: Project Recovery, tab 11; Msgs, Bunker to Sec State, 2 and 3 Feb 68, tabs 16 and 24; Memo, Bunker for COMUSMACV, Dir USAID, Dir Joint U.S. Public Affairs Office (JUSPAO), 5 Feb 68, sub: GVN Organization for Relief of Destruction Caused by VC, tab 28; Msg, Bunker Saigon 17922 to Sec State, 4 Feb 68, Cable Chron-State (Jan–May 68), CMH; MACV History, 1968, vol. 1, pp. 536–37.

[20] For overviews of Project Recovery, see MACV History, 1968, vol. 1, pp. 537–44, and tab 91, Westmoreland History file no. 29 (1–29 Feb 68), CMH. Quotation is from Komer, Item for [Bunker] Cable, 7 Feb 68, Chronological File: Komer (1968); DepCORDS files, CMH. Also Memo, Komer for Bunker, 23 Apr 68, Bunker—Memos for RWK (1967–68); and Msg, Komer to Corps SAs [senior advisers], 25 May 68, Cable Chron-Military (1968). Politics of Thieu's replacement of Ky are recounted in Hammond, *Military and the Media, 1962–1968*, pp. 354–55.

Forces, National Police, and civilian Revolutionary Development cadres to the province and district capitals for defense and relief work, leaving the countryside open to Viet Cong recruiting, taxation, and propagandizing. Fortunately, the Viet Cong also had pulled their own local force and guerrilla units out of the villages to attack the towns, where they suffered heavy losses and remained engaged. Thus, the countryside after Tet constituted a power vacuum that both sides had to race to fill. General Westmoreland told Admiral Sharp late in March: "We unquestionably suffered a real setback [in pacification], but the enemy suffered grievous losses, too. The real question is whether we can recover and forge ahead more quickly than he."[21]

Ambassador Komer recognized this fact long before the final reports were in. From the first days of the offensive, he and General Westmoreland hastened to push government troops and pacification cadres out of the towns and back into the hamlets. On 9 February, Westmoreland, in a message drafted by Komer, directed corps senior advisers and CORDS deputies to exert "maximum advisory pressure" on their counterparts to that end, lest a "major pacification setback" occur "largely through default." Both men repeated this exhortation regularly thereafter and induced President Thieu and General Vien to do the same. At American urging, the Joint General Staff instituted special "show-the-flag" operations by Regional Force companies with attached intelligence personnel and civilian cadre to restore a government presence in hard-pressed villages. Komer and his CORDS advisers oversaw the revision of province Revolutionary Development plans to accelerate recovery and adopted a simplified set of objectives emphasizing security, psychological warfare, elimination of the Communist infrastructure, and local self-defense. All elements of the American mission maintained pressure on President Thieu to replace province chiefs and military commanders who had proven inadequate in the crisis.[22]

Government forces gradually moved back into the countryside. Early in April, according to Komer, 545 of 629 Revolutionary Development teams had returned to their hamlets and 519 regularly stayed over-

---

[21] Overviews of the pacification setback can be found in Sharp and Westmoreland, *Report*, pp. 160–61, 235; MACV History, 1968, vol. 2, pp. 888, 902, 905; and II FFV Tet Offensive AAR, 31 Jan–18 Feb 68, p. 25. Quotation is from Msg, Westmoreland MAC 08814 to Sharp, 29 Mar 68, Cable Chron-Military (1968), DepCORDS files, CMH. In this collection, see also Msg, Bunker Saigon 21382 to Sec State, 7 Mar 68, Cable Chron-State (Jan–May 68); Memos, Komer for Bunker, 14 and 21 Feb 68, Chronological File: Komer (1968). Also, Msg, Palmer ARV 344 to Gen Johnson, 12 Feb 68, Abrams Papers, CMH; Graham Interv, 24 May and 3 Nov 82, sess. 1, pp. 34–37.

[22] Davidson Interv, 24 May and 30 Jun 82, sess. 1, pp. 69–70, credits Komer's early correct assessment of pacification. Quotation is from Msg, Westmoreland MAC 04132 to Corps SAs and DepCORDSs, 9 Feb 68, Cable Chron-Military (1968), DepCORDS files, CMH. In same collection, see Msgs, Westmoreland to Corps SAs, 10 Mar 68; Westmoreland MAC 08814 to Sharp, 29 Mar 68. Memo, Komer for Minister Tri, 28 Mar 68, sub: Revolutionary Development Cadre, tab 57, Westmoreland History file no. 30 (1–31 Mar 68); MFR, Chaisson, 1 Jun 68, sub: MACV Commanders' Conf, 19 May 68, tab 55, Westmoreland History file no. 32 (1–31 May 68). Both in CMH.

night there. Of 51 South Vietnamese battalions assigned to support pacification, 46 were operating in their assigned areas. President Thieu replaced two corps commanders and fifteen province chiefs, to the net advantage of pacification. According to the CORDS Hamlet Evaluation System, the percentage of the South Vietnamese urban and rural population living in relatively secure areas, which had fallen immediately after Tet, began gradually rising during the spring and was approaching pre-offensive levels by the middle of the year. A government-sponsored hamlet self-defense movement made headway in some areas, and there were indications of peasant disillusionment at the Viet Cong's failure to achieve their promised great victory at Tet. The rural economy recovered quickly, with no long-lasting shortages or price inflation. The progress achieved was fragile, and advisers in the hardest-hit provinces estimated that it would take six to nine months to restore the program to full momentum (pessimists doubted it ever had much momentum). Nevertheless, contrary to alarmist reports immediately after Tet in both the news media and official channels, pacification, thanks in part to timely MACV and CORDS efforts to revive it, was far from dead.[23]

I Corps: MACV Versus the Marines

While taking steps to control the situation in the rest of the country, General Westmoreland throughout February and March focused much of his attention on northern I Corps, where he expected enemy forces to launch the next and potentially most dangerous phase of their offensive. The MACV commander told General Wheeler on 9 February that "the only really serious threat that faces me now" was in the area between the Demilitarized Zone and Hai Van Pass. There the rain and fog of the northeast monsoon and the enemy's cutting of Highway 1, the allies' sole land supply line, intensified the threat posed by massed North Vietnamese divisions.[24]

Events strengthened the MACV commander's concern. At Hue, the North Vietnamese augmented their initial attack force and waged a bitter month-long battle to hold the city. At Khe Sanh, besides continuing rocket and artillery bombardment, they assaulted two of the Marine garrison's hilltop outposts and were repulsed only after hand-to-hand fighting. On 7 February, using tanks for the first time in South Vietnam, they overran the Special Forces camp at Lang Vei 14 kilometers southwest of the Marine combat base. General Westmoreland

---

[23] Statistics are from Msg, Komer Saigon 24361 to Bunker, 9 Apr 68, Cable Chron-State (Jan–May 68), DepCORDS files, CMH. In same file, see Msg, Bunker Saigon 21382 to Sec State, 7 Mar 68. Memo, Komer for Bunker, 23 Apr 68, Bunker—Memos for RWK (1967–68); Msg, Komer to Westmoreland, MAC 9389, [ca. Jul 68], Backchannel file (1967–68). All in DepCORDS files, CMH. MACV History, 1968, vol. 1, pp. 519–20, 527–29. Command changes are described in Clarke, *Final Years*, pp. 308–13.

[24] Msg, Westmoreland MAC 01858 to Wheeler and Sharp, 9 Feb 68, Westmoreland Message files, Feb 68, CMH.

President Johnson reviewing the relief map of Khe Sanh

and General Abrams, who activated MACV Forward headquarters at Phu Bai in mid-February, viewed these events, and the buildup of additional North Vietnamese forces in striking distance of Hue and Da Nang, as presaging a full-scale Communist offensive aimed at seizing all of Quang Tri and Thua Thien Provinces, possibly to establish a position of strength from which to enter negotiations.[25]

President Johnson and his advisers anxiously watched the developing siege of Khe Sanh. The president, disturbed by ominous press reports that likened the marines' situation and probable fate to those of the French at Dien Bien Phu, repeatedly pressed Westmoreland, through General Wheeler, for reassurance that the base would not fall. The MACV commander in response reiterated his conviction that airpower and artillery would crush any North Vietnamese assault, as well as his assertion that the outpost must be held for both military and morale reasons. On 4 February, the president secured from the Joint Chiefs of Staff their written concurrence with Westmoreland's views. At

---

[25] Msgs, Westmoreland MAC 01592 to Sharp info Wheeler and Bunker, 3 Feb 68 and MAC 01975 to Sharp and Wheeler, 12 Feb 68; and Abrams PHB 169 and PHB 231 to Westmoreland, 26 Feb 68 and 5 Mar 6. All in Westmoreland Message files, Feb and Mar 68, CMH. MFR, Chaisson, 18 Feb 68, sub: Unit Deployments, tab 65, Westmoreland History file no. 29 (1–29 Feb 68), CMH. Also Enemy plans: CIA Rpt, 20 Feb 68, copy in CMH; Ford, "Tet 1968," pp. 152–62, 168–77, 275–77. Battles for Hue and Khe Sanh are described in detail in Shulimson et al., *Marines in Vietnam, 1968*, chs. 9–12 and 14.

Johnson's direction, Westmoreland, beginning on 5 February, made a special daily report on operations at Khe Sanh and in the Demilitarized Zone area, including statistics on B–52 and tactical air strikes, tons of supply delivered to the base, and American casualties. While seeking reassurance and military details, the president left the conduct of this battle to his field commander. Johnson and his advisers, Wheeler told Westmoreland, recognized that "you are the responsible commander and that no one can direct tactical operations in the field from Washington."[26]

Among President Johnson's greatest worries about Khe Sanh was that the military might ask permission to use tactical nuclear weapons there to prevent disaster. Reassurances to the contrary from Wheeler and Westmoreland were less than convincing. Westmoreland, for example, on 3 February, after the usual expression of confidence, added that "should the situation in the Demilitarized Zone area change dramatically," the United States must be "prepared to introduce weapons of greater effectiveness against massed forces," with "either tactical nuclear weapons or chemical agents" as "active candidates for employment." During the first weeks of February, CINCPAC, MACV, and III Marine Amphibious Force continued the top-secret contingency planning, code-named FRACTURE JAW, which they had begun late in January for using tactical nuclear weapons around Khe Sanh. On the ninth, General Westmoreland approved a MACV operational plan for this purpose. By that time, however, the issue had become public in the United States, with Senator Eugene McCarthy and others charging that the military was preparing to use nuclear weapons in South Vietnam. The administration, facing a domestic and foreign outcry, publicly disavowed any such intent. Secretly, on the twelfth, at Wheeler's direction, Admiral Sharp and General Westmoreland discontinued all FRACTURE JAW planning, placed the documents under tight security control, and instructed the few staff personnel involved not to disclose even the existence of the plans.[27]

With nuclear weapons thus effectively ruled out, the Military Assistance Command used every other means at its disposal to

---

[26] Quotation is from Msg, Wheeler JCS 01316 to Westmoreland info Sharp, 4 Feb 68, Westmoreland Message files, Feb 68, CMH. Msgs, Wheeler JCS 01147, JCS 01305, JCS 01320, and JCS 02885 to Westmoreland, 1, 3, 4 Feb 68 and 13 Mar 68; Westmoreland MAC 01586, MAC 01637, MAC 02018, and MAC 02954 to Wheeler info Sharp, 3, 5, 12 Feb 68, 2 Mar 68; Westmoreland MAC 01666 to Wheeler info Sharp and Bunker, 5 Feb 68. All in Westmoreland Message files, Feb–Mar 68, CMH. MFR, Westmoreland, 16 Feb 68, sub: President's Position on Khe Sanh, tab 60, Westmoreland History file no. 29 (1–29 Feb 68), CMH.

[27] Quotation is from Msg, Westmoreland MAC 01586 to Wheeler info Sharp, 3 Feb 68; Westmoreland Message files, Feb 68, CMH. Msgs, Wheeler JCS 01154 to Sharp and Westmoreland, 1 Feb 68; Wheeler JCS 01272 to Westmoreland info Sharp, 3 Feb 68; Wheeler JCS 01678 to Sharp info Westmoreland, 10 Feb 68; Westmoreland MAC 01900 and MAC 02007 to Cushman, 10, 12 Feb 68; Westmoreland MAC 01902 to Sharp, 10 Feb 68; Sharp to Wheeler info Westmoreland, 2 Feb 68; Sharp to Westmoreland et al., 6 and 12 Feb 68. All in Westmoreland Message files, Feb 68, CMH. Controversy in the United States is covered in Hammond, *Military and the Media, 1962–1968*, pp. 361–63.

strengthen northern I Corps against the coming blow. Despite worsening weather, the command kept up round-the-clock air and artillery bombardment of the North Vietnamese divisions besieging Khe Sanh. With fighting still going on all over South Vietnam, General Westmoreland took the calculated risk of thinning American forces in II and III Corps to obtain additional reinforcements for northern I Corps, notably the aforementioned shift of the 101st Airborne Division from the Saigon area to Thua Thien. He told General Cushman on 23 February, "I have no more reserves" and warned the Marine commander, "you will have to go on extreme economy of force s[outh] of the Hai Van [and] cut corners everyplace" if still more troops were needed in the north. Reacting to the appearance of North Vietnamese tanks at Lang Vei, Westmoreland set the MACV staff to work augmenting I Corps anti-armor weaponry. In cooperation with Admiral Sharp, he resumed planning for an amphibious feint above the Demilitarized Zone to divert North Vietnamese troops from the battle in Quang Tri.[28]

As February gave way to March, the great North Vietnamese attack still did not materialize. The allies continued hammering the enemy with airpower, further expanded their logistical base north of the Hai Van, and deployed their reinforcements. They also began planning a counteroffensive to destroy Communist forces in the coastal lowlands and then break the siege of Khe Sanh.[29]

As the crisis in the north intensified, so also did General Westmoreland's doubts about the competence of III MAF's leadership. His discontent came into the open on 7 February, at a meeting at III MAF headquarters to deal with the fall of Lang Vei and with an apparent new North Vietnamese threat to Da Nang. Discerning what he considered to be an "absence of initiative" among the marines, Westmoreland gave direct instructions to General Cushman's subordinate commanders for organizing the rescue of the surviving Lang Vei defenders and for deploying battalions from the Americal Division to reinforce Da Nang. This experience, and other irritations, strengthened Westmoreland's resolve to set up a new headquarters to oversee the

---

[28] Khe Sanh bombardment is summarized in Shulimson et al., *Marines in Vietnam, 1968*, pp. 475–86. See also Memo, Col D. A. Gruenther, Dir Operations Research/Systems Analysis, Hqs MACV (MACEVAL), for COMUSMACV, 5 Apr 68, sub: An Analysis of the Khe Sanh Battle, Westmoreland History file no. 31 (1–30 Apr 68), CMH. Quotation is from Chaisson Diary, 23 Feb 68, box 9, Chaisson Papers, Hoover Institution; see also MFR, Chaisson, 24 Feb 68, sub: Commander's Guidance, tab 76, Westmoreland History file no. 29 (1–29 Feb 68), CMH. Development of amphibious feint is summarized in MACV History, 1968, vol. 2, pp. 781–82; see also Westmoreland Message files, Feb 68, CMH.

[29] Westmoreland History Notes, 1–29 Feb 68, tab 1, Westmoreland History file no. 29 (1–29 Feb 68), CMH; Westmoreland History Notes, 1–31 Mar 68, tab 1; MFR, Chaisson, 3 Mar 68, sub: COMUSMACV Visit to ICTZ, tab 5; Msg, CG III MAF to COMUSMACV, 12 Mar 68, tab 24. All in Westmoreland History file no. 30 (1–31 Mar 68), CMH; Msg, Abrams PHB 218 to Westmoreland, 4 Mar 68; Cushman to Westmoreland, Abrams, Rosson, 8 Mar 68; Abrams PHB 261 to Westmoreland, 9 Mar 68. All in Westmoreland Message files, Feb–Mar 68, CMH. MACV History, 1968, vol. 2, p. 619.

battle for I Corps, as well as his interest in bringing the marines' fixed-wing aircraft under the control of the Seventh Air Force.[30]

The establishment of MACV Forward, decided upon before Tet, went ahead essentially on schedule. The staff, drawn from MACV and USARV headquarters, began arriving at Phu Bai on 3 February and formally activated the new command on the ninth. General Abrams, his move north delayed by the enemy offensive, took up his duties three days later. Abrams carried with him orders from Westmoreland to "provide instructions" to General Cushman "on all tactical matters in I CTZ," to direct the reception and operations of incoming reinforcements, and "to effect such organizational arrangements as necessary to maintain a maximum defense posture, reaction capability, and preparations to apply maximum pressure on the enemy." General Westmoreland declared subsequently that he intended Abrams to give Cushman "whatever instructions he deemed necessary . . . to include assuming direct command of elements in I Corps if he deemed it appropriate." More succinctly, General Chaisson observed that General Abrams "is running the I CTZ show."[31]

Abrams used his sweeping authority with restraint. He attempted to improve coordination of the allied forces fighting to recapture Hue and exhorted the field commanders there to speed up the attack. He ordered intensified reconnaissance of the A Shau Valley base area west of Hue, closely supervised efforts to reopen lines of communication in northern I Corps, and helped initiate planning for the relief of Khe Sanh. The effect of his efforts was uncertain. The marines at III Marine Amphibious Force complained that at Hue, for example, MACV Forward merely complicated an already difficult command situation by giving orders directly to subordinate units. For the most part, General Cushman and his division commanders conducted the defense of Khe Sanh and the battle for Hue much as they had before Abrams took charge. Nevertheless, the deputy MACV commander was in position in I Corps, ready to take over operations if III Marine Amphibious Force faltered under the climactic enemy assault.[32]

---

[30] The 7 February meeting is described in Westmoreland, *Soldier Reports*, pp. 341–43; Westmoreland History Notes, 1–29 Feb 68, tab 1, Westmoreland History file no. 29 (1–29 Feb 68), CMH; and Chaisson Diary, 7 Feb 68, box 9, Chaisson Papers, Hoover Institution; see also entry for 23 Feb 68, ibid. Other indications of COMUSMACV's irritation at III Marine Amphibious Force are in Msgs, Westmoreland MAC 01604 and MAC 02128 to Cushman, 4, 15 Feb 68, Westmoreland Message files, Feb 68, CMH.

[31] First quotation is from Ltr, Westmoreland to Abrams, 16 Feb 68, sub: Letter of Instructions, tab 58, Westmoreland History file no. 29 (1–29 Feb 68), CMH; second is from Westmoreland History Notes, 28 Dec 67–31 Jan 68, tab A–1, Westmoreland History file no. 28 (27 Dec 67–31 Jan 68), CMH; third is from Ltr, Chaisson to Mrs Chaisson, 18 Feb 68, box 7, Chaisson Papers, Hoover Institution. Msgs, Westmoreland MAC 02270 and MAC 02452 to Sharp, 17, 21 Feb 68, Westmoreland Message files, Feb 68, CMH; Msgs, Abrams MAC 01446 and MAC 01591 to Cushman, 31 Jan 68 and 3 Feb 68, Abrams Papers, CMH. MACV History, 1968, vol. 1, pp. 217–18.

[32] Msgs, Abrams PHB 056, PHB 085, PHB 154, and PHB 169 to Westmoreland, 14, 16, 23, 26 Feb 68; Abrams PHB 086, PHB 087, PHB 126, PHB 171, and PHB 196 to Cushman info Westmoreland,

General Abrams spent much of his time at MACV Forward planning for his headquarters' demise. When General Westmoreland activated MACV Forward, he also announced his intention to convert it, around mid-March, into a corps headquarters to command U.S. forces north of the Hai Van Pass under operational control of General Cushman. This reorganization, Westmoreland claimed, would improve coordination of the Army and Marine forces in northern I Corps while reducing the number of subordinate headquarters with which III Marine Amphibious Force had to deal. The new headquarters, designated Provisional Corps, Vietnam, went into operation on 10 March under the command of Lt. Gen. William B. Rosson, who moved north to Phu Bai from his previous post as commanding general of I Field Force. Under terms of reference worked out by Generals Abrams and Cushman in consultation with the service component commanders, Provisional Corps controlled the operations of the 3d Marine, 1st Cavalry, and 101st Airborne Divisions and had responsibility for most of Thua Thien and all of Quang Tri Provinces. General Cushman, besides exercising operational control of Provisional Corps, directly commanded the 1st Marine and American Divisions in southern I Corps and retained his corpswide advisory and pacification functions. To assist Cushman, who now acted in effect as a field army commander, in handling his enlarged Army contingent, General Westmoreland assigned additional Army officers to the III MAF staff. At the same time, he augmented the Army-dominated Provisional Corps staff with Marine officers, including a Marine deputy corps commander.[33]

With the activation of Provisional Corps as a subordinate command under III Marine Amphibious Force, General Westmoreland seemingly backed away from his initial threat to supersede the marines in control of I Corps. General Chaisson expressed relief that his commander had remedied an initially "real bad" reorganization by "putting Rosson in under Cushman and easing Abe out." General Rosson, who earlier had worked under III MAF operational control as commander of Task Force OREGON (forerunner of the American Division), lost no time in establishing harmonious relations with the marines. On his part, General Cushman declared later that he "got along just fine with Bill Rosson and the other Army commanders. . . ." Nevertheless, suspicion of MACV's

16, 20, 26 Feb 68, 1 Mar 68; Abrams PHB 128 to Maj Gen John J. Tolson, CG, 1st Cav Div, info Westmoreland, 20 Feb 68. All in Westmoreland Message files, Feb–Mar 68, CMH. Chaisson, Oral History, pp. 219–20, MCHC. Command problems at Hue are summarized in Shulimson et al., *Marines in Vietnam, 1968*, pp. 237–38.

[33] Msgs, Westmoreland MAC 02270 and MAC 02452 to Sharp, 17 Feb, 21 Feb 68; Westmoreland MAC 03188 to Abrams and Cushman, 7 Mar 68; Westmoreland MAC 03022 and MAC 03430 to Gen Johnson, 3, 12 Mar 68; Westmoreland MAC 03291 to Gens Johnson and Chapman, 9 Mar 68; Abrams PHB 111, PHB 175, PHB 199, and PHB 234 to Westmoreland, 19, 27 Feb 68, 1, 6 Mar 68; Palmer to Westmoreland, 27 Feb 68. All in Westmoreland Message files, Feb–Mar 68, CMH. MFR, Chaisson, 11 Mar 68, sub: COMUSMACV Visit to ICTZ, tab 25, Westmoreland History file no. 30 (1–31 Mar 68); MACV History, 1968, vol. 1, pp. 219, 245.

General Rosson (right) *accompanied by Lt. Col. Hugh J. Bartley*

intentions persisted among Marine officers, in Washington as well as at Da Nang. One Marine Corps headquarters staff officer opined: "It is obvious that there are other moves in this chess game to come, and don't believe they are meant to be advantageous to our Corps."[34]

Seeming to justify Marine suspicions, as Provisional Corps went into operation, General Westmoreland challenged the marines on one of their most cherished points of doctrine: control of airpower. With Army and Marine divisions intermingled in I Corps and a desperate battle in prospect, Westmoreland became increasingly uneasy about the existing improvised air control system and receptive to General Momyer's continuing arguments for fundamental reorganization. In mid-February, he concluded, he told Admiral Sharp, that it was "essential that I look to one man to coordinate this air effort and bring this firepower to bear on the enemy in the most effective way in line with my day-to-day guidance." That man could only be his deputy for

[34] First quotation is from Ltr, Chaisson to Mrs Chaisson, 14 Mar 68, box 7, Chaisson Papers, Hoover Institution; second is from Cushman Interv, 13 Sep 73, pp. 37–38, MCHC; third is from Ltr, Brig Gen Earl E. Anderson, USMC, to McCutcheon, 19 Feb 68, box 20, McCutcheon Papers, MCHC. Msg, Westmoreland MAC 05919 to Wheeler, Gen Johnson, and Sharp, 5 May 68, Westmoreland Message files, May 68. Interv, Lt Col James E. Smith and Lt Col Edward P. Smith with Gen William B. Rosson, 1981, pp. 388–90, Senior Officers Oral History Program, MHI (hereafter cited as Rosson Interv).

air operations, General Momyer. Admiral Sharp, who Westmoreland saw to it was thoroughly briefed on the proposal, this time accepted Westmoreland's reasoning, primarily out of recognition, in Sharp's words, "of the necessity for maximum effective application of total air assets and for certain changes in light of the new ground force arrangements."[35]

On 7 March, Westmoreland issued an order drafted by Momyer, which Sharp had approved with minor amendments, requiring General Cushman to place his fixed-wing strike and reconnaissance aircraft and the Marine tactical air control system under the "mission direction" of General Momyer in his capacity as deputy COMUSMACV for air operations. III Marine Amphibious Force was to retain command of its helicopters and transport aircraft. Requests for air support from III Marine Amphibious Force and Provisional Corps were to be collated by those headquarters and their direct air support centers and passed to the MACV Tactical Air Support Element, which allocated airpower throughout South Vietnam. Under direction from the Tactical Air Support Element, the Seventh Air Force Tactical Air Control Center then would issue the detailed mission orders. Marines would be added to the staffs of both those agencies. As a minor concession to mollify the III Marine Amphibious Force, Westmoreland declared that he would review the working of the system after its first 30 days in operation. In practice, it took the Seventh Air Force and III Marine Amphibious Force a few weeks to combine their two air control systems and to resolve details, including the location of the I Corps Direct Air Support Center, which had been left unsettled in the original directive. The first missions under what came to be called single management were not flown until 21 March.[36]

Despite Westmoreland's reassurances, the entire Marine chain of command perceived the new system as an Air Force attempt to separate their aircraft from their ground forces, as had happened in the Korean

[35] First quotation is from Msg, Westmoreland MAC 02365 to Sharp info Wheeler, Momyer, Abrams, Cushman, 19 Feb 68, Abrams Papers, CMH; second is from Msg, Sharp to Wheeler and Westmoreland, 3 Mar 68, Westmoreland Message files, Mar 68, CMH. Msgs, Westmoreland MAC 02364 to Cushman info Abrams, 19 Feb 68; Westmoreland MAC 02771 to Sharp info Wheeler, 27 Feb 68. Both in Westmoreland Message files, Feb 68, CMH. Interv, Project CORONA HARVEST with Adm Ulysses S. Grant Sharp, 19 Feb 71, pp. 646–48, Air Force Chief of History Office (AFCHO) (hereafter cited as Sharp Interv); Ltr, Anderson to McCutcheon, 4 Mar 68, box 20, McCutcheon Papers, MCHC. Westmoreland retrospectively explains his decision in *Soldier Reports*, pp. 342–44.

[36] Msgs, Sharp to Wheeler and Westmoreland, 3 Mar 68; Westmoreland MAC 03276 to Abrams, 8 Mar 68; Westmoreland Message files, Mar 68, CMH. Ltr, Westmoreland to CG III MAF, 7 Mar 68, sub: Single Management of Strike and Reconnaissance Assets, tab 13; Ltr, Westmoreland to DepCOMUSMACV for Air Operations, 8 Mar 68, same sub, tab 14. Both in Westmoreland History file no. 30 (1–31 Mar 68), CMH. MACV Fact Sheet on Preplanned Close Air Support, 4 Apr 68, tab 19, Westmoreland History file no. 31 (1–3 Apr 68), CMH. Msgs, Abrams PHB 225 to Momyer, 5 Mar 68; Abrams PHB 234 to Westmoreland, 6 Mar 68. Both in Westmoreland Message files, Mar 68, CMH; MACV History, 1968, vol. 1, p. 437.

Secretary of Defense Clifford (right) *and presidential adviser Walt W. Rostow.*

War. The marines began their war on single management as soon as Westmoreland announced his intention to institute it and never let up thereafter. Their commandant, General Leonard F. Chapman, told Marine officers: "The integrity of our air/ground team concept and possibly even our force structure is at issue. We must all face this challenge resolutely to forestall any future inroads on the Marine air/ground team." General Cushman and General Victor H. Krulak, commander of Fleet Marine Force Pacific, campaigned continuously at their respective levels, while General Chapman took the marines' case to the Joint Chiefs of Staff. Through informal and formal channels, the marines brought the issue to the attention of President Johnson, the incoming secretary of defense, Clark M. Clifford, and the news media.[37]

The Marine leaders attacked single management on both doctrinal and practical grounds. They contended that Sharp and Westmoreland had exceeded their authority by imposing an air command arrangement contrary to Defense Department doctrine for organizing joint forces. They claimed that single management deprived the Marine divisions in Vietnam, which relied on tactical air support to compensate for limited

---

[37] Quotation is from Commandant, Marine Corps (CMC) Green Letter 4–68 to all General Officers, 9 Apr 68, sub: Air Control in I Corps, CMC Green Ltr Book, 1968; and Memo, CMC for JCS, 4 Mar 68, sub: Single Management, HQMC DC/S (Air) Single Manager File, Jan 68–15 Aug 70, MCHC; Anderson Interv, 17 Mar 81, pp. 196–97. Msgs, Wheeler JCS 3602 and JCS 3665 to Westmoreland, 2 Apr 68 and 3 Apr 68, Westmoreland Message files, Apr 68, CMH; Sharp Interv, 19 Feb 71, pp. 642, 648–49.

quantities of organic artillery and helicopter gunships, of an important element of their inherent firepower. They insisted that the change was unnecessary, because the two air control systems in I Corps had coexisted without major difficulty, and unified command for specific operations could be arranged when required, as at Khe Sanh. Finally, the marines declared, on the basis of a steady stream of data from III Marine Amphibious Force, that single management had made the securing of air support slower and more complicated for ground commanders by inserting additional headquarters into the process and by replacing a "consumer-oriented" Marine strike request and control system with the Air Force's "producer-oriented" one. In conclusion, the marines asked Admiral Sharp and the Joint Chiefs of Staff to direct General Westmoreland to restore the previous arrangement under which III Marine Amphibious Force had controlled its own aircraft and provided those sorties it could spare to the Seventh Air Force. General Cushman went so far as to suggest that, if a single manager for airpower were needed in I Corps, it should be himself, since he commanded a considerable air force and his strike request and control system easily could handle aircraft of other services.[38]

General Westmoreland strongly defended single management. He disavowed any intention to revise current joint doctrine or break up the Marine air-ground team, and he promised that Marine airplanes would continue to fly missions for Marine ground troops unless urgent tactical needs dictated otherwise. Citing Seventh Air Force evaluations, he insisted that the system, after initial adjustment problems, was working with steadily increasing efficiency. He noted that the Army provided the Marine divisions in I Corps with helicopter, artillery, reconnaissance, engineer, and communications support; hence, the marines could not legitimately object to sharing their airpower with the other services. Above all, Westmoreland emphasized the need for unified control of MACV's airpower given the intermingling of Army and Marine units in I Corps, the creation of Provisional Corps, and the need to concentrate forces in situations like the defense of Khe Sanh. Under these conditions, he told Wheeler, "the continuation of dual strike support systems was operationally unacceptable" to him as "the responsible commander in Vietnam." Increasingly irritated at what he considered the marines' "parochial inflexibility," Westmoreland declared in retrospect that single management was the only issue during his tenure at MACV over which he considered resigning.[39]

---

[38] Typical Marine arguments are in Marine Corps Brief for JCS, Single Management, 9 Apr 68, encl. 1 to CMC Green Ltr 4–68, CMC Green Ltr Book, 1968, MCHC; Msg, CG III MAF to COMUSMACV, 20 Feb 68, tab 72, Westmoreland History file no. 29 (1–29 Feb 68), CMH; Msg, CG III MAF to COMUSMACV, 22 Apr 68, in MACV History, 1968, vol. 1, p. 439. The detailed development of the marines' arguments and their campaign against single management can be followed through the HQMC DC/S (Air) Single Manager File, Jan 68–15 Aug 70, MCHC.

[39] Phrases quoted are from Msgs, Westmoreland MAC 04266 and MAC 04367 to Wheeler, 29, 31 Mar 68, Westmoreland Message files, Mar 68, CMH. In same files, see Msgs, Westmoreland

*An F–4B Phantom of Marine Attack Squadron 542 completes
a bombing run on a heavily fortified enemy position.*

When the issue reached the Joint Chiefs of Staff, the Navy, Marine, and—to Westmoreland's disgust—the Army chiefs came out against single management. All were reluctant to upset existing hard-won roles and missions agreements, and they distrusted Air Force intentions toward their own air arms. Only General John P. McConnell, the Air Force chief of staff, along with General Wheeler, upheld Westmoreland. Wheeler's support came with qualifications. The chairman of the Joint Chiefs of Staff late in April advised the secretary of defense against vetoing single management, on the premise that it was "militarily unsound to dictate to responsible senior commanders of the level of COMUSMACV and . . . CINCPAC, how to organize their forces and exercise command and control of them." Wheeler added, however, that single management in Vietnam should not be seen as a precedent governing the future control of Marine air units. Instead, it was an

MAC 02674 to Wheeler, 25 Feb 68; Westmoreland MAC 02771 to Sharp, 27 Feb 68; Westmoreland MAC 04545 to Cushman, 5 Apr 68. Memo, Westmoreland for Wheeler, 24 Feb 68, sub: Single Management . . . , tab 85. Both in Westmoreland History file no. 29 (1–29 Feb 68), CMH. Seventh Air Force views are summarized in MACV History, 1968, vol. 1, pp. 437–38. Westmoreland's anger at the marines is reflected in *Soldier Reports*, pp. 343–44.

"expedient adopted to meet a situation imposed by the enemy," which Westmoreland "can and should" adjust as the situation changed.[40]

Even as Wheeler made his recommendation, circumstances compelled General Westmoreland to modify the workings of single management. As the time for the first thirty-day review approached, it was apparent that single management was slower and more cumbersome than the old system in handling requests for ground force support and had resulted in the Marine divisions receiving fewer tactical air sorties—facts that III Marine Amphibious Force and the 1st Marine Aircraft Wing documented in great detail. Admiral Sharp, increasingly concerned about III MAF complaints on this point, early in May over Westmoreland's protests dispatched a CINCPAC team to Vietnam to evaluate the system. The team, after consultation with all the concerned commanders, essentially affirmed the validity of Marine criticisms of single management's workings. At the same time, General Wheeler also expressed unease about single management's reported unresponsiveness to ground commanders.[41]

Before the CINCPAC team made its report, Westmoreland and Momyer, under pressure from all sides, agreed to change single management in practice to save it in principle. Following MACV commanders' conferences on the subject on 2 and 8 May, Momyer, at Westmoreland's direction, developed a revised air strike request and control procedure that went into effect later that month, after thorough review and approval by Admiral Sharp. Under it, the Seventh Air Force allocated large blocs of sorties weekly to each corps area commander, who then could employ them as he saw fit. This meant in practice that III Marine Amphibious Force regularly received back about 70 percent of the Marine sorties it turned over to the Seventh Air Force. Other changes at the same time enhanced the system's speed and flexibility in responding to support requests from ground commanders. These alterations alleviated Sharp's and Wheeler's concerns about single management, though they did not fully satisfy the marines.[42]

---

[40] Quotation is from Msg, Wheeler JCS 4560 to Westmoreland, 27 Apr 68, Westmoreland Message files, Apr 68, CMH. In same files for Mar 68, see Msgs, Wheeler JCS 3422 and JCS 3562 to Westmoreland, 27 and 31 Mar 68. Msg, CMC to CG Fleet Marine Force, Pacific (FMFPAC), 26 Mar 68, McCutcheon folder, Memos for the Record, 1966–68; Ltr, McCutcheon to Brig Gen Earl E. Anderson, USMC, and Maj Gen Norman J. Anderson, USMC, 9 Apr 68, box 20. Both in McCutcheon Papers, MCHC. General Westmoreland later referred to General Johnson's vote against him as "an amazing thing." See Interv, Maj Paul L. Miles, Jr, with William Westmoreland, 6 Mar 71, Paul L. Miles Papers, MHI, p. 14.

[41] Msg, National Military Command Center to COMUSMACV, 30 Mar 68, tab 64, Westmoreland History file no. 30 (1–31 Mar 68), CMH; Msg, CG FMFPAC to CMC, 3 May 68, HQMC Message files, MCHC; Ltr, Hutch to McCutcheon, [May 68]; CINCPAC Evaluation Team, Draft Report, sub: Single Management of Air Support, HQMC DC/S (Air) Single Manager File, Jan 68–15 Aug 70. Both in MCHC. Msg, Wheeler JCS 5196 to Westmoreland info Sharp 13 May 68, Westmoreland Message files, May 68, CMH; Ltr, Chaisson to Mrs Chaisson, 2 May 68, box 7, Chaisson Papers, Hoover Institution.

[42] Msgs, Westmoreland MAC 6075 and MAC 6343 to Sharp, 9 May 68, 15 May 68; Kerwin

Not coincidentally, the Office of the Secretary of Defense issued its final decision on single management only after these changes were under way. On 15 May, Deputy Secretary of Defense Paul H. Nitze, acting for Secretary Clifford, endorsed Wheeler's view that COMUSMACV, as the unified commander on the scene, must be allowed to organize his own forces as he deemed necessary to meet the threat. Nitze, however, also repeated Wheeler's dictum that single management was not a precedent for centralized control of airpower under "other combat conditions"; and he declared further that MACV should "revert to normal command arrangements for III MAF when the tactical situation permits." Taking note of Marine Corps complaints about the workings of single management and of the changes MACV was making, Nitze directed General Wheeler to continue to review "personally" the operation of the system and to determine, in conjunction with Sharp and Westmoreland any additional revisions needed to "minimize delays between requests for air support and their execution."[43]

Nitze's ruling represented a partial victory for both sides. Westmoreland and Momyer gained the principle, and to a degree the reality, of centralized Seventh Air Force direction of fixed-wing airpower. MACV also ended the dual air control system in I Corps, an action that even General Cushman acknowledged in retrospect had been necessary. The marines, if only for doctrinal reasons, continued their campaign for formal termination of single management. Nevertheless, under the May revisions of the system and through later incremental changes, they were assured of the availability of their airplanes to support their own ground troops. Army forces throughout South Vietnam perhaps benefited most from single management. The changes the Seventh Air Force made in its strike request and control system to defuse III Marine Amphibious Force complaints made the Air Force system work more like that of the marines, ensuring Army division commanders highly responsive close air support. As a result, the Army in Vietnam became a strong defender of single management.[44]

---

to Westmoreland, Abrams, et al., 11 May 68; Sharp to Westmoreland info Momyer and Cushman, 11 May 68; Westmoreland MAC 6342 to Wheeler info Sharp, 15 May 68; Sharp to Wheeler info Westmoreland, 25 May 68. All in Westmoreland Message files, May 68, CMH. Westmoreland History Notes, 1–31 May 68, tab 1, Westmoreland History file no. 32 (1–31 May 68), CMH; Msgs, CG III MAF to CMC, 4 May 68; CG FMFPAC to CMC, 22 and 26 May 68. All in HQMC Message files, MCHC.

[43] Quotations are from Memo, Dep Sec Def Paul H. Nitze for CJCS, 15 May 68, sub: Opcon of III MAF Aviation Assets, HQMC DC/S (Air) Single Manager File, Jan 68–15 Aug 70, MCHC; in same file, see Memo, CJCS for Dep Sec Def, 15 May 68, sub: Single Management . . . , and Msg, CJCS to CINCPAC and COMUSMACV, 20 May 68. Wheeler transmits Nitze's ruling to Sharp and Westmoreland in Msg, JCS 5378, 17 May 68, Westmoreland Message files, May 68, CMH. MACV History, 1968, vol. 1, pp. 439–40.

[44] The marines' continuing campaign against single management can be followed through the HQMC DC/S (Air) Single Manager File, Jan 68–15 Aug 70 and HQMC Message files for the same period, all in MCHC. Ltr, Cushman to McCutcheon, 10 Jul 70, box 12, McCutcheon Papers, MCHC, contains the III Marine Amphibious Force commander's acknowledgement of the need for air command

By the time the single management controversy was resolved, the question largely had lost its urgency. During March, the North Vietnamese, battered by American airpower, gradually abandoned their siege of Khe Sanh. Army units employing airmobile tactics and Marine units advancing along Highway 9 linked up with the defenders on 6 April. Similarly, the Communist threat to overrun Quang Tri and Thua Thien withered under allied counterattacks. Greater changes in the war also were in progress. Generals Westmoreland and Momyer and Admiral Sharp, three principals in the airpower controversy, were preparing to end their tours at MACV, Seventh Air Force, and CINCPAC. A partial cessation of the bombing of North Vietnam, ordered by President Johnson on 31 March, reduced demands on MACV's airpower resources. When Secretary Nitze issued his ruling, the United States and North Vietnam were preparing to begin peace negotiations. These events stemmed largely from the political and psychological impact of the Tet offensive in the United States, an impact MACV's actions inadvertently intensified.[45]

Losing the Battle of Perceptions

Besides repairing physical damage and trying to recover the military and pacification initiative in South Vietnam, MACV and the rest of the U.S. mission struggled to counteract the psychological devastation the Tet offensive had inflicted in the United States. Of all their post-Tet efforts, this one proved the least successful. The nationwide Communist attacks, coming as they did after months of optimistic reporting from MACV and the U.S. Embassy in Saigon, profoundly shocked the American press, public, and government. The more than 600 reporters in South Vietnam, and their editors in the United States and around the world, generally portrayed the offensive as a disastrous allied defeat. Their stories emphasized the death, destruction, horror, and confusion of the post-Tet fighting; their commentaries presented the setback as probably irreversible and the war as unwinnable by the United States.[46]

changes in I Corps. Brig Gen Henry W. Hise, USMC, Comments on Draft History of *U.S. Marines in Vietnam 1969*, 3 Sep 86, Vietnam Comment File, MCHC; Ltr, McCutcheon to Lt Col C. G. Dahl, USMC, 18 Jul 68, box 20, McCutcheon Papers, MCHC.

[45] The relief of Khe Sanh is summarized in Sharp and Westmoreland, *Report*, pp. 164, 186–87, and Shulimson et al., *Marines in Vietnam, 1968*, pp. 283–90. General Momyer's replacement is discussed in Msgs, McConnell to Westmoreland, 22 Apr 68, and Westmoreland MAC 05392 to McConnell, 23 Apr 68, Westmoreland Message files, Apr 68, CMH.

[46] General Wheeler expresses anxiety over the state of U.S. public opinion in Msg JCS 2721 to Westmoreland and Sharp, 8 Mar 68, Westmoreland Message files, Mar 68, CMH. News media coverage of Tet is analyzed in great detail and its defeatism criticized in Peter Braestrup, *Big Story: How the American Press and Television Reported and Interpreted the Crisis of Tet 1968 in Vietnam and Washington*, 2 vols. (Boulder, Colo.: Westview Press and Freedom House, 1977). The impact of the offensive on both official and unofficial America is well summarized in Hammond, *Military and the Media, 1962–1968*, chs. 15 and 16, and Oberdorfer, *Tet!* chs. 5 and 7.

Among American officials and political leaders, the Tet crisis provided a justification for long-term doubters to break with administration policy; and it turned many supporters of the war into new doubters. A flow of undigested, often alarmist, early reports from lower echelons of MACV and the U.S. mission intensified official concern and undermined the credibility of General Westmoreland's and Ambassador Komer's assessments. Reflecting the gloom of the time, the secretary of defense's systems analysis office, in its February Southeast Asia report, pronounced that the offensive had "killed" the pacification program "as currently conceived."[47]

From the first day of the offensive, General Westmoreland and his senior staff worked to get their version of events over to the news reporters in Saigon. Following his impromptu press conference at the U.S. Embassy the morning of the thirty-first, Westmoreland held a more extended formal session on 1 February. Thereafter, the MACV commander, Ambassador Komer, and members of the senior staff met frequently with reporters individually and in groups. General Chaisson wrote to his wife on 2 March: "More reporters. Every day now I have one. [Brig. Gen. Winant] Sidle [the MACV chief of information] is my booking agent." Besides trying to sell the press MACV's assessment of the offensive, the command also enforced more strictly its rules on release of military information, especially concerning casualties and damage from rocket and artillery bombardments, so as to deny the enemy knowledge of the effects of their attacks. Westmoreland, as had been his pre-Tet practice, used selected visitors to the command as conduits for his views. Although the Defense Department curtailed trips to South Vietnam in response to the enemy offensive, Generals Wheeler and Westmoreland arranged for a previously scheduled visit by retired General Bruce C. Clarke to go forward in hopes that Clarke would "report his impressions in appropriate channels and media." In a new departure, Westmoreland, with Generals Chaisson and Davidson, on 21 February briefed the assembled foreign ambassadors to Saigon in order, as he put it, "to counter misimpressions based on rumors or extreme press reports."[48]

---

[47] Westmoreland, *Soldier Reports*, p. 334, retrospectively claims the administration lost its nerve after Tet. Low-level reporting is denounced in Memo, Komer for Bunker, 9 May 68, Bunker—Memos to RWK (1967–68); quotation from Southeast Asia report is from Msg, Komer MAC 4188 to Alain C. Enthoven, Assistant Secretary of Defense for Systems Analysis, 26 Mar 68, Backchannel file (1967–68). Both in DepCORDS files, CMH. Other official expressions of pessimism about pacification can be found in *United States–Vietnam Relations*, sec. 4.C.6.(c), pp. 26, 33.

[48] Transcript, Gen Westmoreland's Press Conference, 1 Feb 68, tab 3, Westmoreland History file no. 29 (1–29 Feb 68), CMH. Amb Komer's Press Backgrounder, 24 Feb 68, Chronological File: Komer (1968), DepCORDS files, CMH. Chaisson quotation is from Ltr to Mrs. Chaisson, 2 Mar 68, box 7, Chaisson Papers, Hoover Institution. Information control: Msgs, Sharp to Westmoreland info Wheeler, 24, 29 Feb 68; Westmoreland MAC 02766 to Sharp info Wheeler, 27 Feb 68; Westmoreland Message files, Feb 68, CMH; visits: Msgs, Wheeler JCS 1304 and JCS 1315 to Sharp and Westmoreland, 3, 4 Feb 68 (quotation from latter message); Westmoreland MAC 01625 to Wheeler and Sharp,

The tone of MACV's public relations became more restrained early in March, as the result of guidance from newly installed Secretary of Defense Clark Clifford. Concerned lest overoptimistic statements produce another public backlash if the enemy attacked again in force, Clifford instructed the Military Assistance Command through General Wheeler to be "conservative" in assessing the situation and avoid denigrating the enemy, forecasting his plans, and predicting allied victory. The command instead should "express the view that there is tough fighting ahead and that the enemy has residual capabilities not yet committed"—a view Westmoreland had been expressing all along. Westmoreland pointed out to Wheeler that he needed to maintain an optimistic tone to keep up the morale of his own and the South Vietnamese forces. Nevertheless, he privately passed Clifford's instructions on to his staff and senior commanders.[49]

Within the government, MACV and the U.S. Embassy used every available channel to reassure their superiors in Washington that all was far from lost in Vietnam and that the enemy was taking a severe beating. Yet their reports met much official skepticism. MACV's statistics on enemy casualties, for example, came into question, especially as the claimed number of enemy killed and wounded approached the estimated total strength of the Viet Cong and North Vietnamese Tet attack force. After a review of unit reports by his inspector general, Westmoreland defended the accuracy of MACV's body counts. Enemy sources that subsequently became available indicated that Communist losses were indeed extremely high, 50 percent or more in some battalions. Nevertheless, controversy and recrimination over the estimates of enemy casualties and strength persisted within the government and indeed within the MACV J–2 section, where junior intelligence officers continued to claim that the command was understating the enemy's numbers and overstating his losses.[50]

After Tet, the Central Intelligence Agency revived its longstanding order-of-battle controversy with MACV. In September of the previous

---

4 Feb 68. All in Westmoreland Message files, Feb 68, CMH. Final quotation is from Westmoreland History Notes, 1–29 Feb 68, tab 1, Westmoreland History file no. 29 (1–29 Feb 68), CMH.

[49] Quotation is from Msg, Wheeler CJCS 2721 to Westmoreland and Sharp, 8 Mar 68; see also CJCS 2626, 5 Mar 68; Msgs, Westmoreland MAC 03280 to Wheeler info Sharp, 8 Mar 68; Sharp to Wheeler info Westmoreland, 10 Mar 68. All in Westmoreland Message files, Mar 68, CMH. Chaisson Diary, 9 Mar 68, box 9, Chaisson Papers, Hoover Institution; Hammond, *Military and the Media, 1962–1968*, pp. 367–68.

[50] Msg, Sharp to Westmoreland info Wheeler, 23 Mar 68, Westmoreland Message files, Mar 68, CMH; and Memo, Komer for Bunker, 8 Apr 68, Chronological File, Komer (1968), DepCORDS files, CMH. Casualties: MFR, Bryan, 3 Feb 68, sub: CIIB Meeting, 3 Feb 68, tab 17, Westmoreland History file no. 29 (1–29 Feb 68), CMH. Msgs, Wheeler JCS 1439 to Westmoreland and Sharp, 6 Feb 68; Westmoreland MAC 01754 to Wheeler info Sharp, 7 Feb 68; Westmoreland Message files, Feb 68; Jones, *War Without Windows*, ch. 17; Msg, COMUSMACV MAC 11551 to Address Indicator Group 7055, Director National Security Agency (DIRNSA), et al., 24 Apr 68, tab 59, Westmoreland History file no. 31 (1–30 Apr 68); and CIA Intelligence Information Report, 13 Aug 70. Both in CMH.

year, after a lengthy and acrimonious controversy, the agency and MACV had reached a compromise on the Communist order of battle. In the compromise, the CIA representatives agreed to delete from the order of battle the 150,000 or so part-time Viet Cong self-defense troops and to accept a strength of about 300,000 for the remaining military categories. Many CIA analysts regarded this arrangement as a sellout of their agency position, and they took the Tet offensive as an occasion to renew the fight for what they considered to be the truth. During February, the agency asserted (and leaked to the press) that the Communist force in South Vietnam in fact numbered between 400,000 and 600,000 men, nearly double the earlier agreed-upon total. CIA analysts added back into the order of battle the irregular categories earlier excluded at the insistence of MACV, claiming that those elements had played a major role in the Tet assaults. The Military Assistance Command and CINCPAC rejected this estimate on the same substantive and public relations grounds they had used the previous year. Westmoreland argued in addition that no members of the contested enemy categories had been captured during the offensive and that the enemy units contacted in the fighting all previously had been listed in the MACV order of battle.[51]

In contrast to the compromise reached in 1967, this time neither side in the controversy was willing to alter its position for the sake of presenting a public united front. In mid-April, an interagency order-of-battle conference at CIA Headquarters in Langley, Virginia, ended in deadlock, with the CIA and State Department supporting an estimate of 480,000–615,000, MACV and CINCPAC holding to 278,000–328,000, and the Defense Intelligence Agency and the Joint Chiefs of Staff vainly trying to promote a compromise. Early in May, the directors of the CIA and Defense Intelligence Agency agreed not to publicize any new enemy strength figures until interagency differences could be resolved. At the same time, the Office of the Secretary of Defense launched a review of the entire order-of-battle issue. Despite these efforts, the dispute dragged on without resolution.[52]

---

[51] Memo, Enthoven for Sec Def, 26 Apr 68, sub: Differences in the Estimates of Enemy Forces in SVN, CMH. Msgs, Westmoreland MAC 5301 to Sharp and Wheeler, 22 Apr 68; Sharp to Wheeler, 26 Apr 68. Both in Westmoreland Message files, Apr 68. Memo, Sidle for COMUSMACV, sub: Release of 1st Quarter 1968 Enemy Strength Figures, 11 Apr 68, CMH, illustrates the public relations element of the argument. For other views, see Davidson, *Vietnam Secrets*, pp. 51–53; and Graham Interv, 30 Mar 82, sess. 1, p. 16, and 30 Jun 82, sess. 2, pp. 34–36. Cosmas, *Years of Escalation, 1962–1967*, ch. 13, describes the 1967 debates.

[52] Msgs, Davidson MAC 04572 to Westmoreland, 5 Apr 68; Wheeler JCS 4816 to Sharp and Westmoreland, 4 May 68; Westmoreland MAC 06055 to Wheeler and Sharp, 9 May 68; Sharp to Wheeler info Westmoreland, 11 May 68. All in Westmoreland Message files, Apr–May 68, CMH. Memos, Thomas L. Hughes, Bureau of Intelligence Research for Sec State, 29 Apr 68, sub: Conflicting MACV and CIA Assessments of Enemy Strength in South Vietnam; Enthoven for Sec Def, 26 Apr 68, sub: Differences in the Estimate of Enemy Forces in SVN; and Nitze for CJCS, 3 May 68, sub: VC/NVA Order of Battle, and for Director CIA, 6 May 68, same sub; all in CMH.

Well before the order-of-battle dispute reached its inconclusive denouement, senior American officials in Vietnam realized that, all their public and private efforts notwithstanding, they were losing the war of perceptions. General Abrams, just returned from a trip to Washington, told a MACV commanders' conference on 31 March that "while the enemy failed in RVN, he won in the U.S. This is manifested by the loss in political support suffered by the President in recent weeks." In a memorandum to Ambassador Bunker soon thereafter, Robert Komer was even more direct:

Despite our efforts, official Washington (not to mention the Congress and the public) has totally misread the real situation here. Washington has focused on our own losses, not on the enemy's. It has been swayed far more by the press than by our own reporting. It has counseled with its fears rather than its hopes. As a result, all too many see cutting our losses as the only way out of a painful impasse. . . .[53]

Reinforcement Request and Policy Decision

The Military Assistance Command and the Joint Chiefs of Staff unintentionally intensified the administration's defeatist mood. They did so by reopening during the Tet offensive the issue of further American troop deployments to Vietnam and its companion question of mobilizing the reserves. In mid-1967, the administration, in its reinforcement Program Five, in effect leveled off MACV's American troop strength at the highest point sustainable without a reserve call-up. In addition, by year-end, President Johnson was well on the way to adopting a policy of holding both ground force strength and the bombing of the north at existing levels while gradually turning the fighting over to the South Vietnamese. General Westmoreland accommodated himself to the policy that he saw taking shape, expressing confidence that he could accomplish his mission with the troops that he had and announcing his intention to begin shifting the war's burden to Saigon's forces. However, he continued to assert that with more men and broader authority to attack the enemy's Laotian and Cambodian bases and supply routes he could prevail in much less time. General Wheeler and the Joint Chiefs of Staff were even less satisfied with the Program Five decision. They persisted in advocating a more aggressive strategy in Southeast Asia and viewed with increasing dismay the effects of failure to mobilize for the Vietnam War on America's worldwide military posture.[54]

---

[53] Abrams quotation is from MFR, Chaisson, 5 Apr 68, sub: MACV Commanders' Conference, 31 Mar 68, tab 68, Westmoreland History file no. 30 (1–31 Mar 68), CMH. Komer quotation is from Memo for Bunker, 8 Apr 68, Chronological File: Komer (1968), DepCORDS files, CMH.

[54] Earlier debates and decisions on reinforcements are recounted in Cosmas, *Years of Escalation, 1962–1967*, chs. 12 and 13.

By early 1968, in General Wheeler's view, the mobilization issue had reached the crisis stage. Influenced by the apprehension that the Tet offensive had created in Washington, the Joint Chiefs of Staff chairman viewed the situation in South Vietnam with less confidence than did Westmoreland, Bunker, and Komer. Wheeler was even more pessimistic about the ability of the American armed forces to deal with any additional threats that might develop. In February 1968, the strategic reserve in the United States consisted, aside from divisions earmarked for NATO, only of the 82d Airborne Division and parts of two Marine divisions and aircraft wings. All American forces, including those deployed overseas, had been stripped of skilled specialists and subjected to constant personnel turnover to sustain the units in South Vietnam, with deleterious effects on combat readiness. Even with these sacrifices, the services, especially the Army and the Marine Corps, could barely maintain their strength in Vietnam; and they faced new demands for men to replace heavy Tet casualties. From the Joint Chiefs' viewpoint, immediate mobilization was necessary to restore worldwide American military strength. General Wheeler sought to use the Tet emergency to bring it about.[55]

To do this, Wheeler needed a request from General Westmoreland for substantial reinforcements. Such a request, however, was not immediately forthcoming. Westmoreland was confident that he could defeat the Tet offensive with the troops on hand and knew that he already had or had been promised most of what the United States could provide without mobilization. Hence, he regarded further reinforcements as desirable but not essential. His only major concern was the possibility that the South Koreans, if the *Pueblo* crisis worsened, might want to withdraw their two divisions and marine brigade from South Vietnam, which would require their replacement "man for man" with American or other non-Vietnamese troops. Beyond his immediate situation, the general knew that President Johnson wanted to top off the American commitment and had publicly endorsed that position.[56]

Westmoreland's immediate post-Tet requests were modest. On 3 February, in response to a presidential inquiry, he asked only for additional air transport squadrons and air drop equipment for resupply of Khe Sanh; for accelerated issue of M16 rifles, M60 machine guns, and

---

[55] Wheeler's concerns are summarized in Herbert Y. Schandler, *The Unmaking of a President: Lyndon Johnson and Vietnam* (Princeton, N.J.: Princeton University Press, 1977), pp. 107–09. The Army's difficulties are summarized in Col Reamer Argo, Talking Paper, 12 Aug 69, sub: The World Situation Dec 67–Feb 68 vs the U.S. Army's Capability to React, tab 94, Westmoreland History file no. 29 (1–29 Feb 68), CMH. The problem of casualties and replacements is addressed in Msg, Palmer ARV 393 to Gen Johnson, 16 Feb 68, Westmoreland Message files, Feb 68, CMH.

[56] Quotation is from Msg, Westmoreland MAC 01599 to Sharp info Wheeler et al., 4 Feb 68; see also Msgs, Sharp to Wheeler et al., 31 Jan 68; Westmoreland Message files, Jan–Feb 68, CMH. Westmoreland outlines his tactical and strategic concerns in paper, "The Origins of the Post-Tet 1968 Plans for Additional Forces in RVN," 18 Apr 70, passim, copy in CMH. See also Westmoreland, *Soldier Reports*, pp. 352–53.

mortars to the South Vietnamese Army; for replacement helicopters and reconnaissance aircraft; and for early shipment of a Navy Seabee battalion already part of Program Five. He also urged the administration to do its utmost to prevent any Korean withdrawals and to speed up negotiations with Seoul, begun before Tet, for an additional Korean light infantry division. Finally, in a supplementary message on the seventh, Westmoreland suggested that the administration reduce or slow down the effort, initiated under Program Five, to replace 12,000 military logistic personnel with Vietnamese civilians. He claimed that the Tet offensive had demonstrated that local workers could not be relied upon in emergencies, such as the Viet Cong attacks on the cities and American bases.[57]

With Westmoreland slow to request additional troops, General Wheeler took the initiative. Besides moving immediately to meet Westmoreland's equipment requirements, Wheeler on 8 February, via a personal backchannel message, asked the field commander: "Do you need reinforcements?" Wheeler told Westmoreland that the administration could provide the bulk of the remaining national reserve, namely the 82d Airborne Division and about half a Marine division. He also declared that if Westmoreland considered reinforcements "imperative," he "should not be bound by earlier agreements." "In summary, if you need more troops, ask for them." Reinforcing Wheeler's question, Admiral Sharp at about the same time suggested to Westmoreland that this might be an opportune moment to ask for additional men and equipment. Both Wheeler and Sharp directed Westmoreland to keep his replies within the backchannel, presumably to allow orchestration of the military's approach to the president and secretary of defense.[58]

On 8 February, responding to these proddings from his superiors, General Westmoreland submitted both a short-range reinforcement request and a statement of possible additional requirements, over and above Program Five, for the rest of 1968. He asked that the 82d Airborne Division and the Marine division be prepared for deployment in the unlikely but possible event of the fall of Khe Sanh or other important positions in northern I Corps, which would require MACV to counterattack to regain the lost ground. To ease the strain on allied logistics in the area, Westmoreland suggested that the units, if deployed, come

---

[57] Msgs, Westmoreland MAC 01586 and MAC 01717, to Wheeler info Sharp, 3 Feb 68 and 7 Feb 68, Westmoreland Message files, Feb 68, CMH. Negotiations between Washington and Seoul about the light infantry division are summarized in MACV History, 1968, vol. 1, pp. 346–47. See ibid., vol. 1, pp. 228–29, for background on civilianization.

[58] Schandler, *Unmaking of a President*, pp. 95–99, emphasizes Wheeler's role in eliciting reinforcement requests from MACV. Quotation is from Msg, Wheeler JCS 01529 to Westmoreland info Sharp, 8 Feb 68; see also JCS 01303 (same addressees), 3 Feb 68; Sharp to Westmoreland, 5 Feb 68; and Westmoreland MAC 01718 to Sharp, 7 Feb 68. All in Westmoreland Message files, Feb 68, CMH.

in over the beach near Quang Tri City in April when weather and sea conditions would permit such an operation.[59]

In a second message, Westmoreland furnished Wheeler a preliminary list of "the additional resources required in the coming year if we are to achieve our national purpose in South Vietnam," predicated "on the assumption that the 525,000 force structure ceiling will be lifted." Westmoreland accorded "number one priority" in this list to provide still more equipment for the South Vietnamese armed forces, including helicopters and armored personnel carriers, to accelerate their modernization so that they could assume "a greater share of the burden of defeating the enemy." Next in importance came securing the Korean light infantry division or a U.S. equivalent for deployment in northern II Corps and early dispatch of the remaining Program Five forces, followed by mention of the need for another jet airfield near Hue and Phu Bai. Turning finally to "restoration of items eliminated by the 525,000 force structure ceiling," Westmoreland stated a requirement for an additional American infantry division "particularly if operations in Laos are authorized," a four-battalion engineer group to help with post-Tet reconstruction, enough helicopter units to convert one of his infantry divisions into a second airmobile division, more air transport and fighter squadrons, and vessels to expand the Mobile Riverine Force that operated in the Mekong Delta. He also repeated his request for reduction of the civilianization program.[60]

These requests were still not immediate and urgent enough for Wheeler's purposes. Observing that the administration could handle only one major problem at a time, the Joint Chiefs of Staff chairman on 9 February instructed Westmoreland to delay formal submission of his supplementary program until early March and concentrate instead on "your immediate requirements stemming from the present situation in South Vietnam." Wheeler made clear to Westmoreland that the immediate requirement should be for the earliest possible deployment of the 82d Airborne Division and the marines to insure against the chance that the South Vietnamese Army might "falter here and there" and to "assist in defense or pursuit operations." He concluded:

Please understand I am not trying to sell you on the deployment of additional forces which in any event I cannot guarantee, and I do not want to minimize the problems which would be encountered and the difficulties of all kinds associated with such a decision. However, my sensing is that the critical phase of the war is upon us, and I do not believe that you should refrain from asking for what you believe is required under the circumstances.[61]

---

[59] Msg, Westmoreland MAC 01810 to Sharp and Wheeler, 8 Feb 68, Westmoreland Message files, Feb 68, CMH. Westmoreland, "Additional Forces," pp. 3–9, CMH, retrospectively summarizes the rationale for this request.

[60] Msg, Westmoreland MAC 01812 to Wheeler info Sharp, 8 Feb 68, Westmoreland Message files, Feb 68, CMH; Westmoreland, "Additional Forces," pp. 11–16.

[61] Msgs, Wheeler JCS 01589 and JCS 01590 to Westmoreland info Sharp, 9 Feb 68, Westmoreland Message files, Feb 68, CMH.

Responding to Wheeler's guidance, Westmoreland promptly deferred his longer range request and asked for immediate dispatch of elements of the 82d Airborne Division and part of a Marine division. This request itself required careful shaping by General Wheeler. In a series of exchanges with Sharp and Westmoreland, Wheeler between 9 and 12 February guided the MACV commander from a statement that he would "welcome" additional troops to a "firm request" for immediate dispatch to I Corps of a brigade of the 82d Airborne Division and a Marine regimental landing team (roughly equivalent in size to an Army brigade), a total reinforcement of about 10,500 troops. He asked that the remainder of the 82d Airborne Division and of a Marine division be prepared for possible later deployment.[62]

With an "emergency" reinforcement request from Westmoreland at last in hand, Wheeler then led the Joint Chiefs of Staff in a paradoxical maneuver aimed at forcing a reserve call-up. On 12 February, the Joint Chiefs warned McNamara, then in his last days as defense secretary, that dispatch of the additional troops would dangerously deplete the United States' combat-ready strategic reserve. The Joint Chiefs suggested that the emergency deployment be "deferred at this time," although the 82d Airborne Division and two-thirds of a Marine division and air wing should be prepared for possible later movement to Vietnam. They urged in addition that any further deployments to South Vietnam be compensated for by an equivalent or larger mobilization of reserves and by an extension of active-duty terms of service, for both of which the administration immediately should seek congressional authorization. The Joint Chiefs thus linked the supposed urgent need for more troops in Vietnam to the rebuilding of the strategic reserve so as to push the president into precisely what he so long had avoided: a national mobilization.[63]

President Johnson declined to be pressured. On 12 February, at a White House meeting with his senior civilian and military advisers, Johnson directed the dispatch to Vietnam of Westmoreland's emergency reinforcements. At the same time, the president, at Secretary McNamara's recommendation, postponed a decision on calling the reserves and directed further Defense Department study of the issue. Wheeler's maneuvering had resulted to this point only in further reduction of the already inadequate strategic reserve.[64]

[62] Msgs, Wheeler to Westmoreland info Sharp, JCS 01633, JCS 01691, and JCS 01695, 9, 11, 12 Feb 68; Westmoreland MAC 01849, MAC 01858, and MAC 01975 to Wheeler and Sharp, 9, 12 Feb 68; Westmoreland MAC 01924 and MAC 02018 to Wheeler info Sharp, 11, 12 Feb 68; Sharp to Wheeler info Westmoreland et al., 10, 11, 12 Feb 68. All in Westmoreland Message files, Feb 68, CMH.

[63] The JCS recommendation is reproduced in *United States–Vietnam Relations*, sec. 4.C.6.(c), pp. 2–6. See also Schandler, *Unmaking of a President*, pp. 99–101.

[64] *United States–Vietnam Relations*, sec. 4.C.6.(c), p. 6; Schandler, *Unmaking of a President*, p. 101; Msg, Wheeler JCS 1725 to Sharp and Westmoreland, 12 Feb 68, Westmoreland Message files, Feb 68, CMH.

Deployment of the reinforcements went forward without delay. Air and sea movement of the 3d Brigade, 82d Airborne Division, and the 27th Marine Regimental Landing Team began on 14 February and was completed by the end of the month. The 27th Marine Regimental Landing Team bolstered defenses south of Da Nang and freed other III MAF units to reopen Hai Van Pass. The 82d Airborne Division's brigade, after assembling at Chu Lai, moved to Phu Bai to round out the 101st Airborne Division, which had left one of its brigades behind in III Corps when it moved north. Reflecting the parlous state of the nation's strategic reserve, the new units entered Vietnam in what General Westmoreland described as "marginal shape." For example, the 3d Brigade had been hastily brought up to strength by reducing the other two brigades of its parent division almost to cadre level. Although containing a large contingent of Vietnam veterans, the brigade had to undergo a shakedown period, a period of refresher training and other preparations, at Chu Lai before it could enter combat. [65]

With the "emergency" reinforcement question decided, President Johnson, faced with continued agitation from the Joint Chiefs for a reserve call-up, sent General Wheeler to South Vietnam to assess the longer term military requirements. The Joint Chiefs of Staff chairman arrived in Saigon on 23 February with minimal public fanfare, accompanied by Philip C. Habib of the State Department, Maj. Gen. William E. DePuy, the chairman's assistant for counterinsurgency, and a small staff. Wheeler's purpose, he told General Westmoreland, was to "get a comprehensive view of where we stand today," including results of the Tet offensive, the state of friendly and enemy forces, and the capability of MACV's combined forces to accomplish their basic tasks under current conditions. The administration, Wheeler declared, "must face up to some hard decisions in the near future regarding the possibility of providing you additional troops, recouping our strategic reserves in CONUS [continental United States], and obtaining the necessary legislative support in terms of money and authorities." He implied that President Johnson and Secretary McNamara would base those decisions largely on his findings. [66]

[65] Sharp and Westmoreland, *Report*, p. 184. Quotation is from Westmoreland History Notes, 1–29 Feb 68, tab 1, Westmoreland History file no. 29 (1–29 Feb 68), CMH. Msgs, Abrams PHB 083 to Cushman info Westmoreland, 16 Feb 68; Abrams PHB 046 to Westmoreland, 13 Feb 68; Lt Gen Robert H. York, CG XVIII Abn Corps, BRG 158 to Westmoreland, 19 Feb 68; Westmoreland MAC 02454 to York, 21 Feb 68. All in Westmoreland Message files, Feb 68, CMH. The 27th Marine Regimental Landing Team's deployment problems are described in Shulimson et al., *Marines in Vietnam, 1968*, pp. 572–74.

[66] JCS pressure for mobilization is covered in *United States–Vietnam Relations*, sec. 4.C.6.(c), pp. 6–12 and Schandler, *Unmaking of a President*, pp. 102–03. Quotations are from Msg, Wheeler JCS 1974 to Westmoreland info Sharp, 17 Feb 68, Westmoreland Message files, Feb 68, CMH. In same file, see Msgs, Wheeler JCS 1695, JCS 02087, and JCS 02113 to Westmoreland info Sharp, 12, 21 Feb 68; Westmoreland MAC 02018, MAC 02381, and MAC 02512 to Wheeler info Sharp, 12, 20, 22 Feb 68.

Wheeler's visit was brief and informal, infused with a sense of urgency. The Joint Chiefs of Staff chairman, recovering from a severe heart attack suffered the previous year, seemed to Westmoreland and others at MACV to be haggard, nervous, and close to exhaustion, his view of the Vietnam situation heavily colored by Washington and media pessimism. On the night of his arrival, a Communist rocket fell near Wheeler's Saigon lodgings, inducing him to move in with General Westmoreland who was still living at MACV headquarters. At Wheeler's request, MACV during his two-day visit dispensed with much of the customary ritual of formal briefings and trips around the country. Except for a flight to Da Nang to meet with Generals Abrams and Cushman, Wheeler and his entourage spent all their time in Saigon conferring with General Westmoreland, his senior commanders and staff, and President Thieu, Vice President Ky, and General Vien.[67]

The discussions centered on development of a large reinforcement request intended to serve several purposes. The request would provide MACV with reserves to counter a possible second wave of nationwide Communist attacks. It would make available troops for what General Westmoreland hoped would be expanded, more decisive operations in Southeast Asia. Finally, the request would advance General Wheeler's purpose of strengthening the national reserve. According to General Chaisson, who accompanied Wheeler and Westmoreland on their trip to Da Nang, the Joint Chiefs of Staff chairman emphasized that "we have to mobilize to handle long term small wars . . . and multiple contingencies" and declared that "the President must act or we are all in trouble." Westmoreland, for his part, "wants what he thinks he needs; no more discount jobs." The two generals agreed to request forces adequate for the worst contingency: complete collapse of the South Vietnamese Army, a renewed and expanded enemy offensive, and a South Korean pullout from Vietnam. They also agreed to request forces for the best contingency: continued South Vietnamese stability and military improvement plus authorization for ground attacks on the Ho Chi Minh Trail, the Laotian and Cambodian sanctuaries, and enemy bases in North Vietnam above the Demilitarized Zone. Both generals believed that the administration, in the crisis atmosphere created by Tet, would be receptive to proposals for such actions, especially with Clark Clifford, a man of supposedly hawkish views on the war, due to replace the de-escalation-minded McNamara as secretary of defense. Each for his own reasons, the two commanders wanted what General

---

[67] Msgs, Westmoreland MAC 02366 to Wheeler info Sharp, 19 Feb 68; Wheeler JCS 2024 to Westmoreland info Sharp, 19 Feb 68. Both in Westmoreland Message files, Feb 68, CMH. Msg, Kerwin to Abrams, Komer, Momyer, et al., 22 Feb 68, Abrams Papers, CMH. For atmosphere and incidents of visit, see Westmoreland, *Soldier Reports*, p. 354; Davidson, *Vietnam at War*, pp. 501–02; Davidson Interv, 30 Mar and 30 Jun 82, sess. 1, p. 68; Westmoreland History Notes, 1–29 Feb 68, tab 1, Westmoreland History file no. 29 (1–29 Feb 68), CMH; Interv, LBJL with Earle G. Wheeler, 7 May 70, pp. 2–3 (hereafter cited as Wheeler Interv).

Westmoreland later called "reserves in the rack," and they designed their reinforcement plan to obtain them.[68]

In its details, the troop request was a hasty improvisation. It had some basis in MACV's 8 February supplemental requirement for 1968, which had called for two additional divisions and many support units, and in lists from the component commands of troops needed to fill out Program Five and support the emergency reinforcements. Beyond these specifics, however, the request appears to have been based more on the need to come up with a certain overall number rather than a careful unit-by-unit justification. According to General Davidson, the MACV chief of intelligence, "the staff was just getting together two hundred thousand troops; for what they were going to be used I don't think even the Chief [of Staff] knew. . . . There wasn't any great foresight to it." In contrast to the usual procedure with reinforcement requests, this one was developed without consultation with Admiral Sharp; although General Westmoreland on the twenty-fifth, after the end of the meetings with Wheeler and his group, sent an officer to Honolulu to brief CINCPAC on the proposal. On his way back to Washington, Wheeler discussed the plan at length with Sharp during a stopover in Honolulu.[69]

The troop request, as outlined in General Wheeler's trip report, which he and General DePuy drafted en route to Honolulu, added up to 206,700 men over and above Program Five and the brigade and regimental landing team dispatched in February. These forces were to be deployed in three packages. The first, dubbed Immediate, Priority One, consisted of a brigade of the 5th Infantry Division (Mechanized), the 5th Marine Division less one regimental landing team, an Army armored cavalry regiment,[70] eight Air Force tactical fighter squadrons (three previously part of Program Five), and various support units, all to reach Vietnam before 1 May 1968. The second package, Immediate, Priority Two, to arrive in Vietnam by 1 September, was built around

[68] Quotations are from Ltr, Chaisson to Mrs Chaisson, 26 Feb 68, box 7, Chaisson Papers, Hoover Institution. See also Schandler, *Unmaking of a President*, pp. 109–11; Wheeler Interv, 7 May 70, pp. 3–6. Westmoreland retrospectively explains his thinking in "Additional Forces," pp. 17–20, 22. "In the rack" phrase is taken from Interv, Charles B. MacDonald with Gen William Westmoreland, 19 Feb 73, in MacDonald Notes, CMH. Westmoreland's continued interest in operations in Laos and Cambodia is indicated in Msg, Westmoreland MAC 2962 to Wheeler info Sharp, 2 Mar 68, Westmoreland Message files, Mar 68, CMH.

[69] Memo, Lt Cdr B. A. Robbins, III, for Commander, Naval Forces, Vietnam (COMNAVFORV), 22 Feb 68 sub: Additional Force Requirements, Ltr Chronological File, Jan–Mar 68, box 471, COMNAVFORV Records, Naval Historical Center (NHC), Washington, D.C.; MACV History, 1968, vol. 1, pp. 225–26; Davidson Interv, 30 Mar and 30 Jun 82, sess. 1, pp. 65–68; quotation is from pp. 67–68. Wheeler Interv, 7 May 70, pp. 6–7; Sharp Interv, 19 Feb 71, pp. 587–88; Msg, Westmoreland MAC 2658 to Sharp, 25 Feb 68, Westmoreland Message files, Feb 68, CMH.

[70] Westmoreland, after consultation with General Abrams, decided to ask for an Army mechanized division instead of the 82d Airborne Division, because the mechanized unit would add mobility and firepower in northern I Corps without further straining MACV's limited helicopter resources. Msg, Kerwin MAC 2629 to Abrams, 24 Feb 68, Abrams Papers, CMH.

the remainder of the 5th Infantry Division and four fighter squadrons. It also would include the South Korean light division, if it could be obtained. The third package, dubbed Follow-on, consisted of a U.S. infantry division, three fighter squadrons, and more support units, to be in Vietnam by the end of 1968. Wheeler and Westmoreland understood that provision of these units would require a major activation of reserves. According to General Palmer, the USARV deputy commander, even with such a mobilization, the forces contemplated could not have deployed before 1969 or even 1970, because the Army would have encountered delays in procuring necessary equipment. Wheeler and Westmoreland agreed between themselves that only the first package definitely would go to Vietnam. The others were to deploy only if the situation worsened or the president expanded the war; otherwise, they would rebuild the strategic reserve in the United States.[71]

In retrospect, General Westmoreland declared that, from his point of view, this request was a "contingency plan," not a demand per se for the deployment of additional forces." He considered it a statement of "forces that would be required to accomplish approved military objectives"—those of the expanded strategy he and Wheeler had discussed. "In other words," according to Westmoreland, "the requirements would actually materialize only if certain objectives keyed to a new strategy were approved." For his part, Wheeler echoed Westmoreland's characterization of the proposal as a "contingency plan." He declared that "the only firm request that Westmoreland really made was for the first increment; the second and third increments would have been deployed only on the decision of the President, in the light of circumstances that prevailed at that time." The administration, however, and eventually the American press and public came to perceive the proposal in quite a different light.[72]

General Wheeler cabled his report ahead of him to Washington on the twenty-seventh and the following day elaborated on it in person at a White House meeting with President Johnson and his senior advisers. The Joint Chiefs of Staff chairman's report differed significantly in emphasis from his discussions with General Westmoreland. Wheeler made no mention of reconstitution of the national reserve or expanded operations in Southeast Asia. Instead, he gave the impression that the Military Assistance Command needed all 206,000 additional troops merely to defeat the enemy offensive and to restore the allies' pre-Tet position. Wheeler pictured the enemy as damaged in the initial Tet attacks but recovering rap-

---

[71] Wheeler's proposal is reproduced in *United States–Vietnam Relations*, sec. 4.C.6.(c), pp. 12–16 and summarized in Westmoreland, "Additional Forces," p. 21. For its preparation, see Schandler, *Unmaking of a President*, pp. 109–11; MACV History, 1968, vol. 1, p. 226. General Palmer's comments are in his USARV Exit Interview, reproduced in his 1975 Interv, p. 273.

[72] Quotations are from Westmoreland, "Additional Forces," pp. 21 and 23; and Wheeler Interv, 7 May 70, p. 9. Contemporaneous expressions of this view are lacking in the sources, but Westmoreland's 8 February estimate of force requirements over and above Program Five has a similar contingent flavor; see Msg, Westmoreland MAC 01812, to Wheeler info Sharp, 8 Feb 68, Westmoreland Message files, Feb 68, CMH.

idly and likely to renew his nationwide assaults in great force. The South Vietnamese government and armed forces were holding on but shaken physically and psychologically, largely driven from the countryside, and of uncertain staying power. MACV, with its U.S. units stretched thin protecting the cities, defending northern I Corps, and trying to revive pacification, "does not have adequate forces at this time to resume the offensive . . . , nor does it have adequate reserves against the contingency of simultaneous large-scale enemy offensive action throughout the country." Wheeler thus rested his case for the huge reinforcement, and the reserve mobilization it would require, entirely upon an alleged military crisis in South Vietnam rather than the new contingencies and opportunities that Westmoreland was contemplating. In fact, under the proposed schedule, none of the reinforcements could have reached Vietnam in time to help defeat a second enemy offensive if it followed soon upon the first. (The enemy's second wave actually came in early May and was weaker than the Tet assault.)[73]

Wheeler's report struck the president and his advisers like the proverbial bombshell. Some officials, notably Secretary of State Rusk, were skeptical of the Joint Chief of Staff chairman's basic premise: the need for large reinforcements to cope with the Tet offensive. Most were dismayed by Wheeler's gloomy assessment of the Vietnam situation, as well as by the size of the troop request and the economic and political implications of trying to fulfill it. Wheeler had confronted an administration already shaken in its confidence and resolve with a choice between military defeat and full-scale national mobilization in a presidential election year. He also had called into question Johnson's earlier decision to level off the American commitment to Vietnam. In response, the president undertook a major review of his entire war policy. On 28 February, Johnson directed the incoming defense secretary, Clark Clifford, who was to take office at the beginning of March, to take a fresh look at the entire reinforcement and reserve question and recommend a course of action.[74]

The review took up a week of frenetic meetings and memorandum-writing. Although the State and Treasury Departments, the CIA, and the Joint Staff provided analyses and policy papers, a group of civilian Defense Department officials, former McNamara assistants, dominated the drafting of what became Clifford's recommendation. These individuals, who included Deputy Secretary of Defense Paul H. Nitze and Assistant Secretary of Defense for International Security Affairs Paul C. Warnke, had helped to shape McNamara's opposition to continued

[73] Quotations are from *United States–Vietnam Relations*, sec. 4.C.6.(c), pp. 12–16. Schandler, *Unmaking of a President*, pp. 111–16, analyzes Wheeler's shifting of emphasis. Westmoreland, *Soldier Reports*, pp. 356–57, and Interv, MacDonald with Westmoreland, 19 Feb 73, MacDonald Notes, CMH, interprets Wheeler's motives.

[74] Unless otherwise noted, the following account of the administration's policy review and the Clifford task force is drawn from *United States–Vietnam Relations*, sec. 4.C.6.(c), pp. 16–51 and Schandler, *Unmaking of a President*, pp. 116–76, 182–84.

escalation of the American effort in Southeast Asia. They set to work to convince Clifford of the same proposition. Supported by submissions from the State Department and the CIA as well as the Defense Department's systems analysis office, they repeated the earlier argument that more U.S. troops would increase American casualties and war costs without producing victory. Proclaiming existing American military objectives in South Vietnam to be unattainable, the drafters recommended adoption of a more modest ground strategy oriented toward protecting population centers rather than destroying enemy forces—a strategy they believed MACV could implement with the troops it already had and one which would buy time for reform of the Saigon government and improvement of its armed forces.

The Defense Department "doves" found a receptive audience in Clifford. A Washington lawyer with wide business and political contacts and a long-time friend and adviser of Johnson, Clifford had begun to have doubts about the war even before assuming his Defense post. The Tet offensive, Wheeler's troop request, and the arguments of his assistants confirmed the new defense secretary in the view that the war was probably unwinnable and that its costs to the United States—strategic, economic, political, and social—had become excessive in relation to the stakes involved. The only solution for the United States, Clifford concluded, was to "level off our involvement, and . . . work toward gradual disengagement" through negotiations. From this point on, he vigorously advocated de-escalation in administration councils, at some cost to his friendship with President Johnson.[75]

At General Wheeler's request, General Westmoreland on 2 March attempted to influence the Clifford deliberations by specifying what dangers the proposed reinforcements would avert and what objectives they would advance. Constrained to conform to the approach of Wheeler's report, Westmoreland could discuss the reinforcements only in terms of existing operations in South Vietnam, with no mention of the wider strategy for which the MACV commander had thought the additional troops were intended. Hence, he declared merely that the new forces would help to secure northern I Corps and strengthen allied positions elsewhere in South Vietnam while permitting MACV to free two divisions, probably the 1st Cavalry and 101st Airborne Divisions, to function as a "highly mobile exploitation force" throughout the country. His explanation thus served only to buttress the Defense civilians' contention that the additional troops would have no really decisive effect on the war. Further weakening the force of Westmoreland's arguments, Admiral Sharp on 3 March chimed in with the opinion that

---

[75] Evolution of Clifford's views is recounted in Schandler, *Unmaking of a President*, pp. 213–17, 241–55, 311–12; quotation is from p. 216. Msg, Wheeler CJCS 2721 to Westmoreland and Sharp, 8 Mar 68, Westmoreland Message files, Mar 68, CMH, recounts Clifford's concern with Tet's effect on American public opinion.

MACV could get along with a much smaller reinforcement provided ROLLING THUNDER were stepped up, a course Sharp as usual strongly advocated.[76]

Secretary Clifford's recommendation, forwarded to the president on 4 March, went as far as its drafters believed expedient toward a call for de-escalation. Clifford proposed immediate deployment of part of the first reinforcement increment, about 22,000 men, which could be done from existing resources. Decision on the bulk of the reinforcement should be deferred, subject to week-by-week review of the situation in South Vietnam. However, the administration should mobilize enough reservists at once to meet the full troop request and restore the strategic reserve. At the insistence of the Joint Chiefs, who rejected any imposition of new objectives on the field commander, Clifford offered no fresh campaign guidance for the ground war but called for a "study in depth" of the subject in the context of overall U.S. Vietnam policy. He did, however, urge renewed efforts to strengthen the South Vietnamese government and armed forces. In summary, Clifford's proposals constituted a restatement of the McNamara positions of 1966 and 1967: send the modest reinforcements that are readily available and give higher priority to preparing the South Vietnamese to assume more of the burden of the fight.[77]

Clifford's recommendation was also in line with President Johnson's already well-established inclination to level off the American effort in Vietnam. Hence, the president accepted it. On 5 March, at Johnson's direction, General Wheeler informed Westmoreland that he was unlikely to receive any reinforcements beyond the 22,000 Clifford proposed, and he added that there was "tremendous interest" in Washington in MACV's plans for strengthening the South Vietnamese armed forces. On the ninth, the president increased the planned reinforcement to 30,000 men upon learning the services could furnish that many. These were in addition to the Program Five units, still in the process of deployment, and the emergency regiment and brigade, considered to be on temporary loan to MACV. Johnson also deferred the Program Five civilianization program, in effect adding some 12,000 military spaces to Westmoreland's forces. Subsequently, the administration increased the reinforcement by another 13,500 troops, which Westmoreland indicated that he needed for combat and logistical support of the units sent in February. To provide these forces, the administration planned to call nearly 100,000 reservists beginning in March.[78]

---

[76] *United States–Vietnam Relations*, sec. 4C.6.(c), pp. 44–46. Msgs, Westmoreland MAC 02951 and MAC 02956 to Wheeler info Sharp, 2 Mar 68; Sharp to Wheeler info Westmoreland, 3 Mar 68. All in Westmoreland Message files, Mar 68, CMH. Sharp Interv, 19 Feb 71, pp. 590–92.

[77] *United States–Vietnam Relations*, sec. 4.C.6.(c), pp. 51–64.

[78] Msgs, Wheeler JCS 2590, JCS 2766, JCS 2767, JCS 2847, and JCS 02896 to Westmoreland info Sharp, 5, 9, 12, 13 Mar 68; Westmoreland MAC 03092 to Sharp, 5 Mar 68; Westmoreland MAC 03230 and MAC 3385 to Wheeler info Sharp, 7 and 11 Mar 68. All in Westmoreland Message files, Mar 68, CMH. *United States–Vietnam Relations*, sec. 4.C.6.(c), pp. 64–65, 71–73; Schandler,

On the basis of these decisions, the Military Assistance Command developed a troop list featuring an Army infantry brigade (to replace the 27th Marine Regimental Landing Team), an Army mechanized brigade, an armored cavalry squadron, a military police battalion, and four tactical fighter squadrons. At Secretary Clifford's direction, Marine ground units were excluded from the package, because the Marine Corps at its existing strength simply could not sustain any additional forces in Vietnam. After the president, on 13 March, approved the reinforcement package, MACV, the Joint Chiefs, and the Department of the Army turned to refining troop lists and deployment schedules, aiming to have most of the units in Vietnam by late summer. General Westmoreland also furnished a deployment schedule for the "optimum" 206,000-man augmentation, apparently against the unlikely event of revival of the larger plan.[79]

All this activity turned out to be wasted motion. Political events during March—the *New York Times* revelation of the 206,000-man request, mounting congressional opposition to further troop commitments, steadily worsening public opinion polls, Senator Eugene McCarthy's near-victory in the New Hampshire Democratic primary, and Robert F. Kennedy's entry into the presidential race—led President Johnson further to scale down the reinforcement. On 22 March, he and his advisers decided to drop the 30,000-man increase and dispatch only the 13,500 troops needed to support the units sent in February, which Westmoreland would be allowed to retain. This augmentation would bring total American military strength in South Vietnam to 549,500 men, 24,500 more than the Program Five ceiling. Johnson would back up this deployment with a minimum mobilization of 62,000 reservists. The president based his decision, he declared later, on reported improvements in the military situation in Vietnam and in the effectiveness of the South Vietnamese Army, on his government's growing fiscal difficulties, and on the impossibility of overcoming domestic opposition to further enlargement of the U.S. commitment.[80]

Before announcing this decision, the president sent General Wheeler back across the Pacific to secure General Westmoreland's assent to it. At a hurriedly arranged meeting on 24 March at Clark Air Force Base in the Philippines, Wheeler informed Westmoreland that political conditions

Unmaking of a President, pp. 177–80, 229–31.

[79] Msgs, Wheeler JCS 02925 to Westmoreland info Sharp, 14 Mar 68; Wheeler JCS 03024 to Westmoreland info Sharp and Gen Johnson, 16 Mar 68; Westmoreland MAC 03552 and MAC 03698 to Wheeler info Sharp, 14, 17 Mar 68; Gen Johnson to Westmoreland, WDC 3874, 15 Mar 68; Westmoreland MAC 03651 to Gen Johnson info Wheeler and Palmer, 16 Mar 68; Abrams MAC 3901 to Wheeler info Gen Johnson, Sharp, Westmoreland, 21 Mar 68; Abrams MAC 3902 to Gen Johnson info Wheeler and Westmoreland, 21 Mar 68. All in Westmoreland Message files, Mar 68, CMH. *United States–Vietnam Relations*, sec. 4.C.6.(c), p. 76; MACV History, 1968, vol. 1, p. 226.

[80] Political events are summarized in *United States–Vietnam Relations*, sec. 4.C.6.(c), pp. 65–73; Hammond, *Military and the Media, 1962–1968*, pp. 375–82; and Schandler, *Unmaking of a President*, pp. 194–228, 231–32. The president recounts his reasons in Lyndon B. Johnson, *The Vantage Point: Perspectives of the Presidency, 1963–1969* (New York: Holt, Rinehart, and Winston, 1971), p. 415.

President Johnson meets with his "Wise Men."

in the United States ruled out any major reinforcement or expansion of ground operations. The MACV commander, whom Wheeler had kept up to date on the deteriorating U.S. domestic situation, replied on cue that under those circumstances he could carry out his mission provided he could keep the February reinforcements or replacements for them, and provided he received all his Program Five troops plus the 13,500-man augmentation.[81]

While Wheeler, accompanied by General Abrams, Westmoreland's designated successor as COMUSMACV, took this message back to Washington, Westmoreland on 27 March dispatched a formal request for two Army brigades, an armored cavalry squadron, two fighter squadrons, and the support units. Of the two brigades, one was the 3d of the 82d Airborne Division, already in Vietnam; the other, a mechanized brigade, would replace the 27th Marine Regimental Landing Team, which was to be withdrawn by mid-July. Westmoreland intended to use both brigades in northern I Corps. He declared that, in the light of the enemy's heavy Tet losses, the "exceptional recovery" of the South

---

[81] Msgs, Wheeler JCS 2767 and JCS 2848, to Westmoreland info Sharp, 9, 12 Mar 68; JCS 3024 to Westmoreland info Sharp and Gen Johnson, 16 Mar 68; JCS 3303 to Westmoreland and Abrams, 23 Mar 68. All in Westmoreland Message files, Mar 68, CMH; Johnson, *Vantage Point*, p. 415; Westmoreland History Notes, 1–31 Mar 68, tab 1, Westmoreland History file no. 30 (1–31 Mar 68), CMH; Wheeler Interv, 7 May 70, pp. 9–10; Schandler, *Unmaking of a President*, p. 236.

Vietnamese, and other indications of an improving military situation, this reinforcement would provide MACV "the means necessary to contain further enemy-initiated actions while continuing forward progress in most areas." On the twenty-eighth, President Johnson approved this final Vietnam reinforcement package. In due time, it became the Defense Department's Program Six, the last U.S. force augmentation for Vietnam.[82]

On 31 March, in a broadcast address to the American people, heard in Saigon at 1000 hours on 1 April local time, President Johnson announced the Program Six deployment. He announced also that as of 1 April the United States would cease air attacks on all but the southern panhandle of the Democratic Republic of Vietnam and that he had decided not to run for another term as president. The partial bombing halt was the product of an intra-administration debate that proceeded alongside the reinforcement deliberations but largely bypassed both General Westmoreland and Admiral Sharp. After considerable hesitation, President Johnson and his advisers finally decided to go ahead with the pause more to quiet domestic dissent than because they expected a positive response from Hanoi. General Wheeler emphasized the domestic political aspect in his message of 31 March, informing Sharp, Westmoreland, and other Pacific commanders of the partial bombing halt. This "unilateral initiative to seek peace" was necessary, Wheeler explained, "to reverse the growing dissent and opposition within our society to the war"; without it, public support might become "too frail to sustain the effort" in Southeast Asia.[83]

To the end, General Westmoreland remained a strong supporter of ROLLING THUNDER for its value in reducing the flow of North Vietnamese men and supplies into South Vietnam. On 2 March, he advocated heavier bombing of the Haiphong area, and as late as the twenty-seventh he declared that "relentless pressure" on the north was "complementary" to his reduced reinforcement package. Nevertheless, at Admiral Sharp's direction, he passed on the pause order to his field force and component commanders along with General Wheeler's explanation of its political purpose. Westmoreland noted in addition that "of course, our

---

[82] Msgs, Westmoreland MAC 4192 to Wheeler and Sharp info Abrams, 27 Mar 68 (quotations are from this message); Westmoreland MAC 4242 to Wheeler and Sharp, 28 Mar 68; Wheeler JCS 3449 to Westmoreland, 28 Mar 68; Sharp to Wheeler info Westmoreland et al., 29 Mar 68. All in Westmoreland Message files, Mar 68, CMH. Msg, COMUSMACV MAC 9031 to JCS and CINCPAC, 31 Mar 68, tab 83, Westmoreland History file no. 30 (1–31 Mar 68), CMH; in same file, see Westmoreland History Notes, 1–31 Mar 68, tab 1. MACV History, 1968, vol. 1, pp. 226–27; *United States–Vietnam Relations*, sec. 4.C.6.(c), pp. 76–79, 90.

[83] Quotation is from Msg, Wheeler JCS 3561 to Sharp, Westmoreland, et al., 31 Mar 68; see also Msg, Sharp to Westmoreland et al., 31 Mar 68. Both in Westmoreland Message files, Mar 68, CMH. *United States–Vietnam Relations*, sec. 4.C.6.(c), pp. 80–90, and sec. 4.C.7.(b), pp. 141–203; Schandler, *Unmaking of a President*, pp. 184–93, 237–40. Sharp complains of being bypassed on the decision in Sharp Interv, 19 Feb 71, pp. 601–04. Westmoreland History Notes, 1–30 Apr 68, tab 1, Westmoreland History file no. 31 (1–30 Apr 68) describes how the Mission Council heard the speech.

airpower will be concentrated south of the 20th parallel," the administration's unpublicized northern bombing limit. He instructed his commanders to inform their Vietnamese counterparts of the American decision and the Saigon government's concurrence in it. They were to reassure the South Vietnamese that the reduction of ROLLING THUNDER meant no diminution of offensive operations in the south. "Indeed," Westmoreland concluded, "maximum pressure on the aggressor is required even more."[84]

In retrospect, President Johnson's decisions of 31 March, followed by North Vietnam's announcement early in April of conditional willingness to open negotiations, marked the start of an irreversible process of American disengagement from Vietnam. At the time, this was not so certain. Johnson's decisions of late March were incremental, intended more to facilitate continuation of the war rather than its termination. On the reinforcement issue in particular, the administration essentially reaffirmed its 1967 decision to top off American strength in Vietnam at a level just below that requiring mobilization and to devote more attention and resources to building up the South Vietnamese forces in hopes ultimately of reducing the U.S. role in the war. As yet, however, no firm plan existed for such a reduction, nor had the administration revised MACV's mission or military objectives. Nevertheless, the March decisions, especially as interpreted and implemented by Secretary Clifford, constituted for practical purposes an American abandonment of any hope of genuine victory in South Vietnam. From then on, the objective became extrication on acceptable terms.[85]

A War Lost in the Mind

In 1912, a British military observer of the Balkan Wars wrote:

In large-scale modern battles there must often be a period when the confusion is so great that none of the actors really know which side is winning or which side has lost. . . . If that is so, then there must often be a period when the result hangs in the balance, when those who can be made to <u>think</u> that they are winning will win; and those that think that they are losing will be lost—whatever be the real state of affairs as a whole.[86]

---

[84] Msgs, Westmoreland MAC 2962 to Wheeler info Sharp, 2 Mar 68; MAC 4192 to Wheeler and Sharp info Abrams, 27 Mar 68; MAC 4366 to Field Force and Component Cdrs, 31 Mar 68. All in Westmoreland Message files, Mar 68, CMH. See also Fact Sheet, sub: Seventeen Questions Posed by AP and Gen Westmoreland's Answers, 24 Feb 68, tab 77, Westmoreland History file no. 29 (1–29 Feb 68), CMH.

[85] Movement toward negotiations is summarized in *United States–Vietnam Relations*, sec. 4.C.6.(c), pp. 90–91; and Sharp and Westmoreland, *Report*, pp. 186–88. Schandler, *Unmaking of a President*, pp. 301–03, 313–19, emphasizes the tentative nature of the March decisions and Clifford's effort to interpret them into a real change of direction.

[86] The observer's remarks are quoted in Col. Theodore L. Gatchell, USMC, "Can a Battle be Lost in the Mind of the Commander?" *Naval War College Review* 23 (January–February 1985): 96.

The British observer referred to the large-scale conventional battles of the pre-World War I era, but his words apply with even more force to the events of early 1968 in the unconventional conflict in Vietnam. Militarily, the North Vietnamese and Viet Cong General Offensive–General Uprising was a major defeat for their side, one that, as MACV early perceived, inflicted severe and possibly crippling damage on Communist forces. Nevertheless, the enemy in February 1968 won the battle where it counted most: in the American news media, among influential elements of the general public, and in the minds and emotions of key government officials, including the president of the United States. The Johnson administration, frustrated by years of unproductive effort, distressed by growing dissent and disunity at home, and shocked by the Tet offensive, in effect decided that its war in Vietnam had been a failure or at best had become too expensive to be worth pursuing and turned to a search for a way out.[87]

Without intending to, the American military leadership contributed to this perceptual defeat. The Military Assistance Command's optimistic reporting—although encouraged, even demanded, by its civilian masters—recoiled upon it when the supposedly beaten enemy attacked. Then General Westmoreland, after attempting to reassure the American government and public that the enemy offensive had failed and that he had the situation well in hand, was drawn by General Wheeler into requesting a huge troop reinforcement, which the Joint Chiefs of Staff chairman presented to the president and his advisers as necessary to stave off disaster. The troop request all but nullified General Westmoreland's claims of victory. More important, the military leaders by making the request confronted the administration with an apparent choice between further escalation at unacceptable domestic political and economic cost, with no guarantee of victory, and a major scaling down of objectives. In fact, there was, of course, a third alternative: continuation of the existing strategy, which it could be argued plausibly, was only coming into full effect when the Tet offensive broke; but the military leaders gave the impression that this alternative was no longer available.[88]

Thus, Generals Wheeler and Westmoreland, by trying to use the Tet crisis to secure enlarged forces and expanded military action, managed to push their civilian superiors in just the opposite direction. MACV would have to live with the results. Under a new commander and soon a new administration, MACV would soldier on, attempting to execute a new American war strategy as it gradually emerged.

---

[87] For a typical view that the enemy won the psychological war at Tet, see Interv, Lt Col Bill Mullen and Lt Col Les Brownlee with William E. DePuy, Senior Officers Oral History Program, 1979, pt. 5, p. 12, MHI.

[88] The administration's confrontation with the war's economic and political costs as a result of the 206,000-man troop request is emphasized in *United States–Vietnam Relations*, sec. 4.C.6.(c), pp. 91–92.

4

General Abrams Takes Charge

On 31 March 1968, the United States entered a prolonged period of transition in its conduct of the Vietnam War. The Johnson administration devoted its last months to negotiating with the North Vietnamese and ultimately also with its South Vietnamese ally about the terms under which substantive peace talks could begin. At the same time, the administration avoided new decisions on the conduct of the war in South Vietnam. The Military Assistance Command, under General Creighton W. Abrams, Westmoreland's successor, thus was left to reformulate its own operational concepts, guided only by the realization that no more American reinforcements were coming and that the administration wanted movement toward turning the war over to the South Vietnamese.

General Westmoreland Departs

At a press conference on 22 March, President Johnson made an important announcement concerning high-level military commands. He declared that General Wheeler, whose regular tenure as chairman of the Joint Chiefs of Staff was soon to end, would remain at his post for another year, an arrangement that would permit the next president to select his own chairman for a full term. At the same time, in accordance with plans made late in the previous year, Johnson announced that General Westmoreland would leave MACV in mid-summer to replace the retiring General Harold K. Johnson as chief of staff of the Army.[1]

General Wheeler informed Westmoreland of the decision by secure telephone call on 23 March (simultaneously with the announcement in Washington) while the MACV commander was at Clark Air Base in the Philippines for his annual physical examination and a brief visit with his family. In the same call, Wheeler set up his meeting with Westmoreland on the reinforcement question. Westmoreland at once flew back to Saigon, where he informed Ambassador Bunker, President Thieu, and General Vien of his impending departure, then returned the next day to Clark Air Base to talk with Wheeler. In a message to the president

---

[1] Schandler, *Unmaking of a President*, p. 234.

Korean troops parade at General Westmoreland's farewell.

and in a brief press statement at Tan Son Nhut Airport, Westmoreland expressed appreciation of his new assignment along with "reluctance to leave the battlefield before the battle is over." Privately, he confided to General Chaisson that he would have preferred to become CINCPAC (a possibility the administration had briefly considered) and stay "in the main stream of the war."[2]

A succession of Washington visits preceded the naming of Westmoreland's replacement. After Westmoreland returned to Saigon from his 24 March conference with Wheeler, General Abrams, viewed by all as his probable successor, flew to Clark Air Base and returned with the chairman to Washington for two days of briefings and conferences with President Johnson and his senior advisers. With Abrams back in Saigon, General Westmoreland made a trip of his own to Washington on 6 and 7 April. He made a final report to the president and coordinated plans for his confirmation hearings as Army chief of staff. During this visit, Westmoreland recommended Abrams to succeed him at MACV—something of a formality under the circumstances. President Johnson then, on 11 April, announced Abrams' forthcoming elevation

[2] First quotation is from Msg, Westmoreland MAC 04091 to President, 25 Mar 68. See also Msgs, Westmoreland MAC 03981 and MAC 03993 to Wheeler and Sharp, 23 Mar 68. All in Westmoreland Message files, Mar 68, CMH; Westmoreland History Notes, 1–31 Mar 68, tab 1, Westmoreland History files no. 30 (1–31 Mar 68), CMH. Second quotation is from Ltr, Chaisson to Mrs Chaisson, 23 Mar 68; see also Ltr, 26 Mar 68. Both in box 7, Chaisson Papers, Hoover Institution.

General Goodpaster (left) *with Lt. Gen. Richard G. Stilwell*

to COMUSMACV and named Lt. Gen. Andrew J. Goodpaster, who was to receive a fourth star, as the new deputy MACV commander.[3]

General Westmoreland remained in command in Saigon through late May, with Abrams continuing as his deputy but asserting his own views more positively on many issues. The transition period was at times awkward. General Chaisson observed in mid-April: "Our little circle here is very interesting. Abe now is officially in. Westy isn't about to let go. I am in the middle." On 29 May, after a final commanders' conference and a round of ceremonial and social farewells, General Westmoreland left for the United States to attend his Senate confirmation hearing. Carefully orchestrated by the administration, the hearing went smoothly. He returned to Saigon on 7 June for another round of farewells and departed for the United States with his family on the 11th. For practical purposes, General Abrams assumed command when Westmoreland left Saigon on 29 May. He served as acting COMUSMACV until 3 July, when Westmoreland was sworn in as Army chief of staff.[4]

---

[3] Sorley, *Thunderbolt*, pp. 221–23; Schandler, *Unmaking of a President*, pp. 261–62. Msgs, Wheeler JCS 3487 to Westmoreland info Sharp, 28 Mar 68; Wheeler JCS 3691 to Westmoreland info Sharp et al., 3 Apr 68; Gen Johnson WDC 5311 to Major Cdrs, 11 Apr 68. All in Westmoreland Message files, Mar–Apr 68, CMH. Also Westmoreland History Notes, 1–30 Apr 68, tab 1, Westmoreland History files no. 31 (1–30 Apr 68), CMH; Westmoreland, *Soldier Reports*, p. 362.

[4] Quotation is from Ltr, Chaisson to Mrs Chaisson, 13 Apr 68; see also Ltrs, 23, 30 Mar 68, and 28 May 68, box 7; Chaisson Diary, 21–23 Mar 68, box 9; Chaisson Papers, Hoover Institution. Westmoreland History Notes, (1–31 May 68), tab 1, Westmoreland History files no. 32 (1–31 May 68) and (1–30 Jun 68), tab 1, Westmoreland History files no. 33 (1–30 Jun 68), CMH; in latter file,

General Westmoreland could claim some significant achievements during his four and one-half years in Vietnam. He built up a modern combat force and logistical base in an undeveloped country and managed MACV's transition from an advisory and assistance headquarters to an operational command. He instituted a system of cooperation with South Vietnamese and allied forces that provided for at least minimal unity of action while respecting Asian political sensitivities. His combat operations prevented the enemy from finishing off the Saigon regime through large-unit warfare and heavily damaged the enemy's forces and base areas. Westmoreland contributed substantially to the reestablishment of stable, constitutional government in South Vietnam and to the development of an effective American organization for supporting a revival of pacification. Although Westmoreland, like most American officials, failed to anticipate the nature and scale of the enemy's Tet offensive, his countermoves before and during the attack were sufficient to deny the Communists major success and to preempt a possible overrunning of northern I Corps. By the time Westmoreland left MACV, the allied forces were in position for a broad-front attack on a weakened enemy.[5]

Unfortunately, Westmoreland's accomplishments, impressive as they were, did not produce a military decision or break Hanoi's will to continue the struggle. Westmoreland, along with the rest of the U.S. mission, could find no immediate remedy for Saigon's endemic weak leadership, corruption, and inefficiency. His participation in President Johnson's optimism campaign undermined the credibility of his reports and estimates; the Tet offensive thoroughly discredited the views of both the general and his command. Having made himself a symbol of the war in the eyes of the American people, Westmoreland inevitably came in for bitter criticism as Americans became disillusioned with the costly, prolonged, and inconclusive conflict. Thus, while it could be argued with some validity that Westmoreland by mid-1968 was winning the military war, it could be argued with equal force that he was losing, or had already lost, the psychological and political one.

It must be noted finally that in all that Westmoreland did, he faithfully carried out the wishes of his president and subordinated himself to the restraints placed on him by civilian authority. An inveterate team player, he tailored his actions to the desires of the administration he served. He retained to the end the confidence of President Johnson and Defense Secretaries McNamara and Clifford. Johnson declared after Tet: "Westy did everything he was expected to do, and more. I will not

see also tabs 18 and 22. For preparations for the hearing, and other arrangements for Westmoreland's return, see Westmoreland Message files, Apr–May 68, CMH; Sharp and Westmoreland, *Report*, p. 188.

[5] Westmoreland gives his own version of his accomplishments in MFR, 21 Jun 68, sub: Remarks to Quarterly Review Meetings in the Four Corps, 23–26 Apr 68, tab 88, Westmoreland History files no. 31 (1–30 Apr 68), CMH, and in Sharp and Westmoreland, *Report*, pp. 292–94.

have him made a scapegoat." Although disillusioned with America's prospects in the war, McNamara and Clifford attributed the lack of success to the inherently unwinnable character of the conflict rather than to the policies of their field commander. As a *Washington Post* editorial on the occasion of Westmoreland's reassignment concluded, he had "been a good soldier in an almost impossible spot."[6]

Continuing the Fight

President Johnson's curtailment of ROLLING THUNDER had little effect on the Military Assistance Command's air operations since the restriction did not apply to the southernmost route package in North Vietnam and to the infiltration trails in Laos. If anything, the bombing halt simplified air command relations by effectively terminating the CINCPAC-controlled part of the air war; and it freed more sorties for MACV's use in the south, the Demilitarized Zone area, and along the Ho Chi Minh Trail. The command became involved in the diplomacy of the pause. At Secretary Clifford's direction, General Westmoreland in April dissuaded General Ky from employing the Vietnamese Air Force's new F–5 jet squadron in raids north of the Demilitarized Zone, an action the administration feared would upset its negotiations with North Vietnam. Late in May, General Westmoreland advocated bombing North Vietnamese cities in retaliation for the Communists' urban attacks in South Vietnam; but the administration ignored this proposal, as it did Admiral Sharp's repeated demands for a full resumption of ROLLING THUNDER.[7]

In South Vietnam, there was no diminution of the allied effort. On 31 March, at a conference of senior U.S., South Vietnamese, and allied commanders, General Westmoreland called for an all-out offensive against Communist forces exposed and weakened by their Tet repulse. Westmoreland declared that the allies must use the "means at hand" to destroy the enemy "across the spectrum," including political cadres, hamlet and village guerrillas, Viet Cong local and main forces, and North Vietnamese units. He emphasized as well mobilization and modernization of Saigon's forces so that the South Vietnamese could demonstrate to the world that they were "fighting their own battles to

[6] Quotation is from Schandler, *Unmaking of a President*, pp. 234–36. See also Msg, Lt Col Whitlach MAC 04052 to Westmoreland, 24 Mar 68, Westmoreland Message files, Mar 68, CMH. McNamara's and Clifford's views are cited in Samuel Zaffiri, *Westmoreland: A Biography of General William C. Westmoreland* (New York: William Morrow, 1994), pp. 314–15. See also *The Washington Post*, 24 Mar 68, p. B6, tab 79, Westmoreland History files no. 30 (1–31 Mar 68), CMH.

[7] The ramifications of the bombing halt can be followed in Westmoreland Message files, Apr–May 68, CMH. Westmoreland, Sharp, and Sharp's successor Admiral McCain advocate renewed bombing in Msgs, Westmoreland MAC 06891 to Sharp info Wheeler, 26 May 68; Sharp BNK 1383 to Wheeler, 14, 16 Jun 68; Westmoreland Message files, May–Jun 68; and Msg, McCain to Wheeler info Abrams, 18 Aug 68, Abrams Papers. All in CMH. Also Westmoreland History Notes, 1–30 Apr 68, tab 1; MFR, Bryan, 14 Apr 68, tab 35. Both in Westmoreland History files no. 31 (1–30 Apr 68), CMH. *United States–Vietnam Relations*, sec. 4.C.7.(b), pp. 203–04.

the extent they can." Westmoreland directed new attention to military support of pacification. He declared that "all our efforts in RVN have a pacification victory as the ultimate objective."[8]

After announcement of the bombing cutback, Westmoreland told U.S. commanders to reaffirm to their Vietnamese counterparts that the offensive in the south would continue and that the allies must prevent the enemy from gaining politically exploitable battlefield successes. President Thieu and his corps commanders echoed this theme in meetings with their own subordinates. The practical effect of these injunctions on the fighting is difficult to measure, given the regionally variegated nature of the war. Nevertheless, in these directives, the MACV commander confirmed his adherence to the new American policy that had been evolving gradually since late 1966 and culminated in the March 1968 reinforcement cutoff: MACV could and would fight with what it had; it would work to expand the South Vietnamese effort; and it would wage a balanced military and pacification campaign.[9]

While MACV, with full administration support, pressed the offensive in South Vietnam, it also, at administration urging, tried to describe these activities in less bellicose terms so as to deflect charges by American war opponents that the president was talking peace but escalating the fighting. Accordingly, in April General Westmoreland, with the approval of General Wheeler and Admiral Sharp, stopped using the term "search and destroy" to denote offensive operations against enemy units and base areas. Noting that the phrase was "over-used and often misunderstood particularly in lay circles," Westmoreland instructed his commanders to substitute in their communications such standard military terms as "spoiling attack" and "reconnaissance in force." At the same time, the MACV commander, at administration direction, attempted to keep at low key public affairs presentations of new large offensives, such as Operation PEGASUS to relieve Khe Sanh and the 90-battalion Operation TOAN THANG ("Total Victory") aimed at clearing the environs of Saigon. He instructed General Cushman, for example, to describe PEGASUS "as being merely the usual run of offensive operations . . . and nothing colossal." In sum, the administration wanted to fight while talking but did not want its field commander to talk too loudly about fighting.[10]

---

[8] Quotations are from MFR, Chaisson, 5 Apr 68, sub: MACV Commanders' Conference, 31 Mar 68, tab 68, Westmoreland History files no. 30 (1–31 Mar 68), CMH. See also Ltr, Chaisson to Mrs Chaisson, 3 Apr 68, box 7, Chaisson Papers, Hoover Institution.

[9] The principal COMUSMACV directives on the offensive are reproduced in MACV History, 1968, vol. 1, pp. 26–30. Also Msgs, Weyand HOA 0434 to Westmoreland, 1 Apr 68; Westmoreland MAC 4534 to Field and Component Cdrs, 4 Apr 68; Abrams MAC 04610 to Westmoreland, 6 Apr 68; Westmoreland MAC 6966 to Goodpaster, 28 May 68. All in Westmoreland Message files, Apr–Jun 68, CMH. Other examples of directives are in tabs 29, 47, 48, and 51, Westmoreland History files no. 31 (1–30 Apr 68) and tab 28, Westmoreland History files no. 32 (1–31 May 68), CMH.

[10] Quotations are from Msgs, Westmoreland MAC 4241 to Wheeler, 28 Mar 68; and MAC 4362

The Military Assistance Command pushed forward its own offensive partly to disrupt Communist preparations for another nationwide attack. General Westmoreland and his intelligence officers estimated that the enemy, if only to gain psychological and propaganda successes and to strengthen their negotiating position, would try to continue the offensive it had begun at Tet. While doubting that the enemy had the capability or the intention to launch assaults and take casualties on the scale of Tet, the command expected the North Vietnamese and Viet Cong to renew ground and artillery harassment of the cities, especially Saigon, and to maintain as much pressure as they could on the South Vietnamese and American forces in hopes of undermining the South Vietnamese government and stimulating antiwar sentiment in the United States. The command's estimates were on the mark. On 24 April, the Politburo in Hanoi, after reviewing results of the Tet "activity cycle," called for continuous attack and encirclement of South Vietnam's cities, liberation of the rural areas, and relentless offensives against the "puppet" army and administration and U.S. troops.[11]

The North Vietnamese and Viet Cong launched their second nationwide offensive on 5 May, just before the opening of peace talks in Paris. This offensive, less ambitious in objectives than its Tet predecessor, was aimed at inflicting casualties on American and South Vietnamese forces, disrupting urban life, and maintaining at least the appearance of the military initiative. In contrast to Tet, the allies expected the attack and had learned much of the enemy's plan from defectors and other sources. American and South Vietnamese operations preempted entirely some Communist assaults; other enemy units were intercepted and broken up before they reached their objectives. Such was the fate of the enemy's major effort, a multi-battalion drive on Saigon. Nevertheless, small North Vietnamese and Viet Cong elements got into parts of the capital, and the fight to eliminate them caused more destruction and created more refugees in Saigon than had the Tet offensive.[12]

to Cushman info Rosson, 31 Mar 68; see also Msgs, Wheeler JCS 3563 to Westmoreland info Sharp, 31 Mar 68; Wheeler JCS 3564 to Westmoreland, 31 Mar 68; Westmoreland MAC 4363 to Wheeler, 31 Mar 68; Wheeler JCS 3965 to Westmoreland, 11 Apr 68; Westmoreland MAC 4856 to Wheeler and Sharp, 12 Apr 68; Westmoreland MAC 4899 to Wheeler, 12 Apr 68; Sharp to Wheeler and Westmoreland, 18 Apr 68. All in Westmoreland Message files, Mar–Apr 68, CMH. Westmoreland History Notes, 1–30 Apr 68, tab 1, Westmoreland History files no. 31 (1–30 Apr 68), CMH; MACV History, 1968, vol. 1, p. 371.

[11] Msgs, Westmoreland MAC 4192 to Wheeler and Sharp info Abrams, 27 Mar 68; Westmoreland MAC 5298 to III MAF and Field Force Cdrs, 21 Apr 68; Westmoreland Message files, Mar–Apr 68, CMH. Msg, COMUSMACV MAC 9322 to CINCPAC info JCS, 3 Apr 68, tab 15. All in Westmoreland History files no. 31 (1–30 Apr 68), CMH. Politburo directive is summarized in War Experiences Recapitulation Committee, *Resistance War*, pp. 106–07; see also Ford, "Tet 1968," pp. 205–06.

[12] MACV was informed of the scope and approximate timing of the offensive by a high-ranking enemy defector; see Msg, Westmoreland MAC 5298 to III MAF and Field Force Cdrs, 21 Apr 68, Westmoreland Message files, Apr 68, CMH; and Msg, COMUSMACV MAC 11551 to AIG 7055, DIRNSA, and Commander, Naval Intelligence Command (COMNAVINTCOM), 24 Apr 68, tab 59, Westmoreland History files no. 31 (1–30 Apr 68), CMH. General Westmoreland's reports and evaluations of the offensive are in his Msg files, May 68. Retrospective analyses are in MACV Hq, " 'One

In central I Corps, a North Vietnamese division attacked Kham Duc, a Special Forces camp southwest of Da Nang near the Laotian border. On the evening of 10 May, the enemy overran one of the camp's outposts and brought the base under mortar and machine-gun fire. After consultation with Generals Abrams and Cushman, Westmoreland ordered evacuation of the camp rather than face another Khe Sanh–type siege. He explained to Admiral Sharp, "At this time forces and resources that would be required for defense of Kham Duc can be much more profitably utilized in other areas." Aware of the public relations implications of this apparent retreat, Westmoreland and his chief of public affairs, General Sidle, carefully planned the presentation of the decision to the press, seeking to keep the story at "low key" while explaining the action to newsmen in background briefings. Under cover of round-the-clock B–52 and tactical air strikes, the air extraction of the beleaguered garrison under fire was successful but cost the allies heavily in lost men, aircraft, and equipment.[13]

Overall, however, the Communists had little to show for the 30,000 casualties MACV estimated they suffered in a month of heavy fighting. The May offensive diverted few South Vietnamese security forces from the villages to the towns and cities and thus had almost no effect on rural pacification. By late May, enemy main force units, under aggressive allied air and ground pursuit, were withdrawing to their base areas and cross-border sanctuaries to rest and refit. Nevertheless, small Communist units hung on around Saigon. Until late June, they kept up an intermittent rocket and mortar bombardment of the capital. Their indiscriminate strikes at military installations and civilian districts inflicted relatively minor casualties and damage but created the impression of a city still under siege.[14]

The Military Assistance Command and the South Vietnamese government redeployed forces and created a new headquarters to counter the enemy's persistent pressure on Saigon. On 3 June, after prolonged American urging, President Thieu finally unified command of all his forces protecting the capital and its immediate environs under a military governor of Saigon and Gia Dinh Province. Simultaneously, General Westmoreland, in one of his last acts as COMUSMACV, established a Capital Military Assistance Command under Maj. Gen. John H. Hay, deputy commander of II Field Force, who exercised operational control over all U.S. units and advisory teams in Saigon–Gia Dinh and acted as senior adviser to the new military governor. To counter the rocket bombardment, General Abrams established surveillance zones

War': MACV Command Overview, 1968–1972," ch. 3, pp. 9–10, and ch. 4, pp. 19–24, 27–28; and MACV History, 1968, vol. 1, pp. 38, 132–33.

[13] Westmoreland History Notes, 1–31 May 68, tab 1, Westmoreland History files no. 32 (1–31 May 68); Quotation is from Msg, Westmoreland MAC 6210, to Sharp info Wheeler and Goodpaster, 12 May 68; see also Westmoreland MAC 6222, MAC 6264, and MAC 6568 to same addressees, 12, 13, 19 May 68; Westmoreland Message files, May 68, CMH.

[14] Msgs, Abrams MAC 7605 and MAC 8128 to Sharp, 9 Jun 68 and 19 Jun 68, Abrams Papers, CMH.

A view of mud ramps with enemy rockets in position

surrounding Saigon, each with Army helicopter or Air Force fixed-wing gunships assigned for rapid response to firings. This system, combined with constant infantry sweeps around the city and the capture of many rocket caches, prevented the Communists from fulfilling their promise to hit Saigon with "100 rockets for 100 days."[15]

With the enemy's shift to attacking South Vietnam's cities, their protection—especially that of Saigon, the nation's political center—inevitably became one of COMUSMACV's top priorities, on a par with the continuing battle for northern I Corps. General Abrams declared in mid-June: "The enemy has made Saigon/Gia Dinh his number one effort at this time; I have made it mine." By late June, twenty-seven U.S. and South Vietnamese maneuver battalions were concentrated in Gia Dinh Province. Counting additional troops interdicting infiltration routes and attacking enemy base areas farther from the capital, General Abrams estimated that "over 50 percent of allied maneuver battalion

[15] MACV History, 1968, vol. 1, pp. 219–21; MACV Hq, "One War," ch. 4, pp. 25–27. Msgs, Abrams MAC 7708 and MAC 8887 to Wheeler and Sharp, 11 Jun 68 and 3 Jul 68, Abrams Papers, CMH. For background on the command reorganization of the South Vietnamese Army, see tab 10, Westmoreland History files no. 29 (1–29 Feb 68), and tabs 51, 53, and 86, Westmoreland History files no. 31 (1–30 Apr 68), CMH. The Saigon defense system at full development is described in Memo, Wheeler CM–3896–69 for Sec Def, 26 Jan 69, sub: Protection of Population Centers in South Vietnam, box 064, National Security Council (NSC) files, Richard M. Nixon Presidential Papers, National Archives and Records Administration (NARA), College Park, Md.

assets are involved in the defense of Saigon/Cholon," a deployment that "degrades our flexibility and our potential to accomplish other missions" but nevertheless was a political necessity.[16]

The Military Assistance Command led the way in efforts to repair the damage caused by the May fighting in the capital, which left almost 20,000 homes in ruins and over 130,000 people in need of emergency assistance and new shelter. Fortunately, the Central Recovery Committee set up after Tet remained in operation and quickly instituted emergency relief efforts. To speed the reconstruction of housing in the worst-hit districts, the Americans and South Vietnamese, under a plan developed by General Westmoreland and Ambassador Komer and approved by President Thieu, deployed military engineer units to clear rubble, lay concrete foundations for houses, and set up thousands of prefabricated dwellings manufactured in a U.S. Army factory. This operation, code-named Dong Tam ("United Hearts and Minds"), was intended both to accelerate the restoration of shelter and enhance the prestige of President Thieu's government and its U.S. allies. By the end of June, the rebuilding projects were well under way.[17]

Besides assisting civilian war victims, MACV and the Joint General Staff (JGS) tried to ensure that future urban fighting would produce fewer of them. Generals Westmoreland and Abrams and Ambassadors Bunker and Komer all recognized that allied firepower had caused most of the devastation in Saigon in the course of rooting out small enemy units that had infiltrated commercial and residential areas. Accordingly, on 13 May, Westmoreland, after consultation with the Mission Council, instituted a combined MACV and JGS review of urban combat tactics, aimed at finding ways to eliminate the enemy while minimizing collateral damage. When he took acting command, General Abrams confined to only the most senior commanders the authority to use helicopter gunships, tactical air support, and indirect fire artillery in urban areas. On 2 June, a stray rocket from an American helicopter supporting South Vietnamese Rangers in street fighting in Cholon—on a mission authorized by the III Corps commander, General Khang—killed the chief of the Saigon Military Police and five other high-ranking South Vietnamese officers and wounded three. This incident further dramatized the problem. In response to it, and to embassy and news media

---

[16] First quotation is from Msg, Abrams MAC 7766 to Weyand, 12 Jun 68; second is from Msg, Abrams MAC 8128 to Sharp, 19 Jun 68. Both in Abrams Papers, CMH. Weyand, Debrief, 15 Jul 68, p. 11, reflects the increased U.S. emphasis on defense of Saigon and other principal South Vietnamese cities. See also Chaisson, Oral History, pp. 156–58.

[17] MACV History, 1968, vol. 1, pp. 540, 542–43; Sharp and Westmoreland, *Report*, pp. 173, 235; MFR, Bryan, 14 May 68, sub: Evaluation of Saigon Situation, tab 22; MFR, Chaisson, 1 Jun 68, sub: MACV Commanders' Conf, 19 May 68, tab 55; MFR, Brig Gen A. P. Rollins, Jr, sub: Saigon Emergency Housing, 17 May 68, tab 58. Last three in Westmoreland History files no. 32 (1–31 May 68), CMH.

reports of the extensive destruction in Saigon, Secretary Clifford added his authority to the demand for a review of MACV's urban tactics.[18]

The joint study, completed on 14 June, recommended maximum reliance on direct-fire weapons and riot gas in street fighting. It called for improved urban combat training of South Vietnamese units and the immediate issue to them of 90-mm. and 106-mm. recoilless rifles. It emphasized the need for unified planning and action by all South Vietnamese military and police organizations involved in city defense and called for creation of people's civil defense groups to provide intelligence on enemy infiltration and help with post-battle disaster relief. The study urged that the authority to call for artillery, helicopter gunships, and tactical air in urban

U.S. soldier trains members of Platoon 186 of the Popular Forces on how to fire the M16 rifle.

areas continue to be limited to corps and field force commanders. General Abrams promptly endorsed these recommendations and put them into effect insofar as they applied to his forces. In particular, he maintained tight control on airpower and artillery. On 22 June, Abrams rejected a request from General Weyand that authority for use of these weapons in designated built-up areas of Saigon be delegated to division commanders. He declared that "our military forces must find the way to save Saigon without destroying it." Worthy though these sentiments were, the MACV-JGS study acknowledged, as did General Abrams, that if the enemy got into the cities in great enough force, massive destruction inevitably would result. Hence, the "key

[18] Concern over damage inflicted in clearing the cities dated back to the Tet offensive; see Msg, Sharp to Westmoreland, 9 Mar 68, Westmoreland Message files, Mar 68, CMH, and Msg, Westmoreland MAC 6458 to Wheeler info Sharp, 17 May 68, ibid., May 68. Westmoreland History Notes, 1–31 May 68, tab 1; Westmoreland Schedule, 13–14 May 68, tab 2; MFR, 14 May 68, sub: Evaluation of Saigon Situation, tab 22; MFR, Westmoreland, 20 Jun 68, sub: Mission Council Meeting, 20 May 68, tab 55; Westmoreland History files no. 32 (1–31 May 68); Msg, MACV to JCS and CINCPAC, 8 Jun 68, tab 16, Westmoreland History files no. 33 (1–30 Jun 68), CMH. Clifford's intervention is recounted in William M. Hammond, *Public Affairs: The Military and the Media, 1968–1973*, U.S. Army in Vietnam (Washington, D.C.: U.S. Army Center of Military History, 1996) pp. 26–31.

objective" in city defense continued to be "to intercept and engage the enemy prior to his reaching major urban areas."[19]

The enemy's third try at a nationwide offensive, which began on 17 August, scarcely tested the allies' new city fighting tactics. Forewarned, as in May, of the enemy's plans, American and South Vietnamese forces completely preempted major Communist assaults on Saigon and Da Nang. The offensive quickly tailed off into ineffectual ground and fire attacks on lesser positions. As in May, the North Vietnamese and Viet Cong suffered heavy casualties for little gain.[20]

The three offensives of 1968, each weaker than the last, left Communist forces in South Vietnam depleted and in many cases demoralized. According to defector reports and captured documents, enemy field commanders complained openly that the general offensive had been planned on the basis of unrealistic information, clumsily executed, and barren of results commensurate with its cost in men and materiel. The commanders considered the May and August attacks, made without the advantage of surprise, to have been especially ill-advised and disastrous. By drawing local force units in to keep up pressure on the cities, the continuing offensives attenuated revolutionary control in the villages and hamlets. A North Vietnamese official history later acknowledged:

Because the enemy's situation and our situation had changed we had to fight continually and to concentrate on the cities. In the rural areas we were vulnerable and were strongly counterattacked by the enemy, so our forces were depleted and in some places the liberated area was reduced. The revolutionary movement in the Nam Bo lowlands encountered many difficulties and our offensive posture weakened. When the enemy launched a fierce counteroffensive our weaknesses and deficiencies caused the situation to undergo complicated changes.[21]

Between the May and August offensives, the Military Assistance Command carried out the tactically complex and politically delicate task of disengaging from Khe Sanh. Such disengagement was under consideration well before units of the 1st Cavalry and 3d Marine Divisions reestablished ground contact with the base early in April in Operation PEGASUS. By that time, Generals Abrams, Cushman, and Momyer all

---

[19] First quotation is from Msg, Abrams MAC 8249 to Weyand, 22 Jun 68; second is from Msg, Abrams MAC 8035 to Wheeler, 18 Jun 68. Both in Abrams Papers, CMH. In same files, see Msg, Abrams MAC 7871 to Wheeler, 14 Jun 68.

[20] MACV Hq, "One War," ch. 4, pp. 32–37; MACV History, 1968, vol. 1, pp. 38, 133–36. Msgs, Abrams to Wheeler info Sharp, MAC 10181, 28 Jul 68; Abrams MAC 10260 to Wheeler, 30 Jul 68; Abrams MAC 11181 to Wheeler info McCain, 18 Aug 68; Abrams MAC 12145 to Field Force and Component Cdrs, 8 Sep 68. All in Abrams Papers, CMH.

[21] Quotation is from War Experiences Recapitulation Committee, *Resistance War*, p. 110. Duiker, *Road to Power*, pp. 276–77; Ford, "Tet 1968," pp. 196–200; CIA Intelligence Information Report, 13 Aug 70, CMH. Despite the subject, this report, from an enemy defector, describes bitter criticism of the offensives by Communist field commanders and by observers from the People's Republic of China.

had gone on record in favor of abandoning the fixed position at Khe Sanh at some point after the lifting of the siege. They advocated instead defending the northwestern corner of Quang Tri Province by airmobile operations from bases farther to the east and less vulnerable to North Vietnamese ground and artillery attack, a course of action made possible by the presence in northern I Corps of the 1st Cavalry and 101st Airborne Divisions and by the expansion of the logistical base in the region.[22]

General Westmoreland, however, remained reluctant to give up Khe Sanh if only because the enemy (and U.S. war critics) would proclaim such a withdrawal as an American defeat. At a senior I Corps commanders' meeting at Provisional Corps headquarters on 14 April, Westmoreland angrily rejected a proposal by Generals Cushman and Rosson to dismantle Khe Sanh by the end of the month to regroup forces for a major assault on the enemy's important A Shau Valley base area west of Hue and for other operations. Nevertheless, the MACV commander agreed in principle to a gradual reduction of the position in the context of continued search-and-destroy operations around it, with a view to closing Khe Sanh by early September. By that time, of course, General Abrams would be in command and make the final decision. The mid-May evacuation of Kham Duc, in which Westmoreland, Abrams, Cushman, and Momyer all concurred, clearly signaled MACV's determination to avoid another siege in a remote place of limited value.[23]

When he took acting command of MACV in late May, General Abrams decided to move the Khe Sanh evacuation forward to counter threatening new maneuvers by enemy divisions in northern I Corps and to maintain strong American forces on the western approaches to Hue. Abrams realized, however, that he must avoid the appearance of a retreat forced by the enemy. After 3d Marine Division units had mauled a North Vietnamese division south of Khe Sanh, giving MACV a victory to cover the withdrawal, Abrams on 21 June, with Ambassador Bunker's concurrence and administration approval,

[22] Msgs, Abrams PHB 181 and PHB 197 to Westmoreland, 28 Feb 68 and 1 Mar 68, Westmoreland Message files, Feb and Mar 68; Msg, Kerwin MAC 2929 to Abrams, 1 Mar 68. All in Abrams Papers, CMH. Shulimson et al., *Marines in Vietnam, 1968*, p. 312. Chaisson Diary, 9 Mar 68, box 9, Chaisson Papers, Hoover Institution. Interv, Col D. A. Doehle with Gen Walter T. Kerwin, Senior Officers Oral History Program, 1980, pp. 351–52, MHI, (hereafter cited as Kerwin Interv). Logistics progress is discussed in Msg, COMUSMACV MAC 09322 to CINCPAC info JCS, 3 Apr 8, tab 15, Westmoreland History files no. 31 (1–30 Apr 68), CMH.

[23] The Provisional Corps meeting and its decisions are described in MFR, Chaisson, 17 Apr 68, sub: Report of Visit by COMUSMACV to Hq PCV, 14 Apr 68, tab 34, Westmoreland History files no. 31 (1–30 Apr 68), CMH. This document contains handwritten amendments that make Westmoreland's opposition to evacuating Khe Sanh appear less adamant than in the original text. For other accounts of the meeting, see Ltr, Chaisson to Mrs Chaisson, 17 Apr 68, box 7; and Chaisson Diary, 14 Apr 68, box 8, Chaisson Papers, Hoover Institution. Msg, Westmoreland MAC 02391 to Abrams, 1 Mar 68, Westmoreland Message files, Mar 68, CMH. Chaisson, in Ltr to Mrs Chaisson, 14 May 68, box 7, Chaisson Papers, Hoover Institution, relates the Kham Duc evacuation to Khe Sanh.

authorized Generals Cushman and Rosson to begin demolishing the base's airstrip and defenses and removing men and equipment. The Saigon and Washington authorities carefully crafted the public presentation of the withdrawal, attempting to portray it as a redeployment of forces brought about by changing circumstances. They kept General Westmoreland informed about the operation and secured his public and private endorsement of it. This public relations effort fell short of success. Inevitably, the press, annoyed by Abrams' attempt to delay the filing of stories on the pullout until it was well under way, interpreted the redeployment as a tacit admission that MACV had been wrong to defend Khe Sanh in the first place. On the ground, however, the operation went smoothly. By 5 July, allied forces had vacated the plateau, leaving behind only small reconnaissance elements.[24]

In November 1968, the Thieu administration, at the urging and with the assistance of MACV and the U.S. mission, undertook an ambitious new pacification campaign, to exploit what American officials believed was the vacuum in the countryside created by the enemy's concentration on the cities. Circumstances late in the year favored the endeavor. Pacification had been making a slow but steady recovery since Tet. The government's Regional and Popular Forces were increasing in size and improving in quality under MACV and CORDS programs instituted in late 1967, and the government's post-Tet effort to create a mass People's Self-Defense Force (PSDF) showed promise in both cities and countryside. Political considerations also came into play. MACV, the U.S. mission, and the Johnson administration all saw indications that the enemy, after the failure of its three offensives, was trying to establish political and military control over as much of the countryside as possible, in preparation for confronting the next U.S. president with a call for a cease-fire and a coalition government or territorial partition of South Vietnam. A successful pacification campaign would counter this ploy, and it also would demonstrate to the U.S. home front that the allies were making real progress and that the war was not stalemated.[25]

---

[24] Msgs, Abrams MAC 7016 to Rosson, 28 May 68; Abrams MAC 8023 to Cushman info Rosson, 17 Jun 68; Abrams MAC 8046, MAC 8206 and MAC 8719 to Wheeler and Sharp, 18, 21, 30 Jun 68; Wheeler JCS 06844 to Abrams, 20 Jun 68; Wheeler JCS 06867 to Sharp and Abrams, 21 Jun 68; Abrams MAC 8180 to Anderson, 21 Jun 68; Abrams MAC 8250 to Wheeler, 22 Jun 68; Abrams MAC 8394 to Westmoreland, 25 Jun 68; Westmoreland HWA 2153 and HWA 2165 to Abrams, 27 Jun 68. All in Abrams Papers, CMH. Hammond, *Military and the Media, 1968–1973*, pp. 34–38; Shulimson et al., *Marines in Vietnam, 1968*, ch. 16.

[25] Pacification gains during 1968 are summarized in MACV Hq, "One War," ch. 3, pp. 3–6, 11–14, 17, and Ltr, Komer to William Leonhart, 17 Jul 68, Chronological file, Komer (1968), DepCORDS files, CMH. For political and diplomatic considerations, see Clarke, *Final Years*, pp. 304–05; Msg, Abrams MAC 12067 to Wheeler info McCain, 6 Sep 68, Abrams Papers; MFR, Chaisson, 5 Apr 68, sub: MACV Commanders' Conference, 31 Mar 68, tab 68, Westmoreland History files no. 30 (1–30 Apr 68), CMH. Also Memo, Komer for Abrams, 15 Sep 68, and Ltr, William P. Bundy, Asst Sec State for East Asian and Pacific Affairs, to Samuel D. Berger, Deputy Ambassador to South Vietnam, 7 Oct 68, Accelerated Pacification Campaign Jan–Mar 69 file. Both in DepCORDS files, CMH.

Taking these factors into account, MACV and the U.S. mission during September and early October persuaded President Thieu to launch an Accelerated Pacification Campaign. Initially, Thieu favored a primary emphasis on consolidating Saigon's control over already relatively secure areas. Komer, however, convinced Thieu and the American mission to concentrate instead on rapid if superficial expansion into contested parts of the countryside. The deputy for CORDS reasoned that the allies could "achieve greater results more quickly by seeking to expand a diluted form of government control while destroying enemy forces and infrastructure than by seeking a high degree of security and efficient administration" in regions currently dominated by Saigon. Komer argued that his approach would be more effective than Thieu's as a counter to the enemy "if he plans any ceasefire/partition/coalition gambit."[26]

As finally worked out, the campaign was to run from 1 November 1968 through 31 January 1969, the end date coinciding conveniently with the Vietnamese Tet holiday and with the inauguration of the new U.S. president. It consisted of six subcampaigns, each, at Komer's insistence, focused on simple, specific goals. The centerpiece was a drive to raise between 1,000 and 1,100 hamlets from contested or Viet Cong–controlled status (D and E in the CORDS Hamlet Evaluation System) to partially government-controlled (C) status by occupying them with Regional and Popular Force units, setting up village and hamlet administrations, and organizing PSDF groups. An "intensive military spoiling campaign" was to keep enemy units away from the areas being pacified, and other campaigns were aimed at bringing in enemy defectors and killing or capturing political cadres. A vigorous new information program was to convince the people that the allies had the initiative and were moving rapidly to win the war. While Vietnamese civilian ministries and military forces were to carry out the campaign, the MACV and CORDS staffs drafted the plans and directives for it and closely monitored its progress.[27]

President Thieu and his administration pushed the campaign with what was, by Saigon government standards, great vigor. Thieu created a new Central Pacification and Development Council under his prime minister, Tran Van Huong, to give unified direction to this and subsequent pacification campaigns. The president visited each corps to encourage activity and make sure that the regional authorities cor-

---

[26] MACV Hq, "One War," ch. 3, pp. 18–21. Memos, Komer for Abrams, 15 Sep 68, and 22 Sep 68, sub: The Counter-Offensive—How to Make It Work, Komer-Abrams file, 1968; Memo, Komer for Abrams, n.d., sub: Counteroffensive; Memo, n.d., sub: Feasibility Study for Accelerated Pacification Campaign, Accelerated Pacification Campaign Mar–Sep 68 file; DepCORDS files, CMH.

[27] Memo, Col N. A. Parson, Jr, for Acting Chief Plans & Policy Div, n.d., sub: Counteroffensive Directives; Memo, MACV Office of AC/S CORDS for Distribution List, 23 Oct 68, sub: Planning Memorandum 807, Special Pacification Campaign; Msg, COMUSMACV MAC 32362 to SAs I, II, III, and IV Corps, 31 Oct 68, Accelerated Pacification Campaign Oct 68 file. All in DepCORDS files, CMH.

rectly understood the plan. At MACV's direction, U.S. forces worked with the South Vietnamese Army and the Regional and Popular Forces in cordon and search and other security operations.

Begun on schedule on 1 November, the Accelerated Pacification Campaign essentially had achieved its objectives by its 31 January 1969 cutoff date. Overcoming light and scattered Viet Cong resistance, the government more than met its quota of 1,100 hamlets occupied. Its programs for increasing Viet Cong and North Vietnamese defections and uprooting the enemy's clandestine administration respectively exceeded and came close to their numerical targets. Organization and training of new PSDF units went well, although arming of the militia lagged in most areas. American officials recognized that in the newly occupied hamlets pacification in the full social and political sense had hardly begun and that the campaign owed much of its success to the absence of systematic enemy opposition. Nevertheless, they believed that they had at least raised the government flag over much of the countryside and had significantly damaged the enemy's rural apparatus. Perhaps most important, the South Vietnamese had gained from the campaign new confidence in their own capacities. The Accelerated Pacification Campaign thus laid the foundation for more thorough follow-up efforts during 1969.[28]

As the military and pacification campaigns went forward, MACV during the last half of 1968 carried out and partially modified reinforcement Program Six. One of the two Army brigades involved, the 3d of the 82d Airborne Division, part of the February "emergency" reinforcement, was already in I Corps. The other, the 1st Brigade, 5th Infantry Division (Mechanized), arrived in July, replacing the 27th Marine Regimental Landing Team, and began operations in northern Quang Tri. Two tactical fighter squadrons had deployed in May; and a stream of Army combat and combat service support units, including some reserve field artillery and engineer battalions, entered Vietnam during September and October. In September, at General Abrams' recommendation, the Defense Department deleted from Program Six a reserve armored cavalry squadron and an evacuation hospital so that MACV could use the more than 1,400 personnel spaces thus saved for purposes Abrams deemed more urgent, such as provision of more advisers and helicopter door gunners. The equipment of the deleted armored cavalry squadron went to outfit a new South Vietnamese squadron. Throughout the year, Abrams campaigned for reduction of the Program Five requirement to replace 12,545 military personnel with locally hired civilian workers, contending that its implementation would reduce the efficiency and mobility of many

---

[28] MACV Hq, "One War," ch. 3, pp. 21–24, 26–27, ch. 4, pp. 38–39. Msg, COMUSMACV MAC 36703 to CINCPAC, 20 Nov 68, Accelerated Pacification Campaign Nov 68 file; Msg, Pacification and Development Council of CTZ 2 to Distribution List, 24 Dec 68; Msg, COMUSMACV MAC 44492 to CINCPAC info JCS et al., 26 Dec 68; Paper, 28 Feb 69, sub: Summary of APC 1 Nov–31 Jan, Accelerated Pacification Campaign Jan–Mar 69 file. All in DepCORDS files, CMH.

support units. The Defense Department, however, kept the program in effect, since it was needed to bring MACV's total strength down to the Program Six ceiling of 549,500. By the end of 1968, all the services were well on the way to civilizing the required billets.[29]

Building Up the RVNAF

General Abrams' rejection of a U.S. armored cavalry squadron in Program Six in favor of equipment for a South Vietnamese one reflected MACV's increased emphasis, dictated from Washington, on expanding and improving Saigon's armed forces. The South Vietnamese government showed promising signs of strength after Tet. Its soldiers fought creditably during the offensive and in subsequent engagements. President Thieu took advantage of the Tet crisis to replace several of his weaker commanders and province chiefs, in the process strengthening his military faction at the expense of that of Vice President Ky. Thieu also seized the occasion to implement, and secure National Assembly assent to, a mobilization decree prepared earlier that extended the draft to 18- and 19-year-olds and recalled some 20,000 reservists to the colors. With volunteers and draftees flowing into its induction centers, the RVNAF rather rapidly replaced its Tet losses and seemed able to secure men for further expansion.[30]

In response to the Tet offensive, the Military Assistance Command accelerated its previously planned rearmament of the South Vietnamese with M16 rifles and secured as well additional M60 machine guns, mortars, and other weapons for the regular and territorial forces. The command made large new requests for trucks, helicopters, and armored personnel carriers. Encouraged by the comparative success of South Vietnam's post-Tet manpower mobilization, MACV on 9 March completed a two-year plan for expanding Saigon's armed forces to nearly 780,000 men in 1969 and 801,000 by 1970—substantially higher goals than those of the command's pre-Tet plans—and for adding combat and support units to make the South Vietnamese forces more nearly self-sufficient operationally and logistically. About half the strength increase would be in the Regional and Popular Forces, and the plan provided for formation of Regional Force battalions.[31]

[29] MACV History, 1968, vol. 1, pp. 228–33. Msgs, Palmer ADV 1569 to Abrams, 9 Jun 68; Gen Johnson WDC 8527 to Palmer, 11 Jun 68; Abrams MAC 7755 to Beach and Palmer, 12 Jun 68; Palmer ARV 1622 to Gen Johnson, 14 Jun 68; Abrams MAC 12189 to McCain info Wheeler et al., 9 Sep 68; Abrams MAC 12521 to Westmoreland info Wheeler et al., 16 Sep 68; Westmoreland WDC 13937 and WDC 14065 to Abrams info Wheeler, 12, 13 Sep 68; Westmoreland WDC 14398 to Abrams, 20 Sep 68. All in Abrams Papers, CMH.

[30] Sharp and Westmoreland, *Report*, pp. 164–65, 170–71, sum up RVNAF post-Tet accomplishments. See also tab 68, Westmoreland History files no. 30 (1–31 Mar 68) and tabs 15 and 28, Westmoreland History files no. 31 (1–30 Apr 68), CMH; Clarke, *Final Years*, pp. 307–14.

[31] Sharp and Westmoreland, *Report*, pp. 215–16; Msg, Westmoreland MAC 02952 to Wheeler info Sharp, 2 Mar 68, Westmoreland Message files, Mar 68, CMH; Msgs, Abrams MAC 00273 to Gen Johnson, 7 Jan 68; Gen Johnson WDC 423 to Abrams, 9 Jan 68. Latter two in Abrams Papers,

Defense Secretary Clifford promptly approved MACV's March plan but soon set more ambitious goals. Committed to the most rapid possible U.S. disengagement from the war, Clifford pressed strongly for transfer of the combat burden to the South Vietnamese. The bombing cutback of 31 March and the opening of negotiations, which raised the prospect of an early cease-fire and mutual U.S. and North Vietnamese troop withdrawals, increased the administration's sense of urgency about preparing the South Vietnamese to stand alone, at least against a residual Viet Cong threat. Accordingly, on 16 April, Clifford directed the Joint Chiefs of Staff to prepare a "comprehensive, feasible action plan" with time-phased goals to make the RVNAF self-sufficient as soon as possible in logistics and air and artillery support. He declared: "We have embarked on a course of gradually shifting the burden of the war to GVN forces." Hence, "There is an urgency to accomplishing these objectives."[32]

The Military Assistance Command, to which the Joint Chiefs delegated the planning task, in May produced a detailed RVNAF Improvement and Modernization Plan. The planners assumed that after any mutual withdrawal of North Vietnamese and U.S. combat forces, five years would be needed to develop a RVNAF able to hold its own against the Viet Cong, who were expected to continue receiving North Vietnamese manpower and logistical support. In the interim, an American "residual force" would remain to assist the South Vietnamese. The plan called for a force buildup along the lines proposed in March, with the South Vietnamese reaching their peak combat strength in 1970. Thereafter, gradual reductions in regular and territorial infantry would release manpower for new fixed-wing and helicopter air units and an enlarged seagoing and riverine navy. To support the plan, MACV prepared delivery schedules for large quantities of equipment ranging from M16s to M48 tanks. Assuming negotiated withdrawals began on 1 July 1968, the plan's U.S. residual force would decline from 61,500 men in June 1969 to 20,000 by June 1973 and remain at a level of about 16,600 indefinitely thereafter to perform tasks still beyond RVNAF capabilities. In late June, the Defense Department approved those parts of the May plan that covered re-equipping the existing

CMH. Also Clarke, *Final Years*, pp. 286–87, 293–94.

[32] Quotations from Clifford directive are in MACV History, 1968, vol. 1, pp. 252–53. Gen. William B. Rosson, USA (Ret), "Four Periods of American Involvement in Vietnam: Development and Implementation of Policy, Strategy and Programs, Described and Analyzed on the Basis of Service Experience at Progressively Senior Levels" (Ph.D. diss., New College, Oxford, England, 1979), pp. 224–25 (hereafter cited as Rosson, "Involvement in Vietnam"), and Westmoreland, *Soldier Reports*, p. 382, comment on Secretary Clifford's concern with disengagement from Vietnam. Msg, Westmoreland MAC 05010 to Wheeler and Sharp, 15 Apr 68, Westmoreland Message files, Apr 68, CMH. Clarke, *Final Years*, pp. 292, 294–95, emphasizes the relationship between the bombing cutback and the opening of peace talks on the one hand and the new impetus for RVNAF improvement on the other.

South Vietnamese forces and activating the additional combat units called for in 1969 and 1970.[33]

The administration then moved the goal posts again. As the Paris talks immediately deadlocked and the prospect faded of an early negotiated withdrawal, President Johnson, to defuse domestic antiwar sentiment, shifted his emphasis to securing a prompt, conspicuous increase in the South Vietnamese forces' combat role. To facilitate this, Secretary Clifford, during a July visit to Saigon, instructed General Abrams to expand South Vietnamese ground combat elements at the expense of creating support units for self-sufficiency, on the assumption that U.S. participation in the war would continue for some time. MACV responded with a two-phase revised improvement and modernization plan. Phase I provided for maximum RVNAF combat forces based on an indefinite American presence at Program Six strength. Phase II incorporated the additions required for a force able to deal on its own with the Viet Cong. MACV and the administration rejected out of hand, as unrealistic and too expensive, the Joint General Staff's independently prepared Plan Six, which envisioned a much more nearly self-sustaining establishment heavy in modern aircraft, armor, and artillery. Later in the year, as South Vietnam's mobilization pushed RVNAF strength toward 800,000 well ahead of schedule, General Abrams proposed merging Phases I and II back together again into a single plan calling for a self-sufficient force of 877,000, to be achieved two years ahead of the previous target date. On 18 December, Clifford accepted this revision, which became known as the Accelerated Phase II Improvement and Modernization Plan.[34]

The improvement and modernization plans gave concrete form to ideas that had been in the air since late 1967, but they still left vital questions unanswered. For one, the exact relationship between RVNAF improvement and the pace of American withdrawal remained to be worked out. General Abrams and the Joint Chiefs realized that a too-rapid U.S. departure could impose burdens that the South Vietnamese were not yet ready to assume. Then there was the question of what type self-sufficient force was being built. MACV's plans simply added units and materiel to the existing RVNAF structure without much analysis of its suitability. Some officials, notably Deputy Secretary of Defense Nitze, claimed that the projected force was oriented too much toward conventional warfare rather than toward defeating the insurgency likely to remain after a U.S.–North Vietnamese withdrawal. On the other hand, the Joint General Staff, as indicated in their Plan Six, believed they needed if anything a more conventional force.[35]

[33] Clarke, *Final Years*, pp. 295–96, 298.
[34] Ibid., pp. 298–301, recounts the evolution of the Accelerated Improvement and Modernization Plan. Msg, Abrams MAC 9713 to Wheeler, 18 Jul 68, Abrams Papers, CMH, reviews and rejects the JGS's Plan Six.
[35] These issues, and Nitze's views, are recounted in Clarke, *Final Years*, pp. 301–04.

Finally, could the RVNAF ever be expected to go it alone? In a December study, the CIA answered no, citing the familiar, endemic South Vietnamese failings: inadequate leadership, high desertion rates, rampant corruption, and overdependence on U.S. air and artillery support. Responding to the CIA study, General Abrams cited MACV's continuing efforts to remedy RVNAF deficiencies. He also reiterated that the planned force was designed to "go it alone" only against the "internal threat." It would not be able, he acknowledged, to defeat North Vietnamese divisions remaining in cross-border sanctuaries; and "it obviously could not cope, without external assistance, with an invasion by the forces of NVN." MACV would continue to wrestle with these questions as it tried to prepare the South Vietnamese to fight their own war.[36]

The Paris Talks and the Bombing Halt

As the planning for RVNAF improvement and the launching of the Accelerated Pacification Campaign indicated, the Military Assistance Command conducted operations during the last half of 1968 with one eye always on the possibility of an agreement at the Paris talks. MACV also directly supported the American negotiating team with information, advice, and recommendations; and its commander took part in the deliberations that led up to the cessation of all American bombing of North Vietnam.

Information demands, from both Washington and Paris, were frequent and heavy. Even before the negotiations started, the administration required MACV to submit daily reports on military activity in northern I Corps, information that could be used to detect possible North Vietnamese escalation or de-escalation in that sensitive region. After the Paris meetings began on 10 May, the American negotiators regularly called on MACV for detailed reports, with frequent updates, on such subjects as allied offensive operations, North Vietnamese infiltration across the Demilitarized Zone and through Laos and Cambodia, North Vietnamese units in South Vietnam, and the attacks on Saigon. Along with the information demands came requests for MACV comments and recommendations on issues, including mutual troop withdrawal, re-demilitarization of the Demilitarized Zone, and how to respond if the Communists called for an immediate cease-fire.[37]

---

[36] Quotations are from Msg, Abrams MAC 17134 to Wheeler info McCain, 15 Dec 68, Abrams Papers, CMH; see also in same collection Msg, Wheeler JCS 14581 to Abrams info McCain, 12 Dec 68. Clarke, *Final Years*, pp. 335–36.

[37] Msgs, Wheeler JCS 04785 to Sharp and Westmoreland, 3 May 68; Wheeler JCS 04014 to Westmoreland info Sharp, 12 Apr 68; Westmoreland Message files, Apr–May 68, CMH. Examples of information requests can be found throughout Westmoreland's Message files for May 68 and in the Abrams Papers. For examples of requests for policy views, see Msgs, Wheeler JCS 04270 to Sharp and Westmoreland, 19 Apr 68; Westmoreland MAC 05388 to Sharp, 23 Apr 68; Lt Gen Berton E. Spivy, Jr, DJS/JCS 05639 to Sharp info Westmoreland, 23 May 68; Westmoreland MAC 6836 to

The Military Assistance Command made its own organizational arrangements to support the talks. The command communicated with the American delegation through its senior military member—initially General Goodpaster, the new deputy COMUSMACV—who passed requests from Chief Delegates W. Averell Harriman and Cyrus R. Vance to Saigon either directly or through General Wheeler.[38] In May, MACV dispatched the first of a series of liaison officers to Paris. Generally colonels from the J–2 section, these officers each spent two or three weeks with the delegation, briefing the diplomats on the current military situation and collecting information requests to take back to Saigon. Within MACV headquarters, General Westmoreland on 3 May established an International Affairs Division under the J–5 section. Composed of six officers chosen for extensive joint staff experience and knowledge of international relations, this division drafted MACV's fact sheets and position papers on matters related to the negotiations. Much of the International Affairs Division's output found its way into the series of messages, code-named Bamboo, through which General Abrams and Ambassador Bunker, beginning in October, jointly presented their views to the administration and the Paris delegation. These arrangements continued essentially unchanged when the Nixon administration took office early in 1969 and Henry Cabot Lodge replaced Ambassador Harriman as head of the U.S. negotiating team.[39]

As the negotiations developed, MACV, usually with the concurrence of the embassy, took a hard line on the issues. In April, both General Westmoreland and Ambassador Bunker, on trips to Washington, urged President Johnson to adopt a firm negotiating stance based on the premise that the allies were winning on the ground in South Vietnam. General Abrams declared that a cease-fire unaccompanied by a political agreement and North Vietnamese withdrawal from South Vietnam and the Laotian and Cambodian sanctuaries would be tantamount to allied defeat. If the enemy proposed one, it would be "as an attempt to circumvent the obstacle of our military force in order to further his political purposes"—an action Abrams and Ambassador Bunker both uneasily anticipated since they believed it would be in their adversaries' best interests. Similarly, Abrams emphasized that any U.S.–North Vietnamese troop withdrawal agreement must include

Sharp info Spivy, 25 May 68. All in Westmoreland Message files, Apr–May 68, CMH.

[38] President Johnson wanted General Goodpaster to be "in on the opening stages" of the talks before going on to Saigon. He was replaced in Paris after a few weeks by Maj. Gen. George M. Seignious from the JCS staff. In turn, General Weyand replaced Seignious in February 1969. Johnson, *Vantage Point*, p. 505; Msg, DCSPER DA WDC 2397 to Senior Cdrs, 11 Feb 69, Abrams Papers, CMH.

[39] Johnson, *Vantage Point*, p. 505, describes the initial composition of the Paris delegation. Also MACV History, 1968, vol. 2, pp. 788, 793; ibid., 1969, vol. 1, ch. 2, p. 23; Msgs, Westmoreland MAC 6521 to Goodpaster info Wheeler and Sharp, 18 May 68; Westmoreland MAC 6882 to Goodpaster, 26 May 68; Goodpaster PAR 010 to Westmoreland, 28 May 68, Westmoreland Message files, May 68, CMH. Msgs, Abrams MAC 7079 to Goodpaster, 29 May 68; Maj Gen George Seignious CROC 040 to Abrams, 21 Jun 68 and 30 Nov 68; Abrams MAC 8319 to Seignious, 23 Jun 68; Wheeler JCS 12997 to Abrams info McCain, 8 Nov 68. All in Abrams Papers, CMH.

North Vietnamese forces in Laos and Cambodia and North Vietnamese "fillers" in Viet Cong units, as well as the North Vietnamese formations in the South, and must provide for reliable verification of compliance. However, he indicated that MACV could accept a more limited, perhaps tacit, withdrawal arrangement so long as it allowed the United States to retain enough forces in South Vietnam to balance the North Vietnamese remaining there.[40]

Throughout 1968, the negotiations, and MACV's recommendations, centered on the question of a complete U.S. cessation of its bombing of North Vietnam. Generals Westmoreland and Abrams, along with Admiral Sharp during the remaining months of his tenure as CINCPAC, argued consistently against stopping air attacks on southern North Vietnam; instead, they suggested expansion of the bombing in retaliation for the enemy's offensives. Typically, General Abrams in August warned that a bombing halt would allow the enemy to mass additional forces in and above the Demilitarized Zone, to the point where the allied positions in northern Quang Tri would become "untenable." Nevertheless, the military leaders accepted the fact that political considerations might force a bombing halt. As early as April, they began planning for that eventuality. In September, Abrams directed the commanders of III Marine Amphibious Force and XXIV Corps (as Provisional Corps had been renamed on 15 August) to make recommendations for repositioning U.S. forces in northern I Corps when air attacks were stopped north of the Demilitarized Zone.[41]

During October, the negotiators at Paris moved toward agreement on a U.S. bombing halt in return for a North Vietnamese commitment to engage in prompt substantive talks that would include the Saigon government and the National Liberation Front. In addition, the Americans, partly on Soviet assurances, assumed that "understandings" existed under which the North Vietnamese, if the bombing were stopped, would cease violating the Demilitarized Zone, refrain from attacks on Saigon and other large South Vietnamese cities, and permit continued U.S. aerial reconnaissance over their territory. General Abrams, consulted on these terms in mid-October, declared them

[40] Westmoreland's and Bunker's efforts are recounted in Westmoreland, *Soldier Reports*, p. 362, and Ltr, Berger to Westmoreland, 9 Apr 68, with attached paper by Amb Bunker, tab 27, Westmoreland History files no. 31 (1–30 Apr 68), CMH. Abrams quotation is from Msg, MAC 10907 to Wheeler and McCain, 22 Aug 69, Abrams Papers, CMH. In latter collection, see Msgs, Wheeler JCS 12997 to Abrams info McCain, 8 Nov 68; Abrams MAC 12150 to Wheeler info McCain and Bunker, 8 Sep 68; Abrams MAC 14480, MAC 14481, and MAC 17265 to Wheeler info McCain, 27 Oct 68, 19 Dec 68; Abrams MAC 7494, MAC 11165, MAC 11166, and MAC 16244 to McCain and Wheeler, 12 Jun 69, 27 Aug 69, 16 Dec 69. All in Abrams Papers, CMH.

[41] Johnson, *Vantage Point*, pp. 513–15, and Duiker, *Road to Power*, p. 276, conveniently summarize the negotiations. For military views, see Msg, Sharp to Wheeler info Westmoreland, 29 May 68, Westmoreland Message files, 27 May–11 Jun 68, CMH. Msgs, Abrams MAC 10330 to Wheeler info Sharp, 31 Jul 68; Abrams MAC 11409 to W. W. Rostow, 23 Aug 68; Abrams MAC 12130 to Wheeler info McCain and Bunker, 8 Sep 68; Abrams MAC 12989 to Cushman info Stilwell, 25 Sep 68. All in Abrams Papers, CMH.

acceptable provided that he retained authority to react promptly to enemy violations of the Demilitarized Zone and continue reconnaissance flights over the north. In answer to administration inquiries, he affirmed, as did Ambassador Bunker, that the allies could keep up the morale of their troops and the momentum of their operations in the south during a complete bombing halt. As the day of decision approached, Abrams, hurriedly flown to Washington, repeated these assurances in person to President Johnson at a predawn White House meeting on 29 October.[42]

Besides advising the administration on the bombing halt, MACV took part in bringing the South Vietnamese, who balked at the last minute, into the negotiations. At General Wheeler's instructions, General Abrams informed President Thieu that he had sufficient authority to protect allied forces in the Demilitarized Zone area, that MACV would continue to carry the fight to the enemy in the south, and that the air forces which had ceased bombing North Vietnam would be shifted to "great effect" against the trails in Laos. Thieu, however, remained adamantly opposed to an agreement that accorded the Viet Cong equal status at the negotiating table with his government. After President Johnson unilaterally announced the bombing halt on 31 October, MACV worked to maintain military cooperation with the South Vietnamese armed forces despite the diplomatic impasse. Abrams reported on 5 November that he and General Goodpaster were "on a program of getting around the country to as many people as we possibly can—US and Vietnamese—encouraging, pushing, pulling, listening and smelling." Allied military cooperation in fact was unaffected by the intergovernmental disagreement. The Accelerated Pacification Campaign, for example, opened on schedule on 1 November. After the Thieu government finally joined the talks, MACV helped establish a secure communications link between Saigon and its Paris delegation. In February 1969, MACV and the Joint General Staff set up a combined working group to exchange views and information on the talks and coordinate advice to their respective military representatives at Paris.[43]

Except for the Demilitarized Zone, the 1 November bombing halt had little inhibiting effect on MACV's operations in South Vietnam. It soon became apparent that North Vietnamese troops were continuing

[42] Duiker, *Road to Power*, p. 276; Henry Kissinger, *The White House Years* (Boston: Little, Brown, 1979), p. 237; Johnson, *Vantage Point*, pp. 515–21. Memo, Wheeler CM–4433–69 for Sec Def, 14 Jul 69, sub: The Role of the Soviet Union in the Paris Negotiations; Memo, Gen Goodpaster for Kissinger, 14 Apr 69 with attached chronology, box 098, NSC files, Nixon Papers, NARA. Msgs, McCain to Wheeler info Abrams, 21 Sep 68; Abrams MAC 14482 to Wheeler info McCain and Bunker, 27 Oct 68; Abrams to Goodpaster and Corcoran, 30 Oct 68. All in Abrams Papers, CMH.

[43] Quotation is from Msg, Abrams MAC 14904 to Wheeler and McCain, 5 Nov 68, Abrams Papers, CMH. In same collection, see Msgs, Wheeler JCS 12492 to Abrams info Goodpaster, 30 Oct 68; Abrams MAC 14712 to Field Force and Component Cdrs, 1 Nov 68; Abrams MAC 14738 to Vice Adm Nels C. Johnson info McCain, 1 Nov 68; Wheeler JCS 12737 to Abrams info McCain, 5 Nov 68; and Abrams MAC 14936 to Wheeler, 6 Nov 68. Also MACV History, 1969, vol. 1, ch. 2, p. 23.

to harass allied forces from the southern half of the Demilitarized Zone. General Abrams, who already had the right to fire artillery into the area, promptly requested authority to conduct ground attacks into the zone to destroy these elements. The Johnson administration, unwilling to jeopardize its understandings with North Vietnam, refused that request; but it did permit MACV to send squad-size reconnaissance patrols into the southern half of the Demilitarized Zone and to use platoon-size forces, if necessary, to extract them if they came under attack. Abrams, citing escalating North Vietnamese violations of the Demilitarized Zone, continued to urge that he be allowed to operate in the southern half of the zone with forces "appropriate to the enemy threat involved."[44]

Elsewhere in South Vietnam, the accent remained on the offensive. During General Abrams' brief 29 October visit to Washington, President Johnson warned that if the allies reduced their military efforts the Communists never would negotiate seriously and directed his field commander to maintain maximum pressure on the enemy. According to Abrams, Johnson told him to "pour it on and keep pouring it on." In a message announcing the bombing halt to his commanders, Abrams declared: "the order of the day is to intensify your offensive against infrastructure, guerrillas, and local force units, while maintaining unrelenting pressure on the VC/NVA main force units. We must carry the fight to the enemy and complete his destruction." Nevertheless, while proclaiming the continuation of war as usual, General Abrams took the peace talks and their possible results into account as he formulated and promulgated his concept for defeating the enemy in South Vietnam.[45]

"One War": The Abrams Approach

General Abrams' concept for fighting the war in South Vietnam was based on his own experience and on the policies, forces, and situation he inherited. Abrams entered upon his command with a solid grounding in all the major aspects of the conflict. As Army vice chief of staff, Abrams had helped direct his service's buildup and deployments for the war and had become familiar with the Army staff's Program for the Pacification and Long-Term Development of South Vietnam (PROVN) study, which argued that winning the people's allegiance to the Saigon government was the principal prerequisite for victory. During his year as deputy COMUSMACV, he had immersed himself in the problem of improving the South Vietnamese forces and also had

---

[44] Orders and rules of engagement for the bombing halt are in Msgs, JCS to AIG 7077, 1 Nov 68, box 105, NSC files, Nixon Papers, NARA. Quotation is from Msg, Abrams MAC 2500 to McCain info Wheeler, 26 Feb 69, Abrams Papers, CMH. Demilitarized Zone authority can be traced in same collection, Nov–Dec 68.

[45] Johnson, *Vantage Point*, p. 523. First quote is from Msg, Abrams MAC 14904 to Wheeler and McCain, 5 Nov 68. Second is from Msg, Abrams MAC 14710 to All General Officers, 1 Nov 68. See also Msg, Abrams MAC 14936 to Wheeler, 6 Nov 68. All messages are in Abrams Papers, CMH.

overseen portions of the main force war at Dak To and in northern I Corps. Abrams inherited a MACV strategy that was evolving toward a broad-front, simultaneous attack on all elements of the enemy. He knew that no more American reinforcements were coming and that the administration wanted MACV to begin turning the war over to the South Vietnamese in preparation for eventual American disengagement from the conflict. He recognized that the Paris talks at any time might result in a speedup of that disengagement and in curtailment of MACV's operations.[46]

Abrams' immediate battlefield situation was favorable. He possessed a balanced American combat force and a completed logistical base, as well as a vastly expanded intelligence system. A unified American organization for promoting pacification was in place. The South Vietnamese government and armed forces had withstood the shock of Tet and seemed to be improving in stability and effectiveness. The enemy had come into the open in his repeated offensives and was suffering severe, possibly crippling, losses. Up to this point, COMUSMACV perforce had concentrated on the immediate problems of assembling his forces, stabilizing the Saigon government, and countering enemy offensives. As General Abrams took command, he seemed well positioned to advance beyond day-to-day improvisation toward systematic seizure of the initiative in all phases of the conflict.[47]

On most matters, the new MACV commander shared the views of his predecessor. General Abrams, while cautious in his public statements, assessed the war in generally optimistic terms. He believed that the South Vietnamese had fought well at Tet, that the enemy offensives were being defeated, and that allied forces were making progress in most aspects of the war. While aware of the importance of pacification, Abrams was a strong proponent of the use of American firepower, including the B–52s, which he regarded as his mobile reserve; and he believed, as he declared after Dak To, that "when the enemy comes forth from Cambodia or Laos with his principal formations looking for a fight we must go out and fight him." Abrams was at best a reluctant supporter of the cessation of the bombing of North Vietnam. He regularly joined with Ambassador Bunker in urging both the Johnson and the Nixon administrations to retaliate against North Vietnam for continuing Communist attacks on South Vietnamese cities. Like General Westmoreland before him, Abrams campaigned continuously for authority to strike the enemy's Cambodian and Laotian bases with

---

[46] Abrams' relationship to the Program for the Pacification and Long-Term Development of South Vietnam (PROVN) is emphasized in MACV Hq, "One War," ch. 2, pp. 9, 13. For his service as vice chief of staff, see Sorley, *Thunderbolt*, pp. 178–91.

[47] Abrams assesses the battlefield situation as favorable in Msg, MAC 14710 to All General Officers, 1 Nov 68, Abrams Papers, CMH. For South Vietnamese government improvement, see Clarke, *Final Years*, pp. 361, 507.

artillery, airpower, and ground forces, citing the value of such attacks in preventing future Communist offensives.[48]

Abrams stood firm for the established MACV position in the continuing dispute with the CIA over enemy strength. After the deadlocked April 1968 conference, the CIA and the Defense Intelligence Agency (DIA) reached an agreement on an estimate of enemy main and local forces, administrative services, and guerrillas considerably higher than MACV's. The two agencies also agreed to assign a number to the irregular self-defense forces but not to include them in the military strength total. MACV continued to oppose any quantification of the irregulars. Early in November, General Wheeler asked General Abrams to adopt the CIA-DIA estimate of North Vietnamese troops in South Vietnam in preference to MACV's, so that the government could speak with "one voice" on enemy strength in public statements and in the Paris talks. Abrams in reply declared that he would continue to rely on his J–2, in whose accuracy and objectivity he had full confidence, for the intelligence on which he fought the war and would take full responsibility for the military results of his doing so. Hence, he declined to change MACV's official estimates for the sake of intergovernmental harmony. However, in all MACV public statements, Abrams would employ the compromise figures proposed by Wheeler. Abrams' forthright stand avoided a repetition of the unseemly interagency horsetrading of the previous year, but it did nothing to resolve the fundamental conflict of estimates based on different methodologies and definitions. The incoming Nixon administration as a result was confronted with the disquieting fact that its civilian and military agencies still could not agree on the size of the enemy the United States was facing in Vietnam.[49]

While following established lines of MACV policy, Abrams lost no time in developing his own variations on many themes. The allied Combined Campaign Plan for 1969, issued on 30 September 1968, the first prepared under Abrams, restated the standard objectives of defeating enemy forces and extending government control and population security. However, the plan assumed no increase in American troops. It contained for the first time explicit provision for defense of cities and province capitals, and it emphasized pacification and the enlargement

---

[48] This outline of Abrams' views and policy positions is based on his message files for 1968 and 1969 in the Abrams Papers, CMH. Unless otherwise noted, all messages cited below are from that source. The first quotation is from Msg, Abrams MAC 11239 to Wheeler info Sharp and Westmoreland, 22 Nov 67. A strong statement on the South Vietnamese Army is in MFR, Chaisson, 5 Apr 68, sub: MACV Commanders' Conference, 31 Mar 68, tab 68, Westmoreland History files no. 30 (1–31 Mar 68), CMH. Abrams' recommendation for the Cambodia strike is in Msg, Abrams MAC 1782 to Wheeler and Nazarro, 9 Feb 69; see also Abrams MAC 2264 to Wheeler and McCain, 20 Feb 69.

[49] CIA Memo, 7 Feb 69, CMH; Memo, Jeanne W. Davis, NSC Secretariat, for Offices of Vice President, Sec State, Sec Def, Director Emergency Preparedness, 22 Mar 69, sub: Revised Summary of Responses to NSSM 1: The Situation in Vietnam, NSSM 1 (29 Questions), 1969 file, DepCORDS files, CMH. Msgs, Wheeler JCS 12650 and JCS 12932 to McCain and Abrams, 1, 7 Nov 68; Abrams to Wheeler and McCain, MAC 14821, 3 Nov 68. All in Abrams Papers, CMH.

and improvement of South Vietnamese forces. In its most important departure from the past, the plan, in order to prepare the RVNAF "for the time when it must assume the entire responsibility," eliminated the division of functions under which the Americans had fought the enemy's big units while the South Vietnamese Army concentrated on pacification support. Henceforward, all allied units were to participate equally in the four primary military missions—attacking enemy main forces and base areas, guarding the borders and the Demilitarized Zone, defending the cities, and supporting pacification. Under the new dispensation, South Vietnamese infantry divisions were to be relieved from territorial security tasks by the Regional and Popular Forces as rapidly as the improvement of the territorial forces permitted. The South Vietnamese regulars were to direct their "primary efforts" to destruction of the North Vietnamese and Viet Cong main forces, alongside the Americans and eventually replacing them.[50]

With the Program Six forces nearly all in hand, General Abrams in July 1968 established territorial priorities for the deployment of his U.S. divisions. He gave first priority to western III Corps and northern IV Corps, the region surrounding Saigon, which he labeled a "minimum risk" area. Second priority went to the whole of I Corps and third to the II Corps highlands, which were to be protected by minimum American forces backed by the South Vietnamese and the South Koreans along the coast. These priorities represented more a reaffirmation of existing policy than a radical change; hence, they resulted in few major relocations of troops. As noted previously, Abrams removed American forces from Khe Sanh in favor of a mobile posture in northwest Quang Tri. Late in October, with the North Vietnamese threat to northern I Corps diminishing as a result of allied operations and with an enemy buildup under way in Cambodia opposite Saigon, Abrams shifted the 1st Cavalry Division from I Corps to the border provinces of III Corps. There the division would operate against Communist bases and infiltration routes and preempt any new offensive against the capital. These rearrangements, in Abrams' estimation, placed U.S. forces "in a position to counter likely enemy threats with a minimum of changes." Like Westmoreland, Abrams kept no American units in reserve because their "superior tactical mobility . . . permits any ground forces out of contact to constitute the reserve."[51]

---

[50] Republic of Vietnam Armed Forces/Free World Military Assistance Force (RVNAF/FWMAF) Combined Campaign Plan, 1969, AB 144, 30 Sep 68, pp. 7–8; see also pp. 1–6 and 9–14; MACV History, 1969, vol. 1, ch. 2, p. 5; Clarke, *Final Years*, p. 305, emphasizes how closely AB 144 resembled its predecessors. President Thieu had suggested to General Westmoreland back in April 1968 that expansion of the territorial forces should release South Vietnamese units for "more military operations." See MFR, Westmoreland, 20 Jun 68, sub: Meeting with Thieu on 10 Apr 68, tab 84, Westmoreland History files no. 31 (1–30 Apr 68), CMH.

[51] Quotations are from COMUSMACV Response to NSSM–1 Question 25, Jan 69, folder 20, Thayer Papers, CMH; MACV History, 1969, vol. 1, ch. 2, p. 18; MACV Hq, "One War," ch. 4, pp. 31, 37; Chaisson, Oral History, pp. 147–49; Msgs, Abrams MAC 14472 to McCain info Wheeler,

In northern I Corps, Abrams modified Westmoreland's strongpoint obstacle system in the direction of a mobile, technology-based defense. He retained the bases and strongpoints already built in the eastern half of the barrier and arranged for troops of the South Vietnamese 1st Division to garrison most of them. However, he discontinued construction of the remaining fortifications and barriers, which already had been suspended during the Tet offensive. In their place, Abrams established a network of electronic sensors across the entire southern edge of the Demilitarized Zone, tied in with the Air Force's IGLOO WHITE sensor system in Laos and monitored by a central surveillance facility. He planned to rely on the sensors, along with aerial reconnaissance and other means, to detect enemy forces moving out of the Demilitarized Zone and then strike the intruders with air, artillery, naval gunfire, and mobile ground forces. Abrams considered this revised system "more attuned to present requirements in that it provides for anti-infiltration hardware being utilized in complementary fashion to existing and anticipated tactical operations."[52]

During his first months as COMUSMACV, General Abrams urged his U.S. commanders to seek out and destroy the enemy units exposed by the Communist offensives. He strongly rejected administration suggestions, transmitted through Wheeler, that MACV cut back on offensive operations to reduce casualties. The best way to keep American losses down, he argued, was to "interpose a formidable array of combat power where the enemy is planning to fight." Abrams stated at his first commanders' conference that the "critical problem" was to "determine a practical way to inflict significant attrition on [the enemy], to grab hold of him and to destroy him. This is the payoff—to kill the enemy." Anticipating the enemy's August offensive, Abrams directed his commanders to preempt the Communists by launching attacks of their own. He declared:

I intend to accommodate the enemy in seeking battle and in fact to anticipate him wherever possible. . . . We must anticipate him, fix his major forces as far away as possible from our vital areas, and defeat him decisively. . . . We must concentrate every last element of available combat power on the enemy when he is located. . . . We must defeat his forces, then pursue them and destroy them.[53]

---

27 Oct 68; Abrams MAC 14496 to Cushman, 20 Oct 68. Both in Abrams Papers, CMH. It should be noted that when Abrams ordered the movement of the 1st Cavalry Division, he already knew of the impending agreement on the bombing halt and de-escalation along the Demilitarized Zone.

[52] Quotation is from Msg, Abrams MAC14168 to McCain info Wheeler, 21 Oct 68, Abrams Papers, CMH; MACV History, 1969, vol. 2, ch. 7, pp. 1–5.

[53] First quotation is from Msg, Abrams MAC 8892 to Wheeler, 4 Jul 68; Abrams Papers, CMH. Second is from MACV Hq, "One War," ch. 4, p. 30; see also ch. 4, pp. 31–32, 37. Third is from Msg, Abrams MAC 10181 to Wheeler info Sharp, 28 Jul 68; see also Msg, Abrams MAC 12535 to Wheeler and McCain, 17 Sep 68. Both in Abrams Papers, CMH. MACV History, 1968, vol. 2, pp. 30–32. See Abrams message files for Jun through Sep 68, Abrams Papers, for numerous other communications emphasizing the offensive.

After the defeat of the August offensive, and even more after the 1 November bombing halt and the simultaneous launching of the Accelerated Pacification Campaign, General Abrams changed his emphasis. In his operational guidance to his commanders for the final quarter of 1968, Abrams directed them to cooperate with the South Vietnamese in "an intensive drive against the VC infrastructure and political apparatus aimed at eliminating it just as rapidly as possible; not suppress, but eliminate." At his direction, American units supported the Accelerated Pacification Campaign both by conducting spoiling operations on the fringes of the pacification areas and by working directly with South Vietnamese regular and territorial forces in antiguerrilla and anti-infrastructure actions. After the Saigon government, capitalizing on the success of the accelerated campaign, issued a comprehensive annual pacification plan for 1969, Abrams ordered his commanders to give first priority to supporting it. Early in 1969, he told his commanders that the "most important objective, the one with the highest payoff" was to maintain the momentum of the pacification campaign. He declared later in the year that U.S. forces must consider "the protection of the populace" as their "primary role" and that "all of our actions, wherever they take place, are designed to accomplish this mission."[54]

Abrams had several reasons for this change of operational emphasis. He believed, with the Army authors of PROVN, that restoration of Saigon's control of the rural population, and of the rural population's allegiance to Saigon, was central to the long-term survival of South Vietnam. As of late 1968, North Vietnamese and Viet Cong big units were disappearing from the battlefield into remote base areas or cross-border sanctuaries. The time thus was ripe and the troops available to go after the guerrillas and infrastructure, which now lacked their main force shield. Abrams recognized that enemy large-scale operations depended on prepositioned supplies and on intelligence and other support from the guerrillas and the clandestine Communist administration, known as the Viet Cong Infrastructure, so destruction of the Viet Cong's rural network would help preempt future Communist offensives. Finally, Abrams took into account the political and diplomatic situation. He suspected, as did Ambassador Bunker and other American officials, that the enemy was trying to expand his control of territory in preparation for a call for a cease-fire, which would inhibit large-unit operations but not political subversion, terrorism, and guerrilla activity. Hence, the allies must intensify their own pacification and territorial control

---

[54] First quotation is from Msg, COMUSMACV MAC 28710 to Cdr 7AF et al., 28 Sep 68 in MACV History, 1969, vol. 1, ch. 2, pp. 14–16. Second is from Msg, COMUSMACV MAC 3345 to Cdr 7AF et al., 17 Jan 69, ibid., pp. 18–19. Third is from Msg, CG III MAF to COMUSMACV info CG USARV, 29 Jul 69, Abrams Papers, CMH. MACV Hq, "One War," ch. 3, pp. 24–30, ch. 4, pp. 34–35, 38–41. MACV History, 1969, vol. 1, ch. 2, pp. 4–5; COMUSMACV Response to NSSM–1 Question 25, Jan 69, folder 20, Thayer Papers, CMH.

efforts so as not to "get ourselves into a position where we can lose the war strategically after having defeated the enemy on the battlefield."[55]

The new pacification emphasis did not produce a drastic change in the activities of U.S. troops and was not intended to. American soldiers and marines, increasingly joined by South Vietnamese regulars, continued to devote most of their efforts to seeking out and destroying main force units and base areas. In November 1968, even as the Accelerated Pacification Campaign began, Abrams ordered III Marine Amphibious Force to prepare a large operation against the enemy's Base Area 112 southwest of Da Nang, where two North Vietnamese divisions were believed to be lurking. Early in 1969, marines swept the remote Da Krong Valley in a major airmobile assault, and General Abrams endorsed a II Field Force plan for "opening up" War Zones C and D with "tank-heavy forces." In response to a new Communist offensive early in 1969, Abrams again urged his commanders to pursue and annihilate the attackers. The task of uprooting the Viet Cong guerrillas and infrastructure and securing the population, Abrams emphasized, should be primarily the responsibility of the South Vietnamese territorial forces, police, and pacification cadre.[56]

Abrams viewed the continuing search-and-destroy operations—for public relations reasons, labeled "reconnaissances in force" or "spoiling attacks"—as contributing to pacification by keeping the Communist big units away from the populated areas. In mid-April 1969, he told a visiting Army historian that it was

essential to get out into the difficult western part of Vietnam in order to meet the enemy even as he begins his trek from sanctuaries in Cambodia and Laos. This way we destroy his tediously-prepared logistical arrangements and thus in the end deny large-scale attacks on the populated areas. We have insufficient numbers to protect the population centers in a passive defense. Furthermore, when we have maintained the initiative—whether the enemy is technically on the offensive or not—our kill ratio is spectacular.[57]

---

[55] Quotation is from Msg, COMUSMACV MAC 28710 to Cdr 7AF et al., 28 Sep 68, in MACV History, 1969, vol. 1, ch. 2, pp. 14–16; see also pp. 16–17. Msg, Abrams MAC 14143 to Cushman et al., 20 Oct 68, Abrams Papers, CMH. Abrams assesses enemy post-bombing halt strategy in Msg, MAC 37666 to Field Force and Component Cdrs, 24 Nov 68, Accelerated Pacification Campaign, Nov 68 file, DepCORDS files, CMH.

[56] Msgs, Abrams MAC 16032 to Cushman, 20 Nov 68; Abrams MAC 3806, MAC 4035 and MAC 16766 to Wheeler and McCain, 25, 30 Mar 69; 26 Dec 69; Abrams MAC 5970 to McConnell and McCain, 11 May 69; Abrams MAC 6112 to Lt Gen Julian J. Ewell, CG, II FFV, 14 May 69. All in Abrams Papers, CMH. Chaisson's successor as MACV COC director notes the continuation of search-and-destroy operations under Abrams; see Interv, Marine Corps Historical Program with Lt Gen John N. McLaughlin, USMC, 1980, p. 18, MCHC (hereafter cited as McLaughlin Interv). The Da Krong Valley offensive, Operation DEWEY CANYON, is described in detail in Charles R. Smith, *U.S. Marines in Vietnam: High Mobility and Standdown, 1969* (Washington, D.C.: History and Museums Division, Headquarters, U.S. Marine Corps, 1988), chs. 3 and 4.

[57] Memo, Charles B. MacDonald for SJS MACV, 15 Apr 69, sub: Luncheon Meeting with COMUSMACV, MACV files, MHI.

Trying to give his command an understanding of how all types of operations fitted together, General Abrams promulgated his "one war" concept. He used the phrase as early as March 1968 and used it regularly after becoming COMUSMACV. Repeatedly, he reminded his commanders, his civil and military superiors, and his allies that the enemy knew "no such thing as a war of big battalions, a war of pacification, or a war of territorial security"; for the enemy it was all "just one, repeat one, war." Since there was only one war, "friendly forces have got to . . . carry the battle to the enemy, simultaneously, in all the areas of the conflict," bringing all types of power to "bear against the enemy in every area, in accordance with the way the enemy does his business." Airpower, regular forces, territorial forces, and pacification cadre "all are to be part of the plan aimed at the VC/NVA and the VC infrastructure. All types of operations are to proceed simultaneously, aggressively, persistently, and intelligently. . . ." Abrams declared further: "The full spectrum of allied operations" was to be directed against "the full spectrum of Communist forces, organizations, activities, and facilities. The latter constitute, and are attacked, as a single coordinated system."[58]

The "one war" concept bore a close family relationship to what General Westmoreland had called his "balanced" or "two-fisted" strategy, and indeed to every American strategic plan for Vietnam since 1961, in that it envisioned simultaneous allied pressure on every echelon of the enemy's system from main force units to hamlet party officials. Reflecting the new direction from Washington, Abrams added improvement and modernization of the South Vietnamese forces as a third leg of the policy. He also incorporated his proposals for attacks on the out-of-country sanctuaries. These he regarded as "a pool of options" with which to supplement his "foundation" programs—pacification and RVNAF improvement—"as the climate permits to increase the odds that the foundation programs . . . are enough to give this country and ours the . . . objective we seek." Above all, Abrams emphasized that the "one war" concept involved operational and tactical flexibility:

The one war concept puts equal emphasis on military operations, improvement of RVNAF, and pacification—all of which are interrelated so that the better we do in one, the more our chance of progress in the others. The concept is a flexible one. As a practical matter, the relative priorities accorded these three efforts will vary with time and the requirements of any particular area.

Pressure is put on the enemy wherever and whenever he is found, using tactics best suited to the situation. . . . At the same time, we are working hard to improve RVNAF

[58] First quotation is from Msg, COMUSMACV MAC 30430 to Cdr 7AF et al., 13 Oct 68, in MACV History, 1969, vol. 1, ch. 2, pp. 16–17; see also p. 3. Second is from Msg, Abrams MAC 2127 to CAS Paris for Weyand, 17 Feb 69, Abrams Papers, CMH; in same collection, see Msg, Abrams MAC 14329 to Wheeler info McCain, Bunker, 24 Oct 68. COMUSMACV Response to NSSM 1, Question 25, Jan 69, folder 20, Thayer Papers, CMH. MACV Hq, "One War," ch. 4, pp. 20, 35–36.

performance, often by means of combined military operations, and are supporting pacification wherever required.[59]

Besides promulgating the "one war" concept, General Abrams took steps to provide the Military Assistance Command with a long-range strategic plan based upon it. This plan was to constitute a framework for the annual campaign plans and guide MACV in its allocation of resources. To draft the plan, Abrams during the summer of 1968 brought into the MACV J–5 section a group of field grade officers who had participated in the Army staff's 1966 PROVN study. This Long Range Planning Task Group, headed by Lt. Col. Donald S. Marshall, was to "provide COMUSMACV with an overall plan to carry out and achieve his mission" and to make recommendations "that will influence the optimum allocation and utilization of [MACV's] resources." Working under Abrams' close supervision, the group completed an initial concept for a MACV Strategic Objectives Plan late in November and finished a longer final draft early in 1969.[60]

The resulting MACV Strategic Objectives Plan included many familiar ideas and reflected the strong influence of General Abrams' "one war" philosophy. For example, it incorporated in their entirety Abrams' geographical priority areas and his call for a constant, coordinated attack on the entire enemy structure. It also reaffirmed the existing division of labor between regular and territorial forces. The plan's originality lay in its analysis of the parameters within which MACV had to work and in its attempt to define attainable levels of success linked closely to a progressive reduction of U.S. forces in Vietnam.

The planners assumed that the level of American resources committed to South Vietnam had reached its peak and must be expected to decline under pressure of increasing home-front antiwar sentiment. That same sentiment likely would compel the incoming Nixon administration to move quickly toward disengagement, which meant that MACV had only limited time in which to achieve its goals. Under these circumstances, Marshall's group asserted, MACV could not achieve the "ultimate" U.S. war objective, "A free, independent and viable . . . South Vietnam that is not hostile to the United States, functioning in a secure environment both internally and regionally," the more so since

---

[59] First quotation is from Msg, Abrams MAC 3910 to Wheeler and McCain, 27 Mar 69, Abrams Papers, CMH; see also Msg, Abrams MAC 10629 to Palmer, 7 Aug 68. Second quotation is from Memo, Wheeler JCSM–443–69 for Sec Def, 18 Jul 69, an. E, box 76, NSC files, Nixon Papers, NARA. Clarke, *Final Years*, p. 363, notes the parallel between the Westmoreland and Abrams approaches.

[60] Quotation is from MACV CSAM 68–125, 31 Aug 68, in Long Range Planning Task Group (LRPTG), Briefing Given to COMUSMACV on 20 Nov 68 [and] for the MACV Staff on 26 Nov 68; see also MFR, Lt Col Donald S. Marshall, 23 Nov 68, sub: Briefing for COMUSMACV on the MACV JSOP; both in MACV Strategic Objectives Planning file, CMH; MACV Hq, "One War," ch. 2, pp. 14–16; Davidson, *Vietnam at War*, p. 613.

only the Saigon government could make the political, economic, and social changes required for national viability.

Hence, the planners defined more limited "immediate" and "intermediate" American objectives based on the gradual expansion of secure territory within which Saigon could conduct pacification and national development. The "immediate" goal—securing the most important population centers—should be achieved no later than July 1970, at which time major American troop withdrawals could begin. The "intermediate" goal of extending security to most of the inhabited area of South Vietnam must be reached by July 1972, which would permit reduction of American forces to the level of an advisory group. Accomplishment of these objectives, the planners suggested, might convince the American public the war was not hopelessly stalemated and hence gain MACV more time to work toward its ultimate goal; but they warned that the presidential election year 1972 must be assumed to be the end point of the American effort.[61]

The keystone of the Marshall group's proposed military strategy was an Area Security System that had as its objective "security up to the borders of South Vietnam, which is not dependent on the continued presence of US combat forces." To keep up pressure on all elements of the enemy structure, the Area Security System would divide South Vietnam's territory into four zones. In the Securing and Consolidation Zones, where government military and political influence predominated, territorial forces, police, and civil authorities would conduct pacification operations. In the outer Clearing and Border Surveillance Zones, American, allied, and South Vietnamese regulars would pursue enemy forces, sweep base areas, and drive back cross-border incursions. As enemy strength dwindled under this combined attack, the first two zones would expand to include most of South Vietnam's people. If all worked as envisioned, Hanoi, with its main forces unable to operate safely in the South and its revolutionary organization there being uprooted, might weaken in its resolve to continue the war and agree to an acceptable settlement. Even if that did not occur, the United States could gradually transfer the Area Security System to the South Vietnamese, thereby achieving success "evidenced by a withdrawal of substantial numbers of US forces without a subsequent collapse of the GVN."[62]

In May 1969, General Abrams proclaimed the MACV Strategic Objectives Plan and its Area Security System to be authoritative "overall guidance to the command." MACV and the Joint General Staff subsequently published a combined version of the plan, for the most

---

[61] LRPTG Briefing; LORAPL Marshall Committee, MACV Strategic Objectives Plan, ca. Mar 69, pp. 7–10, 66, 102, 104–05, 196–97, 210–23, CMH.

[62] First quotation is from LORAPL, MACV Strategic Objectives Plan, n.d., p. 133. Second quotation is from p. 11. The Area Security Concept is described in detail on pp. 125–45, 157–58, and 193.

part a Vietnamese translation of the original American document. The two headquarters incorporated the Area Security System into their annual combined campaign plans, beginning with that for 1970. Both the MACV and combined Strategic Objectives Plans underwent periodic revision. The later versions placed increasing emphasis on South Vietnamese self-reliance, for example by proposing military tactics less dependent on American firepower and logistic support. As so often happened with plans in Vietnam, the dates for achieving the immediate and intermediate objectives receded into the future with each new edition.[63]

When promulgated in the combined campaign plans, the Area Security System met criticism from American field commanders and from the CORDS staff. The critics objected that the system's division of territory into Securing, Consolidation, Clearing, and Border Surveillance Zones did not take sufficient account of the fluid nature of control and security in many parts of South Vietnam. Lt. Gen. Julian J. Ewell, the II Field Force commander, for example, observed that "the enemy controls the actual security situation to some extent and as a result it tends to be fluid and dynamic rather than static." In addition, the dissenters argued that the system threatened to undermine the "one war" concept by allowing the divorce of large-unit operations from territorial security. While he acknowledged the importance of these concerns and the need for local flexibility in implementing the concept, General Abrams nevertheless defended the overall scheme. He declared that it would "fix primary responsibility for security" in each zone and thereby make it "more difficult to evade this responsibility than has been the case in the past." The field commanders dutifully incorporated the concept into their planning and to some degree at least into their operations.[64]

An additional deficiency in the long-range plan would become apparent only in retrospect: the Marshall group's assumption that enemy strategy would not change. Marshall and his planners projected that the most "realistic" option for the North Vietnamese and Viet Cong to counter the Area Security Strategy would be to continue their existing combination of main force, guerrilla, and terrorist activity, possibly punctuated by "a sudden dramatic stroke" against Saigon, Hue, Da

[63] Abrams declares the plan authoritative in Memo for Distribution List, sub: Promulgation of MACV Strategic Objectives Plan, in LORAPL, MACV Strategic Objectives Plan. MACV Revised Strategic Objectives Plan, May 70, CMH; JGS/MACV Joint Objectives Plan, 7 Nov 71, CMH. For incorporation of Area Security into the combined campaign plan, see RVNAF/FWMAF Combined Campaign Plan, 1970, AB 145, 31 Oct 69, an. B, CMH.

[64] Davidson, *Vietnam at War*, pp. 613–14, describes American commanders' coolness toward the plan. See also Memo, AC/S CORDS for MACV J5, 22 Apr 69, sub: The MACV Objectives Plan, MACV Strategic Objectives Plan file, CMH. Quotation is from Ewell HOA 3454 to Abrams, 19 Nov 69; see also Msg, Maj Gen Roderick Wetherill, Senior Adviser, IV Corps, CTO 1822 to Abrams, 28 Sep 69; Abrams quotation is from Msg, Abrams MAC 12996 to Wetherill, 5 Oct 69. All in Abrams Papers, CMH.

Nang, or a province capital. The enemy's immediate objective would be to undermine Saigon's pacification effort and promote antiwar sentiment in the United States. Marshall's group believed that major military escalation would expose the enemy's forces to "great losses" and run the risk of provoking the United States to resume bombing North Vietnam. Given these considerations, the Communists were most likely to keep up a steady but relatively low level of military activity in support of a political "fight-talk-fight" strategy. The Marshall group failed to address the possibility that the North Vietnamese, as the American military presence in Southeast Asia diminished, might decide to wage a different kind of war. During the years following Abrams' adoption of the Strategic Objectives Plan, the command, and also the administration in Washington, would develop and execute policy on the basis of the Marshall group's assumptions.[65]

Taken as a whole, General Abrams' approach to the war was an evolutionary expansion upon that of his predecessors. His achievement was one of synthesis. He drew together conceptually, with clarity and force, the basic strands of policy that had emerged during the previous six years. His "one war" concept and the Area Security System could trace their ancestry back to the "two-fisted" strategy and the "spreading-oil-spot" theory of pacification. Responding to Washington's demands for movement toward turning the war over to the South Vietnamese, Abrams emphasized RVNAF improvement and modernization and looked ahead to American troop withdrawals with or without a cessation of hostilities. Stronger allied forces, a relatively stable Saigon government, and a weakened enemy permitted Abrams, for the first time in the war, to mount the balanced military and pacification offensive which Americans had envisioned since the early 1960s. In the end, however, the conflict was not to be resolved on the South Vietnam battlefield alone. Decisions in Washington and Hanoi, and diplomacy in Paris, ultimately would do more to shape the outcome than the "one war" concept.

---

[65] LORAPL Marshall Committee, MACV Strategic Objectives Plan, n.d., ca. Mar 69, pp. 76–77, CMH.

5

Redeployment and Vietnamization

When he inherited the Vietnam War from his Democratic pre-decessor, President Richard M. Nixon inherited also a general course of action and limited room for maneuver. President Johnson had stopped the bombing of North Vietnam, committed the United States to the Paris negotiations, topped off the American force in South Vietnam, and set the goal of reducing American involvement and turn-ing the fighting of the war back to the South Vietnamese. The state of American public opinion made any reversal of this course unthink-able. In addition, the new administration faced a Congress controlled by Democrats, who were free as they had not been under Johnson to take radical antiwar positions. Hard-line anti-Communist though he had been throughout his political career, Nixon understood from the start that he had to disengage the United States from Vietnam or see his administration destroyed. Nevertheless, he and his advisers were determined to extricate the United States on terms that would give the Saigon regime at least a chance to survive and that would demonstrate to allies and enemies alike America's will and ability to maintain its international commitments.[1]

Nixon Sets His Course

Nixon and his foreign policy team—National Security Adviser Henry A. Kissinger, Secretary of State William P. Rogers, and Secretary of Defense Melvin R. Laird—lost no time in reviewing the Vietnam situ-ation and the available policy choices. Immediately after the inaugura-tion on 20 January 1969, the administration issued National Security Study Memorandum (NSSM) 1. Addressed to the State and Defense Departments and the Central Intelligence Agency, NSSM 1 posed a set of detailed questions on six aspects of the war: negotiations, the enemy situation, the condition of the South Vietnamese armed forces, the status of pacification, South Vietnamese politics, and American objec-

---

[1] The administration's overall approach is summarized in Kissinger, *White House Years*, pp. 227–28, 298. Early administration reviews of options are described in Msg, Goodpaster JCS 01029 to Abrams, 24 Jan 69, Abrams Papers, CMH.

Nixon and Kissinger

tives. Both General Abrams and Ambassador Bunker responded to this questionnaire through respectively the Joint Chiefs of Staff (JCS) and the State Department, and their evaluations were incorporated in those agencies' replies.[2]

The agency answers, presented to the senior policymakers in mid-March, reflected consensus on some points but also many disagreements in fact and interpretation. The general agreement was that the allied position in Vietnam "has been strengthened recently in many respects" and that the enemy had suffered military and pacification reverses. Nevertheless, the North Vietnamese and Viet Cong had the capacity to continue the war for a long while yet and had gone to Paris not out of weakness but in hopes of winning in the political arena the victory the United States was denying them on the battlefield. On many issues, the now-familiar lineup of optimists (the JCS, MACV, CINCPAC, and the U.S. Embassy in Saigon) and pessimists (Pentagon civilians, the CIA, and the State Department, Bureau of Intelligence and Research) appeared. The former group believed the government's recent pacification gains were substantial and likely to be lasting; the latter considered the gains inflated and fragile. Similar differences existed

[2] Kissinger, *White House Years*, p. 238; Clarke, *Final Years*, pp. 341–42. Msgs, Gen George S. Brown, USAF, to Abrams, 21 Jan 69; McConnell JCS 01649 to Gen Joseph J. Nazzaro, CINC, Pacific Air Forces, and Abrams, 7 Feb 69. Both in Abrams Papers, CMH.

over how much the Republic of Vietnam Armed Forces was progressing under the Improvement and Modernization program. MACV and the CIA rehearsed once more their arguments over the enemy order of battle and the importance of the Sihanoukville supply route. In sum, the responses to NSSM 1 indicated that the allies were in no danger of defeat but also were far from anything resembling decisive victory, and that Saigon's present and future capabilities still were very much in question.[3]

During its first year in office, the Nixon administration gradually developed a two-track policy of negotiation and what came to be called "Vietnamization"—that is, unilateral withdrawal of American combat troops combined with a major effort to strengthen Saigon's armed forces. Nixon and his advisers hoped that this course of action would simultaneously increase chances of an acceptable settlement at Paris, maintain the allies' relatively favorable battlefield situation in South Vietnam at less cost to the United States, and weaken or neutralize the domestic antiwar movement. At maximum, this policy would give a non-Communist South Vietnam a chance to survive, the preferred result from Nixon's point of view. At minimum, the administration could disengage on acceptable terms without betraying an allied government that was still trying to carry on the fight, ensuring what Kissinger later called a "healthy interval" between America's departure and Saigon's ultimate fate.[4]

On the negotiation track, Nixon and Kissinger early initiated secret discussions with Hanoi and continued the open sessions at Paris. They also attempted, unsuccessfully, to obtain Soviet help in bringing Hanoi to terms. Nixon soon was compelled by domestic pressures to offer major political concessions. In a May 1969 Vietnam policy speech, the president publicly disavowed any intention to seek military victory (Lyndon Johnson had not sought such a victory either, but had not openly announced the fact.) and reduced the U.S. overall objective from securing a non-Communist South Vietnam to ensuring "self-determination" for the South Vietnamese people. He called for mutual withdrawals of U.S. and North Vietnamese troops under international supervision, to

---

[3] Memo, Jeanne W. Davis, NSC Secretariat, for Offices of Vice President, Sec State, Sec Def, and Director of Emergency Preparedness, 22 Mar 69, sub: Revised Summary of Responses to NSSM 1: The Situation in Vietnam, NSSM 1 (29 Questions) 1969 file, DepCORDS files, CMH; Historical Division, Joint Secretariat, U.S. Joint Chiefs of Staff, "The History of the Joint Chiefs of Staff: The Joint Chiefs of Staff and the War in Vietnam, 1969–1970," CMH, pp. 9–13 (hereafter referred to as "Joint Chiefs of Staff and the War in Vietnam, 1969–1970"); Kissinger, *White House Years*, pp. 238–39. Clarke, *Final Years*, pp. 342–46, notes MACV's optimistic assessments of RVNAF progress.

[4] Nixon laid out his basic strategy in National Security Decision Memorandum (NSDM) 9, sub: Vietnam, 1 Apr 69, box 1008, NSC files, Nixon Papers, NARA. In same records, see Memo, Kissinger for the President, [Mar 69] sub: Vietnam Situation and Options, box 142; Memo, Kissinger for the President, 11 Sep 69, sub: Vietnam Options, box 091. Kissinger used the "healthy interval" phrase in a Draft Memo for the President, [Sep 71], sub: Vietnam, box 1013. Nixon's first complete public statement of his policy came in a televised speech on 3 Nov 69. This speech is reviewed in Kissinger, *White House Years*, pp. 304–07; see also pp. 311 and 1480–82.

be followed by a cease-fire and free internationally monitored elections with National Liberation Front participation. President Thieu, under American pressure, echoed the latter offer. Nixon pledged to accept any government in South Vietnam, including a Communist one, if it were installed by a free vote of the people. The North Vietnamese were unimpressed by these concessions. They persisted in their long-standing demands that the United States unilaterally remove its troops from South Vietnam and accept replacement of the Saigon regime by a coalition including the National Liberation Front, and in fact weighted in favor of the Communists, before the holding of elections. The latter demand, which Nixon, his advisers, and President Thieu considered tantamount to forcing Saigon's surrender to the Communists, kept the Paris negotiations stalemated for the next two years.[5]

Both complement and alternative to negotiation was the second policy track—Vietnamization, a term coined by Defense Secretary Laird. The concept was hardly new. It traced its ancestry all the way back to the Comprehensive Plan for South Vietnam of 1963 and had been revived as a goal by the Johnson administration during 1967 and 1968, although without implementing plans. In turning the concept into active policy, Nixon and his advisers hoped to achieve several objectives. By gradually removing U.S. troops and turning the fighting over to the improved South Vietnamese armed forces, they would increase pressure on North Vietnam to negotiate flexibly before it lost the leverage of American battle casualties and war costs. At the same time, Saigon would have stronger incentive to improve its combat and pacification performance and seek political accommodation with the Viet Cong. Finally and perhaps most importantly, troop withdrawals, by reassuring the American people that their country was on its way out of Vietnam, would undermine the antiwar movement and secure more time for the administration to build up Saigon's position and pursue its negotiating strategy at Paris. Secretary Laird summarized for the Senate Foreign Relations Committee:

By strengthening the capability of the South Vietnamese to defend themselves rather than depending on American troops, we provide an additional incentive to Hanoi to negotiate. If, on the other hand, Paris continues stalemated, Vietnamization provides the means for the orderly disinvolvement of American troops from combat without having to sacrifice our . . . objective—the right of self-determination for the people of Vietnam.[6]

[5] Kissinger, *White House Years*, pp. 258–71, 277–83, 303; MACV History, 1969, vol. 1, ch. 2, pp. 38, 40–42, 44–45, and ch. 3, pp. 69–70; MACV Hq, "One War," ch. 8, pp. 3–5, 7–8; MACV J–3, Force Planning Synopsis for Gen Abrams, 2:33–35, 213–14.

[6] Quotation is from Statement of Sec Def Melvin R. Laird before the Senate Foreign Relations Committee on 19 November 1969, p. 2, copy in CMH. Kissinger, *White House Years*, pp. 271–72, credits Laird with inventing the term "Vietnamization" at a 28 Mar 69 NSC meeting. Memo, Kissinger for the President, 8 Jul 69, sub: SEQUOIA NSC Meeting on Vietnam, box 091, NSC files, Nixon Papers, NARA.

While the Nixon administration implemented negotiation and Vietnamization, it held open a third possibility: escalation of the war by massive air strikes on North Vietnam or large-scale air and ground attacks on the Cambodian and Laotian sanctuaries. More political than military in purpose, these campaigns could be used to retaliate for Communist violations of the 1968 bombing halt understandings or to shock and batter Hanoi toward a diplomatic settlement. The sanctuary attacks also would assist Vietnamization by disrupting enemy offensive preparations. Early in 1969, after the Communists launched a nationwide offensive that included renewed bombardment of Saigon and other South Vietnamese cities, the administration put the JCS, CINCPAC, and COMUSMACV to work on contingency plans for bombing North Vietnam and mining its ports. In response to this offensive, and as a signal of resolve to the Communist powers, President Nixon in mid-March began a publicly unacknowledged bombing of the Cambodian base areas. Aside from the Cambodian bombing, however, during the administration's first year, escalation remained an option only, although one which ultimately would shape the final act of the war.[7]

Redeployment Planning Begins: NSSM 36

Vietnamization, in both its troop withdrawal and RVNAF improvement aspects, came to dominate the Military Assistance Command's planning and operations. Troop withdrawal was not a new concept for MACV. Since July 1968, the headquarters, in coordination with Pacific Command, had been developing so-called T-Day (for termination of hostilities day) plans for withdrawing American forces in the context of a cease-fire and a parallel North Vietnamese pullback. These plans called for removing troops in increments over periods of six or twelve months and for leaving behind a "residual force" of more than 100,000 men to continue supporting the South Vietnamese. Troop withdrawals during hostilities also had been under consideration. General Westmoreland had raised the possibility in public in November 1967. Late in March 1968, he directed the MACV J–3 section to determine when a successful South Vietnamese mobilization might permit a "token phase down (B[riga]de size) of U.S. forces without weakening overall posture." General Abrams' long-range strategic plan also envisioned American disengagement.[8]

[7] Kissinger, *White House Years*, pp. 239–47, 249, 284–85. Memos, Rosson for Asst to the President for National Security Affairs, 20 Feb 69, sub: Vietnam Package, box 164; Laird to Kissinger, 21 Feb 69, box 1007; Kissinger to the President, sub: Vietnam Options, 11 Sep 69, box 091. All in NSC files, Nixon Papers, NARA. These plans and operations are discussed in more detail below in ch. 9, pp. 280–83.

[8] Clarke, *Final Years*, pp. 302–04; Msg, Abrams MAC 14387 to McCain info Wheeler, 25 Oct 68, Abrams Papers, CMH. Westmoreland quotation is from MFR, Bryan, 31 Mar 68, sub: CIIB Meeting, 30 Mar 68, tab 63, Westmoreland History file no. 30 (1–31 Mar 68), CMH.

The South Vietnamese, whether anticipating American action or expressing post-Tet self-confidence, themselves raised the issue. Beginning in spring of 1968 and continuing into early 1969, President Thieu, Vice President Ky, and Premier Huong periodically suggested that their armed forces had become strong enough to start replacing Americans on the battlefield; hence, withdrawal of at least one U.S. division might be feasible during 1969. The Vietnamese began pressing MACV to join them in preliminary planning for such an eventuality.[9]

General Abrams and his Washington superiors responded conservatively to these South Vietnamese overtures. President Nixon during January 1969 instructed Abrams to forbid any public discussion within MACV of unilateral withdrawals so as to avoid undermining the administration's negotiating stance at Paris. Abrams complied, and he and Ambassador Bunker also vainly attempted to dissuade Thieu and his associates from pursuing the subject. In private conference, Abrams informed President Thieu and General Vien that the time was not yet right for major U.S. withdrawals and that significant improvement of Saigon's forces was a prerequisite for them. Abrams did initiate tentative discussions with the Joint General Staff of conditions that would permit removal of American troops. At his direction, the MACV staff during February developed a "matrix" of "indicators," built around the enemy threat, pacification progress, and the rate of RVNAF improvement, to guide withdrawal decisions.[10]

Even as he tried to rein in South Vietnamese speculation about American troop redeployments, General Abrams, in conjunction with Admiral John S. McCain, Jr., Sharp's successor as CINCPAC, began planning for them. Believing that some form of American disengagement from Vietnam was inevitable, Abrams at the beginning of 1969 established a small redeployment planning group, numbering at the outset less than five men, within the MACV J–3 section. Working in utmost secrecy, the details of its activities known only to Abrams and a few other key MACV staff officers, the group, headed initially by Col. Donn A. Starry, established the redeployment criteria that Abrams discussed with Thieu and Vien. They also outlined tentative plans for a one-division, later enlarged to a two-division, withdrawal during 1969. Pacific Command headquarters, meanwhile, adapted the automated

---

[9] Vietnamese statements are summarized in MACV, Force Planning Synopsis, pp. 2–4, 6–7. Thieu broached this subject to Westmoreland as early April 1968; see Msg, Berger Saigon 24425 to Sec State, 10 Apr 68, tab 29, Westmoreland History file no. 31 (1–30 Apr 68), CMH; Clarke, *Final Years*, pp. 346–47.

[10] Msgs, Abrams MAC 766 to Wheeler and Nazzaro info Bunker et al., 17 Jan 69; Abrams MAC 1751 to Wheeler and Nazzaro, 8 Feb 69; Nazzaro to Abrams, 19 Jan 69; Brown to Abrams, 21 Jan 69; Abrams MAC 967 to Nazzaro, 21 Jan 69; Wheeler JCS 00867 to Abrams info Bunker et al., 22 Jan 69; Wheeler JCS 01080 to Nazzaro and Abrams, 25 Jan 69; Wheeler JCS 01184 to Abrams info Nazzaro, 28 Jan 69; Abrams MAC 1360 to Field Force and Component Cdrs, 31 Jan 69; Abrams MAC 3388 to Wheeler, 16 Mar 69. All in Abrams Papers, CMH. MACV, Force Planning Synopsis, pp. 4–5, 9.

troop and equipment database it had been using for T-Day planning to work out the logistics of incremental unilateral withdrawals.[11]

While he planned for redeployments, Abrams argued against their early implementation. MACV and the embassy jointly considered that U.S. troops were the "mainstay of our investment" in South Vietnam and "the primary, if not the only major negotiable element in our position"; hence, their presence "must be used to maximum advantage if there is to be a viable settlement." Abrams, in his response to NSSM 1, stated firmly: "Under present conditions in South Vietnam, any significant reduction in current [U.S.] force levels will result in a significant decrease in combat capability." He and his staff told Secretary Laird the same thing during Laird's first visit to Vietnam in early March.[12]

The new secretary of defense rejected that conclusion. Laird, a politically astute former congressman, appreciated the depth of American popular disillusionment with the war. He entered office convinced that the administration, in order to maintain public support for engagement in Southeast Asia and secure resources to rebuild American military strength throughout the world, had to reduce Vietnam's cost to the United States in men and money. During his March visit to Saigon, Laird told Ambassador Bunker, General Abrams, and President Thieu that for most Americans a satisfactory outcome of the war meant "the eventual disengagement of American men from combat" and that the "key factor" in sustaining American domestic support for the effort was to "find the means by which the burden of combat may promptly, and methodically, be shifted to the South Vietnamese." He suggested that MACV and the mission "start doing some planning ourselves on numbers" for an early American troop reduction.[13]

On 13 March, in his trip report to the president, Laird declared that "it is essential that we decide now to initiate the removal from Southeast Asia of some U.S. military personnel." He considered this course to be required by "our national interests, in the light of our military commitments worldwide" and indispensable to Saigon's achievement of

[11] Interv, Abrams Project with Amb Samuel Berger, 17 May 77, pp. 3, 7, MHI (hereafter cited as Berger Interv); Interv, Abrams Project with Gen Donn A. Starry, 14 Dec 76, MHI, pp. 32–34 (hereafter cited as Starry Interv). Msgs, McCain to Gen Ralph E. Haines, CG, USARPAC, et al., 10 Nov 68; Nazzaro to Abrams, 19 Jan 69; Abrams MAC 3388 to Wheeler, 16 Mar 69; McCain to Wheeler info Abrams, 28 Mar 69; Abrams Papers, CMH; MACV History, 1969, vol. 1, ch. 2, pp. 22–23.

[12] First quotation is from Msg, Abrams MAC 17265 to Wheeler, 19 Dec 68, Abrams Papers, CMH. Second is from COMUSMACV Response to NSSM 1 Question 26, Jan 69, folder 20, Thayer Papers, CMH. Memo, Laird for the President, 13 Mar 69, sub: Trip to Vietnam and CINCPAC, March 5–12, 1969, box 142, NSC files, Nixon Papers, NARA.

[13] Laird's political views and concerns are summarized in Kissinger, *White House Years*, p. 262; Douglas Kinnard, *The Secretary of Defense* (Lexington: University Press of Kentucky, 1980), pp. 125, 127–28, 149–51; and Hammond, *Military and the Media, 1968–1973*, pp. 56–57. Quotations are from Memo, Laird for the President, sub: Trip to Vietnam and CINCPAC, March 5–12, 1969, 13 Mar 69, box 142, NSC files, Nixon Papers, NARA; and MACV, Force Planning Synopsis, pp. 10–12. Historical Division, "Joint Chiefs of Staff and the War in Vietnam, 1969–1970," pp. 14–15, describes Laird's trip to Southeast Asia.

"true pacification and . . . control over its own population." As the South Vietnamese forces improved, the United States should be able to reduce its share of the total military effort while still containing the enemy and putting pressure on him. Noting that the South Vietnamese leaders had expressed readiness for a sizeable American withdrawal, Laird declared that the Saigon forces' improvement, "although perhaps less than desired," was sufficient to justify the removal of 50,000 to 70,000 troops from Southeast Asia during 1969. Laird urged the administration to make such a withdrawal and also recommended the development of long-range plans for methodical replacement of American with Vietnamese forces.[14]

General Abrams, alerted by General Wheeler to Laird's recommendations, informed Wheeler on 16 March that he was aware of "no valid evidence" to justify an American troop reduction during 1969 of the size proposed by Laird. Nevertheless, in the wake of Laird's visit and in anticipation of what now seemed inevitable, Abrams accelerated the MACV withdrawal planning effort and enlarged the staff group to include representatives of the component commands. He was urged on by General Wheeler, who informed him that the subject of troop reductions was "an exceedingly hot one" in Washington.[15]

By early April, Abrams' staff group, in conjunction with Admiral McCain's representatives, had completed plans for removing two divisions during 1969, one in the third quarter and the other in the fourth. They nominated the 3d Marine Division as the first to go. The division was a major combat unit, removal of which would demonstrate the reality of redeployment. The strong South Vietnamese 1st Division could fill in for the marines in northern I Corps; and the Marine division, if returned to its former base on Okinawa, could re-enter Vietnam quickly if necessary. Second to leave would be the Army's 9th Infantry Division, then operating in the northern Mekong Delta, a region in which it long had been MACV and mission policy to minimize American troop presence. General Abrams urged that these and any subsequent withdrawals be carried out gradually, with the effect of each redeployment on the conditions MACV earlier had identified—pacification progress, RVNAF improvement, and the enemy threat—carefully assessed before beginning the next. He also suggested that expanded air and ground attacks on the Laotian and Cambodian sanctuaries would reduce enemy capabilities and thus open the way for more rapid removal of American troops.[16]

[14] Memo, Laird for the President, 13 Mar 69, sub: Trip to Vietnam and CINCPAC, March 5–12, 1969, box 142, NSC files, Nixon Papers, NARA.

[15] First quotation is from Msg, Abrams MAC 3308 to Wheeler, 16 Mar 69; second is from Msg, Wheeler JCS 03787 to Abrams info McCain, 27 Mar 69. Both in Abrams Papers, CMH. See also Msgs, Wheeler JCS 03596 to Abrams, 24 Mar 69; and Abrams MAC 3910 to Wheeler and McCain, 27 Mar 69. All in Abrams Papers, CMH.

[16] Msg, Abrams to Goodpaster (transmitted to San Clemente from White House Situation Room), 23 Mar 69, box 065, NSC files, Nixon Papers, NARA. Msgs, Abrams MAC 3693 to McCain, 22 Mar

These preliminary steps were soon overtaken by a more ambitious administration initiative. On 28 March, after a National Security Council review of Laird's trip report, President Nixon decided to begin comprehensive redeployment planning. Implementing this decision, Dr. Kissinger on 10 April issued NSSM 36, which directed the secretary of defense, in coordination with the secretary of state and the director of the CIA, to prepare "a specific timetable for Vietnamizing the war." Kissinger called for preparation of four alternative timetables, ranging from 18 to 42 months, for transferring all combat to the South Vietnamese and reducing the American role to support and advice. The planners were to assume that redeployments would start on 1 July 1969, that enemy strength in South Vietnam would remain at its existing level, that there would be no diminution of allied military efforts except as it resulted from U.S. withdrawals not fully compensated for by the South Vietnamese, and that equipping and training the RVNAF would receive the "highest national priorities." The president, Kissinger declared, wanted a preliminary plan, with specific troop withdrawal alternatives for the rest of 1969, by 1 June and a final overall plan by 1 September.[17]

At the direction of the Joint Chiefs, the Military Assistance Command, in consultation with the Saigon Embassy and Pacific Command, prepared what became the core of the Joint Chiefs' response to NSSM 36. In a preliminary version in May and a final version briefed to CINCPAC on 22 July, MACV's NSSM 36 plan called for gradual withdrawal of about half the U.S. force from South Vietnam in conjunction with the transfer of combat to the South Vietnamese military while hostilities continued. The American troops were to leave in six increments on alternative schedules of 18, 24, 30, and 42 months. The MACV planners tentatively identified the divisions that would compose each increment. As provided in MACV's earlier planning, the 3d Marine Division and the 9th Infantry Division would be the first to withdraw. The duration of each increment could vary depending on which overall redeployment schedule was adopted. At the end of the withdrawals, a residual American force of nearly 270,000 men would remain. That force was to consist of air and ground units furnishing combat, logistical, and advisory support to the South Vietnamese, as well as two and two-thirds infantry divisions to protect U.S. bases and reinforce the RVNAF in emergencies.[18]

69; Abrams MAC 3878 to Wheeler, 27 Mar 69; Wheeler JCS 03837 to McCain info Abrams, 28 Mar 69; McCain to Wheeler info Abrams, 30 Mar 69; Abrams MAC 4231 to McCain, 4 Apr 69; McCain to Abrams, 12 Apr 69; Abrams MAC 5238 to Wheeler and McCain, 24 Apr 69. All in Abrams Papers, CMH. MACV, Force Planning Synopsis, pp. 12–15; MACV History, 1969, vol. 1, ch. 4, p. 11; Rosson, "Involvement in Vietnam," pp. 233–35.

[17] Kissinger, *White House Years*, pp. 271–72; Clarke, *Final Years*, pp. 341, 348–49; NSSM 36, Kissinger to Secs State and Def and DCI, [10 Apr 69], sub: Vietnamizing the War, box 1009, NSC files, Nixon Papers, NARA.

[18] Rosson, "Involvement in Vietnam," pp. 233, 240–41; MACV, Force Planning Synopsis, pp.

The Military Assistance Command was cautious in assessing the risks and feasibility of withdrawal. It emphasized that all the key variables—pacification progress, enemy opposition, and RVNAF improvement—were difficult to forecast and subject to rapid change. Tentatively, MACV concluded that the military risks of a 50,000-man withdrawal during the last half of 1969 were acceptable, but warned against any larger pullout during that period. As to the overall schedule, the command declared that the 18- and 24-month options posed severe dangers to both pacification and military security. Whatever the timetable, MACV emphasized the need to draw the South Vietnamese into the planning as soon as possible so as to give them time to reposition their forces and adjust politically and psychologically to the Americans' departure. The command cautioned that if the other Free World allies reduced their forces as the Americans redeployed, the Americans would have to revise their plans for the residual force; and it urged that American forces in Thailand be kept at their existing level. Above all, MACV and the U.S. Embassy emphasized that American redeployments should be "based on a cut and try approach, and on a thorough evaluation of the effects of preceding redeployments and of the feasibility of further reductions."[19]

The Joint Chiefs submitted their final response to NSSM 36 on 29 August, after incorporating submissions from the CIA and the State Department as well as MACV and the Saigon mission. Their proposed withdrawal schedules and size and composition of what now was called the transitional support force substantially followed the Military Assistance Command's plan. As MACV had recommended, the Joint Chiefs urged that withdrawal schedules remain flexible, with the decision on each succeeding increment based on evaluation of the effects of the previous one in relation to MACV's three criteria. Secretary Laird endorsed the Joint Chiefs' plan on 4 September. He and the Joint Chiefs recommended that the administration adopt the 24-month timetable for planning purposes, notwithstanding MACV's assessment that such a short schedule posed severe risks of military and pacification setbacks. President Nixon made no definitive decision on the overall timetable, but he accepted in principle the Joint Chiefs' "cut-and-try," one-increment-at-a-time approach. The NSSM 36 concept formed the basis of the administration's subsequent redeployment planning and

62, 76.1, 83, 83.1; Memo, Brig Gen A. J. Bowley, USAF, Chief Strategic Plans and Policy Division, J–5, JCS, for Distribution List, 12 May 69, sub: Working Draft for Initial Report NSSM 36, folder 35, Thayer Papers, CMH; USARV Fact Sheet, AVHGC-P, 17 Jul 69, sub: Update on NSSM 36—Vietnamization; USARV Talking Paper, AVHGC-P, sub: NSSM 36—Vietnamization, 17 Jul 69, CMH; MACV, NSSM 36 Briefing of Final Report, CINCPAC 22 Jul 69, in MAC J303 Briefing Book No. 1, MACV Collection, MHI.

[19] Quotation is from MACV NSSM 36 Briefing, 22 Jul 69. MACV, Force Planning Synopsis, pp. 86–87; USARV Fact Sheet, AVHGC-P, 17 Jul 69, sub: Update on NSSM 36—Vietnamization, CMH.

decisions, and Secretary Laird incorporated its 24-month schedule into his Defense budget projections.[20]

During their NSSM 36 planning, the JCS, CINCPAC, and MACV developed specific withdrawal proposals for the last half of 1969, encompassing what would become the first two of the overall time-table's six increments. Late in April, representatives of MACV and CINCPAC briefed Secretary Laird on the finished version of General Abrams' plan for withdrawing the 3d Marine Division during the third quarter followed by the 9th Infantry Division during the fourth. With support elements, each increment would include about 25,000 men. Both Abrams and McCain continued to emphasize the need for caution and for thorough evaluation between the two increments. Not fully satisfied with this plan, Laird early in May, to give President Nixon "a broader range of alternatives," directed the military to prepare troop lists for a possible 100,000-man withdrawal during 1969 as well as those for their 50,000 proposal. MACV, while warning that such a large redeployment would have catastrophic results, developed the required list by adding a third increment built around the 4th Infantry Division from II Corps.[21]

In mid-May, President Nixon summoned General Abrams to Washington for consultations on withdrawal planning. Evidently cultivating Abrams as a source of information and advice independent of Laird, Nixon and Kissinger told the MACV commander that they wanted him to proceed with redeployment and Vietnamization in a "systematic and orderly fashion" and did not expect him to accept "undue risks" to the security of American forces. They enjoined Abrams not to succumb to "the pressures which will develop for premature U.S. disengagement" but instead to base his recommendations on his own analysis of the situation in South Vietnam. Abrams in response reiterated that a two-division withdrawal during the last half of 1969 "could" be feasible, but he urged that a decision and public announcement be delayed until July or August to give time for an up-to-date estimate of enemy activity. He again explained MACV's three criteria for determining the feasibility of withdrawals and also declared that tactical air and B–52 operations must be maintained at their current rates during any ground force drawdown.[22]

[20] Historical Division, "Joint Chiefs of Staff and the War in Vietnam, 1969–1970," pp. 106–07, 120–23. Memo, Laird for the President, 2 Jun 69, sub: Vietnamizing the War (NSSM 36), box 089; Memo, Wheeler CM 4536–69 for Sec Def, 29 Aug 69, sub: Vietnamizing the War, box 091; Memo, Wheeler JCSM–522–1–69 for Sec Def, 29 Aug 69, sub: Vietnamizing the War, box 091; Memo, Laird for the President, sub: Vietnamizing the War (NSSM 36), 4 Sep 69, box 091. All in NSC files, Nixon Papers, NARA.

[21] Kissinger, *White House Years*, p. 275. Historical Division, "Joint Chiefs of Staff and the War in Vietnam, 1969–1970," pp. 107–13. Msgs, Abrams MAC 4808 to McCain, 16 Apr 69; Abrams MAC 4967 to Wheeler, 19 Apr 69; McConnell JCS 05630 to Abrams info McCain, 7 May 69; Abrams MAC 5970 to McConnell and McCain, 11 May 69; McCain to Wheeler info Abrams, 13 May 69. All in Abrams Papers, CMH. MACV, Force Planning Synopsis, pp. 22.

[22] Quotations are from Memo, Kissinger for the President, sub: Talking Points for Use in Private

(Left to right) *General Wheeler, General Abrams,*
and Secretary of Defense Laird

Despite Abrams' advocacy of delay, Nixon and Laird, under intense political pressure, went ahead with plans for an early withdrawal. On 2 June, after further exchanges with the Joint Chiefs, Abrams, and McCain, Laird recommended to the president that planning for 1969 be based on a maximum of 50,000 troops with an immediate decision only on the first installment of 25,000, removal of which would begin in July. General Abrams meanwhile, in response to the Joint Chiefs' concern about the threat to northern I Corps, revised the first increment to include only one regiment of the 3d Marine Division and the headquarters and two brigades of the 9th Infantry Division.[23]

With military planning for the initial withdrawal on the way to completion, President Nixon moved to secure the Saigon government's

Discussion with Gen Abrams, 9 May 69, box 137, NSC files, Nixon Papers, NARA. MACV, Force Planning Synopsis, pp. 29–32.

[23] Msgs, Abrams MAC 6542 to McCain info Wheeler, 22 May 69; Abrams MAC 6987 to Wheeler and McCain, 1 Jun 69; Abrams MAC 7021 to Wheeler and McCain, 2 Jun 69; Abrams MAC 7206 to McCain, 6 Jun 69; Wheeler JCS 07142 to McCain and Abrams, 9 Jun 69; Abrams Papers, CMH. Memo, Laird for the President, 2 Jun 69, sub: Vietnamizing the War (NSSM 36), box 089, NSC files, Nixon Papers, NARA; MACV Force Planning Synopsis, pp. 36–43, 47–49. Westmoreland, *Soldier Reports*, p. 381, claims that his protests to the Joint Chiefs and Henry Kissinger initiated the change in divisions in the first increment.

endorsement, and also that of his field commanders, before making a public announcement. He arranged to meet with President Thieu on 8 June at the U.S. Pacific outpost of Midway, a site chosen because it had not been used for similar conferences by President Johnson and because it lacked inhabitants who might demonstrate against Nixon, Thieu, and the war. En route to Midway, Nixon met on 7 June in Honolulu with his principal civilian and military advisers, and with Ambassador Bunker, General Abrams, and Admiral McCain. Preparatory to this meeting, Wheeler repeatedly urged Abrams and McCain to emphasize for the president "the threat to U.S. forces and the risk involved in force reductions." The chairman's efforts to mobilize his field commanders against redeployment were in vain. At the preliminary gathering, the military commanders, pressed by the civilians who insisted redeployments were a political necessity, agreed to go forward with the first 25,000-man withdrawal. According to Kissinger, they did so with obvious reluctance, since they knew they were committing themselves to a process that likely would be irreversible and deprive them of any real hope of victory.[24]

With the military leaders on board, the rest was anticlimax. At Midway on 8 June, President Thieu agreed without hesitation to the commencement of American withdrawals. Two days later, President Nixon announced that the United States would remove 25,000 troops from South Vietnam by the end of August. As planned, a regiment of the 3d Marine Division and the headquarters and two brigades of the 9th Infantry Division were the principal combat units to depart. Nixon pledged that after completion of the first withdrawal, he periodically would consider additional redeployments in the light of progress in the Paris talks, the pace of RVNAF improvement, and the level of enemy action. The following month, during a trip to Asia, the president expanded Vietnamization into his "Nixon Doctrine," under which he pledged that the United States would protect its Asian allies against nuclear threats but declared that "in cases involving other types of aggression" America would furnish military and economic assistance but would "look to the nation directly threatened to assume the primary responsibility of providing the manpower for its defense."[25]

Once begun, American withdrawals took on a momentum of their own, each increment following the previous one in steady succession. Domestic political pressures, far more than MACV's evaluation criteria, dictated the pace, as Nixon and the Democrats tried to outbid each

[24] Kissinger, *White House Years*, pp. 35, 272. Quotation is from Msg, Wheeler JCS 06337 to Abrams info McCain, 24 May 69, Abrams Papers, CMH. Conference preparations are covered in Msgs, Abrams MAC 6527 to Wheeler and McCain, 22 May 69; Wheeler JCS 06798 to McCain and Abrams, 2 Jun 69; Abrams MAC 7088 to Wheeler and McCain, 4 Jun 69. All in Abrams Papers, CMH.

[25] Quotations are from Kissinger, *White House Years*, pp. 222–25; see also pp. 273–74. Historical Division, "Joint Chiefs of Staff and the War in Vietnam, 1969–1970," pp. 109–10; MACV History, 1969, vol. 1, ch. 4, pp. 10–11.

other on withdrawal size and timing. In June, for example, former Defense Secretary Clark Clifford, writing in the prestigious journal *Foreign Affairs*, urged that the United States pull 100,000 troops out of Vietnam by the end of 1969 and remove all combat personnel by the end of 1970. Nixon, at a 19 June news conference replied: "We have started to withdraw forces. . . . We will withdraw more," and he expressed "hope that we could beat Mr. Clifford's timetable." During the Asian trip on which he promulgated the Nixon Doctrine, the president, in a brief stop in Saigon on 30 July, made it clear to President Thieu that continued withdrawals would be necessary to maintain American public support for the administration and the war.[26]

President Thieu and President Nixon meet at Midway Island.

Even as the troops of the first increment, Phase I, boarded ships and planes, planning for the second redeployment increment, known as Phase II, got under way. Under administration pressure, this increment gradually expanded from 25,000 troops to 40,500. Abrams and McCain protested that such enlargement was unwarranted by the situation. In their final NSSM 36 report, the Joint Chiefs declared that removal of more than 50,000 men during 1969 "would be clearly without justification on military grounds and beyond the threshold of prudent risk." Nevertheless, on 16 September, President Nixon directed the 40,500-man pullout, built around the rest of the 3d Marine Division and the 3d Brigade, 82d Airborne Division, to be completed by 15 December.[27]

---

[26] Quotation is from MACV, Force Planning Synopsis, pp. 65–66; see also pp. 85–86. Kissinger, *White House Years*, pp. 274–77, 282–83. Memo, Kissinger for the President, 8 Jul 69, sub: SEQUOIA NSC Meeting on Vietnam; and Memo, Sec State Rogers for Sec Def, sub: Your Memorandum Transmitting NSSM 36 Final Report . . . , 3 Sep 69, both in box 091, NSC files, Nixon Papers, NARA, illustrate pressures within the administration for continued and larger withdrawals.

[27] Kissinger, *White House Years*, p. 283; MACV, Force Planning Synopsis, pp. 69, 88, 93–94, 96.1, 98–99, 104, 106, 108, 111–12, 115–19, 122.1, 136–37; Historical Division, "Joint Chiefs of Staff and the War in Vietnam, 1969–1970," pp. 113–24; MACV History, 1969, vol. 1, ch. 4, pp. 12–13. For Abrams' and McCain's views, see Msgs, Abrams MAC 9967 to McCain, 2 Aug 69; McCain to Wheeler info Abrams, 13 Aug 69 and 23 Aug 69. Both in Abrams Papers, CMH. Quotation is from Memo, Wheeler JCSM–522–1–69 for Sec Def, 29 Aug 69, box 091, NSC files, Nixon Papers, NARA.

First U.S. Marines leave Vietnam under President Nixon's withdrawal program.

Well before that date, planning started for Phase III, a 50,000-man withdrawal during the first three months of 1970. In November, after reporting an increased rate of enemy infiltration into South Vietnam and declaring that indications were mounting that the Communists might try another countrywide offensive around the time of Tet, General Abrams warned that "the situation is such that it would not repeat not be militarily sound to recommend further U.S. troop redeployments at this time." Nixon nevertheless announced this third withdrawal on 15 December. In a partial concession to the field commanders' concerns, he set 15 April 1970 as the completion date for Phase III, thereby allowing Abrams to delay removal of the major combat units involved—the 1st Infantry Division, a brigade of the 4th Division, and a Marine regimental landing team—until after the dangerous Tet period. By the end of 1969, the administration had withdrawn, or was committed to withdraw, 115,500 troops from Vietnam. While this pace was in line with the NSSM 36 two-year schedule, the steady sequence of announcements indicated definitely that "cut-and-try" was to be honored more in the breach than in the observance.[28]

---

[28] Decision-making on Phase III can be traced in Historical Division, "Joint Chiefs of Staff and the War in Vietnam, 1969–1970," pp. 127–29; Abrams Message files, Oct–Dec 69, Abrams Papers, CMH; MACV, Force Planning Synopsis, pp. 150, 153–54, 161–66, 178–80, 184–88, 192–201, 206, 212–15; and MACV History, 1970, vol. 1, ch. 4, p. 10. Quotation is from Msg, Abrams MAC 15171 to McCain and Wheeler, 23 Nov 69, Abrams Papers, CMH; in same collection, see Msgs, Abrams MAC 13589 to McCain and Wheeler, 19 Oct 69; McCain to Wheeler info Abrams, 23 Nov 69; and Abrams MAC 15267 to Wheeler, 25 Nov 69.

Raising the Stakes in Vietnamization

Even as the administration put into effect the U.S. withdrawal part of Vietnamization, it set more ambitious goals for the improvement and modernization of the South Vietnamese armed forces. The Accelerated Phase II Improvement and Modernization Plan that President Nixon and Secretary Laird inherited from the Johnson administration was aimed at preparing the RVNAF to cope only with the Viet Cong after U.S. and North Vietnamese troops had left South Vietnam. During the first months of the new administration, the Joint Chiefs, Admiral McCain, and General Abrams continued to see this as the only achievable objective. Their planning under NSSM 36 assumed that a large residual American force would remain in South Vietnam as long as hostilities continued. Secretary Laird considered this prospect unsatisfactory. He declared in his March trip report:

I do not believe we can accept the proposition that U.S. forces must remain in substantial numbers indefinitely to contain the North Vietnamese threat, if political settlement proves unobtainable. The heavy expense of RVNAF modernization cannot be justified as a measure merely to permit the GVN to cope with local insurgency.[29]

President Thieu took the initiative in planning for a South Vietnamese force able to hold against both the Viet Cong and the North Vietnamese. At Midway, he presented to President Nixon a JGS proposal, based on their earlier Program Six, for enlarging the RVNAF to more than one million men and adding armor, heavy artillery, air defense, commando, and coastal and riverine units. The expansion would include the Regional and Popular Forces, which were to receive their own artillery, to free the South Vietnamese Army for mobile operations. Thieu also asked for American assistance in improving the living standards of his servicemen. General Abrams, as he had with Program Six, rejected most of Thieu's proposal as too expensive and beyond the ability of the South Vietnamese to implement. He did recommend an increase of the RVNAF to more than 992,000 over the next three years, but favored only limited addition of heavy equipment and advised that the U.S. support new units only as Saigon demonstrated that it could organize and maintain them at no cost to the readiness of its existing forces. Abrams thus wanted to keep the RVNAF, an essentially light force, dependent on the U.S. residual contingent for its air support and heavy sophisticated weaponry.[30]

---

[29] Quotation is from Memo, Laird for the President, 13 Mar 69, sub: Trip to Vietnam and CINCPAC, March 5–12, 1969, box 142, NSC files, Nixon Papers, NARA. Msgs, Abrams MAC 5970 to McConnell and McCain, 11 May 69; and McCain to Wheeler info Abrams et al., 4 Jul 69, all in Abrams Papers, CMH, reiterate the established military view. Memo, W. H. Sullivan for Sec State, 19 Sep 69, sub: Vietnamizing the War, copy in CMH, argues that NSSM 36 all along implied a self-sufficient RVNAF.

[30] Clarke, *Final Years*, pp. 351–53.

South Vietnamese President Thieu meets with his troops.

After Midway, the American military leaders persisted in their assertion that the South Vietnamese could not stand alone. Late in July, General Wheeler, in a review for Secretary Laird of NSSM 36 planning, declared that "the resulting structure is not designed to provide the South Vietnamese armed forces the capability to deal with both the full enemy guerrilla force in country and cope with the North Vietnamese armed forces." Unless the North Vietnamese could be induced to withdraw from South Vietnam and their Laotian and Cambodian bases, a U.S. residual force would have to remain "for some years to come." Wheeler concluded: "RVNAF alone cannot in the near future maintain the integrity of South Vietnam."[31]

In mid-August, Secretary Laird approved Abrams' post-Midway proposals for expanding Saigon's armed forces, with the proviso that the services would have to fund the increases out of their own budgets and furnish the equipment from their own stocks or from redeploying American units. At the same time, Laird directed the Joint Chiefs and the services to review the entire improvement and modernization program "with the goal of developing an RVNAF with the capability to cope successfully with the combined Viet Cong–North Vietnamese Army threat." The review should consider, besides force increases, such qualitative issues as leadership improvement, desertion reduction, strengthening of intelligence and logistics, and "most important, development of strategy

---

[31] Msg, Wheeler JCS 09112 to Abrams, 23 Jul 69, Abrams Papers, CMH.

and tactics best matched with RVNAF capabilities." Early in September, General Abrams and Admiral McCain replied, in effect, that RVNAF self-sufficiency was unattainable. No feasible qualitative and quantitative improvements, they argued, could enable the South Vietnamese to cope with the entire enemy threat; they would continue to need substantial American forces to assist them.[32]

Secretary Laird rejected this conclusion and further increased the stakes. On 10 November 1969, he instructed the Joint Chiefs to develop a Phase III Improvement and Modernization Plan designed to "raise RVNAF effectiveness to the point where the government of Vietnam . . . can maintain at least current levels of security" while U.S. forces were reduced first to a support force of 190,000–260,000 by 1 July 1971 and then, "by continuing steps," to the level of a Military Assistance Advisory Group by 1 July 1973. Laird called for development of RVNAF air, artillery, transportation, and supply units to replace the American residual force previously assumed; and he repeated his demand for programs for improvement in South Vietnamese training, leadership, and morale. The Defense Secretary thus wiped out any long-term American supplementation of South Vietnamese strength even as he demanded that Saigon shoulder the entire burden. With considerable understatement, General Wheeler observed that this instruction represented "a substantial departure from the [Vietnamization] concept as we have known it up to now."[33]

Under Laird's prodding, MACV and the Joint Chiefs in December developed a Phase III Improvement and Modernization Plan for a more nearly self-sufficient RVNAF. Assuming that the existing expansion programs, due to be completed in July 1970, would succeed and that continuing advances in pacification and territorial security would weaken the Viet Cong and make more manpower available to Saigon, they decided that the South Vietnamese forces could be enlarged sufficiently to meet the entire threat if they received continuing American materiel and financial support. Under the Phase III Improvement and Modernization Plan, the RVNAF would grow to more than one million men by mid-1973; and it was to receive new support units, including field artillery battalions, truck companies, and helicopter squadrons, to replace the departing American forces. After a visit to Saigon by Laird in February 1970, the Joint Chiefs of Staff amended the plan to incorporate Vietnamese requests for more heavy artillery for the South Vietnamese Army, a separate field artillery force for the Regional and Popular Forces, and subsidies for soldier food and housing—all elements of Thieu's Midway proposal. The revised plan, completed in

---

[32] Quotations are from Memo, Laird for Secs Army, Navy, and Air Force and the Chairman of the Joint Chiefs of Staff, 12 Aug 69, sub: Government of Vietnam Proposals Presented at the Midway Conference . . . , CMH. Clarke, *Final Years*, pp. 353–54; MACV, Force Planning Synopsis, p. 107.

[33] First quotation is from MACV, Force Planning Synopsis, pp. 178–80. Second is from p. 181; see also pp. 182–83. Clarke, *Final Years*, p. 355.

April, became known as the Consolidated RVNAF Improvement and Modernization Plan (CRIMP).[34]

Throughout this discussion, and indeed throughout the planning that followed, the exact nature of the North Vietnamese threat that Saigon should be prepared to ward off by its own efforts was not specified. As with MACV's long-range plan for South Vietnam, the participants in both Washington and Saigon appear to have had in mind the existing North Vietnamese reinforcement of the Viet Cong with light infantry divisions and fillers for depleted southern units, not a full-scale conventional invasion. Secretary Laird, for example, repeatedly emphasized the desirability of preparing the South Vietnamese to operate without the lavish firepower used by U.S. forces—an approach that made sense only in the context of the mixed conventional and guerrilla conflict then in progress. Despite these uncertainties, the implementation of the CRIMP, in the context of continuing U.S. force reductions, was to be the Military Assistance Command's main task for the next three years.[35]

Redeployment Accelerates

In his November directive setting the goal of military self-sufficiency for Saigon, Laird did more than enlarge the objectives of American military assistance to the South Vietnamese. He also established a firm timetable for removing American troops from the war. By setting 1 July 1971 as the date for reaching the 260,000-man transitional support force level, Laird for practical purposes adopted the NSSM 36 two-year option; and he allowed only two more years for reducing the transitional force to an advisory and assistance group. A master of Washington bureaucratic warfare, Laird kept up the pressure within the administration for withdrawing troops as rapidly as could be done without causing Saigon's immediate collapse. To give personal direction to the Vietnamization program, he set up a special Vietnam Task Force within the Defense Department, including officials who previously had advised the de-escalation-minded McNamara and Clifford. Every six months or so, Laird visited Vietnam and returned with reports of progress in military operations, pacification, and RVNAF improvement, which he then cited to justify continuing U.S. troop withdrawals.[36]

---

[34] Clarke, *Final Years*, pp. 355–59. Abrams elaborates on the pacification rationale in Msg, Abrams MAC 1232 to McCain info Wheeler, 27 Jan 70, Abrams Papers, CMH.

[35] For an example of Laird's view, see MFR, Phil A. Odeen, sub: Vietnamization Meeting with Secretary Laird, 1 Nov 71, folder 78, Thayer Papers, CMH.

[36] Kinnard, *Secretary of Defense*, pp. 128–29, 230. Minutes of Laird's task force are in folders 75–78, Thayer Papers, CMH. Typical of Laird trip reports is Memo, Laird for the President, 17 Feb 70, sub: Trip to Vietnam and CINCPAC, Feb 10–14, 1970, box 144, NSC files, Nixon Papers, NARA. The U.S. intention to withdraw combat forces at a rate somewhere between minimum military risk and a threat to Saigon's survival is stated in MACV, Force Planning Synopsis, pp. 261–63.

Laird's approach, with which Secretary of State Rogers concurred, differed from that of President Nixon and his national security adviser, Henry Kissinger. Nixon and Kissinger, while committed to Vietnamization, preferred a more gradual American withdrawal as a means of maintaining the U.S. negotiating posture in Paris and ensuring the position of the South Vietnamese on the ground. Both men distrusted the Defense and State bureaucracies as disloyal nests of Johnson administration holdovers. Kissinger repeatedly warned the president that Laird's plans rested on questionable assumptions about the rate of South Vietnamese progress and took little account of possible increases in enemy forces or activity. As withdrawal planning developed, Kissinger, usually with Nixon's support, attempted to insert more time and greater flexibility into Laird's program.[37]

Laird frustrated most of these efforts through his management of the Defense budget. From the time Nixon took office, his administration faced a strong bipartisan congressional drive to reduce military spending and shift funds to domestic programs. In this climate, the administration had to allocate steadily diminishing defense resources among the war, other military missions, and the increasingly urgent need of the services for new equipment. Early in 1970, making a virtue of this necessity, Laird directed the Joint Chiefs of Staff to base their budget projections for fiscal year 1971[38] and beyond on a steady drawdown of troops and decline of military activity in Vietnam. He instructed them to assume a force level of no more than 260,000 (and possibly less) by 30 June 1971 and an advisory group of no more than 43,000 by 30 June 1973. Regularly, he warned the Joint Chiefs, Admiral McCain, and General Abrams that, given the budget stringency, any redeployment slowdown would have to be compensated for by reductions elsewhere in the military establishment.[39]

Kissinger succinctly summarized the effects of Laird's action. "Currently," he told the president early in 1970, "budget ceilings are being used to determine the pace of Vietnamization." Vietnamization programs were "competing with all other priorities—NATO programs,

---

[37] Kinnard, *Secretary of Defense*, p. 134. Memo, Kissinger for the President, 9 Mar 70, sub: The Risks of Vietnamization, box 091; Memo, Laurence E. Lynn, Jr, for Kissinger, 26 Mar 70, sub: Secretary Laird's Trip Report, box 144; Memo, Kissinger for the President, 16 Apr 70, sub: Problems on Vietnamization, box 145; Memo, Kissinger for the President, [June 70], [sub:] Review of Vietnamization, box 091; Memo, Haig for Kissinger, 4 Apr 70, sub: Vietnam, box 1009. All in NSC files, Nixon Papers, NARA.

[38] In this period, the government's fiscal year ran from 1 July to 30 June, so that fiscal year 1971 encompassed the period 1 July 1970 through 30 June 1971.

[39] Kissinger, *White House Years*, pp. 212–15; Historical Division, "Joint Chiefs of Staff and the War in Vietnam, 1969–1970," pp. 62–63, 133–39, 381, 386–88; MACV, Force Planning Synopsis, pp. 282–85, 322–24. Memo, Laird for the President, 17 Feb 70, sub: Trip to Vietnam and CINCPAC, February 10–14, 1970, box 144; Memo, Laird for the President, 27 Feb 70, sub: FY 1970–71 Budget Situation for Vietnam, box 091; Memo, Laird for the President, 4 Apr 70, sub: Vietnam, box 145; Memo, Sec Army Stanley R. Resor for Sec Def, 12 Aug 70, sub: . . . Vietnam Trip, box 245, NSC files, Nixon Papers, NARA. Msg, Wheeler JCS 03939 to McCain and Abrams, 1 Apr 69, Abrams Papers.

new weapons systems, etc.," with the Joint Chiefs and the services being "asked to adjudicate among the priorities" and possibly to "forego programs to which they have long-standing operational or political commitments." The services, to save other forces and programs, increasingly allied themselves with Laird in favor of rapid withdrawal. While Kissinger understood Laird's strategy, given the budget stringency, he had no way to counter it. The Defense budget set the parameters of redeployment planning during the next two years.[40]

Discussion of the next redeployment (Phase IV) began even as the units designated for Phase III were standing down from operations and preparing for departure. During February 1970, General Abrams informed General Wheeler that he considered the 260,000 level by mid-1971 to be a "realistic planning objective." On the basis of MACV staff studies, he told his component and field force commanders at the same time that if the military and political situations remained stable, "by carefully assessing the situation as we go along, it might well be possible to redeploy 150,000 U.S. troops from Vietnam in 1970." MACV planners had ready a detailed outline of how such a redeployment, and its accompanying repositioning of the South Vietnamese Army, could be carried out.[41]

Nevertheless, during February and March, Abrams, with the support of Admiral McCain and the Joint Chiefs, argued for a delay in starting Phase IV. He cited increased supply movement in Laos, a shift of five regiments from III to IV Corps, and the discovery of substantial caches near Saigon as indications of a possible major enemy offensive during the spring and early summer. He declared in addition that American withdrawals thus far had stretched to the limit the South Vietnamese ability to take over new areas of responsibility while still maintaining adequate corps- and national-level reserves. Hence, the Vietnamese needed a "breathing spell" after Phase III. Declaring that another large withdrawal on the heels of Phase III would upset the "military and psychological balance" in South Vietnam, Abrams recommended against additional U.S. redeployments during the spring and early summer of 1970. The MACV commander protested as well the growing dominance of the budget in redeployment considerations. He expressed concern that the United States was abandoning its cut-and-try withdrawal criteria and violating understandings with the South Vietnamese about the level of support they could expect to receive. "In summary," he cabled

---

[40] Quotations are from Memo, Kissinger for the President, 19 Mar 70, sub: The Risks of Vietnamization, box 091, NSC files, Nixon Papers, NARA. In same collection, see Memo, Lynn for Kissinger, 13 Mar 70, sub: The Risks for Vietnamization, and Memo, Lynn for Kissinger, 1 Jul 70, sub: Vietnamization, box 092; and Memo, Kissinger for the President, 3 Aug 71, sub: Air Activities in Southeast Asia, FY 1972 and FY 1973, box 156. The latter document reflects Abrams' realization that the services "want out of the Vietnam war." Kinnard, *Secretary of Defense*, p. 133.

[41] Quotations are from Msg, Abrams MAC 1517 to Component and Field Force Cdrs, 1 Feb 70, Abrams Papers, CMH.

Wheeler on 8 March, "I must report that this is not the direction nor the program I had believed we were on."[42]

During March and April, Laird, the Joint Chiefs, McCain, and Abrams exchanged views on a range of Phase IV troop packages and time schedules. Nixon and Kissinger, however, set the course. The president and his national security adviser sympathized with General Abrams' desire to retain as much combat power as possible through the summer, especially in the light of a new Communist offensive in Laos and the upheaval in Cambodia following the overthrow of President Norodom Sihanouk in March by an anti-Communist faction. They also wanted to slow the momentum of withdrawal and gain flexibility in managing it. Nixon accordingly adopted a plan, advanced by Kissinger, to announce in April a withdrawal of 150,000 men, to be completed by 30 April 1971. This redeployment, which would reduce American strength in Vietnam to about 284,000, in fact would maintain the NSSM 36 two-year schedule; but removal of most of the troops would occur late in the period, on a timetable based on Abrams' assessments. No more than 60,000 men would leave Vietnam during the rest of 1970.[43]

Outflanking Laird and the rest of the Cabinet, Kissinger on 6 April, using CIA communications, secretly sought the views of Abrams and Bunker on the proposal. Abrams already knew of the plan through military backchannel exchanges with Admiral McCain and the Joint Chiefs. At a hastily called midnight meeting, Abrams and a few key staff officers discussed the plan. They all were reluctant to commit themselves to such a large redeployment over such a long period, thereby finally abandoning MACV's cherished principle of "cut-and-try" gradualism. Abrams nevertheless recognized that the president was under intense political pressure on the issue and that the plan offered MACV some room for maneuver. He finally telephoned his assent to Bunker, who informed the White House through the CIA channel. Nixon then had Bunker secure President Thieu's agreement, again while keeping both Laird and Rogers ignorant of the plan and allowing them to transmit different proposals through their departments' channels. Only late in the afternoon of 20 April, the day set for the announcement, did Kissinger tell Laird and Rogers what was afoot. That evening, Nixon in a televised address to the nation announced that "we have now reached a point where we can confidently move from a period of 'cut and try'

---

[42] First quotation is from Msg, Abrams MAC 2009 to McCain, 12 Feb 70; the second is from Msg, Abrams MAC 3081 to McCain info Wheeler, 8 Mar 70. Both in Abrams Papers, CMH. In same collection, see Msgs, Abrams MAC 3303 to McCain and Wheeler, 13 Mar 70, and McCain to Wheeler info Abrams et al., 16 Mar 70. Historical Division, "Joint Chiefs of Staff and the War in Vietnam, 1969–1970," pp. 383–85.

[43] Msg, Abrams MAC 4527 to McCain info Wheeler et al., 6 Apr 70, Abrams Papers, CMH, is an example of the various plans. See also MACV, Force Planning Synopsis, pp. 271–73, 279–80, 296–97. Kissinger, *White House Years*, pp. 475–83, describes the development of the 150,000-man withdrawal plan.

to a longer-range program for the replacement of Americans by South Vietnamese troops" and that 150,000 American soldiers would leave Vietnam over the next year.[44]

Planning for the 150,000 redeployment took place against the background of the American–South Vietnamese incursions into Cambodia and the resulting revival of antiwar agitation in Congress and the streets. General Abrams suggested the slowest possible implementation—20,000 troops by 1 September, another 30,000 by the end of the year, and the remaining 100,000 during the first half of 1971. On 24 April, Secretary Laird directed the Joint Chiefs of Staff to prepare a plan for removing 50,000 troops by 15 October but declared that total withdrawals during 1970 need not exceed 60,000. The Joint Chiefs late in May proposed two plans. Alternative A, which reflected Abrams' preference, would remove 60,000 troops during 1970, with 50,000 out by 15 October, and the remaining 90,000 during the first four months of 1971. Alternative B called for two redeployments, of 60,000 and 40,000, during 1970, followed early in 1971 by one of 50,000. The Joint Chiefs declared that both alternatives involved "substantial risks which are beyond prudent levels" but favored Alternative A as the lesser evil even though it would cost one billion dollars more than currently budgeted for Vietnam. General Abrams and Admiral McCain also endorsed Alternative A. Abrams declared it would "facilitate accomplishment of tasks essential to Vietnamization" during the last half of 1970, including the continuation of South Vietnamese cross-border operations to assist the beleaguered anti-Communist government of Cambodia.[45]

On 3 June, the president publicly announced that 50,000 troops would redeploy by 15 October; but budget constraints soon forced the administration to abandon the rest of Alternative A. Late in July, the secretary of the Army informed Secretary Laird that, due to budget limitations and reduced draft calls (previously ordered by Laird), the Army could meet the Vietnam troop requirements of Alternative A only through deep cuts in its worldwide forces, including those committed to NATO. It also would have difficulty supporting the Joint Chiefs' Alternative B. In response, Laird on 30 July, after again ruling out any attempt to increase the fiscal year 1971 budget, directed the

---

[44] The messages between the White House and Bunker are in box 410, NSC files, Nixon Papers, NARA. Msgs, Abrams MAC 4582 to Moorer and McCain, 8 Apr 70; Abrams MAC 4619 to Moorer and McCain, 8 Apr 70; and McCain to Moorer info Abrams, 8 Apr 70. All in Abrams Papers, CMH. MACV, Force Planning Synopsis, pp. 301–03. Abrams' chief of staff describes Abrams' decision in Interv, Abrams Project with Lt Gen Donald H. Cowles, 20 Dec 75, pp. 29–30, MHI (hereafter cited as Cowles Interv). Nixon quotation is from *Public Papers of the Presidents of the United States. Richard Nixon, 1970* (Washington D.C.: U.S. Government Printing Office, 1971), p. 374.

[45] Msg, Abrams MAC 5495 to Wheeler, 25 Apr 70, Abrams Papers, CMH; MACV History, 1970, Supp., p. 9; Historical Division, "Joint Chiefs of Staff and the War in Vietnam, 1969–1970," pp. 385–86, 390–92. Quotations are from MACV, Force Planning Synopsis, pp. 315–17; see also pp. 303–06, 318.

Joint Chiefs to develop a new plan "to continue the momentum of the redeployments beyond October 15th to the end of the year."[46]

After mulling over various alternatives, late in August the Joint Chiefs accepted a proposal from General Abrams to withdraw 50,000 men by 15 October, another 40,000 by 31 December, and 60,000 by 30 April 1971. Abrams and Admiral McCain considered that this schedule, labeled Alternative C, entailed severe risks of military and pacification setbacks in I and II Corps, would cause difficult logistical problems, and would reduce South Vietnamese ability to continue operations in Cambodia. Both men preferred Alternative A as "militarily the only prudent redeployment program," but they accepted Alternative C as the best available compromise "designed to accommodate imposed manpower and budgetary constraints." When consulted, President Thieu acquiesced in the new scheme, although he pointed out that it would force withdrawal of a South Vietnamese task force from Cambodia. On 20 August, Secretary Laird recommended Alternative C to the White House. Nixon and Kissinger, recognizing that the plan represented a reversal of their original intent, sought but failed to find an alternative to it. On 12 October, as the 50,000-man redeployment was nearing completion, President Nixon announced that another withdrawal, of 40,000 men, would be completed before the end of the year. Meanwhile, the Joint Chiefs, Admiral McCain, and General Abrams prepared plans for the final 60,000-man increment.[47]

At the end of April 1971, with completion of the last increment of the 150,000-man withdrawal, U.S. military strength in Vietnam was approaching the NSSM 36 transitional support force level. In Vietnam, the decline of American troop strength to this point had caused no apparent military or pacification setbacks. In the United States, the Nixon administration was working under intensifying congressional pressure to set a final withdrawal date, continuing budgetary and manpower limitations, and an awareness of approaching South Vietnamese and American presidential elections. Given these pressures, and the favorable battlefield situation, redeployments could only accelerate.[48]

Defense Department fiscal planning assumed a steady force drawdown in Vietnam. The Joint Chiefs of Staff, expecting further funding reductions and declining draft calls, in mid-December 1970 reduced

---

[46] Historical Division, "Joint Chiefs of Staff and the War in Vietnam, 1969–1970," pp. 392–98; Kissinger, *White House Years*, pp. 984–85. Quotation is from MACV, Force Planning Synopsis, p. 334; see also pp. 319–21, 333, 335.

[47] Quotation is from Msg, Abrams MAC 12215 to McCain info Moorer, 9 Sep 70, Abrams Papers. In same collection, see Msgs, McCain to Moorer info Abrams et al., 9 and 10 Sep 70. MACV, Force Planning Synopsis, pp. 336–39, 341, 343–44, 346–47, 351–52, 359; Historical Division, "Joint Chiefs of Staff and the War in Vietnam, 1969–1970," pp. 398–400; Memo, 20 Oct 70, [sub:] Conversation between Kissinger, Bunker, and William R. Smyser, 3:00 p.m., Oct 19, 1970, box 149, NSC files, Nixon Papers, NARA.

[48] Memo, Haig for Kissinger, 15 Jan 71, sub: Your Meeting with Secretary Laird . . . , box 083, NSC files, Nixon Papers, NARA, illustrates the continuing influence of budget pressures.

their projected U.S. force in Vietnam at the end of fiscal year 1971 (mid-1971) from 260,000 to 255,000, and they proposed a strength of 200,000 for mid-1972. General Westmoreland, the Army chief of staff, declared that, under current budget and draft call projections, his service could maintain the contemplated force levels in Vietnam only through "serious degradation" of Army units elsewhere. The Joint Chiefs, while acknowledging the Army's difficulties, nevertheless held to the 200,000 level for mid-1972, arguing that it would provide enough American troops to prevent major military setbacks, respond to contingencies, and permit continued South Vietnamese operations in Cambodia. General Abrams and Admiral McCain also endorsed that strength goal. During February 1971, however, Secretary Laird, in his budget guidance for fiscal years 1973 through 1977, directed the Joint Chiefs to plan on the basis of a mid-1972 strength in Vietnam of no more than 153,600.[49]

Even before issuing this directive, Laird instructed General Abrams to begin planning for a still more drastic force reduction. In early January 1971, Laird made another of his periodic journeys to Vietnam. He returned with his usual optimistic assessment of progress and recommended continuation and acceleration of American withdrawals. While in Saigon, Laird told American and South Vietnamese officials that the United States was "working against time in that *a de facto withdrawal timetable has been established*," under which "by 1972 we must have all but a military assistance group redeployed from South Vietnam." Pursuant to this goal, Laird directed Abrams to prepare, on a close-hold basis, a contingency plan for reducing the American force in South Vietnam to 60,000 men by 1 September 1972.[50]

General Abrams' staff completed the required plan, labeled Contingency Plan 208, on 8 March; and a MACV team briefed Secretary Laird on it on the sixteenth and seventeenth. The plan was based on the assumptions that American tactical air and B–52 operations would continue at a high level at least until mid-1973; that cross-border operations into Cambodia and Laos would reduce enemy offensive capability; and that there would be no major political upheavals in South Vietnam, Laos, and Cambodia. It included a four-phase schedule for removing 224,000 troops between 1 May 1971 and 31 August 1972 and

[49] Historical Division, "Joint Chiefs of Staff and the War in Vietnam, 1969–1970," pp. 401–02; Historical Division, Joint Secretariat, Joint Chiefs of Staff, "The Joint Chiefs of Staff and the War in Vietnam, 1971–1973," Sep 1979, CMH, pp. 114–22, 136–39 (hereafter referred to as "Joint Chiefs of Staff and the War in Vietnam, 1971–1973"; MACV, Force Planning Synopsis, pp. 363, 368, 373–74, 377–78. Memo, Westmoreland for CJCS, 4 Jan 71, sub: RVN Force Levels, End FY 71 and FY 72, box 1001; Memo, Adm Robinson for Kissinger, 8 Jan 71, sub: Size of Residual MAAG Force in South Vietnam, box 152. Both in NSC files, Nixon Papers, NARA.

[50] Quotation is from Memo, Laird for the President, 16 Jan 71, sub: Trip to Paris, Bangkok, South Vietnam, and CINCPAC, January 5–15, 1971, box 083, NSC files, Nixon Papers, NARA; italics in original. Historical Division, "Joint Chiefs of Staff and the War in Vietnam, 1971–1973," pp. 141–42.

prescribed the composition of a minimum U.S. force able to protect and support itself, conduct the air war, manage the removal of supplies and equipment, and provide intelligence, combat, and logistical assistance to the South Vietnamese.[51]

Abrams, who earlier had declared the Joint Chiefs' 200,000-man force "appropriate" for the end of 1972, informed Kissinger's assistant, Brig. Gen. Alexander M. Haig, that he considered the 60,000-man force an "acceptable risk." He pointed out that after the end of 1971, when most American combat units would be gone, there was "little point in quibbling" about the size of the residual force since it no longer would have any impact on the ground war. From that point on, American strength should be based on what was needed to advise and assist the South Vietnamese and remove U.S. equipment and supplies. Observing that the "U.S. national environment" probably would force the reductions at any event, Abrams recommended to the Joint Chiefs that they adopt Contingency Plan 208 for planning purposes as soon as possible to give MACV the necessary lead time for the complicated logistical preparations the drawdown would require.[52]

While Laird, the Joint Chiefs, and the Pacific commanders examined various withdrawal timetables for 1971, including MACV Contingency Plan 208, Nixon and Kissinger again seized the initiative. As part of a new military and diplomatic effort to end the war, they decided to announce another large, long-term withdrawal—100,000 men between May and December. Such an announcement would stop what Kissinger called "the endless maneuvering over withdrawal rates," and it would allow the administration to fulfill President Thieu's request to keep at least 200,000 American soldiers in South Vietnam through that country's presidential election in September. Although the number nearly coincided with Laird's proposed withdrawal total of 105,000 for the year, Nixon and Kissinger again kept their figure secret from all but Secretary of State Rogers while clearing it with Ambassador Bunker and President Thieu. Possibly because of displeasure with General Abrams over Operation LAM SON 719, the abortive South Vietnamese drive into Laos, the president this time kept the MACV commander ignorant of the plan until he publicly announced it. On 7 April, Nixon told the nation of the new 100,000-man pullout. He declared as well that "the American involvement in Vietnam is coming to an end," "the day the South Vietnamese can take over their own defense is in sight," and

[51] Historical Division, "Joint Chiefs of Staff and the War in Vietnam, 1971–1973," pp. 141–42. Msgs, Haig SGN 566 to Kissinger, 16 Mar 71, box 084; Haig SGN 593 to Kissinger, 18 Mar 71, box 1013, NSC files, Nixon Papers, NARA. MACV, Force Planning Synopsis, p. 394. OPLAN 208A Briefing Presented to Sec Army, 10 Jan 72 in CIIB, MACV Collection, MHI.

[52] First quotation is from MACV, Force Planning Synopsis, pp. 377–78. Second is from Memo, Kissinger for the President [Mar 71] sub: Troop Withdrawals, box 1013, NSC files, Nixon Papers, NARA. Third is from Historical Division, "Joint Chiefs of Staff and the War in Vietnam, 1971–1973," pp. 142–43. MACV, Force Planning Synopsis, p. 394.

that the administration's goal was "total American withdrawal from Vietnam," to be reached "through our program of Vietnamization."[53]

The rest of 1971 was devoted to carrying out the 100,000-man withdrawal and refining the Military Assistance Command's plan for reaching a force of 60,000 during 1972. Redeployments took place in three increments on a schedule recommended by Abrams on the basis of Contingency Plan 208. More than half the departing troops left Vietnam after 1 September so as to keep American strength at around 200,000 through the South Vietnamese election.[54]

Meanwhile, General Abrams and his staff, in coordination with the component commanders, revised Contingency Plan 208. To ensure adequate air mobility for the South Vietnamese Army, President Nixon in August, at Dr. Kissinger's suggestion, directed the inclusion of more helicopter companies in the residual force. At the same time, Secretary Laird called for a plan to reach the 60,000 level by 30 June, the end of fiscal year 1972, instead of the previous deadline of 1 September. In response, MACV during September and October prepared two new contingency plans, J208 and J208A. Both provided for a drawdown to a 60,000-man force that could conduct air operations, support the RVNAF, protect the remaining U.S. installations, and ship out large quantities of equipment and supplies. As the president had directed, the plans provided for enlarged helicopter contingents. They differed only in that J208A compressed the withdrawal schedule to meet Laird's 30 June 1972 deadline.[55]

The administration lost no time in implementing this plan. As part of their overall strategy, Nixon and Kissinger intended to follow up the 100,000-man withdrawal with smaller increments, conducted over shorter periods of time, until they reached the 60,000 level. Accordingly, on 12 November, the president announced another withdrawal of 45,000 troops, to be completed by the end of January 1972, which would leave only 139,000 American soldiers in South Vietnam. This redeployment put into execution MACV's plan J208A. During December, General Abrams set the new pullout in motion and also

[53] Kissinger, *White House Years*, pp. 985–86. Historical Division, "Joint Chiefs of Staff and the War in Vietnam, 1971–1973," pp. 143–47; MACV, Force Planning Synopsis, pp. 397–98. Msg, Kissinger to Bunker, 27 Mar 71, box 085; Msg, Bunker SGN 0938 to White House, 2 Apr 71, box 412; Memo, Laird for the President, 3 Apr 71, sub: Redeployment of U.S. Forces from Southeast Asia, box 084; Msg, Kissinger SCWH 90161 to Bunker, 3 Apr 71, box 084. All in NSC files, Nixon Papers, NARA. Quotations are from MACV History, 1971, vol. 2, an. F, p. F–7.

[54] Historical Division, "Joint Chiefs of Staff and the War in Vietnam, 1971–1973," pp. 147–48, 151; MACV, Force Planning Synopsis, pp. 400–01, 404.

[55] Historical Division, "Joint Chiefs of Staff and the War in Vietnam, 1971–1973," pp. 153–58; MACV, Force Planning Synopsis, pp. 417–19, 422–26, 432. Memo, Kissinger for the President, [June 71], sub: Mid-1972 Force in Vietnam, box 155; Memo, R. L. Sansom for Kissinger . . . , 14 Jul 71, sub: U.S. Helicopter Support, box 156; Memo, Kissinger for Sec Def, 2 Aug 71, sub: U.S. Helicopters for Vietnam, box 156; Memo, Laird for Kissinger, 26 Aug 71, sub: U.S. Helicopters for Vietnam, box 157. All in NSC files, Nixon Papers, NARA. Msg, Abrams MAC 10696 to Laird, 10 Nov 71, Abrams Papers, CMH.

prepared troop lists for two more increments in early 1972 that would complete the drawdown to 60,000.[56]

Throughout the planning and execution of the redeployments, General Abrams paid close attention to two related issues: the maintenance of a high level of air support for his forces and the question of American troop withdrawals from Thailand. In common with Admiral McCain and the Joint Chiefs, Abrams considered continued American air support "vital if Vietnamization is to succeed" and repeatedly made it a condition for his endorsement of rapid troop withdrawals.[57]

Abrams, McCain, and the Joint Chiefs faced steady pressure to reduce sortie rates. Redeployments removed air squadrons and budget cuts diminished the supply of munitions. The services, notably the Air Force, themselves tried to reduce their Southeast Asia costs by cutting back on combat activity. Secretary Laird and his staff considered that much of the interdiction effort in Laos was not cost-effective and that MACV could get by with less fighter-bomber support by using improved fixed-wing and helicopter gunships. They also suspected that many tactical air missions were being flown more to keep usage rates up, and hence justify higher sortie levels, than in response to combat necessities. Air operations, in Laird's view, thus could be reduced, significantly cutting the costs of the war, without deleterious battlefield effects.[58]

The Defense Secretary made substantial reductions in tactical air and B–52 activity. During 1969, Laird cut tactical air sorties from an average of 24,000 a month to 20,000 and B–52 sorties from 1,800 a month to 1,400. The following year, over protests from Dr. Kissinger, the Joint Chiefs, Admiral McCain, and General Abrams, Defense Secretary Laird cut sortie rates to 10,000 per month (with an emergency ceiling of 14,000) for tactical aircraft and 1,000 for B–52s. In 1971, Laird's office, with Air Force support, proposed to reduce tactical air and B–52 sortie rates respectively to 7,500 and 800 per month during fiscal years 1972 and 1973. On this occasion, however, President Nixon, determined to

[56] Historical Division, "Joint Chiefs of Staff and the War in Vietnam, 1971–1973," pp. 158–60. Memo, Laird for the President, 8 Nov 71, sub: Trip to Vietnam, November 2–8, 1971, box 158; Msg, Kissinger WHS 1132 to Bunker, 10 Nov 71, box 412; Memo, Kissinger WHS 1133 for Bunker, 11 Nov 71, box 412; Memo, Laird for CJCS, 15 Nov 71, sub: U.S. Redeployments from South Vietnam, box 158. All in NSC files, Nixon Papers, NARA. MACV, Force Planning Synopsis, pp. 433–36, 440–41, 443–44; OPLAN 208A Briefing Presented to Sec Army, 10 Jan 72 in CIIB, MACV Collection, MHI.

[57] Quotation is from Msg, Abrams MAC 1946 to McCain info Moorer, 10 Feb 70, Abrams Papers, CMH.

[58] An example of Office of Secretary of Defense thinking is Memo, Dep Sec Def David Packard for the President, 18 Jun 70, sub: Air Operations in Southeast Asia, box 147, NSC files, Nixon Papers, NARA. In same collection, see also Memo, Laird for Kissinger, 23 Jul 70, sub: Vietnam Special Study Group Study on U.S. Air Activity in Southeast Asia, box 148; Memo, Lynn for Kissinger, 29 Apr 70, sub: Laird's Views on Air Support for Vietnam, box 145; and Memo, Kissinger for the President, 3 Aug 71, sub: Air Activities in Southeast Asia, FY 1972 and FY 1973, box 156. MFR, Phil Odeen, 17 Jun 71, sub: Vietnamization Meeting with Secretary Laird, folder 77, Thayer Papers, CMH. Historical Division, "Joint Chiefs of Staff and the War in Vietnam, 1969–1970," pp. 63–66; MACV, Force Planning Synopsis, pp. 281, 288–89.

keep sufficient airpower in Southeast Asia for possible renewed attacks on North Vietnam as well as operations in South Vietnam, overruled Laird. After a direct appeal from General Abrams to Kissinger, Nixon in August 1971 directed that sortie rates be maintained, and budgeted for, at rates recommended by Abrams and the Joint Chiefs: 10,000 per month for tactical aircraft and 1,000 for B–52s during fiscal year 1972 and 8,000 and 1,000 respectively during 1973. Laird nevertheless had the last word. In budget guidance to the Joint Chiefs in December, he instructed them to program funds for only 6,000 tactical air sorties a month in fiscal year 1973 while retaining sufficient forces in Southeast Asia to support 7,100.[59]

Most of the American air strikes against the Ho Chi Minh Trail and in aid of the Royal Laotian government in its war against the Pathet Lao and North Vietnamese were flown by aircraft based in Thailand. As of early 1969, these squadrons constituted about one-third of the U.S. Air Force's tactical air strength in Southeast Asia. For this reason, Admiral McCain and General Abrams, from the beginning of NSSM 36 planning, took the position that there should be no reduction of the 48,000-man American contingent in Thailand until late in the Vietnamization process. Evoking what they called the "one air war" principle, Abrams and McCain insisted that the squadrons in Thailand were a critical element of the military balance in Southeast Asia, essential to interdict enemy infiltration into South Vietnam, sustain the Laotian government, maintain the threat of retaliation against North Vietnam, and in emergencies intervene in the war in the south. Any reduction of these forces, they concluded, would endanger the success of Vietnamization. The American ambassadors in Bangkok and Vientiane endorsed this military judgment.[60]

Secretary Laird nevertheless insisted on withdrawals as part of his effort to reduce American military costs in Southeast Asia. The Air Force, under its own budget pressures, supported his initiatives. At Laird's direction, Admiral McCain in consultation with General Abrams and Maj. Gen. Louis T. Seith, USAF, Commander, U.S. Military Assistance Command, Thailand, planned and carried out a 6,000-man withdrawal in late 1969 and another of 10,000 during 1970 and 1971. The three commanders did their best to retain as much airpower as possible

[59] MACV, Force Planning Synopsis, pp. 256–57, 260–61, 322–24, 337–40, 409–10, 413, 415; MACV History, 1970, Supp., p. 24. Memo, Kissinger for the President, 16 Apr 70, sub: Problems on Vietnamization, box 145; Memo, Kissinger for the President, 3 Aug 71, sub: Air Activities in Southeast Asia, FY 1972 and FY 1973, box 156; Memo, Kissinger for Sec Def, 6 Aug 71, sub: Air Activities over Southeast Asia, FY 1972 and FY 1973, box 156. All in NSC files, Nixon Papers, NARA. Historical Division, "Joint Chiefs of Staff and the War in Vietnam, 1971–1973," pp. 185–207.

[60] MACV, NSSM 36 Briefing, 22 Jul 69, MHI. Msgs, Abrams MAC 4686 to McCain info Nazzaro et al., 13 Apr 69; McCain to Vice Adm Johnson info Abrams, 27 May 69; Abrams MAC 10803 to McCain info Nazzaro et al., 20 Aug 69; McCain to Abrams info Nazzaro et al., 20 Aug 69; Abrams MAC 11803 to McCain info Maj Gen Louis T. Seith, USAF, et al., 10 Sep 69; McCain to Wheeler info Abrams et al., 24 Sep 69; Abrams MAC 3243 to McCain info PACOM Cdrs, 12 Mar 70; Seith BNK 0575 to McCain info Abrams et al., 16 Mar 70. All in Abrams Papers, CMH.

during these reductions but still had to accept a steady diminution of Thailand-based aircraft. Early in 1971, Laird called for withdrawals that would bring American strength in Thailand to 27,900 men, more than 21,000 of them Air Force, by mid-1972. This strength, according to Admiral McCain, would not be sufficient to supplement dwindling American air resources in South Vietnam. In Thailand as in Vietnam, redeployment had assumed a momentum of its own, impelled by the budget and American politics.[61]

Implementing the Withdrawals

Each presidential redeployment announcement set in motion a complicated sequence of events. Before an announcement, General Abrams and Admiral McCain had to provide the Joint Chiefs and Secretary Laird, usually on short notice, with troop packages for redeployments of differing sizes and durations. After the announcement, General Abrams set small planning groups to work at MACV and the component and field force headquarters on detailed lists of units to be removed or inactivated, with proposed dates for their standdowns from operations as well as schedules for shipping out men and equipment. Admiral McCain and his service component commanders reviewed the MACV list and recommended destinations for units to remain in Pacific Command. The Joint Chiefs of Staff and the service departments then established personnel policies, inactivation schedules, destinations for units leaving Pacific Command, instructions for equipment disposition, and public relations plans. With this information in hand, MACV developed a tentative program for moving men and materiel. Finally, Admiral McCain convened a conference of representatives of all concerned commands and agencies to complete a detailed program. Throughout the process, large volumes of data, much of it in punch-card form, passed between the various headquarters. Until the very last stages, the planning took place under tight security restrictions, with knowledge limited to a small number of hard-worked officers on each staff.[62]

From the beginning of redeployment discussions in the spring of 1969, the MACV staff developed and kept up-to-date long-range plans

---

[61] Historical Division, "Joint Chiefs of Staff and the War in Vietnam, 1969–1970," p. 380. Msgs, McCain to Abrams et al., 19 Aug 69; McCain to Wheeler info Abrams et al., 24 Sep 69; McCain MAC 2573 to PACOM Cdrs, 26 Feb 70; McCain to PACOM Cdrs, 7 Mar 70; Abrams MAC 4430 to McCain, 4 Apr 70. All in Abrams Papers, CMH. MACV, Force Planning Synopsis, pp. 268, 280, 322–24, 378–79.

[62] For examples of the planning process, see MACV, Force Planning Synopsis, pp. 319–20; and Msgs, Abrams MAC 11844 to McCain info Wheeler, 10 Sep 69; Abrams MAC 01726 to Field and Component Cdrs, 17 Feb 71, both in Abrams Papers, CMH. Donald A. Seibert, "The Regulars," p. 1039, Donald A. Seibert Papers, MHI, gives a view from the I Field Force G–3 section. The planning process generally can be followed in MACV, Force Planning Synopsis, and the Abrams Message files, Abrams Papers, CMH.

for the drawdown and the residual forces. Seeking to anticipate presidential decisions, the headquarters assembled a variety of troop packages and time schedules, all based on the NSSM 36 plan. In late 1969, at General Abrams' direction, the J–3 staff drew up two overall force reduction plans: Operations Plan (OPLAN) 183–69, a general outline of the standdown and shipping-out process that could be adapted to each successive increment; and OPLAN 186–69, which established the size and composition of the 260,000-man transitional support force. As the transitional force level was reached and passed in early 1971, MACV added the 208 series of plans for the drawdown to a residual force of 60,000. Parallel to this planning, MACV and Pacific Command kept current their T-Day plans for withdrawal in the event of a cessation of hostilities. All the plans, in General Abrams' words, were "dynamic" documents that changed frequently in response to the military situation, new staff studies and war games, advice from component and field force commanders, and intervention by higher authority. At many points, the staff planners had to work without full information as to the administration's ultimate intentions.[63]

General Abrams early sought to include the South Vietnamese in this long-range planning. The American redeployment decisions, like those which had dispatched troops to Vietnam in the first place, were reached unilaterally; although President Nixon made a practice of clearing major announcements in advance with President Thieu. Nevertheless, from the beginning of work on NSSM 36, Abrams realized that, to ensure an orderly American turnover of bases and tactical areas of responsibility to the South Vietnamese Army, as well as to give Vietnamization as a whole a fair chance to succeed, combined advance planning was imperative. For the Americans, the problem—given Saigon's notoriously lax security—was how to provide their allies the information they needed for realistic planning without risking premature leaks of U.S. intentions to the enemy and the news media.[64]

In mid-July 1969, General Abrams secured permission from General Wheeler and Secretary Laird to reveal to the RVNAF Joint General Staff the substance of NSSM 36 but not the existence or high-level origins of that plan. Abrams then described the plan to General Vien, Defense Minister Lt. Gen. Nguyen Van Vy, and a handful of other senior Joint General Staff officers as a hypothetical one originated by his and Admiral McCain's headquarters. Whether the Vietnamese believed this subterfuge is not known. Detailed discussions began late in July between Maj.

---

[63] MACV History, 1969, vol. 1, ch. 2, p. 26. Msgs, Abrams MAC 6685 to McCain and Vice Adm Johnson, 25 May 69; Abrams MAC 14468 to Wheeler info McCain, 8 Nov 69; Lt Gen William J. McCaffrey, Dep CG, USARV, 2972 to Abrams, 10 Sep 71; Abrams MAC 09652 to Component and Regional Assistance Grp Cdrs, 7 Oct 71; Abrams MAC 10029 to Component and Regional Assistance Grp Cdrs, 19 Oct 71; Abrams MAC 10403 to McCaffrey, 1 Nov 71. All in Abrams Papers, CMH. MACV, Force Planning Synopsis, pp. 99–100, 121–22, 140, 160, 176–77, 349, 369–71, 375, 379–81.

[64] Msgs, Abrams MAC 4966 to Wheeler and McCain, 19 Apr 69; Abrams MAC 9420 to McCain info Wheeler, 21 Jul 69. All in Abrams Papers, CMH.

Gen. Edward Bautz, Jr., the MACV J–3, and Bautz's Joint General Staff counterpart, Maj. Gen. Ngo Dinh Dzu, with the content known on the Vietnamese side only to Dzu, Vy, Vien, and presumably President Thieu. The Vietnamese then incorporated this information into instructions to their own planners without indicating its source. By September, through this channel, the Military Assistance Command and the Joint General Staff had reached agreement on American redeployment packages and the composition and stationing of the residual force; and the Vietnamese were developing plans, ostensibly on their own initiative, for repositioning their forces as the Americans left.[65]

The Vietnamese raised few objections to the American withdrawals, apparently appreciating their inevitability. Abrams declared himself "very gratified" at the manner in which the Vietnamese conducted their side of the planning. He told Wheeler and McCain late in 1969 that Generals Vien and Dzu

have made meaningful suggestions, many of which have been incorporated into our planning. They have done considerable thinking about their own problems. . . . They have been operating under extremely close-hold conditions; they are doing the planning personally, and have even gone so far as to produce no written material that would identify the US side of the planning.[66]

From then on, Abrams kept Joint General Staff redeployment planning in step with his own while carefully avoiding full disclosure of the U.S. timetable for disengagement. Early in 1970, for example, he and Ambassador Bunker, without mentioning Laird's 1973 deadline, urged the Vietnamese to base their planning on an American drawdown to an advisory group within a few years. During each redeployment increment, Abrams, once U.S. withdrawal schedules were set, revealed the details to General Vien and authorized his field commanders to do the same for their Vietnamese and third-country counterparts.[67]

After setting the size and time period of each withdrawal, the Nixon administration ordinarily deferred to the views of General Abrams and Admiral McCain on the composition of redeployment increments and the scheduling of unit departures. Typically, General Wheeler, at White House suggestion, in April 1970 assured Abrams that in plan-

[65] Msgs, Abrams MAC 5238 to Wheeler and McCain, 24 Apr 69; Abrams MAC 9548 to McCain info Wheeler, 24 Jul 69; Wheeler JCS 09232 to McCain info Abrams, 25 Jul 69; Abrams MAC 09642 to Wheeler and McCain, 26 Jul 69; Abrams MAC 11579 to Wheeler and McCain, 5 Sep 69; Abrams MAC 13888 to Wheeler and McCain, 26 Oct 69. All in Abrams Papers, CMH.

[66] Quotation is from Msg, Abrams MAC 11579 to Wheeler and McCain, 5 Sep 69, Abrams Papers, CMH.

[67] Msgs, Abrams MAC 0555 to McCain and Wheeler info Weyand, 13 Jan 70; McCain to Abrams info Wheeler, 16 Jan 70; Abrams MAC 0808 to McCain and Wheeler, 19 Jan 70; Wheeler JCS 01317 to McCain info Abrams, 28 Jan 70; Abrams MAC 7175 to Wheeler and McCain, 26 May 70; Abrams MAC 12721 to McCain info Bunker, 22 Sep 70; Abrams MAC 07010 to Vann info McCaffrey, 21 Jul 71. All in Abrams Papers, CMH. MACV, Force Planning Synopsis, pp. 81–82, 351, 353.

ning the 150,000-man drawdown "you are under no constraints from Washington concerning the composition of the respective increments. . . . I am certain that your judgment in this regard will continue to be fully supported at all levels back here." The president, however, occasionally violated this principle, as in his August 1971 intervention to add more helicopters to MACV's 60,000 residual force.[68]

In composing the successive withdrawal increments, General Abrams took account of a number of considerations. Starting from the principle that *"What goes out is not important . . . what stays is,"* Abrams and his subordinate commanders planned backward from the desired composition of the transitional support force. For this reason, Abrams early rejected Defense Department suggestions that he redeploy "balanced" slices of combat and service units. Instead, he deliberately weighted the initial increments toward combat forces so as to retain combat support and combat service support units needed to sustain the South Vietnamese until completion of their modernization program. At the same time, Abrams redeployed American maneuver battalions as late as possible in each increment so that they would be available to back up the South Vietnamese both physically and psychologically as they assumed wider battlefield responsibilities. He reduced American combat forces first in areas, such as northern I Corps, where strong South Vietnamese units could replace them and where the allies were making progress in pacification and military operations. For the sake of morale and unit integrity, Abrams whenever possible redeployed entire divisions at one time rather than reducing them piecemeal over several increments.[69]

Service interests and budgetary considerations influenced the composition of the redeployments, notably in the case of the marines. From the start of redeployment in mid-1969, General Abrams wanted to clear the 81,000 marines out of Vietnam as rapidly as possible. Redeployment of all the marines would simplify command and control in I Corps, and it would allow Abrams to substitute Marine aviation units for Army infantry battalions in the critical early phases of the American withdrawal. Accordingly, the 3d Marine Division left northern I Corps in the first two redeployment increments in 1969; and Abrams planned to send out the rest of III Marine Amphibious Force—the 1st Marine

---

[68] Msg, Wheeler JCS 05242 to McCain and Abrams, 16 Apr 70, Abrams Papers, CMH. The White House role is illustrated in Memo, Haig for Kissinger, 16 Apr 70, box 410, NSC files, Nixon Papers, NARA. See also Msgs, Moorer JCS 06688 to McCain info Abrams, 29 May 69; and Wheeler JCS 16470 to McCain and Abrams, 31 Dec 69. Both in Abrams Papers, CMH.

[69] Quotation is from USARV Talking Paper, AVHGC-P, 17 Jul 69, sub: NSSM 36—Vietnamization, CMH; italics in original. MACV History, 1971, vol. 2, an. F, p. F–3. Msgs, Abrams MAC 6685 to McCain and Vice Adm Johnson, 25 May 69; Abrams MAC 6746 to McCain, 27 May 69; Abrams MAC 7021 to Wheeler and McCain, 2 Jun 69; Abrams MAC 7181 to McCain info Wheeler, 6 Jun 69; Abrams MAC 16766 to McCain and Wheeler, 26 Dec 69; Abrams MAC 1232 to McCain info Wheeler, 27 Jan 70. All in Abrams Papers, CMH. MACV, Force Planning Synopsis, pp. 232–33.

Division and the 1st Marine Aircraft Wing—in Increment Three during the first half of 1970.[70]

This plan met opposition from the Army, the Marine Corps, and the Joint Chiefs of Staff. The Army complained that, under projected funding and draft calls, it could not sustain the units Abrams wanted to keep instead of the marines. Headquarters Marine Corps argued that too-rapid redeployments would create insurmountable logistical and personnel management problems for the Corps. Less openly stated, the Marine commandant and his staff feared that being the first service out of combat in Vietnam would leave the marines at a disadvantage in political battles over the budget and roles and missions. The Joint Chiefs, respecting the marines' concerns, ruled at the end of 1969 that it was "desirable to retain appropriate combat representation from all services" in Vietnam until redeployments reached the transitional support force level. In response, Abrams included only one Marine regiment in Increment Three and agreed to keep a 13,800-man Marine Amphibious Brigade in Vietnam until late in the withdrawals. Nevertheless, during the spring of 1970, his plans for the 150,000-man redeployment included removal of all marines but the Marine Amphibious Brigade by the end of the year.[71]

In August, the same Army budgetary and manpower deficiencies that forced acceleration of the 150,000-man withdrawal also required Abrams to retain more marines longer so as to keep up his ground combat strength. Under hastily revised MACV schedules, only one Marine regiment with air and support units redeployed during the remaining months of 1970. The rest of III Marine Amphibious Force departed between 1 January and 30 April 1971 in the final increment of the 150,000-man pullout, leaving behind the Marine Amphibious Brigade. Even as these redeployments went forward, General Westmoreland proposed keeping the Marine brigade in Vietnam through mid-1972 to ease the strain on Army resources. General Abrams was amenable to the proposal, but Admiral McCain and the Marine commandant objected that it would disrupt the reconstitution of Pacific Command's strategic reserve. In Vietnam, the XXIV Corps commander argued that keeping the Marine Amphibious Brigade would complicate command relationships in his area. Agreeing with the objectors, the Joint Chiefs of Staff, with Westmoreland dissenting, rejected the Army proposal. The Marine

---

[70] Graham A. Cosmas and Lt. Col. Terrence P. Murray, USMC, *U.S. Marines in Vietnam: Vietnamization and Redeployment, 1970–1971* (Washington, D.C.: History and Museums Division, Headquarters, U.S. Marine Corps, 1986), pp. 12–13; Msg, Abrams MAC 16766 to McCain and Wheeler, 26 Dec 69, Abrams Papers, CMH.

[71] Cosmas and Murray, *U.S. Marines in Vietnam, 1970–1971*, pp. 13, 58–59. Quotation is from Msg, Wheeler JCS 16146 to McCain and Abrams, 22 Dec 69, Abrams Papers, CMH. In same collection, Msgs, Abrams MAC 16561 to McCain and Wheeler, 23 Dec 69; CG III MAF to COMUSMACV, 7 Feb 70; McCain to Abrams info PACOM Cdrs, 16 Mar 70; Abrams MAC 3665 to McCain info PACOM Cdrs, 20 Mar 70. MACV, Force Planning Synopsis, pp. 265–67, 275–77, 286–87, 292, 300–01.

A self-propelled 155-mm. howitzer backs onto the ramp of the Landing Ship Tank Pitkin County *(LST 1082) at Da Nang as the marines in 1971 continue their redeployment from Vietnam.*

Amphibious Brigade redeployed during May and June 1971, leaving in Vietnam only 542 marines—members of an air and naval gunfire liaison company, advisers to the Vietnamese Marine Corps, guards at the Saigon Embassy, and officers of the MACV staff.[72]

Between 1 July 1969 and 31 January 1972, the Military Assistance Command carried out ten redeployment increments, which reduced American strength in Vietnam by 410,500 troops, including 102 infantry and other maneuver battalions, 66 artillery battalions, and 33 attack and fighter squadrons as well as support units of all services. General Abrams arranged the sequence of force departures so as to leave ground combat units longest in I Corps, where the enemy threat was greatest. When the transitional support force level was reached in June 1971, I Corps contained seven of the nine American brigades that remained in Vietnam. Of

[72] Cosmas and Murray, *U.S. Marines in Vietnam, 1970–1971*, pp. 86–88, 187–90, 237–47. Msgs, Westmoreland WDC 19733 to Abrams, 27 Oct 70; Westmoreland WDC 20048 to Rosson info Abrams, 31 Oct 70; Sutherland DNG 2602 to Abrams, 9 Nov 70; Palmer WDC 20818 to Rosson and Abrams, 12 Nov 70; Abrams MAC 14691 to Sutherland, 14 Nov 70. All in Abrams Papers, CMH. MACV, Force Planning Synopsis, pp. 365–66.

175

the other two brigades, one reinforced II Corps and the other III Corps. In the autumn of 1971, the 23d (Americal) Infantry Division redeployed from I Corps, followed in February 1972 by the 101st Airborne Division (Airmobile), the last American division to leave Vietnam. Only two U.S. brigades then remained: the 3d of the 1st Cavalry Division at Bien Hoa and the 196th Infantry Brigade at Da Nang. Support forces also stayed, including Army aviation companies and engineer units, as well as sufficient Air Force tactical fighter squadrons to provide, when combined with Thailand-based Air Force units and Navy carrier squadrons, 10,000 attack sorties per month.[73]

The withdrawal of U.S. forces from Vietnam was more complex than simply marching units to ships and planes. Each redeployment, although translated into lists of units, actually consisted of a reduction in MACV's authorized personnel strength. MACV, Pacific Command, and the Joint Chiefs, following a principle established in earlier T-Day planning, made up each increment by redeploying individuals who had the least amount of time left in their one-year tours "in-country." After transfer or redeployment of their personnel, many organizations slated for each increment were inactivated in Vietnam or went home as command groups and color parties. The service components "mix-mastered" their personnel to fill departing units with short-time men and reassign those with the most months left until rotation to organizations remaining in Vietnam. This policy caused great turbulence within units and exacerbated the discipline and racial problems from which MACV suffered during the withdrawal period. On the positive side, it allowed the Military Assistance Command to carry out redeployments using its existing personnel system, which staffs and troops understood; and in theory each new MACV strength level then could be maintained by proper adjustment of the flow of replacements.[74]

In practice, the authorized levels were not maintained. The Military Assistance Command's actual strength—the number of men in South Vietnam on any given day—invariably was less than authorized as a result of unpredictable variations in losses from combat and other causes. When redeployments began in June 1969, MACV had an authorized strength of 549,500 but only about 537,000 people on board; and it had been on the average 9,000 men short in each of the past five

---

[73] Historical Division, "Joint Chiefs of Staff and the War in Vietnam, 1971–1973," p. 161. Major unit withdrawals are summarized in MACV History, 1969, vol. 1, ch. 4, pp. 10–13; ibid., 1970, vol. 1, ch. 4, pp. 10, 12; and ibid., 1971, vol. 2, an. F, pp. F–14 and F–1–1. Redeployments may be followed graphically in Shelby L. Stanton, *Vietnam Order of Battle* (New York: Galahad Books, 1986), pp. 375–82. Initial plans are in USARV Talking Paper, AVHGC-P, 17 Jul 69, sub: NSSM 36—Vietnamization, CMH; and Msg, Abrams MAC 7175 to Wheeler and McCain, 26 May 70, Abrams Papers, CMH. MACV, Force Planning Synopsis, p. 348.

[74] Msgs, Abrams MAC 4743 to McCain info Wheeler, 15 Apr 69; Abrams MAC 10808 to McCain and Wheeler, 20 Aug 69; Gen Haines HWA 4101 to McCain info Abrams and Westmoreland, 26 Sep 70. All in Abrams Papers, CMH. Memo, Laird for the President, 18 Jun 69, sub: CINCPAC Redeployment Planning Conference, 12–14 Jun 1969, box 138, NSC files, Nixon Papers, NARA. MACV History, 1969, vol. 1, ch. 4, pp. 13–25.

months. After each succeeding increment, MACV had fewer people on hand than the new, lower authorization. The administration, seeking to avoid news reports of any increases in the number of Americans in Vietnam at any point in the withdrawals, periodically enforced actual manpower ceilings below the authorized ones. When it did not, the services, increasingly short of funds and personnel, often had difficulty keeping up their programmed flow of replacements. During the summer of 1970, for example, the Army fell short by about 10,000 men of meeting replacement requirements for U.S. Army, Vietnam. General Abrams protested repeatedly against both the double ceilings and the service defaults. He pointed out that they amounted to additional withdrawals above and beyond the planned increments, which he considered risky in themselves, and that they left many units, notably advisory teams and infantry rifle companies, dangerously understrength. Nevertheless, political and budgetary realities once again prevailed.[75] *(Table)*

Besides conducting the redeployment of American forces, General Abrams helped to negotiate the withdrawal of the allied contingents. As the Americans departed, the Australian, New Zealand, Thai, and South Korean governments—all under varying degrees of domestic pressure to disengage—prepared to follow suit. The Nixon administration, through direct government-to-government diplomacy, and through lower-level contacts by Ambassador Bunker, Admiral McCain, and General Abrams, worked to keep allied soldiers in Vietnam as long as possible to support the South Vietnamese and maintain the image of a multinational anti-Communist effort. Abrams, besides assisting in the diplomatic campaign, worked out with the allied commanders and defense ministers withdrawal schedules for their forces and arrangements for the South Vietnamese to replace them. His efforts, and those of the administration, held the major allied contingents in place until the American drawdown reached the transitional force phase. The Australian, New Zealand, and Thai troops withdrew in increments, the bulk of them during 1971.[76]

Withdrawal of the large South Korean contingent became the subject of debate within the Nixon administration. When the Seoul government began planning for disengagement early in 1971, General Abrams, supported by Secretary Laird and the Joint Chiefs, advocated

[75] Msgs, Abrams MAC 7794 to McCain info Wheeler, 18 Jun 69; Wheeler JCS 09539 to McCain info Abrams, 1 Aug 69; Abrams MAC 10808 to McCain and Wheeler, 20 Aug 69; Abrams MAC 11001 to Wheeler info McCain, 23 Aug 69; Wheeler JCS 07344 to McCain and Abrams, 27 May 70; Abrams MAC 7837 to Westmoreland, 10 Jun 70; Westmoreland WDC 11742 to Abrams info McCain et al., 27 Jun 70. All in Abrams Papers, CMH. Historical Division, "Joint Chiefs of Staff and the War in Vietnam, 1969–1970," pp. 389–90, 490; MACV History, 1970, Supp., pp. 7–8.

[76] Msgs, Abrams MAC 4200 to Wheeler and McCain, 1 Apr 70; Abrams MAC 12395 to McCain info Moorer and Bunker, 14 Sep 70; Abrams MAC 13652 to Seith info McCain, 16 Oct 70; Abrams MAC 08017 to McCaffrey, 20 Jul 71. All in Abrams Papers, CMH. Msg, Bunker SGN 12242 to Sec State, 30 Jul 70, box 148, NSC files, Nixon Papers, NARA. MACV, Force Planning Synopsis, pp. 261–63, 358, 395, 422; MACV History, 1970, vol. 1, ch. 4, pp. 34, 37–38; ibid., 1971, vol. 2, an. F, p. F–15.

TABLE—U.S. TROOP REDEPLOYMENTS

Increment	Date	Army Reduction	Air Force Reduction	Navy Reduction	Marine Corps Reduction	Total Reduction	Remaining (549,500)[1]
I........	Jul–Aug 69	15,712	(+321)	1,222	8,387	25,000	524,500
II........	Sep–Dec 69	14,092	2,532	5,412	18,464	40,500	484,000
III........	Feb–Apr 70	29,396	5,614	2,110	12,880	50,000	434,000
IV	Jul–Oct 70	15,932	7,362	9,666	17,040	50,000	384,000
V	Oct–Dec 70	38,054	613	1,328	5	40,000	344,000
VI	Jan–Apr 71	41,848	1,194	5,600	11,358	60,000	284,000
VII......	May–Jun 71	15,030	164	516	13,590	29,300	254,700
VIII......	Jul–Sep 71	21,769	5,700	1,122	109	28,700	226,000
IX	Sep–Nov 71	35,000	5,600	1,400	0	42,000	184,000
X........	Dec 71–Jan 72	36,718	6,265	2,017	0	45,000	139,000
XI	Feb–Apr 72	58,096	8,765	4,032	(+893)	70,000	69,000
XII......	May–Jun 72	14,552	4,884	526	38	20,000	49,000
XIII	Jul–Aug 72	8,484	1,354	155	7	10,000	39,000
XIV.....	Sep–Nov 72	7,282	3,208	603	907	12,000	27,000
Total		351,965	52,934	35,709	81,892	522,500	

[1] Highest authorized U.S. military strength, 1968–69.
Source: Army Activities Report: SE Asia, 8 Nov 72, pp. 4–5, CMH.

rapid removal of the Koreans' two army divisions and marine brigade. Abrams argued that the $300 million the United States was spending annually to support the Koreans was not producing sufficient return in combat effectiveness and that the funds would be better used in modernizing the South Vietnamese forces. President Nixon and Dr. Kissinger, however, along with Secretary of State Rogers, favored retaining the Koreans as long as possible, since they constituted a ground force reserve in the endangered northern half of South Vietnam. In July, President Nixon decided to provide support for South Korean forces at least through 1972. After further negotiation with the Americans and South Vietnamese, the Koreans removed their marine brigade from I Corps late in 1971 in conjunction with the departure of the U.S. Marines. However, they agreed to keep their two infantry divisions in place to protect coastal areas of II Corps for at least another year.[77]

A Rear Guard Action

President Nixon's decisions during 1969 and the following two years amounted to a U.S. commitment to disengage from Vietnam. Even while it disengaged, however, the administration sought to buy enough time to weaken the enemy in South Vietnam, equip Saigon to carry on, and perhaps compel Hanoi to agree to an acceptable compromise settlement. President Nixon and his advisers had few illusions about the fragile balance they were trying to maintain, both in Southeast Asia and at home. Yet they saw no alternative except escalation, which might not work and at any event was politically impossible, and forcing the immediate capitulation of their South Vietnamese ally, which they considered strategically and morally unacceptable.[78]

Although the political maneuvers that attended Nixon's public announcements of the withdrawals were complex and confusing, the actual conduct of the redeployments was steady and methodical. Essentially, the administration followed the two-year schedule for removing combat forces that the Joint Chiefs and MACV had proposed in 1969. Then it allowed two more years for drawing down the residual support force to the level of a large assistance and advisory group. By announcing large withdrawals over long periods of time, Nixon both neutralized his domestic political opposition and provided himself and General Abrams with flexibility so that they could retain the maximum combat power as late in each redeployment increment as possible.

---

[77] Memo, Odeen, 25 Jan 71, sub: Vietnamization Meeting with Secretary Laird, folder 76; Memos, Odeen, 28 Apr 71, 1, 10, 15, 21, 25 Jun 71, 20 Jul 71, sub: Vietnamization Meeting with Secretary Laird, folder 77. All in Thayer Papers, CMH. Historical Division, "Joint Chiefs of Staff and the War in Vietnam, 1971–1973," pp. 168–74; MACV, Force Planning Synopsis, pp. 404, 406–07, 412–13, 416–18. Memo, Haig for Kissinger, 3 Feb 72, sub: Discussion between the President and Amb Bunker, box 158, NSC files, Nixon Papers, NARA. MACV History, 1970, vol. 1, ch. 4, p. 36.

[78] Kissinger, *White House Years*, p. 288, emphasizes the lack of acceptable alternatives to Vietnamization.

Initially pessimistic, in mid-June 1971 Abrams expressed to his senior subordinates general satisfaction with the pace of redeployments to that point, declaring that withdrawals were going "fast enough that [the South Vietnamese] are stretching and not so fast that they feel abandoned." [79]

General Abrams, along with Admiral McCain and the Joint Chiefs of Staff, exercised at best limited influence on the development of President Nixon's overall Vietnamization policy. Domestic political considerations, congressional pressures, budgetary limitations, and intra-administration maneuvering, more than military advice, determined Nixon's course. As a military adviser, General Abrams played an ambivalent role. Especially during the first two years of redeployment, he warned of risks, advocated deliberation and cut-and-try, and sought to postpone the loss of his American combat power. Yet privately, according to one of his chief withdrawal planners, Abrams realized almost from the start that "we were going to get out completely" and that all he could do was try to see that the United States disengaged in an orderly fashion and did not "completely bugout on the Vietnamese and leave them flat and unable to defend themselves"—concerns Abrams shared with Nixon and Kissinger. Abrams and his superiors harbored, and expressed, deep doubt that Laird's goal of South Vietnamese military self-sufficiency could be achieved. Nevertheless, when pressed, they produced the necessary plans along with explanations of why they would work and periodic reports of progress. As did Westmoreland before him, Abrams loyally supported and carried out administration strategy, never publicly or privately challenging its basic assumptions.[80]

For the Military Assistance Command, the war became an extended rear guard action. General Abrams pursued his "one war" strategy while presiding over an inexorable diminution of his American combat power, a diminution he sought to slow as much as possible and to manage to the maximum military advantage of his own forces and those of South Vietnam, but which he could not stop. At the same time, he tried to prepare the South Vietnamese armed forces as well as time permitted to assume the entire burden of the war. In the end, Abrams, like the administration he served, saw no real alternative but to do the best he could under the prevailing conditions to ensure an orderly American disengagement and give the South Vietnamese the best possible chance for survival.

---

[79] Notes on Senior Officers Conference, 10–11 Jun 71, folder 2001, MACV Collection, MHI.

[80] First quotation is from Starry Interv, 14 Dec 76, pp. 35–36, 39–40. A typical Abrams warning of the risks of rapid Vietnamization is in MACV History, 1970, Supp., pp. 11–12. Kissinger, *White House Years*, pp. 34–35, observes that senior military officers "rarely challenge the Commander-in-Chief; they seek for excuses to support, not to oppose him."

6

MACV Headquarters: The Drawdown

By the time troop withdrawals and Vietnamization began, the major interservice and interagency conflicts over management of the American effort in South Vietnam had been resolved. MACV's headquarters organization and command structure, the products of evolution and improvisation to meet changing circumstances, had matured and were functioning effectively. The command's relationships with Pacific Command and the Joint Chiefs of Staff were well defined and stable. MACV had accumulated a large database of intelligence about the enemy and experience in fighting him; many of the senior leaders under Abrams were veterans of previous command and staff tours in Vietnam. With minimal organizational change, MACV managed troop redeployments and Vietnamization, even as it continued military and pacification operations in South Vietnam, waged expanding air and ground campaigns in Laos and Cambodia, and prepared for its own ultimate reduction to an advisory group.

Command Relationships under Abrams

When General Abrams took command in Saigon in mid-1968, he was little known to the American public but was already one of the U.S. Army's most highly respected leaders. Abrams had made a brilliant record in World War II commanding armor units in the drive across France and Germany; his tanks led the relief force into Bastogne during the battle of the Ardennes. After the war, he rose steadily through division and corps commands and important staff assignments. In the early 1960s, as a major general and assistant deputy chief of staff for operations for civil affairs, Abrams directed Army forces during civil disturbances over racial integration at the University of Mississippi and Montgomery, Alabama; he displayed impressive ability in dealing with tense, politically charged situations. As vice chief of staff, he oversaw the Army's Vietnam buildup before going to Military Assistance Command as General Westmoreland's deputy and ultimate successor.[1]

---

[1] Abrams' life and career are traced in Sorley, *Thunderbolt*.

Maj. Gen. John Norton (right) *and General Abrams*

A West Point classmate of Westmoreland, Abrams—"Abe" to friends and close associates—was a study in contrast to his predecessor in personality and leadership style. Whereas Westmoreland was formal, reserved, and always perfectly turned out, Abrams cultivated a down-to-earth, unpretentious image. As one of his first acts as commander, U.S. Military Assistance Command, Vietnam, he replaced Westmoreland's suite of executive-style office furniture with a standard-issue gray steel desk, chairs, and conference table. His uniform always rumpled, usually with a cigar in his mouth, Abrams was blunt and at times profane in speech, given to volcanic, often staged, outbursts of temper. A devotee of good whiskey, he was a congenial host and raconteur. Civilian and military colleagues admired Abrams' solid integrity, and to many young officers he was an inspirational leader and example. His rough-hewn manner concealed a fondness for books and classical music and a mind able to move quickly to the essentials of a problem. Although Abrams made his career and combat reputation in armor and mechanized forces, his authorship of the "one war" concept attested to his grasp of the nature and requirements of the revolutionary conflict in Vietnam.[2]

Abrams gave everything he had to his job. He spent long hours in the office or visiting field commands and often stayed up most of the night in his quarters working on problems or awaiting late messages from Washington, where noon coincided with midnight in Saigon. Fifty-four years old when he took command, Abrams suffered during his tour from ulcers and pneumonia and in July 1970 went to Japan to have his gall bladder removed. Later that year, he collapsed, evidently from heat exhaustion, during a ceremony at Vung Tau and had to be hospitalized for a brief period. Despite occasional restorative visits to

---

[2] Abrams' personality is described in Davidson Interv, 30 Mar 82, sess. 1, pp. 13–14; Interv, Senior Officers Debriefing Program with Gen Andrew J. Goodpaster, 9 Jan 76, sec. 4, p. 65, MHI. See also the following interviews by the Abrams Project, MHI: Amb Samuel Berger, 17 May 77, pp. 1–2, 10, 13; Amb Ellsworth Bunker, 2 May 77, pp. 4–5; Col Ted Kanamine, n.d., pp. 6–8; Gen Walter T. Kerwin, 9 Apr 76, pp. 14–15; Maj Gen Elias C. Townsend, 26 Feb 76, p. 60.

his wife and youngest children in Bangkok, the strain of five uninterrupted years in Vietnam told on Abrams. A former MACV chief of staff recalled: "he would recuperate for a little bit locally . . . but he never got all the way back. It seemed to me like he was just constantly draining away." A member of Secretary Laird's staff reported in June 1971 that Abrams "looked very tired and as if he had the 'weight of the world' on his shoulders."[3]

Abrams made only gradual and marginal changes in the way American and allied forces were commanded and administered. While he had reservations about some aspects of the system he had inherited, Abrams realized that it was the product of a complex evolution and was shaped by political and diplomatic as well as strictly military considerations. Accordingly, he avoided any attempts at major revisions that might disrupt established compromises and balances of power. He concentrated on making the existing system work as well as possible.

A strong believer in an orderly chain of command, Abrams was incensed that every U.S. government agency in Vietnam maintained its own channel of communication with its Washington headquarters. Officers in the U.S. Embassy, U.S. Agency for International Development, and the Central Intelligence Agency habitually used these channels to pass on information or promote policies in conflict with those of MACV without the military headquarters having the opportunity to screen or respond to them. Making matters worse, in Abrams' view, junior members of these organizations took advantage of these communication links to transmit dissenting views to counterparts in Washington, who in turn saw to it that those views reached senior policymakers. The senior officials then sent queries to MACV, putting Abrams and his staff constantly "on the rebuttal." Abrams discovered that even within MACV, lower-ranking staff officers, notably in CORDS, regularly exchanged information with counterparts on the Joint Staff and in other Defense Department agencies, bypassing himself and CINCPAC.[4]

Abrams' indignation at these practices brought him into an early collision with Secretary of Defense Clifford. Early in June 1968, Clifford received a report from a junior civilian official, transmitted from the

[3] First quotation is from Townsend Interv, 26 Feb 76, p. 59. The second is from MFR, Odeen, sub: Vietnamization Meeting with Secretary Laird, 17 Jun 71, folder 77, Thayer Papers, CMH; in same collection, see MFR of 13 Oct 70, folder 76. Abrams' working methods are described in Townsend Interv, 26 Feb 76, pp. 59–60; and Interv, Abrams Project with Lt Gen Donald H. Cowles, 20 Dec 75, pp. 37–38, MHI. Abrams' health problems are described in Sorley, *Thunderbolt*, p. 296; Associated Press Dispatch, Vung Tau, Vietnam, 30 Sep 70, box 149, NSC files, Nixon Papers, NARA; and Interv, Lt. Col Douglas R. Burgess with Gen Bruce Palmer, 29 May 75, the Abrams Project, p. 23, MHI.

[4] Interv, Abrams Project with Lt Gen Charles A. Corcoran, 20 Dec 75, pp. 22, 26–27, MHI (hereafter cited as Corcoran Interv). Quotation is from Msg, Abrams MAC 7404 to Wheeler, 5 Jun 68, Papers of Clark Clifford, box 5, Abrams, Creighton (1), LBJL.

U.S. Embassy through the State Department, which described the devastation inflicted by American firepower in Cholon, Saigon's Chinese district, during the enemy's May offensive. Responding to this report, as well as to news media accounts of the destruction, Clifford directed Abrams through Wheeler to make a study of the civilian casualty and property damage problem "on an urgent basis." Abrams answered by describing the study of urban tactics that MACV and the Joint General Staff already had under way and by recounting the tight restrictions that he had imposed on the use of American air and artillery in the Saigon area. He defended his forces' actions in Cholon, citing the tenacity of the enemy there and the ferocity of the fighting. Finally, he eloquently affirmed his own anguish at the suffering that the war inflicted on the innocent. Abrams went on, however, to protest at being placed on the defensive by queries based on raw information from lower-ranking personnel that had been passed to Washington without review by his own headquarters.

Although Abrams saw the issue as a chain-of-command problem, Clifford was angered by what he perceived as insubordination by the MACV commander. In a memorandum to General Wheeler, Clifford rejected the notion that responsible U.S. Embassy officers had to obtain military clearance before reporting matters of concern to the State Department. The secretary also asserted his own right to query the field commander on "a question of great concern" to himself and the president. In a veiled threat to remove Abrams, Clifford added that if the MACV commander had a contrary view, "it is essential we know this now." When he learned from Wheeler of Clifford's displeasure, Abrams perforce disavowed any claim to review communications between the U.S. Embassy and State Department. He reaffirmed his intention to modify his command's urban fighting tactics. Since Abrams and Clifford in fact were in agreement on the need for less destructive tactics, nothing further came of this exchange.[5]

Within his own command, Abrams kept on fighting the chain-of-command problem. Early in 1969, for example, he discovered that members of the CORDS staff were sending internal MACV reports directly to counterparts in the office of the Joint Chiefs of Staff chairman's Special Assistant for Counterinsurgency and Security Activities (SACSA) and receiving and answering directly inquiries from SACSA. Abrams at once ordered the MACV end of the channel shut down. Informing General Wheeler and Admiral McCain of his action, Abrams declared that he was "somewhat concerned about a lot of internal MACV reports being distributed like the 'shopping news' in Washington, bypassing CINCPAC in the process." If Wheeler, McCain, or the Joint Staff needed additional reports from MACV, Abrams promised, "you'll get instant response," but it would be furnished "within the overall chain of com-

---

[5] This incident is described in Hammond, *Military and the Media, 1968–1973*, pp. 28–30. See also Chaisson Diary, 4 Jun 68 [mislabeled 67], box 8, Chaisson Papers, Hoover Institution.

mand by those responsible for the activity concerned." Even more emphatically, during troop redeployment discussions, he reminded his superiors that "in these delicate times I respond only to the direction of the Chairman, CINCPAC, and the Ambassador. My staff will not respond to direction from staffs in Washington or Hawaii." Abrams had some success in disciplining communication to and from his own headquarters, but the multiple channels of the civilian agencies and even of his service components eluded his control. Like his predecessors, he had to work as best he could within the existing system.[6]

Abrams continued General Westmoreland's Saturday morning Weekly Intelligence Estimate Update (WIEU) conferences. Attended by the senior staff department heads, the component commanders, the deputy COMUSMACV, and the deputy for CORDS, with Ambassador Bunker or his deputy and the Saigon CIA station chief frequently sitting in, these meetings began with intelligence and operations briefings, which occasionally brought forth displays of Abrams' famous temper. Then followed discussion and decisions on various issues. As an innovation of his own, Abrams once a month enlarged the WIEU to include the I and II Field Force and III Marine Amphibious Force commanders and their G–2s and G–3s. Lt. Gen. Frank T. Mildren, deputy commander of U.S. Army, Vietnam, considered that these sessions "really did a lot for that theater. Everybody was oriented on where we were going, and had a complete briefing of what had happened the previous week, and what was expected to happen the following week."[7]

In addition to the WIEU, Abrams regularly held smaller meetings with component commanders or staff section heads on particular problems. Typically, Abrams, his deputy, and his chief of staff might gather in Abrams' quarters late in the evening to review the day's activities. Abrams delegated extensive administrative authority to his chief of staff, who drafted and dispatched most of Abrams' messages except those dealing with major assessments and policies; and he also allowed the chief of staff to select, with Abrams' approval, the senior MACV staff officers. As had Westmoreland, Abrams employed his staff and component and field commanders in extensive contingency planning and war-gaming. MACV headquarters, the service components, and the regional commands, for example, all participated in an elaborate

---

[6] Quotations are from Msgs, Abrams MAC 3996 and MAC 5760 to Wheeler and McCain, 29 Mar 69 and 29 Apr 70; see also Msg, Wheeler JCS 04506 to Abrams info McCain, 12 Apr 69; all in Abrams Papers. Interv, Abrams Project with Maj Gen Roderick Wetherill, 27 Jan 76, pp. 18–19, MHI (hereafter cited as Wetherill Interv).

[7] Msgs, Abrams MAC 9620 to Field Force and Component Cdrs, 17 Jul 68; Abrams MAC 4224 to Field Force and Component Cdrs, 4 Apr 69. Both in Abrams Papers, CMH. Weekly Intelligence Estimate Updates (WIEUs) are described in Davidson Interv, 30 Mar and 30 Jun 82, sess. 1, pp. 11–13; Berger Interv, 17 May 77, p. 5; Interv, Abrams Project with Lt Gen Michael S. Davison, 20 Feb 76, p. 27, MHI (hereafter cited as Davison Interv); and Interv with Lt Gen Frank T. Mildren, 24 Feb 76, the Abrams Project, p. 24, MHI. Final quotation is from Interv, Lt Col James T. Scott with Lt Gen Frank T. Mildren, Senior Officers Oral History Program, 1980, p. 254, MHI.

exercise late in 1971 to test the feasibility of redeployment OPLAN J208A.[8]

Following Westmoreland's precedent, Abrams insisted that his deputy COMUSMACV be an Army four-star general "fully qualified to take over from me." The four-star rank, Abrams believed, was necessary to give the deputy sufficient authority in a command replete with three-star generals and flag officers and with an ambassador as deputy for CORDS. Abrams' first deputy, General Goodpaster, spent much of his one-year tour observing and consulting at the Paris peace conference. General William B. Rosson, who succeeded Goodpaster in May 1969, possessed Vietnam experience dating back to the French war; he had served as MACV chief of staff during the 1965–66 American force buildup and commanded successively I Field Force and Provisional Corps. General Frederick C. Weyand, who replaced Rosson in August 1970 after a stint as military adviser to the U.S. delegation at Paris, also was a Vietnam veteran. He had commanded the 25th Division and the II Field Force under Westmoreland. Secretary Laird, in consultation with Abrams, selected Weyand as the man best qualified to replace Abrams if the MACV commander's health problems necessitated his relief. Weyand served as deputy COMUSMACV for two years before finally succeeding Abrams.[9]

General Abrams employed his deputies on a wide range of missions. General Rosson recalled that as Abrams' deputy, he received "no written guidance whatever." Instead, Abrams informed him that "I should be prepared at all times to take over for him should the situation require, and that I should consider myself his alter ego." Rosson in fact spent much of his time visiting the field and working on improvement and modernization of the South Vietnamese forces. General Weyand performed much the same functions, oversaw MACV support of Cambodia, and also eventually took over direction of CORDS.[10]

Abrams' outwardly cordial relations with Ambassador Komer, deputy COMUSMACV for CORDS, whom Abrams inherited from Westmoreland, concealed personal and institutional tensions. From the time Abrams and Komer arrived in Saigon in May 1967, the two strong-willed, outspoken men had resembled a pair of large bulls confined in a too-small pasture. The unconventional nature of

---

[8] Corcoran Interv, 1975, pp. 29–30; Cowles Interv, 20 Dec 75, pp. 20–25, 55–56; Exercise Briefing Presented to COMUSMACV 30 Oct 71 at WIEU, tab G, MACV Briefing Book no. 4, MACV Collection, MHI.

[9] Quotation is from Msg, Abrams MAC 1736 to Westmoreland, 8 Feb 69, Abrams Papers, CMH; in same collection, see also Msg, Abrams MAC 1878 to Westmoreland, 12 Feb 69. Memo, Haig for Kissinger, 20 Jul 70, sub: Personnel Changes in Saigon, box 148; Memo, Haig for Kissinger, 23 Jul 70, box 1002. Both in NSC files, Nixon Papers, NARA.

[10] Quotation is from Rosson Interv, 1981, pp. 416–17. Msgs, Abrams MAC 8347 to McCain info Wheeler, 29 Jun 69; Abrams MAC 11637 to Westmoreland, 27 Aug 70; Abrams MAC 15448 to McCain, 2 Dec 70. All in Abrams Papers, CMH. For General Weyand's takeover of CORDS, see below, p. 214.

Komer's organization, its assertions of independence from the rest of the MACV staff, and its frequent disregard of command channels, which provoked complaints from field force commanders, offended Abrams' sense of military order. Komer later observed that Abrams, "a surprisingly organization man as far as administration is concerned," viewed CORDS as "sort of an odd-ball outfit alien to the Army system." Abrams lost no time in indicating his dissatisfaction with the way Komer ran CORDS. Although Abrams and Komer worked together effectively to launch the Accelerated Pacification Campaign, when President Johnson offered Komer the American ambassadorship to Turkey, Komer accepted without hesitation. He left Vietnam in November 1968.[11]

William Colby
(Photograph taken in 1975 when he was director of the Central Intelligence Agency.)

Komer's replacement as head of CORDS was his personally selected deputy, Ambassador William E. Colby. A long-term CIA functionary, Colby had spent the previous year understudying Komer as assistant chief of staff for CORDS, the second-ranking man in the organization. Colby, whose operating style was less abrasive and unorthodox than Komer's and who lacked Komer's White House connections, during nearly three years in his position established a harmonious working relationship with the MACV staff, at some cost to CORDS independence. General Abrams, for example, severed CORDS' direct reporting channel to Washington and required CORDS staff members on inspection trips in the field to communicate with their Saigon headquarters through the military chain of command. Such changes led one veteran pacification practitioner to characterize the status of CORDS under Abrams as "a long, sad story of general loss of power

[11] Quotations are from interview of Robert W. Komer in *Organization and Management of the New Model Pacification Program, 1966–1968* (Rand Corporation Doc no. D(L)-20104-ARPA, 7 May 70), p. 92, copy in CMH; see also pp. 91, 192. Other indications of Abrams-Komer friction can be found in Ltr, Komer to Abrams, 28 Jul 68, Chronological File, Komer (1968), DepCORDS files, CMH; and Kerwin Interv, 9 Apr 76, p. 12; Townsend Interv, 26 Feb 76, p. 48; and Wetherill Interv, 27 Jan 76, pp. 31–33. For field force complaints, see Msgs, Peers NHT 1279 to Wetherill, 3 Sep 68; and Peers NHT 2040 to Goodpaster, 6 Dec 68; William R. Peers Papers, MHI.

and influence. . . ." On the positive side, Abrams defended the basic CORDS principle of single management of pacification and helped Ambassador Bunker block efforts by other government agencies to split off some CORDS functions. In keeping with his "one war" concept, he treated pacification as a primary objective of MACV and enjoined military commanders to coordinate their operations closely with the province and district CORDS teams.[12]

Single management of pacification thus survived under Abrams, and so did single management of MACV's fixed-wing airpower. The departure in mid-1968 of General Westmoreland, Admiral Sharp, and General Momyer raised Marine leaders' hopes that Abrams and the new CINCPAC, Admiral McCain, might be more receptive to the Corps' arguments against the system. Those hopes were quickly dashed. General Abrams, like other Army commanders in Vietnam, believed that single management provided more responsive Air Force support to Army ground units. More broadly, Abrams regarded airpower as his principal theater reserve, which he must control as "one great pool." "The air," Abrams declared, "is really a powerful weapon, but to use this power effectively, you need both integrated all-source intelligence and an integrated all-source reaction." In September 1968, both Abrams and McCain affirmed their intention to retain single management; and the Defense Department, Marine appeals to the Joint Chiefs notwithstanding, accepted its field commanders' judgment. The Marine Corps commandant continued to agitate, but for practical purposes the question was decided.[13]

While the doctrinal dispute persisted, Air Force and Marine commanders in Vietnam developed practical, harmonious working relations under which the marines gradually regained in practice much of what they had lost in principle. Momyer's successors at Seventh Air Force, Generals George S. Brown and Lucius D. Clay, Jr., took a pragmatic rather than a doctrinaire approach to the problem, as did their counterparts at III Marine Amphibious Force and the 1st Marine Aircraft Wing. Typically, Lt. Gen. Keith B. McCutcheon, a veteran Marine aviator who commanded III Marine Amphibious Force during most of 1970, declared: "single management is here, and the way to beat it is to join it and outmanage them." By the time the last Marine aircraft

---

[12] Quotation is from Richard A. Hunt, *Pacification: The American Struggle for Vietnam's Hearts and Minds* (Boulder, Colo.: Westview Press, 1995), pp. 180–81; see also pp. 214 and 273–74. Rosson Interv, 1981, pp. 432–36, describes his working relations with Colby. Abrams' support for CORDS is illustrated in Msgs, Abrams MAC 12111 to Field Force Cdrs and Sr Adviser IV Corps, 7 Sep 68; and Abrams MAC 4336 to McCain et al., 6 Apr 69. Both in Abrams Papers, CMH.

[13] Quotations are from MFR, Col Elizabeth H. Branch, 20 Apr 71, sub: COMUSMACV Remarks in Connection with History Briefing, in folder, same title, MACV Collection, MHI; and MACV History, 1970, vol. 1, pp. 6–19. Msgs, CG FMFPAC to CMC, 16 and 22 Jun 68; CG III MAF to CMC and CG FMFPAC, 16 Sep 68. Both in HQMC Msg files, MCHC. McCutcheon to Quilter, 15 Jul 68, box 20, McCutcheon Papers, MCHC. McCutcheon, Draft of CMC Memo for CJCS, 14 Nov 68, sub: Single Management System, McCutcheon folder, MFRs, MCHC. Msg, McCain to Abrams info Wheeler and Chapman, 7 Sep 68, Abrams Papers, CMH.

Admiral McCain and General Abrams

squadrons left Vietnam in mid-1971, McCutcheon and his successors, by manipulating technicalities of the system, had recovered control of a large proportion of their sorties. They also had inserted wording in a revision of MACV's basic air command directive that reaffirmed the unity of the Marine air-ground team even under single management. On their side, the Seventh Air Force commanders tolerated the marines' encroachments because the marines invariably cooperated in genuine emergencies, and because a general decline in the level of combat reduced MACV's need to borrow the marines' jets.[14]

Under Abrams as under Westmoreland, single management of airpower meant management by COMUSMACV, not the Air Force component commander. From the bombing halt of November 1968 until the resumption of air attacks on North Vietnam in spring 1972, Abrams directed a unified Southeast Asia air war, including aerial reconnaissance of southern North Vietnam and, in conjunction with the ambassador in Vientiane, bombing of the Ho Chi Minh Trail and the Plain of Jars in Laos. He also nominated targets to Washington for the secret B–52 strikes on enemy base areas in Cambodia. To the continuing displeasure of the Seventh Air Force, Abrams kept the crucial decisions on

---

[14] The evolution of single management is recounted in Cosmas and Murray, *U.S. Marines in Vietnam, 1970–1971*, pp. 273–79; quotation from McCutcheon is on pp. 275–76 and that from the commandant is on p. 278. See also Interv, Project CORONA HARVEST with Gen George S. Brown, 19–20 Oct 70, pp. 17–18, AFCHO (hereafter cited as Brown Interv).

targeting and allocation of resources in his own hands and those of his Army-dominated MACV staff, with the Air Force headquarters limited to nominating targets and carrying out the missions. He personally supervised targeting of the B–52s, whose importance as MACV's mobile reserve increased as American ground strength dwindled. As General Brown acknowledged, "the chief targeteer was one General Abrams, and to try and take it away from him . . . would have been like taking his right arm."[15]

General Abrams retained his second "hat" as Commanding General, U.S. Army, Vietnam; although he delegated most Army logistical and administrative matters to his deputy commanding generals of USARV, successively Lt. Gens. Mildren and William J. McCaffrey. Abrams claimed late in 1971 that he held onto the USARV command primarily because "I wanted control over assignment of General Officers." He personally reviewed and approved all assignments and reassignments of Army generals in Vietnam and exercised a strong influence over which generals the Department of the Army sent to his command. As the Army's internal problems of race, drugs, and discipline intensified during the withdrawal, Abrams also perforce involved himself in a series of politically sensitive cases. On all Army matters, he dealt with his former Vietnam superior, General Westmoreland, the Army chief of staff. Westmoreland, isolated and all but ignored in the Nixon administration because the president regarded him as Johnson's general, scrupulously avoided interfering in operations in Vietnam; and he usually deferred to Abrams' wishes on officer assignments to MACV and USARV.[16]

Abrams' relationship to U.S. Army, Pacific (USARPAC), the Pacific Command's Army component headquarters, at times was contentious. MACV's Army component was under the command of USARPAC for all except operational matters and depended on the Honolulu headquarters for administrative and logistical support. Abrams, however, considered USARPAC an unnecessary link in his line of communications to the Department of the Army, and he resented the USARPAC commander's frequent visits to Vietnam and occasional attempts to

[15] Wayne Thompson, "From Rolling Thunder to Linebacker: The Air War over North Vietnam, 1966–1973" (Draft MS [Washington, D.C.:], Office of Air Force History, 1995), ch. 6, pp. 17–18; MACV History, 1970, vol. 1, ch. 6, p. 19. Msgs, Abrams MAC 4153 to McCain and Wheeler, 2 Apr 69; Abrams MAC 13410 to McCain and Wheeler, 16 Oct 69. All in Abrams Papers, CMH. Cowles Interv, 20 Dec 75, pp. 31–32; Townsend Interv, 26 Feb 76, p. 41; Interv, Marine Corps Historical Program with Lt Gen John N. McLaughlin, USMC, 1980, pp. 21–22, 31–32, MCHC (hereafter cited as McLaughlin Interv). Quotation is from Brown Interv, 19–20 Oct 70, pp. 37–40.

[16] Quotation is from MFR, Cdr Peter K. Fitzwilliam, USN, 23 Aug 71, sub: Briefing to Command Group and General Staff, in folder, Briefing to Command Group and General Staff—Significant Impacts MACV Transition to VAC Hqs . . . , MACV Collection, MHI. Msgs, Abrams MAC 8822 to Mildren, 2 Jul 68; Abrams MAC 5806 to Maj Gen Charles M. Gettys, 15 Jun 71; Abrams Papers, CMH; Cowles Interv, 20 Dec 75, p. 66. Kerwin Interv, 9 Apr 76, pp. 2–3. Mildren Interv, 24 Feb 76, pp. 8–13, 22–23. Westmoreland's situation and relationship with Abrams are described in Kissinger, *White House Years*, pp. 1004–05; and Palmer Interv, 29 May 75, p. 24.

Admiral Zumwalt
(Photograph taken in 1970 when we was Chief of Naval Operations.)

intervene in areas that Abrams believed were in the purview of MACV. General Mildren recalled that when General Ralph E. Haines, the USARPAC commander, visited USARV, Abrams treated him with bare courtesy. At conferences, Abrams "would cut [Haines] off half the time. . . . [He] just didn't want him interfering."[17]

Abrams exercised more distant supervision of his Navy and Air Force service components. In 1968, the Navy, with the approval of the Joint Chiefs, CINCPAC, and COMUSMACV, upgraded the post of commander Naval Forces, Vietnam (NAVFORV) from a rear admiral to a vice admiral. The first incumbent in that rank, Vice Adm. Elmo R. Zumwalt, enhanced the status of his command by gaining direct access to General Abrams, whereas his predecessors had had to deal entirely through the MACV chief of staff. Zumwalt further strengthened his position with Abrams by improving NAVFORV's riverine operations and aggressively building up the Vietnamese Navy. Abrams interfered little in the internal workings of NAVFORV and the Seventh Air Force. His only instruction to General John D. Lavelle when Lavelle took over operation of Seventh Air Force in September 1971 was to run his air force and resolve a dispute between the Seventh Air Force and MACV intelligence staffs. The Navy, Air Force, and Marine Corps routinely sought Abrams' approval when they changed component commanders and their principal officers on the MACV staff. Abrams as regularly accepted their nominees.[18]

---

[17] Mildren Interv, 24 Feb 76, pp. 26–27. See also Palmer Interv, 29 May 75, p. 24.

[18] McLaughlin Interv, 1980, p. 40. Zumwalt's achievements are summarized in Edward J. Marolda, *By Sea, Air, and Land: An Illustrated History of the U.S. Navy and the War in Southeast Asia* (Washington, D.C.: Naval Historical Center, Department of the Navy, 1994), ch. 4. Abrams' instructions to Lavelle are recounted in USAF Oral History Interv, Lt Col John N. Nick, Jr., with Gen John D. Lavelle, 17–24 Apr 78, AFCHO. Msgs, Wheeler JCS 7221 to Abrams info Sharp, 29 Jun 68; CMC to COMUSMACV, 11 Feb 69; Ryan to McCain and Abrams, 24 Apr 70; Lt Gen Robert J. Dixon, Commander, USAF Military Personnel Center, to McCain, Abrams, and Nazzaro, 8 Apr 71; Abrams MAC 03643 to Dixon and McCain, 9 Apr 71, all in Abrams Papers, CMH, are examples of Abrams' dealing with Navy and Air Force command matters.

General Abrams controlled his U.S. combat forces through MACV's established regional commands. In I Corps, the III Marine Amphibious Force directed operations with XXIV Corps, as Provisional Corps had been renamed in August 1968, subordinate to it. The relationship was reversed in March 1970, when the XXIV Corps became the senior American headquarters with III Marine Amphibious Force under it controlling the remaining marines, who were concentrated in Quang Nam Province. In II and III Corps respectively, the I and II Field Forces continued in operation. In IV Corps, the Delta Military Assistance Command, established in April 1969, oversaw the few American units supporting the South Vietnamese Army. The large III Marine Amphibious Force, XXIV Corps, and field force headquarters had matured into what Abrams called "a reproduction in miniature of MACV with a similar CORDS setup but without component commands."[19]

Abrams delegated to his regional commanders much of the planning and conduct of operations, including such politically sensitive ones as the 1970 Cambodian incursions. He also involved them extensively in redeployment planning, pacification, and the improvement and modernization of the South Vietnamese forces. Abrams took pains to protect his field commanders from the flood of inquiries and suggestions from Washington that accompanied every major operation or crisis. Lt. Gen. James W. Sutherland, Jr., who commanded XXIV Corps, recalled: "He shielded us and protected us. He absorbed all of it." To give guidance to his commanders, Abrams used the same devices Westmoreland had used—annual and quarterly combined campaign plans, occasional special directives, periodic commanders' conferences, and frequent visits to their headquarters. On his field trips, Abrams received situation briefings from his commanders and gave operational direction. He also took every opportunity to see and be with his soldiers in their camps and firebases.[20]

Under Abrams, the Military Assistance Command's relationships with the South Vietnamese and allied forces did not change. General Abrams, like Westmoreland before him, understood the political imperatives that dictated "cooperation and coordination" between his forces and the Republic of Vietnam Armed Forces rather than combined command. President Nixon's Vietnamization policy made

---

[19] Quotation is from Memo, Charles B. MacDonald for SJS MACV, 15 Apr 69, sub: Luncheon Meeting with COMUSMACV, in folder, same title, MACV Collection, MHI; Maj. Gen. George S. Eckhardt, *Command and Control, 1950–1969*, Vietnam Studies (Washington, D.C.: Department of the Army, 1974) p. 81; I FFV Organization and Functions Manual, 2 Mar 69, Peers Papers, MHI.

[20] Quotation is from Interv, Abrams Project with Lt Gen James W. Sutherland, n.d., p. 37, MHI, see also pp. 23–24 (hereafter cited as Sutherland Interv). Corcoran Interv, 1975, pp. 69–71; Davison Interv, 20 Feb 76, pp. 17–18, 23–25; Kerwin Interv, 9 Apr 76, pp. 3–4; Wetherill Interv, 27 Jan 76, pp. 31, 34. Significance of campaign plans is noted in Lt Gen Arthur S. Collins, Jr, CG I FFV, Debriefing Report, 7 Jan 71, p. 1, Arthur S. Collins Papers, MHI. For other examples of operational guidance, see MACV History, 1969, vol. 1, ch. 2, p. 14; Msg, Peers NHT 933 to Abrams, 6 Jul 68, Peers Papers, MHI; and the Abrams Message files, Abrams Papers, CMH.

those imperatives all the more compelling. During his year as deputy COMUSMACV, Abrams had worked closely with the South Vietnamese military. He understood well its strengths and weaknesses and had developed rapport with its leaders, including his direct counterpart, General Vien, chief of the Joint General Staff, with whom Abrams conferred regularly. Abrams, as the highest level American adviser to the RVNAF, labored diligently to persuade his allies to correct their many deficiencies; but, like his predecessors, he found the South Vietnamese hard to move. Unlike Westmoreland, he at least had the advantage of a stable government and high command with which to work. Abrams dealt with the South Koreans, Thais, Australians, and New Zealanders through the American field force commanders and through the MACV Free World Military Assistance Office until those contingents redeployed.[21]

As with the South Vietnamese government, Abrams enjoyed the advantage of stability at the head of the U.S. mission. Ambassador Ellsworth Bunker, who came out to Vietnam with Abrams in May 1967, remained at his post until after the cease-fire agreement in early 1973. The two theoretically coordinate directors of the American effort worked together closely and continuously. Abrams was a full member of Bunker's mission council, which brought together the heads of all the U.S. agencies in Vietnam, and regularly attended the smaller working luncheons Bunker held with his most senior advisers. Bunker for his part usually came to Abrams' Saturday morning Weekly Intelligence Estimate Updates. The two men regularly conferred together with President Thieu, although Bunker relieved Abrams of much of the burden Westmoreland had borne of overseeing South Vietnamese political affairs; and they prepared joint assessments and policy papers for the administration in Washington.[22]

Abrams and Bunker held each other in the highest personal esteem and generally were in agreement on policy. The MACV commander instructed his staff that "Mr. Bunker was the senior United States representative in Vietnam, and we would defer to Mr. Bunker under any and all circumstances." Abrams cleared all his major actions and messages with the ambassador, and Bunker did the same with him. This mutual confidence did not extend to the rest of the civilian side of the mission. Since Bunker shared the military view on critical issues,

---

[21] The combined command issue came up again in February 1968, to the same conclusion; see MACV History, 1968, vol. 1, pp. 221–22, and Msg, Sharp to Westmoreland, 14 Feb 68, Westmoreland Message files, Feb 68, CMH. A former MACV J–3 and chief of staff recalls Abrams' views in Cowles Interv, 20 Dec 75, pp. 30–31. Abrams' advantages and difficulties as an adviser are described in Sorley, *Thunderbolt*, pp. 254–56, and Clarke, *Final Years*, pp. 361–62, 507.

[22] The mission council is described in MACV History, 1970, vol. 1, ch. 4, p. 3. Abrams' relationship to the ambassador is recounted in Bunker Interv, 2 May 77, pp. 3–4; and Berger Interv, 17 May 77, p. 14. Msgs, Abrams MAC 17004 to Wheeler and McCain, 12 Dec 68; and Abrams MAC 7753 to Moorer and McCain, 8 Jun 70, both in Abrams Papers, CMH, describe typical Abrams meetings with Thieu.

General Abrams with General Vien

for example the Cambodian bombing, to a greater degree than many of his State Department colleagues, he and Abrams frequently worked around what Abrams called the "weak side of [the] mission." Aware of this, some mission civilians complained that Bunker depended more heavily on Abrams and MACV for information and advice than he did on his embassy staff.[23]

Under Abrams, the Military Assistance Command remained a subordinate unified headquarters reporting to Admiral McCain, CINCPAC. On the doctrinal level, Abrams shared the view, widespread in the Army, that CINCPAC was an unnecessary link in the chain of command to Southeast Asia. In practice, he and Admiral McCain maintained a close, friendly working relationship facilitated by their common

---

[23] First quotation is from Cowles Interv, 20 Dec 75, pp. 28–29. See also Bunker Interv, 2 May 77, pp. 15–16; Corcoran Interv, 20 Dec 75, pp. 22–23, 25–26; Townsend Interv, 26 Feb 76, p. 45; and Rosson Interv, 1981, p. 440. Abrams describes his working relations with the embassy in Msg, MAC 11780 to Wheeler and McCain, 31 Aug 68, Abrams Papers, CMH. Second quotation is from Msg, Abrams MAC 15485 to Wheeler and McCain, 30 Nov 69, Abrams Papers, CMH. For a civilian view, see Interv, Foreign Affairs Oral History Program with Robert A. Lincoln, 1989, pp. 7–8 (hereafter cited as Lincoln Interv) in Charles S. Kennedy, comp., "A Vietnam Reader: Selections from Oral Histories of the Foreign Affairs Oral History Program" (MS, Foreign Affairs Oral History Program, Georgetown University, 1993).

penchant for cigar smoking and plain speaking. The end of ROLLING THUNDER removed McCain from the day-to-day conduct of operations in Indochina until the last year of the war. As had his predecessor, Admiral Sharp, McCain allowed COMUSMACV a free hand, subject to dictates from higher authority, to fight the war in South Vietnam and its environs; he and his staff concentrated on supporting MACV and interpreting its needs to the Joint Chiefs and the Defense Department. They also helped coordinate support for the South Vietnamese force buildup and did much of the detailed logistical planning for the successive American troop withdrawals. Abrams and McCain took pains to maintain a united front on policy matters. They coordinated all their assessments and staff studies and kept up a continuous exchange of information. On his frequent visits to MACV, McCain received intelligence and operations briefings, often attended Abrams' WIEUs and Ambassador Bunker's mission council meetings, and closeted himself with Abrams to talk over problems amid clouds of cigar smoke.[24]

From CINCPAC, the chain of command ran to the secretary of defense and ultimately the president. Secretary Laird communicated with Abrams through the Joint Chiefs of Staff chairman but also contacted him directly through separate message channels and secure telephone calls. On his periodic visits to South Vietnam, Laird, who developed a close personal rapport with Abrams, always reserved time for private talks with the MACV commander. Throughout their association, Abrams supported Laird as loyally as the conflicting demands of the administration allowed. Laird, on his part, consistently expressed confidence in Abrams, whose approach to Vietnamization the secretary considered "completely in line" with his own, and regularly praised his leadership in memoranda to President Nixon. General Wheeler, who served as Joint Chiefs of Staff chairman until July 1970, and his successor, Admiral Thomas H. Moorer, kept up the established practice of addressing their messages on policy matters simultaneously to McCain and Abrams. The two chairmen regularly sought to orchestrate MACV and CINCPAC responses on major issues so as to present a unified military position to Secretary Laird and President Nixon.[25]

[24] Pacific command relationships are diagrammed in MACV History, 1970, vol. 1, ch. 4, p. 2. Interv, Abrams Project with Adm John S. McCain, Jr, n.d., passim, MHI, describes his working relationship with Abrams. See also the following interviews, all in the Abrams Project: Cowles, 20 Dec 75, pp. 25–26, 50–51; Davison, 20 Feb 76, pp. 13–14; Kerwin, 9 Apr 76, pp. 26–27; Mildren, 24 Feb 76, pp. 26–27; Townsend, 26 Feb 76, pp. 46–47; and Palmer, 29 May 75, p. 24. Msgs, McCain to Abrams, 14 Aug 68, 1 Mar 69, 5 Dec 69; Abrams MAC 10994 to McCain info Bunker, 15 Aug 68; Abrams MAC 15782 to McCain, 6 Dec 69; and Abrams MAC 5854 to McCain, 16 Jun 71, all in Abrams Papers illustrate aspects of the COMUSMACV and CINCPAC relationship.

[25] Abrams' relations with the Joint Chiefs of Staff chairmen can be followed in his Msg files, Abrams Papers, CMH. Admiral Moorer's working methods and dealings with Abrams are described in Walter Poole, "Responding to the North Vietnamese Offensive, Spring 1972" (MS [Washington, D.C.]: Joint History Office, 1997), pp. 1–3 and passim. Kissinger, *White House Years*, pp. 34–36, provides characterizations of Wheeler and Moorer. Laird quotation is from MFR, Phil Odeen, sub: Vietnamization Meeting with Secretary Laird, 27 May 70, folder 75, Thayer Papers, CMH; see also MFR of 15 Jun 71,

Admiral Moorer and President Nixon

General Abrams' relationships with the highest national command authority were shaped by the often Byzantine internal workings of President Nixon's administration. When he entered office, Nixon established a foreign policy-making structure centered on a reorganized National Security Council, to which interagency subcommittees transmitted studies and proposals through a Senior Review Group chaired by Dr. Kissinger, the national security adviser. In emergencies, Nixon convened a Washington Special Action Group of senior White House, State Department, CIA, and Defense officials to coordinate policy and review contingency plans.[26]

In practice, Southeast Asia policy, as the maneuvering over redeployment decisions indicated, was the product of a constant tug-of-war between Nixon and Kissinger on the one hand and Secretary Laird on the other, with Secretary of State Rogers a weak third player. President Nixon distrusted the permanent civilian Defense, State,

folder 77, same collection. Typical of Laird's praise of Abrams is Memo, Laird for the President, 8 Nov 71, sub: Trip to Vietnam, Nov 2–8, 1971, box 158, NSC files, Nixon Papers, NARA.

[26] Nixon's foreign policy organization is described in Kissinger, *White House Years*, pp. 38–39, and Poole, "Responding to the North Vietnamese Offensive," p. 1. Typical proceedings of the Senior Review Group are in MFR, 24 Jan 72, sub: Senior Review Group Meeting, box 158, NSC files, Nixon Papers, NARA.

(Left to right) *Secretary of Defense Laird, Vice President Spiro T. Agnew, President-elect Nixon, and Secretary of State Rogers*

and CIA establishments, which he viewed as dominated by disloyal Democrats and left-wingers who wanted to cut and run in Vietnam. He and Kissinger also had less than full confidence in their senior uniformed military advisers, who they considered had lost most of their initiative and aggressiveness during years of carrying out policies in which they did not believe. Distrusting the bureaucracy, Nixon and Kissinger sought independent channels of information and analysis. In September 1969, for example, Kissinger secured establishment of an interagency Vietnam Special Studies Group under his direction to review periodically the state of pacification in South Vietnam. President Nixon, temperamentally adverse to personal confrontation, made his major decisions in such a way as to involve potential dissenters, such as Laird and Rogers, only after the course was irretrievably set. He restricted information so that disaffected State and Defense bureaucrats could not forestall action by leaks to the news media, which Nixon also considered his enemy.[27]

General Abrams' contacts with the administration initially were straightforward, but complication rapidly set in. During 1969 and 1970, Abrams, along with Ambassador Bunker and Admiral McCain, returned to the United States periodically to brief President Nixon and his senior advisers and receive instructions from them. Early in 1969, however, during the first discussions of B–52 strikes against the enemy bases in Cambodia, Nixon and Kissinger began communicating with Abrams and Bunker through Defense and CIA channels, bypassing the State Department. They continued this practice

[27] Nixon's working methods are described in Stephen E. Ambrose, *Nixon: The Triumph of a Politician, 1962–1972* (New York: Simon and Schuster, 1989), pp. 238–39, 410–12; and Kissinger, *White House Years*, pp. 11–12, 24–33, 264, 275–76. Laird's wide-ranging interest in the war can be followed in the MFRs of his Vietnamization meetings, folders 75–78, Thayer Papers, CMH. Illustrative of White House distrust of Laird is Memo, John R. Brown III for Kissinger, 14 Jan 70, and creation of the Vietnam Special Studies Group: NSDM 23, 16 Sep 69, sub: Vietnam Special Studies Group, both in box 118, NSC files, Nixon Papers, NARA. See also Hunt, *Pacification*, pp. 210–11.

the following year in the planning for the ground incursions into Cambodia, except this time they also cut Secretary Laird out of the circuit. Using CIA message channels, Kissinger with increasing frequency transmitted instructions and requests for assessments directly to Bunker and Abrams. This "Bunker channel" became the authoritative one for all sensitive policy directives. Nixon and Kissinger also employed Col., later Brig. Gen., Alexander M. Haig, Kissinger's military assistant, who made periodic visits to Vietnam, as a go-between to Abrams and Bunker. During the first two years of the administration, Abrams managed to retain the confidence of his several contending masters, primarily through maintaining the consistency of his own assessments and recommendations; but his relations with the administration became increasingly difficult and contentious as the war drew toward its complex conclusion.[28]

Changes in MACV Headquarters

When General Abrams took command, the Military Assistance Command headquarters and its associated agencies contained about 3,400 military and civilian personnel. About 2,000 of these were part of the MACV command group and general and special staffs. The rest belonged to the staffs of CORDS, the Studies and Observations Group, the Advanced Research Projects Agency unit, the Armed Forces Radio and Television Service, and the Joint U.S. Public Affairs Office. In both numbers and positions, the Army dominated the headquarters. Army officers and enlisted men accounted for about 60 percent of the total strength; Army officers headed four of the six general staff sections and most of the special staff agencies. Officers of other services held key positions, however. The Marines Corps, for example, continued to supply the deputy J–3 for operations, in charge of the Command Center.[29]

Roughly two-thirds of the headquarters personnel lived and worked at the main MACV complex at Tan Son Nhut Air Base and the rest in Saigon and Cholon. In August 1968, General Abrams and his senior officers relinquished their leased villas in the city for more secure centralized quarters in a newly constructed MACV General Officers' Trailer Park at the

---

[28] The following, all from the NSC files, Nixon Papers, NARA, illustrate the administration's interaction with Abrams: Memo, Haig for Kissinger, 13 Feb 69, sub: Discussions with Mr Laird . . . , box 104; Memo, Kissinger for the President, 9 May 69, sub: Talking Points for Use in Private Discussion with Gen Abrams, box 137; Memo, Kissinger for the President, 19 Dec 69, sub: Your Meeting with Gen Abrams, box 141; Msg, Haig WHS 0011 to Bunker, 31 Mar 70, box 410; Memo, Kissinger for the President, 26 Apr 70, sub: Meeting on Cambodia . . . , box 507; Msg Haig Saigon 572 to Kissinger, 21 May 70, box 1010; Memo, Kissinger for the President, 14 Feb 71, sub: Gen Abrams' Report on Laos Operation, box 081. See also Msg, Abrams MAC 9870 to McCain and Wheeler, 31 Jul 69, Abrams Papers, CMH.

[29] MACV History, 1971, vol. 1, ch. 8, p. 76, summarizes authorized headquarters strengths from 1969 to 1971; see also ibid., 1970, vol. 1, ch. 4, p. 9.

air base. Additional MACV personnel moved out of Saigon or ceased to go there for work and recreation during 1970–71. At the behest of President Nixon, who wanted to minimize American visibility in the capital as a sign of Vietnamization, the U.S. Embassy and MACV carried out Operation MOOSE (Move out of Saigon Expeditiously) II, a sequel to a similarly titled operation with the same purpose conducted during 1966–68. They closed down offices, bachelor officers' quarters, exchanges, and other facilities in the city and rerouted American military traffic around the outskirts.[30]

Except for general officers, the military personnel in MACV head-quarters served standard twelve-month tours (the marines served thirteen-month tours). General officers spent eighteen months on their initial Vietnam tours (twenty-four months if they moved their families to the Philippines or Thailand) and twelve months if they were on second or subsequent assignments. Their time could be split between headquarters duty and command, although General Abrams tried to ensure that command tours would last at least a year. In MACV headquarters, senior staff officers normally remained in their posts for about a year. The chiefs of intelligence (J–2) and communications (J–6) and some special staff officers stayed longer. Col. Robert M. Cook, the MACV inspector general, spent five years in his position.[31]

Like his predecessor, General Abrams had to cope with a steady stream of distinguished visitors. They included President Nixon, Secretary of Defense Laird, Secretary of State Rogers, and lesser administration officials on various missions, as well as congressional delegations and junketing political candidates. Like Westmoreland, General Abrams complained periodically about the strain the visitors imposed on his manpower and transportation resources; but, despite periodic efforts by Secretary Laird, the flow never stopped.[32]

The structure of the MACV staff underwent gradual incremental change. In May 1968, the chief of staff, General Kerwin, instituted a review of the MACV organization by the assistant chiefs of staff and chiefs of special staff agencies to identify and eliminate duplicate, overlapping, and conflicting functions. This effort resulted in some movement of tasks among directorates but no radical reorganization. Other changes followed, in response to new situations and requirements. Until late in the American withdrawal, however, the

[30] Ibid., 1968, vol. 2, ch. 12, pp. 805–06; ibid., 1969, vol. 3, ch. 14, pp. 24–26; ibid., 1970, vol. 2, ch. 9, p. 135; ibid., 1971, vol. 1, ch. 9, pp. 11–12. Memos, Nixon for Kissinger, 12 and 24 Nov 69; and Memo, Kissinger for Sec State, 18 Nov 69; box 140; Memo, Kissinger for the President, 23 Dec 69, sub: Reduction of American Presence in Saigon, box 141. All in NSC files, Nixon Papers, NARA.

[31] Msgs, Westmoreland WDC 8844 to Abrams, 27 May 69; Abrams MAC 6915 to Westmoreland, 31 May 69; Westmoreland WDC 100080 to Abrams, 17 Jun 69. All in Abrams Papers, CMH.

[32] MACV's handling of visitors can be followed in the Abrams Message files, Abrams Papers, CMH. Examples of concern with the burden are Msgs, Abrams MAC 1560 to Wheeler info Nazzaro, 4 Feb 69; Abrams MAC 9673 to Maj Gen Peterson info Sec Army Resor et al., 27 Jul 69; Abrams MAC 9870 to McCain and Wheeler, 31 Jul 69. All in Abrams Papers, CMH; and MFRs, Odeen, 4 Feb 71 and 7 Oct 71, sub: Vietnamization Meeting with Secretary Laird, folders 76 and 78, Thayer Papers, CMH.

basic structure consisted of the command group—COMUSMACV, his deputies, the chief of staff, the science adviser, the staff judge advocate, the inspector general, and the Office of Information; the general staff, which included the six J sections, the assistant chiefs of staff for CORDS and Military Assistance, and the comptroller; and the special staff—the provost marshal, adjutant general, chaplain, surgeon, construction director, training director, headquarters commandant, and Data Management Agency.[33]

The most important addition to the MACV staff was an Office of the Deputy Chief of Staff for Economic Affairs, headed by an Army brigadier general. Secretary Laird himself ordered the establishment of this agency out of concern that the American redeployment might have adverse effects on Vietnamese prices, wages, and employment that would "under-cut much of our military progress" in South Vietnam and that U.S. civilian agencies were not effectively addressing the problem. General Abrams, also aware of the economic problem, anticipated Laird. In July 1970, he organized an Economics Division in the MACV comptroller's office, with a staff of seven economics-trained officers and enlisted men drawn from MACV and USARV headquarters.[34]

The following month, Secretary Laird directed the Joint Chiefs and the Military Assistance Command to prepare plans for a MACV economics agency headed by a general officer and located high enough in the chain of command to have significant influence on policy. Laird and his assistants closely followed the development of the new agency and canvassed the services for economics-qualified officers to man it. On 17 September, after Laird approved his proposed plan, General Abrams established the Office of the Deputy Chief of Staff for Economic Affairs, which was built around the comptroller's Economics Division. To head the office, Abrams, after reviewing a list of service nominees, selected Army Brig. Gen. William W. Watkin, a former professor of geography at West Point who was already slated for a Vietnam command tour. Laird, after close scrutiny of Watkin's qualifications, approved the appointment.[35]

During the rest of 1970 and 1971, Watkin's office grew rapidly in size and influence. It acquired a staff of twenty-five, including eighteen professional economists whom Laird's office had combed out of the

---

[33] Memo, Kerwin for Distribution List, 7 May 68, sub: Review of HQ MACV Organization and Functions, with staff section responses, Reel 050, MACV Microfilms, MHI; MACV History, 1970, vol. 3, an. A, p. 3; Briefing, 23 Aug 71, sub: Significant Impacts, MACV Transition to VAC Hq, July 71–July 72, in folder, Briefing to Command Group and General Staff—Significant Impacts MACV Transition to VAC Hqs . . . , MACV Collection, MHI.

[34] Quotation is from MFR, Odeen, 11 Aug 70, sub: Vietnamization Meeting with Secretary Laird, folder 76, Thayer Papers, CMH; MACV History, 1970, vol. 2, ch. 9, p. 117.

[35] MACV History, 1970, vol. 2, ch. 9, p. 117. Msgs, Westmoreland WDC 15422 to Abrams, 21 Aug 70; Abrams MAC 12526 to McCain, 17 Sep 70; Dolvin MAC 12655 to Corcoran, 21 Sep 70. All in Abrams Papers, CMH. MFRs, Odeen, 17 Aug 70 and 4, 10, 18, 22, 24, 25 Sep 70, folder 76, Thayer Papers, CMH.

services, organized into branches for commerce, industry, and macroeconomic analysis. As Deputy Chief of Staff for Economic Affairs, General Watkin and his successor, Brig. Gen. John A. Wickham, advised General Abrams on South Vietnamese economic conditions and on the economic impacts of military plans and actions. His office prepared a quarterly report to the Joint Chiefs on economic aspects of Vietnamization, as well as special studies on how the American military could assist South Vietnamese industry, agriculture, and commerce. Working closely with the U.S. Agency for International Development and the U.S. Embassy, the Office of the Deputy Chief of Staff for Economic Affairs during 1971 helped develop and persuade President Thieu to implement a program of exchange rate and tariff reform; and it cooperated with mission efforts to curb inflation and promote economic development. Extending its efforts to the operations side, the Office of the Deputy Chief of Staff for Economic Affairs encouraged the South Vietnamese to use their armed forces to secure areas of commercial, agricultural, and industrial value. Partly as a result of the office's work, the allies' Combined Campaign Plan for 1972 for the first time included an economic annex.[36]

Other MACV staff directorates underwent internal adjustments of their subdivisions and functions. In the J–3 section, for example, General Abrams shifted short-range planning and the issuance of operation orders out of the Command Center, which under Westmoreland had all but supplanted the J–3 proper, to other divisions of J–3. Under a MACV Directive of 12 June 1969, the J–3, through his Psychological Operations Division, assumed the role of staff single manager of the command's psychological warfare activities, which previously had been divided among CORDS and other staff elements. In August 1970, the J–3 formed a Redeployment Control Group, chaired by the Deputy J–3 for Organization, Plans, and Requirements, to coordinate the headquarters' proliferating redeployment-related staff actions and conduct briefings on the status of the effort.[37]

As improvement and modernization of the South Vietnamese armed forces took center stage among MACV's missions, the headquarters centralized much of its advisory effort in the Office of the Assistant Chief of Staff for Military Assistance. Created in September 1967 and headed by an Army brigadier general, the office had a peak strength of sixty-six officers and enlisted men, organized into divisions for Plans and Force Structure, Organization and Programs, and Advisory Affairs. In 1968, the Office of the Assistant Chief of Staff for Military

---

[36] MACV History, 1970, vol. 2, ch. 9, pp. 117–19; ibid., 1971, vol. 1, ch. 8, pp. 84–86, 89–98. MFRs, Odeen, 14 Oct 70 and 4 Nov 70, folder 76; 10 Jun 71 and 18 Aug 71, folder 77; 13 Oct 71, folder 78, Thayer Papers, CMH.

[37] Townsend Interv, 26 Feb 76, pp. 38–41; McLaughlin Interv, 1980, pp. 21–24; Col Anthony Walker, USMC (Ret), Comments on Draft MS, Marine Corps Vietnam for 1970–71, 28 Mar 83, in 1970–71 Comment File, MCHC; MACV History, 1969, vol. 3, ch. 13, p. 5; MACV J–3 Historical Summary for Aug 70, 19 Sep 70, Reel 100, MACV Microfilms, MHI.

Assistance took over from J–3 supervision of the Army, Navy, and Air Force advisory groups. It managed service-funded military assistance to the RVNAF and did most of MACV's programming of equipment and supplies for the South Vietnamese forces. The Office of the Assistant Chief of Staff for Military Assistance exercised general staff supervision of the second major MACV advisory element, the ninety-five-man Training Directorate, which supported the RVNAF schools and training centers. In addition to those offices, every MACV directorate continued to advise and assist its Joint General Staff counterpart. As of 1970, some 390 members of the command group and the general and special staffs were performing advisory tasks.[38]

The Military Assistance Command headquarters by 1969 possessed an extensive, heavily automated reporting and analysis establishment. Its Data Management Agency split off from the J–3 section in July 1969 to become a separate staff element headed by an Army colonel who reported directly to the chief of staff. The agency, which reached a peak strength of eighty-nine officers and men in 1970, generated most of the headquarters' major statistical reports on its then state-of-the-art IBM 360/501 computer. Its products included the CORDS Hamlet Evaluation System reports and the Weekly Intelligence Estimate Update, as well as the detailed troop lists and movement schedules required for redeployment planning. The Data Management Agency served all headquarters agencies but the intelligence section, which had its own computer. As part of the World Wide Military Command and Control System for U.S. forces, it promulgated joint service data processing policies to MACV's subordinate commands. Its chief advised both COMUSMACV and the chief of the RVNAF Joint General Staff on data processing matters.[39]

Among the analysis components, the office of the science adviser, which General Westmoreland had established in 1966, underwent reduction in size and status. After an aborted empire-building attempt by the first incumbent of the position, Dr. William G. MacMillan, the MACV chief of staff in 1969 ordered a review of the office's functions. As a result of the review, MacMillan's successors, Dr. Nels F. Wikner and Mr. John E. Kirk, abandoned their predecessor's attempt to control all research, development, and testing within the command. They confined themselves to advising COMUSMACV on science and technology and supervising the Advanced Research Projects Agency unit in Vietnam. The Operations Directorate oversaw the activities of the

---

[38] MACV History, 1970, vol. 1, ch. 7, p. 64; ibid., 1971, vol. 1, ch. 8, p. 74; MACV, "One War," ch. 7, pp. 4, 49; Brown Interv, 19–20 Oct 70, pp. 86, 89; Briefing, Jul 71, sub: MACV Training Directorate, in MACV Training Directorate Jul 71 folder, MACV Collection, MHI.

[39] MACV General Order no. 3783, 4 Jul 69, Reel 046, MACV Microfilms, MHI; MACV History, 1970, vol. 2, ch. 9, pp. 146–47; ibid., 1971, vol. 2, ch. 10, pp. 53–55.

service component testing agencies, which retained primary responsibility for combat-related research and development.[40]

While the importance of the science adviser diminished, operations research and systems analysis flourished at various points in the headquarters. The MACV Operations Research/Systems Analysis Office, organized in September 1967, grew into an eighteen-man staff of military and civilian analysts and support personnel. Its head, an Army colonel, reported directly to the chief of staff. The MACV Operations Research/Systems Analysis Office provided study groups to examine particular problems assigned by Abrams and constituted "the focal point for information about on-going analysis work within the MACV staff and component commands." In addition to the MACV Operations Research/Systems Analysis Office, the J–3 section maintained its own combat analysis element. The science adviser, the component commands, and CORDS also conducted analytical studies in their own fields.[41]

General Abrams, although he commissioned and employed analytical studies, treated them with caution. He believed that analysis in a combat theater "must be directly responsive to the immediate needs of the commander—long range and highly theoretical studies should be done elsewhere." In this spirit, he tactfully rejected a Defense Department proposal for an elaborate new Vietnam analysis agency with branches in both Washington and Saigon. He bluntly asked General Wheeler to "short stop" an initiative by the Hudson Institute, a private think tank, to establish an advisory and analysis office in South Vietnam. Aware of the difficulty of collecting data in a combat zone, Abrams warned that "some of the effort now going into analysis is wasteful because the data is bad." He was inclined to dismiss study results if they conflicted with his own military judgment. In late 1968, he expressed hope that a planned quantitative analysis to determine future B–52 sortie rates would be used "solely in a supporting role" to his own forthcoming assessment based on "the military experience in the employment of this critical weapons system."[42]

Two perennial problems with MACV's reporting continued to be discussed but not solved: its large volume and its questionable reliability. Early in 1971, Secretary Laird asked his systems analysis office to suggest reports that MACV could discontinue as the command reduced

---

[40] Msgs, McCain to Abrams, 18 Aug 68; Abrams MAC 11903 to Wheeler, 3 Sep 68. Both in Abrams Papers. MACV History, 1969, vol. 3, ch. 12, pp. 3–7. The early years of the office are described in Cosmas, *Years of Escalation, 1962–1967*, pp. 293–94.

[41] The MACV systems analysis agency is described in Msg, Abrams MAC 9649 to Westmoreland, 17 Jul 68, Abrams Papers, CMH. Quotation is from that message. LORAPL Marshall Committee, MACV Strategic Objectives Plan, pp. 90–91, CMH.

[42] Quotations are from Msgs, Abrams MAC 9649 to Westmoreland, 17 Jul 68; and Abrams MAC 13813 to Wheeler info McCain, 12 Oct 68. Both in Abrams Papers, CMH. In same collection, see Msgs, Westmoreland WDC 14063 to Abrams, 13 Sep 68; Abrams MAC 12740 to Westmoreland, 20 Sep 68; and Abrams MAC 7730 to Wheeler, 17 Jun 69.

its headquarters staff. The office produced instead a list of reports to be retained that was "so long that [Laird] wondered if there were any reports that we would let them stop." How well the statistics flowing from MACV and the rest of the mission portrayed the actual state of the war also remained in question. The CORDS Hamlet Evaluation System, for example, the command's comprehensive index of pacification progress, continued to have significant distortions despite several revisions aimed at making it more accurate and objective. If fighting drove peasants from contested hamlets into refugee camps in secure zones, for instance, the Hamlet Evaluation System would record an increase in population security. Administration officials, including Dr. Kissinger, viewed the Hamlet Evaluation System and other such systems with skepticism. Nevertheless, as had been true from the beginning of the war, in the absence of a better alternative, they accepted the results as at least indicating general trends and used them for public relations purposes when the numbers seemed to support their viewpoints.[43]

MACV Intelligence: A Mature Capability

In May 1969, after a month-long orientation period in country, Maj. Gen. William E. Potts replaced General Davidson as MACV J–2. Potts, a World War II European theater and Korean War combat veteran whose career included armor, operations, and intelligence assignments, had a strong background in counterinsurgency and the Vietnam conflict. From 1961 to 1962, while in the Office of the Assistant Chief of Staff for Intelligence, he chaired a special study group on the role of Army intelligence in counterinsurgency. He served as G–3 of U.S. Army, Vietnam, during the buildup from 1965 to 1966, and then had tours as Chief of Staff of the Army Security Agency and G–2 of U.S. Army, Pacific, before joining MACV. General Potts, who stayed in the MACV intelligence slot until August 1972, longer than any of his predecessors, brought continuity to this important function. He enjoyed the confidence of General Abrams, with whom he had served in several previous combat, contingency operation, and peacetime assignments. Testifying to the importance he attached to intelligence as well as his trust in his J–2, Abrams himself once observed that he spent more time with General Potts than with any other of his general staff chiefs.[44]

---

[43] Quotation is from MFR, Odeen, 20 Jan 71, sub: Vietnamization Meeting with Secretary Laird, folder 76, Thayer Papers, CMH. Hamlet Evaluation System (HES) problems are discussed in Hunt, *Pacification*, pp. 261–62. Administration doubts about the HES are illustrated in Memo, Kissinger for the President, 29 Jan 69, sub: Evaluation of Pacification Progress in South Vietnam, box 136; and Memo, Lynn for Kissinger, 28 Nov 69, sub: The Hamlet Evaluation System, box 1009; NSC files, Nixon Papers, NARA. The trend argument is repeated in MACV History, 1970, vol. 1, ch. 8, pp. 15–17.

[44] Memo, Col Sam A. Roberts, USAF for SJS MACV, 17 Apr 69, sub: MACV History Program, Reel 052, MACV Microfilms, MHI; biographical sketch, Lt Gen William E. Potts, CMH. Interv, author with Lt Gen William E. Potts, 29 Apr 97, CMH (hereafter cited as Potts Interv).

Thanks to a buildup during General Westmoreland's tenure, General Potts directed a large, mature organization with extensive collection and production capabilities. With operational control over MACV's theater-level Army intelligence units, Potts coordinated the intelligence activities of other MACV staff agencies and the field and component commands. He codirected with his Joint General Staff counterpart the four combined intelligence centers. Within the J–2, the earlier division between the staff proper and the combined centers had disappeared with time and personnel turnover. The entire intelligence establishment worked as a unified team, staffed by experienced officers who often had served previous Vietnam tours. Potts' section exchanged information with the embassy and other American agencies and received special intelligence support from the National Security Agency element in Vietnam.[45]

Data flowed into the J–2 from captured documents, prisoners of war, defectors, agents, sensors, communications intercepts, and various forms of aerial imaging, as well as combat operations. In 1970, for example, the Cambodian incursion produced, among other booty, more than five tons of enemy documents that contained valuable information on North Vietnamese infiltration, organization, and plans. As the field forces perfected their own intelligence establishments, the J–2 in mid-1968 began decentralizing some of its collection effort to the III Marine Amphibious Force, I and II Field Force, and Delta Military Assistance Command G–2s, who received authority to increase requirements upon collection elements in their areas on behalf of their own commanders and MACV. The J–2 section employed its own computer system to store and retrieve all this information, which constituted a comprehensive, quickly available database on the enemy, as well as to perform various analyses. It continued, for example, to refine its analysis of enemy activity patterns, which permitted more effective targeting of air strikes and ground operations.[46]

The combined intelligence centers, with their mixed Vietnamese and American staffs, provided valuable support to MACV's intelligence output. At the capstone of the system, the Combined Intelligence Center, Vietnam, prepared joint estimates and studies, pattern analyses, and basic information pamphlets for issue to troops and maintained an automated data bank. Two of its most common products were pattern analyses requested by the corps area commands and periodic enemy

[45] MACV History, 1971, vol. 1, ch. 3, pp. 67–69; Msg, Abrams MAC 1232 to McCain info Wheeler, 27 Jan 70, Abrams Papers, CMH; Bfg, Lt Gen William E. Potts, sub: Intelligence Perspectives on the Vietnam War, A Collector's View: The Perspective from J–2, p. 13, CMH. The end of the J–2 and Combined Intelligence Center, Vietnam (CICV), antagonism is noted in Potts Interv, 29 Apr 97.

[46] Potts Interv, 29 Apr 97; DIA Appraisal, sub: Significance of Enemy Documents Captured in Cambodia, box 509, NSC files, Nixon Papers, NARA; Msg, COMUSMACV MAC 12736 to CG USARV et al., 5 May 68, sub: Decentralization of Intelligence Collection Assets, in folder, Decentralization of Intel Collection . . . , MACV Collection, MHI.

base area studies. The Combined Document Exploitation Center by 1970 could receive a captured document from the field one day, translate it, and return it to the capturing unit the next day for use in continuing operations.[47]

The single most important product of this intelligence complex was General Potts' daily briefing for General Abrams, his deputies, and the principal MACV staff officers, which expanded each Saturday morning into the WIEU. In this briefing, Potts and his assistants summarized current developments in North Vietnam, Laos, Cambodia, and South Vietnam, concluding with an estimate of the "nature of the threat." A former USARV deputy commander recalled that in the WIEUs, Abrams "jumped on Potts quite often. But I never remember any time that Potts came up differently the next time." The same information went daily to Admiral McCain and the Joint Chiefs of Staff chairman by secure message. To provide rapid response to queries from headquarters, the field, and Washington, the J–2 section was manned, in three shifts, twenty-four hours a day. General Potts was in his office most days from 0500 to 2200, as well as answering an average of three calls a night during enemy offensives or high points from Washington or the field commanders.[48]

General Potts' briefings for senior officers—which he also gave in modified form to an endless succession of distinguished visitors to MACV—were only one channel through which military intelligence and information were disseminated to MACV headquarters and its subordinate commands. According to a 1969 Military Assistance Command study, all MACV directorates and subordinate commands were receiving and exchanging timely intelligence through a rich network of formal and informal systems. This network had evolved over time and was too complex for centralized regulation, but it was highly effective in furnishing each agency with the information and intelligence it required.[49]

A mature and responsive intelligence capability was one of the foundations of General Abrams' "one war" strategy and made possible the effective use of MACV's diminishing military strength. For example, General Potts and his staff developed the ability to predict, with nearly 100 percent accuracy, when the enemy would launch his periodic offensives or high points, as well as major local attacks. On the basis of this information, General Abrams and his field commanders mounted preemptive operations that blocked the enemy initiatives or greatly reduced their effects. In October 1969, a National Security Council staff member concluded: "The commander in the field is supported by

[47] Potts Interv, 29 Apr 97; Potts, Intelligence Perspectives, p. 14. For a description of CICV in 1970–71, see Cosmas and Murray, *U.S. Marines in Vietnam, 1970–1971*, p. 389. At that time, CICV was directed by a U.S. Marine colonel with a Vietnamese lieutenant colonel as codirector.

[48] Potts Interv, 29 Apr 97. Quote is from Mildren Interv, 24 Feb 76, p. 25.

[49] Memo, Col T. J. DeFranco for Col Roberts, 2 Apr 69, sub: BEIGE BOX Intelligence Flow Survey, in folder, same title, MACV Collection, MHI.

the most sophisticated intelligence apparatus ever assembled. He has, therefore, been able to take advantage of his foreknowledge of enemy intentions . . . to undertake devastating preemptive actions."[50]

Despite the growing sophistication of intelligence, some questions still lacked definitive answers. The exact size of enemy forces in South Vietnam, for instance, long remained a matter of dispute between the Military Assistance Command on one side and the Central Intelligence Agency and Defense Intelligence Agency on the other, with the latter two agencies adhering to the higher estimates. Even when the intelligence community agreed to use strength ranges instead of single figures, disagreements continued over whether, and by how much, enemy strength was declining—an issue that had public relations as well as intelligence implications because it reflected on administration claims of progress and on redeployment criteria. General Abrams and his field commanders gave production of an accurate enemy order of battle a high priority; Abrams personally reviewed and approved each enemy strength report prepared by his staff before forwarding it to higher headquarters. Nevertheless, the problem was complex, in part because small enemy units and replacement groups could enter South Vietnam almost overnight across the long Cambodian and Laotian borders and it took time to make contact with them and identify them. The various estimative methods used by MACV and other agencies were difficult to reconcile, and their differing conclusions caused disquiet among senior officials. As late as March 1971, Secretary Laird, who followed the issue with much interest and concern, cautioned President Nixon to avoid specific numbers in public discussions of enemy strength and "speak only in terms of qualitative trends."[51]

Intelligence, like every other aspect of the allied war effort, underwent Vietnamization. The process was gradual because MACV had to ensure full support of American forces until they departed and then attempt to leave South Vietnamese intelligence in as strong a position as possible. General Potts devoted much attention to the latter task. He secured the appointment of a capable Joint General Staff intelligence chief, Col. Hoang Ngoc Lung. Potts worked closely with Lung and also

---

[50] Quotation is from Memo, Dave McManis for Haig, 8 Oct 69, sub: Predictions of Enemy Offensives, box 089, NSC files, Nixon Papers, NARA. See also Memo, Haig for McManis, 7 Oct 69, sub: Predictions of Vietnamese Offensives; and Memo, Laird for the President, 11 Oct 69, sub: "Batting Average" in Predicting Enemy Activity. Both in box 089, NSC files, Nixon Papers, NARA. Abrams notes the great improvement in intelligence in Memo, Charles B. MacDonald for SJS MACV, 15 Apr 69, sub: Luncheon Meeting with COMUSMACV, in folder, same title, MACV Collection, MHI.

[51] Quotation is from Memo, Laird for the President, 3 Mar 71, sub: Estimates of Enemy Forces in Southeast Asia, box 153, NSC files, Nixon Papers, NARA. Continuing controversy is reflected in Memo, Haig for Brig Gen Robert E. Pursley, 25 Mar 71, sub: NVA/VC Strength Estimates, box 153; Untitled, Undated Paper, [late 69], sub: Enemy Manpower, box 1009; and Memo, Paul V. Walsh for Lynn and Winston Lord, 4 May 70, box 146. All in NSC files, Nixon Papers, CMH. Laird's concern is noted in MFRs, Odeen, 30 Jul 70, 1 Mar 71, and 8 Apr 71, sub: Vietnamization Meeting with Secretary Laird, folders 75 and 77, Thayer Papers, CMH.

with Col. Pham Huu Nhon, who headed the South Vietnamese coun-terpart of the National Security Agency. To a greater degree than his predecessors, Potts regularly exchanged views and estimates with his counterparts on the substance of intelligence. Potts, Lung, and their staffs held weekly meetings; and Potts, according to Colonel Lung, "made himself available for every worthy discussion."[52]

As redeployments proceeded, U.S. intelligence units gradually withdrew from South Vietnam. MACV incrementally removed its personnel from the combined centers so that they ultimately became all-Vietnamese installations. To provide trained personnel for the centers and other agencies, General Potts arranged to send 261 South Vietnamese officers, most of them captains and majors, to the U.S. Army, Pacific, intelligence school in Okinawa and 24 to the Army intelligence school at Fort Holabird, Maryland. While such MACV efforts improved South Vietnamese capabilities, they could not overcome the fragmentation and politicization of the Vietnamese intelligence community. In addition, Vietnamization could not fully compensate for the removal of American technology and expertise. The Vietnamese, for example, even though they sent officers to the United States for computer training and had other personnel instructed on the job in Saigon, could not make full use of the Americans' automated intelligence data-handling system. Recognizing these shortfalls, MACV included in the 69,000-man residual force projected in OPLAN J208A about 6,000 intelligence personnel. MACV plans for its own headquarters reorganization and reduction called for a sizeable directorate of intelligence well into the purely advisory period.[53]

Reducing the Command Structure

As troop withdrawals accelerated, MACV developed and incre-mentally implemented plans for scaling back the American command structure in South Vietnam, including its own headquarters. Under the command's contingency "T-Day" plans, MACV was to revert to a joint Military Assistance Advisory Group capable of providing advice and support to the South Vietnamese forces as well as conducting unilateral U.S. intelligence and communications activities. As part of

---

[52] Quotation is from Lung, *Intelligence*, pp. 82–83. RVNAF military intelligence organization is described in MACV History, 1971, vol. 1, ch. 3, p. 69; Potts Interv, 29 Apr 97.

[53] Msg, Abrams MAC 12568 to McCain, 18 Sep 70, Abrams Papers, CMH; Clarke, *Final Years*, p. 435. Difficulties of Vietnamization are described in Lung, *Intelligence*, pp. 84–86; and in George W. Allen, "Intelligence in Small Wars: Lessons from Vietnam?" (Paper prepared for 1991 Annual Meeting of the American Political Science Association), pp. 14–16, copy in CMH. Memo, Cowles for Distribution, 29 Sep 71, sub: Consolidation of Headquarters . . . , in folder, Minutes of Hq MACV Reorganization Study Group Meeting, 28 Sep 71; and Briefing for Gen Lucius D. Clay, Jr., USAF, 21 Jan 72, sub: U.S. Redeployment Status, tab D, MAC J303 Briefing Book no. 4. Both in MACV Collection, MHI. Number of Vietnamese officers trained is from Potts Interv, 29 Apr 97.

its National Security Study Memorandum (NSSM) 36 submission, the command in mid-1969 indicated that it would gradually draw down headquarters manpower in preparation for the transition to T-Day. It also envisioned reducing or consolidating subordinate headquarters, notably the III Marine Amphibious Force and the Army's 1st Logistical Command.[54]

Actual headquarters reductions were small during the initial redeployment increments, since command, control, and advisory requirements did not diminish. MACV headquarters strength, for example, declined by only about 200 personnel between May 1969 and May 1970. Secretary Laird, concerned at the apparent imbalance between combat and support forces in the withdrawals, continually pressed General Abrams to bring headquarters drawdowns into line with the overall pace of redeployment.[55]

In response to these pressures, during the first half of 1970, General Abrams carried out the III Marine Amphibious Force and 1st Logistical Command reductions called for in the NSSM 36 plan. The first of these—the replacement of III Marine Amphibious Force by XXIV Corps as the senior U.S. headquarters in I Corps—turned out to be more of a command change than a reduction. Given the fact that two corps-level American headquarters existed in the northernmost military region, as well as General Abrams' determination to remove the entire Marine contingent in the early redeployment phases, an Army takeover of I Corps was logical and inevitable. Accordingly, as the 3d Marine Division departed during the summer and fall of 1969, Abrams' staff and that of III Marine Amphibious Force began planning for the turnover. Complicating the task, the marines insisted that, to preserve the integrity of their air-ground team, their 1st Division and 1st Aircraft Wing must operate under a Marine headquarters until they redeployed.[56]

On 26 January 1970, after much consultation with III Marine Amphibious Force and with the Joint Chiefs and the Marine Corps commandant, General Abrams decided simply to place the XXIV Corps in command of all U.S. forces in I Corps. A scaled-down III Marine Amphibious Force, under XXIV Corps operational control, would direct Marine air and ground operations and act as service component command during the short time Marine forces were expected to remain in Vietnam. The turnover, which included movement of XXIV Corps headquarters from Phu Bai to the former III Marine Amphibious Force

[54] MACV History, 1969, vol. 1, ch. 2, p. 23. Msgs, COMUSMACV MAC 22495 to Component Cdrs, 14 Apr 69; COMUSMACV MAC 32821 to CINCPAC, 3 Jun 69. Both on Reel 056, MACV Microfilms, MHI. Msg, Abrams MAC 10110 to McCain info Wheeler, 5 Aug 69, Abrams Papers, CMH.

[55] Headquarters strength is summarized in MACV History, 1971, vol. 1, ch. 8, p. 76; MACV J–3, Force Planning Synopsis for Gen Abrams, vol. 2, pp. 113–14, 352, CMH; MFR, Odeen, 23 Jun 70, sub: Vietnamization Meeting with Secretary Laird, folder 75, Thayer Papers, CMH.

[56] Cosmas and Murray, *U.S. Marines in Vietnam, 1970–1971*, pp. 15–16.

compound at Da Nang, was completed on 9 March. However, it produced no immediate elimination of any headquarters. Because of the stretch-out of Marine redeployments, the III Marine Amphibious Force stayed in operation for another year, with Da Nang and Quang Nam Province as its area of responsibility. It redeployed in April 1971 along with the division and wing, giving way to the short-lived 3d Marine Amphibious Brigade.[57]

During 1970, U.S. Army, Vietnam, carried out the second headquarters consolidation envisioned in NSSM 36 by absorbing the 1st Logistical Command. Both headquarters, located at Long Binh, were engaged in administration and supply of Army forces; their general and special staffs overlapped in many functions. MACV, U.S. Army, Vietnam, and the Department of the Army considered merging the two in 1966 and again in 1968. Each time, they decided against it, on the first occasion because of the rapid troop buildup and on the second out of reluctance to reorganize in the midst of the heavy post-Tet fighting. In June 1969, with redeployment under way, MACV and U.S. Army, Vietnam, decided to proceed with the merger. Implemented gradually, the consolidation was completed a year later. It made no change in the relationship between MACV and the Army component headquarters, but left U.S. Army, Vietnam, in direct control of the four regional Army Support Commands.[58]

As U.S. combat troop redeployments accelerated during 1970, General Abrams set his staff to work on plans for reducing the large field force headquarters and shifting their functions away from military operations toward advice, support, and pacification. The MACV staff in November proposed a plan to combine the field force, Army advisory group, and CORDS staffs in each region into a single headquarters. Each new regional headquarters would contain about 350 personnel in contrast to more than 600 in the existing organization. In January 1971, Abrams adopted the plan. However, at the request of the field force commanders, he left the CORDS staff out of the merger, declaring that such military-civilian integration would be "divisive at this critical time when we all must pull together toward a common goal." Abrams also decided to postpone reorganization of the XXIV Corps, which continued to control large American combat forces and faced a strong enemy threat, until 1972.[59]

---

[57] Ibid., pp. 16–21. Msgs, CG III MAF to COMUSMACV 17 Jan 70; Abrams MAC 1163 to McCain info Wheeler, 26 Jan 70; Zais DNG 644 to Abrams, 18 Mar 70. All in Abrams Papers, CMH.

[58] Paper, sub: Consolidation of Hq USARV and Hq 1st Log Command, Reel 098, MACV Microfilms, MHI; MACV History, 1970, vol. 2, ch. 9, pp. 4–5; MACV J–3, Force Planning Synopsis for Gen Abrams, vol. 2, p. 267.

[59] MACV History, 1971, vol. 1, ch. 8, p. 73; Memo, Cowles for Chief of Staff, Nov 70, sub: Restructuring of Advisory Effort and Integration of Major Headquarters in the Military Regions, in folder, same title, MACV Collection, MHI. Quotation is from Msg, Abrams MAC 01171 to Component and Field Cdrs, 4 Feb 71, Abrams Papers, CMH. See also Msgs, Abrams MAC 14004 to

Reorganization in the other three corps areas went forward. On 30 April 1971, General Abrams redesignated the I and II Field Forces as respectively the Second and Third Regional Assistance Commands and combined them with the Army advisory groups, which simultaneously were being scaled down. At the same time, the Delta Military Assistance Command became the Delta Regional Assistance Command. In II Corps, from which most American combat forces had departed, General Abrams went further in merging civilian and military authority. On 16 May, he converted the Second Regional Assistance Command into the Second Regional Assistance Group and placed it under a civilian, the veteran CORDS regional director John P. Vann. General Abrams made this unusual arrangement to ensure strong American influence over the newly appointed South Vietnamese II Corps commander, General Dzu, whose area was a likely target for any future major Communist offensive and who had learned to depend on Vann's advice in his previous command of IV Corps. Vann, as director of the regional assistance group, oversaw all American military and pacification support functions in II Corps and acted as senior adviser to General Dzu. He had under him a military deputy, who formally commanded the remaining American troops, and a deputy for CORDS.[60]

Even as it reorganized the regional headquarters, the Military Assistance Command accelerated preparations for its own restructuring. During 1970, the J–5 staff completed MACV OPLAN J198, under which the headquarters was to reorganize by mid-1973 into a joint Military Assistance Advisory Group. The group, with about 24,000 American troops under its command and a headquarters staff of about 1,200, was to provide advice and assistance to the RVNAF, manage military support programs, and conduct limited intelligence, communications, pacification, and air operations until its ultimate phasedown and elimination.[61]

Besides refining plans for the Military Assistance Advisory Group, MACV in September 1970 began developing a concept, closely coordinated with that for reduction of the field force headquarters, for an interim transformation into a smaller organization, to be called the Vietnam Assistance Command (VAC). On 15 May 1971, to parallel the work on the J208 series of OPLANs for reducing American strength to about 60,000 by mid-1972, the chief of staff, Maj. Gen. Welborn G. Dolvin, established a VAC planning group chaired by the MACV deputy chief of staff and including representatives of the principal general staff

McCain, 25 Oct 70; Davison HOA 0183 to Abrams, 30 Jan 71; Abrams MAC 01446 to Davison info McCaffrey, 10 Feb 71; Abrams MAC 01952 to McCaffrey et al., 24 Feb 71. All in Abrams Papers, CMH.

[60] MACV History, 1971, vol. 1, ch. 8, p. 73; Letter of Instruction (LOI), Abrams to Vann, 15 May 71, John P. Vann Papers, MHI. The circumstances of Vann's appointment are described in Neil Sheehan, *A Bright Shining Lie: John Paul Vann and America in Vietnam* (New York: Random House, 1988), pp. 748–52. Msg, Funkhouser HOA 1774 to Abrams, 8 Sep 71, Abrams Papers, CMH.

[61] MACV History, 1970, vol. 2, ch. 7, pp. 81–84; ibid., 1971, vol. 1, ch. 8, pp. 71–72.

elements. The group was to make detailed plans for reformation of MACV headquarters into a 950-man VAC, which in turn would phase down into the Military Assistance Advisory Group, renamed the Vietnam Assistance Group (VAG), "the ultimate organization for the long term advisory period."[62]

As envisioned by the planning group, which finished its work in late August, the VAC headquarters would be essentially a scaled-down version of that of MACV. The transitional command would continue as a joint headquarters under CINCPAC with subordinate Army, Navy, and Air Force components. It would remain in existence as long as U.S. combat and combat support units were in South Vietnam and would conduct military and advisory operations. The VAC was to have essentially the same command group and general and special staff structures as MACV, but with the J sections redesignated as directorates and CORDS renamed Civil Operations and Revolutionary Development Assistance. Reducing the total number of headquarters agencies from twenty-three to nineteen, the offices of the J–5 and the Assistant Chief of Staff for Military Assistance, as well as the Construction and Training Directorates, were to be eliminated. Their functions were to be assumed by the J–3 and J–4 sections and, in the case of J–5's strategic planning responsibilities, by Pacific Command headquarters. However, the VAC would retain the recently created Deputy Chief of Staff for Economic Affairs. To perform housekeeping and security tasks for the headquarters complex, the office of the MACV Headquarters Commandant was to combine with the U.S. Army Headquarters Area Command, which provided logistical support for U.S. installations in Saigon, as VAC Special Troops.[63] *(Chart 2)*

Under the VAC plan, the component and regional commands also were to reduce and reorganize. U.S. Army, Vietnam, cut to 350 personnel, would become an Army support command while the Army advisory program continued to be directed by the VAC staff and the regional assistance commands. The Seventh Air Force was to revert to a 775-man air division headquarters and Naval Forces, Vietnam, to a 200-man Naval Advisory Group staff. The regional assistance headquarters were to shrink from about 350 men each to around 150.[64]

[62] Quotation is from MACV History, 1971, vol. 1, ch. 8, p. 72. Bfg, 23 Aug 71, sub: Significant Impacts, MACV Transition to VAC Hq, July 1971–July 1972, in folder, Bfg to Command Group and General Staff—Significant Impacts MACV Transition to VAC Hqs . . . ; Bfg, sub: VAC Structure, tab H. MAC J303 Bfg Book no. 4; Memo, Dolvin for Dist[ribution] List, 15 May 71, sub: Headquarters MACV Staff Reorganization, in folder, Hq MACV Staff Organization. Both in MACV Collection, MHI. Msg, Abrams MAC 06525 to Component and Regional Assistance Cdrs, 7 Jul 71, Abrams Papers, CMH.

[63] Bfg, 23 Aug 71, sub: Significant Impacts, MACV Transition to VAC Hq, July 1971–July 1972, 23 Aug 71, in folder, Briefing to Command Group and General Staff—Significant Impacts MACV Transition to VAC Hqs . . . ; Briefing, sub: VAC Structure, tab H, MAC J303 Bfg Book no. 4, MACV Collection, MHI.

[64] Bfg, 23 Aug 71, sub: Significant Impacts, MACV Transition to VAC Hq, July 1971–July 1972, in folder, Bfg to Command Group and General Staff—Significant Impacts MACV Transition to VAC

CHART 2—PROPOSED VAC HEADQUARTERS ORGANIZATION, 23 AUGUST 1971

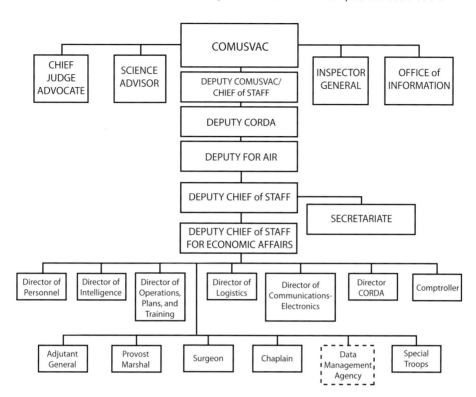

Source: Adopted by author from chart in VAC Bfg, 23 Aug 71, MHI.

Simultaneous with the VAC planning, a working group under the J–5 section refined plans for the VAG. The VAG staff structure, into which the VAC headquarters would phase down as the last American combat and combat support forces redeployed, was to be a reduced version of that of the assistance command. It would exercise control of residual regional assistance agencies and small Army, Navy, and Air Force advisory and component elements.[65]

On 23 August, General Abrams, after a briefing on the VAC plan, approved it with a succinct "Okay, go ahead." His words set the reorganization in motion. To oversee the drawdown, the planning group spawned an "executive committee" chaired by the chief of the J–3 Manpower Control Division, with representatives from the J–1 and the comptroller. This committee in turn established subcommittees to

Hqs . . . ; Memo, Cdr P. K. Fitzwilliam, USN, for Lt Col Muscari et al., 29 Aug 71, sub: Maj Gen Bowley's Hq MACV Study Group Issues, in folder, Minutes of MACV Study Group Meeting, 31 Aug 71, MACV Collection, MHI. Msg, McCaffrey ARV 2403 to Abrams, 16 Jul 71, Abrams Papers, CMH.

[65] Memo, Maj Gen John T. Carley for Asst CofS J–5, 23 Aug 71, sub: Military Advisory Policy, in folder, Military Advisory Policy, 3 Sep 71, MACV Collection, MHI.

work out the details of gradually eliminating personnel spaces, consolidating functions, and disestablishing agencies. The subcommittees' collective objective was to conduct a smooth reorganization with minimum disruption of the headquarters' continuing activities, with the transition to be completed by the end of June 1972.[66]

The executive committee, after exchanges with the staff agencies, developed a joint table of distribution for the VAC headquarters, enlarged from 950 to 1,084 spaces to accommodate staff section demands for additional manpower. During the 45,000-man redeployment that President Nixon ordered on 12 November, the headquarters, on the basis of this joint table of distribution, began reducing its manpower to VAC levels. In November, MACV disestablished the office of the Assistant Chief of Staff for Military Assistance and distributed its personnel and functions to the J–1, J–3, and J–4 sections. It also merged the Headquarters Commandant with the U.S. Army Headquarters Area Command. Elimination of the J–5 section and the Training and Construction Directorates was scheduled for the first half of 1972. Transfer of functions to other headquarters began. The MACV Adjutant General, for instance, turned over most of his Army personnel administration tasks to his USARV counterpart. Simultaneously, MACV's component and regional assistance commands continued their own headquarters reduction planning, which they had begun during the summer, and started to implement their plans.[67]

The headquarters reorganization included the elimination of the civilian deputy COMUSMACV for CORDS. Ambassador Colby, because of family problems, requested relief in June 1971. Prolonged interagency maneuvering ensued as the State and Defense Departments jointly sought a suitable successor. State Department officials wanted to keep a civilian, preferably a Foreign Service officer, in the position but could not find a qualified candidate acceptable to both departments. John Vann, for example, was anathema to the military, who had never forgiven his earlier career in Vietnam as a maverick and dissenter during 1962 and 1963. Finally, in September, Ambassador Bunker and

---

[66] Quotation is from MFR, Cdr P. K. Fitzwilliam, USN, 23 Aug 71, sub: Briefing to Command Group and General Staff, in folder, Briefing to Command Group and General Staff—Significant Impacts MACV Transition to VAC Hqs . . . ; MFR, Cdr P. K. Fitzwilliam, USN, 2 Sep 71, Minutes of MACV Study Group Meeting, in folder, same title, 31 Aug 71, MACV Collection, MHI.

[67] MFR, Lt Col W. P. Baxter, 25 Sep 71, sub: Minutes of Hq MACV Reorganization Study Group Meeting, in folder, same title; Memo, Cowles, C/S MACV, for Distribution, 29 Sep 71, sub: Consolidation of Headquarters . . . , in folder, Minutes of Hq MACV Reorganization Study Group Meeting, 28 Sep 71; MFR, Lt Col W. P. Baxter, 5 Nov 71, sub: Hq MACV Reorganization Study Group Meeting, in folder, same title; Memo, Maj Gen Bowley, USAF for C/S MACV, 11 Nov 71, sub: Reorganization of Hq MACV, in folder, same title, 11 Nov 71; Memo, Cowles for Distribution, 25 Nov 71, sub: Increment 10, in folder, C/S Action Memo no. 71–85—Increment 10. . . . All in MACV Collection, MHI. MACV History, 1971, vol. 1, ch. 8, pp. 73–75, and vol. 2, ch. 10, p. 53. Msgs, McCaffrey ARV 2403 to Abrams, 16 Jul 71; Vann NHT 1542 to Abrams, 19 Jul 71; Gen Lucius D. Clay, Jr, USAF to Abrams, 21 Jul 71; and COMNAVFORV to COMUSMACV, 12 Nov 71. All in Abrams Papers, CMH.

General Abrams jointly recommended Abrams' deputy COMUSMACV, General Weyand. They cited Weyand's excellent rapport with the South Vietnamese; his extensive pacification experience, which dated back to his command of the 25th Division and II Field Force; and his four-star rank, which would maintain the prestige and bureaucratic strength of the organization. The State Department, after initial objection, accepted Weyand since CORDS was due for drastic personnel reductions in 1972 as part of the overall drawdown. In October, accordingly, Weyand, as an additional duty, assumed the post of deputy COMUSMACV for CORDS. The civilians in the organization, many already acquainted with Weyand, received his appointment without demur.[68]

During 1971, another agency closely connected to MACV, the Joint U.S. Public Affairs Office (JUSPAO), came under attack. Since 1965, this agency, staffed by both military and civilian personnel, had coordinated the U.S. mission's public information activities, including those of the MACV Office of Information, and shared with MACV the conduct of psychological warfare operations. In June 1971, Frank Shakespeare, Director of the U.S. Information Agency (USIA), which oversaw JUSPAO, announced his intention to begin phasing down JUSPAO into a normal U.S. Information Agency office, thereby ending both its media relations and psychological warfare roles. Ambassador Bunker, on behalf of the U.S. mission, opposed the change. He declared that, even as JUSPAO had ensured that the mission spoke with "one voice" during the buildup, it was needed to "assure such control during the far more difficult and subtle period of disengagement which lies ahead." Swayed by Bunker's argument, the administration postponed formal dissolution of JUSPAO. Nevertheless, a new JUSPAO chief, at Shakespeare's instructions, during late 1971 began dismantling the agency by reducing civilian positions and neglecting to replace military personnel when their tours ended. The decline of JUSPAO constituted another blow to what was by then a collapsing relationship between MACV, and the mission as a whole, and the news media.[69]

[68] MFRs, Odeen, 23 and 24 Jun 71, 20 Jul 71, 10 and 17 Aug 71, and 27 Sep 71, sub: Vietnamization Meeting with Secretary Laird, folders 77 and 78, Thayer Papers, CMH. Msg, Bunker Saigon 0164 to Kissinger (via CAS channel), 16 Sep 71, box 412; Haig Saigon 256 to Kissinger, 22 Sep 71, box 1014; MFRs, 7 Oct 71, sub: Vietnam Ad Hoc Working Group Meetings, 28 Sep 71, 1 and 5 Oct 71, and Msg, Bunker Saigon 16990 to Amb Sullivan, 25 Oct 71, box 157. All in NSC files, Nixon Papers, NARA. Msgs, Abrams MAC 59162 to Bunker, 18 Jun 71; Bunker PVD 153 to Abrams, 18 Jun 71; Abrams MAC 08819 to McCain and Moorer, 13 Sep 71. All in Abrams Papers, CMH.

[69] Memo, Frank Shakespeare for Kissinger, 30 Jun 71; Msg, Bunker Saigon 10968 to Kissinger, 13 Jul 71, box 155; Memo, Kissinger for Director USIA, 1 Sep 71, box 157. All in NSC files, Nixon Papers, NARA. Lincoln Interv, 1989, pp. 2–3, in Charles S. Kennedy, comp., "A Vietnam Reader: Selections from Oral Histories of the Foreign Affairs Oral History Program" (MS, Foreign Affairs Oral History Program, Georgetown University 1993).

Seasons of Scandal

After 1968, a seemingly endless series of scandals and embarrassing incidents blackened the image of the Military Assistance Command and the U.S. armed forces. Many of these revelations were of deficiencies that had developed during the rapid, disorderly American buildup. Others had their origin in the military and moral ambiguities of fighting a revolutionary war. Adding to the command's travail and generating still more adverse news stories, the discipline and morale of its American soldiers showed signs of breaking down, in part due to conditions in Vietnam and in part as a result of conflicts erupting within the society at home. General Abrams and his subordinates, as they coped with the problems and tried to remedy the deficiencies and abuses, became increasingly bitter at the newsmen who persisted in revealing the extent of their difficulties and the imperfect nature of their solutions.

MACV and the Media: A Breakdown of Relations

In June 1968, General Abrams established his approach to public information. He declared in a message to his principal commanders: "Effective now, the overall public affairs policy of this command will be to let results speak for themselves. We will not deal in propaganda exercises in any way, but will play all of our activities at low key." The Military Assistance Command was to report the bad news as well as the good, in each case after ascertaining the facts. Abrams also insisted on full information for the troops, declaring that "we should never protect our men from the truth because the very system of government for which they fight and sacrifice has its basic strength in its citizenry knowing the facts." While thus enjoining openness, Abrams at the same time directed his commanders to avoid comment and speculation on sensitive national policy matters and to hold closely information on future plans and operations. Abrams deplored and tried to prevent information leaks from MACV headquarters. He attempted, without much success, to embargo news reporting of the evacuation of Khe Sanh. Abrams' approach to information was in accord with those of

Defense Secretaries Clifford and Laird, both of whom instructed MACV to stick to facts and avoid speculation and salesmanship.[1]

Under Abrams, the command tried to make more information available to newsmen. The MACV Office of Information the sole release point in Vietnam for military information, in mid-1969 began supplementing its daily press briefings—known familiarly as the "Five O'Clock Follies"—with off-the-record background sessions between reporters and senior MACV commanders and staff officers. Through these meetings, the command gained advantageous media exposure for its views and analyses.[2]

General Abrams at the outset enjoyed favorable press relations. He held frequent informal off-the-record sessions with newsmen, often over dinner and drinks. He conveyed an impression of candor and realism, which the reporters contrasted favorably with what they regarded as Westmoreland's incessant optimism and salesmanship. Abrams was able to sustain this image in part because President Nixon, unlike his predecessor, refrained from employing his field commander in public promotion of administration policy. Nixon, in accord with pre-Vietnam presidential practice, while he sought favorable information from the embassy and MACV, relied on administration and Republican party figures—notably himself, Dr. Kissinger, and Vice President Spiro T. Agnew—to carry on the rhetorical battle against his critics. Abrams thus was able to resist successfully occasional attempts to draw him and his principal subordinates into the increasingly rancorous public debate.[3]

Abrams' low-key approach gained credibility for what was in fact a continuing MACV emphasis on the positive in public statements and official reporting. Abrams and Ambassador Bunker, along with most other senior mission officials, believed that after Tet 1968 the tide of war in South Vietnam had turned in the allies' favor. Their periodic reports and assessments, as well as their statements to newsmen, affirmed continuing progress in military operations, pacification, and Vietnamization even as they acknowledged persistent problems and South Vietnamese deficiencies. General Abrams enjoined his subordinates to report bad news as well as good, but he at times softened

[1] First quotation is from Msg, Abrams MAC 7236 to Field Force and Component Cdrs, 2 Jun 68; the second is from Msg, Abrams MAC 4619 to Cushman, 6 Apr 68. Both in Abrams Papers, CMH. In same collection, see also Msgs, Abrams MAC 7429 to Field Force and Component Cdrs, 6 Jun 68; Abrams MAC 9496 to Field Force and Component Cdrs, 14 Jul 68; and Abrams MAC 4251 to Field Force and Component Cdrs, 4 Apr 69. The Khe Sanh embargo story is in Hammond, *Military and the Media, 1968–1973*, pp. 34–38; see also pp. 31–33.

[2] MACV History, 1969, vol. 3, ch. 11, pp. 1–2, 5–6.

[3] Msg, Abrams MAC 14468 to Wheeler info McCain, 8 Nov 69, Abrams Papers, CMH, describes Abrams' press backgrounders. Berger Interv, 17 May 77, pp. 10–11; Kerwin Interv, 9 Apr 76, pp. 22–23; and McLaughlin Interv, 1980, pp. 36–37, all describe Abrams' approach to the press. Hammond, *Military and the Media, 1968–1973*, p. 31, notes how reporters contrasted Abrams with General Westmoreland. Msg, Abrams MAC 1688 to McCain info Wheeler, Abrams Papers, CMH, exemplifies his resistance to use his officers to defend the war.

the bad side in the digests he passed up the chain of command. For example, in his answers to National Security Study Memorandum (NSSM) 1, he played down pessimistic adviser comments on the condition and prospects of the South Vietnamese forces. Abrams regularly passed on to CINCPAC and the Joint Chiefs of Staff favorable bits of intelligence and accounts of operational success, and he cooperated with administration efforts to help the South Vietnamese publicize their own achievements.[4]

General Abrams' "honeymoon" with the news media did not last. To the contrary, the Military Assistance Command's relations with the press spiraled downward toward mutual hostility and incomprehension. The causes of the decline were many. Persistent MACV and mission optimism collided, as it had since the command's earliest days, with reporters' more skeptical view of the course of the war. Increasingly, information policy in Vietnam was dictated by President Nixon, who took an adversarial approach to the media and constantly sought to manipulate and intimidate news organizations. An increasingly antiwar media responded with anger and suspicion, which inevitably extended to MACV. As redeployments accelerated, military public affairs personnel in Vietnam declined in numbers and professional competence, a reduction President Nixon himself encouraged in the belief that public affairs officers, like the reporters with whom they dealt, "lean to the left." The MACV Office of Information dropped from sixty-two officers and men in May 1969 to thirty-six in February 1971. A similar decline occurred in the size and experience of the press corps. Operations in Cambodia and Laos produced military-media confrontations, notably General Abrams' prolonged embargo of coverage of the opening phase of the Laos incursion in early 1971.[5]

Symptomatic of the growing alienation, General Abrams abandoned his informal dinners with correspondents, claiming that they were turning into complaint sessions. His subordinates reflected their commander's attitude. The MACV staff became slow and grudging in responding to press inquiries, and some field commanders actively obstructed coverage of their operations. The MACV Office of Information

---

[4] The generally positive tone of Abrams' reporting can best be followed through his Message files, Abrams Papers, CMH, for 1968–1971. Other illustrations of Abrams' viewpoint can be found in MACV History, 1969, vol. 1, ch. 2, pp. 16–17; and MFR, Odeen, 1 Jun 70, sub: Vietnamization Meeting with Secretary Laird, folder 75, Thayer Papers, CMH. Bunker's persistent optimism is traced in Wallace J. Thies, "How We (Almost) Won in Vietnam: Ellsworth Bunker's Reports to the President," *Parameters*, XXI, no. 2 (Summer 1992): 86–95. Clarke, *Final Years*, pp. 342–45, 389–90, analyzes Abrams' response to NSSM 1 and the overall optimism of MACV reporting on the South Vietnamese forces.

[5] The deterioration of MACV press relations is traced in Hammond, *Military and the Media, 1968–1973*; see especially pp. 349–58 and 423–61. Nixon's hatred of the press is described in Ambrose, *Triumph of a Politician*, pp. 411–12, 659–60. Quotation is from Memo, Nixon for Kissinger, 1 Dec 69; see also Memos, Kissinger for Sec Def, 4 Dec 69, sub: Reduction in Armed Services Public Relations Staffs in Vietnam; and Kissinger for the President, 30 Dec 69, sub: Reduction in Public Relations Personnel in Vietnam. All in box 141, NSC files, Nixon Papers, CMH.

in September 1971 discontinued its Sunday press briefings. With less information coming from the command, the press corps, which included a minority of outright antiwar activists, played up every negative story, which in turn intensified military anger.[6]

Scandals Proliferate

A wave of scandals contributed to MACV's deteriorating press relations. Early in 1969, Army and Senate investigations brought to light major racketeering and black market activities in the extensive officer and enlisted clubs, mess, and exchange system, which MACV had established during the buildup to maintain troop morale and reduce pressure

Command Sergeant Major Wooldridge, 1968 (then Command Sergeant Major of the Army)

on South Vietnam's economy. Those indicted included the MACV command sergeant major, William O. Wooldridge. Hard upon the club scandal, General Abrams ordered the arrest of the commander of the 5th Special Forces Group, Col. Robert B. Rheault, and several subordinates on charges of murdering a South Vietnamese double agent.[7]

Even as what came to be called the "Green Beret Case" made headlines, a still more terrible story unfolded. During the summer of 1969, the Department of the Army investigated and substantiated a veteran's report that a company of the Americal Division, during an operation in Quang Ngai Province in March 1968, had murdered several hundred unresisting Vietnamese civilians in My Lai (4) hamlet. During the investigation, it became apparent that the division chain of command had suppressed reports of the incident. The ensuing courts-martial, as well as an inquiry into the cover-up by a board headed by Lt. Gen. William R. Peers, a former I Field Force commander, went on for

[6] Hammond, *Military and the Media, 1968–1973*, pp. 510–18; see also pp. 617–27. MACV History, 1971, vol. 2, ch. 10, p. 48. Plans for reducing support of the media are discussed in Msgs, McCain to Abrams info Daniel Z. Henkin, 13 Oct 70; Abrams MAC 14147 to McCain, 30 Oct 70; and Abrams MAC 14914 to McCain, 19 Nov 70. Both in Abrams Papers, CMH.

[7] These scandals are summarized in Hammond, *Military and the Media, 1968–1973*, pp. 138–44, 191–93. See also MACV History, 1969, vol. 3, ch. 14, pp. 55, 68–69. Ltr, Acting Sec Army Thaddeus R. Beal to Sen Abraham A. Ribicoff, 11 May 71, CMH, explains the origins of the club corruption. The Green Beret case is summarized in Memo, Kissinger for Attorney General John N. Mitchell, 22 Sep 69, sub: Summary of the Green Beret, box 076, NSC files, Nixon Papers, NARA.

Colonel Rheault, 5th Special Forces Group commander,
and some of his men at a press conference

months, accompanied by an international public furor and additional atrocity allegations.[8]

During 1970 and 1971, still more bad news contributed to the witches' brew. The unacknowledged war in Laos, which the Nixon administration finally felt compelled to acknowledge, drew press attention. So did reports of mistreatment of prisoners by the South Vietnamese in the "tiger cages" of Con Son Island. Governmental corruption in South Vietnam and President Thieu's machinations in the 1971 presidential election received constant coverage. Among American forces, combat refusals, racial disturbances, spreading drug use, and attacks on officers and noncommissioned officers ("fragging") made the news. Highly decorated soldiers, notably Lt. Col. Anthony Herbert and Col. David Hackworth, publicly criticized the military conduct of the war; they also leveled specific charges of atrocities and malfeasance. Enemy troops overran an Americal Division firebase called MARY ANN. They inflicted severe American casualties under circumstances that pointed to negligence at all levels of command in a division already tainted by My Lai.[9]

[8] Hammond, *Military and the Media, 1968–1973*, chs. 10 and 11, recounts the public affairs side of the My Lai incident. Lt. Gen. William R. Peers, USA (Ret), *The My Lai Inquiry* (New York: W. W. Norton, 1979) is the standard account of the massacre and the subsequent investigation.

[9] For detailed accounts of these events and the media fallout, see Hammond, *Military and the*

The Military Assistance Command responded to these events on public affairs, administrative, and legal fronts; but it was often a sub-ordinate actor in larger Nixon administration efforts at news management and political damage control. On the organizational side, General Abrams strengthened the headquarters' criminal investigation and inspection arms. Raising the status of the MACV provost marshal, Abrams in August 1969 constituted his office, hitherto a part of the J–1 section, as a full-fledged special staff element, although it remained under general staff supervision of the J–1.[10]

The Office of the MACV Inspector General, headed throughout by Colonel Cook, a long-time Abrams comrade, underwent expansion and reorganization. As its load of major investigations increased from 37 cases in 1968 to 184 in 1971 even as U.S. troop numbers shrank, the office grew from 8 officers and men in 1968 to a maximum of 65 in November 1970. Cook's organization eventually contained divisions for investigations, inspections, complaints, advising the Joint General Staff Inspector General, and combined investigations. Its work covered the range of MACV's troubles: racial incidents, racketeering and corruption, allegations of American and South Vietnamese troop misconduct, operational failures such as the Firebase MARY ANN debacle, and the Herbert and Hackworth charges. Colonel Cook's inspectors cooperated with their Joint General Staff counterparts in a growing number of combined investigations, for example a wide-ranging probe of indiscipline and corruption in the Civilian Irregular Defense Group (CIDG) camps. Formerly a minor element of headquarters, the Office of the MACV Inspector General became MACV's front line of defense against the multiplying scandals.[11]

As incidents occurred, the Military Assistance Command, working in close coordination with its service components, tried to follow General Abrams' formula for dealing with bad news: get the facts, report them fully, and when possible take remedial action. In the Wooldridge case, Abrams, after his inspector general confirmed the sergeant's criminal activities, removed Wooldridge from his post as command sergeant major of MACV and returned him to the United States for trial. The Military Assistance Command cooperated with the mission and the South Vietnamese government in a campaign against black marketeering and currency manipulation.[12]

Media, 1968–1973, chs. 8, 9, 12, 16, and 20.

[10] Memo, Maj Gen Elias C. Townsend for Asst CofS J–3, 4 Jul 69, sub: Examination of Organizational Structure; MACV General Order no. 5077, 24 Aug 69. Both in Reel 046, MACV Microfilms, MHI. Abrams indicates the growing importance of the provost marshal in Msg MAC 10230 to Westmoreland info Mildren et al., 29 Jul 68, Abrams Papers, CMH.

[11] MACV History, 1969, vol. 3, ch. 14, pp. 55–57, 66–67; ibid., 1970, vol. 2, ch. 13, pp. 6–10; ibid., 1971, vol. 2, ch. 10, pp. 24–25, 29–43.

[12] Msgs, Abrams MAC 10234 to Westmoreland info Mildren, 7 Aug 69; Westmoreland WDC 13320 to Abrams info Palmer, 9 Aug 69. Both in Abrams Papers, CMH. MACV History, 1969, vol. 3, ch. 14, pp. 1–2; Berger Interv, 17 May 77, pp. 6, 16–17.

Under his U.S. Army, Vietnam, hat, Abrams initiated criminal proceedings under the Uniform Code of Military Justice against the alleged offenders in the Green Beret murder. After Colonel Rheault lied in answering queries about the incident, an angry Abrams initially confined the defendants in the Long Binh USARV stockade. However, General Westmoreland, in response to protests from Congress and the men's civilian attorneys, directed Abrams to release them while the charges were being adjudicated. The Nixon administration, fearing embarrassing revelations of covert intelligence activities if the case came to trial, gladly dropped the proceedings when the Central Intelligence Agency declined to permit its agents, who had been involved in the affair, to testify. Abrams nevertheless brought in a new 5th Special Forces Group commander. He disengaged the Special Forces from clandestine intelligence operations and, on the basis of the aforementioned combined inspector general investigation, carried out a full-scale housecleaning of the Special Forces and the CIDG program that they advised.[13]

In the Firebase MARY ANN incident, General Abrams, dissatisfied with the XXIV Corps and American Division investigations, turned the case over to Colonel Cook. When Cook's investigation confirmed negligence at brigade and division levels, Abrams relieved the division commander. The Department of the Army ultimately reprimanded the commander and several other officers. General Westmoreland, however, delayed for months public announcement of the resolution of the case, hoping to confine the unfavorable story to "a single bad day of publicity."[14]

The case of Colonel Hackworth, like that of the Green Berets, illustrated the effect of political considerations on the resolution of embarrassing incidents. After the highly decorated Hackworth alleged through the news media that senior Army officers had received undeserved awards, submitted untrue after-action reports, falsified body counts, and committed other derelictions in combat, the Department of the Army instructed General Abrams and his inspector general to interview Hackworth and investigate his charges. The investigation invalidated most of Hackworth's claims. The plot thickened when

---

[13] MACV History, 1969, vol. 3, ch. 11, p. 15, ch. 14, pp. 16–17. Msgs, Abrams MAC 10114 to Palmer, 5 Aug 69; Abrams MAC 10663 to McCain, 17 Aug 69; Abrams MAC 10709 to McCain, 18 Aug 69; Abrams MAC 11027 to McCain, 24 Aug 69; Palmer WDC 14204 to Mildren info Abrams, 26 Aug 69; Abrams MAC 1217 to Westmoreland, 26 Jan 70; Col Michael B. Healy NHT 488 to Abrams, 16 Mar 70. All in Abrams Papers, CMH. Mildren Interv, 24 Feb 76, pp. 17–18, and Townsend Interv, 26 Feb 76, pp. 48–50, both in Abrams Project, MHI. Westmoreland, *Soldier Reports*, pp. 367–68; Statement by Sec Army Resor, 29 Sep 69, box 076, NSC files, Nixon Papers, NARA.

[14] MACV History, 1971, vol. 2, ch. 10, p. 33. Msgs, Abrams MAC 05611 to Westmoreland info Rosson et al., 6 Jun 71; Abrams MAC 06312 to Westmoreland info Rosson et al., 30 Jun 71; Abrams MAC 06497 to Westmoreland info Rosson et al., 8 Jul 71; McCaffrey ARV 2232 to Kerwin, info Abrams, 9 Jul 71. All in Abrams Papers, CMH. Westmoreland, *Soldier Reports*, p. 368. Public relations handling of the case, including the Westmoreland quotation, is covered in Hammond, *Military and the Media, 1968–1973*, pp. 505–10.

Colonel Cook's investigators came upon evidence that Hackworth himself had engaged in large-scale illegal currency transactions and had been involved in drug use, gambling, and prostitution during his own Vietnam tour. Strong grounds existed for prosecution of Hackworth. Perhaps for that reason, after a private talk with Abrams, Hackworth took a more circumspect tone in his public statements. The Army, however, with administration approval, ultimately dropped the case rather than appear to be retaliating against a decorated officer for speaking out against military abuses.[15]

In the case of Colonel Herbert, MACV conducted an investigation of Herbert's charges of misconduct by his former brigade commander and other officers, concluding that most of the allegations were without foundation. In Washington, the Army secretariat saw to it that information reached the news media that called in question Herbert's veracity and emotional stability and cast doubt on the officer's claims of heroic conduct. Herbert's former brigade commander and other officers came forward with misconduct charges of their own against Herbert. Gradually, the Army's campaign reversed the initially favorable media coverage of Herbert's allegations. Completing the reversal, in February 1973, the Columbia Broadcasting System (CBS) aired an exposé of Herbert on its popular "60 Minutes" news program. Reinforced by an equally damaging article in the respected *Atlantic Monthly*, the CBS report "killed whatever lingering credibility Herbert held with the press."[16]

The Impact of My Lai

Of all the unpleasant revelations of the post-Tet period, the My Lai massacre most affected MACV's operations. The command was at best a secondary participant in the investigation. The Peers commission established that in March 1968 neither MACV, USARV, nor III Marine Amphibious Force had received any information about the atrocity, due to suppression of the facts by the Americal Division. Circumstances had facilitated concealment. A widely dispersed aggregation of formerly separate brigades, the division was remote from the Army component headquarters and not closely supervised by its immediately superior command, III Marine Amphibious Force, which was preoccupied at the time with Khe Sanh and the threat to northern I Corps. Hence, the division's sketchy routine report of the engagement, one of scores that took place daily during the heavy

---

[15] MACV History, 1971, vol. 2, ch. 10, p. 33. Msgs, Palmer WDC 11298 to Abrams info McCaffrey, 25 Jun 71; Abrams MAC 06226 to Palmer info McCaffrey, 26 Jun 71; Abrams MAC 06410 to Palmer info McCaffrey, 2 Jul 71; Palmer WDC 11832 to Abrams, 3 Jul 71; and Abrams MAC 06724 to Palmer, 12 Jul 71. All in Abrams Papers, CMH. Hammond, *Military and the Media, 1968–1973*, pp. 498–500.

[16] Hammond, *Military and the Media, 1968–1973*, pp. 496–97.

post-Tet fighting, escaped higher-level notice. By the time the facts were revealed, the personnel involved had left Vietnam.[17]

As a result, the investigations, courts-martial, and public relations actions arising from the incident were directed from Washington by Secretary of the Army Stanley R. Resor and General Westmoreland. MACV collected documents for the Peers commission and supported its inquiries in Vietnam, an effort that included arranging an on-the-ground tour of My Lai (4) as well as visits to all the concerned American and Vietnamese commands. General Abrams and Ambassador Bunker carried out the delicate task of briefing President Thieu on the unfolding results of the investigation. In March 1970, in advance of the public release, members of General Peers' group briefed General Abrams and Admiral McCain on the board's finding that the Americal Division commander, Maj. Gen. Samuel W. Koster, and other officers of the division had been guilty of dereliction of duty in that they failed to investigate the incident fully and report it promptly up the chain of command. The rest of My Lai's complicated legal and political aftermath played itself out in the United States.[18]

For MACV, the My Lai massacre and the Peers board's report made more urgent the long-standing problem of reducing South Vietnamese civilian casualties resulting from American operations. Fought among and for control of the people, the revolutionary war in South Vietnam by its nature blurred the conventional distinction between combatants and noncombatants. As early as 1965, General Westmoreland summarized the dilemma. Although he intended to use his American troops and their firepower primarily against enemy main forces and base areas in thinly populated regions, he acknowledged that

in order to be effective we can not isolate US troops from the population nor deploy them solely in jungle areas where they can be bypassed and ignored by the VC. In the long run, we must use them in areas important to the VC and the [government of Vietnam]. With few exceptions, important areas coincide with heavy population. . . . The final battle is for the hamlets themselves and this inevitably draws the action toward the people and the places where they live.[19]

---

[17] Peers, *My Lai Inquiry*, pp. 241–42; Msg, COMUSMACV MAC 66582 to Secretary of the General Staff, Department of the Army, 3 Dec 69, Reel 044, MACV Microfilms, MHI. Palmer Interv, 1975, pp. 239–42, 422–23, reviews the reasons why the incident failed to come to the attention of MACV and USARV. See also Westmoreland, *Soldier Reports*, pp. 375–80.

[18] MACV History, 1969, vol. 3, ch. 11, pp. 15–16. Msgs, Coats WDC 14852 to Connor, info Abrams, McCain, et al., 5 Sep 69; Resor WDC 20641 to Bunker info Abrams, 26 Nov 69; Abrams MAC 16218 to Mildren et al., 16 Dec 69; Peers WDC 22263 to Abrams, 20 Dec 69; Peers ACD 001 to Resor and Westmoreland info Abrams, 1 Jan 70; Resor and Westmoreland WDC 00085 to Peers info Abrams, Rosson, 3 Jan 70; Palmer WDC 04837 to Bunker, Abrams, et al., 15 Mar 70; Palmer WDC 05071 to Abrams, 18 Mar 70. All in Abrams Papers, CMH. Memo, Maj Cyrus N. Shearer for Insp Gen MACV, 12 Jan 70, sub: AAR for Lt Gen Peers' Visit, Reel 044, MACV Microfilms, MHI.

[19] Msg, Westmoreland MAC 4382 to Wheeler, 28 Aug 65, Westmoreland Message files, CMH.

The action took its toll. About 1.2 million civilians became casualties during the conflict; estimates of the number killed ranged from 195,000 to 415,000. Many of these casualties resulted from enemy actions—terrorism, indiscriminate rocket and mortar shellings, road minings, and deliberate massacres such as that of 3,000 persons at Hue in 1968; but a large proportion also were caused by allied operations. American artillery fire and air strikes, necessary to defeat heavily armed guerrillas and main force units dug into populated areas, killed and injured noncombatants; and there were as well occasional deliberate acts of murder and other crimes by American and allied soldiers.[20]

General Peers

As the antiwar movement in the United States intensified, civilian casualties and alleged atrocities in Vietnam became an issue even before My Lai. War critics, including Senators J. William Fulbright and Edward M. Kennedy, in congressional hearings regularly publicized civilian death and suffering. Communist propaganda—abetted by sympathizers like the British philosopher Bertrand Russell, who organized his own war crimes tribunal—kept up a barrage of atrocity charges. Non-Communist news media in the United States and Europe published accounts of American-inflicted civilian casualties and damage. During the 1968 Tet offensive, American firepower inflicted widespread destruction upon Saigon and other towns in the process of expelling the enemy. Television screens and front pages around the world featured the horrifying picture of the South Vietnamese National Police chief shooting a captured Viet Cong officer in the head. During 1969, American television networks broadcast other stories of South Vietnamese abuse and killing of prisoners. Finally, in November of that year, came the revelation of the My Lai massacre.[21]

---

[20] Civilian casualty figures are from Thomas C. Thayer, "How To Analyze a War Without Fronts: Vietnam 1965–72," *Journal of Defense Research*, Series B, Tactical Warfare Analysis of Vietnam Data, 7B, no. 3 (Fall 1975), ch. 12.

[21] Civilian casualty and atrocity issues can be followed in Hammond, *Military and the Media 1962–1968*, pp. 185–93, 266–70, 274–79, 300–06; and Hammond, *Military and the Media, 1968–1973*, pp. 26–31, 217–53, 493–94. Department of the Army, Deputy Chief of Staff for Military Operations, "Final Report of the Research Project: Conduct of the War in Vietnam," May 71, copy in CMH, was prepared to refute American war critics' charges that General Westmoreland's conduct of

From the start of large-scale American operations, MACV issued and enforced strict rules of engagement designed to minimize civilian casualties and property damage. The rules restricted firing in inhabited areas to positively identified enemy targets and required that commanders obtain clearance from both American and South Vietnamese authorities before using artillery and air strikes in and near towns, villages, and hamlets. General Westmoreland issued directives, incorporated into the orientation of arriving American troops and printed on pocket cards for each individual soldier, calling for humane treatment of prisoners and noncombatants. The standing operating procedures of MACV's subordinate commands repeated the same principles. Given the constant rotation of personnel and the often desperate circumstances of combat, lapses inevitably occurred in enforcement of these rules; and commanders and troops had to be indoctrinated and reindoctrinated in their terms and importance.[22]

Well before the My Lai tragedy came to light, General Abrams moved to reaffirm and tighten the MACV rules of engagement. To prevent a repetition of the urban destruction of the first two 1968 offensives, he withdrew the authority of lower-level commanders to call for indirect fire in built-up areas. In August 1968, he initiated a campaign to reduce casualties among both American troops and South Vietnamese civilians caused by "carelessness and a lack of professionalism in handling our weapons systems."

On 2 March 1969, he reissued in strengthened form a 1966 MACV directive on minimizing noncombatant battle casualties. Declaring that "the use of unnecessary force and indiscriminate employment of weapons" could embitter the people and drive them to support the Viet Cong, Abrams ordered commanders at all echelons to "establish a balance between the force and weapons necessary to accomplish their missions and the safety of the noncombatant populace" even though that would require "the exercise of restraint beyond that usually required of soldiers on the battlefield." Abrams forbade preparatory air and artillery strikes in friendly populated areas, reconnaissance by fire into hamlets and villages, and "uncontrolled" harassment and interdiction fires. He called on commanders to continually indoctrinate their troops in the importance of minimizing noncombatant casualties. Whenever security considerations permitted, commanders were to plan operations in coordination with South Vietnamese province and district chiefs and exchange liaison officers with them. Advisers were to encourage their Vietnamese counterparts to follow these same principles.[23]

the Vietnam conflict constituted a war crime under international law.

   [22] MACV's rules of engagement are reviewed in Gen William B. Rosson, "Assessment of Influence Exerted on Military Operations by Other Than Military Considerations," ch. 1, CMH; "Extracts of Remarks by General Westmoreland Relating to Noncombatant Casualties" in Westmoreland-CBS Case file folder, MACV Collection, MHI; Department of the Army, "Conduct of War," vol. 1, pp. 3ff; and Peers, *My Lai Inquiry*, pp. 29–30.

   [23] First quotation is from Msg, Abrams MAC 10826 to Field Force and Component Cdrs,

On 9 March, the Military Assistance Command published a full-dress revision of its Directive 525–13, the basic document defining its rules of engagement, which last had been amended in October 1968. Like Abrams' earlier message, the amended directive began with the premise that "all practical means will be employed to limit the risk to the lives and property of friendly forces and civilians." The directive prescribed standing operating procedures, which subordinate commands were not to alter or amend, for the conduct of artillery, tank, mortar, and naval gunfire as well as tactical air and helicopter gunship strikes. Incorporating Abrams' earlier orders, it permitted no one lower than corps and field force commanders to call for indirect fire in city fighting. The new rules emphasized that all fire in populated areas must be against clearly identified enemy targets, clarified requirements and procedures for target clearance by American and South Vietnamese authorities, and declared that all tactical air and helicopter gunship missions must be controlled by observers and approved by the ground commanders. A unit now was considered to be "in contact" only "when it is engaged with an enemy force, being fired upon, and returning fire," a more specific definition than in previous editions of the rules. Advisers were to take "all necessary advisory actions" to ensure South Vietnamese compliance with the MACV rules and were to refuse RVNAF requests for support that violated them.[24]

Following the My Lai revelations, Abrams took additional steps to enforce and elaborate upon MACV's rules of engagement. He reassured Admiral McCain in December that "within the past 36 hours (within the bounds of operational capability), every member present in this command has been reinformed of his obligations with respect to noncombatants, POW's and civilians." At a conference on 22 February 1970, he told his commanders that there was an "absolute requirement" for "real sensitivity" toward the Vietnamese people in the conduct of operations and urged them to pay attention to the political impact of "everything we do" in South Vietnam. Later in the year, after a series of incidents in which American air strikes killed and injured friendly civilians, he enjoined upon his subordinates strict adherence to the rules of engagement and issued an implied threat to impose even more inhibiting restrictions if the existing rules were not rigorously enforced. In May 1971, as offensive American ground operations neared their end, Abrams published a revised rules of engagement directive prescribing even more restraint in the use of firepower. Units that received fire from inhabited places now could shoot back only if they

10 Aug 68; see also Msg, Abrams MAC 11977 to Field Force and Component Cdrs, 4 Sep 68. Both in Abrams Papers, CMH. MACV Directive no. 525–23, 2 Mar 69, sub: Military Operations: Minimizing Noncombatant Battle Casualties, Reel 054, MACV Microfilms, MHI. This directive is summarized in MACV History, 1969, vol. 1, ch. 5, pp. 29–30.

[24] MACV History, 1969, vol. 1, ch. 5, pp. 14–28.

could positively identify the source of the fire and only as required for their own self-protection.[25]

In its investigation of the My Lai massacre, the Peers commission found not only derelictions on the battlefield but also a failure by the Americal Division and its subordinate units to follow the established procedures for investigating serious incidents and reporting them up the chain of command. In response, Abrams and McCain, at the direction of the Joint Chiefs, reissued and reemphasized standing instructions to commands at all levels to report immediately by the fastest means available all events that were "of national political or military interest." After publication of the Peers report, Abrams reviewed MACV's directives on the handling of war crimes and other serious incidents and concluded that they were "as presently published, deemed adequate" if conscientiously applied. MACV and its subordinate headquarters investigated atrocity allegations and when justified prosecuted offenders, as in the case of five marines who murdered 16 Vietnamese in Quang Nam Province in February 1970. MACV inspectors general during inspections of province advisory teams began routinely seeking information about U.S., RVNAF, and enemy war crimes. The MACV Inspector General's office also reviewed every investigation of war crimes and Geneva Convention violations conducted in South Vietnam, to ensure that they were properly conducted and where indicated followed up by command actions.[26]

Enforcement of the rules of engagement was difficult for MACV among American forces, engaged as they were in widespread decentralized operations. It was even more difficult in the case of the allied armies that were not in fact under MACV's command. The South Vietnamese and third-country forces all formally adopted the American rules of engagement but the degree of their actual adherence varied. The South Vietnamese, waging a bitter civil war, committed frequent acts of brutality toward enemy soldiers and their own civilians, too often when American news cameramen were present. Conditions in their military and civil prisons were a perennial concern to MACV and source of scandal. While the highly professional Australian and New Zealand contingents usually conducted themselves properly, the large South Korean force earned a justified reputation for harshness toward the Vietnamese. Ambassador Bunker admitted that "while

---

[25] First quotation is from Msg, Abrams MAC 15789 to McCain, 6 Dec 69, Abrams Papers, CMH. MFR, Odeen, 1 Dec 69, sub: Vietnamization Meeting with Secretary Laird, folder 75, Thayer Papers, CMH. Second quotation is from MACV Hq, "One War," ch. 1, p. 21. MACV History, 1970, vol. 1, ch. 6, p. 20; ibid., 1971, vol. 2, an. D.

[26] Msgs, McCain to PACOM Cdrs, 7 Jan 70; Abrams MAC 650 to Field Force and Component Cdrs, 15 Jan 70; Abrams MAC 3635 to Wheeler info McCain, 19 Mar 70; Abrams MAC 4865 to Palmer info Wheeler, McCain, 14 Apr 70. All in Abrams Papers, CMH. Marine case is described in Cosmas and Murray, *U.S. Marines in Vietnam, 1970–1971*, pp. 344–47. Inspector general efforts are recounted in MACV History, 1970, vol. 2, ch. 13, p. 23 and in MS, Col Robert Sholly, "The Role of the Inspector General Military Assistance Command, Vietnam, 1964–1971," n.d., p. 111, CMH.

the Korean forces in Vietnam have issued directives comparable to MACV's on treatment of civilians in battle areas, . . . we should recognize . . . that by our standards the Koreans are ruthless and during military operations they undoubtedly do not interpret or comply with their directives with the same inhibitions as American forces." Allegations of South Vietnamese and Korean atrocities, periodically published in the American news media, embarrassed the administration and caused congressional and public outcry, although never on the scale of that which surrounded the unfolding My Lai story.[27]

Lacking direct command and court-martial authority over his allies, General Abrams used what means he had to influence their conduct. With the South Vietnamese, he worked through the advisory network and also engaged in direct persuasion of top officials to promote more humane behavior. Similarly, Abrams and Ambassador Bunker periodically remonstrated with the Korean force commander and his country's ambassador. When MACV received reports of alleged misconduct by allied troops, it passed them on to the appropriate national commanders and encouraged them to investigate and if necessary discipline offenders. With increasing frequency, the MACV Inspector General's office carried out combined inquiries with the South Vietnamese and South Koreans. Especially when American forces were involved, these investigations established facts and prescribed remedies. Ambassador Bunker acknowledged, however, that it was all but impossible to conclusively prove or disprove charges of Korean atrocities in operations where U.S. forces were not present, because American officials "are rarely in position to conduct independent investigation into [the] facts" in such cases and had to rely on whatever information, if any, the Koreans or Vietnamese would provide. Despite Abrams' and Bunker's best efforts, the independent allied forces fought by their own rules, not those of the Americans.[28]

When all else failed, Abrams attempted to dissociate American advisers from their allies' derelictions. He warned advisers working in the Phoenix program ("Phung Hoang"), the South Vietnamese effort to capture and kill Communist cadre, that they were bound by the same rules of war as any other soldiers; and he instructed them to refuse to participate in illegal acts and report those acts to higher authority. After

---

[27] Quotation is from Msg, Bunker Saigon 2303 to Sec State, 16 Feb 70, sub: Alleged ROK Atrocities, box 143; a typical complaint about the Koreans is Ltr, F. J. West, Jr, to Rear Adm William E. Lemos, 10 Dec 69, box 1010, NSC files, Nixon Papers, NARA. Msgs, McCain DIASO 15621 to Abrams info Wheeler et al., 12 Dec 69; Abrams MAC 484 to McCain info Wheeler, 12 Jan 70. All in Abrams Papers, CMH. Press and public reaction are covered in Hammond, *Military and the Media, 1968–1973*, pp. 242–43, 359–67.

[28] MACV efforts to improve South Vietnamese prisoner of war procedures and facilities are recounted in Clarke, *Final Years*, pp. 167–69, 227, 320, 376–77; MACV, "Role of the Inspector General," pp. 75–77, 88–89, 92–93. For an example of a successful American–South Vietnamese investigation, see MACV History, 1970, vol. 2, ch. 13, p. 17. Quotation is from Msg, Bunker Saigon 2303 to Sec State, 16 Feb 70, sub: Alleged ROK Atrocities, box 143, NSC files, Nixon Papers, NARA.

the Green Beret case called attention to American military involvement in questionable clandestine intelligence and paramilitary activity,
Abrams began trying to extricate U.S. personnel from those programs.
In December 1969, for example, at the urging of Secretary Laird and
Secretary of the Army Resor, he stopped replacing American advisers
with the South Vietnamese Provincial Reconnaissance Units, key strike
forces under the Phung Hoang program, which the American antiwar
movement charged were assassination squads. The Central Intelligence
Agency, which had originated the units and only transferred their support to MACV in July 1969, protested against this action, claiming that
the Provincial Reconnaissance Units were more effective in eliminating Viet Cong cadres than any other South Vietnamese organization.
Laird and Resor, however, considered that the adverse publicity the
Provincial Reconnaissance Units were receiving in the United States
made them a net liability to the American cause; and Abrams accepted
their judgment. In the case of the Koreans, Abrams recommended
their early redeployment from South Vietnam but the administration
decided otherwise.[29]

Among American forces, MACV's intensified emphasis on the rules
of engagement, combined with public and press attention to issues
such as My Lai, affected both performance and morale. Field force commanders, picking up the cues from Abrams, urged their subordinates to
exercise restraint and discrimination in their use of firepower and took
new steps to prevent noncombatant deaths and injuries. Queried by
Abrams on reaction to the My Lai revelations, the commanders of U.S.
Army, Vietnam, and the field forces reported that officers and men at
all levels showed new interest in the rules of engagement and in what
constituted an atrocity. Junior officers in particular expressed concern
that they could face legal action for battlefield mistakes and doubt that
the Army would stand by them in such cases. In planning and executing operations, commanders were following the rules of engagement
more precisely, relying more heavily on written orders, and when possible avoiding maneuver and engagement in populated areas. Men of
all ranks expressed bitterness at what they considered unfairly negative media reporting of My Lai and dismay at the public opprobrium
that was falling on the American soldier in Vietnam. The II Field Force
commander reported that his company commanders "feel a sense of
frustration over the lack of support by the press and the public" and
that many "can be expected to resign when they have completed their
service obligation."[30]

---

[29] Msgs, Westmoreland WDC 17694 to Abrams, 15 Oct 69; McCain BNK 2821 to Abrams info
Wheeler, 29 Oct 69; Abrams MAC 14145 to McCain and Wheeler, 31 Oct 69; Abrams MAC 14585
to Westmoreland, 11 Nov 69; Abrams MAC 16592 to McCain, Wheeler, and Weyand, 24 Dec 69.
All in Abrams Papers, CMH. The Provincial Reconnaissance Unit (PRU) affair is recounted in Hunt,
Pacification, pp. 245–46; and Hammond, *Military and the Media, 1968–1973*, pp. 144–46. For
Abrams' recommendation on the Koreans, see ch. 5, pp. 177–79.

[30] For examples of field emphasis on discrimination in use of firepower, see Lt Gen Melvin Zais,

Race, Drugs, and Discipline

Many of the scandals that plagued the Military Assistance Command stemmed from a general deterioration in the professional standards, leadership, discipline, and morale of American forces in Vietnam. The problem had multiple causes, some peculiar to the war and others rooted in change and conflict in American society. Military manpower policy, specifically the early decision not to employ the National Guard and reserves and the adoption of the one-year tour, had resulted—especially for the Army and Marine Corps—in the war being fought by a "Vietnam-only" force of short-term enlisted men and equally short-term junior officers and noncommissioned officers with only a small professional cadre of senior noncommissioned officers and higher-grade officers. The one-year tour, while considered essential to troop health and morale, produced constant turnover within units, compounded after 1969 by the turbulence created by redeployments.

This short-term, constantly changing force was uniquely susceptible to disruptive political and social influences. The withdrawal of American units from combat left large numbers of soldiers crowded in rear base areas with idle time on their hands. Increasing numbers of the men, aware that the United States was disengaging and influenced by the antiwar movement at home, no longer saw any purpose in the conflict; some actively protested against the war. Successive waves of replacements brought with them the racial militancy, drug culture, and youth rebellion then permeating American society. Equally ominous was an apparent breakdown in the ethical standards of the professional cadre, as evidenced by the club scandals, the My Lai cover-up, and the Green Beret murder case.[31]

Taken together, these forces began to dissolve the long-standing mechanisms of leadership and discipline that held the armed services together. They produced in particular a growing alienation between career senior officers and noncommissioned officers ("lifers" in troop parlance) and the short-term junior leaders and soldiers. A

Opening Remarks at XXIV Corps Commanders' Conference, 22 Mar 70, Speeches box, Zais Papers, MHI; and Memo, Lt Col Clifford Crossman for John P. Vann, 22 Oct 70, sub: Interim Report, DMAC Fire Support Committee, Vann Papers, MHI. Evaluations of My Lai effects are in Msgs, McCain to Abrams and Haines info Wheeler and Mildren, 25 Apr 70; Abrams MAC 5563 to Mildren and Field Cdrs, 26 Apr 70; Mildren ARV 1221 to Abrams, 30 Apr 70; Maj Gen Hal D. McCown, Senior Adviser, Delta Regional Assistance Command, CTO 0465 to Abrams, 30 Apr 70; Zais DNG 995 to Abrams, 1 May 70; Collins NHT 803 to Abrams, 1 May 70; Abrams MAC 5990 to McCain info Haines et al., 4 May 70; and Davison HOA 1045 to Abrams, 1 May 70. All in Abrams Papers, CMH. Quotation is from final message.

[31] Useful studies of the deterioration of morale and discipline and its causes are Ronald H. Spector, "The Vietnam War and the Army's Self-Image," in John Schlight, ed., *Second Indochina War Symposium: Papers and Commentary* (Washington, D.C.: U.S. Army Center of Military History, 1986), pp. 169–85; and BDM Corp., *A Study of Strategic Lessons Learned in Vietnam,* vol. 7, *The Soldier* (McLean, Va.: BDM Corp., 1980). For a contemporary view of the effects upon the Army of the failure to call the reserves, see Memo, Lt Gen Arthur S. Collins, Jr, Asst CofS for Force Development, for the Chief of Staff, 20 Feb 68, Arthur S. Collins Papers, MHI.

A soldier wearing long hair, love beads, and peace tattoo

CINCPAC study in September 1971 acknowledged that "a distinct dichotomy of dedicated life styles exists between a significant portion of the young, first term military members, and the older, career-oriented noncommissioned and commissioned officers. As a result, many leaders do not know their men and vice versa." Alienation at times led to violence, in the form of attacks on officers and noncommissioned officers ("fragging") and racially motivated assaults and disturbances. In a few instances, small units refused orders to move into combat. A tiny minority of black and leftist militants actively attempted to promote disorder and defiance of authority. More common were minor acts of rebellion, typically neglect of military courtesies and the wearing of peace symbols and nonregulation long hair. The military justice system, which many lower-level leaders considered cumbersome and unworkable, and which equally many enlisted men believed was biased against them, threatened to break down under a growing burden of drug and disciplinary cases.[32]

MACV, like other American military commands, only gradually became aware of the extent of the internal problems it faced. Typically, command spokesmen dismissed early news media reports of widespread racial trouble, drug use, and indiscipline as sensationalist and exaggerated. Then, as the facts became obvious over time, they gradually acknowledged the existence and scale of the problems. The MACV command history for 1969 proclaimed that troop morale had remained "at a high state" throughout the year. The history for the following year, however, declared that "unusual psychological pressures were placed upon US military personnel in the Republic of

---

[32] Quotations are from Memo, Col Harry C. Holloway, Medical Corps, and Cdr George P. Fitzgibbons, USN, for CINCPAC, 1 Sep 71, sub: CINCPAC Study for Evaluation of PACOM Drug Abuse Treatment/Rehabilitation Programs, pp. 30–31, CMH.

Vietnam . . . during 1970," and that there had been "some loss of a sense of mission," reflected in various forms of troop misconduct.[33]

MACV dealt with most problems of discipline and morale through its service component commands, which possessed court-martial authority and were responsible under the joint system for internal administration. The components, often following policies established by their parent services, thus bore the burden of handling the comparatively rare instances of public antiwar activity and combat refusals. They also took the lead in preventing and punishing "fraggings" and other soldier-on-soldier violence. MACV monitored their activities, making reports as required to higher authority, and investigating—or directing subordinate headquarters to investigate—major incidents. Until 1969, MACV also delegated the task of troop information to the individual services. Its Office of Information was limited to publishing the command newspaper, *The Observer*, managing the Armed Forces Radio and Television Service stations, and issuing quarterly suggestions to commanders on information topics they might cover in their own programs.[34]

Gradually, the headquarters became more active in the morale field. In 1969, General Abrams required biweekly Commanders' Calls for officers, noncommissioned officers, and enlisted men in all units, with discussion topics prescribed each month. In May 1970, in a letter to his component commanders, he emphasized the "necessity" for "creative and imaginative programs to meet the diversified needs and interests of our personnel during . . . redeployment" and to "raise morale and build esprit." Colonel Cook, the inspector general, enlarged his Complaints Division, which responded to individual soldier grievances, and reorganized it into two branches, one to handle complaints and the other to analyze trends in troop discontent for the guidance of the commander. In May 1971, General Abrams instituted a program of inspector general audits of unit command effectiveness aimed at providing him with a broad picture of the situation and the quality of leadership.[35]

MACV's expanding racial and drug problems required still more active intervention and new command and organizational approaches.

---

[33] Hammond, *Military and the Media, 1968–1973*, pp. 171–89, recounts the initial military reaction to the emerging problems. Quotations are from MACV History, 1969, vol. 3, ch. 14, p. 29; ibid., 1970, vol. 2, ch. 12, p. 1. The commander of U.S. Army, Pacific (USARPAC), recognizes the emerging morale problem in Msg, Haines HWA 3856 to Westmoreland info Abrams, 11 Sep 70, Abrams Papers, CMH.

[34] Msg, Abrams MAC 06514 to Rear Adm R. S. Salzer, COMNAVFORV, 6 Jul 71, Abrams Papers, CMH, outlines the shared functions of MACV and the component commands. Abrams' handling of various incidents can be followed through his Message files, Abrams Papers, CMH. MACV History, 1969, vol. 3, ch. 11, pp. 2, 22–23, describes MACV Office of Information's troop information functions. For a detailed account of how one service, the Marine Corps, dealt with its morale and racial problems, see Cosmas and Murray, *U.S. Marines in Vietnam, 1970–1971*, ch. 20.

[35] MACV History, 1969, vol. 3, ch. 11, pp. 22–23; ibid., 1970, vol. 2, ch. 13, pp. 9–10; ibid., 1971, vol. 2, ch. 10, pp. 26–27, 35–36. Quotation is from Ltr, Abrams to DCG USARV, 7 May 71, sub: Morale and Welfare Activities, Abrams Papers, CMH.

Since the outbreak of major urban riots in the United States in 1967, MACV had anticipated the appearance of racial conflict among its troops. By 1969, trouble was all too evident, in manifestations of black pride and militancy such as Afro haircuts and black power salutes; in more or less peaceable confrontations with authority; and in individual and group attacks by black personnel on whites and by whites on blacks. Black servicemen complained of racial bias in promotions, duty assignments, and military justice; they demanded respect for their new-found racial identity in the form of permission to wear the Afro and provision of "soul" food and music in messes and clubs. In November 1969, Mr. L. Howard Bennett, Acting Assistant Secretary of Defense for Civil Rights, after spending a week interviewing black personnel in Vietnam, called all these grievances to General Abrams' attention. He reported also that communication and mutual confidence had broken down between the majority of African American personnel and the "white" chain of command, which the blacks considered unresponsive to their concerns and complaints.[36]

Well before Assistant Secretary Bennett made his report, General Abrams had addressed the racial problem. In October 1968, in response to a series of incidents around Da Nang, Abrams directed the commander of III Marine Amphibious Force to form a "watch committee," composed of senior representatives from each service in the Da Nang area, "with the mission of monitoring and taking appropriate action on racial tensions and incidents." Acting on Bennett's recommendations, Abrams in December 1969 dispatched a letter to every Army, Navy, Marine, Air Force, and Coast Guard unit commander in Vietnam, in which he emphasized their responsibility to keep open channels of communication to their troops and directed them to "eliminate unnecessary incursions on individual aspirations and identity."[37]

During 1970, MACV issued Directive 600–12, outlining its approach to race relations. The directive reiterated the obligation of subordinate commanders to ensure equal treatment and opportunity for all their personnel. It declared that, second only to mission performance, the primary duty of every officer and noncommissioned officer was to improve his subordinates' welfare; and it called upon them to maintain open channels of vertical and lateral communication throughout their commands. To the latter end, and to improve interracial understanding and head off conflict, MACV required every unit to appoint a human

---

[36] Msgs, Westmoreland MAC 8729 to Component and Field Force Cdrs, 15 Sep 67; Rosson NHT 1486 to Westmoreland, 30 Nov 67. Both in Westmoreland Message files, Sep and Nov 67, CMH. Msg, Abrams MAC 04599 to Component and Field Force Cdrs, 6 Apr 68, Abrams Papers, CMH. The Bennett visit is described in MACV History, 1969, vol. 3, ch. 14, p. 20; and Msg, CG III MAF to COMUSMACV 27 Nov 69, Abrams Papers, CMH. MACV History, 1971, vol. 2, ch. 10, pp. 9–11, 29, discusses racial incidents and black complaints.

[37] First quotation is from Msg, Abrams MAC 14059 to Component Cdrs, 18 Oct 68; see also Msg, Abrams MAC 14839 to Component Cdrs, 16 Nov 69. Both in Abrams Papers, CMH. Second quotation is from MACV History, 1969, vol. 3, ch. 14, pp. 20–21.

relations officer and establish a human relations council representing all ranks and races to assist and advise the commander. Viewed with suspicion by some officers and noncommissioned officers as undermining established chains of command, the councils were often of more cosmetic than practical effect. Nevertheless, they did constitute a forum for the orderly airing of racial grievances. The MACV inspector general investigated major racial disturbances and distributed to the command lessons learned reports based on his findings. MACV also adopted and issued to all services a Marine Corps pamphlet on the small unit leader's role in improving race relations. These measures, combined with individual service programs and with a delicate mixture of repression and conciliation by unit commanders, kept racial turmoil contained during the American forces' last years in Vietnam but fell well short of restoring genuine intergroup harmony.[38]

As much or more than racial conflict, soldier drug abuse absorbed command attention at all levels of MACV and the services. Indeed, the antidrug campaign over time expanded into a virtual war within the war. Relatively rare before 1968, troop drug use—primarily marijuana smoking—expanded rapidly thereafter, driven by a lethal combination of cheap, plentiful narcotics and bored, idle, alienated soldiers already part of their generation's drug culture. After initially denying media reports that drug use was widespread, by late 1969 MACV and its service components were compelled to acknowledge that the problem was extensive and serious. In August 1970, General Abrams declared that drug abuse was "a big and serious problem, . . . in fact, the biggest among all those that we have, including black marketeering and currency manipulation."[39]

Statistics on the amount of drug use were difficult to obtain, of questionable reliability, and subject to constant dispute. However, the trends all went upward. For example, arrests of military personnel on drug charges, which represented only a small proportion of users, increased from 344 in 1966 to 1,722 in 1967, 4,352 in 1968, and 8,446 in 1969. By early 1970, possibly a majority of American military personnel in Vietnam had at least experimented with drugs, principally marijuana. A sizeable proportion of military personnel were regular users. Even more ominous, a heroin epidemic, fueled by the importa-

---

[38] MACV History, 1971, vol. 2, ch. 10, pp. 11–15, 29. For examples of unit-level efforts, see Msg, Maj Gen Charles P. Brown, CG I FFV, NHT 0259 to Abrams and McCaffrey, 30 Jan 71, Abrams Papers; and Cosmas and Murray, *U.S. Marines in Vietnam, 1970–1971*, pp. 353–59.

[39] Early military denials and public relations damage control are covered in Hammond, *Military and the Media, 1968–1973*, pp. 182–89, 385–92. MACV concern is expressed in Msg, Westmoreland MAC 01227 to Sharp info Wheeler, 26 Jan 68, Westmoreland Message files, Jan 68, CMH. Berger Interv, 17 May 77, pp. 15–16, comments on how the drug problem crept up on the mission and MACV. Memo, Holloway and Fitzgibbons for CINCPAC, 1 Sep 71, sub: CINCPAC Study for Evaluation of PACOM Drug Abuse Treatment/Rehabilitation Programs, pp. 11–12, CMH, summarizes reasons for troop drug abuse. Abrams quotation is from Msg, MAC 11711 to McCain, 28 Aug 70, Abrams Papers, CMH.

tion into Vietnam from elsewhere in Southeast Asia of cheap, high-potency narcotics, began in spring 1970 and rapidly spread to involve, according to a 1971 Army survey, as many as 20 percent of the soldiers in some commands and possibly as high as 50 percent in a few rear bases.[40]

Pressed by an increasingly concerned Nixon administration, the Military Assistance Command gradually developed an antidrug offensive based on law enforcement, education, and rehabilitation—the same strategies being applied in the United States. In December 1970, the command codified its program, many elements of which already were in operation, in its Directive 190–4. On the enforcement side, the directive called for establishment at the national and military region levels of combined U.S.-Vietnamese investigative, police, and customs organizations. These initiatives were aimed at inducing the South Vietnamese to strengthen their antidrug laws, crack down on smuggling and trafficking, and halt domestic marijuana growing. Among American forces, provost marshals were to search out and apprehend drug sellers and users. Law enforcement was to be combined with intensive antidrug education in every unit and with service developed and administered programs of amnesty and rehabilitation for users who voluntarily turned themselves in. To improve information, the directive required continuing drug abuse surveys, data from which would be fed into an automated Drug Abuse Reporting System serving MACV and the component commands.[41]

MACV entrusted most implementation of these programs to its service components. U.S. Army, Vietnam, for example, had responsibility for organizing and operating a Joint Customs Group and a Joint Narcotics Investigation Detachment and for conducting the nationwide drug abuse survey. The MACV provost marshal was to "monitor, coordinate, and assist" the services in carrying out their drug suppression programs, both those mandated by MACV and those prescribed by the military departments. Further to coordinate the effort, MACV required every command down to battalion/squadron level to organize a Drug Abuse Suppression Council with representation from the concerned staff agencies and from junior officers, noncommissioned officers, and enlisted men. The council was to meet monthly, review the antidrug

[40] Arrest statistics are from MACV History, 1970, vol. 2, ch. 12, p. 4. See also MACV History, 1968, vol. 2, ch. 12, pp. 839–40; ibid., 1969, vol. 3, ch. 14, pp. 4–5, 8; ibid., 1971, vol. 2, ch. 10, pp. 15–16, 23–24. Fact Sheet, DCSPER-SARD, 19 Jan 71, sub: Drug Abuse; Memo, Dep Asst Sec Army John G. Kester for Sec Army, 25 May 71, sub: Use of Heroin in Vietnam, pp. 1–7, 13–17; Memo, Davison for McCaffrey, 17 Sep 71, sub: Marijuana and Drug Suppression. All in CMH.

[41] Memos, President for Kissinger, 13 Apr 70, and Kissinger for Sec Def, 14 Apr 70, box 145, NSC files, Nixon Papers; and MFR, Odeen, 16 Nov 70, sub: Vietnamization Meeting with Secretary Laird, folder 76, Thayer Papers, CMH, illustrate administration concern. MACV History, 1968, vol. 2, ch. 12, p. 839; ibid., 1969, vol. 3, ch. 14, pp. 5–6; ibid., 1970, vol. 2, ch. 12, pp. 4–6; ibid., 1971, vol. 2, ch. 10, pp. 17, 47–48. Msgs, Abrams MAC 14089 to McCain info Moorer et al., 28 Oct 70; Abrams MAC 14114 to Sec Def info McCain and Westmoreland, 29 Oct 70. Both in Abrams Papers, CMH.

campaign within the unit, and when appropriate make recommendations to the commander for its improvement.[42]

Besides putting Directive 190–4 into effect, MACV during 1971 further escalated its antidrug offensive as reports of increasing heroin use alarmed authorities in Saigon and Washington. In June, President Nixon ordered the military services to begin urine testing of all soldiers rotating home from Vietnam and hold those found positive for heroin for detoxification and treatment before returning them to the United States. MACV and its component commands immediately implemented this program, and they instituted unannounced random testing within units in Vietnam. They also intensified their education, amnesty, and rehabilitation efforts. In a letter to the command on 17 August, General Abrams declared his "personal endorsement and support" of the services' treatment and rehabilitation programs. He urged drug users to take advantage of the programs and promised that "no punitive action will be taken against you." Abrams designated his director of personnel, Maj. Gen. James B. Adamson, as MACV Drug Abuse Control Coordinator and took steps to centralize the public release of drug abuse and rehabilitation statistics. With the news media regularly alleging high-level South Vietnamese official involvement in the drug trade, Abrams and Ambassador Bunker urged President Thieu to enlarge his government's antidrug effort, warning that South Vietnam could lose American aid if he did not. Thieu responded by replacing his Director General of Customs, ousting a number of other allegedly corrupt officials, and improving customs and security at Tan Son Nhut Air Base and the ports. He also established national and provincial interministerial drug-suppression committees, as well as participated in MACV joint organizations.[43]

These efforts had at best limited success, as was indicated by continuing high percentages of men testing positive at rotation. Enforcement was hampered on the American side by overcrowded, understaffed military courts. On the Vietnamese side, Thieu's initial flurry of activity soon gave way to business as usual among Vietnamese agencies and commanders, for some of whom business included the very drug traffic they were supposed to suppress. The component commands' drug rehabilitation programs had a higher success rate than similar programs in the United States, primarily because their patients were otherwise in good health and usually had been addicted for less than a

[42] MACV Directive no. 190–4, 10 Dec 70, sub: Drug Abuse Suppression Program, pp. 1–4, box 1011, NSC files, Nixon Papers, NARA.

[43] Memo, Laird for Secs of Military Depts and CJCS, 17 Jun 71, CMH. Msgs, Abrams MAC 06460 to Component Cdrs, 4 Jul 71; Salzer to Abrams, 5 Jul 71; Abrams MAC 06527 to Component Cdrs, 7 Jul 71, Abrams Papers, CMH; MACV History, 1971, vol. 2, ch. 10, pp. 16–23. Quotation is from Ltr, Abrams to the Command, 17 Aug 71, folder 2001, MACV Collection, MHI. Allegations against the South Vietnamese are recounted in Hammond, *Military and the Media, 1968–1973*, pp. 392–99; MFRs, Odeen, 15 Jun 71 and 10 Aug 71, sub: Vietnamization Meeting with Secretary Laird, folder 77, Thayer Papers, CMH.

year. On the other hand, the service amnesty programs suffered from inconsistent administration and in some instances outright hostility at lower command echelons. Drug education appeared to have little effect on troop behavior due to heavy-handed instructional methods, factual inaccuracies (many senior officers and noncommissioned officers knew less about drugs than did their soldiers), and the generation gap. A CINCPAC study in September 1971 concluded that commanders' efforts at antidrug indoctrination were foundering on "hair, the war, and marijuana." MACV continued its antidrug offensive as long as U.S. troops remained in Vietnam; but the drug problem among its forces, as among Americans at home, resisted solution.[44]

The interlocking maladies of race, drugs, dissent, and the generation gap, while they attracted a great deal of command attention from General Abrams on down, were of uncertain effect on American military capability. One field force commander declared in early 1971 that "we have a serious disciplinary problem which has resulted in operational slippages," but he also praised the "dedication and performance" of American servicemen in Vietnam in the face of public, news media, and congressional hostility to the war. Most common was the view that the force was holding together despite a serious drug problem, continuing racial tension, and the difficulty of leading the new generation of soldiers. The MACV inspector general's command audits reached essentially this conclusion. So did the young captains who, at Department of the Army direction, conducted anonymous field interviews with more than 800 officers, noncommissioned officers, and enlisted men during the spring of 1971. They reported that, while morale and discipline were better in combat than in support units, nevertheless "the American soldier <u>in general</u> is a responsible individual" who "still performs magnificently when led by men who are both technically competent and who communicate a sense of concern for the soldier's welfare."[45]

It seems evident that the majority of American personnel in Vietnam—including many of the drug users, black activists, and men who questioned the purpose of the war—continued to do their duty. Many problems, notably the drug epidemic, peaked after U.S. forces

---

[44] Memo, Kester for Sec Army, 25 May 71, sub: Use of Heroin in Vietnam; Memo, Holloway and Fitzgibbons, for CINCPAC, 1 Sep 71, sub: CINCPAC Study for Evaluation of PACOM Drug Abuse Treatment/Rehabilitation Programs. Both in CMH. Quotation is from latter document, pp. 36–37. Memo, MACV Provost Marshal for Chief of Staff, MACV, 10 Sep 72, sub: MACV Drug Abuse Control Program—Talking Points Paper, CMH, describes the command's continuing antidrug effort.

[45] First quotation is from Collins, Debriefing Report, 7 Jan 71, pp. 12–13, Collins Papers, MHI. Second quotation is from Memo, Capt Barry R. McCaffrey for Lt Gen George I. Forsythe, sub: Visit to USARV from 7 April to 15 May 1971, pp. 7, 32, CMH. For origin of this study, see Msg, Westmoreland WDC 04105 to Abrams info Rosson, 10 Mar 71, Abrams Papers, CMH. Msgs, McCaffrey ARV 0061 to Abrams, 7 Jan 71; CG III MAF to COMUSMACV, 7 Jan 71; and Palmer WDC 02173 to Abrams, 6 Feb 71; all in Abrams Papers, CMH, are generally positive in tone. Inspector general assessments are summarized in MACV History, 1971, vol. 2, ch. 10, pp. 27–28.

were out of ground combat, so that the remaining operational burden fell upon the more mature and professional elements of the command, such as the advisers and aviators. Internal troubles notwithstanding, the Military Assistance Command was able to carry out its complex tasks of redeployment and RVNAF improvement and modernization while simultaneously waging General Abrams' "one war" in South Vietnam and launching new offensives in Cambodia and Laos.

8

South Vietnam: Waging the One War

In the struggle for South Vietnam, the first three years of the Nixon administration were years of apparent progress for the allies. The Military Assistance Command and the South Vietnamese government and armed forces put General Abrams' "one war" concept into execution against a weakened enemy who—from policy, necessity, or both— offered only diminishing resistance. The South Vietnamese armed forces took over a steadily growing proportion of the fighting as American troops withdrew, with no significant setbacks in either combat or pacification; they appeared to be on the way to achieving Secretary Laird's goal of combat and logistical self-sufficiency. The Saigon government, its legitimacy enhanced by a series of local and national elections, enlarged its administrative and military presence in the countryside and undertook ambitious social and economic programs, notably a comprehensive and long-needed land reform. Yet General Abrams, Ambassador Bunker, and most other American officials observed these developments with only guarded optimism. They realized that South Vietnam's fundamental military, political, and social weaknesses still persisted; that much of the progress they were reporting depended on a high level of American support, which was not going to continue; and that while the Viet Cong were much weaker, North Vietnam remained strong and determined to prevail.

The Enemy Returns to Protracted War

The North Vietnamese and Viet Cong, despite their costly military defeats in the three general offensives of 1968, and despite indications that their forces in South Vietnam were diminishing in numbers and quality, attempted to continue the general offensive into 1969. Their fourth nationwide offensive, launched on 23 February, consisted primarily of small ground probes and rocket and mortar bombardments, which included shelling of Saigon for the first time since the November 1968 bombing halt. Aside from its psychological value as a show of strength, this effort brought the Communists little gain for many casualties. Allied forces anticipated the offensive, preempted much of it with attacks of their own, and easily repelled the enemy assaults. Still weaker offensives in May and June had even less military effect.[1]

During the summer of 1969, in response to these setbacks and to the growing political and military disarray of their forces in the south, the North Vietnamese Politburo directed a change in tactics. Until 1968, those Lao Dong Party leaders who favored a drive for quick, decisive victory through big-unit war and the General Offensive–General Uprising had seemed to be in the ascendant. During 1969, the balance shifted to the proponents of a less costly campaign, which would use small-scale guerrilla and sapper attacks combined with renewed rural and urban political activity to bleed American and South Vietnamese forces, disrupt pacification, and rebuild the revolution's southern power base in anticipation of a negotiated settlement and American withdrawal. By fighting a less expensive southern campaign, the Communists also could devote more resources to economic reconstruction in North Vietnam, a goal that party leaders publicly declared to be of equal importance to the liberation of the south. Nevertheless, Hanoi's objective remained victory, defined at this stage as complete American withdrawal and replacement of the Thieu government with a National Liberation Front–dominated coalition as an intermediate step to unification. Some North Vietnamese leaders, notably Defense Minister Vo Nguyen Giap, continued to assert that large-unit offensives were essential to final achievement of the revolution's objectives.[2]

Resolution Nine, published in July 1969 by the *Central Office for South Vietnam* to guide operations in the southern half of South Vietnam, typified the new enemy tactics. The resolution made the customary claims of victory in the General Offensive–General Uprising. It also, however, cited Communist failures in military proselytizing, guerrilla warfare, recruiting, and building political associations; and it reprimanded lower-level party leaders for failing to understand that the general offensive required intensive action over a relatively long period of time. Resolution Nine defined the party's mission as rebuilding its military and political forces to defeat the Nixon administration's policy, which the resolution's authors accurately characterized as an effort to "de-Americanize and de-escalate the war step by step, to preserve their manpower and material as they de-escalate, . . . and to compete with us [in territory and population control] so . . . they can end the war on a definite strong position." The revolution must press forward on all three strategic fronts—the cities, the rural lowlands, and the mountains—employing appropriate political and military methods in each

---

[1] Duiker, *Road to Power*, pp. 277–78. Msgs, Abrams MAC 11672 to Wheeler and McCain, 29 Aug 68; Abrams MAC 13146 to Wheeler, 28 Sep 68; Abrams MAC 7391 to McCain info Wheeler, Bunker, 10 Jun 69. All in Abrams Papers, CMH. RVNAF/FWMAF Combined Campaign Plan, 1969, pp. 1–3, 6, CMH; CIA Directorate of Intelligence, Intelligence Memorandum, Aug 69, box 138; Msg, Abrams MAC 2385 to McCain and Bunker, 24 Feb 69, box 065, NSC files, Nixon Papers, NARA. Enemy offensives are summarized in MACV History, 1969, vol. 1, ch. 3, pp. 116–19, 123–24.

[2] Duiker, *Road to Power*, pp. 278–83, 368; MACV History, 1969, vol. 1, ch. 3, pp. 2, 19, 116.

with the objective of defeating pacification and forcing the Americans to withdraw troops more rapidly than the RVNAF could replace them, thus causing the collapse of the Saigon government. While calling as usual for employment of both main force and guerrilla warfare, *COSVN Resolution Nine* clearly gave priority to the latter. It emphasized the use of guerrillas, sappers, and mortar and rocket units to inflict damage on the Americans and South Vietnamese at minimal cost to the revolutionary forces; and it called as well for renewed political organization and agitation in both rural and urban areas.[3]

As outlined in *COSVN Resolution Nine* and documents elaborating upon it, this was not a strategy of sitting back and waiting for the Americans to leave. Instead, the revolutionary forces were to "fight vigorously and for a sustained period of time, to become stronger as we fight and to win greater victories as we fight." While using forces economically, the North Vietnamese and Viet Cong would exploit opportunities for concentrated large-scale attacks as allied troops dispersed to counterguerrilla activity and protect pacification. They would be alert to moments for "seizing, creating and taking advantage of opportunities in order to produce leaps forward." Nevertheless, the accent was on a prolonged, difficult struggle against an enemy acknowledged to be powerful, with victory "limited" rather than "clear-cut [and] complete" and coming in a "difficult and complicated way."[4]

General Abrams, Admiral McCain, and their Washington superiors grasped the nature of the enemy's tactical shift almost as soon as it went into effect. As early as March 1969, McCain was aware of the improving fortunes of Hanoi's protracted war faction. General Abrams and his commanders, from their analysis of the enemy's activity and their review of captured documents, soon spotted the trend away from large unit to guerrilla and sapper operations, a trend that in fact had begun in late 1968. Final confirmation of the new enemy tactics came in mid-October 1969, when an element of the 199th Light Infantry Brigade captured a complete copy of *COSVN Resolution Nine*. The American leaders believed that the enemy had been compelled to this change by the heavy losses of his failed offensives and by a steady decline in the size and quality of his forces. Abrams declared that the Communists were "attempting to devise a formula for tactical action that will give [them] the maximum psychological and military gains from a military force whose overall effectiveness becomes poorer with each of his . . . coordinated offensive efforts." Nevertheless Abrams, especially during discussion of American troop withdrawals, regularly reminded his

---

[3] Resolution Issued by the 9th Conference of *COSVN*, Jul 69, translated copy in folder, Overview 9th Conference *COSVN*, Jul 69, MACV Collection, MHI, pp. 6–11, 25–35; quotation is on p. 12. The resolution is analyzed and extensively excerpted in MACV History, 1969, vol. 1, ch. 3, pp. 127–34.

[4] First quotation is from Resolution, *COSVN*, 9th Conference, p. 21; see also pp. 31–32. Other quotations are from MACV History, 1969, vol. 1, ch. 3, pp. 121, 130–33; see also pp. 120, 122–23, 126–27.

superiors that the enemy still possessed strong main force units, mostly located in cross-border sanctuaries, and hence retained the capacity for large-scale attacks. He thus saw no need to alter his flexible "one war" concept to counter the enemy's new initiative.[5]

A Change of Mission for MACV

Even as the North Vietnamese altered their tactics, the Nixon administration undertook a review of the mission and operational approach of its command in South Vietnam. Since 1965, there had been dissent against the Military Assistance Command's emphasis on mobile offensive operations. Retired Army Lt. Gen. James M. Gavin, for example, advocated a more defensively oriented strategy of occupying coastal enclaves in order to improve population security and reduce American losses. In March 1968, Secretary of Defense Clifford's staff, in their draft response to General Wheeler's request for 206,000 more troops for Vietnam, recommended that General Westmoreland be directed to withdraw from remote interior positions such as Khe Sanh and concentrate his forces for mobile defense of the "demographic frontier" nearer the coast. General Wheeler vehemently objected to this proposal, claiming it would simply bring the fighting closer to the population centers; and Clifford dropped it from his final recommendation to President Johnson. Discussion of strategic alternatives ceased when it became apparent that the Military Assistance Command could continue its existing pattern of operations without major reinforcement.[6]

From the time he took command of MACV in mid-1968, General Abrams, supported by Admiral McCain and General Wheeler, consistently argued against any curtailment of American offensive operations. The chief of the MACV operations center reported in May 1968 that Abrams "won't stay if they cut back on friendly actions like [in] Korea." Abrams acknowledged that the enemy largely controlled both his own and allied casualties by his ability to vary the tempo of action, but Abrams insisted that the best way to minimize friendly losses was through constant offensive pressure to preempt major Communist attacks. Preemption was especially necessary as the enemy shifted from infantry assaults to standoff rocket and mortar bombardments, which could best be forestalled by aggressive allied sweeping and patrolling as well as by larger operations to disrupt Communist base areas and

[5] Quotation is from Msg, Abrams MAC to Wheeler and Bunker, 7 Jun 69; Msgs, McCain to Wheeler info Abrams, 5 Mar 69; Abrams MAC 11810 to Wheeler info McCain, 10 Sep 69; Abrams Papers, CMH; MACV History, 1969, vol. 1, ch. 3, pp. 134, 127, 135–36. Memo, John Holdridge for Kissinger, 14 Oct 69, sub: Enemy Strategy in SVN, box 139; Memo, Holdridge for Kissinger, 20 Oct 69, sub: Hanoi's War Problems, box 140; Special National Intelligence Estimate 14.3–70, 5 Feb 70, sub: The Outlook from Hanoi: Factors Affecting North Vietnam's Policy on the War in Vietnam, box 144, NSC files, Nixon Papers, NARA.

[6] *United States–Vietnam Relations*, sec. 4.C.6.(c), pp. 37–51, describes the Clifford group's proposals.

supply routes. Reiterating a theme of General Westmoreland's, Abrams pointed to the interdependence of pacification success and allied offensives. He declared in March 1969: "The accelerated pacification program, which we feel is progressing quite favorably, is made possible largely by friendly military initiative which keeps the enemy from concentrating his forces against our pacification program." Further emphasizing the offensive, Abrams took every occasion to suggest that attacks on the enemy's bases in Laos and Cambodia would reduce their combat capability and hence American casualties and would "go far toward making a U.S. force reduction feasible."[7]

President Nixon and his advisers initially accepted the military point of view. A few days after the inauguration, General Goodpaster, the deputy COMUSMACV, who had been sounding out members of the new administration, reassured Abrams that "there appears to be no support . . . for 'deescalating the violence' or reducing the pressure of our operations in Vietnam." The president's national security adviser, Dr. Kissinger, argued against any negotiated or tacit de-escalation of the fighting except in the context of mutual withdrawals of U.S. and North Vietnamese troops. Kissinger considered that any de-escalation would leave the other side free to continue terrorism and subversion, intensify pressure in the United States to bring the troops home, and create morale and discipline problems in Vietnam among idle American soldiers. Heeding these arguments, Nixon stated in his first major Vietnam policy decision memorandum on 1 April that there would be "no de-escalation except as an outgrowth of mutual troop withdrawal." If the North Vietnamese raised the issue in the Paris talks, "the U.S. side will listen but only discuss it in the context of mutual withdrawal."[8]

Calls for reduction of the violence continued, however, especially among the increasingly antiwar Democrats in and out of Congress. Former Johnson administration officials, notably Clark Clifford and Averell Harriman, as well as Senators Fulbright and Kennedy, urged the new administration to seek openings for peace by curtailing American offensive operations. In May, Senator Kennedy and others criticized a bloody attack by the 101st Airborne Division on North Vietnamese troops entrenched on Dong Ap Bia Mountain in

[7] First quotation is from Chaisson Diary, 29 May 68, box 9, Chaisson Papers, Hoover Institution; second is from Msg, Abrams MAC 3806 to Wheeler and McCain, 25 Mar 69; third is from Msg, Abrams MAC 4035 to Wheeler and McCain, 30 Mar 69. Both in Abrams Papers, CMH. In same collection, see Msgs, Wheeler JCS 05824 to Abrams info Sharp, 28 May 68; Abrams MAC 8892 to Wheeler, 4 Jul 68; Abrams MAC 1469 to Wheeler, 2 Feb 69; Wheeler JCS 03805 to McCain and Abrams, 28 Mar 69; McCain to Wheeler info Abrams, 30 Mar 69.

[8] Quotation is from Msg, Goodpaster JCS 01029 to Abrams, 24 Jan 69, Abrams Papers, CMH. In same collection, see Msg, Goodpaster DIASO/SPO to Abrams, 3 Mar 69. Memo, Kissinger for the President, 7 Mar 69, sub: Considerations Surrounding the Issue of Deescalation in Vietnam, box 136; Memo, Kissinger for the President, sub: Vietnam Situation and Options, box 142; National Security Decision Memorandum 9, 1 Apr 69, sub: Vietnam, box 1008, NSC files, Nixon Papers, NARA. Second quotation is from last-cited document.

Troops charge at Hamburger Hill.

the A Shau Valley, an engagement that American soldiers and newsmen labeled the battle of "Hamburger Hill" and Senator Kennedy pronounced "both senseless and irresponsible." The 101st Airborne Division commander, Maj. Gen. Melvin Zais, who claimed later that General Abrams at the time endorsed his decision to press the attack, replied that he fought the North Vietnamese at Dong Ap Bia as part of his mission to destroy enemy forces and installations and insisted the fight had been a "tremendous, gallant victory." Public outcry over the engagement continued, however, with many important newspapers taking Kennedy's side or calling for a lowering of the level of violence.[9]

The proponents of de-escalation had a sympathizer in Secretary of Defense Laird, who was preoccupied with reducing the human and financial costs of the war to the United States. Commenting on Hamburger Hill, Laird noted that the attack was in accord with the guidance to U.S. field commanders to keep maximum pressure on the enemy. He suggested that they could be given alternative guidance to "ease the search-and-destroy pressure and probably, at least in the

[9] Pressure on the administration is summarized in Historical Division, "Joint Chiefs of Staff and the War in Vietnam, 1969–1970," pp. 81–90, and Kissinger, *White House Years*, pp. 262–63. Quotations on Hamburger Hill are in MACV History, 1969, vol. 1, ch. 5, pp. 56–57, which also summarizes the results of the fight. Msg, Wheeler JCS 06172 to Abrams info McCain, 21 May 69, Abrams Papers, CMH. Press reaction is summarized in Hammond, *Military and the Media, 1968–1973*, pp. 85–89. Zais, Draft MFR, 24 Jul 69, sub: Dong Ap Bia, Zais Papers, MHI, contains Zais' claim that Abrams approved of his decision.

246

General Zais is greeted by a fellow officer.

short run, reduce friendly casualties." Laird acknowledged the military commanders' insistence that offensive pressure kept overall casualties down, but declared: "I am convinced there is no way to ascertain the validity of this thesis."[10]

Pursuant to his concerns, Laird on 3 July directed the Joint Chiefs of Staff and through them Admiral McCain and General Abrams to conduct a "broad and deep reassessment" of U.S. military strategy and force employment in Southeast Asia. They were to take into account a number of major changes in American policy and the overall situation: the enemy's adoption of economy of force tactics; the assumption by South Vietnam of major responsibility for its own security; the beginning of American troop withdrawals; the reduction in the American military budget; President Nixon's scaling down of America's Vietnam objective; and the fact that "General Abrams was ordered to conduct the war with a minimum of American casualties."[11]

Abrams and McCain promptly responded that no change in strategy or tactics was needed or desirable. Abrams on 9 July asserted that his "one war" concept enabled his forces to respond to changing enemy tactics by varying their own operational priorities. He repeated that

[10] Kissinger, *White House Years*, pp. 264–65, notes Laird's interest in de-escalation. Memo, Laird for the President, 21 May 69, sub: Combat Activity Related to Hill 937 (Hamburger Hill), box 067, NSC files, Nixon Papers, NARA, contains the Laird quotations.

[11] Msg, JCS 3957 to CINCPAC and COMUSMACV, 3 Jul 69, box 070, NSC files, Nixon Papers, NARA. This message also can be found in MACV J–3 Force Planning Synopsis for Gen Abrams, vol. 2, pp. 73–75, CMH.

constant pressure on the North Vietnamese and Viet Cong, besides keeping American casualties down, also supported pacification and allowed American forces to improve South Vietnamese military performance through combined operations. In a later comment on one of the perennial cease-fire studies, Abrams declared that "we have got where we are [in Vietnam] by the exercise of powerful force." The improvements in pacification, RVNAF effectiveness, and general security, and the reduction of enemy capabilities, had been gained by "exploiting mobility and fire power. . . . We hold the initiative and the enemy is confronted with serious military problems." McCain echoed Abrams' arguments and cited as well indications that the enemy was engaged in a logistical buildup to support future offensives.[12]

Even as Abrams and McCain prepared their replies to Laird, President Nixon decided to explore the possibility of changing, if not the conduct of operations, at least the statement of General Abrams' mission. That statement had evolved over the years, derived from guidance of the Secretary of Defense and the Joint Chiefs of Staff, from terms of reference issued by CINCPAC, and from presidential decisions, such as the one in 1967 making COMUSMACV the single manager for pacification. As of early 1969, CINCPAC's and COMUSMACV's overall task, as defined by the Joint Chiefs, was "to assist the Government of Vietnam and its armed forces to defeat externally directed and supported communist subversion and aggression and attain an independent non-communist . . . South Vietnam functioning in a secure environment." To this end, the commands were to make as difficult and costly as possible North Vietnam's support of the Viet Cong; maintain plans for a full-scale air and naval campaign against North Vietnam; "defeat" the North Vietnamese and Viet Cong in South Vietnam and "force the withdrawal" of the North Vietnamese; extend Saigon's "dominion, direction, and control over all of South Vietnam"; and deter or defeat Chinese Communist intervention. Nowhere were improvements of the South Vietnamese forces or a shift of the burden of the fighting to them even hinted at. General Abrams, when he first took over as COMUSMACV, himself considered revising the statement. He then realized, however, that it would be a "basket of horror" to obtain concurrence for a change from the U.S. Embassy, CINCPAC, and higher authority and discontinued the project.[13]

On 7 July 1969, Nixon met with Kissinger, Laird, Secretary of State Rogers, General Wheeler, and other senior advisers on board the presidential yacht *Sequoia*. After a review of a temporary lull in fighting in

[12] Abrams' and McCain's views are in MACV, Force Planning Synopsis, pp. 77–80, CMH. Quotation is from Msg, Abrams MAC 10174 to McCain and Wheeler, 6 Aug 69, Abrams Papers, CMH.
[13] MACV History, 1971, vol. 1, ch. 2, p. 7. Mission statement quotations are from Memo, Kissinger for the President, 8 Oct 69, box 139, NSC files, Nixon Papers. Abrams' attempt to revise the mission statement is recounted in MFR, Branch, 20 Apr 71, sub: COMUSMACV Remarks in Connection with History Briefing, MACV Collection, MHI.

*The Joint Chiefs of Staff meeting with President Nixon
and members of his staff at the White House*

South Vietnam, Nixon decided to revise Abrams' instructions, if only to deflect domestic political criticism that the administration was ignoring a possible enemy diplomatic signal. Laird then directed Wheeler to pursue the question with McCain and Abrams, with a view not to alter the actual way MACV was operating but to indicate that the command's mission in the war had changed. Wheeler, perhaps reflecting his own inclinations more than Laird's, emphasized to the Pacific commanders that the issue concerned "semantics," and that any revision must still allow maximum pressure on the enemy.[14]

Wheeler, Abrams, and McCain quickly went on record against a change of either mission or tactics. At Laird's request, Wheeler went to Vietnam on 16 July to consult the field commanders and assess the military situation. After conferring with McCain and Abrams, Wheeler cabled to Washington that they all saw "inherent dangers" in any revision of MACV's mission statement. Wheeler argued that General Abrams' credibility with newsmen, then still high, would be damaged when reporters observed that a new mission statement was not followed

<hr />

[14] Kissinger, *White House Years*, p. 276. Memo, Kissinger for the President, 8 Jul [1969], sub: SEQUOIA NSC Meeting on Vietnam, box 091, NSC files, Nixon Papers, NARA. Historical Division, "Joint Chiefs of Staff and the War in Vietnam, 1969–1970," pp. 90–91. Former Ambassador Henry Cabot Lodge also urged a mission change; see Note by Amb Lodge for Use in Meeting with President, Kissinger, and Lodge on 24 Jun 1969 in the President's Office, box 138, NSC files, Nixon Papers, NARA.

by any change in field operations. At the same time, a change would undermine the morale of U.S. and South Vietnamese troops and cause the Saigon government to believe the Americans were preparing for a precipitate withdrawal. By the same token, the enemy would interpret a change as indicating a weakening of American resolve and take a more aggressive stance both at Paris and on the battlefield. Wheeler, and Abrams in a separate statement, repeated their previous arguments about how essential it was to retain the military initiative. Before leaving Saigon on 20 July, Wheeler told the press that he saw no evidence in the battlefield lull of any enemy peace signal, that the American tactics of relentless pursuit of the enemy remained in effect, and that he approved of those tactics.[15]

While Wheeler was still in Southeast Asia, the Joint Chiefs of Staff, on the basis of his and Abrams' cabled views, advised Laird on 18 July against any change in MACV's mission statement. However, "recognizing the political pressures involved," the Joint Chiefs offered two alternatives. The first, which the Joint Chiefs preferred, retained the commitment to defeat aggression and attain a stable, non-Communist South Vietnam but with new subordinate undertakings to provide "maximum assistance in training and equipping the RVNAF as rapidly as possible"; support nation building and pacification; conduct "military operations to reduce the flow of materiel and manpower support for enemy forces" in South Vietnam; and maintain plans for a comprehensive air and naval campaign against North Vietnam. The second alternative changed the mission to assisting the South Vietnamese armed forces to "take over an increasing share of combat operations" aimed at defeating aggression and allowing the South Vietnamese people "to determine their own future without outside interference." It repeated the four tasks of the first alternative and added a new one: "Conduct military operations designed to accelerate improvement in the RVNAF and to continue to provide security for U.S. forces."[16]

Secretary Laird rejected the Joint Chiefs' arguments against a mission change. In a meeting with Wheeler on 22 July, after the chairman returned from Vietnam, Laird again disavowed any desire or intent to alter the conduct of operations in Southeast Asia. However, he insisted that the current MACV mission statement did not square with Nixon's change in America's national goals in Vietnam. If a new mission statement created a major credibility problem, which Laird doubted it would, the administration, not the military, would deal with it. On the twenty-eighth, Laird informed the Joint Chiefs that he had decided

[15] Historical Division, "Joint Chiefs of Staff and the War in Vietnam, 1969–1970," pp. 92–95; Memo, McConnell JSCM–443–69 for Sec Def, 18 Jul 69, sub: Statement of Mission of US Forces in Southeast Asia, box 076, NSC files, Nixon Papers, NARA. This memo has appended comments of Generals Wheeler and Abrams.

[16] Memo, McConnell JCSM–443–69 for Sec Def, 18 Jul 69, sub: Statement of Mission of US Forces in Southeast Asia, box 076, NSC files, Nixon Papers, NARA; Historical Division, "Joint Chiefs of Staff and the War in Vietnam, 1969–1970," pp. 93–94.

to propose to the president a new MACV mission statement based on the language of their second alternative. The Joint Chiefs two days later declared that Laird's draft was "suitable if the President wishes to modify the goals upon which military directives and operations for Southeast Asia are premised" but again expressed concern that a publicized change in the mission statement "could jeopardize the credibility of the Administration and military because no substantial change in the pattern of operations in South Vietnam would follow from the mission change."[17]

On 7 August, Laird presented the new mission statement to President Nixon with the declaration that it "reflects your policy guidance much more accurately than does the current mission statement" and was more closely in line with "what our forces in Southeast Asia are actually doing." The statement defined America's objective as assuring the South Vietnamese people's right "to determine their future without outside interference." To that end, CINCPAC and COMUSMACV were to assist the South Vietnamese armed forces "to take over an increasing share of combat operations" aimed at defeating subversion and aggression. The commands were to provide maximum assistance for the rapid development, training, and equipment of the RVNAF. They were to continue military support for accelerated pacification, civic action, and security programs. They were to conduct military operations designed to accelerate RVNAF improvement, protect U.S. forces, and reduce the flow of materiel and manpower to the enemy in South Vietnam, as well as maintain plans for "a comprehensive air and naval campaign in Vietnam." In a concession to the Joint Chiefs' concerns about credibility, Laird proposed to issue the new instructions and incorporate them in appropriate joint documents but make no public announcement of the change. "Rather," he told Nixon, "we plan to handle the matter in a low-key manner."[18]

Nixon, at Kissinger's recommendation, agreed to Laird's approach. At Laird's direction, the Joint Chiefs on 21 August relayed the new mission statement to Admiral McCain and General Abrams and inserted it in joint publications. In October, Abrams included the new language in a formal Military Assistance Command statement of mission "for use as a basic frame of reference" to guide MACV planners. In addition, he stated that "the application of U.S. military power, and the provision of civil and military support will be executed in the name of the Republic of Vietnam and with the approval of Vietnamese officials and agencies," whom MACV was to assist "in assuming full responsibility

[17] Historical Division, "Joint Chiefs of Staff and the War in Vietnam, 1969–1970," pp. 95–97. Memo, Wheeler JCSM–474–69 for Sec Def, 30 Jul 69, sub: Statement of Mission of US Forces in Southeast Asia, box 076, NSC files, Nixon Papers, NARA. Quotations are from this memorandum.

[18] First and last quotations are from Memo, Laird for the President, 7 Aug 69, sub: Statement of Mission of U.S. Forces in Southeast Asia, box 139, NSC files, Nixon Papers, NARA. Quotations from mission statement are from MACV History, 1969, vol. 1, ch. 2, pp. 3–4. Historical Division, "Joint Chiefs of Staff and the War in Vietnam, 1969–1970," pp. 97–98.

for the planning and execution of national security and development programs at the earliest feasible date."[19]

The new instructions soon became public and produced at least some of the confusion about which the Joint Chiefs had warned. On 3 November, in a major nationally televised speech explaining his Vietnam policy, Nixon declared that he had "changed General Abrams's orders" to the effect that "the primary mission of our troops is to enable the South Vietnamese forces to assume the full responsibility for the security of South Vietnam." The very day of the speech, a story in the *Washington Star* pointed out that Vietnamization had made no real difference in the way American forces fought. After the speech, CBS News reported that General Abrams disapproved of the new orders and soon would be replaced by a "logistical type general." Abrams, in a 7 November message to his commanders, denied "any division between COMUSMACV, CINCPAC, the Chairman JCS, Sec Def, and/or the Commander-in-Chief." He declared that he had "accepted completely, and is executing to the best of his ability, all orders of the President" and directed his commanders to get on with the "cohesive pursuit and accomplishment of U.S. objectives." Six days later, Admiral McCain issued a message to all Pacific commanders reaffirming and disseminating the revised mission statement but adding that "a change in current operations or emphasis has not been directed by, nor is expected to result from this message."[20]

During the following months, the Nixon administration emitted conflicting signals as to what, if any, implications the mission change was to have for Military Assistance Command's operations. President Nixon, in the fall of 1969 after the first two American troop redeployments, expressed the desire that "remaining U.S. ground forces be deployed so that a major enemy offensive would involve early contact" with them. In February 1970, Kissinger urged Nixon to inform Laird and Wheeler, who were about to leave for Vietnam, "that you anticipate General Abrams will utilize this period, when U.S. strength is still strong [sic], to initiate the maximum number of spoiling attacks designed to keep the enemy attrition high." Three months later, Nixon committed American ground forces to an offensive against the enemy's Cambodian base areas. As the Cambodian operations were ending,

---

[19] Memo, Kissinger for the President, 11 Aug 69, sub: Statement of Mission of U.S. Forces in Southeast Asia, box 076; Memo, Laird for CJCS, 15 Aug 69, sub: Statement of Mission of U.S. Forces in Southeast Asia, box 1004, NSC files, Nixon Papers, NARA. Historical Division, "Joint Chiefs of Staff and the War in Vietnam, 1969–1970," p. 98. Quotation is from MACV Revised Strategic Objectives Plan, May 70, pp. 33–34, CMH. See also MACV History, 1971, vol. 1, ch. 2, p. 7.

[20] Nixon quotation is from Msg, Wheeler JCS 13701 to Bunker, McCain, and Abrams, 4 Nov 69; Abrams quotation is from Msg MAC 14418 to all Commanders info Bunker and Rosson, 7 Nov 69; CINCPAC quotation is from Msg, McCain to Pacific Commanders, 13 Nov 69; see also Msg, Wheeler JCS 13789 to Abrams info McCain, 5 Nov 69. All in Abrams Papers, CMH. *Washington Star* report is discussed in Hammond, *Military and the Media, 1968–1973*, pp. 137–38.

Nixon told Abrams to plan for an incursion into Laos, continuation of South Vietnamese ground and American air operations in Cambodia, and a summer offensive in South Vietnam. The enemy, Nixon said, "cannot be led to believe that we have shot our wad." Yet Nixon also urged Abrams to "get the South Vietnamese to move offensively and at the same time keep our casualties low."[21]

Secretary Laird seemed to be pushing MACV in the opposite direction. Late in 1969, he stated publicly that American units in South Vietnam had adopted a policy of "protective reaction" instead of "maximum pressure," although newsmen in the field could see little practical difference between the two. In guidance to the Joint Chiefs on 16 May 1970, Laird declared that the two long-term objectives of the Cambodian incursion were to facilitate Vietnamization and allow "continuing and even accelerated" U.S. redeployments, with success measured in lower American casualties and accelerated Vietnamization and troop withdrawals. On 21 August, he instructed McCain and Abrams that American combat operations "are to be steadily decreased, commensurate with the increasing capability of RVNAF to assume combat and support responsibilities, and commensurate with the security of remaining forces." Laird nevertheless stopped short of directing Abrams to discontinue offensive operations or give up maintaining maximum pressure on the enemy.[22]

In the end, what did the new mission statement mean? Its wording was loose enough to justify any offensive action Abrams chose to take or that the administration ordered him to take. The other side, contrary to administration expectations, displayed no interest in tacit or negotiated battlefield de-escalation. However, Laird's new mission statement better reflected the administration's policy objectives; and it gave President Nixon something with which to counter his political critics without tying his hands operationally. For Laird, it was a means of nudging MACV toward less aggressive or at least less costly tactics. In the end, continuing troop redeployments and tight budgets, as well as a persistent low level of enemy activity, did more than the new MACV mission statement to shape the pattern of operations in South Vietnam.

---

[21] First quotation is from Memo, Kissinger for Sec Def, sub: Future Operations in Vietnam, box 1008; second is from Memo, Kissinger for the President, 7 Feb 70, sub: Presidential Meeting with Secretary of Defense, Chairman JCS, and President's Advisor for National Security Affairs . . . , box 143; third is from Haig, Memo of Conversation, 31 May 70, San Clemente, box 146. All in NSC files, Nixon Papers. NARA.

[22] "Protective reaction" episode is recounted in Hammond, *Military and the Media, 1968–1973*, p. 138. Cambodia guidance is in MACV, Force Planning Synopsis, pp. 309–10. Memo, Odeen, 28 Jul 70, sub: Vietnamization Meeting with Secretary Laird, folder 75, Thayer Papers, CMH. Final Laird quote is from MACV History, 1970, Supp., pp. 1–2.

Military Operations, 1969–1971

Between 1969 and 1971, the fighting in South Vietnam gradually diminished. The North Vietnamese and Viet Cong, despite the exhortations of *COSVN* Resolution Nine and other directives, accomplished little more in most of the country than harassment of the allies, insufficient to disrupt pacification or American redeployments. The allies maintained offensive pressure on enemy main forces, base areas, guerrillas, and political infrastructure even as U.S. troops progressively turned over the ground battle to the South Vietnamese. General Abrams and his field commanders kept their shrinking American combat forces in action while trying to keep down casualties and push the South Vietnamese Army to the front. In an effort to reduce both American costs and Vietnamese civilian death and suffering, they modified or abandoned some long-standing Vietnam War military practices.

Enemy operations in III and IV Corps, and to a lesser extent in I and II Corps, followed the principles of *COSVN* Resolution Nine. The number of battalion and larger size attacks declined from the levels of 1968; but smaller assaults, increasingly directed against the government territorial forces, continued at about the same rate, and acts of antipacification terrorism against civilians and village and hamlet officials became more frequent. To reinforce the guerrilla campaign, the enemy broke down a number of main force regiments into smaller elements and placed them under control of its local party committees. He retained divisions in remote base areas and across the border in Cambodia and Laos, and he continued to move men and supplies down the Ho Chi Minh Trail. Keeping up a main force threat, he tested the South Vietnamese Army during 1969 in sustained engagements at Ben Het and Bu Prang–Duc Lap in the II Corps highlands. On several occasions, the enemy compelled American and South Vietnamese units in western I Corps to evacuate isolated firebases. Overall, however, Communist offensive activity of all sorts, including terrorism, declined in frequency and effectiveness throughout 1970 and 1971. General Abrams attributed much of this decline in III and IV Corps to the effects of the allies' 1970 incursions into Cambodia, which at least temporarily disrupted the Communists' supply system and forced their troops away from the South Vietnamese border.[23]

American and South Vietnamese military operations continued to be guided by the annual combined campaign plans. Those plans, and their supplemental corps area plans, changed little over the years in basic principles. While acknowledging that U.S. strength in Vietnam

---

[23] Memo, Laird for the President, 28 May 70, sub: Enemy Activity in South Vietnam, box 146, NSC files, Nixon Papers, NARA. Msgs, Abrams MAC 3303 to McCain and Wheeler, 13 Mar 70; Abrams MAC 13231 to Moorer and McCain, 6 Oct 70; Abrams MAC 6538 to Moorer and McCain, 14 May 70; Abrams Papers, CMH. Enemy operations are summarized in MACV History, 1969, vol. 1, ch. 3; ibid., 1970, vol. 1, ch. 3; ibid., 1971, vol. 1, ch. 1, pp. 8–9, and ch. 3, passim. A firebase siege and evacuation are described in MACV History, 1970, vol. 3, an. G.

gradually would diminish, the plans retained as fundamental objectives the defeat of enemy forces and the extension of Saigon's authority throughout the countryside. They listed as subordinate tasks the destruction of enemy units and base areas, the expansion of territorial security, protection of the cities, and the opening of lines of communication. They included as well a commitment to organize, train, and equip the South Vietnamese armed forces and use them in accord with their assigned missions and capabilities. The latter phrase denoted in particular the replacement of South Vietnamese regulars by territorials in security and pacification missions, so that the South Vietnamese could take over from the Americans the waging of mobile warfare against enemy main forces and base areas. Beginning with the 1970 edition, the plans incorporated the area security concept developed by the Marshall Committee with its concentric secure, consolidation, clearing, and border surveillance zones. The 1971 plan, in the wake of the Cambodian offensive, added operations outside South Vietnam to block enemy infiltration.[24]

In all four corps areas, U.S. and South Vietnamese units devoted much effort to what formerly were called search-and-destroy missions. For example, in I Corps the allies repeatedly swept areas in the mountains and piedmont, with special attention to the A Shau Valley and other key enemy supply and infiltration corridors. In 1970 and 1971, the allies extended their search-and-destroy missions into the enemy's Cambodian and Laotian sanctuaries. There was, however, a shift of emphasis in these operations away from attacking enemy units, which continued to be hard to find and engage, toward keeping the main forces away from the populated lowlands and uprooting the Communists' supply system by searching out caches and blocking infiltration routes. As U.S. redeployments gained momentum, American and South Vietnamese commanders in I and II Corps gradually moved their remaining forces eastward, adopting a variant of the "demographic frontier" strategy, which Clifford's staff had proposed back in 1968.[25]

Behind the shield of the regulars, the Regional and Popular Forces, National Police, People's Self-Defense Force, Provincial Reconnaissance Units, and other pacification elements, supported by CORDS advisers,

---

[24] The plans are summarized in detail in MACV History, 1969, vol. 1, ch. 2, pp. 5–12; ibid., 1970, vol. 1, ch. 2, pp. 2–8; ibid., 1971, vol. 1, ch. 2, pp. 6–9, ch. 4, pp. 5–7, ch. 7, p. 11, and vol. 2, an. H, pp. 1–3. Full texts of the plans are Combined Campaign Plan 1969, AB 144, 30 Sep 68; Combined Campaign Plan 1970, AB 145, 31 Oct 69; and Combined Campaign Plan 1971, AB 146, 31 Oct 70. All in CMH.

[25] Operations are summarized in MACV History, 1969, vol. 1, ch. 5; ibid., 1970, vol. 1, ch. 1, p. 1, ch. 2, pp. 9–17, ch. 5; ibid., 1971, vol. 1, ch. 1, pp. 7–8, ch. 4, pp. 8–10, 21–25, ch. 5, and vol. 2, an. H, p. 3. Memo, Resor for Sec Def, 12 Aug 70, sub: Sec of the Army Vietnam Trip, box 245, NSC files, Nixon Papers, NARA. Msgs, Corcoran NHT 0610 to Abrams, 14 Apr 69; Ewell HOA 2764 to Abrams, 10 Sep 69. Both in Abrams Papers, CMH. Zais, Debriefing for CINCPAC, Jun 70, Zais Papers, MHI.

conducted small-unit operations to secure the villages and hamlets and eliminate the remaining guerrillas and Communist political cadre. While the allies emphasized in their plans and operations bringing security to the people, they also systematically depopulated certain strategic enemy-dominated zones. In Quang Nam Province, 1st Marine Division elements, supported by Army Rome plow units, between May and July 1969 leveled Go Noi Island, a Viet Cong stronghold south of Da Nang. Allied forces in III Corps similarly sanitized large parts of the enemy war zones menacing Saigon. A State Department official described the results:

A great circular swath around greater Saigon has been literally "cleared" of jungle foliage and resident population. This includes the classic Viet Cong concentration and military infiltration regions . . . War Zone C, War Zone D, and the "Iron Triangle." They are now visibly empty, pockmarked by innumerable bomb craters and scarred by vehicle tracks. There is literally hardly any place for the Viet Cong to hide in this region. . . .[26]

As long as they remained in South Vietnam, American combat units took part in offensive operations of all types. During 1970, they devoted the bulk of their efforts, measured in battalion days, to what were described as "combat operations," including the drive into Cambodia. On the average, pacification and security activities accounted for less than 30 percent of American battalion days each month. Abrams, however, expanding on the efforts of his predecessor, tried to reduce the public visibility of continuing American offensives. In July 1969, at General Wheeler's suggestion, Abrams began referring to such activities as "pre-emptive operations." He directed MACV public affairs officers to stop releasing the code-name of every new American operation.[27]

While pressing the attack, General Abrams and his field commanders displayed increasing concern with minimizing American casualties. At a 5 April 1969 commanders' conference, Abrams instructed his generals to keep as much pressure as possible on the enemy but also to avoid unnecessary losses. Field commanders picked up the cues. When he took over XXIV Corps in March 1970, Lt. Gen. Melvin Zais, while he urged his subordinates to remain aggressive, also enjoined them to "recognize the atmosphere in our own country, recognize the political climate, recognize the difficulties under which the administration is operating insofar as public support is concerned, and recognize the impact

[26] The clearing of Go Noi Island is described in Smith, *U.S. Marines in Vietnam, 1969*, pp. 174–87. Quotation is from Msg, Ray S. Cline Saigon 303 to Kissinger, 9 Mar 70, box 410, NSC files, Nixon Papers, NARA.

[27] Battalion day figures are from MACV History, 1970, vol. 2, ch. 7, p. 105. Historical Division, "Joint Chiefs of Staff and the War in Vietnam, 1969–1970," pp. 94–95; Msgs, Abrams MAC 10176 to Lt Gen Herman Nickerson, Jr, CG, III MAF, 6 Aug 69; Nickerson to Abrams, 7 Aug 69. Both in Abrams Papers, CMH.

of heavy casualties." Commanders must "remember that it can be very counter-productive to win a battle if it costs you too much in the present environment in which we are operating."[28]

The effect of such injunctions is difficult to measure precisely. However, Zais' forces during their 1970 summer offensive into the enemy's base areas declined several opportunities for pitched battles. In July, for example, elements of the 101st Airborne Division evacuated Firebase RIPCORD in the A Shau Valley when it came under siege by North Vietnamese troops. The MACV annual history declared candidly that the decision to evacuate was based in part on "the domestic and foreign political implications of another U.S. firebase undergoing a Khe Sanh or Dien Bien Phu siege. Firebase RIPCORD, if given an inordinate amount of adverse publicity, might well have jeopardized the entire Vietnamization program."[29]

A sure way to reduce American casualties was to turn more of the fighting over to the South Vietnamese—a central goal of Vietnamization. General Abrams continually pressed his commanders on this point. Even before Secretary Laird inaugurated Vietnamization, Abrams told General Weyand, then II Field Force commander, "the goal is a continued increase in ARVN participation." A year later, he declared to Weyand's successor, General Ewell: "We have to get ARVN to shoulder more of the load. . . . A major effort has to be directed toward that end."[30]

In response to Abrams' urging, the field commanders used various expedients to place the South Vietnamese in the forefront of the fight. While U.S. troops remained, the I and II Field Forces paired American and South Vietnamese units in combined offensives and territorial security operations aimed at getting the South Vietnamese into the field and improving their tactical capabilities. American forces regularly provided the South Vietnamese with B–52, tactical air, helicopter, artillery, and logistical support. During the battles of Ben Het and Bu Prang–Duc Lap, I Field Force deployed American units on security missions to free South Vietnamese battalions for the major engagements. Gradually, as American divisions departed, the South Vietnamese assumed the predominant combat role. By late 1971, the South Vietnamese Army and territorial forces were conducting most

[28] Hammond, *Military and the Media, 1968–1973*, p. 82. Msgs, Abrams MAC 6179 to Nickerson, 15 May 69; Nickerson to Abrams, 17 May 69. Both in Abrams Papers, CMH. Quotation is from Zais, Opening Remarks at XXIV Corps Commanders' Conference, 22 Mar 70, Speeches box, Zais Papers, MHI; in same collection, see Zais, Commanders' Briefing, 24 May 70.

[29] Quotation is from MACV History, 1970, vol. 3, an. G, pp. 4–6. For another instance of avoiding a fight, see Cosmas and Murray, *U.S. Marines in Vietnam, 1970–1971*, pp. 75–76. For an earlier avoidance of "another Khe Sanh," see Msg, Nickerson to Abrams info Zais, 10 Sep 69, Abrams Papers, CMH.

[30] First quotation is from Msg, Abrams MAC 9198 to Weyand, 11 Jul 68; second is from Msg, Abrams MAC 4813 to Ewell, 16 Apr 69; see also Msg, Abrams MAC 8028 to Ewell info Wetherill and Hollis, 23 Jun 69. All in Abrams Papers, CMH.

ground operations in South Vietnam and its environs; the Vietnamese Air Force was flying the majority of tactical air strike missions in South Vietnam; and the Vietnamese Navy had taken over riverine and most coastal surveillance tasks.[31]

As a result of diminishing enemy activity, more cautious tactics, and above all falling U.S. troop strength, American combat deaths in South Vietnam declined both in absolute numbers and in relation to total allied losses. In 1969, more than 9,100 Americans were killed in action; in 1970, the toll fell to 4,100 and in 1971 to about 1,300. By mid-1970, South Vietnamese combat deaths outnumbered American in every military region but I Corps, where the numbers were about equal. This trend continued into 1971, as did a general decline in the war's intensity as measured in overall friendly and enemy casualties. President Nixon and his advisers, who closely monitored the casualty figures, welcomed these numbers as a sign that Vietnamization was working and that their effort to calm domestic antiwar agitation by cutting the war's costs was paying off.[32]

Nixon and his advisers eagerly anticipated the day when they could announce the end of American offensive ground combat in Vietnam. As early as May 1970, Secretary Laird declared in a public hearing of the Senate Armed Services Committee that the American combat role would end in mid-1971 as redeployments brought U.S. forces down to the transitional support level. The remaining Americans would continue to assist the South Vietnamese, "but those support functions under our program will also be Vietnamized." Laird, and Secretary of State Rogers, repeated that promise at intervals thereafter. General Abrams, however, insisted that his forces could not assume a totally passive posture. Instead, all the units in South Vietnam "must participate actively in combat operations consistent with their capabilities." Assumption of a "guard-type security posture," Abrams declared, would be "detrimental to the security of the command."[33]

[31] Clarke, *Final Years*, pp. 391–417; MACV History 1969, vol. 2, ch. 6, pp. 147–48; ibid., vol. 1, ch. 1, p. 5; ibid., 1971, vol. 1, ch. 1, pp. 1–3, ch. 4, p. 11; MACV J3–06 Command Briefing, 28 Nov 71, in folder, J3 Command Briefing, 28 Nov 71, MACV Collection, MHI; Zais, Opening Remarks, XXIV Corps Commanders' Conference, 22 Mar 70, Speeches box, Zais Papers, MHI. Msgs, Corcoran NHT 1159 to Abrams, 6 Jul 69 and NHT 1489 to Abrams, 25 Aug 69; Ewell HOA 2077 to Abrams info Colby and Maj Gen Richardson, 10 Jul 69. All in Abrams Papers, CMH.

[32] Casualty figures are from MACV History, 1970, vol. 1, ch. 5, p. 12; ibid., 1971, vol. 1, ch. 10, pp. 69–72. Memo, Odeen, sub: Vietnamization Meeting with Secretary Laird, 29 Jul 70, folder 75, Thayer Papers, CMH. MFR, Brig Gen J. C. McDonough, 12 Nov 70, sub: U.S. Casualties in South Vietnam, box 150; Memo, Laird for the President, 6 Apr 71, sub: Tempo of the War, box 153; Chart 5, Apr 71, box 084; Memo, Kissinger for the President, 15 Sep 71, sub: U.S. Combat Deaths, box 157; Memo, J. D. Negroponte for Kissinger, 2 Dec 71, sub: Declining Intensity of the Vietnam War, box 158. All in NSC files, Nixon Papers, NARA.

[33] First quotation is from Msg, Paul M. Kearney, OCJCS, JCS 06659 to Wheeler info McCain, Abrams, 13 May 70, Abrams Papers, CMH. Memo, Kissinger for the President, 31 May 71, sub: Statements on Ground U.S. Combat Role in Vietnam, box 154, NSC files, Nixon Papers, NARA, reviews of the promises of Laird and Rogers. Quotation from Abrams is in MACV, Force Planning Synopsis, p. 386.

During the first half of 1971, the administration conducted a muted repetition of the 1969 debate over changing MACV's mission statement. President Nixon, Dr. Kissinger, and Secretary Laird, desiring to forestall congressional movements to set a deadline for American withdrawal or cut off war funding, wanted to announce publicly that American troops were out of the ground fighting. The Joint Chiefs of Staff argued against tying down U.S. forces in passive defense and warned of a credibility gap if in fact the troops became involved in combat after the public announcement. All sides finally agreed on a formula proposed by General Abrams. Under it, American troops would conduct active operations, primarily small-unit patrolling, in "dynamic defense" of their bases and of elements supporting the South Vietnamese; but they would not engage in large-unit offensives against enemy formations beyond striking distance of American positions. In June, Abrams formally directed his commanders to adopt this posture while continuing to provide operational support to the South Vietnamese forces "within our narrowing capabilities." The remaining U.S. combat units gradually shifted to "dynamic defense," which in some instances—notably that of the 101st Airborne Division in northern I Corps—still involved considerable offensive action.[34]

In January 1972, Secretary of the Army Robert F. Froehlke told a Pentagon press briefing that "basically, the responsibility for offensive operations in Vietnam has been taken over by the ARVN" while the remaining U.S. combat troops performed "defensive security tasks." He noted that this mission still involved "some very real hardship and danger and fighting" because "good security is not provided by ducking down behind a fortification or hiding in a pill box." By the time Froehlke spoke, the two American combat brigades still operational in Vietnam, the 196th Infantry Brigade and the 3d Brigade, 1st Cavalry Division, were deployed respectively to protect Da Nang and the Saigon–Bien Hoa–Long Binh complex. Except for the remaining advisers with South Vietnamese units, active American ground combat participation in the war had come to an end.[35]

As American ground troops left the battlefield, General Abrams turned to American airpower as his principal instrument for influencing the course of combat. "While air is powerful," Abrams said, "it is

---

[34] Historical Division, "Joint Chiefs of Staff and the War in Vietnam, 1971–1973," pp. 219–33; MACV, Force Planning Synopsis, p. 407, CMH. Msgs, Bunker Saigon 943 to Kissinger, 22 May 71, box 412; Memo, R. C. Robinson for Moorer, sub: Mission Change for United States Forces in Southeast Asia, box 1004. All in NSC files, Nixon Papers, NARA. Msg, Abrams MAC 06474 to Component and Regional Assistance Cdrs, 5 Jul 71, Abrams Papers, CMH; MACV History, 1971, vol. 1, ch. 4, p. 10. MACV J–3–06 Command Briefing, 28 Nov 71, in folder, J–3 Command Briefing, 28 Nov 71; AAR, Opn OPORD 11–71, 101st Abn Div, both in MACV Collection, MHI.

[35] Excerpts from Pentagon News Briefing by Sec Army Robert F. Froehlke, 28 Jan 72, in *Command Comment*, no. 88, Feb 72, in Speeches-Miscellaneous file, Peers Papers, MHI. As of early 1972, the South Korean Capital and 9th Divisions continued security operations in Military Region 2; see MACV History, 1971, vol. 1, ch. 1, p. 5.

also flexible. . . . Where the enemy puts the heat on, whether it's the Plain of Jars or Duc Lap, it's only a matter of hours until tremendous shifts of power can be made." Even as aircraft numbers and sortie rates were reduced by redeployments and budget cuts, U.S. Air Force, Navy, and Marine fighter-bombers and Thailand-based B–52s supported American and allied units in contact, pounded enemy troop concentrations and base areas in South Vietnam, and sought to stem the flow of supplies through Laos and Cambodia. Complementing the combat operations, American fixed- and rotary-wing aircraft continued the less dramatic but still essential daily work of reconnaissance, transport, and resupply of allied forces. General Abrams, exploiting the flexibility of single management, regularly shifted the weight of air attack between targets inside and outside of South Vietnam in response to weather and the combat situation. As fighting in South Vietnam lessened, he committed an increasing proportion of both fighter-bomber and B–52 sorties to interdiction in Laos and support of the new allied battlefront in Cambodia.[36]

While the Military Assistance Command continued to make maximum use of its airpower, it cut back employment of other weapons, notably artillery, in response to budgetary and political considerations. As early as mid-1968, the Defense Department directed the command to try to reduce its expenditures of artillery ammunition. The department especially questioned the value of harassment and interdiction fire directed at suspected enemy movement routes, supply caches, and concentration points. Such fire missions accounted for nearly 30 percent of the artillery ammunition used during the early months of 1968. Secretary Laird, who suspected that artillery fire, like air strikes, was being used excessively in Vietnam, continued the drive for ammunition economy. By late 1970, MACV's field commanders had sharply reduced their monthly shell expenditures, mainly by an almost complete termination of harassment and interdiction fire. The 1st Marine Division, for example, in October 1970, stopped artillery fire at targets within 500 meters of inhabited areas except in support of troops in actual contact. Such measures, besides conserving ammunition, reduced civilian casualties and property damage and increased the people's sense of security as the sound of artillery was heard less frequently.[37]

The Military Assistance Command also phased out its use of herbicides as a result of budget cuts and political pressure. Since 1962, the command had used commercial weed killers, sprayed from fixed-

---

[36] Quotation is from MACV History, 1970, vol. 1, ch. 6, p. 1. MACV's air operations are summarized in ibid., 1969, vol. 1, ch. 5; ibid., 1970, vol. 1, ch. 6; ibid., 1971, vol. 1, ch. 6.

[37] Msg, Wheeler JCS 05567 to Westmoreland and Sharp, 22 May 68, Westmoreland Message files, May 68, CMH. Msgs, Abrams MAC 6870 to Wheeler and Sharp, 26 May 68; Abrams MAC 8148 to Cushman et al., 20 Jun 68; Moorer JCS 11461 to McCain info Abrams, 18 Aug 70; Abrams MAC 11529 to McCain, 24 Aug 70. All in Abrams Papers, CMH. MFRs, Odeen, 3 and 10 Aug 70, 1 Feb 71, 25 Mar 71, sub: Vietnamization Meeting with Secretary Laird, folders 76 and 77, Thayer Papers, CMH; Cosmas and Murray, *U.S. Marines in Vietnam, 1970–1971*, pp. 105–06.

*Four U.S. Air Force C–123s spray defoliant
during Operation* RANCH HAND.

wing aircraft and helicopters and from the ground, to clear fields of fire along roads and around firebases and camps, as well as to wither Viet Cong crops in remote, unpacified areas. Crop-destruction missions were closely restricted, requiring prior authorization by the ambassador or COMUSMACV. In 1969, MACV defoliated 4,907 square kilometers of woods and brush and destroyed 256 square kilometers of crops. General Abrams, Ambassador Bunker, Secretary Laird, and the Joint Chiefs of Staff considered the herbicide program essential to the war effort because it denied the enemy cover and concealment and complicated his food supply problems. North Vietnamese and Viet Cong propaganda, on the other hand, charged that the chemicals were causing birth defects in humans as well as damage to plants and animals. At home, the antiwar movement and the growing environmental crusade by 1969 were picking up the issue; and scientists were questioning the safety of the chemicals for use in the United States as well as South Vietnam.[38]

The political furor coincided with new scientific findings and declining defense resources to bring a gradual end to the program. In September

---

[38] MACV History, 1969, vol. 2, ch. 7, pp. 17–24; ibid., 1970, vol. 2, ch. 14, pp. 5–7, 10–13. Hammond, *Military and the Media, 1968–1973*, pp. 374–75. Memo, Laird for the Assistant to the President for National Security Affairs, 18 Jul 70, sub: United States Anticrop Warfare Program in Vietnam, box 148, NSC files, Nixon Papers, NARA, summarizes Defense arguments for the program.

1969, to accommodate projected reductions in procurement of the agents, Admiral McCain ordered General Abrams to reduce herbicide operations by 30 percent by 1 July 1970. The Department of Defense budget for fiscal year 1971 included only $3 million for herbicide procurement, whereas MACV had requested $27 million. On 15 April 1970, the Defense Department discontinued use of one of the three most commonly used herbicides, Agent ORANGE, after a report to the Department of Health, Education, and Welfare indicated that one of its main ingredients did indeed cause birth defects in experimental animals. MACV continued operations with two other agents, BLUE and WHITE; but under the restricted budget, stocks of those chemicals rapidly diminished. With herbicide supplies dwindling and the Air Force beginning to redeploy its UC–123 spray planes, General Abrams on 10 July terminated all fixed-wing defoliation operations, although he allowed commanders to continue helicopter and ground spraying around defensive positions. He concentrated the remaining fixed-wing aircraft for crop destruction in I and II Corps in conjunction with a summer campaign against enemy base areas.[39]

Additional curtailment steps followed during 1970, even as a committee from the American Association for the Advancement of Science visited South Vietnam to investigate the effects of herbicides. In October, General Abrams placed the remaining stocks of Agent ORANGE under strict centralized control after his inspector general confirmed a press report that elements of the American Division had made unauthorized use of the agent. In November, at Ambassador Bunker's and General Abrams' direction, an interagency mission committee, composed of representatives of the U.S. Embassy, U.S. Agency for International Development, Joint U.S. Public Affairs Office, CORDS, and the MACV intelligence and operations directorates, conducted a review of the crop destruction program in the light of changing circumstances, namely dwindling supplies of chemicals and the Saigon government's expanding control over food-producing areas. While the committee endorsed at least limited continuation of the campaign, Abrams and Bunker in December decided to phase it out by May 1971 and thereafter to use up the remaining stocks of BLUE and WHITE in helicopter and ground spraying around camps and firebases. They planned no public announcement of the decision so as to preserve "our option to reinstitute [the] program if necessary in the future."[40]

[39] MACV History, 1969, vol. 2, ch. 7, pp. 24–26; ibid., 1970, vol. 2, ch. 14, pp. 5, 7–10.

[40] Msg, McCain to Abrams info Moorer, 29 Jul 70, Abrams Papers, CMH; MACV History, 1970, vol. 2, ch. 14, pp. 13–15. Unauthorized use incident is described in MACV History, 1970, vol. 2, ch. 13, p. 18; and Hammond, *Military and the Media, 1968–1973*, p. 375. Quotation is from Msg, Bunker Saigon 19374 to Sec State, 9 Dec 70, sub: Herbicide Policy Review; see also Msgs, Bunker Saigon 18557 to Sec State, 23 Nov 70, sub: Herbicide Policy Review; box 150; and Bunker Saigon 20011 to Sec State, 21 Dec 70, sub: Herbicide Policy Review, box 151. All in NSC files, Nixon Papers, NARA.

As 1970 neared its end, the administration anticipated a critical report from the American Association for the Advancement of Science and faced in addition a congressionally mandated National Academy of Sciences study of the environmental and health effects of herbicide use in South Vietnam. The Senate had scheduled hearings on ratification of the 1925 Geneva Protocol against chemical warfare. For political reasons, therefore, the White House promptly made the mission's decision public. On 29 December, it announced that an "orderly and rapid" phase-out of herbicide operations was under way and would be completed by the following spring. The Defense Department in January 1971 ordered immediate termination of all crop destruction spraying and directed that defoliation around bases end by 1 May.[41]

The latter directive brought a protest from General Abrams. Supported by Ambassador Bunker, the Joint Chiefs, and Secretary Laird, Abrams insisted that spraying around installations must continue in order to protect American lives because defoliation was the only safe way to keep mined perimeters free of brush. He requested authority to spray at least until December, when defoliant stocks would run out. Secretary of State Rogers, however, opposed any extension for fear that it would cause a domestic political uproar.[42]

President Nixon hesitated to make a decision until requests from Laird and Abrams became urgent and rumors spread that soldiers returning to Vietnam from leave were bringing back weed killer for their units. Finally, on 18 August, Nixon authorized helicopter and ground spraying through 1 December in situations where commanders considered it essential for protection of their forces and other means could not be used. Nixon forbade any public announcement of the extension. MACV public affairs officers, if queried, were to say that herbicides were being phased out except for limited spraying around bases under the same health and safety restrictions then in force in the United States. On this basis, MACV used up its stocks of Agents BLUE and WHITE while the Defense Department arranged to ship the remaining Agent ORANGE back to the United States for destruction. No public furor erupted over the extension. Only after the end of the war would persistent scientific, political, and legal controversy arise over Agent ORANGE's possible damage to the health of Vietnam veterans.[43]

[41] Msg, Sec State 188497 to Am Emb Saigon and COMUSMACV, 18 Nov 70, sub: Herbicide Policy Review, box 150; Memo, Michael A. Guhin for Kissinger, 19 Dec 70, sub: Dr David's Proposed Vietnam Herbicide Policy and Draft Announcement; Memo, Kissinger for Sec Def, 28 Dec 70, sub: Policy Regarding Herbicides in Vietnam, with attached documents, box 151, NSC files, Nixon Papers, NARA; MACV History, 1971, vol. 1, ch. 6, pp. 20–21.

[42] Msg, Sec State 072220 to Am Emb Saigon, 27 Apr 71, sub: Herbicides; Msg, Bunker Saigon 6463 to Sec State, 28 Apr 71, sub: Herbicides, box 154; Memo, Laird for the President, 13 May 71, sub: Policy Regarding the Use of Herbicides in Vietnam; Memo, Rogers for the President, 24 Jun 71, sub: DOD Request for Authority to Continue Use of Herbicides in Vietnam, box 155; Memo, Rear Adm Robert O. Welander for Haig, 9 Aug 71, sub: Herbicides in Vietnam; Memo, Kissinger for the President, 13 Aug 71, sub: Herbicides in Vietnam, box 156. All in NSC files, Nixon Papers, NARA.

[43] Memo, Kissinger for Secs State and Def, 18 Aug 71, sub: Herbicides in Vietnam; Msg, Sec

MACV's reductions in artillery fire and phasing out of defoliation and crop destruction, like its post–My Lai tightening of the rules of engagement, were aspects of the command's effort to reduce damage to South Vietnamese civilians from American operations. Whether because of these initiatives or due to other factors, suffering attributable to American actions appears to have declined after 1968. According to a Defense Department analysis, civilian casualties, as measured by hospital admission rates, fell from 7,000 per month in 1968 to 3,000 in 1971. In the same period, the percentage of injured from bombing and shelling—those almost certain to have been victims of American weapons—dropped from 43 to 22. The Defense Department analysts attributed most of this decline to the general lowering of the intensity of combat and even more to movement of the main force fighting, with its heavy use of air and artillery, away from population centers. In 1969, for example, 32 percent of all tactical air strikes occurred within 3 kilometers of hamlets; by 1971 only 16 percent did. Despite MACV's conscientious efforts to enforce restraint, reduction of the war's cruelty thus was largely out of the command's control. Whatever the rules of engagement, if the enemy returned in force to the populated areas, civilians again would suffer.[44]

Pacification

Alleviation of civilian suffering was essential to the success of the pacification program, to which MACV and the rest of the American mission, along with the Saigon government, devoted increasing attention and resources. Ambassadors Bunker and Colby, General Abrams, and President Thieu all anticipated a final political struggle between the government and the Communists, possibly after a military cease-fire. To prepare for it, they followed up the Accelerated Pacification Campaign of late 1968 with a sustained effort to reoccupy the countryside and attract the peasantry to the government. Following a well-established strategy, Regional and Popular Forces and Revolutionary Development cadres moved into contested villages and hamlets, expelled or suppressed the Viet Cong guerrillas and political infrastructure, and set up elected local governments and People's Self-Defense Force units. Behind this shield of security were to come land reform and other economic improvements aimed at giving the people a stake in Saigon's system.[45]

State 153250 to Am Emb Saigon, CINCPAC, COMUSMACV, 20 Aug 71, sub: Use of Herbicides, box 156. Both in NSC files, Nixon Papers, NARA; MFR, Odeen, 20 Sep 71, sub: Vietnamization Meeting with Secretary Laird, folder 78, Thayer Papers, CMH; MACV History, 1971, vol. 1, ch. 6, pp. 20–21; Hammond, *Military and the Media, 1968–1973*, pp. 375–76.

[44] Analysis is in Thayer, "War Without Fronts," pp. 863–67. See also MFR, Odeen, 7 Oct 71, sub: Vietnamization Meeting with Secretary Laird, folder 78, Thayer Papers, CMH.

[45] Hunt, *Pacification*, pp. 214–17, provides an overview of allied pacification strategy. Colby expressed the view that the war was moving toward a political phase in MFR, Odeen, 31 Aug 70, sub:

The allies embodied their strategy in annual pacification and development plans, joint products of President Thieu's Central Pacification and Development Council, the Saigon government ministries, MACV, and CORDS, which dovetailed with the military combined campaign plans. Beginning with the first pacification and development plan, that for 1969, the Vietnamese agencies did most of the drafting of these plans, although with much behind-the-scenes advice from CORDS. General Abrams regularly instructed his American forces to treat the plans as authoritative guidance for their own support of pacification. Like the campaign plans, the national pacification plans were supplemented by corps area and province plans, the latter signed jointly by the province chief and his American province senior adviser.[46]

The annual plans translated the broad concepts of pacification into specific, usually quantitative, goals. Typical were the eight objectives of the 1969 plan: to control and secure 90 percent of the population; to eliminate 33,000 Viet Cong cadre under Phoenix and other programs; to establish elected local governments in all villages throughout the country; to recruit the People's Self-Defense Force to 2 million members and arm 400,000 of them; to bring in 25,000 enemy defectors under the *Chieu Hoi* ("Open Arms") program; to resettle at least 300,000 refugees; to expand village-level propaganda and information efforts; and to improve the rural economy and increase rice production. The 1970 plan kept the same basic objectives and added several special programs, notably land reform. For 1971, the South Vietnamese dropped the word "pacification" from the title of the plan. They renamed it the Community Defense and Local Development Plan to reflect the claim that "pacification"—wresting the people from enemy control—had been completed. They also reduced the eight objectives to three—self-defense, self-government, and self-development—to demonstrate greater national self-sufficiency as the Americans withdrew. During 1971, in what would turn out to be a premature expression of confidence, the Vietnamese began writing a four-year Community Defense and Local Development Plan for 1972 and beyond.[47]

Like every other aspect of the war, pacification underwent Vietnamization between 1969 and 1972. Much more than the military effort, pacification from the beginning had been Vietnamese in command and operation. Nevertheless, the 7,500 CORDS military and civilian advisers in Saigon, the corps areas, the provinces, and the districts played a vital role. They helped with planning, monitored

Vietnamization Meeting with Secretary Laird, folder 76, Thayer Papers, CMH.

[46] Drafting process for the 1969 Pacification and Development Plan (P&D) is described in MACV History, 1969, vol. 2, ch. 8, pp. 5, 8–9. CORDS role in drafting the 1970 plan may be followed in detail in CORDS, 1970 Pacification and Development Plan After-Action Report, CMH. A typical Abrams endorsement is in Memo, Abrams for Distribution List, sub: GVN 1970 Pacification and Development Plan, attached to 1970 P&D Plan, CMH.

[47] P&D plans are summarized in MACV History, 1969, vol. 1, ch. 2, pp. 4–5, vol. 2, ch. 8, pp. 9–17; ibid., 1970, vol. 1, ch. 2, pp. 3–4, ch. 8, pp. 4–10, 94–95; ibid., 1971, vol. 1, ch. 7, pp. 1, 7–10.

execution, encouraged, persuaded, and worked to replace corrupt or incompetent Vietnamese officials. MACV and the mission accordingly delayed CORDS personnel reductions for as long as possible so as to sustain the momentum of pacification. Nevertheless, during 1970 and 1971, CORDS cut its advisory strength by about two-thirds, principally by eliminating its mobile training teams for the Regional and Popular Forces and its district advisory teams. CORDS also turned over to the Vietnamese key administrative functions, including operation of the Hamlet Evaluation System, MACV's main device for measuring pacification results.[48]

As measured by the Hamlet Evaluation System and other statistical indicators, the allies made steady progress toward their pacification objectives. Territorial security showed impressive gains. By the end of 1971, close to 95 percent of South Vietnam's population lived in places rated relatively secure under the Hamlet Evaluation System, compared to 60 percent in February 1968 when the Hamlet Evaluation System criteria had been less stringent. Some of this gain resulted from movement of people from contested and fought-over villages to government-controlled towns and refugee camps, but much was due to actual expansion of security into the countryside. To provide this security, the government enlarged its Regional and Popular Forces in the period from 300,000 men to 520,000, the National Police from 74,000 to 121,000 (many for the first time occupying village and hamlet stations), and the People's Self-Defense Force—more useful as a source of intelligence and a means of committing people to the government than as a fighting force—from 1.4 million to 3.9 million. Most years, the government met its quota of Communist defectors and deserters. However, the Phoenix campaign to identify and "neutralize" by death or capture underground Viet Cong leaders fell short, hampered by corruption, poor administration, and the unwillingness of South Vietnamese agencies to pool information. Many American officials questioned whether the accomplishments of Phoenix compensated for the bad publicity the program received in the United States.[49]

---

[48] The Vietnamese character of pacification is emphasized in interview of Robert W. Komer, *Organization and Management of the New Model Pacification Program—1966–1969* (Rand Corporation Doc no. D(L)–20104–ARPA, 7 May 70) pp. 6–7, CMH; Memo, Dean Moor for Kissinger, 21 Aug 69, sub: Status of Pacification in South Vietnam, box 138, NSC files, Nixon Papers, NARA. Hunt, *Pacification*, pp. 261, 272–73. MACV History, 1971, vol. 1, ch. 7, pp. 1, 3–5, ch. 8, p. 77.

[49] Hunt, *Pacification*, pp. 253–54. Thayer, "War Without Fronts," pp. 871–82, concludes that the Hamlet Evaluation System was a valid measurement system and that the increase in secure population after 1969 did represent government authority reaching into the countryside. For the view that part of the security gain resulted from people fleeing or forced to leave contested areas, see Memo, Col Charles A. Wilson, Jr., for Potts, 23 Nov 70, sub: VC Guerrilla and Local Force Erosion, in folder USMACV (J–2) CICV St. 70–02, MACV Collection, MHI; and Ltr, Zais to Abrams, 12 Jun 70, Zais Papers, MHI. MACV claims are in MACV History, 1969, vol. 2, ch. 8, pp. 34–35, 48–50, 70–73; ibid., 1970, vol. 1, ch. 1, pp. 2–3, vol. 2, ch. 8, pp. 1–2, 94–99; ibid., 1971, vol. 1, ch. 1, pp. 3, 9, ch. 7, pp. 11–12.

Personal observations and impressions, often from former skeptics and pessimists, seemed to confirm the statistical evidence of progress. John P. Vann, who had trumpeted MACV's military and pacification failures during his tour as an Army adviser in 1962–63 and later returned to Vietnam as a civilian corps area deputy for CORDS, as early as March 1969 informed William P. Bundy, Assistant Secretary of State for East Asian and Pacific Affairs, that "the situation is very much improved, and . . . the improvement is solid." Observers from the National Security Council and analysts from the State Department and Central Intelligence Agency, with varying degrees of qualification, reached similar conclusions. Visitors could sense the improving security. A member of Kissinger's staff reported after a December 1970 trip to Vietnam: "Roads once closed are open, in some cases 24 hours a day. One no longer hears bombs and artillery every night in Saigon. Trade and commerce flow more freely." From the enemy side, prisoners, defectors, and captured documents admitted to significant losses in people and territory.[50]

Partly a cause and partly a consequence of improving territorial security was a steady decline in enemy guerrilla and local force strength. In late 1970, a MACV J–2 study estimated that enemy guerrilla strength had fallen from about 80,000 in December 1967 to 43,800 in January 1970. Local force numbers in the same period dropped from about 30,700 to 20,300. The enemy appeared to have succumbed to a vicious cycle. Years of hard fighting, culminating in the heavy casualties of Tet 1968 and the subsequent general offensives, had worn down the Viet Cong, allowing the government to reoccupy many villages and hamlets. This pacification success in turn denied the enemy the recruits he needed to recover from the military attrition, ensuring that enemy strength would continue to decline. In an effort to compensate for these losses, the enemy began introducing North Vietnamese into Viet Cong local force and guerrilla units, even in the Mekong Delta where the war previously had been a South Vietnamese fight on both sides. The northerners, however, lacked the Viet Cong's knowledge of the terrain and rapport with the people; their increasing dominance of the revolutionary organizations demoralized many veteran southern fighters and cadres.[51]

[50] First quotation is from Memo, Haig for Kissinger, 29 Mar 69, sub: MFR on John Vann's Views, box 136; second is from Memo, W. R. Smyser for Kissinger, 23 Dec 70, sub: A Few Observations on Pacification . . . , box 1011; see also Study, State Department, Bureau of Intelligence and Research, 24 Jul 70, sub: South Vietnam: Pacification Holding the Line, box 148, NSC files, Nixon Papers, NARA. Enemy viewpoints are reported in Memo, Wilson for Potts, 23 Nov 70, sub: VC Guerrilla and Local Force Erosion, MACV Collection, MHI; and Orrin DeForest and David Chanoff, *Slow Burn: The Rise and Bitter Fall of American Intelligence in Vietnam* (New York: Simon and Schuster, 1990), pp. 100–01, 186.
[51] Memo, Wilson for Potts, 23 Nov 70, sub: VC Guerrilla and Local Force Erosion, MACV Collection, MHI. Typical views of Viet Cong weakness are MFR, Col Amos A.

Subsequent Vietnamese Communist analysts acknowledged that the allies' pacification programs after Tet 1968 had hurt the revolution badly in the countryside. As they saw it, the party during 1968 and early 1969 had made a major strategic error by concentrating its forces around the cities in a vain attempt to continue the general offensive. The allies' rural counterattack had caught the revolution off balance. When Nixon initiated Vietnamization and the buildup of Saigon's forces, especially the territorials and People's Self-Defense Force, the Communist Party underestimated the threat posed by the American president's "very dangerous plans." In particular, as a former *COSVN* general put it,

When we saw the Americans shift to their "Vietnamization" strategy, . . . our thoughts were focused on our hopes for our military proselyting operations. We tried to turn the enemy into a watermelon, "Green on the outside but Red on the inside,". . . because we thought that our people were very good people at heart. We did not realize the extent of the stubbornness, the viciousness, and the cunning guile of the enemy, who used demagoguery, bribery, and oppression to control the population.[52]

As the balance of armed force in the countryside swung to the government, political and economic development produced mixed results. Between 1969 and 1972, South Vietnam established elected governments in about 98 percent of its villages and hamlets and carried out successful elections for provincial councils and for both houses of its national legislature. The presidential election of October 1971, however, disappointed the mission and the Nixon administration. Despite strenuous American efforts to ensure a fair, contested campaign—albeit one which Thieu would win—Thieu maneuvered his major rivals out of the race and secured overwhelming voter endorsement in a one-man referendum. The outcome cast doubt on the reality of South Vietnamese democracy and called in question Thieu's commitment to a broad-based representative political system. In fact, most governmental power down to the district level remained in military hands; and President Thieu headed an administration of soldiers, civil servants, and technicians. Relatively efficient compared to previous Saigon regimes, though still riddled with corruption at all levels, Thieu's government lacked both a popular political base and institutions for mobilizing one. Some American officials, including Dr. Kissinger, considered that Thieu was doing as

Jordan, Jr, Oct 69, sub: Qualitative Observations on Territorial Security, Vann Papers, MHI; and Msg, Abrams MAC 13298 to Moorer and McCain, 7 Oct 70, Abrams Papers, CMH; MACV History, 1969, vol. 1, ch. 3, pp. 84, vol. 2, ch. 8, p. 54; ibid., 1970, vol. 1, ch. 3, pp. 185–86. Hostility of southern cadres to the North Vietnamese Army is reported by a CIA operative in DeForest and Chanoff, *Slow Burn*, pp. 186–87.

[52] Sr. Gen. Hoang Van Thai, "A Few Strategic Issues in the Spring 1968 Tet Offensive and Uprising," *Military History Magazine [Tap Chi Lich Su Quan Su]*, Issue 2 (26), 1988, published by the Ministry of Defense's Military Institute of Vietnam. Trans. Merle Pribbenow. Copy in CMH.

much to promote democracy as could reasonably be expected during a civil war; but opponents of the war in the United States branded Thieu a dictator unworthy of continued American support.[53]

If the presidential election disappointed American officials, President Thieu's efforts at land reform were more encouraging. Under the Land to the Tiller Act, which Thieu pushed through the national legislature in 1970, South Vietnam during the next three years transferred title to 2.5 million acres of rice land from landlords (who received compensation) to the farmers who actually tilled the fields. The program, assisted by American aerial surveys and computerized record keeping and administered at the local level by village committees to ensure fairness, all but eliminated farm tenancy in South Vietnam and created a new class of small landowners with, presumably, a stake in the regime. Land reform's immediate effectiveness in winning peasants to the government was uncertain, but it constituted a major contribution to the nation's long-run political stability and social well-being. Unfortunately, this land reform, one of the most ambitious and extensive in Asia and conducted in the midst of war, attracted less public attention in the United States than did the botched presidential election.[54]

South Vietnam also made progress in other economic fields. American military engineers by 1971 were finishing construction of a national road network that facilitated both military movements and civilian commerce. The regime, its efforts assisted and monitored by the MACV Assistant Chief of Staff for Economic Affairs, had some modest success in curbing inflation, expanding agricultural production, and reviving industry. South Vietnam nevertheless remained heavily dependent on U.S. economic support, especially in financing its swollen military budget.[55]

By the end of 1971, Ambassadors Bunker and Colby and General Abrams, as well as Washington officials such as Secretary Laird, were convinced that the allies were winning the pacification side of the war. Yet they also recognized the potential fragility of their achievement. The South Vietnamese government, for all its improvement, still lacked a solid popular political base; poor leadership and corruption persisted in both the civil administration and the armed forces; and the genuineness of the regime's commitment to American-sponsored reforms remained in question. Saigon's pacification gains in the countryside had resulted as much from weak opposition, which stemmed primarily from the bleeding of enemy forces in years of fighting, as

---

[53] Hunt, *Pacification*, pp. 265–67; Clarke, *Final Years*, pp. 361, 479–481. Hammond, *Military and the Media, 1968–1973*, pp. 518–23, describes administration disappointment and American domestic reaction; on same theme, see Msg, Kissinger WHS 1096 to Bunker, 10 Sep 71, box 412, NSC files, Nixon Papers, NARA. Kissinger defends Thieu in *White House Years*, p. 273, as does Ray S. Cline in Msg Saigon 303 to Kissinger, 9 Mar 70, box 410, NSC files, Nixon Papers, NARA.

[54] Hunt, *Pacification*, pp. 263–65; Thayer, "War Without Fronts," pp. 928–33.

[55] MACV History, 1971, vol. 1, ch. 1, pp. 3–4, 9–11, ch. 2, p. 4, ch. 8, p. 99.

from government strength or efficiency. As a Rand Corporation analyst put it, "Attrition is pushing pacification, not vice-versa." Much of the Viet Cong political infrastructure remained in place, though temporarily driven into hiding by the government's military domination of the countryside. It could arise again if the balance of force changed, and American troop redeployments were in fact changing the balance. The permanence of pacification thus depended in the end on whether the South Vietnamese armed forces could replace the departing Americans both in maintaining territorial security and in keeping the upper hand in the main force war.[56]

A Self-Defending South Vietnam?

As U.S. troops left South Vietnam, the Military Assistance Command and the Joint General Staff put into effect the Consolidated RVNAF Improvement and Modernization Plan (CRIMP). Their objective, set by Secretary Laird, was to create an indigenous armed force able to defend South Vietnam and defeat the insurgency with minimal American assistance. The final plan, which Laird approved in June 1970, called for expansion of the South Vietnamese forces to 1.1 million men—about half in the regular army, navy, and air force and half in the territorial elements—by the end of fiscal year 1973. With improved training and modern equipment, this force was to take over in successive phases—first ground combat and then air, naval, and logistical operations—as the American presence dwindled to a military advisory mission.[57]

The Military Assistance Command and the Joint General Staff (JGS) set up combined organizations to carry out the plan. An overall coordinating committee, composed of the MACV Assistant Chief of Staff for Military Assistance, the heads of the Training Directorate and the CORDS Territorial Security Directorate, and the chiefs of the Air Force and Navy advisory groups along with the JGS Assistant to the Chief of Staff for Planning and the chiefs of staff of the Vietnamese Navy and Air Force, met weekly to review progress and identify problems. It also conducted periodic field inspections. Within MACV headquarters, a military assistance service-funded program watch committee oversaw materiel assistance to the Vietnamese by the American armed services. A subcommittee under it reviewed and approved all changes to RVNAF tables of equipment. Other MACV and combined committees worked on desertion control and South Vietnamese logistical improvement. MACV's subordinate commands and combat and support units all took part in training Vietnamese counterparts and transferring equipment

---

[56] Hunt, *Pacification*, pp. 252, 255, 258–63, 267–68, summarizes the pluses and minuses. Quotation is from Ltr, F. J. West to Lemos, 10 Dec 69, box 1010; see also Memo, Holdridge for Kissinger, 29 Nov 71, sub: New Communist Emphasis on Countering Pacification . . . , box 158; NSC files, Nixon Papers. Komer Interv, 7 May 70, pp. 89–90, 226, also ties pacification success to military attrition.

[57] MACV History, 1970, vol. 2, ch. 7, pp. 3, 15–16; ibid., 1971, vol. 1, ch. 8, p. 1.

to them. Expansion of the Vietnamese Air Force helicopter force, for example, was a cooperative effort of U.S. Army, Vietnam, the Army 1st Aviation Brigade, and the Seventh Air Force, as well as Army helicopter pilot training facilities in the United States.[58]

General Abrams, while he aggressively pushed forward the expansion and improvement of the South Vietnamese armed forces, tried to minimize changes in their basic organization and deployment. Supported by Ambassador Bunker and Admiral McCain, Abrams argued that radical changes would upset power relationships and institutional balance in the Saigon government and cause confusion and loss of momentum. On similar grounds, Abrams rejected periodic JGS proposals to equip their forces with advanced jets, heavy tanks, self-propelled artillery, and other sophisticated weapons that he believed they did not need and could not maintain. Abrams supported marginal changes and improvements, such as establishment of a separate artillery force for the Regional and Popular Forces and provision of additional 175-mm. gun battalions and air defense units. He also worked with the Joint General Staff to incorporate the Special Forces–advised Civilian Irregular Defense Groups, hitherto outside the RVNAF, into the armed forces as Regional Force units and Border Defense Ranger Battalions, a change completed by the end of 1970.[59]

The overall structure of the armed forces, however, remained unchanged. The chain of command continued to run from the Joint General Staff to the four corps, which President Thieu in July 1970 redesignated as military regions. In an effort to disengage the regular forces from territorial security functions, he gave each military region commander two deputies—one for military operations and the other for Regional and Popular Force operations and pacification. In practice, the reorganization made little difference in the corps and military region commanders' discharge of their dual military and political functions. The nine South Vietnamese divisions and most other regular ground force units, as well as the territorials, answered to the military region commanders; and the regular units for practical purposes continued to be anchored to their regions, if only by the fact that their men were native to them. The Joint General Staff directly controlled the marine and airborne divisions of the general reserve, the air force and navy, the base logistic depots, and the training centers and military schools.[60]

Measured against the CRIMP's statistical goals, the improvement and modernization effort made encouraging, even dramatic, progress. In late March 1971, Secretary Laird reported to President Nixon that

---

[58] MACV History, 1969, vol. 1, ch. 4, pp. 25–26; ibid., 1970, vol. 2, ch. 7, pp. 85–87; Clarke, *Final Years*, pp. 427–44.

[59] MACV History, 1969, vol. 1, ch. 4, pp. 49–52; ibid., 1970, vol. 2, ch. 7, pp. 2–5, ch. 14, pp. 1–3; Clarke, *Final Years*, pp. 378, 381–83, 455–56.

[60] MACV History, 1970, vol. 2, ch. 7, pp. 16–20; Clarke, *Final Years*, pp. 378–79, 384.

the South Vietnamese forces had met their fiscal year 1973 manpower expansion goals two years ahead of time. Provision of major new equipment items, either directly from American production lines or transferred from redeploying U.S. units, also was on or ahead of schedule. The Saigon government, through conscription and voluntary enlistment, was able to provide the manpower for its new units; its training centers, according to their American advisers, steadily improved the quantity and quality of their instruction. By late 1971, the South Vietnamese were close to completing their takeover of ground, air, and naval combat operations within their borders. At the same time, they were performing a growing proportion of their own logistical support, including supply storage and distribution, port operations, and equipment maintenance; although they still relied on U.S. forces or private contractors for the more technically sophisticated functions, including communications-electronics.[61]

South Vietnamese battlefield performance, although uneven, appeared to be adequate and steadily improving. General Abrams assessed South Vietnamese Army conduct of the battle of Ben Het in the Central Highlands in July 1969 as giving "justification for confidence"; although MACV advisers noted that the South Vietnamese Army had depended heavily on U.S. fire support and displayed many lapses in staff work, operational coordination, and logistics, as well as a lack of aggressiveness in pursuing the defeated enemy. By 1970, the South Vietnamese had remedied some of these deficiencies to the point where they could undertake multiregiment operations against enemy bases in Military Regions 3 and 4. In the Cambodian incursion of the same year, the South Vietnamese Army successfully planned and conducted mobile operations at considerable distance from their home bases, and they supplied their forces with minimal American assistance. The territorial forces in Military Regions 3 and 4 proved able to maintain security in the regulars' absence. While lightly opposed, the Cambodian invasion, in Abrams' view, was well conducted and improved South Vietnamese morale. "Their pride is up," he privately told President Nixon. The 1971 South Vietnamese Army offensives in Laos and Cambodia, which met heavier North Vietnamese opposition, went less well and revealed continuing South Vietnamese operational deficiencies. Nevertheless, by the end of 1971, American and South Vietnamese commanders were expressing confidence that the South

---

[61] Laird's March 1971 report is summarized in Memo, Kissinger for the President, 26 Mar 71, sub: RVNAF Expansion and Modernization, box 153; see also Memo, Laird for the President, 8 Nov 71, sub: Trip to Vietnam, November 2–8, 1971, box 158, NSC files, Nixon Papers, NARA. For an earlier, similar view by Abrams, see Msg MAC 3303 to McCain and Wheeler, 13 Mar 70, Abrams Papers, CMH. Clarke, *Final Years*, pp. 377–78, 390; MACV History, 1971, vol. 1, ch. 1, pp. 2–3, ch. 8, p. 1; Bfg, MACV Training Directorate, Jul 71, in MACV Training Directorate Jul 71 folder, MACV Collection, MHI.

Vietnamese forces could hold their own, provided they received continuing American air and materiel support.[62]

As RVNAF improvement and modernization progressed, the Military Assistance Command redefined the functions of its advisers with the South Vietnamese forces and gradually reduced their numbers. In 1969, the command converted its tactical advisory teams with South Vietnamese divisions, regiments, and battalions to combat assistance teams. Reflecting an established fact of life, the name change denoted that the teams' mission was no longer offering advice—which South Vietnamese commanders did not need—but instead providing "combat support coordination" and liaison with U.S. forces. During 1971, General Abrams, believing that "we Americans can take a Vietnamese unit only so far," began withdrawing the combat assistance teams first from battalions and then from regiments. MACV in the same period reduced its advisory contingent at the RVNAF schools and training centers by not replacing men as they ended their tours.[63]

In October 1971, Abrams informed Admiral McCain and the Joint Chiefs that the military advisory effort had gradually changed emphasis, as the South Vietnamese forces improved, from tactical operations to functional areas such as logistics and pacification. The number of advisers would continue to decline as the South Vietnamese gained expertise. Nevertheless, Abrams emphasized that the advisory effort must continue. The Vietnamese still needed assistance in command and control, personnel management, logistics, some aspects of training, communications-electronics, and intelligence. Abrams and his field commanders relied heavily on the advisers' reports for information on their ally's situation and performance; and they realized that the advisers reinforced the South Vietnamese command structure by using their own network to ensure coordination between Vietnamese headquarters. Accordingly, adviser strength in South Vietnam by the end of 1971 had declined by only 22 percent, whereas overall U.S. strength had fallen by 66 percent.[64]

---

[62] First quotation is from Msg, Abrams MAC 8347 to McCain info Wheeler, 29 Jun 69; see also Msgs, Abrams MAC 1232 to McCain info Wheeler, 27 Jan 70, and Abrams MAC 15447 to McCain, 2 Dec 70. All in Abrams Papers, CMH. Second quotation is from Haig, Memo of Conversation, 31 May 70, San Clemente, box 146; see also Memo for the files, 17 Nov 71, sub: Vietnam Ad Hoc Working Group Meeting, November 16, 1971, box 158, NSC files, Nixon Papers, NARA. Clarke, *Final Years*, pp. 401, 418–20, 472–76; MACV History, 1969, vol. 3, an. H; ibid., 1970, vol. 1, ch. 1, p. 4, ch. 7, p. 103.

[63] Quotation is from Sutherland Interv, n.d., pp. 27–28. MACV History, 1969, vol. 1, ch. 4, p. 26; ibid., 1970, vol. 1, ch. 7, pp. 77–79; ibid., 1971, vol. 1, ch. 8, pp. 79–80; Clarke, *Final Years*, pp. 368–69, 372, 449–50, 452. For a field commander's view that advisers can be reduced, see Collins, Debriefing Report, 7 Jan 71, pp. 9–10, Collins Papers, MHI.

[64] Abrams' views on adviser roles can be found in MACV History, 1971, vol. 1, ch. 8, pp. 81–83. For commanders' views on continuing adviser functions, see Msgs, Sutherland DNG 2555 to Abrams, 3 Nov 70; Collins NHT 2128 to Abrams, 4 Nov 70; and Wagstaff HOA 1328 to Abrams, 12 Jul 71. All in Abrams Papers, CMH. Clarke, *Final Years*, p. 450.

Taking all the positive indicators into account, Secretary Laird, Ambassador Bunker, and General Abrams regularly expressed confidence that the South Vietnamese were successfully assuming the burden of their own defense. Other American officials, both in Washington and in Vietnam, were less sanguine. Dr. Kissinger and members of his National Security Council staff regularly expressed skepticism at Laird's optimistic projections. They pointed out that the level of enemy activity in South Vietnam was too low to provide a real test of RVNAF fighting ability; that American troop withdrawals inexorably were shifting the force ratio against Saigon; and that Laird's assessments of RVNAF adequacy were founded on only "best case" estimates of the enemy threat.[65]

Much of the official optimism was based on reports produced by the Military Assistance Command's automated System for Evaluating the Effectiveness of RVNAF (SEER). Established in 1968, the SEER collated field advisers' periodic statistical reports and subjective evaluations of the performance of Vietnamese units. Like the Hamlet Evaluation System, the SEER was supposed to identify weak points for corrective action. However, also like the Hamlet Evaluation System, the SEER became a measurement of progress and at times a public relations tool. Its unit reports showed general improvement, for example in ratios between friendly and enemy killed and weapons lost and captured; but they compared units only against their own past performance rather than against mission requirements or the strength of enemy resistance. Hence, while MACV evaluations based on the SEER regularly indicated increasing RVNAF effectiveness, the actual meaning of the changes in the numbers was questionable. For instance, a highly aggressive South Vietnamese regiment might have a low kill ratio due to heavy mine and booby trap casualties. Often, the apparent upward trends were contradicted by specific critical situation reports from the field. In sum, the SEER measured achievement of program goals rather than actual present or future South Vietnamese ability to defeat the enemy.[66]

General Abrams, while positive in his overall evaluations, had to admit in mid-1971 that "some weaknesses in the overall RVNAF structure and doctrine" still required "corrective attention." The South Vietnamese armed forces in fact continued to suffer from most of the fundamental deficiencies that had plagued them since the early 60s: overreliance on air and artillery rather than infantry fire and maneuver

---

[65] Typical expressions of Laird and mission confidence are in Memos, Kissinger for the President, 26 Mar 71, sub: RVNAF Expansion and Modernization, box 153; and Laird to the President, 8 Nov 71, sub: Trip to Vietnam, November 2–8, 1971, box 158. Both in NSC files, Nixon Papers, NARA. Bunker expresses confidence in Memo, Odeen, 10 Aug 71, sub: Vietnamization Meeting with Secretary Laird, folder 77, Thayer Papers, CMH. Skeptical views are in Memos, Kissinger for the President, 19 Jan 70, sub: Reporting on Vietnamization, and 19 Mar 70, sub: The Risks of Vietnamization, box 091; and Memo, K. Wayne Smith for Kissinger, 19 May 71, sub: Secretary Laird's Memo on RVNAF Improvements, box 154. All in NSC files, Nixon Papers, NARA.

[66] Problems with SEER are analyzed in Clarke, *Final Years*, pp. 387–89, 512–13.

to destroy the enemy; weak leadership at all command levels; chronic high desertion rates; low pay and lack of social services and amenities for troops and their dependents; and a promotion system dominated by corruption, personal patronage, and bias in favor of the urban upper class. American advisers from Abrams on down continually pressed the Vietnamese for reform in these areas. The Vietnamese continually agreed that something must be done, but little actually changed.[67]

General Abrams persistently urged President Thieu to replace incompetent and corrupt corps, division, and lower commanders who constituted a major obstacle to other reforms. Like Westmoreland, however, Abrams considered it necessary to be circumspect in pressing for command changes, which usually had political as well as military implications. During the years of Vietnamization, President Thieu replaced many senior commanders, some in response to MACV recommendations but others as part of a campaign to place men loyal to himself in key military positions. These shakeups, in the view of General Abrams, resulted in a significant improvement of corps and division leadership. In November 1971, Abrams told Secretary Laird that the commanders in Military Regions 1 and 4 were "excellent" and those in Military Regions 2 and 3 adequate and improving, and that only one South Vietnamese division commander still needed to be replaced. Field advisers' evaluations of the same officers often were less favorable. The many command changes notwithstanding, politics and personality still dominated RVNAF promotions. Well-connected incompetents usually were transferred laterally to other senior posts rather than being retired or cashiered. They crowded the upper echelons of the officer corps, blocking advancement of abler juniors.[68]

In view of persistent South Vietnamese failure to reform, many American advisers and senior officials, Secretary Laird among them, questioned whether their ally possessed the will to prevail in the struggle. Typical of this viewpoint, Lt. Gen. Arthur S. Collins, who commanded II Field Force during most of 1970, declared: "The GVN has been given everything it needs to do the job. They could win this war in three months if they just wanted to. The one thing the military lacks

[67] Quotation is from Msg, Abrams MAC 6474 to Component and Regional Assistance Commanders, 5 Jul 71, Abrams Papers, CMH. Clarke, *Final Years*, pp. 372–76, 385–87, 422–24, 464–69, summarizes the faltering course of RVNAF institutional reform. MACV History, 1970, vol. 1, ch. 7, p. 98. South Vietnamese Army tactics are criticized in Memo, Collins, Fall 70, sub: Ideas on Vietnam; see also Memo, Collins, 10 Dec 70, sub: Assessment of Situation in MR 2. Both in Collins Papers, MHI.

[68] Clarke, *Final Years*, pp. 364–68, 476–79. A typical expression of official American concern about Vietnamese leadership is Memo, Resor for Sec Def, 12 Aug 70, sub: Secretary of the Army Vietnam Trip, box 245, NSC files, Nixon Papers, NARA. In same collection, Memos, Kissinger for the President, 4 Mar 71, sub: Situation Report from Gen Abrams, box 084; and Laird for the President, 8 Nov 71, sub: Trip to Vietnam, November 2–8, 1971, box 158, contain Abrams' evaluations of senior South Vietnamese commanders. Contrasting views of South Vietnamese leadership are in MACV History, 1970, vol. 1, ch. 7, p. 24, and Collins, Debriefing Report, 7 Jan 71, pp. 5–7, Collins Papers, MHI.

is the desire or the will, and this is something that advisors cannot provide."[69]

These allegations of lack of determination ignored other significant obstacles to South Vietnamese victory—notably the existence of North Vietnam and its army. While the South Vietnamese had their failings, their American mentors' house also was far from in perfect order. In particular, the statistical progress of RVNAF improvement and modernization concealed fundamental confusion in Washington and Saigon about what missions the forces ultimately should be able to perform. Secretary Laird envisioned that the South Vietnamese at some point must defend themselves without direct American help, even in such highly technical tasks as interdiction of the Ho Chi Minh Trail; but were the forces being built actually capable of doing that?[70]

Particularly in question was the readiness of the South Vietnamese Army to counter a North Vietnamese renewal or expansion of main force warfare. Under the MACV and Joint General Staff combined campaign plans, the territorial forces were progressively to relieve the South Vietnamese divisions of all pacification and local security missions so that the regulars could take over mobile large-unit operations from the departing Americans. Not all Nixon administration officials endorsed this role for the South Vietnamese Army. President Nixon himself, as well as Secretary Laird, occasionally expressed concern that MACV was developing an army too heavy and conventional for counterinsurgency operations. General Vien, chief of the Joint General Staff, and other South Vietnamese officials, as they had since the beginning of Vietnamization, saw the problem in reverse. They believed that their forces needed more heavy equipment than MACV was willing to furnish if they were to stand alone against the North.[71]

In practice, MACV fell between the extremes. The command to a degree extricated the South Vietnamese Army from territorial security tasks, at least within the military regions. However, in keeping with Abrams' preference for not rocking the organizational boat, it made no

---

[69] Quotation is from Msg, Collins NHT 2128 to Abrams, 4 Nov 70, Abrams Papers, CMH. Laird expresses his concern in Memo for the Assistant to the President for National Security Affairs, 1 Jul 71, sub: Suggested Topics for Discussion in the Republic of Vietnam, box 155, NSC files, Nixon Papers, NARA. See also MFR, Odeen, 17 Jun 71, sub: Vietnamization Meeting with Secretary Laird, folder 77, Thayer Papers, CMH.

[70] Laird emphasizes total South Vietnamese self-sufficiency to his staff in MFR, Odeen, 1 Oct 71, sub: Vietnamization Meeting with Secretary Laird, folder 78, Thayer Papers, CMH. See also Memo, Laird for Assistant to the President for National Security Affairs, 1 Jul 71, sub: Suggested Topics for Discussion in the Republic of Vietnam, box 155, NSC files, Nixon Papers, CMH.

[71] Clarke, *Final Years*, pp. 424, 456. MACV plans for the regulars are summarized in MACV History, 1969, vol. 1, ch. 2, pp. 12–13; and MFR, Odeen, 31 Aug 70, sub: Vietnamization Meeting with Secretary Laird, folder 76, Thayer Papers, CMH, which quotes Colby on this point. Concern that the South Vietnamese Army is becoming too conventional is expressed in Memos, Nixon for Kissinger, 2 Mar 70; Haig for Lynn, 6 Mar 70, sub: Vietnamization, box 144; Lynn for Kissinger, 22 May 70, sub: Imminent Vietnamization Decision, box 146; NSC files, Nixon Papers, NARA.

attempt to separate the South Vietnamese divisions from their regional ties to the point where they could function as a unified, mobile national army. Abrams remained conservative also on the issue of heavy weaponry. After the Laos invasion of 1971, the Joint General Staff renewed its requests for main battle tanks, antitank missiles, more self-propelled artillery battalions, and other units and materiel to match the equipment the North Vietnamese had employed. Abrams again vetoed most of these proposals. He argued that the South Vietnamese Army did not need this equipment for its principal missions: defense of South Vietnam and limited cross-border raids. In mid-1971, Abrams agreed only to establish one battalion of M48 tanks; and he endorsed later in the year activation of a new South Vietnamese 3d Division, formed from existing units in I Corps, to strengthen the defense of the Demilitarized Zone.[72]

These modifications notwithstanding, the South Vietnamese Army that MACV created under the CRIMP was essentially a localized territorial defense force, supported by an air force of helicopters and short-range fighter-bombers and a logistical organization configured for an area counterinsurgency campaign. Its only mobile reserve consisted of the marine and airborne divisions and a newly organized nine-battalion ranger force. Against full-scale conventional attack by large units with heavy tanks and artillery, it would have to rely on the Americans, principally their air forces, for rapidly deployable reinforcements, a fact Abrams readily acknowledged and seemed to regard as unalterable. In sum, the results of Vietnamization approximated closely what General Abrams, Admiral McCain, and other military commanders always had considered feasible—a force capable of defeating the internal insurgency but requiring American aid to counter a North Vietnamese invasion. Through the end of 1971, the American leaders in both Washington and Saigon persisted in assuming that the enemy would continue with a guerrilla campaign punctuated by occasional light infantry main force attacks, culminating in some sort of political denouement. Throughout the period, enemy action in South Vietnam conformed to that pattern and gradually diminished in intensity. Accordingly, the ambiguities of Vietnamization could be overlooked amid the steady flow of encouraging numbers and reports.[73]

[72] Clarke, *Final Years*, pp. 384–85, 456–58; MFR, Odeen, 15 Jun 71, sub: Vietnamization Meeting with Secretary Laird, folder 77, Thayer Papers, CMH; MACV History, 1971, vol. 1, ch. 4, p. 23, ch. 8, pp. 11–12; vol. 2, an. H, pp. 3–7; National Security Decision Memorandum 118, 3 Jul 71, sub: Improvements in South Vietnamese Forces, box 155, NSC files, Nixon Papers, NARA.

[73] These themes are fully developed in Clarke, *Final Years*, pp. 445, 455, 508, 517–58. Laird sees the RVNAF having a limited, defensive mission in Memo for Assistant to the President for National Security Affairs, [Mar 71], sub: RVNAF Expansion and Modernization, box 153, NSC files, Nixon Papers, NARA.

An Appearance of Success

As 1971 came to an end, the Military Assistance Command could look back on what seemed to be three years of success in every element of General Abrams' "one war." A J–3 briefing in November 1971 concluded that the enemy had been prevented from defeating South Vietnam and had not won "a single important campaign," including the 1968 Tet offensive. As a result of allied military success, pacification had made remarkable strides, providing the people with the security they needed to achieve progress in political, social, and economic development. Finally, the South Vietnamese, with U.S. assistance, had built a "strong, broadly based" military establishment "which will be difficult for any aggressor to defeat on its home ground."[74]

The briefer's assertions had a strong foundation in fact. Since 1968, the military and political balance within South Vietnam clearly had swung to the allies. The southern insurgency was a declining force, no longer by itself a threat to the regime's survival. The Saigon government had achieved relative stability. Its military forces were replacing those of the United States on the battlefield, and it was exercising increasingly effective authority throughout the populated regions of South Vietnam. Its land reform program held out the promise of future stability and social equity.

Balancing these encouraging developments were two adverse circumstances that the J–3 briefer neglected to mention. First, as had been true since Tet 1968, battlefield and pacification progress in South Vietnam, even when accompanied by a sharp decline in American casualties, did not add up to victory in what had become the critical arena: the minds and hearts of the American people. On the home front, the drumbeat of scandal and controversy and the persistent reports of atrocities, race riots, spreading drug use, and South Vietnamese corruption drowned out official claims of success in a war many Americans no longer believed their country should be fighting.

A second circumstance lent validity to the public's doubts. The allies' achievements in South Vietnam had taken place in the absence of a full-strength enemy challenge. Whether through policy or circumstance, the North Vietnamese and Viet Cong in this period of the war were unable to apply enough force, on the battlefields and in the villages, to disrupt allied programs; although they did extract a price in American and South Vietnamese casualties and compel Saigon to maintain a military effort it could not afford on its own in the long run. South Vietnam had yet to meet the test of a renewed North Vietnamese main force offensive. The absence of such an offensive, and enemy inactivity in South Vietnam, in turn resulted at least in part from the course of the conflict beyond the republic's borders in Laos and Cambodia.

---

[74] MACV J–3–06 Command Briefing, 28 Nov 71, in folder, J–3 Command Briefing, 28 Nov 71, MACV Collection, MHI.

9

Across the Borders: Cambodia

Even as the Nixon administration withdrew American forces from South Vietnam, it expanded U.S. and South Vietnamese military operations in Laos, Cambodia, and North Vietnam. The administration by its actions acknowledged the longstanding fact that the enemy treated the Indochina conflict as one war and systematically used the territory of South Vietnam's nominally neutral neighbors as a base and line of communications for his attack on the southern republic. Nixon expanded the allies' cross-border actions, at considerable domestic political cost to his administration, for two principal reasons. He believed that, by disrupting the enemy's sanctuaries, he could gain a respite in the war in South Vietnam for redeploying American forces and strengthening Saigon. He also hoped that the threat, and actuality, of escalation would push North Vietnam toward a diplomatic settlement acceptable to the United States. The Military Assistance Command played significant roles as advocate, planner, and implementer of the administration's cross-border offensives.

The Situation in Early 1969

As the Nixon administration entered office, MACV's American forces were operating under various authorities and rules of engagement in North Vietnam, the Demilitarized Zone, Laos, and Cambodia. Air operations over North Vietnam, after the 1 November 1968 bombing halt, were limited to unarmed reconnaissance flights, although MACV had authority to send fighter escorts as well if the enemy fired on the reconnaissance planes. With the end of ROLLING THUNDER, MACV terminated its Operations Plan 34A maritime harassment and psychological warfare operations in the north; but it continued to insert intelligence agent teams there, most of which the North Vietnamese quickly eliminated or brought under their control.[1]

In the Demilitarized Zone, where North Vietnamese forces continued to move and operate despite the November 1968 understandings,

---

[1] Msg, CJCS JCS 4649 to CINCPAC, CINCSAC, COMUSMACV, 1 Nov 68, box 105, NSC files, Nixon Papers, NARA; MACV History, 1968, an. F, pp. 2–5 and app. 3.

MACV's ground activities were limited to squad-size reconnaissance patrols supported by platoon-size reaction forces. The command could fire artillery and conduct air strikes against the enemy in the southern half of the zone; and it could bomb and bombard hostile forces north of the zone if they fired on allied troops. MACV could engage and destroy North Vietnamese units of battalion or smaller size that attacked from the Demilitarized Zone, but American ground forces could maneuver into the zone itself only with special authorization from the "highest authority." If the North Vietnamese assaulted through the Demilitarized Zone in major force, COMUSMACV was to seek authority immediately from the Joint Chiefs of Staff for "appropriate counter actions."[2]

In Laos, General Abrams' forces were engaged in two separate active air campaigns and a major ground reconnaissance and raiding effort. The Seventh Air Force flew bombing and reconnaissance missions in northern Laos, code-named BARREL ROLL, at the request of the U.S. Embassy in Vientiane and under the embassy's rules of engagement, in support of Meo guerrillas and the Royal Laotian Army. In the Laotian panhandle, known as STEEL TIGER, the Seventh Air Force, under MACV's direction, waged a systematic interdiction campaign against the Ho Chi Minh Trail, using fighter-bombers, gunships, and B–52s against trucks, roads, bridges, way stations, and storage areas. Supporting and supplementing the air campaign, MACV continued its PRAIRIE FIRE ground reconnaissance program. The command regularly sent twelve-man teams recruited from the area and led by American Special Forces personnel into an authorized zone up to twenty kilometers deep in the panhandle; and it also could dispatch platoon-size reaction forces, of similar composition, to assist the reconnaissance teams or attack vulnerable targets. In addition to PRAIRIE FIRE, MACV provided limited fixed-wing and helicopter support to CIA-recruited Laotian irregulars who also watched and harassed the Ho Chi Minh Trail.[3]

In contrast to Laos, MACV carried on only reconnaissance operations in Cambodia, although its forces in South Vietnam could fire and maneuver across the border in self-defense if attacked from the Cambodian side. On the ground, MACV continued its DANIEL BOONE reconnaissance program, initiated in 1967 and renamed SALEM HOUSE during 1969, under which twelve-man teams regularly penetrated up to thirty kilometers into Cambodia, strictly to gather information about

---

[2] Memo, Wheeler CM–3895–69 for Sec Def, 29 Jan 69, sub: Additional Authorities Recommended for Operations in South Vietnam Border Areas, box 100, NSC files, Nixon Papers, NARA.

[3] Msgs, Wheeler JCS 04332 to Westmoreland info Sharp, 22 Apr 68; Sharp to Wheeler info Westmoreland, 24 Apr 68; Westmoreland Message files, Apr 68, CMH. Msgs, Abrams MAC 10218 to Maj Gen Royal N. Baker, USAF, 29 Jul 68; Abrams MAC 15605 to McCain info Nazarro, 11 Nov 68. All in Abrams Papers, CMH. Msg, Am Emb Vientiane 2616 to Sec State et al., 27 Apr 69, box 545, NSC files, Nixon Papers, NARA; MACV History, 1968, an. F, app. 4, pp. 1–2, 5–7, tab A. Irregular operations in Laos are described in Brig. Gen. Southchay Vongsavanh, *RLG Military Operations and Activities in the Laotian Panhandle*, Indochina Monographs (Washington, D.C.: U.S. Army Center of Military History, 1981), pp. 33–40.

enemy troops and bases. As of late 1968, the command was conducting an average of forty-six of these missions per month. An aerial reconnaissance effort called DORSAL FIN, also begun in 1967, had reached a rate of thirty missions per month plus thirty airborne radio direction finding flights, in a cross-border zone twenty kilometers deep. Supplementing DORSAL FIN was GIANT DRAGON—Strategic Air Command–controlled U–2 missions, which covered all of eastern Cambodia except the vicinity of the capital, Phnom Penh. Through these operations, MACV steadily enlarged its mass of evidence documenting Cambodia's essential role in supporting Communist operations in South Vietnam.[4]

The Military Assistance Command's organization for planning and conducting cross-border operations was well established and stable. MACV's Studies and Observations Group, a separate joint headquarters with its own intelligence, operations, and logistical directorates and its own army of American Special Forces–led indigenous irregulars, carried out the PRAIRIE FIRE and DANIEL BOONE/SALEM HOUSE campaigns as well as the attempted infiltration of North Vietnam. Planning and conduct of all air operations were the tasks of the Seventh Air Force commander, who received missions, depending on the country and operational area, from COMUSMACV, CINCPAC, and the U.S. Air Attaché in Vientiane. General Abrams allocated sorties and set the priority of effort. To coordinate the several American wars in Southeast Asia, Abrams, Admiral McCain, and the American ambassadors to South Vietnam, Laos, and Thailand continued their periodic Southeast Asia Coordinating Committee sessions. They and their subordinates also met less formally to work out operational problems.[5]

From the time he took command, General Abrams campaigned for expansion of American operations outside South Vietnam. Indeed, only in Laos was he satisfied with the extent of his operating authority. Joined by Admiral McCain and usually by the Joint Chiefs, Abrams regularly urged resumption of ROLLING THUNDER as retaliation for the enemy's 1968 offensives. Even after the final November 1968 bombing halt, which both he and McCain in retrospect considered a mistake, Abrams persisted in advocating air strikes against the north

---

[4] Memo, Wheeler CM–3895–69 for Sec Def, 29 Jan 69, sub: Additional Authorities Recommended for Operations in South Vietnam Border Areas, box 100, NSC files, Nixon Papers, NARA. Msgs, Abrams MAC 7601 to Peers, 9 Jun 68; Wheeler JCS 13019 to McCain and Abrams, 9 Nov 68; CJCS JCS 13020 to SACRECON info CINCPAC, COMUSMACV, 9 Nov 68. All in Abrams Papers, CMH. MACV History 1968, an. F, app. 4, pp. 2–3, 7–9.

[5] Corcoran Interv, 20 Dec 75 pp. 40–41. Msgs, Abrams MAC 11708 to Wheeler and McCain, 30 Aug 68; McCain to Wheeler info Abrams et al., 4 Sep 68; Abrams MAC 14798 to McCain, 3 Nov 68; Abrams MAC 16167 to Sullivan info McCain, Brown, 23 Nov 68; McCain to Chargé d'Affaires Robert Hurwitch info Wheeler, Abrams, 13 May 69; McCain to Wheeler info Abrams, 5 Mar 70, all in Abrams Papers, CMH, are examples of command and coordination relationships. Organization and operations of the Studies and Observations Group are detailed in MACV History, 1968, an. F.

as "an essential ingredient for effective counter actions" to any major new enemy offensive in South Vietnam.[6]

Abrams repeatedly asked for an end to the restrictions on his ground operations in the Demilitarized Zone. Citing extensive enemy activity in the zone and the risk to allied forces posed by attacks from it, he, McCain, and General Wheeler recommended that MACV be permitted, as it had been before November 1968, to send troops into the southern half of the zone "as necessary to counter enemy activity." They also proposed that the command be given standby authority to preempt major enemy attacks by artillery, naval gunfire, and air strikes on targets throughout the Demilitarized Zone. The Johnson administration, unwilling to risk disrupting the Paris negotiations for anything other than the most severe provocation, rejected the military's proposals.[7]

General Abrams persistently advocated air and ground attacks on the enemy's Cambodian sanctuaries. Upon succeeding General Westmoreland, he took up without a pause his predecessor's campaign for bombing and bombardment of North Vietnamese troops and supplies in the triborder area where South Vietnam, Laos, and Cambodia came together. During the autumn of 1968, with encouragement from General Wheeler, he had his staff develop plans for limited ground incursions into the Cambodian bases, three to five days in duration and penetrating no more than twenty kilometers, to be conducted in response to any new enemy offensive. Supported by Admiral McCain, Abrams repeatedly requested permission to launch such raids; and he added a proposal for a naval quarantine of Cambodian ports. Action against the Cambodian bases, Abrams argued, would have a decisive impact in reducing the threat to III Corps and Saigon. He declared:

Should the enemy be denied sanctuary in these base areas, a major portion of the threat to SVN [South Vietnam] could be neutralized. Should such action result only in driving the enemy deeper into Cambodia, it would be beneficial to the allied cause, as it would push him further from SVN borders, disrupt his well constructed and organized base area system, and force him nearer the populated areas of Cambodia where his presence would be obvious and unwelcome. The denial of these base areas by some means appears to me to be a prerequisite for the realization of U.S. objectives in SVN.[8]

[6] Quotation is from Msg, Abrams MAC 1208 to Wheeler info Nazzaro, 27 Jan 69; see also Msgs, Abrams MAC 7605 to Sharp, 9 Jun 68; Abrams MAC 10330 to Wheeler info Sharp, 31 Jul 68; and Abrams MAC 14808 to Wheeler info McCain, Bunker, 3 Nov 68. All in Abrams Papers, CMH. McCain Interv, n.d., pp. 8–9, recalls the two commanders' view of the bombing halt.

[7] Memo, Wheeler CM–3895–69 for Sec Def, 29 Jan 69, sub: Additional Authorities Recommended for Operations in South Vietnam Border Areas, box 100, NSC files, Nixon Papers, NARA. Msgs, Abrams MAC 17672 to Wheeler info McCain, Bunker, 29 Dec 68; Abrams MAC 2500 to McCain info Wheeler, 26 Feb 69. Both in Abrams Papers, CMH.

[8] Quotation is from Msg, Abrams MAC 1102 to Wheeler and Nazarro, 24 Jan 69; see also Msgs, Wheeler JCS 05825 to Abrams, 28 May 68; Abrams MAC 7350 to Wheeler, 4 Jun 68; Wheeler JCS 09245 to Abrams info McCain, 15 Aug 68; Abrams MAC 11819 to Wheeler and McCain, 1 Sep 68; McCain to Wheeler info Abrams et al., 30 Sep 68; Abrams MAC 14477 to Wheeler and McCain,

The outgoing Johnson administration, however, remained determined not to expand the war into Cambodia. Besides domestic and international political considerations, a long-standing interagency dispute over Cambodia's significance as an enemy supply conduit inhibited action. The Military Assistance Command persisted in its assertion that most of the weapons and ammunition for North Vietnamese and Viet Cong forces in III and IV Corps were coming in through Sihanoukville and being trucked from there to the border bases. The CIA and the State Department, while they acknowledged the extent and importance of the base areas, declared MACV's evidence for the Sihanoukville route to be unpersuasive. They held to the position that the bases were being stocked via the Ho Chi Minh Trail. In November 1968, a special State Department, Central Intelligence Agency, and Defense Intelligence Agency delegation visited South Vietnam and reviewed the evidence but found against MACV, a conclusion that may have reflected as much agency policy preferences as the facts. Whatever its cause, the intelligence deadlock persisted into the new administration and with it a lack of action on Cambodia.[9]

MENU and PRUNING KNIFE

From the start, President Nixon was receptive to military proposals for stronger action outside South Vietnam's borders. While preparing to take office, he requested a study of enemy facilities in Cambodia and told Kissinger that "a very definite change of policy" toward that country "probably should be one of the first orders of business when we get in." Entering the White House amid predictions from MACV of another Tet-period nationwide Communist offensive, Nixon directed the Joint Chiefs of Staff to prepare contingency plans for retaliating against North Vietnam for attacks on Saigon and other major South Vietnamese cities. The Joint Chiefs, after consultation with Admiral McCain and General Abrams, late in January submitted a plan for an intensive forty-eight-hour air and naval assault on North Vietnamese military targets south of the 19th Parallel, to be executed if the other side bombarded Saigon or another comparable center. They also submitted plans for more limited reprisals if the enemy damaged lesser towns and cities. Nixon, Rogers, Laird, and Kissinger, however, were reluctant to strike North Vietnam even if strongly provoked, for fear

27 Oct 68; Abrams MAC 1166 to Nazzaro, 26 Jan 69. All in Abrams Papers. Early planning for a Cambodian offensive is described in Townsend Interv, 26 Feb 76, pp. 42–43, 55–56.

[9] Memo, Hughes for Sec State, 3 Feb 69, sub: Comments on Abrams' Reports on Cambodia, box 505; Msg, Abrams MAC 2775 to McCain info Wheeler, 4 Mar 69, box 065; Memo, Hughes for Sec State, 29 Mar 69, box 065; in NSC files, Nixon Papers, NARA, illustrate the continuing disagreement. Msgs, Wheeler JCS 12931 to McCain info Abrams, 7 Nov 68; Msg, McConnell JCS 13502 to McCain and Abrams, 18 Nov 68; McCain to Wheeler, 21 Nov 68. All in Abrams Papers, CMH. Kissinger, *White House Years*, pp. 241–42 attributes political motives to the interagency study, as does the MACV J–2 at the time. Davidson Interv, 30 Jun 82, pt. 2, pp. 31–33.

of the domestic and foreign political furor they knew would result. Hence, they looked for other retaliatory options.[10]

The Military Assistance Command provided them with one. On 7 February 1969, General Kerwin, the II Field Force commander, heard a briefing by officers of the Combined Intelligence Center, which pinpointed the location of the *COSVN* just across the border in Cambodia in an area nicknamed the Fishhook. On the basis of this information, Kerwin proposed to General Abrams a "short duration, concentrated" B–52 strike to destroy this major enemy headquarters, simultaneous with a similar attack on the North Vietnamese *7th Division's* Cambodian base area, which also was located in the Fishhook. Kerwin declared that these targets could be hit without harming Cambodian citizens and that destruction of *COSVN* "would . . . have a very significant impact on enemy operations throughout South Vietnam." He urged that the attack be carried out covertly. "A cover plan should be devised and knowledge of the operation held as closely as possible."[11]

General Abrams adopted the *COSVN* part of Kerwin's proposal. On 9 February, he informed General Wheeler that MACV possessed "hard intelligence," which he attributed to photographic reconnaissance and an enemy defector, on *COSVN's* position. Citing his command's extensive evidence that the enemy was preparing for another nationwide offensive in the near future, Abrams recommended that if the offensive occurred, among other retaliatory measures, he be authorized to strike *COSVN* with B–52s. Abrams claimed that *COSVN's* destruction "in a single blow" would help disrupt the Communist attack as well as "have its effect on future military operations which *COSVN* may desire to undertake." Ambassador Bunker, after a briefing by Abrams' intelligence officers, on 12 February cabled to the State Department his endorsement of the plan. He argued that the United States could not continue to permit attacks to be planned and mounted from Cambodia, which had forfeited any rights of neutrality by permitting the enemy to use its territory as a base for aggression. Both Bunker and Abrams emphasized that, due to *COSVN's* border location, the bombing was unlikely to strike Cambodian civilians.[12]

---

[10] Quotation is from Kissinger, *White House Years*, p. 241; see also pp. 232–40. Memo, Wheeler CM–3892–69 for Sec Def, 28 Jan 69, sub: Response to Major Attack on Population Centers; see also Memo, McConnell CM–3903–69 for Sec Def, 3 Feb 69, sub: Responses to Minor Attacks on Population Centers in South Vietnam. Both in box 100, NSC files, Nixon Papers, NARA. Msgs, Lt Gen Meyer JCS/J–3 01374 to Nazzaro info Abrams, 31 Jan 69; Abrams MAC 1465 to Nazzaro, 2 Feb 69; Abrams MAC 1778 to Wheeler info Nazzaro, 9 Feb 69. All in Abrams Papers, CMH.

[11] Msg, Kerwin HOA 398 to Abrams and Davidson, 8 Feb 69, Abrams Papers, CMH.

[12] Quotations are from Msg, Abrams MAC 1782 to Wheeler and Nazzaro, 9 Feb 69; see also Msg, Abrams MAC 1844 to Nazzaro info Wheeler, 11 Feb 69; Abrams MAC 1910 to McConnell info Nazzaro, 13 Feb 69. All in Abrams Papers, CMH. The informant failed a polygraph test on his information, but Abrams considered that other sources confirmed *COSVN's* location. Msg, Abrams MAC 2512 to Wheeler, 26 Feb 69, Abrams Papers, CMH; Msg, Bunker Saigon 2830 to Sec State, 12 Feb 69, box 065, NSC files, Nixon Papers, NARA.

Ironically, Bunker's endorsement, by alerting the State Department to the plan, prevented its immediate implementation. Nixon and his advisers were concerned that leaks from the department would make denial of the bombing impossible to sustain. Accordingly, Nixon on 14 February sent instructions to Bunker through State Department channels to drop the entire matter. At the same time, he directed Abrams via Defense Department channels to ignore the State Department message, continue planning the operation, and dispatch a team to Washington to brief the administration on it. The MACV team on the eighteenth explained the proposal to Kissinger, Laird, their personal military assistants, and General Wheeler. The group decided that a covert strike against *COSVN* would be more useful as a signal of resolve to the Soviets than as retaliation for an assault in South Vietnam by the North Vietnamese and Viet Cong. On the nineteenth, at Kissinger's recommendation, President Nixon, in order to "set the stage" and "clear the books" within the bureaucracy, authorized Abrams to conduct air strikes right up to the Cambodian border in III Corps and to continue contingency planning for the *COSVN* bombing. The president then could order execution of the raid, on Abrams' recommendation, if "a suitable local action" developed in III Corps that could be used as a justification.[13]

The suitable action came almost at once, in the form of the fourth and weakest of the enemy's series of nationwide offensives that had begun with Tet 1968. On 22–23 February, the North Vietnamese and Viet Cong launched attacks by fire and conducted a few ground probes against more than one hundred civilian and military targets throughout South Vietnam. The attacks included a seven-round rocket bombardment of Saigon, a clear violation of the understanding, which the North Vietnamese claimed did not exist, that the Communists would avoid attacks on major cities if the Americans stopped bombing the North. Occurring just as Nixon was embarking on his first presidential trip to Europe, the offensive seemed to be a direct challenge to the new administration. General Abrams, encouraged by General Wheeler and with the concurrence of Ambassador Bunker and Admiral McCain, on the twenty-third called for retaliation in the form of a ninety-six-hour air and naval gunfire bombardment of North Vietnam below the 19th Parallel, employing all available ships and aircraft.[14]

---

[13] Msg, Rogers State 023875 to Bunker, 14 Feb 69, box 065; Memo, Haig for Kissinger, 13 Feb 69, sub: Discussions with Mr Laird . . . regarding *COSVN* Matter; Memo, Kissinger for the President, 19 Feb 69, sub: Consideration of B–52 Options Against *COSVN* Headquarters; Memo, Kissinger for Laird, 22 Feb 69, sub: *COSVN* Matter, box 104. All in NSC files, Nixon Papers, NARA. Kissinger, *White House Years*, p. 242.

[14] Msg, Wheeler JCS 02252 to Abrams and McCain, 23 Feb 69; McCain to Wheeler and Abrams, 23 Feb 69; Abrams MAC 2372 to Wheeler and McCain, 23 Feb 69. All in Abrams Papers, CMH. Msg, Bunker Saigon 3429 to Sec State, 23 Feb 69, box 065, NSC files, Nixon Papers, NARA. Democratic Republic of Vietnam denial of the existence of the understanding is noted in MACV History, 1969, vol. 1, pp. 3–11.

Nixon and his advisers unanimously ruled out any bombing of North Vietnam during the president's European tour. Instead, they turned to Abrams' *COSVN* proposal. On 23 February, Nixon ordered execution of the operation, code-named BREAKFAST. He cancelled the mission three days later, however, before it could be launched, for fear news of it would leak and cause a public furor while he was in Europe. At General Wheeler's direction, MACV continued to refine its tactical, security, and public affairs plans for the raid.[15]

During the last days of February and the first two weeks of March, the enemy continued his offensive, including sporadic bombardment of South Vietnam's cities; and the administration continued to deliberate about retaliation. President Nixon issued public warnings that the United States was nearing the end of its patience with North Vietnam's violation of the November 1968 understandings, but he and his advisers remained unwilling to face the political consequences of attacking the North or Cambodia. General Abrams and Ambassador Bunker kept up the pressure for retaliation against either or both North Vietnam and the Cambodian sanctuaries. Abrams declared that the city attacks and North Vietnamese activity in the Demilitarized Zone constituted "a fabric of bad faith, deception, and exploitation which we can no longer tolerate as a nation." Besides repeating his earlier arguments, Abrams indicated that Cambodian operations, by reducing enemy offensive capabilities, could open the way for the U.S. troop withdrawals the administration then was considering. Secretary Laird, although opposed on political grounds to bombing the North, on 9 March declared that the BREAKFAST plan had "merit" as an additional response to the continuing enemy attacks. He informed Nixon that he was "prepared to recommend that we go ahead with that proposal."[16]

On 15 March, in response to another rocket firing on Saigon, Nixon ordered the immediate implementation of BREAKFAST. The next day, General Wheeler, after a final review of alternative strike plans, instructed Abrams to hit the presumed *COSVN* site with forty-eight B–52 sorties. As cover, twelve other sorties would attack targets near the border within South Vietnam. Abrams was to confine knowledge of the raid to as few headquarters personnel as possible. He was to inform the press only that B–52s had struck within South Vietnam. If the Cambodians issued a public protest, the United States would investigate, apologize, and offer compensation for damages. Executed

[15] Kissinger, *White House Years*, pp. 242–44. Memo, Laird for the President, 25 Feb 69; Memo, Haig for Pursley, 26 Feb 69, sub: Breakfast Plan; Msg, Wheeler MAC 2945 to Abrams, McCain et al., 7 Mar 69, box 104, NSC files, Nixon Papers, NARA.

[16] Kissinger, *White House Years*, pp. 244–45. First quotation is from Msg, Abrams MAC 2836 to Wheeler and McCain, 5 Mar 69; see also Msg, Abrams MAC 3308 to Wheeler, 16 Mar 69. All in Abrams Papers, CMH. Msg, Bunker Saigon 4320 to Sec State, 6 Mar 69, box 067; Memo, Laird for the President, 4 Mar 69, sub: Possible Responses to Enemy Activity in South Vietnam, box 136; Msg, Laird MAC 3049 to the President, 9 Mar 69, box 067. All in NSC files, Nixon Papers, NARA. Laird quotation is from last-cited document.

on schedule on 18 March, the B–52 attack resulted in seventy-three large secondary explosions in the target area, which indicated the presence of a major military complex, but no evidence of any damage to *COSVN* headquarters. The Cambodians, North Vietnamese, Chinese, and Soviets made no diplomatic or public response to the attack; and the American press took no notice.[17]

After the initial mission, the B–52 bombings, code-named MENU with each separate base area target denoted by a different meal of the day, soon expanded into a continuing campaign. The strategic bombers systematically hammered six enemy base areas located in a narrow strip along the Cambodian–South Vietnamese border. North Vietnam and the other Communist nations made no public protest against the attacks, probably to avoid having to acknowledge the extent of their own violation of Cambodia's neutrality. Cambodia's chief of state, Prince Norodom Sihanouk, followed the same policy. During 1969, he actually resumed diplomatic relations with the United States, which he had broken off in 1965, and permitted the reopening of the American embassy in Phnom Penh. Taking advantage of his adversaries' silence, President Nixon, who had been prepared for public revelation of the raids, kept them covert, both to prevent opposition in the United States and to facilitate Sihanouk's turning of his diplomatic blind eye. He and Kissinger, however, did brief a few key congressional leaders on the attacks.[18]

General Abrams' headquarters was the principal agent for planning and conducting the missions. Abrams, assisted by a few staff officers, nominated MENU targets through Admiral McCain to the Joint Chiefs of Staff for final approval by Laird, Kissinger, and Nixon. During the first weeks of the campaign, Abrams submitted each target individually. Beginning in late August, the administration allowed him to propose weekly packages, each including three or four attacks. Under a system developed by MACV staff officers, each raid began with the launching of a regularly requested ARC LIGHT strike against targets within South Vietnam. To preserve secrecy, the B–52 pilots and navigators received new target coordinates while in flight for their Cambodian missions. Reported through normal channels, the cover missions allowed inclusion of the MENU sorties in the regular statistical summaries of air activity.

---

[17] Kissinger, *White House Years*, pp. 245–47. Dictated Summary of Telephone Conversations between the President and Henry Kissinger; MFR, Kissinger, 15 Mar 69, sub: March 16 Rocket Attack on Saigon, box 089; Memo, Haig for Kissinger, 16 Mar 69, sub: Joint Chiefs of Staff Military Operations to Support Breakfast Plan; Msg, Wheeler JCS 03298 to Abrams, McCain, et al., 16 Mar 69, box 104; Memo, Kissinger for the President, 18 Mar 69, sub: Breakfast Plan; Memo, Kissinger for the President, 19 Mar 69, sub: Reaction to Breakfast Plan, box 103. All in NSC files, Nixon Papers, NARA. Msg, Abrams MAC 3414 to McCain and Wheeler, 16 Mar 69, Abrams Papers, CMH. Lack of media reaction is noted in Hammond, *Military and the Media, 1968–1973*, p. 70.

[18] Kissinger, *White House Years*, pp. 247–54. Paper, sub: Sihanouk on Cambodian Border Incidents, box 089, NSC files, Nixon Papers, NARA. Stories on the bombing appeared in the U.S. press but did not give rise to a major public furor. See Hammond, *Military and the Media, 1968–1973*, pp. 70–75.

After each strike, MACV used aerial reconnaissance and where possible SALEM HOUSE teams to assess bomb damage. Abrams reported the results to McCain and Wheeler through a special secure channel.[19]

The command took elaborate and successful precautions to maintain the secrecy of MENU. Within the headquarters, General Abrams closely restricted the number of personnel involved in the operations. All message traffic went through limited-distribution backchannels. Officers carried the Cambodian target coordinates by hand to the ground stations that controlled the B–52s just before the strikes. Specially cleared personnel interpreted post-strike photography, and a few similarly cleared SOG teams performed the ground follow-up reconnaissance. Outside MACV headquarters in Saigon, only Ambassador Bunker and President Thieu, whom Abrams and Bunker briefed on the operations, knew of the campaign. The rest of the American mission was kept in ignorance. In Washington, Secretary Laird, the Joint Chiefs, a few officers of the Joint Staff, and the service deputy chiefs of staff for operations were informed. Among State Department officials, Secretary Rogers alone was in the know.[20]

During the MENU campaign's first year, more than 3,100 B–52 sorties dropped over 91,000 tons of munitions—nearly one-fifth of the entire tonnage expended by American air forces in the Pacific theater in World War II—on six North Vietnamese/Viet Cong base areas in Cambodia. Bomber crews and post-strike air and ground reconnaissance regularly reported secondary explosions and extensive damage to enemy fortifications and facilities, with no evidence of injury to Cambodian civilians.[21]

Both the administration and MACV considered the raids successful and valuable. President Nixon and his advisers believed that they had found a way to injure the North Vietnamese and display toughness to the Russians and Chinese while denying to the enemy the propaganda advantage they would have gained if the United States had resumed

---

[19] Department of Defense, "Report on Selected Air and Ground Operations in Cambodia and Laos," 11 Sep 73, pp. 5–18, copy in Chief of Staff Correspondence, Miscellaneous box, Creighton W. Abrams Papers, MHI, (hereafter cited as DoD, "Report on Selected Air and Ground Operations"). Typical MENU-related cables can be found throughout the Abrams Message files for 1969 and 1970, Abrams Papers, CMH. Townsend Interv, 26 Feb 76, pp. 53–54; Memo, Kissinger for the President, 26 Sep 69, sub: B–52 Operations in Cambodia; MFR, 3 Oct 69, sub: B–52 Strikes in Cambodia, box 105. Both in NSC files, Nixon Papers, NARA.

[20] Msg, Abrams MAC 1477 to Wheeler and McCain, 31 Jan 70, Abrams Papers, CMH, describes security procedures. In Abrams Papers, see also Msgs, Abrams MAC 5150 to Wheeler and McCain, 23 Apr 69; Wheeler MAC 5442 to Abrams and McCain, 29 Apr 69; Abrams MAC 6355 to Wheeler and McCain, 18 May 69; and Abrams MAC 2121 to Wheeler, Moorer, and McCain, 15 Feb 70. DoD, "Report on Selected Air and Ground Operations," pp. 15–18. Bruce Palmer, Jr, *The 25-Year War: America's Military Role in Vietnam* (Lexington: University Press of Kentucky, 1984), pp. 96–97, describes MENU security in the Pentagon.

[21] Figures are from Memo, Laird for the President, 24 Mar 70, sub: Assessment of MENU operations, box 104, NSC files, Nixon Papers, NARA. A typical post-strike report is Msg, Abrams MAC 7014 to McCain info Holloway et al., 2 Jun 69, Abrams Papers, CMH.

bombing of the North. For his part, General Abrams believed that Menu, although it had not achieved its initial objective of destroying *COSVN*, was damaging and disrupting the enemy's logistical system and help- ing to preempt and defeat his offensives. In particular, Menu played an essential role in reducing the threat to III Corps and Saigon; and by weakening the enemy it contributed to the success of Vietnamization. In a typical assessment, Abrams declared in October 1969 that Menu "has been one of the most effective campaigns of the war." He recom- mended that "these operations be continued as long as the enemy is present in and utilizing these [Cambodian] areas." The administration accepted his recommendation, extending the raids into 1970.[22]

President Nixon's decision to undertake the Menu operations rep- resented a victory for General Abrams in his campaign for authority to attack the enemy outside South Vietnam's borders. On the persistent issue of Demilitarized Zone operations, the MACV commander achieved much less. Throughout the administration's first year, Abrams and the Joint Chiefs repeatedly asked that MACV be permitted to resume unrestricted air and ground operations in the southern half of the Demilitarized Zone, to counter an enemy force buildup and increasing activity in that area. Just as regularly, Secretary Laird opposed their requests. Laird contended that the level of enemy activity in and around the Demilitarized Zone was lower than it had been before the bombing halt, that MACV's existing authorities were sufficient to protect allied forces and repel attacks, and that expanding allied operations in the zone would merely raise the level of violence in the area and possibly lead to new demands for bombing of North Vietnam. During the year, President Nixon, over objections by Laird, authorized Abrams to use B–52 strikes at his discretion against both observed and intelligence targets in the southern half of the Demilitarized Zone. Otherwise, the limits on MACV's operations remained in place despite continuing remonstrances from Abrams and the Joint Chiefs.[23]

Throughout 1969, President Nixon and his advisers canvassed the possibility of renewed military operations against North Vietnam

---

[22] Quotations are from Msg, Abrams MAC 13011 to Moorer and McCain, 6 Oct 69, Abrams Papers, CMH. In same collection, see Msgs, Abrams MAC 8809 to Wheeler and McCain, 9 Jul 69; Abrams MAC 9195 to McConnell and McCain, 16 Jul 69; Abrams MAC 10993 to Wheeler info McCain et al., 23 Aug 69; and Abrams MAC 3180 to Wheeler and McCain, 11 Mar 70. Kissinger, *White House Years*, p. 249; Memo, Laird for the President, 24 Mar 70, sub: Assessment of Menu Operations; box 104, NSC files, Nixon Papers, NARA.

[23] Historical Division, "Joint Chiefs of Staff and the War in Vietnam, 1969–1970," pp. 41–42, 76–80, 165–70. Msgs, Wheeler JCS 03512 to McCain and Abrams, 21 Mar 69; Abrams MAC 8088 to Wheeler and McCain, 24 Jun 69; Abrams MAC 10453 to McCain and Wheeler info Bunker, 11 Aug 69; Abrams MAC 11188 to Wheeler and McCain, 27 Aug 69; Abrams Papers, CMH. Memo, Wheeler CM–4217–69 for Sec Def, 13 May 69, sub: Vietnam Demilitarized Zone . . . ; Memo, Laird for Assistant to the President for National Security Affairs, 14 May 69, sub: Operations in the Demilitarized Zone . . . ; Memo, Nixon for Laird, 16 May 69, sub: JCS Request for Extension of Authorities . . . , box 070; Msg, JCS 2865 to CINCPAC, 20 Oct 69, box 139. All in NSC files, Nixon Papers, NARA.

which, in Laird's words, "might jar the North Vietnamese into being more forthcoming at the Paris talks." In September, with the negotiations deadlocked, the National Security Council, at Kissinger's urging, began considering an alternative course of action to Vietnamization and diplomacy. The national security adviser's staff developed a political-military scenario, called DUCK HOOK, under which the United States would make Hanoi a generous offer for a peace settlement. If the Democratic Republic of Vietnam rejected the offer, the administration then would stop troop withdrawals and launch heavy, damaging new attacks on North Vietnam. The attacks would be intended to convince Hanoi that it faced major damage to economic and military assets if it continued its intransigence and to give the Russians an incentive— avoidance of dangerous American escalation—to push their North Vietnamese clients toward compromise.[24]

In support of DUCK HOOK, General Wheeler in early September, during Washington visits by McCain and Abrams, instructed both commanders to develop concepts for the contemplated attack. Wheeler then dispatched a group of four officers from the Joint Staff, headed by Rear Adm. Frederick A. Bardshar, the J–3, to Saigon to work with MACV and CINCPAC representatives on a final version of the plan. The plan received the code-name PRUNING KNIFE to reflect its cover designation as a "redeployment contingency planning effort."[25]

In preparation for Admiral Bardshar's visit, General Abrams' staff developed a concept for the air campaign. As envisioned at MACV, the campaign would begin with concentrated attacks by "all available U.S. air and naval bombardment forces committed to Southeast Asia and contiguous waters" on all significant air defense and transportation targets in North Vietnam, aimed at achieving "maximum military and political impact in minimum time." Surprise air strikes would knock out the enemy's entire air defense system, including airfields and surface-to-air missile installations. This action would reduce the risk to American planes in subsequent phases of the operation and leave the Hanoi government and its military forces vulnerable to additional assaults. With North Vietnam's air defenses crippled, American forces would mine the port of Haiphong and systematically bomb bridges, rail lines, storage depots, shipyards, automotive and railroad repair facilities, and concentrations of trucks and railroad cars. While Air Force and Navy fighter-bombers conducted these raids, B–52s would hammer targets along the routes in southern North Vietnam that fed into the mountain passes to Laos. In the event that the North Vietnamese elected to "accept higher levels of destruction before negotiating," the initial

---

[24] Kissinger, *White House Years*, pp. 284–85. Laird quotation is from Memo, Laird for Kissinger, 21 Feb 69, box 1007; Memo, Kissinger for the President, 11 Sep 69, sub: Vietnam Options, box 091. Both in NSC files, Nixon Papers, NARA.

[25] Msgs, McCain to Wheeler info Abrams, 15 Sep 69; Rear Adm Frederick A. Bardshar JCS/J–3 11470 to McCain and Abrams, 17 Sep 69; Abrams MAC 12219 to Wheeler and McCain, 18 Sep 69. All in Abrams Papers, CMH.

massive blow could be followed by "sustained attacks to attain significant cumulative effects."[26]

On 24 September, Admiral Bardshar dispatched to Wheeler the
operational plan for PRUNING KNIFE. Based heavily on Abrams' concept,
the plan called for a concentrated surprise air and naval assault on
North Vietnam to achieve "maximum political, military, and psychological shock" by cutting off the enemy's imports of war material and
then "exacting continuing attrition upon NVN's [North Vietnam's]
war-making capacity and support of aggression in South Vietnam."
The objective was to "cause NVN to terminate its aggression . . . at the
earliest possible date." The plan had two phases. In the first, which
would require five days of operations, all available American aircraft
would be committed to destroy the North Vietnamese air force and
air defenses, hit major supply concentrations and logistical facilities
around Haiphong, conduct aerial mining of Haiphong and other ports,
and cut North Vietnam's railroad line to China. The second phase, of
indeterminate length, would consist of tactical air and B–52 strikes at
a variety of logistical targets in North Vietnam, a naval quarantine of
Sihanoukville, and possible cross-border ground operations as directed
by General Abrams. Admiral McCain would have overall command
of the operation, with Pacific Fleet, Pacific Air Forces, the Military
Assistance Command, and the Strategic Air Command responsible for
planning and executing various portions.[27]

In comments to General Wheeler on the PRUNING KNIFE plan, General
Abrams emphasized that destruction of North Vietnam's air force and
air defenses should have priority in timing and weight of effort, so as to
reduce the cost and increase the effectiveness of the rest of the strikes.
This aspect of the campaign also would constitute in itself "a highly
important part of the impression we intend to create on the North
Vietnamese leadership." Abrams urged as well that "since the price of
admission for resumption of action against NVN is high whatever the
specific U.S. action involved," if PRUNING KNIFE were executed, it should
be with maximum force against "the vital sectors and targets which
offer a significant military and political gain rather than . . . merely
renewed efforts at signals and reprisals."[28]

PRUNING KNIFE in fact never was executed. When Nixon, Laird, and
Kissinger reviewed the plan as presented by General Wheeler, they
found fundamental objections to it. The military planners themselves
noted a major one: the fact that during the next several months, the

[26] Msg, Abrams MAC 12219 to Wheeler and McCain, 18 Sep 69, Abrams Papers, CMH.

[27] Msg, Bardshar MAC 12508 to Wheeler info McCain, Abrams, 24 Sep 69, box 123; Memo,
Moorer JCSM–600–69 for Sec Def, 1 Oct 69 (as revised 7 Oct 69), sub: Air and Naval Operations
against North Vietnam, box 245. Both in NSC files, Nixon Papers, NARA. Msgs, Abrams MAC
12219 to Wheeler and McCain, 18 Sep 69; Bardshar MAC 12441 to Wheeler info McCain, Abrams,
23 Sep 69; Bardshar MAC 12562 to Wheeler info McCain, Abrams, 25 Sep 69; Abrams MAC 13121
to McCain, 8 Oct 69; McCain to Abrams et al., 13 Oct 69. All in Abrams Papers, CMH.

[28] Msg, Abrams MAC 12696 to Wheeler and McCain, 28 Sep 69, Abrams Papers, CMH.

late autumn and winter, the northeast monsoon would limit the days of good flying weather over North Vietnam, making a rapid, sustained attack all but impossible. The five-day first phase alone might take up to three weeks to carry out. Although he strongly favored the DUCK HOOK approach, Kissinger expressed dissatisfaction with the plan for implementing it, claiming that the military in fact was offering nothing but an open-ended, indecisive campaign reminiscent of ROLLING THUNDER. He and Laird both concluded that the operation as proposed was unlikely to achieve military or diplomatic results commensurate with the probable American aircraft losses and domestic and international political costs it would entail. Agreeing with the civilian officials, General Wheeler declared the plan "militarily unsound" because the time it allowed for the raids was too short.[29]

On 11 October, after a conference with Kissinger, Laird, Attorney General John N. Mitchell, and all the Joint Chiefs, President Nixon indefinitely postponed action. Instead, he directed the Joint Chiefs of Staff to revise PRUNING KNIFE so as to target more directly North Vietnam's economy. The staffs in Saigon and Honolulu accordingly produced a new version, PRUNING KNIFE ALPHA; but it had the same inherent problems as the initial plan. In submitting the revised plan to Wheeler, Admiral McCain declared forthrightly that there was "little probability" of achieving the stated objectives of PRUNING KNIFE ALPHA, "destruction of NVN's economy and reduction of NVN's capability to function as a viable entity," during the northeast monsoon season. "To achieve the desired results would require relentless heavy attack for an extended period of time."[30]

During the summer and autumn, the White House emitted a number of hints that it might take drastic action on Vietnam after 1 November, the anniversary of the bombing halt. However, no bombs fell on North Vietnam. In his major Vietnam policy speech on 3 November, Nixon concentrated on negotiation and Vietnamization. Meanwhile, the Pacific commands produced an endless series of refinements and variations of PRUNING KNIFE, including plans for both the all-out strike and lesser retaliatory campaigns. Nevertheless, while DUCK HOOK and PRUNING KNIFE were not implemented, the fundamental concept—a maximum offer to Hanoi backed by a massive assault—remained in Nixon's mind, awaiting a propitious moment for revival.[31]

[29] Memo, Kissinger for the President, sub: JCS Concept for Air and Naval Operations against North Vietnam. Laird's comments are in Memo, Laird for the President, 8 Oct 69, sub: Air and Naval Operations against North Vietnam. Both documents are in box 245, NSC files, Nixon Papers, NARA. Wheeler quotation is from MFR, Moorer, 13 Oct 69, sub: JCS Meeting with the President . . . , 11 October 1969, box 1008, NSC files, Nixon Papers, NARA.

[30] MFR, Moorer, 13 Oct 69, sub: JCS Meeting with the President . . . , 11 October 1969, box 1008, NSC files, Nixon Papers, NARA. Msgs, McCain to Abrams et al., 19 Oct 69; Msg, McCain to Nazzaro and Hyland, 25 Oct 69; McCain to Westmoreland (Acting CJCS) info Abrams et al., 26 Oct 69; McCain to Wheeler info Abrams et al., 26 Oct 69. All in Abrams Papers, CMH. McCain quotation is from last-cited message.

[31] For examples of the continuing planning, see three Msgs, McCain to Wheeler info Abrams et al., 10 Mar 70, Abrams Papers, CMH. Kissinger, *White House Years*, p. 308, in retrospect expresses

Into Cambodia

The next major escalation came in Cambodia, which remained a focus of MACV scrutiny and planning. Even as MENU proceeded, General Abrams kept a few staff officers at work on plans for air and ground raids on the enemy's border bases. Abrams, Admiral McCain, and the Joint Chiefs persisted in advocating such operations. The Joint Chiefs, at Dr. Kissinger's request, developed a proposal for an air and sea quarantine of Sihanoukville to cut the Cambodian supply line at its source. Admiral McCain recommended that the United States conduct covert operations inside Cambodia for the same purpose. President Nixon himself expressed interest in "another crack or two" at Cambodia. However, during the rest of 1969 and the first months of 1970, he postponed decisions on the military's recommendations.[32]

A political upheaval in Cambodia made American action both possible and necessary. In January 1970, Prince Sihanouk, who throughout the previous year had seemed to be tilting against the Vietnamese occupiers of his borderlands, left Phnom Penh for Paris on a combined vacation and diplomatic junket. In charge in his absence were Prime Minister Lon Nol and Deputy Prime Minister Sirik Matak, both of whom Sihanouk had installed in office but with whom he subsequently had quarreled over economic policy. Early in March, anti-Vietnamese demonstrations, probably government organized, erupted in provincial towns and in Phnom Penh. On 12 March, Lon Nol officially demanded that all Vietnamese forces leave Cambodia within seventy-two hours. On the eighteenth, the National Assembly by unanimous vote deposed Sihanouk as head of state. Sihanouk's overthrow plunged his country into war. In response to the coup, North Vietnamese and Viet Cong forces in Cambodia began an offensive to secure the border region and isolate Phnom Penh while simultaneously starting to organize and arm local Communist insurgents, the *Khmer Rouge*. By mid-April, the Vietnamese occupied three of Cambodia's seventeen provinces and were operating in strength in five others. Sihanouk, then in Beijing, called for the overthrow of the Phnom Penh regime and publicly associated himself with the Laotian and Vietnamese Communists. They, along with the Chinese, declared their support for his restoration. Lon Nol in response appealed to the United States and other countries for assistance against North Vietnamese aggression.[33]

regret that the administration did not implement the DUCK HOOK concept in 1969.

[32] Nixon words are from handwritten comment on Memo, Kissinger for the President, 25 Mar 69, sub: Quarantine of Cambodia. See also Memo, Kissinger for Laird, 8 Apr 69, sub: Quarantine of Cambodia; and Memo, Moorer for Kissinger, 1 Jun 69. All in box 505, NSC files, Nixon Papers, NARA. Msgs, Abrams MAC 3850 to Wheeler and McCain, 26 Mar 69; Abrams MAC 3910 to Wheeler and McCain, 27 Mar 69; McCain to Wheeler, 15 Feb 70. All in Abrams Papers, CMH.

[33] Msg, Abrams MAC 2439 to Wheeler and McCain, 24 Feb 70, box 143, NSC files, Nixon Papers, NARA, reviews Sihanouk's anti-Vietnamese actions. Kissinger, *White House Years*, pp. 457–75. Brig. Gen. Tran Dinh Tho, *The Cambodian Incursion*, Indochina Monographs (Washington,

Lon Nol and Sirik Matak in Cambodia

The Nixon administration reacted uncertainly to the Cambodian upheaval, which it had neither engineered nor anticipated. With only a chargé d'affaires, a political officer, and a three-man defense attaché office in its Phnom Penh embassy, the American government had difficulty securing up-to-date information. The president was at first suspicious of the new regime, headed as it was by former Sihanouk loyalists who had facilitated and profited from the Communist arms traffic through Sihanoukville. Nevertheless, Nixon soon decided that he had no choice but to uphold the Lon Nol government, since Sihanouk's return under Communist auspices would eliminate any chance of disrupting the North Vietnamese and Viet Cong logistical system in Cambodia. Divisions quickly developed, however, among Nixon's advisers. Secretaries Laird and Rogers, concerned with domestic political reaction and convinced the war would be won or lost in South Vietnam, strove to limit American involvement in the new conflict. Over their opposition, Nixon and Kissinger maneuvered the administration step by step, first to provide military assistance to Phnom Penh and then to a direct invasion of Cambodia aimed at destroying the base areas and reducing enemy pressure on Lon Nol.[34]

D.C.: U.S. Army Center of Military History, 1979), pp. 29–32. Abrams assesses enemy intentions in Cambodia in Msg, Abrams MAC 7583 to Wheeler and McCain, 4 Jun 70, box 147, NSC files, Nixon Papers, NARA.

[34] For embassy size, see Tho, *Cambodian Incursion*, pp. 196–98, 209–10. Administration divi-

The initial American military response reflected the administration's uncertainty. General Abrams on 18 March informed his field force and component commanders that a coup might be occurring in Phnom Penh. "The precise nature is unknown." He directed them to adhere strictly to the established rules of engagement for the Cambodian border and to report to MACV headquarters at once any overtures by Cambodians for military assistance. On the twenty-first, Secretary Laird temporarily suspended the MENU bombing in view of the uncertain situation, expressing concern that some faction in Phnom Penh might publicize the attacks. General Wheeler asked Abrams and McCain to consider possible reactions to a wide range of Cambodian contingencies.[35]

General Abrams' command gradually became involved in the Cambodian fighting. Late in March, South Vietnamese commanders along the frontier, under local arrangements with Cambodian counterparts, began providing artillery support to beleaguered Cambodian Army (*FANK—Forces Armées Nationales Khmères*) units and also launched battalion and smaller-size cross-border incursions of their own. At General Abrams' direction, U.S. forces withheld support from these operations, and unit advisers remained in South Vietnam. The Nixon administration, after initially halting the South Vietnamese Army forays for fear of American domestic opinion, gave its assent to them provided the Saigon government kept them small in scale, conducted them only after consulting with Cambodian authorities, and explained them as "protective reaction" for their forces in South Vietnam. With Ambassador Bunker, General Abrams transmitted this guidance to President Thieu and General Vien. Abrams instructed his own forces not to assist the South Vietnamese incursions in any way and to reject artillery fire requests from the *FANK*. He and the commanders of II Field Force and the Delta Military Assistance Command closely monitored the South Vietnamese activities and worked to keep them low in visibility and within President Nixon's guidelines.[36]

The Military Assistance Command during April took other steps to assist the Cambodians, whose poorly equipped and ill-trained 32,000-man army was little match for the Vietnamese Communist forces moving against it. At the administration's direction, Bunker and Abrams arranged with President Thieu for the South Vietnamese air

sions are discussed in Kissinger, *White House Years*, pp. 487–98. Msg, Moorer JCS 05634 to McCain and Abrams, 23 Apr 70, Abrams Papers, CMH, informs the field commanders of "strong dissenting opinions" on Cambodia in "high levels of our government."

[35] Msgs, Abrams MAC 3574 to Field Force and Component Cdrs, 18 Mar 70; Wheeler JCS 03958 to McCain info Abrams, 20 Mar 70; Wheeler JCS 03993 to Abrams and McCain, 21 Mar 70. All in Abrams Papers, CMH.

[36] Msg, Rosson MAC 3838 to McCain info Wheeler, 23 Mar 70, box 506; Haig WHS 0011 to Bunker, 27 Mar 70, box 410; Haig to Bunker, 28 Mar 70, box 101; Haig WH 0012 to Bunker, 31 Mar 70, box 410. All in NSC files, Nixon Papers, NARA. Msgs, Wheeler JCS 04424 to McCain and Abrams, 1 Apr 70; Abrams MAC 4276 to Field Force and Component Cdrs, 1 Apr 70; Abrams MAC 4390 to Wheeler and McCain, 3 Apr 70; Abrams MAC 4587 to McCain and Moorer, 8 Apr 70; Moorer JCS 04851 to Abrams info McCain, 9 Apr 70. All in Abrams Papers, CMH.

force to ship AK47 rifles, ammunition, and other Communist materiel captured in South Vietnam to the largely Soviet-equipped Cambodians. MACV also organized and trained battalions of ethnic Cambodians recruited from CIDG units in South Vietnam for transport to Phnom Penh to reinforce the *FANK*.[37]

General Abrams conducted a growing American air campaign in Cambodia. After the initial suspension, the administration quickly resumed MENU operations. Abrams selected targets for the B–52s that would assist the Cambodians and also prepare the way for large-scale ground attacks under consideration. Since B–52 strikes were of little effect against maneuvering troops, General Abrams on 18 April requested, and the administration two days later granted, authority to use tactical aircraft throughout the SALEM HOUSE reconnaissance zone in northeastern Cambodia. On 25 April, the administration expanded this authority to a thirty-kilometer-deep strip along the entire Vietnamese-Cambodian border. MACV conducted these strikes, code-named PATIO, under secrecy arrangements similar to those of MENU, using cover targets in Laos and special mission request and reporting channels. In addition to these air operations, the United States on 23 April established naval surveillance of the port of Sihanoukville.[38]

Paralleling these steps, the Military Assistance Command made contingency plans for division-size American and South Vietnamese assaults on the enemy's Cambodian base areas. President Nixon set this planning in motion on 25 March for "potential execution in the event the Communists attack Phnom Penh." During the following month, small groups of officers from MACV and the I and II Field Forces, working with representatives of the Joint General Staff and the South Vietnamese III and IV Corps, developed plans for both unilateral and combined cross-border offensives. By late April, two of these operations had moved from contingency to preparation for execution status. The first, code-named SHOEMAKER, called for a combined drive into *COSVN's* Fishhook hideout aimed at destroying the elusive headquarters and other installations. The second, TOAN THANG 42, was an all–South Vietnamese converging attack on bases in the Parrot's Beak region of the border, an operation that the Vietnamese thought would eliminate

---

[37] Msgs, Wheeler JCS 05037 to Abrams info McCain, 11 Apr 70; Kearney JCS 05161 to McCain and Abrams, 15 Apr 70; Wheeler JCS 05160 to Abrams info McCain, 15 Apr 70; Wheeler CJCS/JCS 05285 to Abrams info McCain, 17 Apr 70; Abrams MAC 5365 to McCain and Wheeler, 22 Apr 70; Abrams MAC 5559 to Wheeler and McCain, 26 Apr 70; Abrams MAC 5879 to Wheeler and McCain, 1 May 70; Abrams MAC 6085 to Wheeler and McCain, 6 May 70. All in Abrams Papers, CMH. Msg, Bunker Saigon 6574 to Sec State, 30 Apr 70, box 589, NSC files, Nixon Papers, NARA; MACV History, 1970, Supp., p. 36.

[38] Msg, Wheeler JCS 04447 to McCain and Abrams, 1 Apr 70; Abrams MAC 4297 to Wheeler and McCain, 2 Apr 70; Abrams MAC 5472 to Moorer and McCain, 24 Apr 70; Abrams MAC 6240 to Wheeler and McCain, 8 May 70. All in Abrams Papers, CMH. DoD, "Report on Selected Air and Ground Operations," pp. 21–23.

the most immediate threat to Saigon and that Abrams considered well within South Vietnamese capabilities.[39]

As enemy forces advanced in Cambodia and Nixon and his advisers debated over the U.S. response, General Abrams and Ambassador Bunker weighed in on the side of aggressive action. In joint assessments during April, the two men warned that the fall of Lon Nol, and the installation of a pro-Communist regime, would have dire military and political consequences in South Vietnam and also in Thailand and Laos. In South Vietnam, it likely would mean intensification of the war in III and IV Corps and "force a reexamination of the speed of the Vietnamization process by both the GVN and the US." To assist Lon Nol, Bunker and Abrams recommended, besides the efforts already under way, provision of American air and artillery support to South Vietnamese cross-border raids and the launching of "selective and carefully targeted combined US/GVN military operations against high payoff targets in Cambodia," including *COSVN* headquarters. The general and the ambassador strongly endorsed the Fishhook and Parrot's Beak operations, which Abrams characterized as "the military move to make at this time in support of our mission in South Vietnam both in terms of security of our own forces and for advancement of the Vietnamization program."[40] *(Map 3)*

On 28 April, Nixon finally overrode Laird and Rogers and put the offensive in motion. He directed the execution, as nearly simultaneously as possible, of Toan Thang 42 and Shoemaker, with the latter to jump off on 1 May. Nixon gave general authorization for other unilateral and combined operations penetrating up to thirty kilometers into Cambodia, but he required MACV to submit combined attack proposals that involved American troops for his case-by-case approval. Separately, the president permitted Abrams to send American advisers into the Parrot's Beak on the ground with their South Vietnamese units, an action that Abrams considered essential to ensuring effective coordination and aggressive conduct of the South Vietnamese attack.[41]

---

[39] Msgs, Wheeler JCS 04182 to Abrams info McCain, 26 Mar 70; Wheeler JCS 04213 to McCain and Abrams, 26 Mar 70; Wheeler JCS 04217 to Abrams info McCain, 26 Mar 70; Abrams MAC 4159 to McCain info Wheeler, 30 Mar 70; Abrams MAC 5307 to McCain info Wheeler, 21 Apr 70; Abrams MAC 5336 to McCain info Wheeler, 22 Apr 70; Abrams MAC 5419 to McCain and Moorer, 23 Apr 70; Moorer JCS 05623 to McCain and Abrams, 23 Apr 70; Abrams MAC 5558 to Wheeler and McCain, 26 Apr 70. All in Abrams Papers, CMH. Msg, Rosson MAC 3999 to Wheeler and McCain, 26 Mar 70, box 101, NSC files, Nixon Papers, NARA.

[40] First quotations are from Msg, Bunker Saigon 169 to Kissinger, 22 Apr 70; Abrams quotations are from Msg, Bunker Saigon 251 to the President, 27 Apr 70; see also Msg, Kissinger WHS 0033 to Bunker, 27 Apr 70. All in box 410, NSC files, Nixon Papers, NARA.

[41] Memo, Kissinger for the President, 26 Apr 70, sub: Meeting on Cambodia . . . ; National Security Decision Memo 58, 28 Apr 70, sub: Actions to Protect U.S. Forces in South Vietnam, box 507, NSC files, Nixon Papers. Msgs, Wheeler JCS 05730 to Abrams, 27 Apr 70; Wheeler JCS 05750 to Abrams, 27 Apr 70; Abrams MAC 5610 to Wheeler, 27 Apr 70; Abrams MAC 5618 to Wheeler, 27 Apr 70; Abrams MAC 5675 to Wheeler, 28 Apr 70; Wheeler JCS 05807 to Abrams, 28 Apr 70; Wheeler JCS 05812 to McCain and Abrams, 28 Apr 70. All in Abrams Papers, CMH.

On 29 April, the South Vietnamese Army began its offensive. The following evening, President Nixon announced the incursions to the American people in a televised address. He declared that the attacks were necessary to protect allied forces in South Vietnam, ensure the continuation of Vietnamization, and assist Cambodia against North Vietnamese aggression. At about the time he was speaking, 1 May in Vietnam, allied forces entered the Fishhook in Operation TOAN THANG 43, as SHOEMAKER had been retitled at the request of Lt. Gen. Do Cao Tri, the South Vietnamese III Corps commander.[42]

Once committed, President Nixon rapidly expanded the offensive. On 1 May, General Wheeler, at Nixon's direction, ordered Abrams to submit plans for additional attacks on the enemy's Cambodian bases. The president authorized Abrams to make full use of American and South Vietnamese ground and air forces in these operations, but American ground troops were not to penetrate more than thirty kilometers into Cambodia. In subsequent public statements and directives, the administration required U.S. forces to be out of Cambodia by 30 June. Wheeler told Abrams that Nixon considered the Cambodian offensive his "number one priority" among Southeast Asia operations and desired "a hard hitting campaign . . . carried out using imagination and boldness," so as to deliver "the hardest blow we are capable of inflicting" to the enemy's cross-border sanctuaries. In response, Abrams proposed, and the administration through mid-May approved, six additional base area attacks and a riverine operation to reopen the Mekong for Cambodian government traffic.[43]

As the offensive expanded, so did the Military Assistance Command's authority to use American airpower in Cambodia. Within the thirty-kilometer limit, MACV carried on the full range of fixed-wing and helicopter support of allied forces. In addition, President Nixon on 23 May, on General Abrams' recommendation, authorized the MACV commander to conduct tactical air and B–52 strikes beyond the thirty-kilometer line against enemy logistical targets in a large North Vietnamese-controlled section of northeastern Cambodia, essentially as an extension of the STEEL TIGER campaign against the Ho Chi Minh Trail. Nixon also gave Abrams permission to send B–52s up to sixty kilometers into Cambodia in pursuit of the still-elusive *COSVN* headquarters. As allied forces over-

---

[42] Msgs, Abrams MAC 5692 to Wheeler and McCain, 29 Apr 70; Abrams MAC 5798 to Wheeler and McCain, 30 Apr 70; Abrams MAC 5824 to Wheeler and McCain, 1 May 70. All in Abrams Papers, CMH. Nixon's speech is analyzed in Hammond, *Military and the Media, 1968–1973*, pp. 303–05.

[43] Quotations are from Msg, Moorer JCS 06037 to McCain and Abrams, 1 May 70, Abrams Papers, CMH. Msgs, Abrams MAC 5906 to Moorer and McCain, 2 May 70; Abrams MAC 5996 to Wheeler and McCain, 4 May 70; Wheeler JCS 06214 to McCain and Abrams, 5 May 70; Wheeler JCS 06224 to Abrams, 5 May 70; Abrams MAC 6128 to Wheeler, 6 May 70; Wheeler JCS 06370 to McCain and Abrams, 7 May 70. All in Abrams Papers, CMH. Memo, Kissinger for the President, 5 May 70, sub: Proposal for Attacks on Additional Base Areas in Cambodia, box 507; Memo, Winston Lord for Kissinger, 2 Jun 70, sub: Chronology of June 30 Deadline, box 509. Both in NSC files, Nixon Papers, NARA.

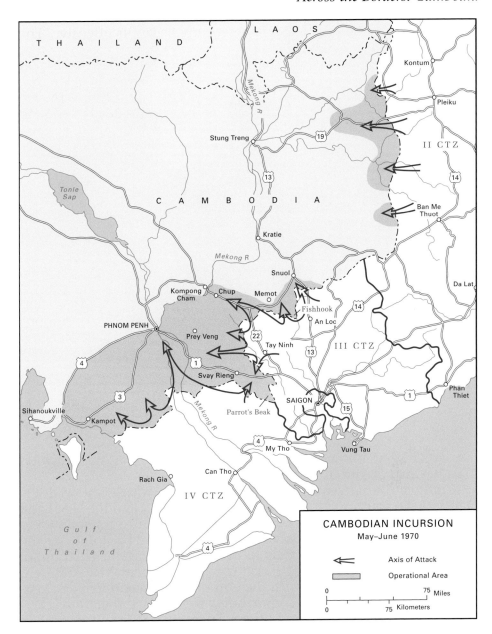

Map 3

ran the MENU target areas, the Joint Chiefs on 27 May discontinued that operation and placed ARC LIGHT strikes in Cambodia under the normal request and reporting procedures. MACV, however, kept the aerial photography, damage assessments, and other documentation of

299

*Armored personnel carriers and M48 battle tanks blast away with
.50-caliber machine guns during the allied sweep into Cambodia.*

the earlier MENU bombings under tight control, to prevent revelation
that they had occurred.[44]

Command arrangements for the operations, which involved elements of the South Vietnamese II, III, and IV Corps and the U.S. I and
II Field Forces, followed the established principle of coordination and
cooperation. The Military Assistance Command and the Joint General
Staff each issued their own Cambodia rules of engagement. Those of
the South Vietnamese Army, based on an agreement Vice President
Nguyen Cao Ky negotiated with the Cambodian government and general staff, authorized corps commanders to conduct operations, unilaterally or with American and Khmer forces, in a strip of Cambodian
territory extending forty to sixty kilometers from the border. Unlike
the Americans, the South Vietnamese set no terminal date for their

---

[44] Memo, Laird for the President, 22 May 70, sub: Use of U.S. Tactical Air in Cambodia; Memo,
Kissinger for Sec Def, 23 May 70, U.S. Air Operations in Cambodia. Both in box 509, NSC files,
Nixon Papers, NARA. DoD, "Report on Selected Air and Ground Operations," pp. 3, 14, 23–25.
Msgs, Abrams MAC 7164 to Wheeler, McCain, et al., 26 May 70; Abrams MAC 7275 to Wheeler
and McCain, 29 May 70; Abrams MAC 7371 to Field Force and Component Cdrs, 31 May 70;
Moorer JCS 07869 to McCain and Abrams, 6 Jun 70; Moorer JCS 09365 to Holloway, Abrams, and
McCain, 9 Jul 70. All in Abrams Papers, CMH.

incursions. Ambassador Bunker and General Abrams, however, through regular contacts with President Thieu, ensured that South Vietnamese Army activities during the combined offensive conformed to American time and territorial limits, with the understanding that the South Vietnamese retained the right to continue operating in Cambodia by themselves after U.S. forces withdrew on 30 June.[45]

General Abrams and General Vien delegated most of the detailed planning, as well as the conduct, of the Cambodia offensive to their respective corps-level commanders, who maintained direct liaison among themselves. Abrams gave his I and II Field Force commanders, Lt. Gens. Arthur S. Collins and Michael

General Collins
(Photograph taken in 1974.)

S. Davison, the freest possible hand to run their campaigns. Abrams heard advance briefings on their plans, visited their headquarters and troops in the field during the operation, conferred with them regularly, and devoted at least one commanders' meeting, on 19 May, to discussion of their progress. At the administration's direction, Abrams required Collins and Davison to submit special twice-daily situation reports and weekly summaries while their attacks were in progress, as feeders for his own reports to McCain and Wheeler. Aside from this requirement, however, Abrams successfully shielded his subordinates from the constant stream of inquiries and suggestions that reached MACV from Washington. "In no instance," Davison recalled, "did he allow any of that to penetrate down to me."[46]

Much of the message traffic from Washington, reflecting continued divisions within the administration, concerned pressure on General Abrams to limit the scope and duration of the offensive, or at least American participation in it. In the United States, Nixon's announcement of the incursion set off widespread, intense antiwar agitation in the streets, on the campuses, and in Congress. Literally besieged in the

---

[45] Tho, *Cambodian Incursion*, pp. 36–39. Msgs, Abrams MAC 6403 to Wheeler and McCain, 11 May 70; Abrams MAC 7175 to Wheeler and McCain, 26 May 70. Both in Abrams Papers, CMH.

[46] Tho, *Cambodian Incursion*, pp. 36, 40–43. Msgs, Wheeler JCS 05958 to McCain and Abrams, 30 Apr 70; Abrams MAC 5867, 6060, and 6765 to Field Force and Component Cdrs, 1, 5, and 18 May 70; Abrams MAC 6210 to Wheeler and McCain, 7 May 70. All in Abrams Papers, CMH. Quotation is from Davison Interv, 20 Feb 76, pp. 23–25; see also pp. 19–22.

White House by thousands of antiwar demonstrators, President Nixon himself publicly promised allied forces would leave Cambodia by 30 June. On 7 May, Laird, seeking to shorten the campaign and reduce the domestic unrest it was causing, informed Abrams that all operations involving American support must be "essentially completed" by 31 May and "terminated in toto" by 15 June. In effect, Nixon countermanded this instruction. Through Kissinger's military assistant, General Haig, the president late in May made clear to Abrams that he wanted "maximum effort in [the] sanctuaries consistent with weather and actions of [the] enemy not artificial restrictions imposed by OSD." Nixon later told Abrams in person: "Do not withdraw for domestic reasons but only for military reasons. We have taken all the heat on this one." Abrams accordingly avoided setting exact withdrawal timetables for his forces while assuring the administration that he would have his troops out of Cambodia by the 30 June deadline.[47]

Before the offensive ended on the scheduled date, a total of 32,000 U.S. and 48,000 South Vietnamese soldiers had participated in unilateral and combined operations that overran all but one of the enemy's border base areas. While no large-scale battles occurred, the Americans and South Vietnamese claimed to have killed more than 11,000 North Vietnamese and Viet Cong in smaller fights and rounded up 2,300 prisoners and defectors. Allied forces lost 976 killed and 4,534 wounded, of which 338 of the dead and 1,525 of the injured were Americans.[48]

General Abrams and his superiors considered the incursion a major success. As early as 26 May, Abrams declared that the cross-border attacks had "disrupted enemy operations, preempted enemy planned activities and removed pressure from the pacification program in the *COSVN* area." The South Vietnamese, in the view of Abrams and other American commanders, in the main performed competently in planning and carrying out large-scale mobile operations, though they still required much American advice and support. The participating South Vietnamese troops displayed improved morale and enhanced self-confidence and aggressiveness. The incursion yielded a bountiful harvest of captured weapons and equipment—more than 22,800 individual and 2,500 crew-served weapons and more than 1,700 tons of ammunition and 6,800 tons of rice, as well as quantities of miscellaneous supplies. Agencies differed in their estimates of how many battalions the captured arms could equip and how many troops the captured rice could feed for how long, but all the estimates were expansive. American

---

[47] First quotation is from Msg, Haig Saigon 572 to Kissinger, 21 May 70, box 1010; second is from Memo of Conversation, San Clemente, 31 May 70, box 146; NSC files, Nixon Papers, NARA. Msg, Laird OSD 06398 to Abrams, 7 May 70; Abrams MAC 8069 to Moorer and McCain, 15 Jun 70. All in Abrams Papers, CMH. Hammond, *Military and the Media, 1968–1973*, pp. 315–19.

[48] Operations are summarized in MACV History, 1970, vol. 3, an. C. Statistics are from Memo, Lt Col Watha J. Eddins, Jr, for Cdr Jonathan Howe, 26 Jun 70, sub: Request for Information, box 510, NSC files, Nixon Papers, NARA; and Tho, *Cambodian Incursion*, pp. 193–94. Memo of Conversation, San Clemente, 31 May 70, box 146, NSC files, Nixon Papers, NARA.

Cambodian war booty

newsmen and some officials noted, however, that most of the captured small arms were older Soviet models long ago replaced in enemy units with the AK47, and that the lost rice easily could be replenished from subsequent harvests. General Abrams believed that the attacks, while they did not capture *COSVN* headquarters, had forced it to make a series of hasty relocations, thereby disrupting the other side's command structure. Enemy activity in South Vietnam remained at a low level during the offensive. Abrams expected that the Communists' loss of supplies in Cambodia and the disruption of their headquarters and personnel infiltration routes would limit their offensive operations for some time to come.[49]

The incursion, and the change of government in Phnom Penh that preceded it, had the side effect of resolving the Sihanoukville dispute in MACV's favor. With Cambodian help, American intelligence officers documented the fact that, between December 1966 and April 1969, Chinese vessels had delivered at least 21,600 tons of military and 5,300 tons of nonmilitary cargo to Sihanoukville, from where it went by truck convoy to North Vietnamese and Viet Cong depots on

[49] MACV History, 1970, vol. 3, an. C, pp. 103–08. Quotation is from Msg, Abrams MAC 7134 to Wheeler and McCain, 26 May 70; Msgs, Abrams MAC 6571 to Moorer and McCain, 14 May 70; Abrams MAC 7581 to Wheeler and McCain, 4 Jun 70. All in Abrams Papers, CMH. Memo of Conversation, San Clemente, 31 May 70, box 146, NSC files, Nixon Papers, NARA. South Vietnamese performance is evaluated in Clarke, *Final Years*, pp. 418–25. Dissenting views are summarized in Hammond, *Military and the Media, 1968–1973*, pp. 327–36.

the border. The military stores included some 222,000 individual and 16,000 crew-served weapons, enough to equip 600 enemy battalions, as well as more than 100 million rounds of ammunition and over half a million mines and hand grenades. After reviewing the documents, the CIA concluded, as MACV long had asserted, that Sihanoukville had been "a primary route for logistic support of the VC/NVA forces in southern South Vietnam, while the Laos route was used primarily to resupply the forces in the northern half of the country."[50]

Aiding the Cambodians

As the 30 June deadline approached, the Nixon administration faced the question of continuing allied operations in Cambodia and finding means to shore up the hard-pressed Lon Nol regime. While the May–June offensive benefited the allies in South Vietnam, it in many respects worsened the threat to Cambodia. The North Vietnamese and Viet Cong, even as they were pushed away from the border, continued advancing westward toward Phnom Penh. Employing relatively small units, they cut lines of communication, captured key towns, and seized nearly complete control of the northeastern half of the country. In preparation for a protracted war, they pushed government forces out of the countryside, thereby opening the way for expansion of the indigenous *Khmer Rouge*. In order to replace Sihanoukville with a southward extension of the Ho Chi Minh Trail, the North Vietnamese strengthened their hold on the southern Laotian panhandle by capturing the strategic towns of Attopeu and Saravane.[51]

Nixon established his long-term Cambodia policy well before the end of the offensive. Determined to keep Cambodia independent and non-Communist, the president nevertheless realized that an advisory and assistance effort even remotely comparable in scale to that in South Vietnam was politically out of the question. Within the limits, he did as much as he could. While ruling out further U.S. ground activity in Cambodia, Nixon directed Admiral McCain and General Abrams to continue American air operations there. They also were to encourage the South Vietnamese to carry out additional cross-border attacks, both to prevent reestablishment of the North Vietnamese and Viet Cong bases and to maintain the threat of deeper intervention if the enemy launched a direct assault on Phnom Penh. Nixon continued the program, already under way, of shipping captured Communist weapons and equipment to the Cambodian armed forces. Under the principles of the Nixon Doctrine, he sought money and arms for Cambodia

---

[50] Memo, Richard Helms, Dir CIA, for Kissinger, 22 Feb 71, sub: The Sihanoukville Route, with attached paper, sub: The Sihanoukville Route, from which quotation is taken, box 512; Memo, Holdridge for Kissinger, 21 Sep 70, sub: A New Estimate of Communist Supplies Delivered through Sihanoukville, box 511. Both in NSC files, Nixon Papers, NARA.

[51] Msg, Abrams MAC 11614 to McCain, 26 Aug 70, Abrams Papers, CMH. North Vietnamese attacks in southern Laos are described in Vongsavanh, *Laotian Panhandle*, pp. 53–58.

from friendly Asian countries, notably Indonesia and Thailand. As Cambodia's need for direct U.S. assistance became apparent, Nixon instituted a Military Assistance Program (MAP) for Phnom Penh. He initially diverted MAP funds from other countries to the program and eventually secured a regular congressional appropriation for it, although on terms that prohibited introduction of U.S. ground troops and military advisers into Cambodia.[52]

For the Military Assistance Command, Nixon's decisions amounted to the opening of a permanent new front in the war. After 30 June, General Abrams closely monitored the continuing cross-border activity of the South Vietnamese Army. Conferring weekly on the subject with General Vien, he sought to dissuade the South Vietnamese from diverting too many troops from their own country and ensure that their Cambodian efforts centered on the border region. Abrams' U.S. ground forces, including advisers and leaders of SALEM HOUSE reconnaissance teams, stayed out of Cambodia. American units in South Vietnam furnished combat, logistical, and advisory assistance to the South Vietnamese up to the border. They fired artillery into Cambodia in support of the South Vietnamese, and they shifted forces within South Vietnam to fill in for Vietnamese units absent on cross-border incursions. At the end of 1970, by General Abrams' count, the South Vietnamese had the equivalent of seventeen battalions operating in Cambodia, as well as elements of their air force and navy.[53]

While American ground activity was restricted, U.S. tactical aircraft and B–52s after 30 June continued bombing enemy troops and logistical facilities in a steadily expanding area of northeastern Cambodia code-named FREEDOM DEAL. These operations were intended to destroy forces and supplies that threatened the allies in South Vietnam. Publicly and in formal instructions, President Nixon forbade American tactical air support of South Vietnamese cross-border attacks; and the South Vietnamese in Cambodia accordingly relied whenever possible on their own fixed-wing aircraft and helicopters. Privately, Nixon instructed Abrams to interpret "interdiction" broadly and to provide tactical air support to the South Vietnamese if their own resources proved insufficient. By late 1970, U.S. fixed-wing aircraft were directly assisting

---

[52] Nixon's domestic problems are described in Hammond, *Military and the Media, 1968–1973*, pp. 322–46; and Kissinger, *White House Years*, pp. 509–19. Memo of Conversation, San Clemente, 31 May 70, box 146; Memo, Col Richard T. Kennedy for U. Alexis Johnson, Under Secretary of State for Political Affairs, 21 May 70, sub: Guidance on GVN Military Activities Relating to Cambodia, box 508. Both in NSC files, Nixon Papers, NARA. Msgs, Wheeler JCS 07308 to McCain and Abrams, 26 May 70; Moorer JCS 08495 to McCain and Abrams, 15 Jun 70; McCain to Abrams info Wheeler, 18 Jun 70; Moorer JCS 14205 to McCain info Abrams et al., 21 Oct 70. All in Abrams Papers, CMH. Historical Division, "Joint Chiefs of Staff and the War in Vietnam, 1969–1970," pp. 310–14.

[53] MACV History, 1970, vol. 1, ch. 2, p. 11; Supp., pp. 2–3, 22; an. B, app. 3, pp. 37–39. Msgs, Abrams MAC 8540 to McCain info Moorer, 24 Jun 70; Abrams MAC 15447 to McCain, 2 Dec 70; Abrams MAC 15809 to McCain info Moorer, 12 Dec 70. All in Abrams Papers, CMH.

South Vietnamese and *FANK* units outside the FREEDOM DEAL area, and they were joined in January 1971 by helicopter gunships.[54]

Besides directing American operations in Cambodia and assisting and influencing those of the South Vietnamese, the Military Assistance Command became heavily involved in building up Phnom Penh's armed forces. Lon Nol's government began expanding its military establishment soon after Sihanouk's overthrow, although it lacked every resource but manpower. Under the U.S. Military Assistance Program, which attempted to rationalize the process, the *FANK* was to reach a strength of about 220,000 by mid-1972. Composed of a light infantry army and a small navy and air force, the Cambodian military, as the Americans envisioned it, was to be capable of protecting the capital and major populated areas, keeping open principal lines of communication, and conducting limited offensive operations with American and South Vietnamese assistance.[55]

MACV and the South Vietnamese armed forces, from April 1970 on, provided indispensable help to the Cambodian buildup. In addition to furnishing Phnom Penh with captured Communist arms and battalions of ethnic Khmers from South Vietnam, the South Vietnamese in July, at Phnom Penh's request, began training Cambodian infantry units and military specialists. During 1970, their training centers instructed over 13,000 Cambodian troops, including 80 infantry companies. MACV's U.S. forces also took part in the effort. Special Forces personnel by the end of the year were training 30 infantry battalions and 3,000 small-unit leaders. The Seventh Air Force and Naval Forces, Vietnam, also instructed elements of their Cambodian counterpart services. The allies planned to continue and enlarge these programs during 1971.[56]

To coordinate military assistance to Cambodia in the absence of a regular advisory group, the administration established a civilian political-military counselor, a retired Army officer holding high Foreign Service rank, in its Phnom Penh embassy. Backing up the counselor and his four-man team in Phnom Penh, General Abrams and his MACV

---

[54] MACV History, 1970, vol. 1, ch. 6, pp. 70–79, and DoD, "Report on Selected Air and Ground Operations," pp. 23–24, summarize air operations. Msgs, Abrams MAC 11389 to McCain info Brown, 21 Aug 70; Abrams MAC 12574 to Amb Emory C. Swank info Clay, 18 Sep 70; Abrams MAC 12627 to McCain info Clay, 20 Sep 70. All in Abrams Papers, CMH. Memo of Conversation, San Clemente, 31 May 70, box 146; Memo, Kissinger for the President, sub: U.S. Tactical Air Support in Cambodia, box 587; Memo, Kissinger for the President, 28 Jan 71, sub: U.S. Tactical Air Strikes in Cambodia, box 587. All in NSC files, Nixon Papers, NARA.

[55] Msgs, McCain to Abrams, 24 Oct 70; Moorer JCS 14429 to McCain info Abrams, 27 Oct 7. All in Abrams Papers, CMH. Details of the Military Assistance Program (MAP) are in MACV History, 1970, Supp., pp. 40–51; ibid., 1971, vol. 2, app. 1, pp. 4–6.

[56] Msgs, Abrams MAC 7729 to Wheeler and McCain, 8 Jun 70; Abrams MAC 7945 to Moorer and McCain, 12 Jun 70; Abrams MAC 8038 to McCain, 14 Jun 70; Abrams MAC 8570 to Wheeler and McCain, 24 Jun 70; Abrams MAC 8571 to McCain info Moorer, 24 Jun 70; Abrams MAC 11206 to McCain info Jonathan F. Ladd, 18 Aug 70; Abrams MAC 11531 to McCain info Moorer, 24 Aug 70. All in Abrams Papers, CMH. MACV History, 1970, vol. 2, ch. 7, pp. 59–60; and Supp., pp. 30–31, 51.

staff assumed much of the burden of planning, managing, and coordinating the military aid effort. Admiral McCain delegated to MACV the preparation of the annual Military Assistance Program for Cambodia, including development of the *FANK* force structure. Most of the personnel for the political-military counselor's office and for expansion of that of the Phnom Penh defense attaché came from MACV. In addition, the command provided technical specialists on twenty-four-hour temporary assignments to augment the embassy's resources while keeping within overall manpower ceilings.[57]

As the incursions began early in May, General Abrams dispatched a MACV liaison officer to Phnom Penh. On 24 May, he established a new MACV staff element, the Special Support Group, under the J–4 to manage military assistance to Cambodia. Eventually including nine officers and six enlisted men in Saigon and two men in Phnom Penh as well as representatives from the Joint General Staff and the U.S. Military Assistance Command in Thailand, the support group handled the details of MAP planning, supply deliveries, and training assistance. It drew on other MACV staff elements as required. By late August, General Abrams estimated that thirty-seven MACV staff members were working full time and one hundred part time on assistance to Cambodia.[58]

While Abrams avoided personal contact with Cambodian officials and never visited Phnom Penh, he devoted much time and attention to coordinating help to the Khmer Republic. He developed a close personal and official relationship with the political-military counselor, Col. Jonathan F. Ladd, a former commander of the 5th Special Forces Group. Through weekly conferences in Saigon, Ladd kept Abrams informed about Cambodian events. Abrams in turn ensured Ladd's access to the senior MACV staff. Through informal contact with the Joint General Staff, Abrams smoothed out rough spots in the cooperation between the South Vietnamese and their new Cambodian allies. He also maintained contact with the U.S. Embassy and military command in Thailand, since that country was providing limited tactical air support and other assistance to the Khmer forces. In December, General Abrams arranged for establishment of a tripartite group of senior American, South Vietnamese, and Cambodian officers, each

[57] Msg, State and Defense Depts 86887 to Am Emb Phnom Penh, 5 Jun 70, box 589; Memo, Col Kennedy for Kissinger, 22 Jun 70, sub: Strengthening the Defense Attaché Office in Phnom Penh, box 510; Msg Swank Phnom Penh 3282 to Marshall Green, 4 Dec 70, and Msg, Sec State 166459 to Am Emb Phnom Penh, 8 Oct 70, box 511. All in NSC files, Nixon Papers, NARA. Msgs, Abrams MAC 8315 to McCain info Moorer, 19 Jun 70; McCain to Moorer et al., 19 Sep 70; McCain to Moorer and Abrams, 25 Oct 70. All in Abrams Papers, CMH. Tho, *Cambodian Incursion*, pp. 223–31; Interv, Abrams Project with Col Jonathan F. Ladd, 26 Feb 77, pp. 3–4, 30–33, MHI (hereafter cited as Ladd Interv).

[58] Msgs, Wheeler JCS 06287 to Abrams info McCain, 6 May 70; Abrams MAC 6287 to Wheeler, 9 May 70; Abrams MAC 7068 to McCain info Wheeler, 24 May 70; Seith BNK 1233 to Abrams info McCain et al., 25 May 70; Abrams MAC 11481 to McCain, 23 Aug 70. All in Abrams Papers, CMH. MACV History, 1970, Supp., pp. 71–72.

supported by a small staff, who met monthly in Saigon and Phnom Penh in rotation to work out day-to-day operational and logistical problems. Abrams assigned his deputy, General Weyand, as the MACV member of this group and at the same time placed Weyand in overall charge of the Military Assistance Command's Cambodian efforts.[59]

As U.S. military aid to Cambodia expanded, Admiral McCain and General Abrams repeatedly recommended to the Joint Chiefs that the Defense Department establish at least a small military assistance group in Phnom Penh. They argued that only a military assistance group or its equivalent could discharge properly the defense secretary's statutory responsibilities for managing the Military Assistance Program and furnish MACV and CINCPAC with adequate information on Cambodian military affairs. These functions simply were beyond the capacity of the political-military counselor's small staff. The Joint Chiefs endorsed McCain's and Abrams' proposal, but it met opposition from the State Department, which insisted on minimizing the American military presence in Phnom Penh.[60]

On 29 December, after considerable interdepartmental jockeying for position, Secretary Laird, at the president's direction, established a Military Equipment Delivery Team for Cambodia. The team, headed by an Army brigadier general provided by MACV, consisted of sixty officers and men, most of them located in Saigon. As Abrams had recommended, the team chief administered the Military Assistance Program under the supervision of the ambassador and Colonel Ladd. He was under the military command of Admiral McCain and worked in coordination with General Abrams. Activated in January 1971, the team, its strength gradually increased to more than one hundred, relieved the Military Assistance Command staff of most details of administering the Cambodia Military Assistance Program. However, the State and Defense Departments engaged in a prolonged wrangle over the authority of the team chief, Brig. Gen. Theodore C. Mataxis, in relation to Ambassador Emory C. Swank and Colonel Ladd. President Nixon finally resolved the issue by reaffirming the political-military counselor's primacy in the embassy on defense matters. General Abrams continued to conduct his own dealings with the Phnom Penh embassy through Ladd. General Weyand's tripartite group, supported by a small element of the MACV J–3 staff, retained its role in coordinating allied operations.[61]

[59] Msg, Haig Saigon 994 to Kissinger, 15 Dec 70, box 410; Msgs, Swank Phnom Penh 80 to Sec State, 8 Jan 71, box 511. All in NSC files, Nixon Papers, NARA. Msgs, Abrams MAC 7166 to Wheeler, McCain, Bunker, 26 May 70; McCain to Wheeler info Abrams et al., 22 Jun 70; Abrams MAC 8786 to McCain, 29 Jun 70; Abrams MAC 12129 to McCain, 7 Sep 70; Abrams MAC 13385 to Ladd, 9 Oct 70; Abrams MAC 15448 to McCain, 2 Dec 70; Abrams MAC 15581 to McCain, 6 Dec 70. All in Abrams Papers, CMH. Ladd Interv, 26 Feb 77, pp. 4–5, 33–37, 44–46, 56–57, 60–61.

[60] Msgs, McCain to Abrams, 23 Aug 70; Abrams MAC 11568 to McCain, 25 Aug 70; Abrams MAC 14998 to McCain, 21 Nov 70; McCain to Moorer info Abrams et al., 22 Dec 70. All in Abrams Papers, CMH. MACV History, 1970, Supp., pp. 71, 73.

[61] Memo, Laird for CJCS, 28 Dec 70, sub: Cambodian Military Equipment Delivery Team . . . and

Cambodia Balance Sheet

American aid to Cambodia ensured the survival of Lon Nol's regime. Although the North Vietnamese by late 1970 occupied nearly half of Cambodia's land area, the government held the cities, the major towns, and the regions containing most of the people. The regime benefited from an initial wave of popular patriotic enthusiasm. Its rapidly expanding armed forces, with American and South Vietnamese help, halted the enemy's territorial gains and even achieved occasional modest offensive successes. Yet the Communists were held back as much by their own small numbers, disorganization, and lack of supplies as by the *FANK*. They seemed more concerned with building a Cambodian guerrilla and political infrastructure and repairing their line of communication to South Vietnam than with immediate overthrow of the Phnom Penh government.[62]

The Lon Nol regime and its armed forces suffered from fundamental weaknesses similar to those which continued to undermine South Vietnamese effectiveness. Cambodia's military establishment had expanded too rapidly for the available trained leadership, which was weak to begin with. At the end of 1970, General Abrams considered the *FANK* "marginally effective at best." The Lon Nol government lacked competent officials at all levels. Lon Nol himself proved an erratic leader, authoritarian in style and tolerant of corruption. He suffered a stroke early in 1971 but clung to power even though physically impaired. Given the regime's limitations and the restrictions on American advice and assistance, the war in Cambodia clearly was at best a holding action, its outcome ultimately dependent on what happened in South Vietnam.[63]

From the viewpoint of the Military Assistance Command and the Saigon government, the Cambodian upheaval and the allied offensive brought significant strategic benefits. The enemy had lost his border base areas, thousands of troops, and huge materiel stockpiles, not to mention his secure, efficient Sihanoukville supply route. The enemy had shifted much of his remaining strength opposite III and IV Corps westward to establish his new Cambodian war front and would have to expend time and resources building a logistical corridor from

---

Msg, Sec State 003780 to Am Emb Phnom Penh et al., 8 Jan 71, box 511; Memo, Haig for Kissinger, 31 May 71, sub: Cambodia, box 512; Msg, Haig to Ladd, 24 Jul 71, box 430. All in NSC files, Nixon Papers, NARA. Ladd Interv, 26 Feb 77, pp. 46–49; MACV History, 1971, vol. 2, an. I, pp. 1–3.

[62] Typical assessments of the situation are Memo, Thomas Karamessines for Haig, 16 Nov 70, quoting Msg from Ladd, box 430, NSC files, Nixon Papers, NARA; and Msg, Abrams MAC 15447 to McCain, 2 Dec 70, Abrams Papers, CMH. Ladd Interv, 26 Feb 77, pp. 35–36, emphasizes enemy confusion.

[63] Quotation is from Msg, Abrams MAC 15447 to McCain, 2 Dec 70, Abrams Papers, CMH. Cambodia's governmental weaknesses are emphasized in Interv, Foreign Affairs Oral History Program with Swank in Charles S. Kennedy, comp., *A Cambodian Reader* (Washington, D.C.: Association for Diplomatic Studies, Aug 1993), passim.

southern Laos into northeastern Cambodia. South Vietnamese forces in III and IV Corps could count on a lengthy period of relief from major enemy attack, a period the allies could use to advance pacification and Vietnamization. Partially offsetting these gains were the allies' own need to extend their forces over a new battlefield and the political damage the Nixon administration had suffered in the United States. Nevertheless, the advantages appeared to American officials in Saigon and Washington to outweigh the disadvantages. As 1970 ended, they were making plans for additional, even more ambitious, cross-border offensives.[64]

[64] The MACV assessment is summarized in Msg, Rosson MAC 10929 to Moorer and McCain, 11 Aug 70, box 511, NSC files, Nixon Papers, NARA; in same box, see Memo, Smyser for Kissinger, 10 Sep 70, sub: Attached Report from Gen Rosson, for a critique of the MACV analysis by a NSC staff member who emphasizes the negative consequences. See also MACV History, 1970, vol. 1, ch. 1, p. 2.

10

Across the Borders: Laos and North Vietnam

Even as the Nixon administration opened a new war front in Cambodia, it continued and expanded air operations in the Laotian panhandle and the Plain of Jars. It also incrementally renewed the air war against North Vietnam, both to protect American aircraft engaged in Laos and to warn Hanoi that it was not immune from punishment for its persistent intransigence in the Paris negotiations. In the wake of the apparent success of the Cambodian incursions, the administration began considering large-scale ground operations in Laos to disrupt the flow of supplies down the Ho Chi Minh Trail. The Military Assistance Command was an influential advocate of all these efforts, as well as a major participant in them.

More Bombs over Laos, 1969–1970

During the first two years of the Nixon administration, MACV and the Seventh Air Force enlarged and refined their bombing offensive against the Ho Chi Minh Trail in the STEEL TIGER operating area of southern Laos. As combat diminished in South Vietnam, General Abrams shifted the weight of his airpower to the interdiction campaign, which he and Admiral McCain considered essential to preventing enemy offensives and buying time for pacification and Vietnamization. At its seasonal peak, the effort absorbed well over half of MACV's available tactical air and B–52 sorties. On the basis of intelligence from sensor arrays, PRAIRIE FIRE teams, and other sources, the Seventh Air Force used fighter-bombers, B–52s, and fixed-wing gunships in a series of integrated annual campaigns, code-named COMMANDO HUNT, aimed at disrupting the enemy's push of supplies through the trail network during the Laotian dry season, which extended from October through the end of April. Continually enhanced and refined, each campaign began with concentrated attacks on the mountain passes leading from North Vietnam into Laos, then followed the traffic along the Ho Chi Minh Trail's many branches with night and day strikes on way stations, storage areas, and moving trucks. According to Seventh Air Force estimates, the successive COMMANDO HUNTs destroyed tens of thousands of vehicles and reduced the amount of supplies reaching South Vietnam

Ambassador Godley

to less than one-fourth of the tonnage that entered the Ho Chi Minh Trail's northern end. The accuracy of these figures, especially the number of trucks destroyed, is open to question. However, at minimum, the interdiction campaign made the enemy's movement of supplies more costly in men and materiel than it otherwise would have been and diminished the flow.[1]

Beginning in early 1969, the Military Assistance Command had to respond to increasingly urgent demands from the U.S. Embassy in Vientiane for air support in the BARREL ROLL area of northern Laos. These demands were the result of two developments. Ambassador William H. Sullivan, who had sought to keep military activity in Laos at the lowest possible level, was replaced in mid-July by G. McMurtrie Godley, a cigar-smoking, pistol-packing veteran of covert operations in the Congo. Although Godley, like Sullivan, jealously guarded his authority over military operations in Laos, he was much more inclined than his predecessor to unleash American airpower against the North Vietnamese and Pathet Lao.[2]

Enemy pressure provided Godley with reason to do so. During the spring and summer, the North Vietnamese and Pathet Lao, breaking their normal seasonal pattern of operations, launched a sustained offensive that went beyond the annual ebb and flow across the Plain of Jars. They seemed intent on isolating the royal capital, Luang Prabang, and destroying the principal strongholds of Maj. Gen. Vang Pao's CIA-supported Meo irregulars, the allies' most effective Laotian fighting force. As the offensive continued into the Laotian rainy season,

[1] Thompson, "Rolling Thunder to Linebacker," ch. 6, pp. 18, 36–37. Msgs, Abrams MAC 3656 to Zais, 20 Mar 70; Abrams MAC 12864 to McCain, 26 Sep 70; Abrams MAC 12929 to Field Cdrs, 29 Sep 70. All in Abrams Papers, CMH. COMMANDO HUNT results are summarized in MACV History, 1971, vol. 1, ch. 6, pp. 28–31. Earl H. Tilford, Jr, *Setup: What the Air Force Did in Vietnam and Why* (Maxwell Air Force Base, Ala.: Air University Press, 1991), pp. 180–85, challenges Air Force statistical claims.

[2] Godley is characterized in Charles A. Stevenson, *End of Nowhere: American Policy Toward Laos since 1954* (Boston: Beacon Press, 1972), p. 225; and in Interv, Foreign Affairs Oral History Program with Nicolas A. Veliotes, in Charles S. Kennedy, comp., "A Laotian Reader: Selections from Oral Histories of the Foreign Affairs Oral History Program" (MS, Washington, D.C., 1993), p. 8.

Ambassadors Bunker and Godley, along with Admiral McCain, became convinced that the North Vietnamese were escalating their operations in Laos to compel Premier Souvanna Phouma to call for a halt to all U.S. bombing in his country, including the interdiction campaign—a request the United States would find embarrassing to refuse and disastrous to accept.[3]

To counter the North Vietnamese offensive, the embassy in Vientiane called for additional U.S. tactical air support. It also, for the first time in the Laotian war, requested B–52 strikes against enemy troop concentrations and supply lines on and around the Plain of Jars. The latter request became the subject of a lengthy debate within the Nixon administration. Secretary of Defense Laird and Secretary of State Rogers opposed the use of the heavy bombers in northern Laos. They contended that suitable targets for the B–52s had not been identified in the area and that it was politically undesirable to escalate the Laotian conflict. On the other side, Ambassadors Bunker and Godley, supported by Admiral McCain, pressed hard for the B–52s and warned that without such reinforcement Souvanna's army and regime might collapse.[4]

From General Abrams' viewpoint, Vientiane's demands threatened to divert airpower from the interdiction campaign, which Abrams considered more important to the struggle in South Vietnam. Abrams accordingly tried to limit the number of tactical air sorties allotted to BARREL ROLL and initially expressed reluctance to use B–52s there. In early April, he recommended that requests for ARC LIGHT strikes in northern Laos "not be favorably considered" because the area contained few worthwhile targets and the bombers could be used more profitably in COMMANDO HUNT and within South Vietnam. As the offensive continued, however, and the rains slowed traffic on the Ho Chi Minh Trail, Abrams shifted more tactical sorties to the north. He also sent officers to Thailand to assist the U.S. Air Attaché in Vientiane in developing targets and planning a campaign to isolate enemy forces on the Plain of Jars. On 29 July, he declared that the allies must "do what is necessary" to prevent further deterioration of the situation in northern Laos, which otherwise might have "wide-spread impact including the loss of US authority for bombing in Laos." He put the Seventh Air Force to work identifying possible B–52 targets around the Plain of Jars and recommended to Admiral McCain that preparations be made to conduct ARC LIGHT strikes there on short notice. Early in August, he informed McCain that, due to a lower level of combat in South Vietnam and the

---

[3] Msgs, McCain to McConnell info Abrams et al., 8 May 69; McCain to Wheeler info Abrams et al., 13 Jul 69; Abrams Papers. Msg, Bunker Saigon 16371 to Sec State, 14 Aug 69, box 138, NSC files, Nixon Papers, NARA.

[4] Memo, Laird for CJCS and Asst Sec Def (International Security Affairs), 29 Jul 69, box 099; Msg, McCain to Wheeler info White House et al., 30 Jul 69, box 545; Msg, Haig WH 91684 to Tony Lake, 30 Jul 69, box 102; Msg, Haig WH 91698 to Kissinger, 31 Jul 69, box 099. All in NSC files, Nixon Papers, NARA.

seasonal decline in traffic on the Ho Chi Minh Trail, he could spare some Arc Light missions for Barrel Roll.[5]

Despite these deliberations, the B–52s did not intervene in northern Laos during 1969. President Nixon in late July personally ordered the conduct of reconnaissance flights to select aiming points for Arc Light missions. After the reconnaissance missions were flown during the first days of August, MACV and Seventh Air Force, in consultation with the U.S. Embassy in Vientiane, nominated a list of targets. However, in the end, no Arc Light strikes were launched. During August, Vang Pao's forces, with heavy American tactical air support, counterattacked and retook much of the Plain of Jars. The State and Defense Departments continued to argue that the military results of escalation in northern Laos would not be worth the political and diplomatic costs. In mid-September, General Abrams concluded that none of the proposed targets were any longer suitable for B–52s. After considering several measures for strengthening Souvanna's regime, Nixon eventually authorized only the dispatch of additional M16 rifles and T–28 aircraft for the royal Laotian forces and the limited, covert introduction of Thai artillery units to reinforce threatened government positions.[6]

The B–52 question arose again the following January. On the twenty-fourth, Ambassador Godley reported that North Vietnamese and Pathet Lao troops were massing to assault the Plain of Jars. With the support of Admiral McCain and General Abrams, Godley asked for a preemptive Arc Light strike on the enemy concentrations. Secretary Laird this time favored the operation, but Secretary Rogers again argued that B–52 strikes were unlikely to be militarily decisive and would have adverse international and domestic political consequences. The administration temporized until mid-February, by which time the offensive was under way and the Laotian and Meo forces were in full retreat. After Souvanna Phouma formally requested B–52 strikes to save his position, and in response to increasingly urgent representations from Ambassador Godley, President Nixon finally authorized a strike, which took place on 17 February 1970.[7]

---

[5] Msgs, Abrams MAC 4153 to McCain and Wheeler, 2 Apr 69; Abrams MAC 9754 to McCain, 29 Jul 69; Abrams MAC 9969 to McCain info Wheeler et al., 2 Aug 69. All in Abrams Papers, CMH.

[6] Memos, Haig for the Sec Def, 31 Jul 69 and 1 Aug 69, box 102; Memos, Laird for the Assistant to the President for National Security Affairs, 31 Jul 69, sub: CINCPAC Proposal for B–52 Strikes in Laos; and Kissinger for the Sec Def, 15 Sep 69, box 545. All in NSC files, Nixon Papers, NARA. Msgs, Abrams MAC 9869 to McCain info Wheeler et al., 31 Jul 69; Abrams MAC 9919 to McCain info Wheeler et al., 1 Aug 69; Abrams MAC 10072 to McCain info Wheeler et al., 4 Aug 69; Abrams MAC 12267 to McCain and Amb G. McMutrie Godley, 19 Sep 69. All in Abrams Papers, CMH. The Meo counterattack is described in Stevenson, *End of Nowhere*, pp. 224–26.

[7] Msgs, McCain to Wheeler info Godley et al., 24 Jan 70; Abrams SPECAT to McCain info Wheeler, 24 Jan 70, Memo, Kissinger for the President, sub: B–52s in Laos, box 102; Memo, Laird for the Assistant to the President for National Security Affairs, 26 Jan 70, sub: Request for B–52 Strikes in North Laos; Memo, Rogers for the President, 26 Jan 70, sub: B–52 Strikes in the Plain of Jars . . . , box 123; NSC files, Nixon Papers, NARA. DoD, "Report on Selected Air and Ground Operations," p. 19.

Once the barrier was broken, B–52 strikes in Barrel Roll soon became a matter of routine. Under procedures prescribed by the administration, the U.S. Embassy in Vientiane nominated targets for each mission, which General Abrams reviewed and passed to the Joint Chiefs through Admiral McCain, using secure backchannel communications. The Joint Chiefs then recommended the operations to Secretary Laird, who regularly approved them. Ambassador Godley considered the raids of great value, both in checking the enemy onslaught and psychologically shoring up Souvanna's government. Assisted by the B–52s, American tactical aircraft, and battalions of Thai "volunteers," the anti-Communist forces maintained the balance of power in Laos throughout 1970. The cost of the intensified fighting to the Laotian people, however, was high. Besides the daily toll of civilian and military dead and wounded, according to some estimates, the lengthy war had turned one-fourth of the small nation's population of three million into refugees.[8]

Following a policy in effect since the mid-1960s, the Nixon administration, in order to protect Souvanna Phouma's facade of neutrality, made no public announcement of the first B–52 strikes in northern Laos. Nevertheless, reports of the attacks soon appeared in the American press. They helped bring to a head a debate within the administration over information policy toward the Laotian war. Since Nixon's inauguration, Defense Department public information officers had urged that the government openly announce and explain its military activities in Laos, which were common knowledge within Congress and the executive branch, not to mention the large, aggressive Saigon press corps. State Department officials in Washington and Vientiane, however, insisted on maintaining official silence. They warned that open discussion of U.S. operations would render Souvanna's position untenable and possibly provoke damaging Communist-bloc diplomatic and military reactions.

With the intensification of the Laotian war during 1969 and 1970, the official policy became steadily less credible. Press coverage of American operations increased, as did congressional demands for a true account of the scale of the effort and opposition to its expansion. Late in December 1969, a bipartisan majority attached a rider to a defense appropriation bill that forbade American ground combat operations in Laos and Thailand although it allowed continuation of the air war. President Nixon, in a December news conference, for the first time admitted that the United States was waging an interdiction campaign in the Laotian panhandle. In late February 1970, Ambassador Bunker

---

[8] DoD, "Report on Selected Air and Ground Operations," pp. 19–20. Msgs, Abrams MAC 2249 to Godley info McCain et al., 18 Feb 70; McCain to Wheeler info Abrams, 27 Feb 70; Godley to McCain and Abrams, 28 Mar 70; Abrams MAC 5100 to Lt Gen Alvan C. Gillem, II, USAF, Cdr 8th AF, 17 Apr 70. All in Abrams Papers, CMH. Statistics on Lao casualties are in Stevenson, *End of Nowhere*, p. 1.

and General Abrams declared that, given the scale and visibility of the operations, the existing information policy could not be implemented "in a meaningful manner and serves only to lessen our overall credibility with the press, the Congress and the American people. . . ." Their declaration drove one of the final nails into the coffin of the official policy of silence.[9]

In March 1970, over continuing objections from the State Department and Ambassador Godley, the administration adopted a new information approach to Laos. President Nixon issued a statement outlining the entire scope of the American effort in that country. On 13 March, the Defense Department instructed MACV to include air operations and losses in STEEL TIGER and BARREL ROLL in its daily military communiqués. However, the command continued to incorporate American personnel casualties in PRAIRIE FIRE into its figures for South Vietnam. General Abrams transmitted this guidance to his subordinate commanders, with instructions to withhold details of operations in Laos until they were released in Saigon. When implemented, the new policy produced no adverse diplomatic consequences. By adopting it, the administration reduced at least one source of friction between MACV and the news media.[10]

"Protective Reaction" over North Vietnam

Although President Nixon declined to execute PRUNING KNIFE, he kept the Commander in Chief, Pacific, and his subordinates at work on contingency plans for large-scale air attacks on North Vietnam. In addition, during 1970 the president with increasing frequency permitted Admiral McCain and General Abrams to launch actual limited, short-duration air raids against North Vietnam. The administration announced these publicly as "protective reaction" strikes to neutralize North Vietnamese air defenses that attacked or threatened U.S. aircraft over North Vietnam and Laos, but it gradually expanded them into brief but intense blows at Hanoi's logistics system.

Throughout 1970, the headquarters in Honolulu and Saigon developed and revised a series of attack plans, all subsumed under the codename PRUNING KNIFE ALPHA. Repeatedly, the staffs altered target lists and force assignments in response to administration demands, new intelligence, and American redeployments. By late 1970, the PRUNING KNIFE ALPHA series included a seven-day all-out air and naval offensive with options for mining Haiphong and other ports, a three-day campaign concentrating on the Haiphong complex, and briefer retaliatory raids on less important targets. In addition, CINCPAC and MACV main-

---

[9] This discussion is based on Hammond, *Military and the Media, 1968–1973*, pp. 261–72. Quotation is from Msg, Bunker and Abrams Saigon 2764 to Sec State, 24 Feb 70, box 143, NSC files, Nixon Papers, NARA.

[10] Hammond, *Military and the Media, 1968–1973*, pp. 272–79.

An F–4 Phantom prepares to land aboard the U.S.S. Midway
off the coast of North Vietnam.

tained plans for limited invasions of North Vietnam and other overt
and covert operations.[11]

For PRUNING KNIFE ALPHA, Admiral McCain kept in effect the route
package command system used in ROLLING THUNDER. Under it, MACV
and Seventh Air Force planned the strikes in Route Package 1, the
southernmost part of North Vietnam; and Admiral McCain designated
General Abrams as coordinating authority for operations in that area.
Late in 1970, McCain extended Abrams' authority beyond the old
Route Package 1, to include most of North Vietnam up to the 19th

[11] Msgs, McCain to Nazzaro and Hyland info Abrams et al., 7 Feb 70; McCain to Nazzaro et al.,
18 Feb 70; McCain to Abrams info Wheeler, 4 May 70; McCain to Wheeler info Abrams, 11 May 70;
McCain to Nazzaro and Hyland info Abrams et al., 10 Sep 70; McCain to Nazzaro and Hyland info
Abrams et al., 10 Sep 70; Abrams MAC 12713 to McCain info Nazzaro et al., 22 Sep 70; McCain to
Moorer info Abrams, 5 Dec 70. All in Abrams Papers, CMH. Memo, Haig for Kissinger, 13 Jul 70,
sub: Contingency Plans for Air Strikes against North Vietnam, box 148, NSC files, Nixon Papers,
NARA.

Parallel. He thereby placed under Abrams' jurisdiction all the mountain passes leading to the Ho Chi Minh Trail. As in ROLLING THUNDER, McCain directed air operations over the rest of North Vietnam through his air and naval component commanders. These arrangements assured Abrams, who disliked the route package system's division of authority and resources, control of air activity in the regions of most interest to him. By informal understanding with Admiral McCain, Abrams exercised something close to a veto on strikes in the other route packages if they conflicted with more urgent requirements in South Vietnam and Laos.[12]

While they prepared contingency plans, Abrams and McCain, supported by the Joint Chiefs, campaigned continuously for expanded authority to attack enemy air defenses, principally surface-to-air missile (SAM) sites, in southern North Vietnam. Since November 1968, MACV had possessed, and periodically exercised, the right to engage and destroy enemy missile and antiaircraft batteries below the 19th Parallel that fired on reconnaissance planes over North Vietnam or tactical aircraft and B–52s over Laos. In August 1969, Abrams, citing a buildup of North Vietnamese air defenses and the prospect of B–52 operations over the Plain of Jars, made the first of many requests for extension of his retaliatory authority at least to the 20th Parallel. Admiral McCain declined to transmit this request to the Joint Chiefs, since the B–52s were not yet flying over northern Laos and he considered the political atmosphere in Washington at the moment unfavorable to proposals for escalation. However, on 19 December 1969, a SAM battery in North Vietnam fired at and missed a formation of B–52s over the Laotian panhandle south of the 19-degree line, the first such enemy attack on the heavy bombers. This event imparted a new urgency to the issue.[13]

On 5 February 1970, with the season's COMMANDO HUNT campaign under way and the North Vietnamese air defense threat continuing to increase, Abrams requested still more expansive attack authority. He asked the Joint Chiefs, through Admiral McCain, for standby permission to strike North Vietnamese missile and antiaircraft installations within twenty-five nautical miles of the Laotian border and the Demilitarized Zone "without regard to firing initiatives by the enemy." With such discretionary authority, Abrams argued, he could launch preplanned strikes against North Vietnam's air defenses in response to current intelligence and in combination with other air operations.

---

[12] Abrams' dislike of the route packages is noted in Cowles Interv, 20 Dec 75, pp. 33–34; see also Corcoran Interv, 1975, pp. 40–41. Msgs, McCain to Abrams info Nazzaro et al., 28 Oct 69; McCain to Nazzaro, Hyland, and Abrams, 24 Nov 70; Abrams MAC 15136 to McCain, 25 Nov 70; McCain to Abrams, 26 Nov 70; McCain to Nazzaro, Hyland, and Abrams info Moorer, 26 Nov 70; McCain to PACOM Cdrs, 19 Dec 70. All in Abrams Papers, CMH.

[13] Msgs, Abrams MAC 7598 to McCain info Wheeler et al., 14 Jun 69; Abrams MAC 10987 to McCain info Brown, 23 Aug 69; McCain to Abrams info Brown, 3 Sep 69. All in Abrams Papers, CMH. Thompson, "Rolling Thunder to Linebacker," ch. 6, pp. 37–40.

Such attacks would disrupt a developing "SAM offensive against our interdiction operations," thereby denying to the enemy "advantages he now possesses and is rapidly increasing."[14]

During several weeks of exchanges with Admiral McCain, General Wheeler, and Secretary Laird, Abrams gained only part of the authority he wanted. On 9 February, the administration altered the rules of engagement to permit MACV to strike at will any SAM and antiaircraft installations in southern North Vietnam that posed a threat to American aircraft. However, it almost immediately rescinded that authority for fear of disrupting a diplomatic initiative then in progress. A month later, after additional urgent representations from Abrams and McCain and more SAM firings, President Nixon authorized destruction of any North Vietnamese batteries south of the 20th Parallel that engaged American aircraft over Laos. These attacks could be made at any time within seventy-two hours of the triggering incident. While keeping this retaliatory authority in effect throughout the year, Secretary Laird, on behalf of the administration, regularly turned down requests from Abrams and McCain for standby permission to conduct preemptive strikes. Laird insisted that existing authorities were sufficient to protect U.S. aircraft and that unprovoked attacks would arouse public and congressional opposition in the United States and give the other side justification for discarding the 1968 bombing halt understandings, perhaps by renewing bombardment of South Vietnam's cities.[15]

Although the administration withheld general permission for preplanned strikes in North Vietnam, during 1970 it authorized several one-time air raids on both antiaircraft installations and the logistical network that fed the Ho Chi Minh Trail, a network the North Vietnamese had been repairing and expanding unmolested since the end of ROLLING THUNDER. President Nixon intended these strikes to reinforce the interdiction campaign in Laos and as signals to Hanoi that its sanctuaries were not inviolable. Publicly, the administration explained the attacks as "protective reaction" in defense of U.S. airmen. The president tried to time the raids to coincide with other escalatory actions, such as the Cambodian incursion, so as to gain the maximum military benefit from each period of intensified domestic political furor.[16]

At Abrams' and McCain's recommendation, Nixon authorized one-day raids in March and again in April, hitting both air defense and logistical targets on the North Vietnamese side of the mountain passes

[14] Msg, Abrams MAC 1692 to McCain info Wheeler, 5 Feb 70, Abrams Papers, CMH.

[15] Memo, Nixon for the Sec Def, 21 Mar 70, sub: Air Operations in Southeast Asia, box 123, NSC files, Nixon Papers, NARA. Msgs, Wheeler JCS 01970 to McCain and Abrams, 9 Feb 70; Abrams MAC 2247 to Brown, 18 Feb 70; Abrams MAC 2419 to McCain info Wheeler et al., 28 Feb 70; McCain to Wheeler info Abrams et al., 28 Feb 70; Abrams MAC 2993 to Brown, 7 Mar 70; Moorer JCS 14354 to McCain info Abrams, 24 Oct 70; Abrams MAC 14844 to McCain info Moorer et al., 18 Nov 70; Moorer JCS 16306 to McCain info Abrams, 8 Dec 70. All in Abrams Papers, CMH.

[16] Thompson, "Rolling Thunder to Linebacker," ch. 6, pp. 2–4, 40–43, ch. 7, pp. 40–44; Historical Division, "Joint Chiefs of Staff and the War in Vietnam, 1969–1970," pp. 352–56, 360–62.

into Laos. From 1 to 4 May, as the Cambodian incursion got under way, MACV and CINCPAC conducted four days of similar air strikes. Admiral McCain claimed that the 700 sorties flown destroyed more than 10,000 tons of supplies that had been awaiting movement into the Ho Chi Minh Trail complex and "may be among the most successful ever conducted against forward elements of the NVN [North Vietnamese] logistics system." Another large attack on air defense installations and supply facilities, code-named Freedom Bait, went in on 21 November, in conjunction with an unsuccessful commando raid to free American prisoners of war in North Vietnam. Since these attacks were concentrated in Route Package 1 and the area of the passes into Laos, General Abrams, in cooperation with the commanders of the Seventh Air Force and the Navy's Task Force 77, planned and conducted the operations. Abrams strongly endorsed the raids. Nevertheless, he and Admiral McCain considered them an inadequate substitute for the standby anti-SAM strike authority they continued to request. The limitations notwithstanding, as 1970 ended, MACV once again was engaged in an incrementally expanding air war against North Vietnam.[17]

The 1971 Dry Season Offensive

By late 1970, the focus of the cross-border war was shifting from Cambodia to Laos. After the loss of the Sihanoukville route and the disruption of their Cambodian bases, the North Vietnamese increased the volume of traffic on the Ho Chi Minh Trail, their sole remaining supply conduit to the south, and extended the trail from Laos into northeastern Cambodia. Air attacks and commando operations by themselves could reduce but not stop the flow of North Vietnamese men and supplies through southern Laos. Accordingly, General Abrams and Admiral McCain considered ways and means of attacking the supply route with ground forces. As early as March 1969, General Abrams suggested the conduct of brief incursions into the enemy's Laotian base areas. During 1970, as the Cambodian offensive unfolded, Abrams and McCain were especially interested in preventing the enemy from extending his logistical network into northeastern Cambodia to replace Sihanoukville. Their options, however, were limited by the congressional ban on using American ground troops in Laos. McCain suggested expanding the Prairie Fire zone of operations westward to Tchepone, a key Ho Chi Minh Trail nexus opposite northern I Corps. Abrams declared this plan impractical because enemy ground and antiaircraft defenses in the area

---

[17] Message traffic for these raids is in Abrams message files, Abrams Papers, CMH. Quotation is from Msg, McCain to Moorer info Abrams et al., 13 May 70, Abrams Papers, CMH. The following illustrate command relationships: Msgs, Abrams MAC 4581 to McCain info Wheeler, 8 Apr 70; McCain to Wheeler info Abrams, 7 May 70; McCain to Abrams et al., info Moorer et al., 15 Nov 70; McCain to Abrams info Moorer et al., 20 Nov 70. All in Abrams Papers, CMH. Msg, Abrams MAC 13883 to McCain info Clay, 22 Oct 70, Abrams Papers, CMH, reiterates the need for preemptive strikes on SAM sites.

were too strong. He and Ambassador Godley also considered unworkable a proposal by McCain to use South Vietnamese, Thai, and Laotian troops to occupy the strategic Bolovens Plateau in southern Laos, arguing that the available allied forces were insufficient for the task. McCain and Abrams continued their exchanges through late autumn, but reached no conclusion other than to continue with COMMANDO HUNT and PRAIRIE FIRE.[18]

President Nixon and Dr. Kissinger meanwhile were contemplating new cross-border attacks. Nixon and his national security adviser anticipated that the North Vietnamese would launch a major offensive sometime in 1971 or 1972, to disrupt pacification and Vietnamization, improve Hanoi's negotiating position, and influence the South Vietnamese and American presidential elections. They believed that the attack most probably would come in northern Military Region 1, where North Vietnamese supply lines were short and where American troop withdrawals were shifting the balance of strength in the enemy's favor. Increasing their apprehension, intelligence reports during October and November indicated that the North Vietnamese were preparing for a southward movement of men and supplies comparable in scale to that before Tet 1968 and that they were assembling troops, including a new corps-level headquarters, just above the Demilitarized Zone for a possible multidivision offensive in Military Region 1 early in the new year. [19]

In the light of this information, Nixon decided to preempt the North Vietnamese by launching offensives of his own in Laos and Cambodia. Employing South Vietnamese ground forces with all-out U.S. air support, the attacks would have the objective of disrupting the enemy's timetable and preventing major North Vietnamese offensives during the rest of 1971 and even into 1972. Nixon and Kissinger considered early 1971 to be the last feasible time for such operations, since strong American combat forces would still be available to support the South Vietnamese and fill in behind them in South Vietnam.[20]

On 6 December 1970, Admiral Moorer set the offensive planning in motion. He informed McCain and Abrams that the president desired concepts for multidivision South Vietnamese offensives in Cambodia and the Laotian panhandle, to be conducted early in the new year with full U.S. air support. General Abrams was to consult with Ambassador

[18] Msgs, Abrams MAC 3066 to McCain, 10 Mar 69; Abrams MAC 5709 to McCain, 29 Apr 70; McCain to Abrams et al., 23 May 70; Abrams MAC 7111 to McCain info Seith et al., 25 May 70; Godley CCF 042 to McCain info Abrams et al., 1 Jun 70; McCain to Moorer info Abrams et al., 16 Aug 70; McCain to Moorer info Abrams, 24 Oct 70. All in Abrams Papers, CMH.

[19] Kissinger, *White House Years*, pp. 986–89. For intelligence background, see Memo, Holdridge for Kissinger, 17 Dec 70, sub: North Vietnamese Strength in Laos, box 548, NSC files, Nixon Papers, NARA; and Msg, Sutherland QTR 0446 to Abrams, 21 Mar 71, Abrams Papers, CMH. Msgs, McCain to Abrams, 7 Nov 70; Abrams MAC 14507 to McCain, 9 Nov 70; Abrams Papers, CMH, also reflect official concern about an enemy offensive.

[20] Kissinger, *White House Years*, p. 990.

Bunker and President Thieu on the operations and obtain Thieu's support for them. Ordering McCain and Abrams to inform only their most senior subordinates of the administration's intentions, Moorer advised them to expect a visit within a week from General Haig, Kissinger's military assistant, who would receive the commanders' initial proposals. Nixon, in a direct follow-up message to Abrams, called upon the MACV commander for "bold and aggressive allied counteractions" to the expected enemy offensive and demanded plans to "carry the battle to the enemy to the greatest extent possible." Both Nixon and Moorer placed primary emphasis on Cambodia, where they wanted to prevent the enemy from reestablishing his border bases. For Laos, they initially envisioned an operation in the lower panhandle, perhaps in the Bolovens Plateau, which would complement the Cambodian offensive.[21]

General Abrams already had in hand a plan for the attack in Cambodia. By early December, MACV and the Joint General Staff were completing a concept for a drive by the South Vietnamese III Corps, with American air support, into the area of the Chup Plantation, about sixty miles northeast of Phnom Penh. The operation, which eventually might involve up to twenty-eight South Vietnamese battalions and last from January through July, would open a key route, Highway 7, from the Vietnamese border to the Mekong River, clear out a base area the enemy was developing, and disrupt any North Vietnamese offensives planned for Military Region 3. Essentially an expansion on what the South Vietnamese already were doing in Cambodia, this proposal met with quick administration acceptance. On 24 December, Abrams received permission to plan on using American tactical aircraft, B–52s, and helicopters in the operation to whatever extent was necessary for its success. On 6 January 1971, Admiral Moorer on behalf of the administration authorized MACV to commit its forces to the attack, which actually began early in February.[22]

Abrams' plan for Laos was the product of more extensive deliberation. Two days after he received Moorer's request for offensive plans, Abrams conferred at MACV headquarters with General Weyand, his deputy; General Sutherland, commander of XXIV Corps; General Davison, commander of II Field Force; and the MACV chiefs of operations and intelligence. After reviewing various alternatives, Abrams directed Sutherland and Davison, without consulting their staffs, to draw up general concepts for drives into Laos, respectively from Military Regions 1 and 3. At a subsequent meeting, Abrams reviewed

---

[21] Msgs, McCain to Abrams, 6 Dec 70; Moorer JCS 16390 to Abrams, 10 Dec 70. Both in Abrams Papers, CMH. Quotation is from latter message. Msg, Kissinger WHS 0064 to Bunker, 10 Dec 70; Msg, Kennedy WHS 0065 to Haig, 15 Dec 70. Both in box 1011, NSC files, Nixon Papers, NARA. The latter message indicates the administration's interest in a Bolovens operation.

[22] Msgs, Abrams MAC 15447 to McCain, 2 Dec 70; Moorer to McCain info Abrams, 24 Dec 70; Abrams Papers. Msg, Abrams SPECAT 68644 to McCain info Moorer, 30 Dec 70; JCS 9395 to CINCPAC info COMUSMACV, 6 Jan 71, box 511, NSC files, Nixon Papers, NARA.

General Lam (left) *with President Thieu*

their proposals and adopted Sutherland's plan for a South Vietnamese attack with XXIV Corps support to cut the Ho Chi Minh Trail near Tchepone. He considered that blocking the trail opposite Military Region 1 would have more decisive effect than any other operation, both in stemming the flow of supplies and preempting enemy attacks during 1971. Abrams then reviewed the concept with Ambassador Bunker, President Thieu, and General Vien, all of whom endorsed it. Later in December, Vien broached the idea to the I Corps/Military Region 1 commander, General Lam, who in turn informed the commander of the South Vietnamese 1st Division, which would constitute a major element of the attack force. The Vietnamese at once began their own planning for the operation.[23]

Abrams' concept, which he transmitted to McCain on 12 December, called for an attack by a South Vietnamese armored brigade and the equivalent of two infantry divisions, with support troops, from northern

---

[23] These meetings are described in Sutherland Interv, n.d., pp. 24–26; and Maj. Gen. Nguyen Duy Hinh, *Lam Son 719*, Indochina Monographs (Washington, D.C.: U.S. Army Center of Military History, 1979), pp. 33–35. The latter account dates the start of discussions as early January 1971, but Sutherland's interview and other American records indicate that Thieu, Vien, and Lam were consulted or learned of the operation in December.

Quang Tri Province to Tchepone to "sever" the Ho Chi Minh Trail at a major junction point and destroy enemy forces and supply stockpiles. The advance, to be supported with "maximum" U.S. airpower, would follow the trace of Highway 9, an east–west highway that roughly paralleled the Demilitarized Zone in South Vietnam and extended into Laos to and beyond Tchepone.

The operation was to develop in four phases. In the first phase, a reinforced U.S. brigade would open and secure Highway 9 to the Laotian border and establish a forward operating base, airfield, and artillery firebases within South Vietnam to support the South Vietnamese advance. American forces also would take position to block enemy counterattacks across the Demilitarized Zone. In the second phase, the South Vietnamese armor, its flanks protected by heliborne air assaulting infantry, would advance rapidly along Highway 9 and seize Tchepone. In the third phase, the South Vietnamese would improve Tchepone's airfield for resupply operations, secure their lines of communications along Highway 9, and fan out to block the Ho Chi Minh Trail and destroy North Vietnamese forces and supplies in the surrounding area, known as Base Area 604. In the fourth phase, the South Vietnamese were to withdraw from Tchepone, either directly eastward along Highway 9 or southeastward through another base area, 611, which they would destroy as they went. Starting in late January or early February, the operation was to last about three months, until the onset of the Laotian rainy season late in April. Abrams told McCain that the operation would deny to the North Vietnamese "the logistic corridor vital for continued prosecution of the war in RVN [Republic of Vietnam], Cambodia and . . . southern Laos" during the peak period of supply movement. It would "significantly disrupt" their timetable for 1971, and restrict their efforts in 1972 by forcing them to laboriously restore their lines of communication and supply stockpiles before they could launch a major offensive.[24] (*Map 4*)

Abrams' concept for the Tchepone operation was hardly new. Throughout America's military engagement in Vietnam, U.S. commanders had proposed incursions into the Laos panhandle to cut the umbilical cord that connected the enemy's "Great Front Line" in South Vietnam with their "Great Rear Area" in the north. In 1965, for example, General Johnson had proposed establishing a permanent cordon of American and allied troops across Laos. On the Vietnamese side, General Vien also advocated the cordon project. General Westmoreland had his staff draw up numerous plans for temporary incursions against the trail, using both American and South Vietnamese forces. Several of these plans included advances from northern I Corps along Highway 9 to and beyond Tchepone. However, Ambassador Sullivan in Vientiane objected to any large operations; and neither Westmoreland nor Admiral Sharp

---

[24] Msg, Abrams MAC 15808 to McCain, 12 Dec 70, Abrams Papers, CMH.

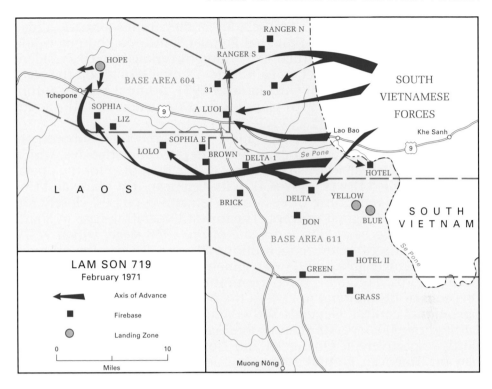

MAP 4

campaigned for them with any real urgency. Indeed, in early 1968, Sharp, in what turned out to be a prescient assessment, predicted that any such operation would run into heavy North Vietnamese resistance and afford the enemy, fighting on favorable ground, a good chance to inflict "abnormally high" allied casualties and thereby gain "a major propaganda victory detrimental to US and Vietnamese morale."[25]

By late 1970, Admiral Sharp's forebodings appear to have been forgotten. Sharp's successor, Admiral McCain, "wholeheartedly" concurred in Abrams' concept, which he forwarded to Admiral Moorer on 15 December. When General Haig reached Saigon in mid-month, he found Bunker, Abrams, Thieu, and Vien unanimous in preferring the Tchepone operation over the proposals Haig had brought from Washington for incursions farther south in the panhandle. According to Haig, "all here are extremely enthusiastic about this operation," which Abrams characterized as "the most significant . . . of the war thus far"

---

[25] For American proposals, see Cosmas, *Years of Escalation, 1962–1967*, pp. 378–79. Vien's concept is summarized in Hinh, *Lam Son 719*, pp. 32–33. Quotation is from Msg, Sharp to Wheeler, 14 Jan 68; see also Msgs, Sharp to Wheeler info Westmoreland et al., 6 Jan 68; and Sharp to Wheeler info Westmoreland, 21 Jan 68. All in Westmoreland Message files, Jan 68, CMH. Sullivan continued to oppose large ground incursions into Laos after returning to Washington; see Memo, Sullivan for Kissinger, 10 Jun 69, sub: Laos, box 545, NSC files, Nixon Papers, NARA.

and "potentially decisive." Ambassador Godley from Vientiane added his endorsement and told Haig that Premier Souvanna Phouma would not object. When he returned to Washington, Haig briefed President Nixon, Dr. Kissinger, Secretary Laird, and Admiral Moorer on the plan; all tentatively approved it. On 7 January 1971, Admiral Moorer authorized Abrams to proceed with planning in conjunction with the South Vietnamese.[26]

During January, XXIV Corps and I Corps, and their subordinate commands, drafted detailed plans and orders for the offensive, which Abrams and Vien reviewed and approved. The final plan for the operation, to be called DEWEY CANYON II in its American first phase and LAM SON 719 in its remaining three South Vietnamese phases, closely followed Abrams' original concept. The forward operating base in South Vietnam was to be at Khe Sanh, site of the 1968 siege, which XXIV Corps would secure and reopen during Phase I. Besides the armored brigade, a Ranger group, and two regiments of the 1st Infantry Division from I Corps, President Thieu committed the airborne and marine divisions of his national reserve to the offensive under General Lam's operational control. Generals Sutherland and Lam were to direct the battle through cooperation and coordination from forward command posts, respectively at Quang Tri and Dong Ha. Under the legislative ban on American ground troops in Laos, the American advisers to South Vietnamese units would remain in South Vietnam. However, the operation depended entirely on massive American air support in all its forms, from B–52 strikes to helicopter lift of troops, artillery, and supplies; and U.S. ground forces would be engaged on the South Vietnamese side of the border.[27]

As they planned LAM SON 719, the Americans and South Vietnamese knew that the enemy had strong forces in the target area—at least three infantry regiments, eight regimental-size *binh trams*, or military way stations, and several hundred antiaircraft weapons of various types—and that they could reinforce with additional infantry and artillery from North Vietnam. Generals Sutherland and Abrams also were aware by late January that the North Vietnamese probably had learned of their plans from South Vietnamese security lapses. Nevertheless, the allied commanders and staffs did not seem to have expected a pitched battle early in the operation. In conversations with President Thieu on 29 and 30 January, as DEWEY CANYON II was getting under way, General

---

[26] First quotation is from Msg, McCain to Moorer info Abrams, 15 Dec 70, box 1012; remaining quotations are from Msg, Haig Saigon 993 to the White House (Kissinger), 15 Dec 70, box 1011. Both in NSC files, Nixon Papers, NARA. Godley's endorsement is recounted in Msg, Haig Saigon 035 to White House (Kissinger), 17 Dec 70, box 1011, NSC files, Nixon Papers, NARA. Kissinger, *White House Years*, pp. 994–95; Sutherland Interv, n.d., pp. 25–26; Hinh, *Lam Son 719*, pp. 33–35.

[27] The final plan is summarized conveniently in Hinh, *Lam Son 719*, pp. 35–52. The change of name in the first phase was designed to divert enemy attention to the Da Krong Valley in South Vietnam, since DEWEY CANYON was the name of a large Marine operation conducted there in 1969. Msg, Sutherland DNG 0251 to Abrams, 30 Jan 71, Abrams Papers, CMH.

Abrams told Thieu that the attack force should cover the thirty-odd miles from the border to Tchepone in one or two days and that the North Vietnamese would not be able to move major forces in to contest the area during the operation's first three weeks. The subordinate commands also assumed light opposition at the outset. Given only a short time to plan, they made few provisions for any other contingency.[28]

By contrast, during December and January, the Central Intelligence Agency, in analyses done in Langley, concluded that the North Vietnamese clearly anticipated an allied ground attack on their infiltration routes, were moving reinforcements into the area with a heavy concentration around Tchepone, and were "in a good posture" to resist an offensive "vigorously and promptly." An agency memorandum, prepared on 21 January at Kissinger's request, concluded that Hanoi would be likely to "do whatever it could to make the position of the South Vietnamese in Laos untenable and . . . be prepared to accept the heavy manpower losses this might entail."[29]

The possibility of fierce North Vietnamese resistance, and questions about whether the South Vietnamese, even with American air support, could overcome it surfaced during the Nixon administration's month-long deliberations over LAM SON 719. Involving the president, Kissinger, and members of the cabinet as well as the national security adviser's Washington Special Actions Group, these discussions went on throughout January even as forces moved into position in Military Region 1 and DEWEY CANYON II began. Nixon's objective throughout was to ensure that all his principal advisers and the bureaucracy were unified behind the decision to go ahead, which he already had made, so that his government could present a solid front to the expected press, congressional, and public opposition.

After a mid-January visit to Saigon, Defense Secretary Laird fully endorsed the operation. On the other hand, Secretary of State Rogers and CIA Director Richard Helms, reflecting the views of their subordinates, expressed doubts. Both men anticipated that the offensive would meet strong North Vietnamese opposition and questioned whether the South Vietnamese Army, fighting without its American advisers, would be able to prevail even with U.S. air support. Rogers also warned that a severe South Vietnamese military defeat in Laos could bring down President Thieu, who faced an election in September. Raising the usual fears of compromising Laotian neutrality, the State Department

---

[28] Abrams' comments to Thieu are reported in Msgs, Bunker Saigon 1375 to Sec State, 29 Jan 71, box 083; and Bunker Saigon 1401 to Sec State, 30 Jan 71, box 080; NSC files, Nixon Papers, NARA. Sutherland Interv, n.d., pp. 25–26, describes lax South Vietnamese security. Hinh, *Lam Son 719*, pp. 53–57, notes the short time available and the general expectation of light opposition as well as other deficiencies in the planning.

[29] The CIA assessment is quoted in Memo, Tom Latimer for Kissinger, 12 Apr 71, sub: CIA and Lam Son Intelligence Failures, box 154, NSC files, Nixon Papers, NARA. The same points are made in Memo, Kissinger for the President, 26 Jan 71, sub: CIA Analysis of Probable Reactions of Various Concerned Parties to Operations in Laos, box 083, NSC files, Nixon Papers, NARA.

attempted to block the operation by inducing the president to seek Premier Souvanna Phouma's approval before proceeding. Souvanna, however, as Godley had predicted he would, privately agreed to the attack although he made a pro forma public protest. The military authorities in Saigon and Washington repeatedly reaffirmed that the offensive would succeed. President Nixon finally steeled himself to go ahead. DEWEY CANYON II jumped off on 30 January. On 2 February, Nixon agreed to the launching of Phase II, the actual beginning of LAM SON 719, and authorized Abrams to commit MACV's airpower to the battle. The South Vietnamese crossed the border into Laos on 8 February.[30]

By the time the South Vietnamese entered Laos, the media and congressional uproar Nixon anticipated was already under way. An action by General Abrams did much to intensify the furor. Abrams and McCain realized that the North Vietnamese, after the Cambodian incursion, almost certainly would expect and prepare to meet a similar attack on their sanctuary in Laos even without the forewarning that they probably had received. Therefore, the American commanders carried out a number of diversionary operations, including a feigned amphibious raid on Vinh in North Vietnam, designed to keep their adversaries uncertain of the actual objective of the buildup in far northwestern Military Region 1.[31]

On 30 January, as part of this effort, MACV ordered newsmen in Saigon not to file stories on the progress of DEWEY CANYON II and the South Vietnamese movement toward the border until permitted to do so by the military command. Although the MACV chief of public affairs, Col. Robert Leonard, briefed the Saigon reporters in background on the impending offensive and the reasons for the embargo, the correspondents, whose relationship with MACV already was deteriorating, reacted with suspicion and indignation. The embargo proved quite porous, both in Vietnam and in Washington. During the first days of February, reports and speculation on the coming invasion of Laos were widespread, as was editorial denunciation of the military's attempt to muzzle the news media. As controversy mounted, Abrams grimly held the embargo in place, insisting that it was protecting the lives of American and South Vietnamese soldiers. Nevertheless, on 4 February, with the floodgates clearly collapsing, Admiral Moorer directed Abrams to lift the restriction. By that time, the damage was done. The media approached LAM SON 719 in a hostile frame of mind, aggravated still fur-

---

[30] Kissinger, *White House Years*, pp. 994–1002, recounts Nixon's decision-making process. Memo, Howe for Haig, 9 Feb 71, box 084, NSC files, Nixon Papers, NARA, lists the meetings by dates, times, and participants. Memoranda of many of the meetings, which give the flavor of the arguments, are in Special Operations file, box 083; authorization for Phase II is issued in Msg, Sec State 019640 to Embassy Saigon info Embassy Vientiane, 4 Feb 71, box 080. Both in NSC files, Nixon Papers, NARA.

[31] The diversion off Vinh is described in Cosmas and Murray, *U.S. Marines in Vietnam, 1970–1971*, pp. 207–09.

ther by inept South Vietnamese management of news coverage of the operation. MACV and the administration could expect critical scrutiny of their every statement and action and maximum press attention to any setbacks.[32]

Setbacks there were in abundance. From the start, LAM SON 719 ran into major difficulties. Highway 9, the South Vietnamese Army's sole ground avenue of advance through the heavily forested mountains of the operational area, was little more than a trail, cut by innumerable streams and heavily cratered by past bombings, which ran along a narrow river valley flanked by steep escarpments. Instead of dashing to Tchepone, the armored column moved along

Colonel Leonard

the road at a slow crawl. On the flanks, the Rangers and the airborne division north of the highway and the South Vietnamese 1st Infantry Division south of it met a high volume of North Vietnamese antiaircraft fire as they air assaulted into their planned firebases. American helicopter losses mounted rapidly, straining MACV's replacement and repair capabilities and limiting the available airlift for supply, reinforcement, and medical evacuation. Well prepared to meet the attack, the North Vietnamese ringed the firebases with antiaircraft guns and infantry and constantly pounded them with mortars and 130-mm. and 152-mm. heavy artillery, which outranged the South Vietnamese 105-mm. and 155-mm. pieces. Most ominous, the North Vietnamese moved infantry and armor into the operational area much more rapidly than American and South Vietnamese commanders had anticipated and attacked persistently and aggressively. Disregarding severe casualties from tactical air and B–52 strikes, the North Vietnamese seemed intent on destroying the South Vietnamese force as well as protecting their trail complex and supply depots.[33]

In fact, the South Vietnamese were facing an enemy that desired a decisive battle and had made extensive preparations for it. As early as

[32] The embargo, news coverage of the operation, and media reaction are covered in detail in Hammond, *Military and the Media, 1968–1973*, chs. 17, 18, and 19.

[33] Aircraft losses and unexpectedly rapid enemy reinforcement are discussed in Msgs, Sutherland DNG 0448 to Abrams, 14 Feb 71; and Sutherland QTR 0135 to Abrams, 23 Feb 71. Both in Abrams Papers, CMH.

*A 175-mm. self-propelled gun fires at enemy targets
in Laos during Operation* LAM SON *719.*

mid-summer 1970, the North Vietnamese General Staff, anticipating that the Americans would follow up the Cambodian offensive with one in Laos, had directed the concentration of forces and preparation of the battlefield in the LAM SON 719 area of operations—a critical nexus of the Ho Chi Minh Trail. During the ensuing months, the enemy secretly redeployed a main force division from Quang Nam Province in South Vietnam to the front. To control that division and four others brought down from North Vietnam, the enemy created a provisional corps headquarters (the one American intelligence had noted in November) capable of directing a large-scale combined arms battle. As the troops assembled, *Group 559*, the headquarters that operated, maintained, and guarded the Ho Chi Minh Trail, prepared its own units for defense, built fortifications, constructed additional truck routes in the area for movement of supplies, and set up depots and a medical evacuation network. Because of allied security breaches, the North Vietnamese learned many details of the LAM SON 719 plan and intensified their preparations.

By the time the South Vietnamese crossed the Laotian border on 8 February, the North Vietnamese, by their own account, had massed some 60,000 troops on what they called the "Route 9–Southern Laos front," about double the strength of the South Vietnamese attack force and well above what allied commanders had expected. Waiting for General Lam's troops were five divisions, two separate infantry regiments, eight artillery regiments, three engineer regiments, three tank battalions, six antiaircraft regiments, and eight sapper battalions, plus logistic and transportation units. North Vietnamese historians called this "our army's greatest concentration of combined-arms forces . . . up to that point." In and within easy reach of the battle area, *Group 559* had stockpiled supplies sufficient to support the force in combat for as long as four or five months.

The North Vietnamese had massed this combat power for more than simple defense of their vital supply route. The leaders in Hanoi saw an opportunity to fight a battle of annihilation on advantageous terms, destroy some of Saigon's best units, and thoroughly disrupt and discredit Vietnamization. Indicating the importance Hanoi assigned to the campaign, Col. Gen. Van Tien Dung, deputy chairman of the Politburo's Central Military Party Committee and chief of the General Staff, journeyed to the front to oversee operations. In a prebattle address to the troops, the Communist Party Central Committee declared: "The coming engagement will be a strategically decisive battle. We will fight not only to retain control of the strategic transportation corridor, but also to annihilate a number of units of the enemy's strategic reserve forces, [and] to . . . deal a significant defeat to a portion of their 'Vietnamization' plot. . . ."[34]

As their search-and-destroy operation turned into a sustained conventional battle, the South Vietnamese soldiers in the main fought well; but weaknesses in the South Vietnamese Army leadership and command control quickly developed. Without their unit advisers, the South Vietnamese had difficulty coordinating their air and artillery support. Their division commanders and staffs lacked experience in managing a large-scale engagement; indeed the marines and airborne had never previously operated as divisions. General Lam, while adequate as a military region commander in low-intensity warfare, was beyond his depth when required to fight a corps-size pitched battle. Compounding his problems, as the campaign's difficulties mounted, the commanders of the airborne and marine divisions, who as part of the national reserve considered themselves responsible directly to the Joint General Staff, often ignored Lam's orders. Adding still further to the confusion, President Thieu personally intervened in key tactical decisions.[35]

---

[34] Enemy preparations and objectives are described in the Military History Institute of Vietnam, *Victory in Vietnam: The Official History of the People's Army of Vietnam, 1954–1975*. Trans. by Merle L. Pribbenow (Lawrence, Kans.: University Press of Kansas, 2002), pp. 272–75.

[35] The course of combat is described in Hinh, *Lam Son 719*, ch. 4; and Dale Andrade, "U.S. Army Combat Operations in Vietnam, 1968–1973" (Draft MS, Washington, D.C.: U.S. Army Center of Military History), chs. 10 and 11. Msg, Abrams MAC 15103 to McCown, 24 Nov 70, Abrams Papers, CMH, describes the Vietnamese Marine division headquarters as "strictly administrative" with no

Faced with unexpectedly severe resistance and losses, the South Vietnamese, with Thieu taking the lead, began reshaping the campaign in the direction of hesitancy and caution. On 12 February, Thieu visited Lam's headquarters and directed the corps commander to halt his westward advance, which had reached a point about halfway to Tchepone. Lam was to shift forces to the flanks to suppress the antiaircraft defenses, contain the developing North Vietnamese counterattack, and secure the Highway 9 line of communications. Thieu reiterated this guidance during a second visit to Lam on the twenty-first. The South Vietnamese accordingly halted in place while enemy pressure increased. On the northern flank, tank-supported North Vietnamese infantry drove the Rangers and airborne division out of four firebases. Overrunning one base on 25 February, the enemy captured the commander and staff of the airborne division's 3d Brigade.[36]

General Abrams had been the principal initiator of the Laos offensive, but once it began he could influence events only through advice and assistance to the South Vietnamese. Abrams closely watched the progress of the attack. He received daily reports from General Sutherland by both message and secure telephone. Abrams and General Weyand frequently visited Sutherland's and Lam's headquarters. In Saigon, Abrams spoke almost daily with General Vien; and he and Ambassador Bunker regularly exchanged views with President Thieu. To improve the speed and responsiveness of American air and artillery support for the operation, Abrams secured the establishment on 1 March of a U.S. Joint Coordinating Group at Lam's advance command post at Khe Sanh. Headed by the commander of the U.S. 108th Artillery Group and composed of representatives of the 101st Airborne Division, the XXIV Corps G–3, and the Seventh Air Force, the group assisted Lam and his staff in planning and using all forms of American airpower and fire support.[37]

As the Vietnamese hesitated, Abrams and General Sutherland worked to keep LAM SON 719 on its planned track. They reluctantly acknowledged the validity of Thieu's reasons for halting the advance on 12 February; but they urged him and Lam to resume the movement to Tchepone as soon as possible so as to retain the initiative and be sure of cutting the enemy's main supply routes, which ran to the west of the town. Abrams repeatedly urged upon Thieu and Vien the military and psychological importance of keeping their troops in Laos through the end of the rainy season, and he pointed out that the battle offered an unprecedented opportunity to destroy major enemy forces and

capability to control tactical operations in the field.

[36] Msgs, Abrams MAC 01554 to Sutherland, 13 Feb 71; Sutherland DNG 0443 to Abrams, 14 Feb 71. Both in Abrams Papers, CMH. Andrade, "Combat Operations, 1968–1973," ch. 11, pp. 11–32.

[37] Msg, Abrams MAC 02193 to Davison and Sutherland, 2 Mar 71, Abrams Papers, CMH; Sutherland Interv, n.d., pp. 26, 30. Coordinating group: Msgs, Abrams MAC 02079 to Sutherland, 27 Feb 71; Sutherland QTR 0172 to Abrams, 28 Feb 71. Both in Abrams Papers, CMH. Hinh, *Lam Son 719*, pp. 147–48.

gain a decisive victory. On 6 March, Abrams suggested to General Vien that he reinforce the attack with elements of the South Vietnamese 2d Division from southern Military Region 1, where U.S. troops of the Americal Division were available to take over the South Vietnamese 2d Division's territorial security responsibilities.[38]

By the time Abrams made this suggestion, the South Vietnamese had had enough. Their troops had been engaged in nearly a month of continuous hard combat, and their army lacked a system for rapidly replacing losses or rotating units. In early March, President Thieu, apprehensive of the political effect within South Vietnam of heavy casualties and fearing that his elite marine and airborne forces might be surrounded and destroyed, decided to cut LAM SON 719 short. Two battalions of the South Vietnamese 1st Division air assaulted into the abandoned ruins of Tchepone for a symbolic three-day occupation. That accomplished, Thieu, Vien, and Lam on 9 March agreed to begin pulling out of Laos within the next ten days. They told Abrams that their forces, after rest and refitting in South Vietnam, would attack into the A Shau Valley and Base Area 611. Informed of this decision, Abrams urged General Vien to hold on in Laos for at least another month and again suggested reinforcing with the South Vietnamese 2d Division. Vien declared that the Vietnamese would do so only if Abrams would send American brigades into Laos, to which Abrams could only respond that "under no circumstances would U.S. ground forces be inserted in Laos."[39]

The South Vietnamese withdrawal began with a pullout from Tchepone on 11 March and then rapidly accelerated. Rather than coming out to the southeastward through Base Area 611, as contemplated in the original plan, the South Vietnamese Army fell back along the axis of Highway 9. Their withdrawal was well planned in General Sutherland's estimation but poorly executed due in no small part to General Lam's deteriorating relationship with the airborne and marine division commanders. Under North Vietnamese attack on both their northern and southern flanks, the South Vietnamese units managed to extricate themselves from the battle, but at a high cost in men and equipment. The armored brigade, particularly hard hit, lost more than half its tanks and armored personnel carriers during its retreat along the highway. By 25 March, all the South Vietnamese troops had left

---

[38] Msgs, Abrams MAC 01554 to Sutherland, 13 Feb 71; Sutherland DNG 0443 to Abrams, 14 Feb 71; Abrams MAC 02372 to Sutherland info Moorer et al., 6 Mar 71; Sutherland QTR 0251 to Abrams, 6 Mar 71; Lt Gen Donn J. Robertson, USMC, QTR 0287 to Abrams, 8 Mar 71. All in Abrams Papers, CMH. Msg, Abrams SPECAT to Moorer and McCain, 16 Feb 71, box 084, NSC files, Nixon Papers, NARA.

[39] Msgs, Robertson QTR 0282 to Abrams, 8 Mar 71; Abrams MAC 02455 to Sutherland, 9 Mar 71. Both in Abrams Papers, CMH. Quotation is from the latter message. Secretary Laird claimed that Thieu had told him in January that the operation would only last five to eight weeks and that Thieu was simply following his own original timetable. See Odeen, MFR, Odeen, 25 Mar 71, sub: Vietnamization Meeting with Secretary Laird, folder 77, Thayer Papers, CMH.

Laos, ending LAM SON 719. The follow-up operations of which Thieu and Vien had spoken did not materialize.[40]

As these events unfolded, the White House bombarded General Abrams with increasingly urgent requests for assessments of how LAM SON 719 was going. Abrams and Ambassador Bunker responded with daily messages, and Abrams conferred frequently by telephone with Admiral Moorer. Throughout their reporting, the Ambassador and the MACV commander maintained an optimistic tone. They took the position that, while unexpected developments had forced changes in movements and time schedules, LAM SON 719 was achieving its purpose of blocking the Ho Chi Minh Trail and destroying enemy forces and supplies. Typically, Abrams admitted on 16 February that the operation was "proceeding to the west more slowly than planned" because of heavy antiaircraft fire, poor flying weather, difficulty resupplying the base at Khe Sanh, and the fact that the enemy "has reinforced faster and is stronger north of Route 9 than anticipated." Nevertheless, he promised that the South Vietnamese would reach and block the main supply routes west of Tchepone and expressed confidence that "the task that was initially laid out will be done." Abrams gave similar reassurances to Admiral Moorer on 4 March and also declared that General Lam was "in good shape—he is tough, determined, careful and his spirits are good." Ambassador Bunker, for his part, in mid-March was still "enthusiastic and confident" about the course of the cross-border operations in both Laos and Cambodia.[41]

Nixon and Kissinger were not reassured. They had been led to expect that the South Vietnamese would move rapidly to Tchepone and remain in Laos through most of the dry season. When the operation deviated from those expectations, and when the press, with what the administration considered almost treasonable relish, began portraying LAM SON 719 as an outright South Vietnamese defeat, Nixon's and Kissinger's consternation and anger mounted daily. The South Vietnamese failure to reach Tchepone early and stay there in force was especially galling, since intelligence reports indicated that the enemy had shifted his main supply effort to routes west of that town and that materiel was continuing to flow southward even as the fighting raged. Thieu's decision to cut the operation short also disappointed Nixon and Kissinger, who vainly urged Bunker and Abrams to secure its rever-

---

[40] The operations are summarized in Hinh, *Lam Son 719*, ch. 5; and in Andrade, "Combat Operations, 1968–1973," ch. 12, pp. 1–30. Sutherland's evaluation is in Msg, Sutherland QTR 0521 to Abrams, 25 Mar 71, Abrams Papers, CMH.

[41] Abrams quotations are from Msg, Abrams SPECAT to Moorer and McCain, 16 Feb 71, and Memo, Kissinger for the President, 4 Mar 71, sub: Situation Report from General Abrams. Both in box 084, NSC files, Nixon Papers, NARA. Bunker is quoted in Msg, Haig to Kissinger, 16 Mar 71, box 1013, NSC files, Nixon Papers, NARA. Msg, Moorer SPECAT to McCain and Abrams, 13 Feb 71, box 080, NSC files, Nixon Papers, NARA, is an example of administration demands for information and assessments.

sal. "We never would have approved the plan," Kissinger complained, "if we thought they were only going to stay for a short time."[42]

Although Abrams and Bunker sent regular assessments, and Kissinger was briefed daily by an officer from the Joint Staff, the president and his national security adviser became convinced that they were receiving late, incomplete, inaccurate information on what was happening in LAM SON 719. Administration statements to the press based on this information repeatedly were contradicted by events, increasing the skepticism of the news media. Seeking more reliable data, Kissinger sent General Haig to Vietnam in mid-March to evaluate the operation. Haig reported that MACV had "badly underestimated" the enemy's ability and willingness to reinforce and fight in the LAM SON 719 area, but he also stated that the South Vietnamese had accomplished as much as could be expected and that the operation should be closed out as soon as possible.[43]

For the allies, LAM SON 719 was costly in men and materiel. Out of about 17,000 South Vietnamese troops committed, more than 1,700 were killed, over 6,600 wounded, and about 680 missing or captured. Materiel losses included 96 artillery pieces, 54 tanks, 87 combat vehicles, and quantities of small arms, radios, trucks, and other equipment, much of it abandoned during the withdrawal. Of the major South Vietnamese units engaged, U.S. advisers rated the armored brigade ineffective for combat after the incursion. They considered the Ranger group and airborne division marginally effective, while the 1st Division and the marine division came out of Laos still in condition to fight. American casualties in the campaign amounted to 215 killed, 1,100 wounded, and 38 missing. The Army reported 82 helicopters destroyed in Laos and more than 600 damaged and recovered, but these statistics obscured the fact that at several points during LAM SON 719 the number of flyable helicopters was barely adequate to support South Vietnamese operations. The U.S. Air Force lost seven tactical aircraft.[44]

---

[42] Kissinger, *White House Years*, pp. 1003–08, recounts the growing concern in the White House. The quotation is from Memo, [sub:] Briefing of Dr Kissinger by Lt Col Martin on 11 Mar 71, box 433, NSC files, Nixon Papers, NARA. Memo, Holdridge for Kissinger, 16 Feb 71, sub: North Vietnamese Effort to Shift Logistical Effort Westward in Lao Panhandle, box 153; Msgs, Kissinger to Bunker via CAS Backchannel, 9 Mar 71, and Kissinger WHS 1018 to Haig, 17 Mar 71, box 084. All in NSC files, Nixon Papers, NARA. The latter two messages reflect the president's desire that the South Vietnamese remain in Laos as long as possible.

[43] Memo, Howe for Kissinger, 24 Mar 71, sub: White House View of Laotian Planning (February 8–March 20), box 1077, NSC files, Nixon Papers, NARA, concludes that the president did not receive timely information on the many changes in the operation. See also Stephen E. Ambrose, ed., *The Haldeman Diaries: Inside the Nixon White House* (New York: Putnam, 1994), pp. 250, 256. Quotation is from Memo, Haig for Kissinger, 21 Mar 71, sub: LAM SON 719, box 085, NSC files, Nixon Papers, NARA. Haig endorsed an early closeout in the latter memo and expressed the same view to the II Field Force commander. See Msg, Davison HOA 0552 to Abrams, 19 Mar 71, Abrams Papers, CMH.

[44] Allied losses are summarized in Hinh, *Lam Son 719*, pp. 127–36. Adviser assessments are recounted in Msg, Weyand SPECAT to McCain, 13 Apr 71, sub: LAM SON 719 Final Report and Assessment, box 080, NSC files, Nixon Papers, NARA.

Over against these costs, Generals Abrams, Weyand, and Sutherland, as well as Ambassador Bunker and Admiral McCain, counted many gains. The North Vietnamese, according to allied estimates, had lost at least 13,000 dead, most of them from first-line combat units or essential logistical organizations, as well as 88 tanks, 2,000 other vehicles, possibly half their antiaircraft guns, thousands of individual and crew-served weapons, and hundreds of tons of ammunition, rice, and petroleum products. Of thirty-three enemy infantry battalions engaged, the American commanders claimed that at least sixteen had been rendered ineffective for combat. Although they acknowledged failure to completely block the Ho Chi Minh Trail, the commanders insisted that they had drastically reduced the flow of North Vietnamese supplies through the operation area, if only by forcing the enemy to consume them in the fighting. Thereby, they had ensured lean logistical times for North Vietnamese and Viet Cong units in Cambodia and lower South Vietnam.[45]

Even more important in the view of Abrams, Weyand, and Sutherland, LAM SON 719 had forestalled any major enemy offensive in Military Region 1 during the rest of 1971. It had forced the North Vietnamese to remove at least one division from South Vietnam and caused them to use up the corps-size force that had threatened to invade Military Region 1. As Weyand put it, "In 1971, RVNAF units fought in Laos against elements of the same enemy divisions that allied forces drove out of Hue and Da Nang during Tet [1968]." As to Vietnamization, the commanders acknowledged South Vietnamese deficiencies in command control, fire-support coordination, and communications security, as well as the disappointing combat performance of the armored brigade. Nevertheless, they concluded that the South Vietnamese, fighting without American advisers on the ground, had acquitted themselves creditably, both in combat and in logistical support, in the largest, most complex, and most heavily opposed operation they had yet attempted. In MACV's view then, LAM SON 719, while not a complete success, had achieved its minimum objectives and had been as well an encouraging demonstration of the South Vietnamese progress toward the ability to stand on its own.[46]

Defense Secretary Laird, who early had endorsed LAM SON 719, accepted the military view of its results, although with some reserva-

[45] Enemy losses are tabulated in Hinh, *Lam Son 719*, pp. 128, 131–32; and Msg, Weyand SPECAT to McCain, 13 Apr 71, sub: LAM SON 719 Final Report and Assessment, box 080, NSC files, Nixon Papers, NARA. Abrams estimates enemy battalion losses in Msg to McCain and Moorer, 22 Mar 71, attached to Memo, Kissinger for the President, 22 Mar 71, sub: Assessment by General Abrams, box 978, NSC files, Nixon Papers, NARA.

[46] Quotation is from Msg, Weyand SPECAT to McCain, 13 Apr 71, sub: LAM SON 719 Final Report and Assessment, box 080; Memo, Kissinger for the President, 22 Mar 71, sub: Assessment by General Abrams, box 978. Both in NSC files, Nixon Papers, NARA. Msgs, Sutherland QTR 0443 to Abrams, 21 Mar 71, and Sutherland QTR 0446 to Abrams, 21 Mar 71. Both in Abrams Papers, CMH. Sutherland in retrospect was less expansive; see Sutherland Interv, n.d., pp. 32–34.

tions. Unlike Nixon and Kissinger, Laird was not disappointed by the reduced duration of the operation. He claimed that when he conferred with President Thieu during his January visit to Saigon, Thieu had predicted that the incursion would last no more than five to eight weeks; hence, LAM SON 719 in fact had ended about on schedule. Laird believed that LAM SON 719 would "prove to be a success, after a period of several months" because the North Vietnamese "had taken heavy casualties and their logistics flow had been hampered." Nevertheless, "it may be some time before the impact will be clear." In the meantime, Laird was concerned that the adverse media coverage would create a "bad image" of the South Vietnamese Army among the American people. Later, he expressed annoyance at the apparent casualness of the South Vietnamese in abandoning expensive equipment that the United States had to replace out of dwindling resources, characterizing that aspect of the operation as a "fiasco."[47]

Publicly, the Nixon administration echoed the Military Assistance Command's assertions that LAM SON 719 had set back the enemy's timetable and inflicted major damage upon his forces and supply network. Administration spokesmen castigated the press and the television networks for their negative reporting of the offensive. Privately, Nixon and Kissinger were less sanguine. They concluded that, while the operation had achieved useful results, it had not been as decisive as it should have been and probably had not been worth the domestic political controversy it had stirred up. They also concluded that they had been "misled by Abrams on the original evaluation of what might be accomplished." According to the president's chief of staff, H. R. Haldeman, on 23 March Nixon and Kissinger decided that "they should pull Abrams out" but then relented after the president "made the point that this is the end of the military operations anyway, so what difference does it make." Abrams thus retained his command, but he no longer enjoyed the president's full confidence.[48]

Admiral Moorer's confidence in Abrams also was shaken. The Joint Chiefs of Staff chairman had faithfully transmitted Abrams' optimistic assessments of the progress of LAM SON 719 to Nixon and Kissinger, and he had borne the brunt of their angry questions when events belied the assessments. As time went on, he concluded that Abrams and the

---

[47] Quotations are from MFR, Odeen, 25 Mar 71, sub: Vietnamization Meeting with Secretary Laird; see also memos of 9 Mar 71 and 15 Jun 71. All in folder 77, Thayer Papers, CMH. Laird, like other administration officials, tried to correct what they considered erroneous news coverage. See Hammond, *Military and the Media, 1968–1973*, p. 485.

[48] The administration's public response is described in Hammond, *Military and the Media, 1968–1973*, pp. 479–92. Examples of internal assessments are Memo, Kissinger for the President, 22 Mar 71, sub: Implications of the Laos Operation for South and North Vietnam and for the U.S., box 549; and MFR of Meeting at Western White House, 1 Apr 71, box 153. All in NSC files, Nixon Papers, NARA. Quotations are from Ambrose, ed., *Haldeman Diaries*, p. 259. Abrams continued to have Laird's full support. See MFR, Odeen, 15 Jun 71, sub: Vietnamization Meeting with Secretary Laird, folder 77, Thayer Papers, CMH.

other Army generals who had planned the operation and sold it to the administration had misled him on critical aspects. In retrospect, Moorer declared that he was "appalled" that his field commanders, who included "two full generals and four [lieutenant generals]," had given him no reason to believe that General Lam might not be able to "hack it." If Abrams and his subordinates had accurately appraised the "limited" competence of Lam and the South Vietnamese in Military Region 1 to conduct such an ambitious offensive, "they never should have let this operation be approved." In the crises to come, Moorer would receive Abrams' reports at less than face value, and he would seek alternative appraisals of the situation from other officers.[49]

The South Vietnamese Army's Cambodian offensive, code-named TOAN THANG 01/71, also produced mixed results. The operation started well on 4 February. Soon after it began, however, General Tri, the capable III Corps commander, was killed in a helicopter crash. His replacement, Lt. Gen. Nguyen Van Minh, while he received positive initial evaluations from Generals Abrams and Davison, failed to keep up the offensive's momentum. His forces, like Lam's, moved slowly and cautiously and gradually surrendered the initiative to the enemy. Nevertheless, the South Vietnamese stayed in the field through May, suffering a gradual decline in unit strengths and morale due to the same deficient replacement system and inability to rotate units that hampered the northern operation. General Abrams found encouraging the fact that, in contrast to LAM SON 719, in TOAN THANG 01/71 the South Vietnamese Air Force provided the bulk of both combat and logistical support for the offensive, requiring supplementation only by U.S. air cavalry troops and B–52s. This relative self-sufficiency was possible because in Cambodia the attack force largely could move and supply itself by road.[50]

The North Vietnamese, although they did not react on the scale that they did in Laos, harassed the South Vietnamese task forces with frequent small ambushes and mortar and rocket bombardments; and they launched occasional battalion and regimental-size counterattacks. Most of these failed with what the South Vietnamese claimed were heavy enemy losses. Late in May, however, in the campaign's most severe action, the North Vietnamese routed a task force of the South Vietnamese 5th Division near Snuol in a battle that rendered that division combat ineffective in the estimation of its American

---

[49] Walter S. Poole, "LAM SON 719: The 'Moment of Truth' " (Draft Paper, Washington, D.C.: Joint History Office, Joint Chiefs of Staff, 2001), pp. 28–29.

[50] The course of the operation is summarized in MACV History, 1971, vol. 2, an. E, pp. 5–11. General Tri's death is reported in Msg, Bunker Saigon 172 to Kissinger, 23 Feb 71, box 412, NSC files, Nixon Papers, NARA. For evaluation of Minh, see Msg, Davison HOA 0347 to Abrams, 24 Feb 71, Abrams Papers, CMH. Also Msgs, Davison HOA 0568 to Abrams, 21 Mar 71; HOA 0648 to Abrams, 1 Apr 71; HOA 0761 to Abrams, 15 Apr 71; HOA 1046 to Abrams, 24 May 71. All in Abrams Papers, CMH. The South Vietnamese Air Force role is discussed in Msg, Abrams to McCain info Moorer, 22 Mar 71, attached to Memo, Kissinger for the President, 22 Mar 71, sub: Assessment by General Abrams, box 978, NSC files, Nixon Papers, NARA.

advisers. When TOAN THANG 01/71 ended early in June, Maj. Gen. Jack J. Wagstaff, Davison's replacement as senior U.S. adviser to III Corps/Military Region 3, declared that it had failed to attain two of its objectives—stopping enemy supply movement across Highway 7 and cleaning out the caches around the Chup Plantation—but had accomplished the third, keeping three Viet Cong divisions out of Military Region 3 during the dry season and inflicting significant casualties upon them.[51]

The 1971 dry season offensives revealed both American and South Vietnamese deficiencies in planning and execution. In LAM SON 719, senior American and South Vietnamese commanders did not anticipate the rapidity and violence of the North Vietnamese response and were caught off balance when the enemy engaged allied forces in a sustained combined arms battle. Although many South Vietnamese units fought hard, the South Vietnamese Army suffered from command failures, performed with uneven effectiveness under attack by armor and artillery, and in some instances fell into panic and confusion during the withdrawal from Tchepone and the battle of Snuol. For the American public, the defining image of LAM SON 719 was that of desperate South Vietnamese soldiers clinging to the skids of evacuation helicopters. South Vietnamese armor and artillery needed strengthening if the South Vietnamese were to engage North Vietnamese heavy divisions without American air support. Still, the offensives could not be considered a definitive test of Saigon's military capacity to stand alone. LAM SON 719 and TOAN THANG 01/71 were predicated upon full-scale U.S. combat and logistical support; no one expected the South Vietnamese Army on its own to conduct cross-border offensives on that scale. The jury thus was still out on the ultimate results of Vietnamization.

General Abrams chose to play down these negatives and ambiguities. Instead, he claimed overall success for the two dry season offensives. Acknowledging that "disappointments and failures" had occurred in both, he nevertheless asserted that the operations had "gone well militarily" and produced "the maximum practical benefits." He noted that the South Vietnamese had planned and executed two simultaneous multidivision offensives, without accompanying American advisers, and "in the main" achieved their goals. This fact, he said, "speaks for the success of the Vietnamization program." Most important, Abrams believed that the operations had forestalled enemy offensives in both South Vietnam and Cambodia and thus helped keep Vietnamization and pacification on schedule. The low level of combat within South Vietnam throughout 1971 appeared to validate his claim.[52]

---

[51] Msgs, Wagstaff HOA 1069 to Abrams, 27 May 71; Wagstaff HOA 1089 to Abrams, 31 May 71; Wagstaff HOA 1093 to Abrams, 31 May 71; Wagstaff HOA 1135 to Abrams, 7 Jun 71. All in Abrams Papers, CMH. Memo, Col Edward F. Astarita for Lt Gen Joseph M. Heiser, Dep CofS Logistics, Dept of the Army, 20 Aug 71, sub: Information on Future Redeployments beyond Dec 71 . . . , in Notebook, Briefing of Future Redeployments beyond Dec 71, MACV files, MHI.

[52] Quotations are from Memo, Kissinger for the President, 22 Mar 71, sub: Assessment by General

Cross-Border Operations Continue

After the dry season offensives, the fighting outside South Vietnam's borders settled back into its established patterns. The North Vietnamese and their allies continued to wage war in Laos and Cambodia in order to control vital base areas and lines of communication and gain political power. Maintaining the threat of a large-scale offensive in northern Military Region 1, the North Vietnamese moved additional SAM batteries into their southernmost provinces and built up forces and supplies just above the Demilitarized Zone and in Laos. In response, MACV kept up its air campaigns over Laos and North Vietnam and supported South Vietnamese and Khmer ground forces fighting in Cambodia.[53]

In southern Laos, MACV and the Seventh Air Force completed COMMANDO HUNT V on 30 April 1971 and followed it with COMMANDO HUNTS VI and VII. The former covered the summer rainy season in Laos and the latter, which began in November, was aimed at disrupting the enemy's 1971–72 dry season supply effort. As part of the Vietnamization program, the Vietnamese Air Force began flying interdiction missions in the far southern panhandle. In conjunction with the air campaigns, the Studies and Observations Group continued PRAIRIE FIRE operations. These incursions received a new code-name, PHU DUNG, during the year to denote the fact that, after LAM SON 719, at the direction of the Joint Chiefs of Staff, no Americans accompanied the reconnaissance teams and reaction forces into Laos. However, MACV continued to furnish fixed-wing and helicopter air support to the teams.[54]

To the north, the ebb and flow of battle continued around the Plain of Jars. The U.S. Embassy in Vientiane regularly requested tactical air and B–52 support, and MACV furnished it. During July and August alone, Vientiane asked for nineteen B–52 strikes in aid of Vang Pao's army. MACV concurred in fourteen of the requests but turned down the other five because it did not consider the targets lucrative enough to warrant diverting aircraft from more important missions. Admiral McCain and the Joint Chiefs seconded the MACV recommendations, and Secretary Laird regularly approved them. As 1971 came to an end, the North Vietnamese and Pathet Lao again were pushing the Meo back; and Ambassador Godley was calling for bombers to stop them.[55]

Abrams, box 978, NSC files, Nixon Papers, NARA.

[53] Enemy strategy is assessed in MACV J–3–06 Command Briefing, 28 Nov 71, MACV files, MHI.

[54] COMMANDO HUNT operations are summarized in MACV History, 1971, vol. 1, ch. 6, pp. 31–33. The change from PRAIRIE FIRE to PHU DUNG is described in MACV History, 1971–72, an. B, pp. 23–26. In the same period, the SALEM HOUSE program, which had used only indigenous personnel on the ground since 1 July 1970, was renamed THOT NOT; ibid., pp. 18–22. South Vietnamese Air Force interdiction operations are discussed in Msgs, Godley Vientiane 09044 to Sec State, 13 Dec 71; and Rogers State 226081 to Embassy Vientiane, 16 Dec 71. Both in box 549, NSC files, Nixon Papers, NARA.

[55] MACV History, 1971, vol. 1, ch. 6, pp. 27–28. Msgs, Deputy Chief of Mission Stearns LAO 413 to Abrams info McCain et al., 16 May 71; Godley LAO 0989 to Abrams info Moorer et al., 18 Dec 71; Godley LAO 0998 to Abrams, 19 Dec 71; Godley LAO 1004 to Abrams info Moorer

In Cambodia, the South Vietnamese continued their cross-border operations, although on a reduced scale, throughout the summer and fall. Their troops helped Khmer forces keep open their Mekong River supply line to Phnom Penh, sought to prevent the North Vietnamese from reestablishing their border bases, and attempted to tie down enemy divisions that threatened Military Region 3. MACV supported its South Vietnamese and Cambodian allies with tactical airpower and B–52s, which ranged throughout the Khmer Republic; and it provided helicopter assistance to the South Vietnamese when necessary to supplement the resources of the South Vietnamese Air Force.[56]

In April, General Abrams, taking advantage of the experience of LAM SON 719, set up an ad hoc group of MACV staff officers and representatives of XXIV Corps and the field forces to study ways to improve American air and artillery support for South Vietnamese units engaged in cross-border operations or other "high intensity contacts" requiring "timely, concentrated assistance." On the basis of this study, each U.S. corps area command organized a joint support group patterned on the one XXIV Corps had established during the Tchepone offensive. Working closely with the South Vietnamese corps and division staffs, these groups helped the South Vietnamese use U.S. tactical aircraft, B–52s, helicopter gunships, and artillery fire to the best advantage in engagements. In the view of the corps senior advisers, they both ensured more rapid American response to South Vietnamese fire requests and brought about improvements in South Vietnamese management of their own and American supporting arms. During heavy fighting along Highway 7 in Cambodia in September and October, one of these coordination groups helped the South Vietnamese win a substantial victory that at least partially avenged the South Vietnamese Army's earlier rout at Snuol.[57]

Throughout 1971, General Abrams and Admiral McCain, supported by the Joint Chiefs, pressed their campaign for authority to make preemptive attacks on the SAM batteries, airfields, and fighter direction centers of the enemy's expanding air defense complex in southern North Vietnam. They insisted that the increasing number of missile firings at American aircraft over Laos, as well as the aggressiveness of the

et al., 21 Dec 71; Lavelle to Abrams, 2 Jan 72. All in Abrams Papers, CMH. Memo, Welander for Haig, 2 Sep 71, sub: ARC LIGHT Support of Vang Pao's Operations, box 549, NSC files, Nixon Papers, NARA.

[56] Msgs, Wagstaff HOA 1196 to Abrams, 19 Jun 71; Wagstaff HOA 1209 to Abrams, 21 Jun 71; Wagstaff HOA 1819 to Abrams, 13 Sep 71; Abrams MAC 10910 to John P. Vann, 18 Nov 71; Abrams MAC 10924 to Swank, 18 Nov 71. All in Abrams Papers, CMH. Air operations are summarized in MACV History, 1971, vol. 1, ch. 6, pp. 23–27.

[57] Memo, Dolvin for Deputy Asst CofS J–3 MACV, 22 Apr 71, sub: LOI to Chairman, Support Coordination Project Group, in folder, same sub, MACV files, MHI; Msg, Abrams MAC 03942 to Component and Field Force Cdrs, 18 Apr 71; Msg, McCown CTO 0433 to Abrams, 21 Apr 71; Wagstaff HOA 1209 to Abrams, 21 Jun 71; Dolvin DNG 1904 to Abrams, 6 Jul 71. All in Abrams Papers, CMH. The autumn battles are described in MACV History, 1971, vol. 2, an. E, p. 11.

enemy's MiG jet fighters, which twice tried unsuccessfully to intercept B–52s, must be countered by a systematic air offensive. Just as consistently, Secretary Laird rejected their requests. He claimed that existing retaliatory authorities were sufficient to protect American aircraft and that escalation would have undesirable political consequences. Laird did not object, however, when Abrams in August construed "protective reaction" as permitting attacks on any portion of a missile defense complex that fired on American planes rather than simply the offending battery.[58]

After the end of LAM SON 719, the North Vietnamese assembled troops, artillery, and supplies above the Demilitarized Zone and in Laos. They also began moving men and materiel through the Demilitarized Zone for attacks on South Vietnamese positions in northern Military Region 1. Under the established rules of engagement, General Abrams could respond to this threat only with squad-size patrols, artillery fire, and air strikes in the southern half of the zone—a response he considered inadequate. Accordingly, during the summer, Abrams, McCain, and the Joint Chiefs sought permission for MACV to conduct tactical air and B–52 strikes against air defense and logistical targets throughout the Demilitarized Zone and in the southernmost part of North Vietnam, either on a regular basis or in a more limited three- to ten-day campaign. Laird responded as he had on the protective reaction issue. He declared that MACV's existing authorities were adequate to safeguard American and South Vietnamese forces and that the enemy threat had not increased sufficiently to justify incurring the political costs of further escalation. Laird also reminded his field commanders that "the key to the military situation in the Republic of Vietnam" was "the complex of will, desire, and determination of the South Vietnamese people," not expanded air operations in North Vietnam.[59]

While the administration thus withheld any permanent enlargement of COMUSMACV's and CINCPAC's authority to strike the north, it continued the pattern of occasional preplanned two- to four-day raids against North Vietnamese air defenses and supply facilities under the "protective reaction" rubric. Since the attacks were concentrated in southern North Vietnam, MACV and Seventh Air Force planned and directed them. The first two of these operations—LOUISVILLE SLUGGER on 20, 21, and 28 February, and FRACTURE CROSS ALPHA on 21 and 22

---

[58] Thompson, "Rolling Thunder to Linebacker," ch. 8, pp. 5–6, 12. Memo, Kissinger for the President, 27 Feb 71, sub: Strikes in North Vietnam, box 153, NSC files, Nixon Papers, NARA. Historical Division, "Joint Chiefs of Staff and the War in Vietnam, 1971–1973," pt. 1, pp. 254–71.

[59] Memos, Moorer CM–995–71 for the Sec Def, 23 Jun 71, sub: Actions which Could Reduce the Risks to MRs 1 and 2 . . . ; Moorer CM 1012–71 for the Sec Def, 27 Jun 71, sub: DMZ Authorities; Laird for the CJCS, 29 Jun 71, sub: Actions which Would Reduce the Risks to MRs 1 and 2 . . . (quotation is from this memo); Laird for the CJCS, 1 Jul 71, sub: DMZ Authorities; Moorer CM 1060–71 for the Sec Def, 19 Jul 71, sub: Air Campaign, DMZ North; Laird for the CJCS, 24 Jul 71, sub: Bombing Campaign, DMZ North; and Haig for Kissinger, 28 Jul 71, sub: Air Campaign against North Vietnam. All in box 155, NSC files, Nixon Papers, NARA.

March—actually were enlarged protective reaction strikes at SAM batteries and supporting facilities, timed to coincide with LAM SON 719.
After the summer rainy season in Laos, which reduced both U.S. air
activity and enemy harassment, Nixon sent the bombers north against
a wider range of targets. In PRIZE BULL, on 21 September, the Seventh Air
Force concentrated entirely on three petroleum storage areas. Finally,
in PROUD DEEP ALPHA, the largest raid on North Vietnam since 1968, Air
Force and Navy planes flew more than 1,000 sorties between 26 and 30
December, against airfields, oil tank farms, barracks, and transportation
networks, some no more than 120 kilometers from Hanoi. To minimize
domestic protest, Nixon timed this raid to take place after Congress
adjourned and during the university Christmas vacation season, when
the campuses would be deserted.[60]

From the viewpoint of the Military Assistance Command, Vietnam,
three years of cross-border operations kept the enemy at bay and won
time in South Vietnam for Vietnamization and pacification to run their
course. The change of government in Cambodia, and South Vietnamese
operations there, cut an important North Vietnamese supply line and
diverted enemy divisions that otherwise would have threatened Saigon
and the Mekong Delta. In Laos, air and ground interdiction reduced
the flow of men and supplies down the Ho Chi Minh Trail and possibly
forestalled a major North Vietnamese offensive in Military Region 1. In
northern Laos, MACV's airpower was instrumental in keeping the non-
Communist forces in being. Although General Abrams did not obtain
the attack authority he wanted in the Demilitarized Zone and southern
North Vietnam, the Nixon administration was cautiously escalating
the northern air war along the lines Abrams advocated.

As 1971 came to an end, the overall effectiveness of the cross-border
campaigns in weakening the enemy seemed likely soon to be put to the
test. The heavy December bombing was only one indication that events
in Southeast Asia might be approaching a climax. With the North
Vietnamese preparing for a new offensive, with the Nixon administration engaged in complex diplomatic maneuvers with the Russians and
Chinese as well as secret talks with Hanoi's representatives at Paris,
with a U.S. presidential election in the offing, and with the American
military withdrawal from South Vietnam nearing completion, the year
1972 held the likelihood of decisive developments on all of the war's
multiple military and political fronts.

[60] Strikes are summarized in MACV History, 1971, vol. 1, ch. 6, pp. 33–34, and Thompson,
"Rolling Thunder to Linebacker," ch. 8, pp. 7–11. Administration political considerations are illustrated in Memos, Kissinger for the President, 10 Dec 71, sub: Your Meeting with Deputy Secretary
of Defense Packard and Chairman of the Joint Chiefs of Staff . . . ; and Kissinger for the President,
n.d., sub: Strikes against North Vietnam. Both in box 123, NSC files, Nixon Papers, NARA. Msg,
Abrams MAC 09104 to McCain, 21 Sep 71, Abrams Papers, CMH, emphasizes Abrams' command
role in the raids.

11

The Easter Offensive

During 1972, the Vietnam War reached a military and diplomatic climax. The North Vietnamese launched a massive main force offensive against South Vietnam. In response, President Nixon threw American air and naval power into the battle to defend his ally even as he continued U.S. troop withdrawals. Seizing the opportunity to force a diplomatic end game, Nixon renewed the bombing of North Vietnam with unprecedented intensity and mined North Vietnamese harbors. Simultaneously, he pursued the secret Paris negotiations and engaged in new initiatives with the Soviet Union and the People's Republic of China. These events and decisions confronted the Military Assistance Command, Vietnam, with conflicting demands and challenges. The command used its remaining American military assets to influence the fighting in South Vietnam and vied for control of the renewed air campaign in the north. At the same time, it reorganized itself and continued redeploying American troops. As the enemy offensive played itself out, MACV, under a new commander, looked forward to the real possibility of a conclusion of the long war.

A War in the Balance

As 1972 began, the outcome of President Nixon's policies, and indeed of the entire American effort in South Vietnam, seemed to be hanging in a delicate balance. In a typical official assessment, Ambassador Bunker told Nixon on 26 January: "The consequences of our endeavors for many years in Vietnam will be on trial this year and next." Washington and Saigon, Bunker said, would be "navigating a narrow and dangerous strait between the enemy's still-formidable capabilities and the political pressures in the United States." The administration's major task would be "to stay the course and continue providing the essential support that will enable the Vietnamese to survive the coming tests."[1]

---

[1] Msg, Bunker Saigon 1175 to the President, 26 Jan 72, box 158, NSC files, Nixon Papers, NARA.

In South Vietnam, the allies' position appeared to be strong and stable, despite the less-than-triumphant outcome of LAM SON 719. The level of military activity had remained low throughout 1971. The enemy's main forces, mostly pushed back into their Cambodian and Laotian bases, were struggling to repair the logistical damage caused by the loss of the Sihanoukville route and the South Vietnamese attack on Tchepone. MACV and the mission reported steady South Vietnamese progress in pacification, economic stabilization, and political development. American disengagement from the conflict had entered its final stage. MACV's troop strength was down to 139,000 men at the beginning of 1972, with additional withdrawals already planned, and American ground combat operations had ceased. South Vietnam's forces had replaced the Americans without any noticeable diminution in security. Redeployments seemed to be alleviating the Military Assistance Command's internal difficulties. In February, General Abrams told the press that U.S. troop morale in South Vietnam had improved and that hard drug use, racial violence, and assaults on officers and noncommissioned officers all were declining in frequency.[2]

The balance's delicacy lay in the political and diplomatic situation outside South Vietnam. Nixon's troop withdrawals, by diminishing the human and material costs of the war, had won him time and political maneuvering room in the United States; but the steady progress of the withdrawals diminished their value as a bargaining counter with Hanoi. Although the American antiwar movement had lost some of its intensity as U.S. casualties diminished and troops came home, the cause remained alive on campuses and in the streets. In Congress, the administration had to beat back, by ever narrowing margins, repeated attempts to legislate firm deadlines for American disengagement from South Vietnam and an end to U.S. military activity in Southeast Asia. Despite military setbacks, the North Vietnamese remained inflexible in Paris and determined to outlast the United States on the battlefield.

During 1971, for both diplomatic and domestic political reasons, the administration offered additional concessions to Hanoi. By the end of the year, it had abandoned its long-standing demand that North Vietnamese troops withdraw from the South as a condition for an armistice. Instead, the administration expressed willingness to set a firm date for removal of all remaining American forces in return for North Vietnam's agreement not to reinforce its units already in the South. The administration also proposed an in-place cease-fire, to be followed by all-party elections under international supervision; and it extracted from Thieu a promise that he would resign the presidency

---

[2] Typical assessments are MACV J–3–06 Command Briefing, 28 Nov 71, in folder, same title, MACV Collection, MHI; Msg, Bunker Saigon 1175 to the President, 26 Jan 72, and Memo, Odeen for Kissinger, 25 Feb 72, sub: Vietnam Control Indicators for 1971, box 158, NSC files, Nixon Papers, NARA. Abrams' comments on morale and discipline are in *New York Times*, 26 Feb 72, p. 1, Newspaper Clippings, Biography, and Miscellaneous box, Abrams Papers, MHI.

of South Vietnam a month before the elections. Nixon and Kissinger viewed these terms as the maximum that they could offer to North Vietnam short of outright abandonment of their Saigon ally. Seeking to change the context of the dialogue with Hanoi as well as to create a new international constellation of forces, Nixon pursued his diplomatic courtship of the People's Republic of China, which would culminate in February 1972 in the president's visit to Beijing; and he and Kissinger prepared for a possible summit meeting in Moscow. With the U.S. presidential election fast approaching, Nixon and Kissinger sought some means of forcing a diplomatic settlement before troop withdrawals or congressional action deprived them of all their bargaining power.[3]

The North Vietnamese also confronted strategic problems. Their return to protracted small-unit warfare had neither produced significant military gains nor materially hindered the advance of pacification. The insurgency in South Vietnam was declining in strength, and the upheaval in Cambodia had compounded the Communists' logistical and operational difficulties throughout the theater of war. American troop withdrawals were depriving Hanoi of a major source of political and diplomatic leverage against the United States as well as strengthening the reelection prospects of President Nixon, North Vietnam's most stubborn adversary. The intensifying hostility between the Soviet Union and China, and China's movement toward a new relationship with the United States, threatened North Vietnam's major foreign sources of military and diplomatic support. Clearly, the North Vietnamese needed to do something to reverse the unfavorable trends and if possible force a settlement before reelection strengthened Nixon's domestic position. Aware of their own and the enemy's difficulties, American officials anticipated that the North Vietnamese would attempt a major military offensive sometime in 1972, to discredit Vietnamization and revive opposition to the war in the United States. Exemplifying a growing official consensus, Ambassador Bunker told Defense Secretary Laird in June 1971 that 1972 would be a "very critical year," featuring a powerful North Vietnamese military effort "in order to influence the U.S. election." For both sides, the established policies seemed to be at the point of diminishing returns. The time for new and risky initiatives was at hand.[4]

Bracing for the Blow

American expectations of a large-scale North Vietnamese attack in 1972 were on the mark. During May and June 1971, the collective

---

[3] The administration's domestic problems and the development of negotiations are summarized in Kissinger, *White House Years*, pp. 1016–46, 1488–90.

[4] Paper [1971], "Assessment of Military Situation in Indochina," box 1004; CIA Intelligence Memorandum, 26 Apr 71, box 154; NSC files, Nixon Papers, NARA. Bunker quotation is from Memo, Phil Odeen, 15 Jun 71, sub: Vietnamization Meeting with Secretary Laird, folder 77, Thayer Papers, CMH.

North Vietnamese artillery

leadership in Hanoi decided to launch a general military offensive early the following year to "win a decisive victory . . . and force the U.S. imperialists to end the war by negotiating from a position of defeat." Reminiscent of 1968, party directives called for a combination of main force attacks, intensified guerrilla activity, and urban uprisings. However, in this assault, the North Vietnamese in fact would rely primarily on conventional regular divisions using concentrated armor and large amounts of heavy artillery. Their objectives were to destroy as much of South Vietnam's army as possible, seize territory, and support guerrillas and local forces in rolling back pacification. The enemy anticipated that President Nixon, preoccupied with his reelection campaign, would be unable to make a decisive military response. With his South Vietnamese allies defeated and Vietnamization discredited, Nixon would be compelled to negotiate a settlement on North Vietnam's terms. Late in 1971, after preliminary offensives in the Plain of Jars and the Laotian panhandle to secure their lines of communication, the North Vietnamese began moving men, tanks, guns, and supplies into position for strikes into Military Regions 1, 2, and 3. They committed ten of their thirteen army divisions to this all-out military gamble. The enemy reinforced his air defenses in southern North Vietnam and Laos with surface-to-air missile and antiaircraft gun batteries and shifted his MiG jet fighters toward the south. This growing air defense complex threatened American aircraft flying missions over Laos, and its reach extended over the northern part of Military Region 1.[5]

---

[5] War Experiences Recapitulation Committee, *Resistance War*, pp. 138–44; quotation is from

The Military Assistance Command J–2 and other U.S. intelligence agencies quickly picked up evidence of these preparations. They noted as well that official North Vietnamese publications and captured documents were calling for a renewed general offensive–general uprising in South Vietnam and asserting the necessity for decisive main force warfare. By late January 1972, the question for American officials in Saigon, Honolulu, and Washington was not whether an enemy offensive would occur but when, where, and on how large a scale. In the light of the accumulating indications, General Abrams expected the coming offensive to "evolve into the maximum military effort the North is capable of making in the next few months."[6]

As the offensive threat developed, President Nixon responded along a number of lines. While continuing troop redeployments from South Vietnam, he began building up American air and naval forces in Southeast Asia. He also intensified his diplomatic effort to separate North Vietnam from its Chinese and Soviet backers and establish a record of U.S. reasonableness and peaceable intentions in contrast to Hanoi's military preparations. Seeking to avoid a repetition of the public relations disaster of 1968, the president and his associates made sure that the news media were fully briefed on the expected enemy offensive. As one of the principal executors of American policy, General Abrams prepared to defend South Vietnam against the coming onslaught while simultaneously drawing down and reorganizing his own command.[7]

The Military Assistance Command could do little to strengthen South Vietnam's forces beyond continuing the improvement and modernization programs already under way. In the wake of the Laotian incursion and after a late-1971 force structure review, MACV and the Joint General Staff made some incremental additions to Saigon's military establishment. These included a new 3d Division and an armor battalion with M48 tanks for northern Military Region 1, a substantial increase in fixed-wing gunships, and the establishment of Ranger groups and battalions. However, General Abrams continued to turn down South Vietnamese requests for large numbers of new tank and artillery units. On the basis of recommendations from his corps area advisers, Abrams urged President Thieu to replace weak commanders, notably those of the two infantry divisions in Military Region 2. Abrams and his regional commanders encouraged and assisted South

p. 138. Dale Andrade, *Trial by Fire: The 1972 Easter Offensive, America's Last Vietnam Battle* (New York: Hippocrene Books, 1995), pp. 34–42; Msg Abrams SPECAT to Moorer and McCain, 8 Mar 72, Abrams Microfilm, MHI; MACV History, 1971, vol. 1, ch. 3, pp. 2–3.

[6] Quotation is from Msg, Abrams SPECAT to McCain info Moorer, 17 Jan 72, Abrams Microfilm, MHI. Msgs, Abrams MAC 0948 to Moorer and McCain, 1 Feb 72; Abrams MAC 1609 to Moorer, McCain, et al., 22 Feb 72; Abrams Papers, CMH; CIA Information Report, 24 Jan 72; Memo, Laird for the Assistant to the President for National Security Affairs, 26 Jan 72, sub: The Current Situation in SVN. All in box 158, NSC files, Nixon Papers, NARA.

[7] Kissinger, *White House Years*, pp. 1099–1108; Hammond, *Military and the Media, 1968–1973*, pp. 534–37.

Vietnamese efforts to shift units to the most threatened areas and supported preemptive attacks on enemy forces and bases. Abrams directed his field advisers to prepare their South Vietnamese units to undergo heavy artillery bombardment, which most of the South Vietnamese Army outside northern Military Region 1 had not previously faced; and he directed the advisers to report promptly and accurately to MACV on the course of the battle when it began. He rearranged withdrawal schedules to retain U.S. combat support units, such as helicopter companies and a 175-mm. gun battalion, to fill in for South Vietnamese units programmed but not yet operational. Through White House and State Department channels, Abrams tried, with only limited success, to persuade the South Koreans to commit elements of their two divisions to reinforce the Central Highlands if that became necessary.[8]

To disrupt enemy offensive preparations, Abrams relied primarily on his American airpower. During January and February, the administration augmented MACV's air force with eighteen F–4 fighter-bombers stationed at Da Nang and in Thailand, dispatched eight additional B–52s to Thailand and twenty-nine to Guam, increased the number of carriers on station off Vietnam from three to four, and lifted all budget-based limits on aircraft sorties. Abrams used these forces in a systematic, continuous effort to disrupt North Vietnamese supply lines and destroy troop and artillery concentrations. He directed his fighter-bombers mainly against the Ho Chi Minh Trail and his B–52s against the enemy forces gathering along the Demilitarized Zone and the borders. On occasion, he massed the bulk of his air strength for brief periods against particular enemy concentrations, for example those menacing Kontum and Pleiku in Military Region 2.[9]

With the support of Ambassador Bunker, Admiral McCain, and the Joint Chiefs of Staff, Abrams renewed his campaign for expanded authority to attack targets in the Demilitarized Zone and southern North Vietnam. In late January, he requested and the administration granted permission to plant sensors throughout the Demilitarized Zone, use U.S. fixed- and rotary-wing aircraft to support South Vietnamese operations in Laos and Cambodia, and fire antiradar missiles at fighter ground control facilities everywhere in North Vietnam outside the Hanoi-Haiphong area whenever MiGs were airborne and appeared to

[8] MACV History, 1972–73, vol. 1, an. C, p. 12; Briefing for Gen Clay, 21 Jan 72, sub: United States Redeployment Status, tab D, MAC J–303 Briefing Book no. 4, MACV Collection, MHI. Msgs, Abrams MAC 1082 to John P. Vann, 4 Feb 72; Abrams MAC 1156 to Dolvin et al., 7 Feb 72; Abrams MAC 1261 to Component and Regional Cdrs, 11 Feb 72. All in Abrams Papers, CMH. Msg, Bunker Saigon 0011 to Kissinger, 13 Jan 72, box 414, NSC files, Nixon Papers, NARA.

[9] MACV History, 1972–73, vol. 1, an. B, pp. 2–4. Memos, Laird for the Assistant to the President for National Security Affairs, 7 Feb 72, sub: Daily Report on Southeast Asia Situation, box 158; Laird for the President, 8 Mar 72, sub: Actions Relative to the North Vietnamese Dry Season Offensive; box 159. Both in NSC files, Nixon Papers, NARA. Msgs, Abrams MAC 0925 to Lavelle et al., 31 Jan 72; Dolvin DNG 0272 to Abrams, 1 Feb 72. All in Abrams Papers, CMH. Msg, Cowles MAC 1114 to Vann, 6 Feb 72, box V, Abrams Papers, MHI.

threaten American aircraft. The administration authorized Abrams to conduct tactical air strikes in the upper half of the Demilitarized Zone and bomb artillery and rocket sites north of the zone within range of friendly forces whenever he determined that the North Vietnamese were preparing to attack southward from those areas. It also gave him complete freedom to attack airborne MiGs anywhere over North Vietnam south of the 18th Parallel once the ground battle began.[10]

However, until the offensive started, President Nixon, at the recommendation of both Laird and Kissinger, turned down Abrams' and the Joint Chiefs' requests for general permission to attack enemy air defenses, troops, supply dumps, and lines of communication in southern North Vietnam. In rare agreement, Laird and Kissinger argued that such attacks would amount to a full-scale resumption of the northern bombing campaign. In the absence of an actual attack, such an escalation would stir up political opposition at home and abroad and possibly disrupt Nixon's diplomatic maneuvers with the Chinese and Russians. Hence, the administration withheld this authority, although it directed the military commands to refine and update their contingency plans for bombing North Vietnam. Through informal channels, Laird and Moorer also encouraged MACV and the Seventh Air Force to take maximum advantage of the authority, which remained in effect, to conduct protective reaction strikes against antiaircraft units in North Vietnam that fired on American planes.[11]

The Seventh Air Force commander, General John D. Lavelle, interpreted the protective reaction rules so liberally as to violate them in both letter and spirit. Between November 1971 and early March 1972, Lavelle's forces conducted twenty-eight preplanned raids on air defense and logistical targets in North Vietnam. Lavelle's headquarters falsely reported these strikes through channels as responses to hostile fire. The general himself informed Abrams that the attacks had occurred but not that they were unprovoked. Since the raids took place in areas of heavy enemy antiaircraft activity, Abrams claimed later, he had no reason to doubt that they were genuine cases of protective reaction. These operations were in addition to the occasional raids on the North directed by President Nixon and were minor in scale. All told, they amounted to less than 150 sorties compared to the

[10] Memos, Laird for the Assistant to the President for National Security Affairs, 26 Jan 72, sub: The Current Situation in SVN; Nixon for the Sec Def, 1 Feb 72, sub: Vietnam Authorities; Kissinger for the President, 8 Feb 72, sub: Secretary Laird's Daily Report on Southeast Asia Situation; and Kissinger for the President, 16 Feb 72, sub: Efforts in Southeast Asia. All in box 158, NSC files, Nixon Papers, NARA.

[11] Msg, Abrams SPECAT to Moorer and McCain, 8 Mar 72, Abrams Microfilm, MHI. Memo, Moorer CM–1625–72 for the Sec Def, 9 Mar 72, sub: Urgent Request for Air Authorities; Memo, Laird for the President, 14 Mar 72, sub: Request for Operating Authorities . . . , box 159; Memo, Kissinger for the President, 18 Mar 72, sub: Request for Operating Authorities . . . ; Memo, Nixon for the Sec Def, 18 Mar 72, box 097. Both in NSC files, Nixon Papers, NARA. On expansive interpretations of protective reaction, see Interv, USAF Oral History Program with Gen John W. Vogt, Jr, USAF, 8–9 Aug 78, Office of Air Force History, pp. 156–57 (hereafter cited as Vogt Interv).

General Lavelle

1,000 used in the officially sanctioned PROUD DEEP ALPHA strike of December 1971.[12]

Lavelle's unauthorized attacks came to an end in early March. An Air Force enlisted man at the base at Udorn, Thailand, who was aware of the false reporting, wrote to his U.S. senator about it. This information, along with other indications, prompted the Air Force chief of staff, General John D. Ryan, to send his inspector general to Vietnam to investigate the allegations of unauthorized bombing. Lavelle and his subordinates admitted that they had conducted and concealed the strikes; but Lavelle insisted that higher officials, including General Abrams, tacitly had approved his breaking of the rules. However, when queried by Secretary Laird, Abrams denied knowing that the attacks were unprovoked. Lavelle's freelancing disturbed Laird and Admiral Moorer, who feared that if the raids became public knowledge, popular and congressional outrage would make it politically impossible to escalate air operations against the North when the enemy offensive actually started. On 23 March, after the inspector general reported, Ryan recalled Lavelle to Washington for consultations. Subsequently, at Laird's direction, Ryan relieved Lavelle of command for what were described publicly as health reasons. Early in April, General John W. Vogt, U.S. Air Force, Director of the Joint Staff, replaced Lavelle as Seventh Air Force commander.[13]

Inevitably, the real reasons for Lavelle's dismissal became public in mid-May, after the enemy offensive was well under way. Much controversy ensued. The Senate and House Armed Services Committees investigated at length but could not establish that Lavelle's superiors ordered or knew of the unauthorized operations. The Air Force retired Lavelle for disability and demoted him. From the available evidence,

---

[12] Thompson, "Rolling Thunder to Linebacker," ch. 8, pp. 1–3, 6–7, 10–13, 16–18. Abrams' denials are reported in the *Washington Post*, 14 Sep 72, p. P–8, Miscellaneous/Calendar Backup box; and *Washington Post*, 17 Sep 72, no pp., Newspaper Clippings, Biography, Miscellaneous box. Both in Abrams Papers, MHI.

[13] Thompson, "Rolling Thunder to Linebacker," ch. 8, pp. 18–23; Joint History Office, "The Chairman of the Joint Chiefs of Staff and Crises: Response to the North Vietnamese Offensive" (MS, Washington, D.C.: Joint History Office, Joint Chiefs of Staff, 1996), pp. 8–10 (hereafter cited as Joint History Office, "CJCS and the North Vietnamese Offensive"); Vogt Interv, 8–9 Aug 78, pp. 152–54.

it seems clear that Lavelle, who had a prior record of impulsive actions, ordered the strikes on his own, probably in response to the high-level official hints that he should stretch his authority and out of impatience with rules of engagement that he (and most other commanders) resented as hindering their operations and endangering the lives of their men.[14]

General Vogt

While preparing to resist the North Vietnamese offensive, the Military Assistance Command planned and carried out additional troop withdrawals. As of the end of January, the command had completed its tenth redeployment increment, involving 45,000 men, which cut MACV's authorized strength to 139,000 and its actual strength to about 136,500. This was the first step in implementing OPLAN J208A for reducing the American force in Vietnam to 60,000 men by 1 July 1972. General Abrams and his staff were preparing further redeployment steps for reaching the 60,000 goal. The Free World allies also were withdrawing. By early March, the Thai division and the Australian task force had left Vietnam, as had the 10,000-man South Korean Marine Brigade and a slice of logistical troops. Under an agreement negotiated by Washington, Saigon, and Seoul, the two Korean infantry divisions would remain in Military Region 2 at least through the end of the year.[15]

On 13 January, driven by domestic political pressures, President Nixon again accelerated U.S. withdrawals. He announced that 70,000 more troops would leave Vietnam by 1 May, reducing MACV's strength ceiling to 69,000, whereas OPLAN J208A had envisioned a force of about 84,000 on that date. The 69,000-man level itself was to be only

---

[14] U.S. Senate Committee on Armed Services, Report of the Committee on Armed Services on the Nomination of General Creighton W. Abrams for . . . Chief of Staff, U.S. Army, with Additional Views of Senator Margaret Chase Smith, copy in Miscellaneous/Calendar box, Abrams Papers, MHI.

[15] Historical Division, "Joint Chiefs of Staff and the War in Vietnam, 1971–1973," pt. 2, p. 442; MACV History, 1972–73, vol. 1, p. 9. Briefing [for Sec Def], sub: Contingency Plan OPLAN J208A, tab F, MAC J–303 Briefing Book no. 4; OPLAN 208A Briefing Presented to Sec Army, 10 Jan 72; Hq MACV J–3 Historical Summary, Feb 72, p. 2. All in MACV Collection, MHI.

transitional, since Nixon also promised another withdrawal announcement before the end of April.[16]

In response to this acceleration of redeployment, General Abrams,
in consultation with his regional commanders, designed an "austere"
69,000-man force. The force would be capable of commanding and
controlling American operations; protecting its own installations; sup-
plying and administering itself; carrying out minimal intelligence and
communications functions; advising the South Vietnamese; and furnishing limited air, helicopter, and logistical assistance to the South
Koreans. It would include two infantry brigades, two artillery battalions, and three fighter/attack squadrons as well as large advisory and
logistical elements. About 10,000 of the logistical troops were designated as a "roll-up" force for shipping out excess American supplies
and equipment. MACV and its service components prepared detailed
troop lists for the new withdrawal, Increment Eleven, which would
remove the 101st Airborne Division, the last American division to leave
South Vietnam. With an eye to the expected enemy offensive, General
Abrams scheduled for redeployment late in the increment those units,
for example helicopter companies, most needed to support the South
Vietnamese. Other units began standing down during February. As they
did so, Abrams and his staff, at Laird's and the Joint Chiefs' direction,
began preparing plans for reducing MACV to 30,000 men by 1 July and
15,000 by 1 November.[17]

As part of the speedup in redeployments, MACV accelerated its own
headquarters reduction and restructuring under the plan for an interim
Vietnam Assistance Command (VAC). On 14 January, General Abrams
directed all headquarters agencies to reconfigure to the VAC level by 1
May instead of the previous target date of 1 July, but with no change in
the designations of the various elements. This required the headquarters to cut its strength from 1,844 spaces to 1,058 in four months. By
early February, the reorganization was well under way. MACV headquarters dissolved the office of the Assistant Chief of Staff for Military
Assistance and distributed its advice and support functions among the
assistant chiefs of staff for personnel, operations, and logistics. The J–3
section took preliminary steps toward its planned absorption of the J–5
office.[18]

[16] Kissinger, *White House Years*, p. 1101; MACV History, 1972–73, vol. 2, an. F, p. 56. Briefing
presented to Gen Abrams, Ambs Bunker and Berger, and Field and Component Cdrs, 22 Jan 72, tab
B, MAC J–303 Briefing Book no. 4, MACV Collection, MHI.

[17] Msgs, Abrams SPECAT to McCain info Moorer, 14 Jan 72; Abrams SPECAT to McCain
info Moorer et al., 17 Mar 72; Abrams Microfilm, MHI. Msgs, Abrams MAC 0424 to Lavelle
et al., 15 Jan 72; Abrams MAC 0829 to Vann, 27 Jan 72; Abrams MAC 0929 to Lavelle and
McCaffrey, 31 Jan 72. All in Abrams Papers, CMH. Briefing presented to Gen Abrams, Ambs
Bunker and Berger, and Field and Component Cdrs . . . , 22 Jan 72, tab B; Briefing for Gen
Clay, 21 Jan 72, sub: U.S. Redeployment Status, tab D. Both in MAC J–303 Briefing Book no.
4, MACV Collection, MHI.

[18] Memo, Maj Gen Bowley, USAF, for Distribution, 24 Jan 72, sub: Increment 11 Drawdown of
HQ MACV, in folder, same title; Memo, Bowley for CofS, MACV, 5 Feb 72, sub: Reorganization

On 19 January, in the light of the fact that MACV was drawing down toward assistance command level faster than anticipated, Admiral McCain asked Abrams for his views on when MACV could revert to an advisory group headquarters and whether an interim VAC was any longer needed. McCain also inquired as to whether command and control of air operations in Southeast Asia, which increasingly were being mounted from bases in Thailand, should be transferred out of South Vietnam. In response, General Abrams took the position that MACV should change into a military assistance group only upon the "termination of a combat role requiring the exercise of operational control of U.S. combat forces by the command," which presumably would not occur until the end of air operations. Abrams declared further that command and control of the air war in Southeast Asia, which likely would continue at high sortie levels for at least another year, should remain in South Vietnam. Transfer of the responsibility to a headquarters in Thailand or the Philippines, he argued, would disrupt the effective working relationship between the U.S. and South Vietnamese air forces and lead as well to diplomatic difficulties and political accusations that the administration was expanding the war.[19]

On 12 February, to ensure that command of the air war remained in Saigon even as American forces shrank below the 69,000 level, Abrams proposed to McCain a modified version of the VAC plan. Under it, MACV would absorb the operational and intelligence elements of the Seventh Air Force headquarters into a restructured VAC headquarters. The commanding general of Seventh Air Force, while retaining his title and operational control of Air Force units in South Vietnam and Thailand, would serve also as deputy COMUSMACV. There would be six general staff directorates—personnel, intelligence, operations (incorporating the Seventh Air Force's Tactical Air Control Center), communications-electronics, logistics, and civil operations and revolutionary development support. The reorganized headquarters would have under it Army, Air Force, and Navy advisory groups. A small joint assistance command in each military region would advise the South Vietnamese commander, coordinate American support of his forces, and report on his operations. U.S. Army, Vietnam, would be reduced to a VAC support command performing Army supply and administrative functions and providing common item support to U.S. forces. Abrams argued that this structure would permit retention of air command and control in South Vietnam while minimizing headquarters overhead. It also would maintain a "viable" advisory effort in training, technical matters, and logistics and could readily adapt to a variety of future U.S. redeployment schedules. Abrams asked McCain's permission to

of HQ MACV, in folder, same title; Hq MACV J–3 Historical Summary, Feb 72, p. 6. All in MACV Collection, MHI.

[19] Msgs, McCain SPECAT to Abrams, 19 Jan 72; Abrams SPECAT to McCain, 21 Jan 72; Abrams SPECAT to McCain info Moorer, 12 Feb 72. All in Abrams Microfilm, MHI.

begin planning at once on the basis of the concept, for implementation sometime in April or May.[20]

On 15 February, Admiral McCain authorized Abrams to proceed with planning and preparations for the reorganization. At Abrams' recommendation, for simplicity's sake and to avoid a need for "adjudication at the Washington level" that might delay implementation of the plan, McCain decided to abandon the VAC designation and continue calling the reorganized command in Saigon the Military Assistance Command, Vietnam, until it became an advisory group. To work out details of the reorganization, Abrams then formed a senior planning group headed by the MACV deputy chief of staff and including the deputy J–3 for plans and representatives of Seventh Air Force; U.S. Army, Vietnam; and Navy Forces, Vietnam. By early March, the planners had refined the functions and command relationships of the proposed new MACV organization, which were the same in general principles as those of the existing one. On 4 April, the Joint Chiefs of Staff approved the new structure, for implementation on a date to be set by Abrams. Meantime, headquarters reductions under previous plans continued. On 19 March, XXIV Corps, denuded of all but one brigade of American combat troops, stood down and was replaced by the First Regional Assistance Command. This change brought the advisory and support organization in Military Region 1 into line with those of the other three military regions. On 31 March, the Studies and Observations Group began the process of phasing down to an advisory team attached to the South Vietnamese Strategic Technical Directorate, Saigon's headquarters for special operations, which would continue the activities of the Studies and Observations Group on a lesser scale.[21]

Attack and Counterattack

On 30 March, the North Vietnamese opened their long-anticipated offensive, which they named "Nguyen Hue" after a hero of an earlier war with China. Americans labeled it the "Easter Offensive." It began with a thunderous artillery bombardment of the South Vietnamese firebases in northern Military Region 1. Under cover of rain and clouds that hampered American air operations, three North Vietnamese divisions, heavily supported by armor, moved to the attack across the Demilitarized Zone and down Highway 9 from Laos. In a month of the severest conventional fighting yet seen in the Vietnam conflict, the North Vietnamese destroyed the new South

---

[20] Msg, Abrams SPECAT to McCain info Moorer, 12 Feb 72, Abrams Microfilm, MHI.

[21] Msgs, McCain SPECAT to Abrams info Moorer, 15 Feb 72; Abrams SPECAT to McCain info Moorer et al., 23 Feb 72 and 6 Mar 72; Abrams SPECAT to McCain, 22 Jun 72. All in Abrams Microfilm, MHI. Msgs, Abrams MAC 1563 to Regional and Component Cdrs, 20 Feb 72; Abrams MAC 2304 to Regional and Component Cdrs, 14 Mar 72; Abrams MAC 1987 to McCaffrey and Dolvin, 4 Mar 72. All in Abrams Papers, CMH. Msg, Col John F. Sadler SOG 237 to USARV et al., 30 Mar 72, box V, Abrams Papers, MHI.

A U.S. Navy A–7 pulls away from a strike on the Hai Duong railway bridge in North Vietnam; below, An enemy T54 tank burns in An Loc, Binh Long Province, South Vietnam, after being struck by a U.S. Army AH–1G Cobra helicopter gunship.

Vietnamese 3d Division, routed other defending forces, and captured most of Quang Tri Province including the capital, Quang Tri City. The enemy then rolled toward Hue, the main prize of the region. By early May, as refugees streamed southward and Saigon's battered units formed a shaky defense line north of the city, the fall of the old imperial capital seemed imminent.

Nearly simultaneous crises developed farther south. In Military Region 3, where the allies had not expected large-scale attacks, two North Vietnamese divisions, also with armor, advanced from Cambodia into Binh Long Province, north of Saigon. By 7 April, they had laid siege to An Loc, the province capital. The South Vietnamese defenders, supported by round-the-clock U.S. tactical air and B–52 strikes, held on through more than two months of savage fighting. In Military Region 2, the Communists opened their offensive by seizing the northern districts of Binh Dinh, a heavily populated coastal province and long-time revolutionary stronghold. The major crisis in this region, however, did not come until early May. Then an armor-supported North Vietnamese force, after overrunning several outlying towns and camps, attacked Kontum, a key Central Highlands province capital, and precipitated another hard fought month-long siege. As at An Loc, American airpower enabled the South Vietnamese defenders to hold. In Military Region 4, the Mekong Delta, the enemy launched a flurry of battalion and smaller-size attacks during April, May, and June. The South Vietnamese, with the Regional and Popular Forces doing much of the fighting, beat back these thrusts and even were able to spare a division to assist Military Region 3 in the battle for An Loc.[22] *(Map 5)*

President Nixon reacted belligerently to the North Vietnamese offensive. With his successful China trip behind him, Nixon decided to risk the breakdown of his diplomacy with Beijing and Moscow, not to mention a domestic political firestorm, rather than accept the defeat of his Vietnamization policy and the attendant humiliation of the United States before the world. On 4 April, Kissinger, speaking for the president, told his interagency crisis response group that Nixon did not expect to lose the fight for Military Region 1, that all previous restraints on American action were subject to removal, and that the United States "must bring as much air and naval force to bear as possible in order to give the enemy a severe jolt." Beyond defeating the immediate attack, Nixon and Kissinger intended to use the crisis as an occasion to do what they had contemplated since 1969—bomb the North Vietnamese into negotiating an end to the war on terms the United States could live with. The North Vietnamese had opened the end game and Nixon was determined to play it to a decision.[23]

---

[22] This summary of events is drawn from Andrade, *Trial by Fire*, and MACV History, 1972–73, vol. 1, an. A, pp. 5–6.

[23] Kissinger, *White House Years*, pp. 1097–99, 1108–11; Historical Division, "Joint Chiefs of Staff and the War in Vietnam, 1971–1973," pt. 1, pp. 352–57. Quotation is from Joint History Office,

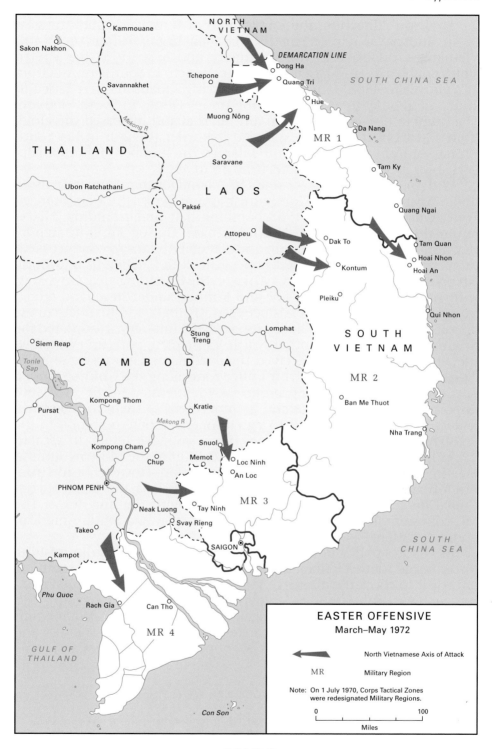

Kammouane

Sakon Nakhon

NORTH
VIETNAM

DEMARCATION LINE

Dong Ha

SOUTH CHINA SEA

Savannakhet

Tchepone

Quang Tri

Hue

Mekong R.

Muong Nông

Da Nang

THAILAND

MR 1

Tam Ky

Saravane

L A O S

Ubon Ratchathani

Paksé

Quang Ngai

Attopeu

Dak To

Tam Quan

Hoai Nhon

Kontum

Hoai An

Pleiku

Qui Nhon

Stung
Treng

Lomphat

S O U T H
V I E T N A M

Siem Reap

C A M B O D I A

MR 2

*Tonle
Sap*

Ban Me Thuot

Kompong Thom

Kratie

Pursat

Mekong R.

Nha Trang

Kompong Cham

Snuol

Chup

Memot

Loc Ninh

PHNOM PENH

An Loc

Neak Luong

Tay Ninh

MR 3

Takeo

Svay Rieng

SAIGON

*SOUTH
CHINA SEA*

Kampot

Phu Quoc

Rach Gia

Can Tho

*GULF
OF
THAILAND*

MR 4

Con Son

EASTER OFFENSIVE
March–May 1972

North Vietnamese Axis of Attack

MR   Military Region

Note: On 1 July 1970, Corps Tactical Zones
were redesignated Military Regions.

0   100

Miles

MAP 5

At Nixon's direction, the Joint Chiefs of Staff accelerated the flow of air and naval reinforcements that had begun before the North Vietnamese offensive. Between January and May 1972, the United States doubled its land-based tactical air strength in Southeast Asia from 212 aircraft to 480. Many of the reinforcing squadrons were based in Thailand in order to avoid exceeding troop ceilings in South Vietnam. The number of B–52s on Guam and in Thailand increased threefold, from 42 to 148. The Navy expanded its carrier strength in the South China Sea from three to six and enlarged the number of gunfire support ships in Vietnamese waters from 16 to 54.[24]

With the increased forces came a freer hand for commanders in using them. Assuming that the Communist assault across the Demilitarized Zone had terminated the 1968 bombing halt understanding, Nixon resumed the air war against North Vietnam. During April, he step by step authorized Admiral McCain and General Abrams to conduct tactical air and naval gunfire attacks up to the 20th Parallel. In mid-April, Nixon directed a one-time B–52 strike on the Haiphong area. On 8 May, with Hue in danger and An Loc and Kontum under siege, and after a fruitless secret meeting in Paris between Kissinger and his Vietnamese opposite number, Le Duc Tho, Nixon took the final step. He ordered the mining of Haiphong and other North Vietnamese ports and extended the air campaign, which received the code-name LINEBACKER, to all of North Vietnam except a narrow buffer zone along the Chinese border. The campaign's military purpose was to interdict North Vietnam's importation of war supplies and its movement of them to the south. Its larger diplomatic aim was to signal American determination to the Russians and Chinese and compel Hanoi to make terms. In escalating as he did, Nixon risked Soviet cancellation of the Moscow summit meeting, then in the final stages of preparation. However, aside from pro forma denunciations and protests, the Russians and Chinese continued their three-sided diplomatic minuet with the Americans. The Moscow summit took place late in May as planned while American bombers battered North Vietnam.[25]

As Nixon's policy unfolded, General Abrams used his diminishing forces inside South Vietnam and his expanding air and naval resources outside it to check the offensive. At the same time, he continued planning and executing troop redeployments and the MACV headquarters reorganization. As the air war against the north expanded, Abrams faced command issues dormant since the end of ROLLING THUNDER and conflicts with the administration over operational priorities.

"CJCS and the North Vietnamese Offensive," pp. 20–21; see also p. 3.

[24] Historical Division, "Joint Chiefs of Staff and the War in Vietnam, 1971–1973," pt. 1, pp. 357–60, 394–96.

[25] Thompson, "Rolling Thunder to Linebacker," ch. 9, pp. 3–4, 16–19; MACV History, 1972–73, vol. 1, an. B, p. 5; Historical Division, "Joint Chiefs of Staff and the War in Vietnam, 1971–1973," pt. 1, pp. 365–91, 406–12. The diplomatic aspects are covered in Kissinger, *White House Years*, pp. 1113–1201.

General Abrams' first task was to monitor and report on the developing offensive. To follow the course of the battle, he relied primarily on daily reports from his American regional commanders and senior advisers and occasional face-to-face conferences with them. He made personal visits to the Vietnamese corps commanders and sent his deputy, General Weyand, on periodic trips to the field. Abrams and Ambassador Bunker met regularly with President Thieu to review the situation and inform Thieu of American efforts on South Vietnam's behalf. As in previous crises, Abrams sent daily appraisals to Admirals McCain and Moorer and special reports to Secretary Laird and President Nixon. Abrams and Bunker briefed Dr. Kissinger's military assistant, General Haig, during Haig's periodic visits to Saigon.[26]

Relatively optimistic at the beginning of the offensive, Abrams' assessments descended rapidly toward alarm, especially as the South Vietnamese forces in northern Military Region 1 neared collapse. Early in April, Abrams reported that the situation in the north was grave but that the South Vietnamese, considering the pressure they were under, were performing "in an orderly and controlled manner." He characterized the Vietnamese corps commanders as "serious, determined and confident" and declared that they were "skillfully adjusting their tactics to the enemy situation in their respective areas." On 24 April, after the South Vietnamese had temporarily stabilized their lines around Quang Tri City, Abrams asserted that overall his allies had "fought well under extremely difficult circumstances" and that "the leadership in MR [Military Region] 1 is outstanding; aggressive and confident." A week later, as the South Vietnamese retreated in disorder from Quang Tri, Abrams' tone changed. On 1 May, he reported to Secretary Laird: "As the pressure has mounted and the battle has become brutal the senior military leadership has begun to bend and in some cases break. In adversity it is losing its will and cannot be depended upon to take the measures necessary to stand and fight." There was "no apparent basis for confidence," Abrams concluded, that Hue could be held.[27]

Aside from providing air support to the South Vietnamese, General Abrams, with only two American combat brigades left in the country, could influence the ground fighting only at the margins. MACV's remaining helicopter units delivered fire support, supplies, and reinforcements to embattled South Vietnamese garrisons. U.S. Army, Vietnam, furnished equipment to refit shattered South Vietnamese

[26] Msgs, Abrams MAC 3029 to Regional Cdrs, 5 Apr 72; Abrams MAC 3143 to Regional Cdrs, 8 Apr 72. Both in Abrams Papers, CMH. Msg, Cowles MAC 4381 to Regional and Component Cdrs, 11 May 72, box V, Abrams Papers, MHI; Msg, Abrams SPECAT to McCain info Moorer, 6 Apr 72, Abrams Microfilm, MHI. Msg, Bunker Saigon 0060 to Kissinger, 10 Apr 72, box 414; Memo, Haig for Kissinger, 19 Apr 72, sub: Southeast Asia Trip Report, box 1014; Msg, Laird OSD 08825 to Abrams, 23 Apr 72, box 117. All in NSC files, Nixon Papers, NARA.
[27] Msgs, Abrams SPECAT to McCain info Moorer, 3 and 6 Apr 72, Abrams Microfilm, MHI. Msgs, Abrams MAC 3757 to Laird, 24 Apr 72; Abrams MAC 4021 to Laird, 2 May 72. Both in Abrams Papers, CMH. Msg, Abrams to Laird, 3 May 72, box 130, NSC files, Nixon Papers, NARA.

units. MACV dispatched advisers to train the Vietnamese in technical specialties, such as counterbattery fire and the air dropping of supplies and heavy equipment. Late in May, to help the South Vietnamese defeat the enemy's armor, MACV introduced the TOW (tube launched, optically tracked, wire guided) antitank missile into the fighting. However, Abrams limited distribution of the sophisticated weapon to only the most reliable South Vietnamese units, such as the marine division. General Abrams engaged in lengthy, frustrating negotiations with the South Korean forces commander, Lt. Gen. Lee Sae Ho, seeking to persuade Lee to assist the South Vietnamese in the Central Highlands. Lee, under orders from Seoul to avoid combat unless directly attacked, responded grudgingly and demanded exorbitant amounts of U.S. helicopter, armor, and artillery support when he did move. In April, the Koreans made slow work of clearing An Khe Pass on the vital supply route from the coast to the highlands. Beyond that, they did little but protect their own areas of operation.[28]

Early in May, as South Vietnamese collapse began to seem possible, Abrams prepared for the worst. He convened a group of representatives from the MACV and component command staffs to prepare contingency plans "to be implemented should the military or political situation in the [Republic of Vietnam] dictate evacuation of U.S. personnel from any threatened area. . . ." Reflecting the sense of impending disintegration, he also issued instructions that "no Vietnamese commander will be airlifted out of a unit defensive position by U.S. fixed-wing aircraft or helicopter" unless the evacuation was directed personally by the Vietnamese corps commander.[29]

The latter directive, as well as General Abrams' 1 May assessment, pointed up the fact that the early South Vietnamese defeats resulted in large part from the inadequacy of Saigon's top-level military leadership. In the April battles for Quang Tri, the Military Region 1 commander, General Lam, whose limitations had been apparent during LAM SON 719, again demonstrated his unfitness to direct large-scale conventional operations. His counterparts in Military Regions 2 and 3 also proved unequal to the demands of high-intensity warfare, as did several division commanders.[30]

---

[28] Msg, McCaffrey ARV 1166 to Abrams, 5 May 72; Maj Gen James F. Hollingsworth, Senior Adviser, First Regional Assistance Command, ARV 1241 to Abrams, 10 May 72; Abrams MAC 4371 to McCaffrey, 10 May 72; Abrams MAC 4372 to Watkins, 10 May 72; Abrams MAC 4458 to Vann, 13 May 72; Vann PKU 539 to Abrams, 8 Apr 72; Vann PKU 586 to Abrams, 18 Apr 72. All in Abrams Papers, CMH. Msgs, CINCUNK/COMUSKOREA SPECAT to Moorer and McCain, info Abrams, 26 Apr 72; Abrams SPECAT to McCain, info CJCS and COMUSKOREA, 8 May 72. Both in Abrams Microfilm, MHI. Andrade, *Trial by Fire*, pp. 191–92, 293–98.

[29] First quotation is from Msg, Abrams MAC 4217 to Component Cdrs, 6 May 72; second is from Msg, Abrams MAC 4040 to Regional Cdrs, 2 May 72. Both in Abrams Papers, CMH.

[30] Lam's failings are summarized in Andrade, *Trial by Fire*, pp. 169–70. Overall South Vietnamese command problems are summarized in Clarke, *Final Years*, pp. 483–86.

On this issue, General Abrams and Ambassador Bunker intervened decisively. On 2 May, at a meeting with President Thieu, Abrams, with Bunker's concurrence, described in unvarnished terms the inadequacies of the senior South Vietnamese generals and warned of an approaching breakdown of command and control, especially in Quang Tri. "All that had been accomplished over the last four years was now at stake," Abrams told Thieu, "and it was the effectiveness of his field commanders that would determine the outcome." Following this meeting, Thieu called together his four military region commanders, the chief of the Joint General Staff, and other senior officers to announce command changes. He replaced Lam in Military Region 1 with Lt. Gen. Ngo Quang Truong, then in charge of Military Region 4. A former commander of the South Vietnamese 1st Division, Truong knew the northern corps area well, and the Americans considered him South Vietnam's most competent field general. Subsequently, Thieu relieved General Dzu, the Military Region 2 commander, although he could not find a successor for Dzu of Truong's caliber. General Minh, commander of Military Region 3, although only marginally effective, survived the shakeup because of his close friendship with President Thieu. In follow-up meetings on the leadership problem, Abrams and Bunker strongly pressed Thieu to replace Minh and counseled the president on the selection and promotion of other commanders.[31]

In Military Region 1, the command change made an immediate, dramatic difference. General Truong quickly restored order among the armed forces and civilian population in Hue, started reassembling broken units, and organized a defense of the city built around the marines and the South Vietnamese 1st Division. Assisted by heavy American air strikes, his troops repelled North Vietnamese attacks and began a counteroffensive to retake Quang Tri Province. In Military Regions 2 and 3, despite the reliefs, Vietnamese leadership remained at best lackluster. Abrams told Vice President Agnew in mid-May that "only about ten" South Vietnamese generals were "earning their pay." The American regional senior advisers, John Vann (killed in a helicopter crash on 9 June) in Military Region 2 and Maj. Gen. James F. Hollingsworth in Military Region 3, braced up wavering counterparts and orchestrated the constant American air strikes that smashed the North Vietnamese attacks at Kontum and An Loc. At the tactical level, unit advisers, whom Abrams characterized as "heroic, smart, and professional in every sense of the word," held the defense together at critical points and compensated by example and action for persistent weaknesses in South Vietnamese command and control.[32]

---

[31] Quotation is from Msg, Abrams MAC 4021 to Laird, 2 May 72, Abrams Papers, CMH. Msgs, Bunker Saigon 0081 to Kissinger, 2 May 72, and Bunker Saigon 0100 to Kissinger, 8 Jun 72, box 414; Msg, Abrams to Laird, 3 May 72, copy in box 130; Msg, Bunker Saigon 6374 to Sec State, 3 May 72, box 160. All in NSC files, Nixon Papers, NARA.

[32] Quotations are from Msg, Abrams MAC 4600 to Vice President Spiro T. Agnew, 17 May 72, Abrams Papers, CMH. Andrade, *Trial by Fire*, pp. 171–72, 187–94, 312–13, recounts

Airpower was the Military Assistance Command's decisive weapon in the 1972 battles. During the crisis, MACV's single management system, tried and perfected since 1968, enabled General Abrams to mass his airplanes where and when they were needed. Each day, Abrams personally allocated the available tactical air, B–52, and fixed-wing gunship sorties among South Vietnam's military regions, on the basis of his own and his staff's reading of the situation, the advice of the Seventh Air Force commander, and requests from the regions. He also apportioned sorties to Laos and Cambodia. The Seventh Air Force tactical air control center then directed flights to the regions, where the South Vietnamese commanders and their senior advisers, working through the corps direct air support control centers and airborne forward air controllers, sent the aircraft where they could best affect the outcome of the battle. As the action developed, Abrams regularly shifted the weight of effort between North Vietnamese troops engaging the South Vietnamese or massing to attack and the enemy's supply routes and cross-border bases. American airplanes kept the North Vietnamese under a round-the-clock rain of destruction. Where the enemy gained ground, he paid a fearful price in dead men and wrecked equipment. Where the South Vietnamese held, American airpower was the mainstay of their defense. Abrams declared on 3 May: "In my judgment, any bleeding off of the tactical air support now being directed into the . . . land battle would result in major defeats of ARVN forces."[33]

Nixon's air war against North Vietnam threatened just such a bleeding off, and it raised also questions of command and control similar to those in ROLLING THUNDER. When the North Vietnamese offensive opened, General Abrams, as he had since 1968, effectively controlled the allocation and targeting of the American air effort throughout Vietnam, Cambodia, and Laos, subject only to restrictions set by national policy. However, as Nixon progressively extended the air campaign northward, CINCPAC once again became involved in air operations, often as the transmitter of administration directives that conflicted with General Abrams' tactical priorities.

The well-established working relationship between Admiral McCain and General Abrams survived these new stresses, as did the close cooperation between their respective staffs. Especially helpful was the line of communication that Abrams' chief of staff, Maj. Gen. Donald H. Cowles, established with his Pacific Command opposite number, Maj. Gen. Charles A. Corcoran, himself a former MACV chief of staff. The two officers spoke by telephone every day, "to make sure we under-

---

Truong's accomplishments and Dzu's relief. Clarke, *Final Years*, pp. 484–86, describes the work of Vann and Hollingsworth.

[33] Quotation is from Msg, Abrams SPECAT to McCain, 3 May 72, Abrams Microfilm, MHI. Msg, Abrams MAC 4316 to Regional Assistance Cdrs, 9 May 72, box V, Abrams Papers, MHI; Bfg, 17 Jun 72, sub: U.S. Air Operations in Southeast Asia, in folder, same title, MACV Collection, MHI. Vogt Interv, 8–9 Aug 78, pp. 261–66, 268–69, contains comments on the role of Seventh Air Force in intelligence and targeting.

stood each other, even if no one else did." Corcoran kept the MACV chief of staff informed of what the president and the Joint Chiefs were telling Admiral McCain. Abrams regularly sat in on the Saigon end of these conversations, and he also talked with McCain "once or twice a week as circumstances dictated." By these means, the two commanders maintained their united front in dealing with a frequently peremptory administration.[34]

McCain and the chairman of the Joint Chiefs, Admiral Moorer, increasingly found themselves trying to mediate between General Abrams and a White House that progressively lost confidence in the MACV commander. Abrams' credit with Nixon and Kissinger had been damaged by LAM SON 719. When the North Vietnamese offensive began, Nixon almost immediately decided that Abrams, and the American military leadership in general, was sluggish and unimaginative in using the additional forces and expanded authorities he was giving them. Early in April, he complained that Abrams was not acting forcefully enough to control the crisis in northern Military Region 1 and directed Admiral Moorer to tell Abrams to commit his entire B–52 strength to that region. Moorer passed this instruction on to Abrams, as a suggestion rather than an order. An enraged Abrams telephoned Moorer and threatened to resign his command if Washington were going to dictate his air allocations. Moorer managed to mollify both Abrams and the White House. Nixon, however, continued to be dissatisfied with the MACV commander's response to the offensive. He suspected that Abrams and Secretary Laird were working together to concentrate American military action on restoring the status quo in South Vietnam while passing up the opportunity to pressure North Vietnam for a definitive settlement. For his part, Admiral Moorer became increasingly convinced that Abrams, tired from having been on the job too long, was taking an overly narrow, localized view of the situation and American strategy.[35]

In an effort to invigorate the air campaign and ensure its responsiveness to his political direction, Nixon personally interceded with General Lavelle's successor in command of the Seventh Air Force, General Vogt, whom Nixon had come to know while Vogt was director of the Joint Staff. An Ivy League–educated officer with more staff than command experience, Vogt had worked on ROLLING THUNDER in the Pentagon and at Pacific Air Force headquarters in Hawaii. He was close to Admiral Moorer and had made Kissinger's acquaintance while taking courses at Harvard. Early in April, before Vogt left for Saigon,

---

[34] Corcoran Interv, 1975, pp. 40–41, 45–47. Quotation is from Cowles Interv, 20 Dec 75, pp. 21–22. McCain Interv, n.d., pp. 17–18.

[35] Kissinger, *White House Years*, pp. 1111–12. Msg, Moorer SPECAT 3492 to McCain and Abrams, 8 Apr 72, box 1016; Memos, Nixon for Kissinger and Haig, 15 and 19 May 72, box 1006, in NSC files, Nixon Papers, NARA, reflect Nixon's irritation with his military commanders. Joint History Office, "CJCS and the North Vietnamese Offensive," pp. 16–18, 23–25, 60, covers Abrams' reaction to the B–52 order and Moorer's view of Abrams.

Nixon summoned the new Seventh Air Force commander to the White House and told Vogt that he was to direct the entire air war in Southeast Asia, apparently without reference to McCain and Abrams. Evidently unaware of the MACV reorganization already in train, Vogt suggested that he be made deputy COMUSMACV rather than merely deputy for air, and that he be freed from answering to a multitude of superiors for different air campaigns. Nixon promised those things would be done. However, when Vogt reached Saigon, he found that neither the White House nor the Defense Department had changed the MACV and Seventh Air Force terms of reference. "So . . . I ran into the same problems that all my predecessors had run into. I had bosses all over the place." Vogt answered to Abrams for operations in South Vietnam, Cambodia, and Laos and to Admiral McCain for the Seventh Air Force role in bombing North Vietnam.[36]

Nevertheless, Vogt clearly was the administration's man in MACV. Admiral Moorer, whose confidence in Abrams' reporting had been shaken during LAM SON 719, turned to Vogt as an alternative source of information on military operations in South Vietnam. At Moorer's direction, Vogt sent the chairman of the Joint Chiefs of Staff daily situation reports and assessments through Air Force channels that bypassed both Abrams and McCain, and he also conferred frequently with Moorer by telephone outside the formal chain of command. Especially as the defense of Quang Tri crumbled, the Air Force general's evaluations of South Vietnamese performance and prospects usually were less optimistic than those coming from MACV. Moorer and Kissinger, to whom Moorer passed copies of the messages, relied heavily on Vogt's reports for their views of the course of the battle.[37]

General Vogt's influence notwithstanding, disputes arose between General Abrams and the White House over the allocation of airpower. While not opposed to bombing North Vietnam, Abrams believed that such attacks would have little immediate effect on the fighting in the South, his principal concern. He argued that, by the time they started their offensive, the North Vietnamese had built up, in South Vietnam and its immediate approaches, enough troops and materiel for an extended campaign. Therefore, air could be most profitably used against the North Vietnamese assault forces and the parts of their logistical pipeline closest to the front. Attacks on the enemy's deeper rear would have effect only after the critical battles for South Vietnam had been decided. Defense Secretary Laird and much of the U.S. intelligence community concurred with Abrams' assessment and with its logical conclusion that American airpower should be concentrated in the South.[38]

---

[36] Thompson, "Rolling Thunder to Linebacker," ch. 9, pp. 4–7; Vogt Interv, 8–9 Aug 78, pp. 63–64; quotation is from pp. 116–17.

[37] Joint History Office, "CJCS and the North Vietnamese Offensive," pp. 27–28, 44n, 66–67.

[38] Msg, Abrams SPECAT to Moorer and McCain, 8 Apr 72, Abrams Microfilm, MHI; Memos,

Nixon and Kissinger, on the other hand, were convinced that defeat of the immediate offensive would lead to nothing but a renewed military and diplomatic stalemate. They wanted to shape the intensified air war so as to push the North Vietnamese, and indirectly the Soviets and the Chinese, toward negotiations that at minimum would secure South Vietnam's survival for Kissinger's "healthy interval." "In effect," Nixon wrote to Kissinger on 30 April, "we have crossed the Rubicon and now we must win—not just a temporary respite from this battle, but if possible, tip the balance in favor of the South Vietnamese for battles to come when we no longer will be able to help them with major air strikes." Caught in the middle, Admiral Moorer acknowledged that Abrams was "absolutely right from a purely military point of view." However, the United States was now "playing a political problem" with the North Vietnamese and the Russians and General Abrams had to take more than his local circumstances into account.[39]

During April and early May, the tug-of-war over allocation of air sorties, particularly those of the B–52s, reached its height. Abrams considered it essential to concentrate the strategic bombers in support of the South Vietnamese at Hue and An Loc, both for tactical reasons and to shore up the will to fight of wavering South Vietnamese commanders. At the same time, Nixon wanted B–52 strikes deep in North Vietnam to show Hanoi he meant business and provide a forceful backdrop for his trip to Moscow. In the first collision, in mid-April, Abrams, citing the crisis at An Loc and appeals from President Thieu, tried to secure postponement of a White House–directed tactical air and B–52 raid on the Haiphong area. The administration overrode his objections and the strike went in as planned on 16 April. Immediately thereafter, Kissinger sent General Haig to Saigon to convey personally to Abrams the importance the president attached to the northern air campaign. After discussions with Abrams, Haig assured Kissinger and Admiral Moorer that the MACV commander appreciated the political requirements and would "divert whatever is necessary to support the diplomatic hand."[40]

Haig's optimism was premature. A second confrontation occurred early in May, against the background of Kissinger's secret Paris meeting with Le Duc Tho, final preparations for the Moscow summit, and battlefield crises at Hue, An Loc, and Kontum. On 3 May, President Nixon

Laird for the Assistant to the President for National Security Affairs, 6 Apr 72, sub: Contingency Plans for Operations against North Vietnam; and Haig for Kissinger, 6 Apr 72, sub: Contingency Planning. Both in box 1014, NSC files, Nixon Papers, NARA.

[39] Nixon quotation is from Memo, Nixon for Kissinger, 30 Apr 72, box 1006, NSC files, Nixon Papers, NARA. Joint History Office, "CJCS and the North Vietnamese Offensive," pp. 26–28; Moorer quotation is from pp. 31–32. See also Kissinger, *White House Years*, p. 1113.

[40] Msgs, Moorer SPECAT 8374 to Moorer et al., 13 Apr 72, Abrams SPECAT to Moorer and McCain, 14 Apr 72, box 1016; Bunker Saigon 0062 to Kissinger, 14 Apr 72, Haig Saigon 0065 to Kissinger, 17 Apr 72, box 414. All in NSC files, Nixon Papers, NARA. Haig quotation is from last-cited message. Joint History Office, "CJCS and the North Vietnamese Offensive," pp. 33–36, 39.

ordered a forty-eight-hour attack, using fighter-bombers and B–52s, on targets close to Hanoi and Haiphong, the timing directly related to the diplomatic maneuvering. Abrams, with Admiral McCain's concurrence, promptly declared that diversion of the B–52s and Seventh Air Force tactical aircraft from the southern battlefield at that point could lead to South Vietnamese military collapse. General Truong had just taken command of Military Region 1 and "we have got to pour the air support to him" to buy time while Truong regained control of the situation. Deferring to his field commanders' urgent recommendations, Nixon cancelled the attack. However, on 4 May, Kissinger informed Ambassador Bunker that Nixon was "nearing the end of his patience" with Abrams' seeming inability to appreciate that "we are playing a most complex game with the Soviets involving matters which extend far beyond the battle in Vietnam crucial as it is." In an effort to circumvent what he, Nixon, and Moorer thought was Laird's contradictory influence on Abrams, Kissinger arranged for the White House to transmit its instructions on critical military operations directly to Abrams through Bunker, bypassing regular State and Defense channels. Abrams was to send his views to the White House by the same route.[41]

The "Bunker channel" received its first test a few days later, when Nixon initiated LINEBACKER and the mining of North Vietnam's harbors. At Nixon's direction, the Joint Chiefs and CINCPAC did the planning for these operations, and the president and the National Security Council decided to launch them, without involving MACV. However, on 6 May, Kissinger, via Bunker, informed Abrams of the administration's intentions. He told the ambassador that there should be "no question in either your or General Abrams' mind that we want to devote the necessary assets to this action" and would send additional air and naval reinforcements if Abrams needed them to meet "tactical exigencies" in the south. Both Bunker and Abrams welcomed the president's decision. On 9 May, Abrams declared that it was "certain to have strong impact on the enemy." To supplement the mining, he recommended that the Seventh Air Force launch immediate and continuing attacks on the railroads between Hanoi and the Chinese border, North Vietnam's only remaining means of importing large quantities of supplies once the ports were closed. He also suggested that he be given the authority "to determine the proper daily application of sorties" so as to achieve "maximum effectiveness . . . both within the rail line interdiction program and the in-country close support."[42]

---

[41] Quotation is from Msg, Abrams SPECAT to Moorer and McCain, 4 May 72; Msgs, McCain SPECAT to Moorer, 4 May 72; Kissinger WHS 2063 to Bunker, 4 May 72; Bunker Saigon 0085 to Kissinger, 5 May 72. All in box 414, NSC files, Nixon Papers, NARA. Moorer's suspicion of Laird's influence is expressed in Joint History Office, "CJCS and the North Vietnamese Offensive," p. 52.

[42] Kissinger message is quoted in *White House Years*, p. 1181. For an account of the president's decision, see pp. 1174–86; Thompson, "Rolling Thunder to Linebacker," ch. 9, pp. 19–20. Abrams quotations are from Msg, Abrams SPECAT to McCain, info Moorer, 9 May 72, Abrams Microfilm, MHI.

Allocation authority, however, belonged to Admiral McCain. To conduct LINEBACKER, McCain reinstituted the route package system. He assigned Route Package 1, the area just above the Demilitarized Zone, to MACV's control and himself directed operations in the other route packages through Pacific Air Force and Pacific Fleet. McCain had the final say in apportioning the available airpower among the northern route packages and Abrams' areas of operation, although he consulted the MACV commander closely and gave high priority to his requirements. In contrast to President Johnson's detailed management of ROLLING THUNDER, in LINEBACKER President Nixon established a list of approved targets and permitted his military commanders to decide when and how to strike them. Nevertheless, the president and his national security adviser frequently intervened to orchestrate the bombing in aid of their diplomacy. Secretary Laird also regularly exercised his authority to limit attacks within the restrictive circles that remained around downtown Hanoi and Haiphong.[43]

Paradoxically, the initiation of LINEBACKER was followed by a reduction in the tension between the Military Assistance Command and the White House over air sortie allocations. This was so even though after 9 May the north received more than 50 percent of the air attack effort compared to 13 percent during the previous month. The burden of the LINEBACKER campaign fell upon the tactical fighter-bombers, which were best suited for precision strikes, some with the new guided "smart" ordnance, against bridges, rail yards, power plants, and other transportation and industrial targets. Abrams thus could concentrate the B–52s in the south where he wanted them. In addition, the steady arrival of air reinforcements made more sorties available for all purposes. Finally, during May and June, the tide of battle turned in South Vietnam. The allies, after stopping the initial enemy attack, prepared their own counteroffensives. Still, the difference in perspective and priorities remained. Nixon and Kissinger pressed constantly for a high level of activity over the North. Abrams, while he acknowledged that attacks on the enemy's logistical system in North Vietnam had achieved "very substantial results," emphasized that "it is not possible to lose the war in the north but it still is possible to lose the war in the south and we must not turn loose of this until the job is done."[44]

As the LINEBACKER campaign and the harbor mining moved into high gear, both Kissinger's National Security Council staff and the Military

[43] MACV History, 1972–73, vol. 1, an. B, p. 5; Thompson, "Rolling Thunder to Linebacker," ch. 9, pp. 25–26, 58–66. Memos, Nixon for Haig, 18 and 20 May 72, box 1006; and Msg, Kissinger WHS 2081 to Haig, 30 Jun 72, box 414, all in NSC files, Nixon Papers, NARA, are examples of the administration's orchestration efforts.

[44] Thompson, "Rolling Thunder to Linebacker," ch. 9, pp. 20–21. Percentages are given in Memo, Laird for the President, 3 Jul 72, sub: Assessment of Campaign against North Vietnam, box 096, NSC files, Nixon Papers, NARA. In this memorandum, Laird concludes that the air attacks in the north have had little immediate impact on the fighting in South Vietnam. Abrams quotation is from Msg, Abrams SPECAT to McCain, info Moorer et al., 6 Jun 72, Abrams Microfilm, MHI.

Assistance Command floated proposals for fundamental changes in the U.S. command structure in Southeast Asia. Kissinger considered the division of responsibility for air operations in North and South Vietnam to be "institutionalized schizophrenia." Early in May, he had his staff develop a plan for a new joint U.S. Southeast Asia Command, built around the existing MACV headquarters. Separate from Pacific Command and reporting directly to the Joint Chiefs, the new organization would control all U.S. air, land, and naval forces operating in and around the two Vietnams, Cambodia, Thailand, and Laos. Secretary Laird and Admiral Moorer promptly objected to this proposal. They argued that it would disrupt well-established, functioning command relationships throughout the Western Pacific at a critical time. In addition, the change would impose on the commander and staff in Saigon a host of regionwide operational, logistical, intelligence, and advice and support tasks that currently were being handled by Pacific Command. The reorganization thus would necessitate enlargement of the headquarters in South Vietnam at a time when the United States was trying to reduce its strength there. Laird and Moorer recommended instead that the administration proceed with the MACV and Seventh Air Force merger already in progress, which would ensure continuity in the direction of the air effort while economizing on headquarters spaces. On 19 May, Nixon accepted Laird's and Moorer's recommendation and directed that the MACV reorganization go forward as planned.[45]

On its part, the Military Assistance Command reached out for control of the entire air war. Early in June, with the MACV and Seventh Air Force merger about to be consummated, General Abrams suggested that Admiral McCain transfer mission tasking for the two route packages covering the rail lines to China from Pacific Air Force to the restructured MACV. Admiral Moorer at once rallied the Joint Chiefs to defeat this proposal. In October, Abrams' successor as COMUSMACV, General Weyand, went further. In connection with plans for continuing LINEBACKER into 1973, Weyand suggested that MACV be given responsibility for the conduct of U.S. operations in both North and South Vietnam, including all targeting of air strikes. The breakthrough in the peace negotiations, which occurred that same month, rendered Weyand's proposal moot and turned MACV's planning in a different direction. Except for the combination of the MACV and Seventh Air

---

[45] Historical Division, "Joint Chiefs of Staff and the War in Vietnam, 1971–1973," pt. 2, pp. 459–62; Joint History Office, "CJCS and the North Vietnamese Offensive," pp. 54, 60, 62. Memos, Odeen for Haig, 5 May 72, sub: Command Structure in SEA; Moorer CM–1820–72 for Laird, 8 May 72, sub: Command Structure in Pacific/Southeast Asia Area; Moorer JCSM–214–72 for Laird, 8 May 72, sub: Command Structure in the Southeast Asia Area; Laird for the President, 10 May 72, sub: Command Structure in the Pacific/Southeast Asia Area; and Kissinger for the Sec Def, 19 May 72, sub: Command Structure in Southeast Asia. All in box 096, NSC files, Nixon Papers, NARA. Quotation is from Kissinger, *White House Years*, p. 1112.

Force headquarters, the existing Southeast Asia command arrangements remained in force until the close of hostilities.[46]

Redeployments and Reorganization

Even as the Military Assistance Command fought to defeat the North Vietnamese offensive, it continued to remove troops from South Vietnam and prepare for reorganization under General Abrams' February plan. During April, Abrams revised his troop list for the eleventh withdrawal increment to retain in the 69,000-man force helicopter companies and other units indispensable in the ongoing battle, as well as to accommodate the Air Force and Marine jet squadrons arriving in the administration's buildup. He kept under the ceiling by redeploying 3,000 logistical troops, most of them Army elements that had been intended for the "roll-up" force. The result, Abrams pointed out to McCain, was to "unbalance" the remaining structure, making it "questionable how long the augmentation forces can be sustained by the supporting base." Despite this caveat, redeployments went forward, bringing MACV's actual troop strength down to 68,100 on 30 April.[47]

Besides managing Increment Eleven, Abrams addressed Secretary Laird's request for plans to reduce MACV to 30,000 men by 1 July and 15,000 by 1 November. On 15 March, he declared that these "rather arbitrary" ceilings, if enforced, would leave MACV unable to control the air war and provide essential advice and support to the South Vietnamese. Abrams recommended instead that the administration set a 1 November strength limit of 23,000 for the Military Assistance Command, the lowest level which would permit MACV to conduct both air operations and the advisory mission, and that he would be allowed to schedule redeployments to reach that goal. If "overriding considerations at the national level" dictated another withdrawal by 1 July, Abrams proposed that the troop level at that time go no lower than 37,000. On 16 April, after the offensive began, Abrams declared the 37,000 strength "unrealistic" in the light of the reinforcements streaming into Southeast Asia and the intensifying combat. He advised postponement of any new redeployments until after 1 July "to permit refined assessments of enemy intentions and capabilities, to regain an

---

[46] Msg, Abrams SPECAT to McCain info Moorer, 6 Jun 72, Abrams Microfilm, MHI; Joint History Office, "CJCS and the North Vietnamese Offensive," pp. 66–67. Msg, Haig Saigon 0176 to Kissinger, 3 Oct 72; Memo (handwritten), and Weyand for Haig [Oct 72]. Both in box 1017, NSC files, Nixon Papers, NARA.

[47] MACV History, 1972–73, vol. 2, an. F, pp. 56–57. Msg, Abrams MAC 3194 to Component Cdrs, 9 Apr 72, Abrams Papers, CMH. Msgs, Abrams SPECAT to McCain, 14 Apr 72; Abrams SPECAT to McCain info Moorer, 16 Apr 72. Both in Abrams Microfilm, MHI. Abrams quotation is from last-cited message. Historical Division, "Joint Chiefs of Staff and the War in Vietnam, 1971–1973," pt. 2, p. 453, gives the actual MACV strength figure.

element of balance in the force, and to provide maximum possible assistance to the RVNAF."[48]

Abrams' recommendation notwithstanding, the administration was committed to keeping up the withdrawals during the enemy offensive, both to demonstrate continuing confidence in Vietnamization and to reduce the adverse effect on American public opinion of the escalation of the air war. There were disagreements, however, over the size and timing of the next increment. On behalf of the Joint Chiefs, Admiral Moorer endorsed Abrams' call for a temporary halt to withdrawals. Secretary Laird advocated setting an end strength for MACV of 15,000, to be reached by 1 December, and permitting Abrams to stretch out the necessary redeployments over the intervening months. As he had done previously, Nixon chose his own course. On 26 April, after sending General Haig to sound out Bunker and Abrams, the president announced a reduction of 20,000 spaces during May and June, to bring MACV down to 49,000 men by 1 July. By taking this approach, Nixon kept up the momentum of withdrawals while retaining flexibility to respond to changes in the military and diplomatic situations. He also held MACV's strength on 1 July well above the 37,000 that Abrams initially had considered acceptable.[49]

In response to this directive, Abrams, in consultation with his regional and component commanders, designed a 49,000-man transitional force that he declared would have "many weaknesses" and suffer from "severe" personnel and logistical turbulence and imbalances in structure. Nevertheless, it would remain marginally capable of performing its basic administrative, operational, and advisory functions. To reach the new ceiling, Abrams made heavy cuts in security forces, by redeploying one of his two remaining combat brigades, and in logistical troops by eliminating the "roll-up" elements. He transferred the Air Force and Marine squadrons based at Da Nang to fields in Thailand, from which they continued to fly missions in North and South Vietnam. These reductions enabled him to retain advisers, helicopter units, and logistical troops essential to supporting the South Vietnamese and managing the flow of new equipment to them. During June, to keep still more of these elements, as well as some air squadrons, he gave up his remaining brigade, the 3d of the 1st Cavalry Division, except for two battalion-size task forces for defense of American installations around Da Nang and Saigon. When completed at the end of June, Increment Twelve left MACV's actual personnel strength at 48,000. Large American forces remained elsewhere in Southeast Asia.

---

[48] Msgs, Abrams SPECAT to McCain info Moorer, 15 Mar 72 and 16 and 21 Apr 72, Abrams Microfilm, MHI. Quotations are from the first two messages.

[49] Kissinger, *White House Years*, pp. 1166–67; Historical Division, "Joint Chiefs of Staff and the War in Vietnam, 1971–1973," pt. 2, pp. 454–57. Memos, Laird for the President, 21 Apr 72, sub: US Force Redeployments from SVN, and 25 Apr 72, sub: US Force Deployments from SVN, box 159; Msg, Haig Saigon 0065 to Kissinger, 17 Apr 72, box 1014; Haig WHS 2053 to Bunker, 23 Apr 72, box 414. All in NSC files, Nixon Papers, NARA.

In response to the North Vietnamese offensive, the United States had increased its strength in Thailand from 32,000 men to about 45,000; and 42,000 more Americans were on Navy ships in the South China Sea.[50]

As the Increment Twelve withdrawal went on, the administration planned for the next one. On 21 June, in response to a query from Laird, both McCain and Abrams, their views endorsed by Moorer, stated that any further reduction below 49,000 would undermine the security of U.S. forces and impair their ability to support the South Vietnamese. Nevertheless, Abrams declared that, if it were imperative to continue withdrawals, he could spare another 10,000 spaces during July and August. Taking the MACV commander at his word, on 28 June, Nixon announced a withdrawal that would bring MACV down to 39,000 men by 1 September. In a further gesture to public opinion, the president declared that no more draftees would be sent to Vietnam unless they volunteered for the assignment. MACV executed this redeployment, Increment Thirteen, on schedule, removing in the process the last Army infantry combat units to leave South Vietnam. On 31 August, the command's actual troop strength stood at 36,800.[51]

The consolidation of the MACV and Seventh Air Force headquarters was an integral part of the spring redeployment plans. However, to avoid disruption of air operations during the height of the enemy offensive, General Abrams postponed the actual combination from its original proposed date of 1 May until late June. In the interim, the Military Assistance Command continued reducing its staff and taking preliminary reorganization steps. These included formal disbandment of the Studies and Observations Group and the organization of MACV Special Troops to replace the office of the Headquarters Commandant and the U.S. Army Headquarters Area Command. On 15 May, MACV established an Army Advisory Group, formed around the old Training Directorate. A counterpart to the Air Force and Navy advisory groups, the Army Advisory Group was to plan and carry out assistance to South Vietnam's land forces. Headed by a brigadier general, the group consolidated under one headquarters all Army advisers to the South Vietnamese except those with units in the field, who remained under the regional assistance commands, and the logistics advisers who stayed under the MACV J–4.

---

[50] MACV History, 1972–73, vol. 2, an. F, p. 57; Historical Division, "Joint Chiefs of Staff and the War in Vietnam, 1971–1973," pt. 2, pp. 457–59. Msgs, Abrams SPECAT to McCain info Moorer, 27 Apr and 9 May 72; Abrams SPECAT to Moorer, 13 May 72; Abrams SPECAT to McCain info Moorer et al., 10 Jun 72. All in Abrams Microfilm, MHI. *New York Times*, 29 Jun 72, p. 1, in Newspaper Clippings, Biography, Miscellaneous box, Abrams Papers, MHI.

[51] Msg, Abrams SPECAT to McCain info Moorer, 19 Jun 72, Abrams Microfilm, MHI; Msg, Kissinger WHS 2077 to Bunker, 14 Jun 72, box 414, NSC files, Nixon Papers, NARA; Historical Division, "Joint Chiefs of Staff and the War in Vietnam, 1971–1973," pt. 2, pp. 462–64; *New York Times*, 29 Jun 72, p. 1, Newspaper Clippings, Biography, Miscellaneous box, Abrams Papers, MHI; MACV History, 1972–73, vol. 2, an. F, p. 58.

During the last half of June, the shift of functions and personnel from the Seventh Air Force headquarters to MACV took place. The intelligence and operations sections of the Seventh Air Force staff moved across Tan Son Nhut air field into the MACV building and were incorporated into the J–2 and J–3 offices of the senior headquarters. On 29 June, General Abrams formally put the consolidation into effect. The administration publicly announced it at the same time.[52]

The restructured MACV headquarters had a personnel strength of about 1,450, larger than the originally contemplated VAC organization but 350 people smaller than the previous aggregate of the MACV and Seventh Air Force staffs. General Vogt served as deputy COMUSMACV while also commanding the Seventh Air Force. Besides Vogt and a civilian deputy COMUSMACV for CORDS, the command group included the chief of staff, a technical assistance coordinator (the renamed science adviser), the deputy chief of staff for economic affairs, the staff judge advocate, the inspector general, the Office of Information, and the secretary of the Joint Staff. The general staff consisted of directorates, as the J sections were retitled, for personnel, intelligence, operations, logistics, communications-electronics, and CORDS plus the comptroller. The special staff included an Office of Administrative Services, the chaplain, the command surgeon, the provost marshal, the Free World Military Assistance Office, and the Data Management Agency. Under MACV, a reduced Seventh Air Force headquarters and a Naval Advisory Group performed service component functions. U.S. Army, Vietnam, redesignated the MACV Support Command, besides acting as Army component, provided common item supply to the other services. The regional assistance commands carried on advice and support of the South Vietnamese military regions.[53]

Reflecting the predominance of airpower in the American effort in Southeast Asia, the Air Force enjoyed enhanced influence in the reorganized MACV headquarters. As deputy COMUSMACV, General Vogt took part in the planning and conduct of ground as well as air operations, in his view to the "dramatic" improvement of air-ground coordination. In the restructured staff, Air Force generals headed the directorates for operations, personnel, and communications-electronics. The Army held on to the MACV chief of staff, the directorates of intelligence and logistics, and all the special staff sections. With possession of the deputy COMUSMACV slot (which the service had coveted

---

[52] Msg, Abrams SPECAT to McCain info Clay, 14 May 72, Abrams Microfilm, MHI; Msg, Abrams MAC 5105 to Vogt, 2 Jun 72, Abrams Papers, CMH; MACV History, 1972–73, vol. 1, p. 37, an. C, pp. 8–9, 32–33; vol. 2, an. I, pp. 3–5; Memo, Cowles for Distribution List, 8 May 72, sub: Establishment of Army Advisory Group, in folder, same title, MACV Collection, MHI; Hq MACV J–3 Historical Summary, Jun 72, MACV Collection, MHI; Thompson, "Rolling Thunder to Linebacker," ch. 9, p. 37.

[53] Msg, Abrams SPECAT to McCain, 22 Jun 72, Abrams Microfilm, MHI; Hq MACV Directory, Jul–Aug 72, folder 2000; Hq MACV Joint Table of Distribution, Aug 72, vol. 1, pp. 1–3, MACV Collection, MHI.

since MACV was established), as well as the operations directorate, the Air Force no longer could claim that it was underrepresented in the joint headquarters.[54]

At Secretary Laird's direction, the MACV reorganization was timed to coincide with the end of General Abrams' tour in command. On 20 June, at Laird's recommendation, President Nixon nominated Abrams to succeed General Westmoreland, who was retiring, as chief of staff of the Army. Dissatisfied with the general's performance in Vietnam, Nixon was reluctant to advance Abrams. In 1969, however, Nixon had promised Laird that as secretary of defense he would have the final word on military and civilian Defense Department appointments, and Laird held Nixon to his pledge. Nixon nevertheless delayed Abrams' nomination until the imminence of Westmoreland's retirement forced his hand. Then the president gave way to Laird's unwavering support of Abrams. A week after announcing Abrams' elevation, the president designated General Weyand to replace him as COMUSMACV. General Abrams left Saigon on 29 June. Befitting the continuing crisis in South Vietnam, he departed with no public change of command or farewell celebration, although President Thieu presented him with a decoration in a private ceremony.[55]

Like Westmoreland in 1968, Abrams left behind in South Vietnam an unfinished work and an uncertain legacy. During his four years in command, Abrams was compelled to fight what amounted to a prolonged rear guard action. He successfully managed the extrication of nearly 500,000 American troops from the battlefield in the midst of continuing hostilities. Under his guidance, the South Vietnamese armed forces were enlarged and improved to the point where they could assume the entire burden of territorial security and conduct major cross-border offensives. Behind their shield, Saigon established military and administrative control over most of its national territory. When the North Vietnamese responded to these gains with a full-throated main force assault, Abrams used his remaining resources—airpower and advisers—to help the South Vietnamese parry the blow. By the time he laid down his command, the North Vietnamese offensive had spent its force, and the South Vietnamese were recovering from their early defeats and beginning to counterattack. Yet fundamental problems remained unsolved. Abrams had not overcome South Vietnam's persistent deficiencies in military leadership, nor had he been able to disentangle the South Vietnamese Army from its territorial responsibilities and turn it

---

[54] MACV History, 1972–73, vol. 2, an. M; Vogt Interv, 8–9 Aug 78, pp. 211, 270–72.

[55] Msg, Sec Def OSD 0675 to Abrams, 20 Jun 72, box V; *New York Times*, 2 Jul 72, p. 1, Newspaper Clippings, Biography, Miscellaneous box; Abrams Papers, MHI; Msg, Moorer SPECAT 1808 to McCain and Abrams, 22 Jun 72, Abrams Microfilm, MHI. Memo, Laird for the President, 31 May 72, sub: Appointments of Key Military Officials; Memo, Haig for Kissinger, 1 Jun 72, sub: Action Items, box 1001; Transcript of White House News Conference, 28 Jun 72, box 1016. All in NSC files, Nixon Papers, NARA. Sorley, *Thunderbolt*, pp. 332–35; Interv, Walter S. Poole with Melvin R. Laird, 15 Jul 98, Joint History Office, Joint Chiefs of Staff, Washington D.C.

into a force capable on its own of mobile conventional combat. While the Viet Cong had been forced underground in most places, their political and military hard core survived; and North Vietnam remained implacable and able to return to the attack at any time. Laird's goal of a militarily self-sufficient South Vietnam still was some distance away. In sum, while Abrams, like his predecessor, registered impressive success in fulfilling MACV's mission, he did so without achieving an acceptable conclusion to the war.[56]

Abrams returned to the United States to face congressional scrutiny over his role in General Lavelle's unauthorized air strikes. The Senate delayed his confirmation as Army chief of staff until October, to allow time for a full investigation of the bombing by its Armed Services Committee. In the end, the committee concluded that Abrams neither ordered nor had knowledge of Lavelle's illegal actions. On 12 October, the full Senate confirmed Abrams' nomination with only two dissenting votes. As chief of staff, Abrams returned to Vietnam almost immediately at the president's direction, to help Ambassador Bunker and General Weyand try to persuade President Thieu to accept the tentative peace agreement Kissinger had negotiated. Then he launched upon the task of rebuilding an Army badly damaged by the Vietnam conflict. Tragically, his death from cancer on 4 September 1974 prematurely terminated his efforts and deprived the Army of one of its most respected leaders.[57]

Abrams' successor as COMUSMACV, General Weyand, possessed extensive Vietnam experience. Fifty-five years old in 1972, Weyand entered the Army through the Reserve Officers Training Corps at the University of California at Berkeley. A veteran of the China-Burma-India Theater in World War II, he commanded an infantry battalion in combat in the Korean War and also held a number of intelligence assignments. In Vietnam from 1966 to 1968, he commanded successively the 25th Infantry Division and II Field Force. In the latter position, he played a critical role in defending Saigon during the Tet offensive. After returning from Southeast Asia, Weyand spent fifteen months, from March 1969 to June 1970, as military adviser to the U.S. delegation at the Paris peace talks. He returned to Vietnam in September 1970 as General Abrams' deputy. Like Abrams, Weyand viewed the Vietnam conflict as a many-faceted struggle that required flexible tactics and

[56] Abrams is cautiously optimistic in Msg, Abrams SPECAT to McCain info Moorer, 21 Jun 72, box 130, NSC files, Nixon Papers, NARA. Also Msg, Laird 06922 to Abrams, 28 Jun 72, box V, Abrams Papers, MHI. Clarke, *Final Years*, p. 508, summarizes Abrams' advisory successes and failures.

[57] Abrams' confirmation struggle can be followed in the newspaper articles in the Newspaper Clippings, Biography, Miscellaneous box, Abrams Papers, MHI. U.S. Senate, Committee on Armed Services, *Report . . . on the Nomination of General Creighton W. Abrams for . . . Chief of Staff, U.S. Army, with Additional Views of Senator Margaret Chase Smith*; *Washington Post*, 13 Oct 72, p. P–2; both in Miscellaneous/Calendar Backup box, Abrams Papers, MHI. Abrams' post-Vietnam activities are covered in Sorley, *Thunderbolt*, pp. 339–78.

constant pressure on all elements of the enemy's political and military system. As it turned out, however, his experience at Paris would prove the most relevant to the problems he was to face as COMUSMACV.[58]

During General Weyand's first four months in command, MACV's activities continued with little change. The command provided fixed- and rotary-wing air support, naval gunfire, and advice to the South Vietnamese as they battled to retake areas the Communists had overrun in the spring offensive. On 16 September, after a prolonged struggle, Vietnamese marines raised the republic's red and gold flag over the rubble of Quang Tri's citadel, signaling the symbolic recapture of that lost province. During the summer and

General Weyand is named Army Chief of Staff after serving as COMUSMACV.

early autumn, under Project ENHANCE and other programs, the Military Assistance Command presided over an influx of American weapons and equipment to replace the combat losses of the South Vietnamese armed forces and complete their expansion under the improvement and modernization plan. At the same time, American troop withdrawals continued. On 29 August, after consultations among Secretary Laird, the Joint Chiefs, and General Weyand, President Nixon announced another redeployment of 12,000 men, to be completed by 30 November. This fourteenth withdrawal increment, which lowered MACV's strength to 27,000, turned out to be the last but one. In December, Nixon held off further reductions pending the outcome of the critical military and diplomatic actions then under way.[59]

The Blow Parried

By the end of summer 1972, the Military Assistance Command and its South Vietnamese allies had fought the enemy's offensive to a stand-

---

[58] Gen Frederick C. Weyand, Biographical Summary, CMH. Weyand's view of the Vietnam War can be found in Weyand Debrief, 15 Jul 68, pp. 3–4.

[59] The recovery of Quang Tri is recounted in Andrade, *Trial by Fire*, chs. 11 and 12. Clarke, *Final Years*, pp. 452–53, details the reequipment effort. Redeployment is discussed in Historical Division, "Joint Chiefs of Staff and the War in Vietnam, 1971–1973," pt. 2, pp. 465–70; MACV History, 1972–73, vol. 2, an. F, p. 59.

still and rolled it back in some areas. Yet the long-run implications of the spring and summer battles were uncertain. The North Vietnamese and Viet Cong had failed to destroy Saigon's army and had been unable to take and hold permanently any important places. They had disrupted pacification in some provinces, but no general political uprising had accompanied the general military offensive. By the end of the summer, the enemy had lost perhaps 100,000 troops killed and much of his stock of tanks and heavy equipment; his units were depleted and exhausted. Although probably of little immediate effect on the fighting in the South, LINEBACKER and the mining campaign had drastically reduced North Vietnam's imports of both civilian and military goods and wrecked a large part of the North's industrial and transportation infrastructure. On the other hand, South Vietnam also had suffered severely. The southern republic's casualties included at least 10,000 soldiers killed and 33,000 wounded, as well as large quantities of tanks, artillery pieces, and other equipment destroyed or captured. About 25,000 civilians died in the fighting and nearly one million were left homeless. North Vietnamese troops held about half the land area of Military Region 1, although only a tiny fraction of the people, and they had established themselves in a strip of lightly populated territory along the borders of Military Regions 2 and 3.[60]

As a test of Vietnamization, the results of the campaign were subject to varying interpretation. General Abrams attributed allied success to the courage and resilience of Saigon's armed forces. Their willingness to stand and fight, he insisted, had enabled American air power to play its critical role in beating back the enemy. In his private assessments for Admiral Moorer, General Vogt painted a less flattering portrait of the South Vietnamese performance, noting for example that in the battle for Quang Tri, South Vietnamese troops repeatedly broke and ran under bombardment by North Vietnamese artillery. Whereas Abrams cited shortcomings in command and control as the principal cause of South Vietnamese setbacks, Vogt asserted that Saigon's troops lacked fighting spirit. American air power alone, Vogt contended, had saved South Vietnam from collapse. On 6 June, he told Moorer: "If it was not for the air and the carriers offshore, the whole ground war would have gone down the drain a long time ago. That is 100 percent truth." In fact, South Vietnamese troops had fought well in some places and poorly in others. The differences in performance often were due to objective tactical and materiel factors, such as North Vietnamese superiority in armor and long-range artillery at particular points, as well as to command failures and lack of morale. In the end, the South Vietnamese had survived a heavy blow, but U.S. air power and advisers

---

[60] Results of the offensive are conveniently summarized in Andrade, *Trial by Fire*, pp. 527–38. For representative contemporary analyses, see State Department, Bureau of Intelligence and Research, Study, 17 Jul 72, sub: Vietnam: The July Balance Sheet on Hanoi's Offensive, box 161, and CIA Intelligence Memorandum, 22 Aug 72, box 097, NSC files, Nixon Papers, NARA.

clearly had provided the margin of success. For the moment, a rough battlefield equilibrium had been established, and neither side possessed the immediate capacity to upset it.[61]

[61] Quotations are from Historical Division, "Joint Chiefs of Staff and the War in Vietnam, 1971–1973." Clarke, *Final Years*, pp. 481–89, gives a balanced summary of South Vietnamese strengths and weaknesses during the offensive.

12

The Final Phasedown

During the autumn of 1972, the Military Assistance Command was preparing for its final drawdown to a 15,000-man Military Assistance Group as General Weyand and his subordinates made plans for continuing the war into 1973. At that point, a sudden breakthrough occurred in the secret Paris negotiations. Dr. Kissinger and his Communist opposite number, Le Duc Tho, achieved a cease-fire agreement that rendered invalid the assumptions about redeployment and Vietnamization under which Weyand and his command had been working up to that time. In this changed political environment, MACV had to plan for and carry out new and difficult tasks even as it dismantled itself at an accelerated pace.

Peace Nearly at Hand

As Nixon and Kissinger had thought likely, once the Easter offensive's inconclusive outcome became evident, the North Vietnamese moved quickly to serious negotiations.[1] In July, Le Duc Tho, a member of the North Vietnamese Politburo, resumed his secret Paris talks with Kissinger. On 8 October, after weeks of diplomatic sparring, the North Vietnamese dropped their long-standing demand for Thieu's removal and the establishment of a coalition government in Saigon. Since the United States previously had abandoned its insistence that North Vietnam withdraw its troops from the south, the stage was set for rapid progress. On 12 October, Kissinger and Le Duc Tho concluded a draft agreement. On the twenty-third, as a gesture of good faith, Nixon stopped the bombing of North Vietnam above the 20th Parallel.[2]

Le Duc Tho's concession, which surprised and dismayed the leaders of the southern Viet Cong, stemmed in large part from North Vietnam's military situation in late 1972. North Vietnamese and Viet Cong forces

---

[1] The following account is based on Kissinger, *White House Years*, pp. 1301–1473; and Walter Scott Dillard, *Sixty Days to Peace: Implementing the Paris Peace Accords, Vietnam 1973* (Washington, D.C.: National Defense University Press, 1982), pp. 5–26.

[2] Thompson, "Rolling Thunder to Linebacker," ch. 9, pp. 64–65, recounts the decision to cut back bombing of North Vietnam.

Kissinger and Le Duc Tho

in the south were exhausted and depleted; they required an extended pause for recovery. The American bombing and mining campaign—a campaign that had elicited no effective response from Hanoi's Russian and Chinese allies—had reduced North Vietnam's economy and air defenses to a shambles. So long as the bombing and blockade continued, North Vietnam could not secure the wherewithal to rebuild its forces. In the United States, Nixon had momentarily faced down the antiwar movement by responding forcefully to the Easter offensive, and he seemed certain to defeat his Democratic opponent, Senator George McGovern, in the coming presidential election. At the same time, the military equilibrium in South Vietnam clearly depended heavily on continued American support of the South Vietnamese Army with air power and materiel. If U.S. attacks on the North could be stopped and American air power removed from the war, Saigon's army might well collapse under renewed Communist attack. Taking all these factors into account, the North was willing to accept the temporary survival of the Thieu regime as the price for removing the American aid that propped it up.[3]

---

[3] Larry Berman, *No Peace, No Honor: Nixon, Kissinger, and Betrayal in Vietnam* (New York: Free Press, 2001), p. 176. For a Communist view of the state of their forces, see Tran Van Tra,

The draft terms of the Paris agreement called for an in-place cease-fire within twenty-four hours of the formal signing of the instrument and withdrawal of all American troops and materiel within sixty days. Simultaneously, American and Vietnamese military prisoners of war, but not Viet Cong civilian detainees, were to be released. Both sides were to refrain from enlarging their armed forces in South Vietnam but could replace equipment on a one-for-one basis. Under the political provisions, Thieu's regime would remain in place until a National Council of National Reconciliation and Concord, composed of equal numbers of representatives of the Saigon government, the Viet Cong Provisional Revolutionary Government, and a neutral "third force," could organize national elections in South Vietnam. However, the National Council was to make decisions on the basis of unanimity and possessed no independent means of enforcing any decrees it managed to issue. All sides pledged to respect the neutrality, sovereignty, and territorial integrity of Laos and Cambodia and to refrain from using those countries as bases for attacking each other. Four-party and two-party military commissions representing the belligerents and an international control commission of neutrals were to implement the agreement and oversee compliance with its terms.[4]

Nixon and Kissinger believed that the agreement would allow the United States to recover its prisoners of war and disengage while still securing its minimum objective in South Vietnam: the continued survival of the Saigon government and its access to American financial and materiel support, at least for a while. President Thieu would be able to keep thousands of Viet Cong in jail, and he would possess a veto over decisions of the National Council. This possibility meant that elections could occur in South Vietnam only when Thieu considered them to his advantage. While the agreement would allow some 150,000 North Vietnamese troops to remain inside South Vietnam, it would leave Saigon with forces many times as large and in control of all the heavily populated areas of the country. When consulted on the agreement, Secretary Laird and General Abrams endorsed it as the best the allies could obtain. Abrams observed that the allies would be no better off militarily if they continued fighting for another year on the same scale, which he doubted that they would be able to do, given congressional pressure to cut back or end U.S. operations.[5]

President Thieu saw the agreement differently. From his perspective, a complete American pullout, in combination with a continued North Vietnamese military presence in the South and recognition of the Provisional Revolutionary Government as a political entity on a

Vietnam: History of the Bulwark B2 Theater, vol. 5, *Concluding the 30-Years War* (Ho Chi Minh City: Van Nghe Publishing House, 1982). Trans. by Foreign Broadcast Information Service, Feb 1983, pp. 33–34 (hereafter cited as Tran Van Tra, *Bulwark B2*).

[4] Texts of the agreement and its protocols are in Dillard, *Sixty Days to Peace*, apps. A–E.

[5] Abrams' views are summarized in Kissinger, *White House Years*, pp. 1365–67, 1374.

par with his government, meant ultimate disaster for his country. In addition, he felt compelled by domestic political considerations to display independence of the Americans. Accordingly, on 18 October, when Kissinger, accompanied by General Abrams, presented the agreement to Thieu, the South Vietnamese leader rejected it. As an act of South Vietnamese self-assertion, Thieu demanded a long list of major and minor changes in the document.

The North Vietnamese had difficulties of their own with their southern allies. Leaders of the National Liberation Front and the Provisional Revolutionary Government, although represented at the formal Paris talks, had been left out of the negotiations between Kissinger and Le Duc Tho. When the southerners learned of the draft terms, they objected to the exclusion of their civilian comrades from the prisoner exchange and to Thieu's continuation in control of Saigon's political apparatus. Like their enemies, the southern Communists wanted to amend the agreement to serve their interests.[6]

There ensued a confusing period of three-sided jockeying between the United States and the two Vietnams. Pressing for an early conclusion of the deal, the North Vietnamese publicized its terms on 26 October. Kissinger responded by telling a news conference that "peace is at hand." During November and early December, in negotiations over Thieu's amendments and over the protocols implementing the agreement, the North Vietnamese hardened their position and made their own demands for American concessions on critical points. In mid-December, the negotiations collapsed. Nixon, a landslide reelection behind him, resumed the mining of North Vietnam's ports. Between 18 and 29 December, he conducted the so-called "Christmas bombing," a series of unprecedentedly heavy B–52 and tactical air strikes on targets in and around Hanoi and Haiphong. At the same time, Nixon pressed Thieu to endorse the agreement. He threatened that if the South Vietnamese remained adamant, the United States would conclude peace without them and terminate military and economic aid.

In the end, both North and South Vietnam gave way. When the Paris talks resumed early in January 1973, the North Vietnamese withdrew their most objectionable alterations to the October terms. On 21 January, Thieu finally endorsed the agreement. On 23 January 1973, Kissinger and Le Duc Tho initialed the Paris Peace Accords and their ancillary protocols.

Preparing for a Cease-Fire

For MACV, the months between the October breakthrough and the signing of the Paris Peace Accords were a hectic period of planning and preparation for the final American withdrawal and the replacement

---

[6] Southern Communist and non-Communist reactions are summarized in Berman, *No Peace, No Honor*, pp. 176–77.

of MACV by other organizations. The process was plagued with difficulties, many of which stemmed from the secrecy that had shrouded Kissinger's diplomacy. From the start of the national security adviser's meetings with Le Duc Tho in 1969, only President Nixon, a few of Kissinger's National Security Council staff, and Ambassador Bunker had been aware of the private negotiations in progress. Until January 1972, the State and Defense Departments, the Joint Chiefs of Staff, and the Central Intelligence Agency were not informed of the talks. MACV had maintained liaison officers with the formal Paris delegation and furnished information to it but had no knowledge of the secret meetings and of the concessions that Kissinger was offering. This ambiguity meant that the military conducted its redeployment and Vietnamization planning, and executed the plans, without reference to the changing U.S. diplomatic position.[7]

MACV received its first inkling that a termination of hostilities might be imminent late in September 1972. At that time, Kissinger directed Bunker and Weyand to encourage the South Vietnamese to "move promptly and seize the maximum amount of critical territory." During Kissinger's and Abrams' mid-October visit to Saigon, Kissinger briefed Ambassador Bunker and General Weyand on the proposed peace terms; but he forbade them to reveal the information to their staffs at that time. MACV's planning began only after the North Vietnamese publicly announced the state of the negotiations. On 30 October, via the special channel the administration had set up for sensitive policy matters, Kissinger instructed Bunker to start MACV working on the details of organizing the four-party commission that was to implement the cease-fire and supervise the exchange of prisoners and the American troop withdrawal. Bunker was to bring Weyand "completely into [the] picture" on the Paris talks and have him form a small staff to do the planning. Without exchanging written documents, Weyand was to include General Vien in the deliberations. Although initially requesting only an organization and staffing plan for the commission, Kissinger soon expanded Weyand's task to defining exactly what a cease-fire would mean in a war without fronts and how to bring it into effect.[8]

To lead the MACV planning group, Weyand turned to his chief of staff, Maj. Gen. Gilbert H. Woodward. Fortuitously, Woodward was uniquely qualified for the task. Having served as staff secretary to the Berlin Command in 1953 and senior member of the United Nations Command Armistice Commission in Korea from 1968 to 1969, the period of the *Pueblo* crisis, Woodward possessed a rich fund of experience in dealing with Communist military negotiators. His planning

[7] Ibid., pp. 43–44.

[8] Dillard, *Sixty Days to Peace*, pp. 8–10, 15–18. Msgs, Kissinger WHS 2212 to Bunker, 28 Sep 72; Kissinger WHS 2305 to Bunker, 30 Oct 72; Haig WHS 2312 to Bunker, 4 Nov 72. All in box 413, NSC files, Nixon Papers.

General Woodward (center)

group initially consisted of a Marine colonel and an Army major from the MACV Operations Directorate. Equipped with a copy of the draft agreement, the two planners set up shop in an office next to Woodward's. They, and others who joined them later, enjoyed direct access to both Woodward and General Weyand. As the planning progressed, Weyand through personal conferences kept General Vien informed and sought his counterpart's views. Despite President Thieu's intransigence, Vien maintained a cooperative attitude and made useful suggestions.[9]

By early November, General Woodward and his team had outlined how the Four-Party Joint Military Commission should be organized and the requirements for an effective cease-fire. They proposed that the commission be headed by a major general or equivalent from each party (the United States, South Vietnam, North Vietnam, and the Viet Cong's Provisional Revolutionary Government), assisted by a staff in Saigon with equal representation from all sides. In the field, four regional control groups, one for each military region, and subgroups at province level and below, would try to enforce the armistice terms. Those terms, Weyand and his planners stated, at minimum must provide for determining the size and positions of opposing forces, defining the territorial limits of each side's control, forestalling last-minute land-grabbing, and establishing monitored entry points for each side's introduction of supplies and replacement equipment. Weyand observed that the purpose of a cease-fire in this unconventional war would be "to stop the shooting and free the political negotiating process from the pressures of armed force." Hence, the armistice terms must allow

[9] Dillard, *Sixty Days to Peace*, pp. 11–12.

Saigon's police and troops the latitude to protect their population from small-scale attacks by Viet Cong guerrillas, who could be expected to continue to operate despite the cease-fire.[10]

MACV's submissions formed the basis of the American position in the Paris negotiations over the protocols to the main agreement. Woodward and his team supported the talks by reviewing North Vietnamese proposals and drafting responses and modifications of the American plan. Early in January, Woodward and one of his chief planners, Maj. Paul L. Miles, traveled to Paris to participate in the last stages of the technical negotiations. The final cease-fire protocol closely followed the principles MACV had outlined. However, in a concession to the Communists, which the South Vietnamese resented, the Americans agreed that the four-party commission's field structure would conform to the enemy's geographical command and administrative organization rather than Saigon's. It would consist of seven regional control groups instead of four and twenty-six subregional ones. While the organizational aspects of the cease-fire were settled at Paris, the negotiators, in both the main agreement and the protocols, avoided the complex political-military question of defining each side's area of territorial control in South Vietnam. Instead, the military commanders in the field were to settle that issue among themselves. Viewed with consternation by Weyand and Woodward, this omission set the stage for future problems in establishing and enforcing the armistice.[11]

While General Woodward and his team worked on the Four-Party Joint Military Commission, other groups in MACV headquarters planned for the final withdrawal of American forces from South Vietnam and for MACV's successor military organizations. None of MACV's many contingency plans for the termination of hostilities envisioned total removal of American forces from South Vietnam; hence, the planners had to start from scratch. Until late in the process, all the planning was done by small, compartmented groups of officers under conditions of extreme secrecy. A limited number of people, unable to communicate with each other because of the tight security, "worked unbelievably long hours doing what the overall staff could have accomplished in a routine manner." As the Paris negotiations alternately progressed and halted, the planners repeatedly had to revise their assumptions and their work. They labored under uncertain deadlines, since no one could predict when the contemplated cease-fire actually would take place and withdrawals begin.[12]

---

[10] Ibid., pp. 13–14. Msgs, Bunker Saigon 0248 to Kissinger, 4 Nov 72; Bunker Saigon 0253 to Kissinger, 7 Nov 72. Both in box 413, NSC files, Nixon Papers, NARA. Quotation is from last-cited message.

[11] Maj Gen Gilbert H. Woodward, Briefing, sub: The Four-Party Joint Military Commission, pp. 4–5, box 1, Gilbert H. Woodward Papers, MHI; Dillard, *Sixty Days to Peace*, p. 13. Berman, *No Peace, No Honor*, pp. 178–79, emphasizes the avoidance of the territorial issue.

[12] Quotation is from Essay, "Cautionary Notes"; see also Memo, sub: Answers to Historical Questions. . . . Both in folder, interview with Col R. L. Branch (Special Planning Groups) MACV

Immediately after Kissinger's mid-October visit, General Weyand put a small steering group to work on a general concept for redeploying all U.S. and South Korean forces within sixty days of a cease-fire. On 27 October, he received instructions from the Joint Chiefs to continue planning for the troop withdrawal and also to prepare proposals for two successor command organizations: an oversized Defense Attaché Office in Saigon, to manage continuing American assistance to the South Vietnamese military, and a joint headquarters in Thailand to conduct post-cease-fire U.S. operations in Vietnam, Laos, and Cambodia. Weyand assigned the task of planning for the headquarters in Thailand to the MACV Directorate of Operations. The MACV Directorate of Logistics took on the planning for the Defense Attaché Office, since that office primarily would perform supply tasks. Each directorate initially formed a small close-held planning group, which gradually drew in the rest of the staff as the approach of agreement in Paris permitted a relaxation of security restrictions.[13]

Planning for the new headquarters in Thailand was punctuated by a final round of interservice debate over command and control of air operations in Southeast Asia. After MACV submitted its initial concept early in November, the Army and Air Force chiefs of staff argued that the new headquarters should have targeting and tasking authority over all American air forces in Southeast Asia, including the Strategic Air Command's B–52s and the Pacific Fleet's carriers. Admiral Moorer, supported by the chief of naval operations and the commandant of the Marine Corps, objected to this proposal as reviving the already rejected concept of a Southeast Asia Command. Instead, Moorer preferred to continue in Thailand the more limited jurisdiction then possessed by MACV. Secretary Laird endorsed Moorer's position.[14]

That argument settled, the Military Assistance Command completed plans for a headquarters entitled U.S. Support Activities Group/Seventh Air Force (USSAG/7AF), to be located at Nakhon Phanom Air Base in Thailand. A "multi-service integrated headquarters" under CINCPAC's operational command, USSAG/7AF was to exercise operational control of Air Force units based in Thailand and was to command the Defense Attaché Office in Saigon, thereby overseeing military aid to South Vietnam. It was to plan and conduct post-cease-fire American air operations in Vietnam, Laos, and Cambodia, for which purpose it could tie in to the South Vietnamese Air Force's air control system. Command of the B–52s was to remain with Strategic Air Command, which would maintain a liaison team at Nakhon Phanom, and that of the carriers with Pacific Fleet. In structure, the 600-man headquarters was essentially a

Collection, MHI. MACV History, 1972–73, vol. 1, p. 103.

[13] Msg, Weyand MAC 10291 to Abrams, 28 Oct 72, box A, Abrams Papers, MHI; MACV History, 1972–73, vol. 2, an. G, pp. 1–2, 8–9.

[14] MACV History, 1972–73, vol. 2, an. G, p. 2; Essay, "Cautionary Notes," in folder, interview with Col R. L. Branch (Special Planning Groups), MACV Collection, MHI; Historical Division, "Joint Chiefs of Staff and the War in Vietnam, 1971–1973," pt. 2, pp. 643–45.

shrunken version of MACV with many of its key officers double-hatted as members of the Seventh Air Force staff, also to be located at Nakhon Phanom. An Air Force general was to command USSAG/7AF with an Army major general as deputy, and Air Force officers would head all the general staff divisions except those for personnel and logistics, which had Army chiefs. Secretary Laird approved this concept on 17 November and authorized the Joint Chiefs and CINCPAC to take the necessary steps for establishing the new headquarters as soon as the cease-fire went into effect. During December, the State Department, through the American ambassador in Bangkok, secured the necessary permission from the initially reluctant Thai authorities.[15]

Within the Directorate of Logistics, a planning group headed by Col. Raymond L. Branch, chief of the Logistics Operations Center, struggled to flesh out the size, organization, and functions of the Defense Attaché Office, which initially went by the cumbersome title, quickly changed, of Defense Resources Surveillance and Termination Office. To continue assistance to the South Vietnamese after a total American military pullout, the planners, with no precedents to guide them, had to construct a unique hybrid civilian-military organization within manpower and functional limits that changed repeatedly with the ebb and flow of the Paris negotiations. They had to identify all the activities, both of the government and private contractors, that had grown up to assist the South Vietnamese and determine which ones U.S. civilian agencies could assume and which must remain under military direction through the Defense Attaché Office. Some activities, a participant recalled, "came out of the woodwork" as the planning proceeded.[16]

Despite these difficulties, between late October 1972 and January 1973, Branch's group gradually filled in the outline of an organization of 50 military personnel and about 1,200 government and contract civilians, which was to occupy the MACV headquarters building at Tan Son Nhut. An Army major general was to head the office and sit on the ambassador's country team as senior American military representative in South Vietnam. In the military chain of command, he was to report to the commander of the USSAG/7AF. The Defense Attaché Office had a division for operations and plans, a division for assistance to each South Vietnamese military service, and directorates for communications-electronics, and support, as well as small field offices around the country. It was to furnish the limited advice and support to Saigon's armed forces permitted under the Paris Peace Accords and plan and administer continuing financial and material assistance by the Defense

[15] MACV History, 1972–73, vol. 2, an. G, pp. 2–4. Msgs, State 223339 to Bangkok, 9 Dec 72; Bangkok 17592 to State, 14 Dec 72. Both in box 1022, NSC files, Nixon Papers, NARA.

[16] MACV History, 1972–73, vol. 2, an. G, pp. 8–9. Interview of Col R. L. Branch, 6 Apr 73, and accompanying documents in folder, interview with Col R. L. Branch (Special Planning Groups), MACV Collection, MHI, describes the planning problems.

Department and the individual U.S. services. It also would report on and evaluate South Vietnamese military operations. Most pacification support functions, however, were to be transferred to the American embassy when MACV closed down.[17]

While the separate planning groups were still refining the details of MACV's successor entities, the headquarters completed its outline plan for the final drawdown. Published on 9 November as OPLAN J215, this plan was initially code-named THUNDERBOLT, in honor of General Abrams, and later renamed, more descriptively, COUNTDOWN. It brought all cease-fire-related redeployments and reorganizations together in a single schedule built around a still hypothetical cease-fire date, designated X-Day.

The plan had three phases. In Phase I, before X-Day, units would begin standing down, the USSAG/7AF advance party would move to Nakhon Phanom, and MACV would complete equipment and facilities transfers to the South Vietnamese. In Phase II, X-Day to X plus 45, most U.S. and Korean troops would leave; the Defense Attaché Office was to be activated, initially under MACV's operational control; the USSAG/7AF headquarters main body would move to Thailand; and MACV would begin turning over its functions to the new agencies and the American embassy. In Phase III, X plus 45 to X plus 60, all remaining American and Korean forces were to depart except for the Defense Attaché Office staff; the successor organizations would go into full operation; and on X plus 60 MACV headquarters would go out of business. Paralleling the MACV standdown, the four Regional Assistance Command headquarters would start closing down on X plus 30. However, regional, division, and other field advisers would remain in place and continue reporting to MACV until X plus 45. MACV would retain enough aircraft and communications equipment in South Vietnam to exercise command and control until X plus 50. The Army, Navy, and Air Force component commands would be responsible for the details of troop redeployments and the transfer of equipment and bases to the South Vietnamese. When the plan was published in early November, the length of Phase I was uncertain. In fact, it lasted nearly three months, time that MACV and its subordinate commands put to good use to perfect their plans and preparations.[18]

Besides planning for its own dissolution, the Military Assistance Command launched a final drive to place the South Vietnamese armed forces in the best possible position before the cease-fire. Between October and January, the command transferred to the South Vietnamese title to all of its bases and facilities, including those still occupied by U.S. units, which became in effect tenants of their ally. This expedient was necessary because the Paris Peace Accords required the dismantling of all bases still under American ownership when the cease-fire went

[17] MACV History, 1972–73, vol. 1, p. 138; vol. 2, an. G, pp. 9–12.
[18] Ibid., vol. 2, an. H, pp. 1–2.

into effect. (To permit this maneuver, U.S. negotiators at Paris had purposely kept the wording of the agreement ambiguous on the issue of what constituted "American" bases.) At the same time, the command oversaw a massive effort to complete the equipping of South Vietnam's forces and building up their materiel stockpiles. The Americans made sure that formal title to all the items was passed to Saigon before X-Day, when the one-for-one replacement provision of the agreement would begin to apply. Supplementing earlier programs for replacing RVNAF combat losses and equipping new units, President Nixon late in October initiated Project ENHANCE PLUS. Under it, between 23 October and 12 December, MACV received and distributed over 105,000 equipment items, including medium and light tanks, armored personnel carriers, artillery pieces, fixed-wing aircraft, and helicopters, many taken from U.S. reserve components or diverted from military assistance programs for other American allies. When the cease-fire went into effect in January, the South Vietnamese possessed reserves of major items well in excess of authorized unit requirements. Much of this materiel was in storage, awaiting the activation and training of the battalions and squadrons that would use it.[19]

On the eve of the cease-fire, South Vietnam's armed forces, their losses from the North Vietnamese offensive made good and their combat capabilities enhanced by additional armor, antitank, and aviation elements, ranked as the fifth largest in the world. They appeared to enjoy overwhelming superiority over the North Vietnamese and Viet Cong. South Vietnam had about 1.1 million men under arms, about half in the regular army, navy, and air force, and the rest in territorial, police, and paramilitary formations. The regular army included eleven infantry divisions and one airborne division, seven Ranger groups, seven nondivisional armored cavalry squadrons, three M48 medium tank battalions (two in training), thirty-three border defense Ranger battalions (descendants of the old CIDG units), five 175-mm. artillery battalions (three in training), forty-one 105-mm. artillery battalions, fifteen 155-mm. artillery battalions, and four air defense artillery battalions (one in training and two still to be activated). The Regional and Popular Forces possessed their own artillery support in the form of 204 platoons of 105-mm. guns. South Vietnam's Air Force had a planned strength of sixty-six squadrons, of which thirty-nine were operational and twelve in training at the time of the cease-fire. Its 1,099 fixed-wing aircraft included jet fighters and fighter-bombers, and its pilots flew 1,098 helicopters of various types. The Vietnamese Navy possessed

[19] Dillard, *Sixty Days to Peace*, pp. 60–61; Clarke, *Final Years*, pp. 452–53; MACV History, 1972–73, vol. 1, p. 104 and an. C, pp. 20–21, 74, 77. Memo, Laird for the Assistant to the President for National Security Affairs, 13 Oct 72, sub: RVNAF Supply Status . . . , box 162; Memo, Sec Def Elliot L. Richardson for the Assistant to the President for National Security Affairs, 17 Mar 73, sub: Replacement of RVNAF Combat Losses, box 163, NSC files, Nixon Papers, NARA.

about 1,500 riverine, coastal surveillance, harbor defense, and logistic and support craft and included as well a division-size marine corps.[20]

As had been true since the days of Ngo Dinh Diem, and despite MACV's best efforts, the impressive facade concealed significant weaknesses. It was questionable whether South Vietnam's available manpower base could sustain its forces over the long term; and its economy could carry the load only with continuing, substantial American assistance. The South Vietnamese still depended heavily on American technical support in areas such as maintenance of the sophisticated equipment, which the United States had poured in under ENHANCE PLUS. Weak top-level leadership, inequitable promotion systems, high desertion rates, and neglect of troop and dependent welfare persisted despite American exhortations and South Vietnamese promises of reform. For all the expansion of its air force, Saigon could not carry on anything like the Americans' interdiction campaign against the Ho Chi Minh Trail.[21]

Perhaps most ominous for the future, Saigon's ground forces, with most of the infantry divisions still closely tied to particular localities, remained without adequate mobile reserves to counter concentrated attacks like those the North Vietnamese had launched in 1972. American airpower had filled the gap during that offensive, but the days of that support's availability were numbered. During the summer of 1972, President Nixon, at Kissinger's urging, prodded the Defense Department for action on this issue. Secretary Laird, however, supported by the Joint Chiefs and Generals Abrams and Weyand, declared that no drastic reorganization or expansion of the South Vietnamese Army was possible at that stage. Instead, Laird said, the United States must rely on a "sequential and evolutionary approach" emphasizing continued improvement of the territorial forces and gradual steps to free regular divisions from static security tasks. There the question rested until the cease-fire. In the end, Vietnamization had prepared the South Vietnamese to hold their own against Viet Cong guerrillas supported by North Vietnamese light infantry. Their capacity by themselves to defeat a major conventional North Vietnamese assault with heavy mechanized and artillery formations was as much in doubt as ever.[22]

---

[20] MACV History, 1972–73, vol. 1, an. C, pp. 19–20, 84. South Vietnam's world ranking is noted in William S. Turley, *The Second Indochina War: A Short Political and Military History, 1954–1975* (New York: New American Library, 1987), p. 161.

[21] Clarke, *Final Years*, pp. 462–69. General Cao Van Vien and Lt. Gen. Dong Van Khuyen, *Reflections on the Vietnam War*, Indochina Monographs (Washington, D.C.: U.S. Army Center of Military History, 1980), pp. 113–14.

[22] Clarke, *Final Years*, pp. 517–18; Vien and Khuyen, *Reflections*, pp. 114–15. Quotation is from Memo, Laird for the Assistant to the President for National Security Affairs, 4 Aug 72, sub: Reserve Forces for the RVNAF, box 161, NSC files, Nixon Papers, NARA. For examples of White House concern, see Memo, Kissinger for the Sec Def, 12 Jul 72, sub: Military Assistance to the RVN, box 1019; and Memo, Odeen for Kissinger, 20 Sep 72, sub: Additional Mobile Reserve Units for RVNAF, box 161. Both in NSC files, Nixon Papers, NARA.

South Vietnam's forces were not severely tested during most of the time between the diplomatic breakthrough in October and the signing of the agreement in January. On the ground, military activity declined. The North Vietnamese and Viet Cong concentrated on refitting their battered forces. They also used guerrillas and small main force elements to establish a presence in as many areas as possible. The South Vietnamese countered these efforts with renewed pacification and population control campaigns. There were upsurges of combat in October and again in late January, as each side attempted last-minute land grabbing in anticipation of the armistice.[23]

During those months, MACV continued its air operations in South Vietnam, Cambodia, and Laos, as well as in North Vietnam below the 20th Parallel. The command played only a subordinate part in the December LINEBACKER II bombing campaign, which was concentrated around Hanoi and Haiphong, in route packages over which MACV had no jurisdiction. Because the B–52s, with their massive bomb loads and all-weather attack capability, played the central role in the campaign, Secretary Laird and the Joint Chiefs placed the Strategic Air Command headquarters at Omaha, Nebraska, in charge of scheduling, targeting, and planning the missions. Strategic Air Command issued operational instructions to the Eighth Air Force on Guam, the carrier Task Force 77 in the Gulf of Tonkin, and the MACV/Seventh Air Force in Saigon. General Vogt's headquarters had little to do but respond, often on short notice, to Strategic Air Command's demands for escort and other missions. As an Air Force historian put it, during LINEBACKER II, Strategic Air Command "was not merely going its own way, but instructing Seventh Air Force to follow along smartly."[24]

The Final Drawdown

On 27 January 1973, at the International Conference Center in Paris, Secretary of State Rogers and the foreign ministers of North and South Vietnam and the People's Revolutionary Government formally signed the "Agreement on Ending the War and Restoring Peace in Vietnam" and its supporting protocols. With that action, a cease-fire went into effect in South Vietnam, and the sixty-day countdown began for final American withdrawal and MACV's inactivation. General Weyand and his subordinates at once put into execution the plans they had carefully worked out during the previous three months.

On 28 January, Weyand activated the U.S. delegation to the Four-Party Joint Military Commission. To head the delegation, the administration, at Weyand's recommendation, selected General Woodward.

---

[23] MACV History, 1972–73, vol. 1, pp. 103–04, an. A, p. 7.

[24] Historical Division, "Joint Chiefs of Staff and the War in Vietnam, 1971–1973," pt. 2, pp. 666–78; Thompson, "Rolling Thunder to Linebacker," ch., 10, pp. 1–3, 23–24, 33–37, 40–49, 50–51. Quotation is from pp. 23–24.

General Wickham, who had been serving as MACV deputy chief of staff for economic affairs, became Woodward's deputy. Like Woodward, Wickham had experience in dealing with Cold War confrontation lines, having served in Berlin and on the Demilitarized Zone in Korea. Personnel from MACV headquarters, most of whom had participated in planning for the commission, constituted the U.S. delegation's central staff in Saigon. Officers and enlisted men from the regional assistance commands formed the delegation's regional and subregional teams. To ensure close coordination between MACV headquarters and the Four-Party Joint Military Commission, General Woodward retained his other "hat" as MACV chief of staff until the new organization was well launched. Woodward reported to Washington through General Weyand and the military chain of command. He also worked closely with Ambassador Bunker, who had final authority on political matters. The Nixon administration gave Bunker, Weyand, and Woodward wide freedom of action and full and prompt support in the unfolding negotiations over implementation of the Paris terms.

During the commission's negotiations, Woodward held regular conferences, outside the plenary sessions, with his South Vietnamese counterpart, General Dzu, and with Dzu's successor, Lt. Gen. Du Quoc Dong, to harmonize the allies' positions. When necessary, which it often was, Bunker and Weyand assisted Woodward in obtaining decisions from President Thieu, who allowed Dzu and Dong little discretion. Further facilitating American liaison with the South Vietnamese, General Wickham established a close working relationship with the influential deputy chief of the Saigon delegation, Brig. Gen. Phan Hoa Hiep, who had close personal ties to Thieu. [25]

General Woodward's task was far from easy. At every stage of the Four-Party Joint Military Commission's existence and every step of its work, he had to contend with the mutual hostility and conflicting political agendas of the two Vietnamese sides. President Thieu had signed on to the Paris agreements only under extreme American pressure, and his government dragged its feet at every point of their implementation. The South Vietnamese reneged on a commitment to provide logistical support for the field elements of the Four-Party Joint Military Commission and the International Commission for Control and Supervision. To fill the gap, the MACV Directorate of Logistics and the regional assistance commands took on the housing, feeding, and transportation of the armistice organizations. For their part, the North Vietnamese and the Provisional Revolutionary Government haggled over the smallest procedural details, usually in order to expand the Provisional Revolutionary Government's organizational presence throughout South Vietnam and enhance its governmental status. They attempted to establish linkages between issues that the Paris agree-

---

[25] Dillard, *Sixty Days to Peace*, pp. 29–49, 181; Msg, Weyand MAC 11038 to Abrams, 21 Nov 72, box A, Abrams Papers, MHI.

ments had clearly separated. For example, they tried to tie the release of Viet Cong civilian detainees to the exchange of military prisoners. Most damaging, on the excuse, which was largely valid, that the South Vietnamese had failed to provide the requisite support and security, the Communists never fully manned their parts of the Four-Party Joint Military Commission's regional and subregional offices, thereby crippling enforcement of the cease-fire.[26]

Through a judicious combination of tact, patience, and firmness, General Woodward kept the Four-Party Joint Military Commission moving forward on the commission's three basic tasks: supervising American and South Korean troop withdrawals, accounting for and exchanging captive military personnel, and attempting to stop the shooting. Of these tasks, the commission fully discharged the first two before it went out of existence on 29 March. Supervising troop withdrawals was a straightforward matter of stationing observers at the ports and airfields to verify the movement of men and supplies. The prisoner exchange was complicated by the aforementioned Communist attempts at linkage. Backed by Bunker, Weyand, and the administration, Woodward countered those ploys by insisting on exact adherence to the Paris agreement. At one point, he withdrew from commission meetings and the administration temporarily halted redeployments in a display of firmness. The other side, interested above all in getting American forces out of South Vietnam, gave way. In the end, the commission managed the return of 587 American military personnel from captivity in North and South Vietnam and Laos; and the two Vietnamese sides also completed an exchange of their military prisoners.[27]

Despite General Woodward's best efforts, the Four-Party Joint Military Commission failed to end military combat in South Vietnam. The American delegation made a good-faith attempt to enforce a cease-fire, but it faced intractable obstacles. The negotiators at Paris had avoided the politically explosive task of determining which side controlled which territory—a nearly impossible endeavor at any event in an unconventional conflict with no fixed front line. One belligerent, North Vietnam, refused to acknowledge that its army even was present on the battlefield. By refusing to deploy their regional and subregional teams, the North Vietnamese and Viet Cong prevented investigation and resolution of the numerous cease-fire violations. The International Commission for Control and Supervision, made up of Canadians, Indonesians, Poles, and Hungarians, had no better success, due to disagreements between its Communist and non-Communist members and to the Viet Cong's refusal to support or protect its teams

[26] Dillard, *Sixty Days to Peace*, pp. 37–38, 54–67; MACV History, 1972–73, vol. 1, pp. 138–39, vol. 2, an. H, p. 18; Woodward, Briefing, pp. 11–13.

[27] Dillard, *Sixty Days to Peace*, pp. 71–99, 178, 180; Woodward, Briefing, pp. 1–2, 26–28. The negotiations can be followed in detail in General Woodward's Handwritten Notes on the Four-Power Armistice Commission, 2 Feb–14 Mar 73, Woodward Papers, MHI.

in contested areas. After much American prodding, Saigon and the Provisional Revolutionary Government organized the Two-Party Joint Military Commission, which was supposed to enforce the cease-fire after the Four-Party Joint Military Commission disbanded. However, the Two-Party Joint Military Commission, hamstrung by a requirement for unanimous decisions, never functioned at all.[28]

More than any other factor, the unresolved issue of territorial control undermined the cease-fire. Even had the negotiators at Paris made more of an effort than they did to establish the opposing military positions, circumstances on the battlefield would have frustrated their efforts. The war had left the contending Vietnamese forces intermingled in a "leopard spot" pattern. In the many contested rural areas, the degree of Saigon government and Communist control continuously fluctuated, depending in some villages on whether it was day or night. The most practical solution might have been a regrouping of military forces into clearly demarcated, geographically contiguous zones of control, on the pattern of the partition of Vietnam in the 1954 Geneva Agreements; but both Vietnamese sides rejected that approach. President Thieu insisted that his government was sovereign throughout South Vietnam; even after the Paris agreements were signed, he persisted in trying to recover the Communist-controlled regions. For their part, the North Vietnamese and Viet Cong recalled that, after the 1954 regrouping of forces, President Ngo Dinh Diem had used his troops and police to destroy the party's political organization in South Vietnam. They preferred the existing intermingling of armies, which allowed their military units to protect and support the revolutionary political structure. In addition, as of early 1973 the Communists controlled more territory than people; they would have to fight and maneuver to enlarge their population base.[29]

What Kissinger and Le Duc Tho could not settle in Paris, Weyand and Woodward, as they had feared, could not settle in Vietnam. The Vietnamese antagonists, regardless of what they had signed at Paris, intended to resolve the issue between them by armed force. During the first three months after the signing of the Paris agreement, combat in South Vietnam showed no noticeable decline from immediate precease-fire levels. Generals Weyand and Woodward were not surprised by this development. Fully appreciating the complex nature of the Vietnam conflict, they had hoped that the so-called cease-fire at least would reduce rather than end the violence. Even that hope, however, went unrealized.[30]

---

[28] MACV History, 1972–73, vol. 1, p. 139; Dillard, *Sixty Days to Peace*, pp. 137–69, 178, 181–82; Woodward, Briefing, pp. 29–30.

[29] The Communist view is summarized in Tran Van Tra, *Bulwark B2*, pp. 38–39, 44–45. Berman, *No Peace, No Honor*, pp. 8–9, 179, argues that Nixon and Kissinger never expected the cease-fire to work. They wanted from the Paris agreements simply the recovery of American prisoners of war and a legalistic rationale for continued U.S. support of South Vietnam in an ongoing war.

[30] MACV History, 1972–73, vol. 1, pp. 139, 141–49, summarizes military operations.

While General Woodward and his staff struggled to implement the cease-fire, the rest of MACV put in motion the troop withdrawals and headquarters reorganizations of Operation COUNTDOWN. As of 28 January, out of an authorized strength of 27,000 officers and men, the command had 23,335 American personnel actually in South Vietnam, most of them in logistical units, air cavalry troops, helicopter companies, and a Marine aircraft group. These troops, along with about 35,000 South Koreans and 100 or so Thais, Filipinos, and Nationalist Chinese, had to leave South Vietnam by the end of March. The American withdrawal took place in four fifteen-day increments, each consisting of about one-fourth of the force, paralleled by outward shipments of cargo by air and sea. Troop movements proceeded steadily, except for a temporary halt during one of the crises in the prisoner exchange negotiations. The final increment boarded ships and planes between 27 and 29 March, simultaneously with the departure of the last American prisoners of war from Hanoi. The Koreans and other allies managed their own withdrawals. All their forces left South Vietnam well before the end of March.[31]

Formation of the USSAG/7AF headquarters and the Defense Attaché Office followed the three phases outlined in the COUNTDOWN plan. The advance echelon of USSAG/7AF moved to Nakhon Phanom on 29 January. Transfer of the main body, drawn largely from the operations and intelligence sections of MACV and Seventh Air Force, began on 10 February. At 0800 on 15 February, General Vogt, as USSAG/7AF commander, took over from MACV control of American air operations. Additional headquarters and support personnel continued moving from Saigon to Nakhon Phanom during the following month as their MACV staff agencies closed down. As the personnel of USSAG/7AF moved out of the MACV headquarters complex at Tan Son Nhut, civilian members of the Defense Attaché Office arrived for orientation and on-the-job training by their MACV counterparts. On 28 January, Maj. Gen. John E. Murray, the MACV director of logistics, whom General Weyand had nominated to head the new office, activated the Defense Attaché Office and took command of it, initially as a subordinate of COMUSMACV. Assembly of the 1,200-person civilian staff was slower than expected, due to difficulty in recruiting civil servants to work in Vietnam. By 29 March, nevertheless, 90 percent of the necessary people had been hired and 58 percent of the staff had arrived in Saigon. On that date, General Murray assumed responsibility for residual American support of the South Vietnamese armed forces.[32]

During COUNTDOWN, the Military Assistance Command staff gradually dwindled. Directorates transferred their functions to USSAG/7AF and the Defense Attaché Office, and headquarters personnel either

---

[31] Ibid., vol. 1, pp. 137–38; vol. 2, an. F, pp. 60–61, an. H, pp. 2–6.
[32] Ibid., vol. 1, pp. 137–38; vol. 2, an. G, pp. 4–5, 10–12; Vogt Interv, 8–9 Aug 78, pp. 252–53.

redeployed or joined the new agencies. Much of the Directorate of Operations moved to Nahkon Phanom, while the Defense Attaché Office absorbed the MACV command center and took over liaison with the Joint General Staff. The Intelligence Directorate withdrew its personnel from the combined intelligence centers and turned the centers over to the South Vietnamese. Civilians of the Defense Attaché Office and employees of American contractors replaced the Logistics Directorate in providing technical assistance to Saigon's forces. MACV's Communications and Electronics Directorate set up communications for USSAG/7AF, supported the Four-Party Joint Military Commission and the International Commission for Control and Supervision, and maintained MACV's contact with the rest of the world until the end of March, when it turned over its mission and much of its equipment to the Defense Attaché Office. The MACV Office of Information, while furnishing public affairs support to General Woodward's delegation, slowly went out of existence. The office held its last afternoon press briefing on 27 January and then progressively turned over public information to the South Vietnamese and the U.S. Embassy. MACV's Office of Civil Operations and Revolutionary Development Support stood down on 27 February. It passed its remaining pacification support and reporting functions, as well as many of its civilian personnel, to the U.S. Embassy's Office of the Special Assistant to the Ambassador for Field Operations and the U.S. Agency for International Development. CORDS field representatives went to newly established Directorates for Resettlement and Reconstruction in the American consulates general at Da Nang, Nha Trang, Bien Hoa, and Can Tho, where they would continue to monitor the situation in the countryside.[33]

MACV's advisory groups and regional assistance commands also gradually went out of business. The regional assistance command headquarters, charged with support of the field elements of the Four-Party Joint Military Commission and the International Commission of Control and Supervision, kept working with minimal staffs until the last days of March. When they disbanded, they turned the task of monitoring South Vietnamese military activity over to the consulates general. After the signing of the Paris Accords, the Army, Navy, and Air Force advisory groups withdrew their personnel from Vietnamese units, training centers, and other facilities and assembled them in Saigon for redeployment. Before disbanding in March, the advisory groups transferred their remaining equipment and bases to the South Vietnamese and their residual advice and assistance functions to the Army, Navy, and Air Force divisions of the Defense Attaché Office.[34]

[33] MACV History, 1972–73, vol. 1, pp. 138–39, an. D, pp. 43–44; vol. 2, an. H, pp. 6–10, an. I, p. 6; Hammond, *Military and the Media, 1968–1973*, pp. 613–14.

[34] MACV History, 1972–73, vol. 1, p. 139; vol. 2, an. H, pp. 15–18; Memo, Col R. R. Battreall for CofS MACV, 26 Mar 73, sub: COUNTDOWN After Action Report, in AAR COUNTDOWN folder, MACV Collection, MHI.

As its forces redeployed and its headquarters closed down, the Military Assistance Command relinquished its responsibilities for the war in Cambodia to other agencies. The Military Equipment Delivery Team, which managed the assistance program for Cambodia, had moved all its personnel from Saigon to Phnom Penh by the end of 1971. During 1972, the United States began shipping military materiel to Cambodia directly through the port of Kompong Som instead of through Saigon. MACV gradually terminated its airlift and logistical support to the Military Equipment Delivery Team and turned those functions over to Pacific Command and the U.S. forces in Thailand. MACV's component commands closed out their training programs for the Cambodian armed forces, leaving that effort to the South Vietnamese. When the cease-fire went into effect in South Vietnam, USSAG/7AF, in conjunction with the American embassy in Phnom Penh, assumed control of air operations in Cambodia, where the war went on. The tripartite American–South Vietnamese–Cambodian operational coordinating group moved its sessions from Saigon to Phnom Penh. Pacific Command took over from MACV provision of the senior U.S. member, with USSAG/7AF and the Defense Attaché Office also sending representatives.[35]

At this final stage of Vietnamization, General Weyand viewed South Vietnam's military prospects with cautious optimism. On 7 March, in a personal assessment prepared at the request of the new secretary of defense, Elliot L. Richardson, who had replaced Laird on 29 January, Weyand declared that the South Vietnamese should be able to hold their own after the Americans left. He anticipated that the North Vietnamese would rebuild their main force units and bases inside South Vietnam, principally in Military Region 1 and the border areas of Military Region 3; but he doubted that they would attempt a "decisive violation" of the cease-fire, at least in the near future. Instead, the North Vietnamese and the Provisional Revolutionary Government would carry on a campaign of political subversion and "low-level" military action to expand their influence and territory. The South Vietnamese, with their existing force structure and weaponry, could deal easily with this threat. Weyand assessed favorably the incumbent South Vietnamese corps and division commanders but noted that the quality of their staff officers and subordinate commanders, as well as that of province and district leaders, remained mixed. He saw encouraging indications that Thieu's government was beginning to take merit as well as politics into account in assignments and promotions. Weyand expressed considerable concern about the persistent inadequacy of South Vietnamese

---

[35] MACV History, 1972–73, vol. 2, an. F, pp. 63–65. Msgs, Abrams SPECAT to McCain, 10 Jan 72 and 14 Feb 72, Abrams Papers, MHI. Maj Gen Howard H. Cooksey, Briefing, n.d., sub: US Air Strikes in Support of the Khmer Republic, Howard H. Cooksey Papers, MHI. Msgs, State 39041 to Phnom Penh, 2 Mar 73; Phnom Penh 3411 to State, 10 Apr 73; box 514, NSC files, Nixon Papers, NARA.

equipment maintenance, which suffered from command neglect and a lack of qualified personnel. Presumably, the Defense Attaché Office and its contractors would have to take up the slack in that area.

Weyand seemed less certain of South Vietnam's ability to defeat another large-unit offensive, for which he estimated the North Vietnamese would be ready by 1974. He acknowledged that the South Vietnamese artillery could not counter North Vietnam's longer-range 130-mm. fieldpieces and that the South Vietnamese had yet to master the tactical coordination of armor and infantry. He admitted as well that the South Vietnamese still lacked sufficient mobile reserves and could shift forces between regions only by creating "unavoidable risks" in the areas from which they were withdrawn. Weyand's proclamation that "Vietnamization has succeeded" notwithstanding, the facts he presented made clear that South Vietnam's survival would depend in large measure on North Vietnamese and Provisional Revolutionary Government willingness to pursue power through means short of all-out war and on American willingness to intervene if the other side again escalated the military conflict.[36]

By 29 March, the only American military personnel left in South Vietnam were the U.S. delegates to the Four-Party Joint Military Commission, themselves in the process of winding up work and departing; the fifty-man Defense Attaché Office military contingent; and a 143-man Marine embassy guard. At 1100 on the twenty-ninth, in a simple ceremony, General Weyand furled the colors of the Military Assistance Command, Vietnam, and formally inactivated it. In a final statement, he declared: "Our mission has been accomplished." "I depart," he said "with a strong feeling of pride in what we have achieved, and in what our achievement represents." In a message read at the ceremony, Admiral Moorer expressed gratitude and admiration for all those Americans who had served in the armed forces in Vietnam. He praised the work of MACV and the "courageous actions" of its members. Immediately after furling the colors, General Weyand himself left for Washington with an intermediate stop at Honolulu. At his departure ceremony at Tan Son Nhut, attended by General Vien and other Vietnamese dignitaries and featuring a band and honor guard, Weyand "astounded all present" by delivering his five-minute farewell remarks in understandable Vietnamese. With that graceful gesture, Weyand boarded his aircraft and MACV's eleven years of war came to an end.[37]

---

[36] Msg, COMUSMACV MAC 39933 to JCS, 7 Mar 73, Historians files, CMH; Clarke, *Final Years*, pp. 493–95.

[37] MACV History, 1972–73, vol. 2, an. G, p. 27; Historical Division, "Joint Chiefs of Staff and the War in Vietnam, 1971–1973," pt. 2, p. 775. Msg, George D. Jacobson Saigon 0878 to Abrams, 30 Mar 73, box A, Abrams Papers, MHI, describes Weyand's departure speech. Maj. Charles D. Melson, USMC and Lt. Col. Curtis G. Arnold, USMC, *U.S. Marines in Vietnam: The War That Would Not End, 1971–1973* (Washington, D.C.: History and Museums Division, Headquarters, U.S. Marine Corps, 1991), p. 216.

The colors of the Military Assistance Command, Vietnam, were officially retired, 29 March 1973, during a deactivation ceremony at MACV headquarters in Saigon.

Epilogue: The Fall of a Nation

Although MACV's war had ended, South Vietnam's war went on. Even as Generals Weyand and Woodward tried to put the Paris agreements into effect, North Vietnam began rebuilding its military strength in the South. As early as February 1973, the North Vietnamese established a new surface-to-air missile complex at the old American base at Khe Sanh, to protect the movement of men and supplies into Military Region 1. During the first year after the signing of the Paris agreements, more than 100,000 North Vietnamese troops entered South Vietnam, along with tanks and artillery to replace the losses of 1972. To support their forces, the enemy built new roads and logistical facilities in Laos, Cambodia, and South Vietnam. Fighting continued in Cambodia. In Laos, a cease-fire, signed on 21 February 1973, soon broke down. In all four of South Vietnam's military regions, Saigon's forces battled with the North Vietnamese and Viet Cong for control of territory and for strategic position. According to one estimate, 80,000 Vietnamese on both sides were killed during the first year of "peace."[38]

---

[38] Military operations are summarized in Turley, *Second Indochina War*, pp. 163–67; and in Col. William E. LeGro, *Vietnam from Cease-Fire to Capitulation* (Washington, D.C.: U.S. Army Center of Military History, 1981), chs. 3–7. The North Vietnamese recount their buildup with pride

In the process of persuading President Thieu to sign the Paris agreements, President Nixon repeatedly promised that he would take stern action, presumably a resumption of U.S. air strikes, if the North Vietnamese violated the terms. Put to the test, he did not keep his word. During March and April 1973, Nixon and his advisers seriously considered bombing North Vietnamese troops and bases in South Vietnam and on the Ho Chi Minh Trail, and the Joint Chiefs of Staff drew up plans for the raids. The administration continued the air war over Cambodia and conducted B–52 and tactical air strikes in Laos in response to Communist breaches of the cease-fire there. However, Nixon took no action in Vietnam. Until the end of March, the president did not want to upset the return of American prisoners of war. Thereafter, the intensifying Watergate scandal undermined Nixon's authority and paralyzed the administration. Finally, in July 1973, Congress passed and Nixon reluctantly signed legislation that prohibited any use of government funds after 15 August to support American combat activities within Cambodia, Laos, and the two Vietnams and in the skies above them.[39]

Whether Nixon ever intended to resume a full-scale air war in Vietnam if the North Vietnamese violated the agreement—as he and Kissinger expected them to do—remains a question. Nixon and his national security adviser gave every indication that they were ready to settle for a "healthy interval" between the Paris agreements and South Vietnam's fall. On 5 March, for example, Kissinger told his Washington Special Actions Group that Nixon "has no intention of letting North Vietnam take over South Vietnam militarily—particularly in 1973; two or three years from now is another matter."[40]

In fact, South Vietnam's fall took two more years. At the outset, South Vietnam's post-cease-fire position was far from hopeless. The Saigon government, according to one authority, "was no longer a fragile colonial rump but a fairly stable regime in possession of the world's fifth largest armed force. . . . It was no longer susceptible to overthrow by political turmoil or Southern-based insurgency." Despite the enemy's buildup, the military balance, in numbers of troops and quantities of supplies and equipment, initially favored Saigon. Besides its strong armed forces, Thieu's government held administrative and military control of the bulk of South Vietnam's population and resources, whereas the Communist-dominated regions were poor and thinly populated. After the Paris agreement was signed, aggressive South Vietnamese "land-grabbing" and pacification operations further reduced the enemy's ter-

in *Victory in Vietnam*, pp. 338–40.
[39] Berman, *No Peace, No Honor*, pp. 254–59.
[40] CJCS M–24–73 for Record, 15 Mar 73, quoted in Historical Division, "Joint Chiefs of Staff and the War in Vietnam, 1971–1973."

ritory. The *COSVN* commander recalled: "[Saigon's forces] stepped up their attacks and exercised even tighter control over the people, thus creating considerable difficulties for us." Faced with defeats and losses, some Communist leaders "concluded that the balance of forces on the battlefield had changed in favor of the enemy, and that the revolution was in danger." Most North Vietnamese and Viet Cong commanders, however, kept their faith in ultimate victory and worked methodically to reverse the unfavorable trends.[41]

Their faith was justified. During 1973 and 1974, the balance of forces in Vietnam gradually tipped in the Communists' favor. The North Vietnamese, while continuing military operations and political agitation in the South, methodically rebuilt their main forces and logistical system in preparation for another sustained offensive. Besides armor and artillery, the buildup included a formidable air defense system that effectively neutralized Saigon's air force. With the Watergate scandal sapping his administration's authority, Nixon could not prevent Congress from progressively reducing appropriations for military assistance to South Vietnam. Nixon's resignation under threat of impeachment in August 1974 closed out whatever chance remained of another American rescue of Saigon. Materially, the aid reductions compelled the Joint General Staff to restrict issues of fuel, ammunition, spare parts, medical supplies, radio batteries, and other consumable items to its troops in the field even as enemy pressure on them increased. Psychologically, the cuts induced a sense of abandonment and defeatism at all levels of South Vietnamese society. The diminution of American support exacerbated all of South Vietnam's long-standing internal weaknesses—uninspired military and civilian leadership, endemic corruption, and political and social disunity. President Thieu, whose increasingly dictatorial rule alienated a wide spectrum of non-Communist elements, proved unable to stop the rot or devise a strategy for national survival suited to the changing circumstances.[42]

In fact, Thieu's political and strategic decisions played a major part in shaping South Vietnam's final tragedy. Thieu adopted a policy toward the Paris agreements of "Four No's"—no negotiations with the enemy, no Communist activity in South Vietnam, no coalition government, and no surrender of territory. The unanimity rule on the National Council of National Reconciliation and Concord permitted Thieu to deadlock the political process as he wished. Implementing his fourth point, Thieu pressed a nationwide military offensive to seize and hold every part of South Vietnam's territory. As noted previously, this offensive produced initial gains. However, it also exacerbated

---

[41] First quotation is from Turley, *Second Indochina War*, p. 161; see also pp. 162, 166–67. Second quotation is from Tran Van Tra, *Bulwark B2*, pp. 32–33.

[42] Stephen T. Hosmer, Konrad Kellen, and Brian M. Jenkins, *The Fall of South Vietnam: Statements by Vietnamese Military and Civilian Leaders* (New York: Crane, Russak & Co., 1980); Turley, *Second Indochina War*, pp. 169–74.

South Vietnam's principal military weakness: the dispersal of its forces in defensive and security missions. The Communists, with an army that was smaller overall than the South Vietnamese Army, thus could concentrate superior strength at any point of attack, and Saigon lacked mobile reserves to counter them. Exploiting this advantage, the North Vietnamese step by step eliminated the outer layers of South Vietnam's defenses, securing their expanding logistical system and compressing the South Vietnamese back into the major population centers.[43]

During 1973 and 1974, the South Vietnamese managed to hold on militarily, but at the cost of a casualty rate in both years that nearly equaled that of 1972. By the beginning of 1975, Saigon's forces were bled out, suffering from shortages of munitions and supplies, territorially overextended, and pervaded, like South Vietnamese society as a whole, by an expectation of inevitable defeat. When the North Vietnamese opened their new main force offensive, featuring a more sophisticated employment of combined arms than in 1972, the South Vietnamese collapse came with stunning rapidity. During March 1975, after initial defeats, President Thieu made an ill-considered last-minute attempt to regroup his forces in Military Regions 1 and 2 for defense of a few key centers. Saigon's shaky command and staff structure was not up to the challenge, and its locally based military units disintegrated as soldiers deserted to save their families. Within a few weeks, the North Vietnamese captured all of Military Regions 1 and 2. In the debacle, the better half of South Vietnam's army ceased to exist. After regrouping, the North Vietnamese advanced into Military Region 3 and closed in on Saigon, only briefly delayed by the valiant stand of the South Vietnamese 18th Division at Xuan Loc northeast of the capital. On 21 April, with Saigon's defenses crumbling, President Thieu resigned. Nine days later, on 30 April, his successor, General Duong Van Minh, who had led the overthrow of Ngo Dinh Diem twelve years before, unconditionally surrendered South Vietnam to the North Vietnamese and the Provisional Revolutionary Government. By the time he did so, Phnom Penh had already fallen to the *Khmer Rouge*. Laos, where the cease-fire of February 1973 had failed to halt the fighting, soon would follow South Vietnam and Cambodia into the Communist fold.[44]

In the United States, government officials and the general public had the impression that South Vietnam was giving up without a fight, but the truth was more complex. Many South Vietnamese and territorial units fought hard until the very end. Especially notable was the stand of the South Vietnamese 18th Division and Long Khanh provincial forces at Xuan Loc, a key town and road junction on the eastern approaches to Saigon. For eleven days, from 9 to 21 April 1975, the

---

[43] Turley, *Second Indochina War*, pp. 166–69; LeGro, *Cease-Fire to Capitulation*, p. 179.

[44] South Vietnamese casualty rates are noted in Thayer, "War Without Fronts," pp. 938–39. Military operations are recounted in LeGro, *Cease-Fire to Capitulation*, passim.

South Vietnamese 18th Division fought a North Vietnamese corps of three divisions to a standstill, repelling attack after attack by Communist armor and infantry supported by heavy artillery and inflicting thousands of enemy casualties. The result was due in good measure to the leadership of the 18th's commander, Brig. Gen. Le Minh Dao. Dao carefully planned his defense, conserved his scarce artillery ammunition for the main battle, deployed and maneuvered his troops with skill, and made effective use of supporting arms and of what was left of South Vietnamese air power. When finally outflanked and forced to withdraw, he brought his troops out in good order. The North Vietnamese corps commander, a veteran of combat against both the French and the Americans, characterized Xuan Loc as the fiercest battle of his career.[45]

South Vietnamese soldiers help the wounded leave the embattled town of Xuan Loc.

Xuan Loc was not an isolated incident. In every corps area, while some South Vietnamese and territorial units disintegrated, others fought until overwhelmed by superior enemy numbers and fire power. The troops of Military Region 4, the Mekong Delta, held together and continued battling the local Communist main force units and guerrillas until ordered to surrender after Saigon fell. Their commander, Maj. Gen. Nguyen Khoa Nam, dutifully transmitted the order to his soldiers, then went into his office and shot himself. The valor of individuals and units, however, could not compensate for the strategic failures of the South Vietnamese high command, in particular Thieu's poorly planned effort to regroup his forces in the northern two military regions. An American officer who closely studied the final campaign concluded: "Unit for unit and man for man, the combat forces of South Vietnam repeatedly proved themselves superior to their adversaries. Missing . . . were inspired civilian and

---

[45] George J. Veith and Merle L. Pribbenow, II, " 'Fighting Is an Art': The Army of the Republic of Vietnam's Defense of Xuan Loc, 9–21 Apr 1975," *The Journal of Military History* 68 (January 2004): 163–213. This detailed account is based on Vietnamese sources from both sides.

Vietnamese refugees line up on the deck of the U.S.S. Hancock *for processing following evacuation from Saigon; below, Vietnamese refugees crowd the decks of the U.S. Merchant Ship* Pioneer Contender.

Aerial view of MACV headquarters on fire

military leadership at the highest levels and unflagging American moral and material support."[46]

As the unraveling proceeded, the American mission and the Defense Attaché Office in Saigon could do little but watch in dismay. President Gerald R. Ford attempted to secure additional assistance for South Vietnam, but the Congress rejected his requests. A fact-finding trip in late March by General Weyand, who had succeeded Abrams as Army chief of staff, accomplished nothing. The American mission evacuated its personnel from Military Regions 1 and 2 during March, and U.S. Navy and commercial vessels offshore picked up thousands of fugitive Vietnamese troops and civilians. In the last days of April, as North Vietnamese divisions closed in on Saigon, Bunker's successor, Ambassador Graham Martin, ordered the execution of previously prepared evacuation plans. Helicopters of the Air Force and the 9th Marine Amphibious Brigade, operating from Seventh Fleet ships in the South China Sea, lifted out of Saigon the remaining Americans in the embassy and Defense Attaché Office, foreign nationals, and thousands

[46] Quotation is from LeGro, *Cease-Fire to Capitulation*, p. 179; see also pp. 171–72. The final days in Military Region 4 are described in Francis Terry McNamara with Adrian Hill, *Escape with Honor: My Last Hours in Vietnam* (Washington, D.C.: Brassey's, 1997), passim. For General Nam's suicide, see p. 211.

of Vietnamese. Tragically, thousands more Vietnamese who had fought and worked for the U.S. and the Saigon government were left behind. Perhaps fittingly, the Defense Attaché Office compound at Tan Son Nhut Air Base, the former MACV headquarters, was one of the two locations where helicopters picked up evacuees, the other being the U.S. Embassy in downtown Saigon. Over 5,000 persons left from the Defense Attaché Office landing zone before the marines shut it down. During the evacuation, under North Vietnamese bombardment of the airbase, a rocket killed two marines of the landing zone security force. The last American combat fatalities in Vietnam thus occurred almost literally on MACV's former doorstep. The rear guard of marines left the Defense Attaché Office compound at 0300 on 30 April. Before departing, they set the buildings afire with thermite grenades.[47]

---

[47] Evacuation operations at the Defense Attaché Office are described in Maj. George R. Dunham, USMC, and Col. David A. Quinlan, USMC, *U.S. Marines in Vietnam: The Bitter End, 1973–1975* (Washington, D.C.: History and Museums Division, Headquarters, U.S. Marine Corps, 1990), pp. 169–97.

13

Conclusion: MACV in Retrospect

As a major participant in the unsuccessful American intervention in Indochina, MACV had a mixed record. The successive MACV commanders worked within the framework of policy set by the nation's civilian leadership. Two elements of that policy were controlling throughout. The first was the decision to minimize American military activity, especially on the ground, outside the borders of South Vietnam and to renounce from the outset the option of invading North Vietnam or threatening the existence of the government in Hanoi. The second was the requirement to maintain the appearance, and as far as possible the reality, of South Vietnamese sovereignty. These imperatives restricted the MACV commander's use of the extensive resources at his disposal, probably to the point of placing anything like decisive military victory out of reach.

Throughout most of the command's existence, its basic mission was the same: in the words of the Joint Chiefs of Staff, "to assist the Government of Vietnam and its armed forces to defeat externally directed and supported communist subversion and aggression and attain an independent non-communist . . . South Vietnam functioning in a secure environment."[1] To that end, MACV was to help the Saigon government defeat the North Vietnamese and Viet Cong armed forces and to extend its political and administrative control throughout the territory of the southern republic. The latter task involved the command in the interwoven civilian and military processes of pacification and "nation-building," the more so as civil authority in South Vietnam rested primarily with the military forces MACV was assisting. Under President Nixon, MACV's mission changed to securing the South Vietnamese people's right to determine their own political future by peaceful means. The implementing tasks, however, remained fundamentally the same, although with more emphasis on building up Saigon's armed forces and a new requirement to disengage American ground troops from combat.

---

[1] Mission statement is quoted in Memo, Kissinger for the President, 8 Oct 69, box 139, NSC files, Nixon Papers, NARA.

The Strategy

From the Military Assistance Advisory Group's Geographically Phased Counterinsurgency Plan of 1961 through General Westmoreland's "two-fisted strategy," General Abrams' "one war," and the Marshall Committee's area security system, MACV's basic approach to fighting the war in South Vietnam changed only in nomenclature and detail. It consisted throughout of two basic elements. The first was a series of variations on the spreading oil-spot approach to pacification. Working outward from relatively secure bases, the allies tried to drive enemy military units from the villages, uproot the Viet Cong political and administrative structure, emplace a pro-government system, and carry out programs to win the allegiance of the peasants. The second element consisted of efforts by regular troops outside the pacification zones to destroy major enemy formations and base areas. Initially intended to assist pacification by forestalling enemy offensives, these operations also acquired the purpose of breaking the other side's will by inflicting heavy casualties on its forces. MACV's emphasis on the two elements—pacification and offensives—shifted over time in response to conditions in South Vietnam, to the actions of the other side, and to policy direction from Washington.

The actions of the enemy were the most significant variable in determining the intensity of the main force war and MACV's distribution of resources between big battles, territorial security, and other endeavors. In South Vietnam, the United States was combating not a new stand-alone insurgency but the continuation of a Vietnamese revolution that had begun in 1945. By the early 1950s, the Viet Minh had advanced through the military stages of Maoist revolutionary warfare to the final level of multidivisional conventional battles, typified by their defeat of the French at Dien Bien Phu. Under the 1954 Geneva agreements, the Viet Minh constituted themselves a state in the northern half of Vietnam, with an effective government and powerful armed forces, even as they remained a guerrilla movement in South Vietnam. From its activation, MACV thus confronted an opponent capable of shifting almost at will through the spectrum of revolutionary warfare, using large- and small-unit operations in opportunistic combinations. Because North Vietnam, its war effort underwritten by the Soviet Union and China, could reinforce its southern forces from bases in Laos and Cambodia, the level of main force combat in South Vietnam did not depend entirely on the state of the guerrilla movement. Indeed, the North Vietnamese launched their largest conventional attacks in 1972, when the southern insurgency was at its lowest ebb of the war.

North Vietnamese actions, combined with the internal vicissitudes of the Republic of Vietnam and changing U.S. national policy, determined MACV's priorities and shaped the stages of the command's war. In the first stage, from 1962 through Ngo Dinh Diem's fall in November 1963, MACV focused on building up Saigon's armed forces and working with other agencies of the U.S. mission to implement the Strategic Hamlet Program. In the second stage, from Diem's overthrow to early 1965, MACV tried to press on with advice and support and pacification while struggling to stabilize the Saigon government and participating in the first steps of American escalation. In the third stage, between 1965 and 1968, the enemy added an expanding main force campaign to his ongoing guerrilla and political subversion efforts. To forestall what appeared to be an imminent collapse of its ally and to pursue success by a massive commitment of U.S. military power, the Johnson administration launched ROLLING THUNDER and sent a large expeditionary force to South Vietnam. In this third stage, General Westmoreland's priorities became managing the American buildup, defeating the Communist main force, and reestablishing a semblance of constitutional government in Saigon as the basis for a renewed pacification effort. The North Vietnamese/Viet Cong Tet offensive of 1968 and its follow-on attacks terminated this third stage of MACV's war and confirmed President Johnson's resolve to level off escalation and try to reduce the U.S. commitment. If the offensive shook the resolution of the U.S. government, however, in South Vietnam the enemy failed to achieve his objectives. The heavy losses that he suffered left his forces, and especially the Viet Cong, much weakened.

The United States' decision to de-escalate and disengage, combined with the temporary enfeeblement of the enemy, shaped the fourth stage of the conflict. During this stage, both sides, for different reasons, stepped back from large-scale combat; and the United States endeavored to reduce the war's cost in blood and treasure while still preventing the fall of South Vietnam to the Communists. Accordingly, General Abrams switched the weight of MACV's effort to providing security for Saigon and South Vietnam's other major cities, solidifying the pacification program, improving South Vietnam's armed forces, and withdrawing American troops. At the same time, he advocated and carried out ground and air offensives against the North Vietnamese bases in Cambodia and Laos. The North Vietnamese put a violent end to this stage and inaugurated a fifth with their 1972 spring offensive, to which President Nixon responded with renewed bombing of North Vietnam. Bereft of American ground combat forces, MACV assisted the Vietnamese with airpower and advisers but continued to withdraw U.S. troops. Early in 1973, the Paris agreement inaugurated a last stage of preparation for the cease-fire and inactivation of MACV. After MACV disbanded and after two more years of fighting, a final North Vietnamese conventional assault decided the issue.

The Generals

As participants in formulating U.S. Vietnam policy, MACV's commanders took a generally consistent line. Except for the first, General Paul D. Harkins, who commanded during the run-up to the anti-Diem coup, they harmonized their advice and recommendations with those of the American ambassadors to South Vietnam, CINCPAC, and the Joint Chiefs of Staff; and they rarely dissented openly from presidential decisions. The commanders advocated a strong American military effort in the south and viewed negotiations and proposals to reduce offensive operations with skepticism. Yet they were also acutely aware of the political limitations within which they had to work. As a result, if they campaigned for attacks on the enemy's cross-border sanctuaries, they never pressed their case to the point of stating that such operations were essential to victory. Concerning the bombing of North Vietnam, Westmoreland, Abrams, and Weyand kept in step with CINCPAC and the Joint Chiefs in advocating the air campaign. However, when questions of sortie allocation arose, they urged, as General Abrams did during the Easter offensive, that the war in South Vietnam have first call on the available aircraft. They also periodically attempted to gain control of the northern air offensive, only to be rebuffed by CINCPAC and the Joint Chiefs.

The four generals who commanded MACV—Paul Harkins, William Westmoreland, Creighton Abrams, and Frederick Weyand—differed in professional background and command style. Each faced different challenges, and each responded to them about as well as circumstances and national policy allowed. None of them, however, achieved anything like complete success. Harkins managed competently the American advisory buildup and the insertion into Vietnam of U.S. combat support units, and he worked diligently with the ambassador at the thankless task of moving President Diem in the directions that Washington wished him to go; but in the end, he was caught in the political wreck of the Diem regime. He ended his tour in bitterness, discredited in the view of the Kennedy administration and the American press.

Westmoreland devoted his first year in command to an attempt to revive pacification while stabilizing the Saigon government. As the war escalated, he managed successfully the buildup of a half-million-man U.S. expeditionary force in South Vietnam, beat back the North Vietnamese/Viet Cong main force offensive, helped Ambassadors Lodge and Bunker establish an at least nominally constitutional South Vietnamese government, and contributed significantly to the unification of the American pacification effort through the creation of CORDS. Yet Westmoreland also ended badly. Although allied forces under his command defeated the Communist Tet offensive of 1968, the nationwide attack invalidated Westmoreland's earlier claims of progress in the eyes of both U.S. officials and the American public. As Americans at home turned against the war, many also turned against Westmoreland as its most prominent symbol. Under Richard Nixon, Westmoreland as Army chief of staff found himself marginalized and largely ignored in the shaping of Vietnam policy.

General Creighton Abrams took command at a favorable point in the war. He inherited from Westmoreland a mature MACV organization, a stable Saigon government, and a severely weakened enemy. Building on these assets, Abrams competently executed Nixon's troop withdrawal policy while simultaneously strengthening Saigon's forces and working with them in the most effective pacification campaign yet conducted in the war.[2] His cross-border offensives damaged the enemy's logistic structure and bought time for redeployment and Vietnamization. Yet for Abrams as for Westmoreland, apparent early success was followed by an ambiguous ending. The LAM SON 719 offensive in Laos that Abrams conceived and sold to the administration turned out badly, causing Nixon and Kissinger to lose confidence in their MACV commander. During the Easter offensive of 1972, the South Vietnamese armed forces buckled at many points under full-scale North Vietnamese attack, casting doubt on Abrams' previous claims of progress of the South Vietnamese armed forces improvement and modernization. Although hard fighting by some South Vietnamese units and the intervention of American air power and advisers ultimately repulsed the assault, the outcome further discredited Abrams in the view of Nixon, Kissinger, and the Joint Chiefs of Staff chairman, Admiral Moorer. Like Westmoreland, Abrams left behind an incomplete task and an uncertain legacy.

The last MACV commander, General Weyand, executed with competence and grace the final drawdown of American forces in Vietnam and the inactivation of his headquarters. He carried out MACV's tasks in implementing the Paris agreements to the best of his ability, although circumstances beyond his control prevented him from achieving a full cease-fire. Weyand, however, also made assessments that were belied by events. His proclamation of March 1973 that Vietnamization had succeeded rang hollow when South Vietnam crumbled in the spring of 1975. Succeeding Abrams as Army chief of staff, as the collapse proceeded, Weyand could only join in the futile efforts of President Gerald Ford to obtain enlarged American material support for South Vietnam.

From beginning to end, the MACV and its leaders purveyed a positive view of the course of the war in reports to higher authority and statements to the news media. Generals Harkins and Westmoreland were more emphatic, and publicly visible, in their optimism than were Abrams and Weyand, whose assessments were lower keyed and contained more caveats. Nevertheless, the command's voluminous reports generally painted a picture of progress in destroying enemy forces, building up those of Saigon, and pacifying the countryside even as they acknowledged persistent problems. This pervasive optimism, which generally was echoed by the American ambassador and his senior assistants, was in part elicited by presidents trying to counter domestic

---

[2] Abrams' successes were such that some authorities have claimed that he all but won the war, at least in South Vietnam. See for example Lewis Sorley, *A Better War: The Unexamined Victories and the Final Tragedy of America's Last Years in Vietnam* (New York: Harcourt, Brace & Co., 1999).

criticism of the war. This was true of Westmoreland's public statements in the period before Tet 1968. In addition, senior military and civilian officials in Saigon seemed to believe in their mission and to have been genuinely convinced that the massive American effort was succeeding, albeit slowly and at high cost. From the beginning, however, lower-level American military men and civilians in Vietnam, along with the Saigon press corps, held a less sanguine view of the war's progress. Doubts also arose and persisted among many high-level officials in the State and Defense Departments and at the Central Intelligence Agency. Episodes like LAM SON 719 did nothing to improve MACV's credibility in these circles. In the face of lengthening American casualty lists, reports of South Vietnamese ineptitude and corruption, and the absence of tangible evidence of progress, coupled with dramatic enemy initiatives like the Tet and Easter offensives, MACV's assertions that the war was going well failed to check the steady erosion of American official and popular will to persist in the seemingly endless conflict.

The influence of the MACV commanders on the development of American policy toward Vietnam is difficult to measure. They provided much of the information on which senior officials acted, but they shared that function with the State Department, the National Security Agency, and the Central Intelligence Agency, not to mention the American news media. Policymakers sought information from all the available sources. McNamara, for example, received regular briefings on the war from Central Intelligence Agency as well as Defense Department officials. On critical decisions, the MACV commanders often appeared to follow rather than set the trends of policy. Westmoreland asked for large American ground forces in 1965 only after receiving indications from General Harold K. Johnson, the Army chief of staff, among others, that the administration would be receptive to such proposals. Similarly, Westmoreland followed General Wheeler's lead in the ill-fated reinforcement request after Tet 1968. General Abrams recognized early that withdrawal was the administration's intention and adjusted his advice accordingly. He also seized the opportunities President Nixon afforded him to attack enemy bases in Laos and Cambodia and was a consistent advocate of such attacks. On questions such as the pace of American disengagement, other considerations than the MACV commander's advice clearly predominated. In sum, COMUSMACV was a significant but subordinate player in American decisions for escalation and de-escalation in Southeast Asia.

Command and Control

MACV's place in the U.S. Pacific Command structure was shaped by both military and political considerations. Pacific Command's insertion as a link between Saigon and Washington reflected not only the national policy of limiting the scope of hostilities in Southeast Asia but also the Navy's interest in maintaining unified control of air and sea forces in the western Pacific. The need to limit the war constituted an immovable obstacle to creation of a full-fledged Southeast Asia Command, since it would have been diplomatically awkward for COMUSMACV to direct U.S. military activity in nations such as Thailand, which were at least nominally nonbelligerent. With MACV a subordinate unified command under Pacific Command, the latter headquarters could look after broader U.S. military interests in the region while MACV fought the war in South Vietnam.

In practice, the extra echelon had little adverse effect on MACV's efforts and in some instances was helpful. Pacific Command relieved the Saigon headquarters of many logistical and administrative chores, for example in conducting troop deployments and withdrawals. CINCPAC and COMUSMACV maintained a united front on most policy issues, and at times the Honolulu commander provided his Saigon subordinate with a buffer against Washington interference. COMUSMACV generally was able to organize his forces and conduct operations in South Vietnam as he saw fit. True, MACV's commanders were denied control of the air campaign in the north. However, that campaign—in both its ROLLING THUNDER and LINEBACKER phases—was primarily an extension of Washington's diplomacy rather than an integral element of the military effort in the south. COMUSMACV controlled air operations over the southernmost part of North Vietnam, and he acquired dominant influence over American military activity in those parts of Cambodia and Laos of most vital interest to him. COMUSMACV's limited freedom of action beyond South Vietnam's borders was an outgrowth of national policy, which in turn determined Pacific Command relationships.

Within South Vietnam, the organization of MACV's headquarters staff and component and field commands evolved and expanded with the U.S. commitment. It followed generally the standard American pattern for joint commands and in the field conformed to the existing South Vietnamese regional military structure. Deviations from regular U.S. doctrine and practice reflected the peculiar political and military conditions of Vietnam. General Westmoreland's decision, which his successors kept in effect, to retain tactical control over his U.S. Army forces and restrict the Army component command to administration and logistics was a case in point. Westmoreland justified this arrangement on the grounds that he could not have two high-level American headquarters both trying to work with the South Vietnamese Joint General Staff, which directed Saigon's army as well as its entire military establishment. Proposals for a new advisory group headquarters under MACV to unify the fragmented Army advisory effort fell afoul of the same consideration. The size and location of American forces led to other deviations, such as the constitution of the III Marine Amphibious Force as a *de facto* fourth service component command and the establishment of an Army corps headquarters under the III Marine Amphibious Force to conduct operations in northern I Corps.

415

The most significant organizational innovation within MACV was the establishment of CORDS to unify American support of pacification. This unorthodox joint civilian and military agency, headed by a civilian deputy COMUSMACV with ambassadorial rank, brought focus and direction to a key element of the American war effort. A drastic departure from bureaucratic business-as-usual that was resisted by many agencies, CORDS owed its existence primarily to the initiative of President Johnson and the urging of Secretary McNamara and Robert Komer; but General Westmoreland gave significant assistance at the birth. He early advocated central management of pacification and strongly supported Komer in putting CORDS into effective operation. Westmoreland's successors maintained MACV's commitment to CORDS and thereby made possible the allies' post-1968 advances in reclaiming the South Vietnamese countryside.

Disputes among the American armed services, and between individual services and MACV, punctuated the expansion of the command. At issue were the conduct of the Vietnam conflict, the validation of service roles and missions, and the setting of critical precedents for future joint operations. The services jockeyed for key positions in MACV headquarters, with the Army winning the lion's share of posts by virtue of the fact that the struggle in Vietnam was primarily a land war. Only at the end, after U.S. ground forces had left Vietnam, did the Air Force gain a predominant position within the headquarters. There were repeated disputes over the organization of service research and testing in the theater. The Army and the Air Force quarreled over the airmobility concept and the control of helicopters. MACV engaged in confrontations with the Marine Corps over command arrangements in I Corps and central management of fixed-wing tactical aircraft. Throughout, the successive MACV commanders sought to maintain as much interservice harmony as possible while ensuring their own ability to carry out their mission. In consultation with CINCPAC and the chairman of the Joint Chiefs, they arrived at compromises and working arrangements on most issues. However, when COMUSMACV asserted his right to organize and control his forces against service prerogatives, as Westmoreland did in his central management dispute with the marines, CINCPAC, the Joint Chiefs, and the secretary of defense supported him, although sometimes with reservations. Their actions foreshadowed the statutory strengthening of the authority of theater joint commanders over the organization of their forces in the Goldwater-Nichols Act of 1986.[3]

General Westmoreland's collision with the Marine Corps over central management pointed up the critical role of airpower in MACV's war. Throughout most of MACV's existence, American airpower con-

---

[3] The impact of the Goldwater-Nichols Act in strengthening joint commanders is summarized in Richard M. Swain, *"Lucky War": Third Army in Desert Storm* (Fort Leavenworth, Kans.: U.S. Army Command and General Staff College Press, 1994), pp. 27–29.

stituted the joint commander's most potent and responsive instrument for influencing the course of combat within South Vietnam. It was very nearly his only means of attacking the enemy beyond the nation's borders. Accordingly, the control of aircraft and the allocation of sorties among the various air campaigns in Southeast Asia were issues on which MACV commanders, in particular Westmoreland and Abrams, waged some of their hardest battles with the individual services and at times the White House and the Joint Chiefs of Staff. Although denied authority over the bombing of North Vietnam, the MACV commanders brought airpower in the rest of the theater under their control and used it as an instrument of their will. While the Seventh Air Force commander issued the tasking orders, COMUSMACV, to the Air Force's discomfort, kept targeting and allocation firmly in his own hands and those of his Army-dominated staff. Westmoreland and Abrams set a lasting precedent. In the Gulf War of 1991, General H. Norman Schwarzkopf, over Marine and Navy objections, designated his Air Force component commander, Lt. Gen. Charles A. Horner, as Joint Force Air Component Commander with authority to assign missions to airplanes of all services through a daily tasking order. However, as had been true in Vietnam, Schwarzkopf, not Horner, made the critical targeting decisions.[4]

MACV's command relationships with its allied forces were conditioned more by political than military considerations. With the South Vietnamese, the sensitivities of a people only recently freed from European colonial rule, along with U.S. preoccupation with maintaining Saigon's sovereignty, reinforced after 1969 by the imperatives of disengagement and Vietnamization, dictated that there be no combined command. Instead, MACV and its American forces worked with the South Vietnamese on the basis of cooperation and coordination. MACV's commanders influenced South Vietnamese operations by means of their advisory network, regular high-level contacts with the Joint General Staff and South Vietnamese political leaders, the promotion of combined campaign plans and other cooperative staff work, and the provision of military assistance. With the other allies, notably the South Koreans, political considerations also prevailed. Given Washington's eagerness to obtain "more flags" in Vietnam, the allies could set their own terms for their presence; and the Koreans in particular did so in a restrictive manner. MACV used persuasion and the provision of U.S. combat and logistical support to influence their operations, often to only limited effect. These arrangements clearly violated the military principle of unity of command, but under the circumstances American officials in Washington and Saigon could find no acceptable alternatives.[5]

---

[4] Col. Edward C. Mann, III, USAF, *Thunder and Lightning: Desert Storm and the Airpower Debates* (Maxwell Air Force Base, Ala.: Air University Press, 1995), pp. 55–60.

[5] A representative criticism of the lack of unity of command can be found in Palmer, *The 25-Year*

Taken as a whole, the command structure in South Vietnam was a fabric of compromises, among the U.S. armed services, American civilian government agencies, and the allied nations. Nevertheless, it was adequate for coordination of the forces in a conflict in which division-size and larger formations were essentially static and operated in fixed areas; and it conformed to the requirements of American national policy. Alternative structures, such as a multinational combined command in South Vietnam and a U.S. Southeast Asia Command, while organizationally neater and potentially more operationally efficient, all possessed seemingly prohibitive political and diplomatic drawbacks. The wars in Indochina were politically and militarily messy and complicated; so, inevitably, was America's organization for waging them.

The cooperation and coordination principle, so frequently condemned in Vietnam, reappeared when the United States again went to war alongside non-European allies with memories of a colonial past. In the Gulf War, a Defense Department report declared, "It became clear [that] an acceptable command structure must reflect the participating nations' national, ethnic, and religious pride." Hence, while American and British forces campaigned under the operational control of General Schwarzkopf's U.S. Central Command, the various Arab contingents were grouped under a separate headquarters with a Saudi prince in charge. The French also answered to their own national authorities. There was no overall coalition commander. General Schwarzkopf worked with his counterparts on a cooperation and coordination basis that Westmoreland, Abrams, and Weyand would have found familiar. Under conditions quite different from those in Vietnam, the multi-headed Gulf War coalition command achieved the swift, overwhelming victory that MACV never did.[6]

In its combat operations within South Vietnam, MACV accomplished the most that was possible within the limits set by U.S. national policy. Although criticized by pacification advocates, the command's concentration of its U.S. troops, while it had them, against the enemy's large units and logistical system made the most productive possible use of American firepower and mobility. At the same time, MACV avoided over-Americanization of the territorial security and pacification effort, which officials expected to continue long after U.S. combat troops left, and which could only be carried on with lasting success by the South Vietnamese. As the war went on, MACV, profiting from experience and from an expanding intelligence capability, grew more effective at grinding down the other side's military forces. The enemy's three failed offensives of 1968 also contributed to the attrition process. By the time

---

War, pp. 193–94.

[6] Department of Defense, Conduct of the Persian Gulf War: Final Report to Congress, Pursuant to Title V of the Persian Gulf Conflict Supplemental Authorization and Personnel Benefits Act of 1991 (Washington, D.C.: Department of Defense, 1992), vol. 1, pp. 55–59; quotation is from p. 55.

U.S. ground troops ceased offensive operations in mid-1971, MACV had driven the North Vietnamese divisions back to South Vietnam's borders, much reduced the southern guerrillas and local units, and severely damaged the Communists' base network. The command's air operations hindered the enemy's movement of supplies down the Ho Chi Minh Trail and made it costly in casualties and materiel, although they could not completely shut off the flow. Even so, the centers of the other side's power remained intact; and MACV's tactical successes came at a high cost in American and Vietnamese lives and in destruction and social disruption within South Vietnam. MACV won many battles, but it could not end the war by military means.

In cooperation with other U.S. agencies, MACV advanced nation-building and pacification. During the long interregnum after Diem's overthrow, General Westmoreland used his advisory relationship to maintain unity among the fractious generals who in practice ran the Saigon government, helping to move them toward restoration of a stable and at least formally constitutional system. Generals Abrams and Weyand had less to do this area since the Thieu regime remained in office throughout their tours. With CORDS leading the way, the command helped South Vietnam repair the social and economic damage of the 1968 enemy offensives. Under General Abrams, it also played a central role in a succession of accelerated pacification campaigns that restored the Saigon government's presence and authority in much of the countryside; and it assisted in projects like the land-to-the-tiller program that promised to enhance long-term social stability and equity in South Vietnam. By the time MACV ceased operations, the insurgency within South Vietnam no longer posed an immediate threat to overthrow the Saigon government. Nevertheless, as in military operations, the extent and permanence of MACV's achievement were uncertain. Although the insurgency was much weakened, its political hard core remained intact throughout South Vietnam. The government's ascendancy seemed to be due more to a temporarily favorable military balance than to its winning the active loyalty and support of the peasantry, and North Vietnam retained the capacity to change the military balance.

The South Vietnamese

Throughout MACV's existence, the strengthening of the South Vietnamese armed forces was one of its principal missions. Between 1965 and 1968, the huge American intervention temporarily eclipsed that effort; but the advent of Vietnamization in 1969 returned advice and assistance to center stage. The command sought to improve Saigon's forces by infusing American advisers into them at every level from the Joint General Staff to battalion and district headquarters. It largely planned the expansion of the South Vietnamese military and managed the provision of American funds, weapons, and equipment

419

to it. In conferences with the chief of the Joint General Staff, and frequently with the president of the republic, MACV commanders tried to influence South Vietnamese military appointments and promotions and to induce their allies to correct their forces' many administrative and operational deficiencies.

The results of this effort and of its culmination in Nixon's Vietnamization program defy simple categorization. In 1973, MACV left the South Vietnamese army, navy, and air force much larger, better equipped, and operationally more capable by several orders of magnitude than it had found them eleven years before. By themselves, those forces could certainly contain, and perhaps ultimately eradicate, the southern insurgency even if that insurgency was reinforced by North Vietnamese troop infiltration. As the Easter offensive demonstrated, with U.S. advice and air support, they could repel a full-scale invasion by North Vietnamese heavy divisions. Yet Saigon's forces still were plagued at the end by the same problems of weak and corrupt leadership, high desertion rates, and uneven tactical performance that had afflicted them at the beginning. They continued to depend on the American advisory network for much of their operational planning and coordination. Because their American sponsors had never fully resolved the issue of what kind of force they were creating, and for what kind of war, the South Vietnamese army was overly heavy and conventional for counterinsurgency and too lightly equipped and erroneously deployed for mobile conventional battle. Saigon's military establishment was also too large, and too reliant on sophisticated weaponry and lavish expenditures of fuel and ammunition, to be sustainable without permanent American subsidies. When both advisers and subsidies were taken away, its decline was inevitable.

Several points should be made about Vietnamization's context and about the situation that gave rise to the effort. First, the policy originated late in the Johnson administration. Nixon picked it up and enlarged upon it in good measure because he and his advisers saw no other acceptable alternative. They refused to surrender South Vietnam to the Communists outright, and they considered escalation through renewed heavy attacks on North Vietnam to be politically unfeasible. Second, circumstances after Tet 1968 favored the effort. The enemy, exhausted by its failed offensives, could not interfere effectively with the gradual U.S. turnover of most military operations in South Vietnam to Saigon's forces. In fact, between late 1968 and early 1972, Hanoi appears to have treated the struggle in the south as a holding action while it concentrated on repairing the damage done by ROLLING THUNDER and building up strength for a new and more conventional offensive. Third, the Nixon administration, although under intense domestic political pressure, managed to keep the pace of U.S. troop withdrawals rapid enough to appease American public opinion and yet gradual enough to allow an orderly transfer of military operations to South Vietnam.

Until shortly before the cease-fire, the architects and implementers of Vietnamization worked on two assumptions that turned out to be wrong. The first of these was that the United States would maintain a large military advisory and support presence in South Vietnam, even after a cessation of hostilities and a political agreement. All of Pacific Command's and MACV's contingency plans provided for such a presence. Secretary Laird based his redeployment plan on drawing MACV down to a permanent 15,000-man advisory and assistance group by mid-1973 and then keeping the U.S. force at that level indefinitely. By requiring the complete removal from Vietnam of all but a handful of American military personnel, the Paris agreement upended this assumption and abruptly truncated the Vietnamization process.

The second assumption was that the Communist threat would remain essentially what it had been since late 1965: a guerrilla insurgency in South Vietnam reinforced by infiltrated North Vietnamese light infantry divisions. After early 1969, the Communists' withdrawal of their main force to the borders and reversion to small-unit military action and terrorism appeared to validate this assumption. As a result, until the Easter offensive, MACV emphasized territorial security in its Combined Campaign Plans, as typified by Abrams' adoption of the Marshall Committee's Area Security System, and in its guidance of the improvement and modernization of Saigon's forces. LAM SON 719 signaled that the North Vietnamese might have something else in mind, but General Abrams in response pressed for only small modifications in South Vietnamese force structure and deployment. After the Easter offensive and with a cease-fire and total American withdrawal imminent, the Nixon administration conducted a last-minute U.S. infusion of heavy equipment into South Vietnam, too late for the South Vietnamese to assimilate it in their organization and training.

Despite these flaws in concept and execution, Vietnamization as a military program produced South Vietnamese armed forces capable on their own of holding the cities and major populated areas against the Viet Cong and North Vietnamese infiltrators. As Xuan Loc and other engagements indicated in 1975, the South Vietnamese armed forces that MACV created could fight successfully against North Vietnamese armor and artillery, at least in the defense, if properly deployed and competently led. Unfortunately, in 1975 neither proper deployment nor effective high-level leadership was present. Combined with the decline of U.S. financial and materiel assistance and with the institutional weakness and political disunity of the South Vietnamese state and society, President Thieu's final military blunders brought about the collapse. Even with this disastrous denouement, one could argue that Vietnamization achieved President Nixon's minimum objectives; it secured for South Vietnam a fighting chance to survive and provided Nixon and Kissinger with their "healthy interval" between American disengagement and Saigon's ultimate fate.

Final Judgments

A combination of circumstances prevented MACV from achieving more than partial, temporary success in South Vietnam. The first of these was the character of its ally. During the long conflict, the Republic of Vietnam displayed remarkable endurance and resilience, considering its origins and circumstances. More than 200,000 South Vietnamese soldiers died in the war, as did perhaps twice that number of civilians.[7] Nevertheless, the southern republic was a collection of political, religious, and ethnic fragments. Many of its leaders were tainted by association with the former French imperial masters. Its national institutions were underdeveloped leftovers from the same French colonialism. Endemic South Vietnamese disunity, corruption, and inefficiency sapped the effectiveness of every allied endeavor, whether in military operations or pacification. Equally and perhaps more damaging, the spectacle of South Vietnam's corruption and disarray disgusted many Americans, citizens and officials alike, and contributed to what eventually became a majority conviction in the United States that the republic was not worth the cost of defending it. Even with total Vietnamese cooperation, which was not often forthcoming, MACV and the U.S. mission would have needed a generation or more to transform South Vietnam into an effective state, let alone one meeting American standards of democracy and social justice.

Unfortunately, South Vietnam's northern rival, the Democratic Republic of Vietnam, already was a militarily and administratively effective state, although not by American standards a democratic one. Its leaders, veterans of the war of independence against the French, were implacable in their determination to "liberate" the south, however long the struggle took and whatever it cost in lives and treasure. As a result of the Soviet-Chinese competition for the allegiance of the rest of the Communist bloc, North Vietnam could count on a steady flow of military and economic aid for its war effort while remaining free to pursue its national objectives with little interference from its great power sponsors. From the early stages, North Vietnam fed the struggle in the south with men and materiel. It countered every expansion of American activity with one of its own. Convinced that they could outlast the United States in a battle of attrition, the leaders in Hanoi persisted despite American bombing, some 850,000 battlefield casualties among their forces,[8] and disastrous defeats that, as at Tet 1968, sometimes resulted from their own arrogant miscalculations.

---

[7] Turley, *The Second Indochina War*, p. 203. About 170,000 South Vietnamese soldiers died between 1965 and 1972 alone. See Thayer, "War Without Fronts," p. 848.

[8] The Defense Department estimated that the North Vietnamese and Viet Cong lost more than 850,000 killed in action between 1965 and 1972. See Thayer, "War Without Fronts," p. 847. The Socialist Republic of Vietnam today officially uses roughly the same figure. See Lewis Stern, "Research Note: North Vietnam's War Dead," *Indochina Chronology*, v. 18, no. 1 (October 1998–January 1999): 27–29.

The geography of Indochina constituted the third immovable obstacle to MACV's success. South Vietnam was flanked on the west by a 900-mile land border, most of it covered by jungle and mountains. Cambodia and Laos, the republic's neighbors on that side, lacked the power to prevent the North Vietnamese from appropriating their frontier regions for military bases and lines of communication. From these cross-border havens, the North Vietnamese could invade South Vietnam at every point from the Demilitarized Zone to the Mekong Delta, presenting Saigon with an almost insoluble defense problem. The same bases provided retreating Communist troops with sanctuaries from American and South Vietnamese ground attack. Intensive American air bombardment and small-unit reconnaissance and raids harassed the bases and supply routes but did not render them unusable. Unable to seal off its battlefield, MACV sought to destroy the enemy's forces within South Vietnam more rapidly than they could be reinforced, but it never reached that goal. The United States might have attempted to resolve this strategic dilemma by blockading or invading North Vietnam or by establishing a cordon of ground forces across Laos to the Mekong River. American officials, however, were unwilling to enlarge the war to that extent and thereby increase the risk of a direct conflict with the Soviet Union and China.

During the war, and over the years following it, alternative American strategies have had their advocates. From the earliest planning for what became ROLLING THUNDER, Air Force leaders, supported by the Joint Chiefs of Staff and CINCPAC, argued for concentrated heavy bombing of North Vietnam, possibly accompanied by blockade or mining of its ports. Such a hard, swift squeeze, they contended, would have brought Hanoi to terms many years before the LINEBACKER campaigns supposedly achieved that result. Supporting this position is the fact that, in 1968 and again in 1972, Hanoi's diplomacy seemed to focus on ending the bombing of the north while leaving the comrades in the south to face continued heavy pounding from the allies. On the other side, Secretary McNamara and his civilian analysts argued that no permissible level of bombing would cause North Vietnam to cease supporting the revolution in the south or render it incapable of doing so. They also came to believe that the military and diplomatic costs of ROLLING THUNDER were excessive in relation to the meager results being obtained. Subsequent researchers—including Air Force officers—contend that the political conditions (Nixon's opening to China) and technological advances (guided "smart" bombs) that allowed the conduct of LINEBACKER I and II and contributed to their apparent success were not present before 1972; hence the hard, swift squeeze was not possible earlier in the war.[9]

---

[9] The case for a stronger air war is made by Admiral Ulysses S. G. Sharp, *Strategy for Defeat: Vietnam in Retrospect* (San Rafael, Calif.: Presidio Press, 1978). For the counter argument, see Mark Clodfelter, *The Limits of Air Power: The American Bombing of North Vietnam* (New York: Free

At various times another alternate strategy was proposed by the Joint Chiefs; General Westmoreland; General Johnson, the Army chief of staff; and General Vien, the chief of the South Vietnamese Joint General Staff. This strategy was the establishment of a cordon of U.S., South Vietnamese, and possibly Laotian and Thai troops across the Laos panhandle to the Mekong River, roughly along the South Vietnamese line of advance in LAM SON 719. Unlike the temporary cross-border incursions of 1970–71, this cordon would have been aimed at permanently severing the Ho Chi Minh Trail. Since this action did not involve an invasion of North Vietnam, it would have entailed minimal risk of direct confrontation with China. If put in place in late 1965 or early 1966 using the first American divisions to arrive in Vietnam, the cordon would in theory have blocked North Vietnam's movement of large troop units and major quantities of supplies into South Vietnam, thereby limiting the escalation of the fighting there. With American advisers and air support, the South Vietnamese forces could then have dealt with the Viet Cong and the few North Vietnamese who managed to slip past the barrier.[10]

Although in retrospect the cordon appears to be a commonsense solution to the problem of infiltration, its implementation entailed formidable practical problems. Establishment and maintenance of the line across Laos would have required lengthy diplomatic negotiations and extensive logistical preparations in South Vietnam and probably in Thailand as well. Hence, Westmoreland, although he endorsed the cordon idea in principle, declined in 1965 to recommend it as an immediate measure. He preferred to use his American divisions within South Vietnam.[11] As the Ho Chi Minh Trail system and its defenses expanded, so did the military difficulty of attacking them, well illustrated by the limited results of LAM SON 719. Throughout the war, the U.S. Embassy in Vientiane and the State Department vigorously opposed all but the smallest allied ground incursions into Laos, claiming that such operations would destroy what remained of that country's neutrality. Intent on containing rather than expanding the war, President Johnson rejected MACV's proposals for even short-term cross-border incursions in both Laos and Cambodia. Nixon authorized them, but only as spoiling attacks to gain time for Vietnamization and U.S. withdrawal.

Given the diplomatic constraints on American action, the geography of Indochina, and the limited capabilities of South Vietnam as a state,

---

Press, 1989). Television and laser-guided bombs became available during the last days of ROLLING THUNDER but did not play a significant part in that campaign. See Wayne Thompson, *To Hanoi and Back: The U.S. Air Force and North Vietnam, 1966–1973* (Washington, D.C.: Smithsonian Institution Press, 2000), pp. 65–66, 230–31.

[10] An argument for the cordon strategy is made in Harry G. Summers, Jr, *On Strategy: A Critical Analysis of the Vietnam War* (Novato, Calif.: Presidio Press, 1982), especially pp. 122–24; and Palmer, *Twenty-Five Year War*, pp. 183–88.

[11] Westmoreland's views are summarized in Cosmas, *Years of Escalation, 1962–1967*, ch. 11, p. 379.

there seemed to be no alternative but the strategy the United States actually followed: to pursue attrition and pacification in the South, harry the enemy's Laotian supply line, and punish North Vietnam with a carefully measured campaign of aerial bombing. At some point, so the official reasoning went, Hanoi's leaders would realize that they could not drive U.S. forces out of South Vietnam or overthrow the Saigon government and that the attempt to do so was costing them too much. At that point, negotiations to end the war might be possible. Failing that, the United States might at least reduce enemy strength in South Vietnam and build up Saigon's forces to the point where American troops could gradually withdraw.

Although the war in South Vietnam was thus probably not winnable within the means the United States was willing to use, it also was not losable as long as America was willing to pay the price of supporting its ally. Indeed, not losing appears to have been President Johnson's unpublicized objective in expanding U.S. involvement in the war. On 18 June 1965, as the administration was approaching its decision to send American combat units to Vietnam, Secretary McNamara told a Cabinet meeting that the U.S. objective was to convince the North Vietnamese Communists that they could not win in the South. He continued:

We think [we] can achieve that objective by moving toward a stalemate, convincing [Hanoi] that the situation in the South will not lead to a military victory, that they can't win while the stalemate continues, they are being forced to absorb the penalty in the North as a result of our bombing of their military targets. So that is our basic strategy. We think that if we can accomplish that stalemate, accompanied by the limited bombing program in the North, we can force them to negotiations . . . that will lead to a settlement that will preserve the independence of South Vietnam.

The basic question, the military question is, how can we accomplish a stalemate, and how can we move from a situation in which they believe they are winning, to one in which they see that there is no hope for the victory that they are endeavoring to accomplish.[12]

As an objective, a military stalemate in Vietnam was consistent with the U.S. global strategy of meeting localized Communist encroachments upon the "Free World" with equally localized force to maintain or restore the status quo. The United States had done this successfully in the Korean War and in other crises that were resolved without actual hostilities. In South Vietnam, the United States simply had to keep a non-Communist government in being in Saigon and help it control the major cities and dominate or at least contest as much of the countryside as possible. For practical purposes, MACV accomplished these objectives

[12] Minutes of the meeting of the President's Cabinet, in the Cabinet Room, the White House, at 11:10 a.m., Jun 18, 1965, folder Cabinet Meetings 6/18/65, p. 43, box 3, Cabinet Papers file, LBJL. I am indebted for this citation to Dr. Edward J. Drea of the Historical Office of the Secretary of Defense.

throughout its eleven-year existence. In addition, in 1973, President Nixon negotiated an agreement that would have allowed the United States and South Vietnam to perpetuate and stabilize indefinitely the political and military stalemate.

Why, then, did containment in Vietnam fail? One reason was the fact that the North Vietnamese, contrary to McNamara's expectations, never accepted the proposition that they could not win in the South. In the view of the leaders in Hanoi, the existence of a battlefield stalemate simply meant that they had taken the heaviest American blows and survived; and the United States with its many commitments around the world could not sustain indefinitely the level of effort that it was making in Southeast Asia. All the Communists had to do, then, was keep the struggle going and make it as expensive for the Americans as they could—objectives well within their capabilities as enhanced by aid from the Soviet Union and China. Combined with the extravagant American approach to fighting the war, and with the well-publicized incompetence and corruption of the Saigon regime, the North Vietnamese strategy had its intended effect. Ultimately, American officialdom and the American public decided that defending South Vietnam was no longer worth the cost.[13]

A second reason for the failure of containment in Vietnam was the Johnson administration's inability to connect its actual political goals with its military means. During the years of escalation, Johnson and McNamara, while speaking of stalemate in private, talked to the Joint Chiefs of Staff, CINCPAC, and COMUSMACV in terms of a "victory" the dimensions of which the civilians and the military never precisely defined. Repeatedly, Johnson through McNamara told his commanders to ask for what they needed to prevail and told them not to "nickel and dime" the effort. This inconsistency may have stemmed from the early U.S. view of the conflict in South Vietnam as primarily an internal insurgency. Pacification, after all, was aimed at the total eradication of the Viet Cong and the securing of the Vietnamese people's allegiance for Saigon, not at a stalemate. As the conflict became a real war after 1965, officials never restated with sufficient clarity their political goals and their corollary military objectives. Even Nixon's announced war aim, to secure the South Vietnamese people's right to determine their own political future without outside interference, required battlefield success more complete than the president's military strategy could deliver.[14]

America's senior military leaders, including those at MACV, either did not understand or refused to accept that the president was in fact playing for a draw. Hence, they made no attempt to shape a low-cost, sustainable military effort. Instead, they promoted and acquiesced

---

[13] Turley, *Second Indochina War*, pp. 86–87, summarizes the North Vietnamese leaders' view of the meaning of stalemate.

[14] The difficulty of linking political goals to military operations is discussed in Colin S. Gray, "Why Strategy Is Difficult," *Joint Force Quarterly*, 34 (Spring 2003): 80–87.

in an incremental escalation that still fell short of their own vaguely defined concept of victory. Simultaneously, they maintained in their reports and evaluations that the insufficient strategy was succeeding.[15] Johnson, McNamara, the Joint Chiefs, and COMUSMACV thus cut off the option of holding on at minimal cost. They left the United States with a military commitment to South Vietnam that was at once too expensive in blood and treasure to sustain for very long and too limited in scope to produce a battlefield decision. When Secretary McNamara belatedly attempted to scale back the effort in favor of a manageable equilibrium in South Vietnam, the military leaders resisted him. After Tet, Wheeler and Westmoreland joined in a huge reinforcement request that finally priced the war off the market. Recognizing political reality, President Nixon took up in earnest the effort to cut the cost of America's commitment so as to sustain South Vietnam over the long run. The continuing decline of domestic political support turned his policy into one of rapid disengagement that set the stage for Saigon's abandonment by the United States and ultimate downfall.

Within the limitations of U.S. policy and the situation in Southeast Asia, MACV accomplished about as much as was possible. At minimum, MACV kept the Republic of Vietnam afloat as long as the United States considered that objective worth pursuing. It can be argued that in the long run, the command's efforts were not in vain. The United States delayed the fall of South Vietnam for about a decade. During that time, the neighboring countries achieved sufficient political stability and economic prosperity to halt the spread of revolution in Southeast Asia. Meanwhile, China turned away from its militant promotion of the people's revolutionary war toward a rapprochement with the United States. Because of these changes, when Saigon's collapse came in 1975 it had minimal effect on the global balance of power. Whether this result justified the terrible cost of the Second Indochina War to all the societies involved, and whether the war was even necessary to achieve the result, will long remain subjects of historical speculation and debate.

During the course of the war, more than two million American men and women served in Vietnam, most of them in MACV and its subordinate commands, and more than 50,000 lost their lives there. For those who came home, there were no victory parades but instead an often bitter legacy of questions about the purpose and worth of the struggle in which they sacrificed so much. MACV's war remains deeply controversial three decades after General Weyand folded the command's colors for the last time and shows little sign of becoming less so. The one certainty is that those who served, at every rank and position, did the best they knew how for their country.

---

[15] An examination of the dysfunctional relationship between Johnson and McNamara and their Joint Chiefs is H. R. McMaster, *Dereliction of Duty: Lyndon Johnson, Robert McNamara, the Joint Chiefs of Staff, and the Lies that Led to Vietnam* (New York: HarperCollins, 1997).

Bibliographical Note

This account of a joint headquarters engaged in the making of theater-level policy and strategy, the conduct of joint and combined military operations, and the provision of advice and support to the South Vietnamese government and armed forces of necessity draws on a wide range of sources. The work is based primarily on the message traffic and other papers of the successive MACV commanders, principally those of Generals William C. Westmoreland and Creighton W. Abrams. These materials are supplemented by documents from the MACV records in the National Archives; from the national security files of Presidents Lyndon B. Johnson and Richard M. Nixon; and from the records of the State Department, the Central Intelligence Agency, the Joint Chiefs of Staff, and the American armed services.

Unpublished Sources

National Archives and Records Administration

Major record groups bearing on MACV are located in the National Archives and Records Administration (NARA) facility at College Park, Maryland. Record Group (RG) 472 (Records of the United States Forces in Southeast Asia, 1950–1975) now contains the main body of MACV headquarters material. This record group also includes the records of the Military Assistance Advisory Group (MAAG), Vietnam, and those of many agencies subordinate or related to MACV. These include headquarters U.S. Army, Vietnam; the Army corps, divisions, brigades, and support organizations; the Army and Air Force advisory groups; the regional assistance commands; the U.S. Military Assistance Command, Thailand; the Defense Attaché Office, Saigon; the Military Equipment Delivery Team to Cambodia; and the U.S. Delegation to the Four-Power Joint Military Commission. Also useful are records of the Army Staff (RG 319), U.S. Army commands (RG 338), and Interservice Agencies (RG 334). Located at College Park are the Richard M. Nixon presidential papers, including the national security files covering Southeast Asia. Most of the State Department, Central Intelligence Agency, and Joint Chiefs of Staff documents for the 1969–1973 period cited in this study were consulted in the Nixon national security files.

U.S. Army Center of Military History

The U.S. Army Center of Military History in Washington, D.C., holds a large and varied mass of documents collected by the historians preparing the Center of Military History's multivolume history of the Army's role in Southeast Asia. Many of these are copies or duplicates of material in other repositories. The Center of Military History will transfer these materials to the National Archives upon completion of the U.S. Army in Vietnam series.

Most important of these for the historian of the Military Assistance Command, Vietnam, are the papers of Generals Westmoreland and Abrams. The Westmoreland Papers are photocopies of those held by the Lyndon Baines Johnson Library in Austin, Texas. They consist of two main collections. The first is a historical diary that the general dictated at intervals to members of his staff describing his day-to-day activities and decisions, supported by copies of messages, memorandums, reports, staff studies, and other documents. The second is a chronological file of the messages between Westmoreland and other senior commanders in Vietnam and between him and his superiors in Hawaii and Washington. Through these messages, the historian can follow the policy dialogue between the theater commander and higher authorities. Less extensive than the Westmoreland collection, the Abrams Papers at the Center of Military History consist entirely of messages which, as in Westmoreland's case, illuminate General Abrams' views and role in the making of U.S. policy and strategy for Southeast Asia. Unfortunately, comparable collections do not exist for Abrams' successor, General Frederick C. Weyand, though the Center of Military History's files contain scattered messages and other documents for his period in command.

Besides the Westmoreland and Abrams papers, the Center of Military History's holdings include more than one hundred linear feet of CORDS documents provided by Ambassador Robert Komer. These messages, memorandums, and reports detail the pacification effort under both Ambassador Komer and Ambassador William E. Colby. The Center possesses a large body of material on the Army's race, drug, and discipline problems that was assembled in support of a projected but never completed study of the American soldier in Vietnam. Other Vietnam holdings include an extensive body of province pacification reports, a complete run of the annual combined campaign plans, manuals for MACV's automated data processing systems, message files of U.S. Army, Vietnam, deputy commanders, and numerous unit operational reports.

U.S. Army Military History Institute

The U.S. Army Military History Institute at Carlisle Barracks, Pennsylvania, holds important collections on the history of MACV.

These include a block of records retired directly from Saigon to the Military History Institute, covering the period 1969–1973, as well as numerous MACV Periodical Intelligence Reports and officer end-of-tour debriefings. Besides these paper documents, the Institute possesses a microfilm collection of documents used to support the annual MACV command histories with a printout of a computer-generated finding aid.

The Military History Institute holds the main body of General Abrams' papers, which include messages, news clippings, and miscellaneous documents, and also a set of microfilms of Abrams' special category (SPECAT) messages. These collections contain many items not found in the Abrams Papers at the Center of Military History. The Army War College, also located at Carlisle Barracks, possesses tape recordings of Abrams' Weekly Intelligence Estimate Updates (WIEUs), but these remain too highly classified for use by most researchers.

Other personal papers collections at the Military History Institute bear on the history of MACV. Most useful for this volume are the papers of Arthur S. Collins, William R. Peers, John P. Vann, Gilbert H. Woodward, and Melvin Zais. The Institute also holds a duplicate set of the Westmoreland historical and message files.

Air Force, Navy, and Marine Corps Documents

This volume draws from materials held by the other service historical offices in the Washington, D.C., area. The Office of Air Force History contains copies of documents and oral histories held at the Air University at Maxwell Air Force Base, Alabama. The Naval Historical Center at the Washington Navy Yard possesses the records of the Commander, U.S. Naval Forces, Vietnam. Among the collections of the Marine Corps Historical Center, also at the Washington Navy Yard, the III Marine Amphibious Force message files, the Marine Corps headquarters file on single management, the Victor H. Krulak Papers, and the Keith B. McCutcheon Papers were of special value for this study.

Other Manuscript Collections

The Lyndon Baines Johnson Library holds the national security files of the Johnson administration. More useful for this volume were the Richard M. Nixon Papers, now located in the National Archives at College Park, Maryland.

The Hoover Institution on War, Revolution, and Peace at Stanford University contains the papers of Maj. Gen. John R. Chaisson, USMC, the officer who headed the MACV combat operations Center from late 1966 until well into 1968. Chaisson's letters to his wife and the notebooks he used during his travels and meetings with Westmoreland provide a rare glimpse of the personalities and inner workings of MACV headquarters during a critical period of the war. They are especially useful when read in conjunction with Westmoreland's history and message files.

Oral History Interviews

Most of the principal figures in this study—the successive Pacific Command and MACV commanders and the ambassadors to South Vietnam—were interviewed at different times by various institutions. While uneven in coverage and candor, these materials are an indispensable supplement to the documentary record, especially for the details they provide concerning official and personal relationships among the senior leaders. For Admiral Sharp, the Naval Historical Center holds the transcript of a lengthy reminiscence. This interview was the basis of Sharp's published memoir, *Strategy for Defeat*; but the transcript contains blunt comments on events and personalities that do not appear in the book. A briefer interview with Sharp by the Air Force's Project CORONA HARVEST is available at the Office of Air Force History in Washington, D.C. An interview with Sharp's successor, Admiral McCain, done by the Military History Institute as part of a project to memorialize General Abrams, contains useful information on the working relations between those two strong personalities. The Lyndon Baines Johnson Library has an interview with General Earle G. Wheeler conducted in 1969.

Of the MACV commanders, the Lyndon Baines Johnson Library conducted an interview with General Westmoreland, which is available at the library. An extensive interview with Westmoreland, done for the Senior Officer Debriefing Program, is available at the Military History Institute. The Center of Military History possesses a copy of the Military History Institute interview and also the notes that Army historian Charles B. MacDonald took while assisting Westmoreland with the writing of his memoirs. As with Admiral Sharp's reminiscences, these notes include revealing material that did not appear in the published volume. General Abrams died while still on active duty; hence, he never was interviewed on his tour as COMUSMACV. To date, General Weyand has declined to discuss his experiences. However, Weyand's Senior Officer Debriefing at the end of his tour as commander, II Field Force, which is available at the Center of Military History, includes insightful comments on the nature of the war.

As to the ambassador, the Military History Institute possesses an interview with Ambassador Bunker concentrating on Bunker's relationship with General Abrams. The Institute also has a similar interview with Bunker's deputy, Samuel Berger.

The Military History Institute contains career and topical interviews with Army officers who played significant roles in the latter period of MACV's history. They include Donald H. Cowles, Harold K. Johnson, Theodore Kanamine, Walter T. Kerwin, Frank T. Mildren, Bruce Palmer, William R. Peers, William B. Rosson, Donn J. Starry, James W. Sutherland, and Elias C. Townsend. Copies of transcripts of many of these interviews are available at the Center of Military History. The Center also possesses a copy of an interview of Ambassador Robert Komer by the Rand Corporation on pacification organization and management, as well as tapes and transcripts of interviews the author conducted with Lt. Gen. William E. Potts (U.S. Army, Ret.) bearing on aspects of intelligence and military operations.

Interviews of value to this study are contained in other service historical collections. The Office of Air Force History possesses transcripts of key officers of Seventh Air Force and other air commands involved in Southeast Asia, including Generals George Brown, David Jones, John Lavelle, John McConnell, and John Vogt. The Naval Historical Center's holdings include the aforementioned reminiscences of Admiral Sharp. The Marine Corps Historical Center contains interviews with almost all the important Marine commanders of the period, as well as numerous lower-ranking Marine officers. Most useful for this study were those of John Chaisson, Robert Cushman, William K. Jones, Victor H. Krulak, Keith B. McCutcheon, and John N. McLaughlin.

In the Lyndon Baines Johnson Library, the interview of General Earle G. Wheeler contains his view of the 1968 reinforcement request. For insights into the interaction of State Department officials with MACV and the military in Southeast Asia, at every level from the embassy to CORDS district offices, researchers should consult the growing collections of the Foreign Affairs Oral History Program, Association for Diplomatic Studies and Training, located at the National Foreign Affairs Training Center, Arlington, Virginia. Nearly 900 transcripts of these interviews have been published on CD-ROM.

Published Primary Sources

Heading the list of published primary sources is the so-called "Pentagon Papers," initially classified histories of Defense Department policymaking on Vietnam from 1945 through early 1968, prepared at Secretary McNamara's direction and leaked to the press in 1971 by Daniel Elsberg. The narrative in these volumes is supplemented by extracts and complete reproductions of many high-level official documents. Throughout, this study cites the original Defense Department version of the papers, which was published as: U.S. Congress, House Committee on Armed Services. *United States–Vietnam Relations, 1945–1967: Study Prepared by the Department of Defense.* 12 vols. Washington, D.C.: Government Printing Office, 1971.

Second in importance for the story of MACV are the command's own annual histories, comprehensive, highly detailed multivolume studies prepared by the headquarters' Military History Branch. Although these histories generally conform in their interpretation to the progress-oriented MACV view of the war, they contain occasional candid observations and large quantities of raw historical data. They are indispensable sources for study of the Military Assistance Command's many functions. Most of them include a special annex, which was published and distributed separately, covering activities of the Studies and Observations Group. Complete citations for the histories consulted for this volume are:

Military History Branch, Headquarters, United States Military Assistance Command, Vietnam (MACV), Command History, 1967. Volumes 1–3. Saigon, 1968.
MACV History, 1968. Volumes 1–2. Saigon, 1969.
MACV History, 1969. Volumes 1–3. Saigon, 1970.
MACV History, 1970. Volumes 1–4. Saigon, 1971.
MACV History, 1971. Volumes 1–2. Saigon, 1972.
MACV History, 1972–73. Volumes 1–2. Saigon, 1973.

From 1964 to 1968, Admiral Sharp and General Westmoreland directed the preparation of an overview of their stewardship, the U.S. Pacific Command, *Report on the War in Vietnam (as of 30 June 1968)*. Washington, D.C.: Government Printing Office, 1969. While it contains useful information, this report is very much a defense of its authors' conduct of the war and should be read as such. Covering most of General Abrams' tenure, MACV headquarters prepared a similar summary: " 'One War': MACV Command Overview, 1968–1972," a copy of which is available at the Center of Military History.

The office of the Joint Chiefs of Staff prepared its own official histories of the Joint Chiefs of Staff role in the Southeast Asia conflict. Now declassified and in the process of editing and preparation for publication, these histories illuminate the higher level policy context within which MACV operated and record the Saigon command's exchanges with its overseers in Washington. The critical volumes for the history of MACV are:

Historical Division, Joint Secretariat, U.S. Joint Chiefs of Staff. "The Joint Chiefs of Staff and the War in Vietnam, 1960–1968." Parts 1–3. The History of the Joint Chiefs of Staff. Washington, D.C., 1970.
_____. "The Joint Chiefs of Staff and the War in Vietnam, 1969–1970." The History of the Joint Chiefs of Staff. Washington, D.C., 1976.
_____. "The Joint Chiefs of Staff and the War in Vietnam, 1971–1973." The History of the Joint Chiefs of Staff. Washington, D.C., 1979.

In addition to these histories, the Joint History Office has compiled a series of as yet unpublished studies of how the chairmen of the Joint Chiefs of Staff responded to various Cold War–era crises. One of these, "The Chairman of the Joint Chiefs of Staff and Crises: Response to the North Vietnamese Offensive," was of particular use in preparing the account of MACV's conduct during the 1972 Easter Offensive.

Pacific Command also issued annual official histories of the Vietnam War period. These volumes are less useful than the MACV and Joint Chiefs of Staff histories for study of the Military Assistance Command since they concentrate heavily on Pacific Command's responsibilities outside the Southeast Asian theater of war and largely duplicate the MACV histories in coverage of the conflict itself.

In 1984, General Westmoreland sued the Columbia Broadcasting System (CBS) for libel in response to a CBS documentary, "The Uncounted Enemy," which charged Westmoreland with falsification of intelligence during the 1967 order of battle controversy. The trial, which ended inconclusively, resulted in the declassification and publication of a large mass of documents, affidavits, and testimony concerning not only the immediate issue of enemy numbers but also the entire intelligence prelude to the 1968 Tet offensive. The Center of Military History possesses copies of the memoranda of law and affidavits assembled by both sides. These are:

U.S. District Court, Southern District of New York. *William C. Westmoreland, Plaintiff, v. CBS, Inc., et. al., Defendants. 82 Civ. 7913 (PNL). Plaintiff General William C. Westmoreland's Memorandum of Law in Opposition to Defendant CBS's Motion to Dismiss and for Summary Judgment.*

_____. *William C. Westmoreland, Plaintiff, v. CBS Inc., et. al., Defendants. 82 Civ. 7913 (PNL). Memorandum in Support of Defendant CBS's Motion to Dismiss and for Summary Judgment.*

_____. *William C. Westmoreland, Plaintiff, v. CBS Inc., et. al., Defendants. 82 Civ. 7913 (PNL). Plaintiff's Counter-Statement of Undisputed Material Facts Pursuant to Local Rule 3(g) and Appendix B—Important Documents Cited in Support of Plaintiff's Opposition to Defendant's Motion.*

In addition, the testimony and documents of the trial are available on microfiche as *Vietnam: A Documentary Collection—Westmoreland vs CBS*, Clearwater Publishing Company, Inc., 1985. Copies of this collection exist, among other places, in the Library of Congress and the U.S. Army Military History Institute. The original documents are in the National Archives.

Two sets of studies prepared under Department of the Army auspices contain primary elements. The first series, the Vietnam Studies, consists of monographs by active and retired Army officers who served in Southeast Asia on subjects of which they had special knowledge. While authored in some instances by subordinates instead of the principals, these studies provide information on many aspects of the war. The monographs of most use in this volume were:

Eckhardt, George S. *Command and Control, 1950–1969.* Washington, D.C., 1974.

Ewell, Julian and Hunt, Ira A., Jr. *Sharpening the Combat Edge: The Use of Analysis to Reinforce Military Judgment.* Washington, D.C., 1974.

Kelley, Francis J. *U.S. Army Special Forces, 1961–1971.* Washington, D.C., 1973.

Larsen, Stanley R., and Collins, James L., Jr. *Allied Participation in Vietnam.* Washington, D.C., 1975.

The second set of studies, the Indochina Monographs, helps to fill in the South Vietnamese side of the history of the war. A series of twenty narratives prepared by former South Vietnamese, Cambodian, and Laotian military leaders under the supervision of Lt. Gen. William E. Potts (U.S. Army, Ret.) and the staff of the General Research Corporation, the monographs are based on records available to the authors but also include much personal comment and experience, thereby acquiring to some extent the character of primary documents. The Center of Military History published these studies for limited distribution and retains copies of them. For this volume, the following monographs were the most useful:

Hinh, Nguyen Duy. *Lam Son 719.* Washington, D.C., 1979.

Lung, Hoang Ngoc. *The General Offensives of 1968–1969.* Washington, D.C., 1981.

_____. *Intelligence.* Washington, D.C., 1982.

Tho, Tran Dinh. *The Cambodian Incursion.* Washington, D.C., 1979.

Vongsavanh, Soutchay. *RLG Military Operations and Activities in the Laotian Panhandle.* Washington, D.C., 1981.

Since the end of the Cold War, published source documents on the North Vietnamese and Viet Cong conduct of the Vietnam conflict are gradually becoming available. The Center of Military History is accumulating a growing body of translated official People's Army of Vietnam operational histories. While highly propagandistic in some respects, especially their handling of statistics, these histories contain valuable information on enemy plans, order of battle, and combat operations. Of direct use in preparing this history of MACV were translations of two other accounts from the revolutionary side which treat high level policy and strategy. They are:

Tra, Tran Van. *Vietnam: History of the Bulwark B2 Theater.* Vol. 5. *Concluding the 30-Years War.* Ho Chi Minh City: Van Nghe Publishing House, 1982. Trans. by Foreign Broadcast Information Service. Joint Publications Research Service, Southeast Asia Report no. 1247, 1983.

War Experiences Recapitulation Committee of the High-Level Military Institute. *Vietnam: The Anti-U.S. Resistance War for National Salvation, 1954–1975: Military Events.* Hanoi: People's Army Publishing House,

1980. Trans. by Joint Publications Research Service. Doc no. 80968, 1982.

Published Official Histories

U.S. Army

The Center of Military History's U.S. Army in Vietnam series currently consists of eight published major histories and a pictorial volume, with additional volumes in progress. The following have been published:

Bergen, John D. *Military Communications: A Test for Technology.* Washington, D.C.: U.S. Army Center of Military History, 1986.

Carland, John M. *Combat Operations: Stemming the Tide, May 1965 to October 1966.* Washington, D.C.: U.S. Army Center of Military History, 2000.

Clarke, Jeffrey J. *Advice and Support: The Final Years, 1965–1973.* Washington, D.C.: U.S. Army Center of Military History, 1988.

Cosmas, Graham A. *MACV: The Joint Command in the Years of Escalation, 1962–1967.* Washington, D.C.: U.S. Army Center of Military History, 2006.

Hammond, William M. *Public Affairs: The Military and the Media, 1962–1968.* Washington, D.C.: U.S. Army Center of Military History, 1988.

_____. *Public Affairs: The Military and the Media, 1968–1973.* Washington, D.C.: U.S. Army Center of Military History, 1996.

MacGarrigle, George L. *Combat Operations: Taking the Offensive, October 1966 to October 1967.* Washington, D.C.: U.S. Army Center of Military History, 1998.

Meyerson, Joel D. *Images of a Lengthy War.* Washington, D.C.: U.S. Army Center of Military History, 1986.

Spector, Ronald H. *Advice and Support: The Early Years, 1941–1960.* Washington, D.C.: U.S. Army Center of Military History, 1983.

U.S. Air Force

The Office of Air Force History is publishing a series on The United States Air Force in Southeast Asia, one volume of which was drawn upon:

Schlight, John. *The War in South Vietnam: The Years of the Offensive, 1965–1968.* Washington, D.C.: Office of Air Force History, 1988.

In addition, the author had access to a manuscript study, Wayne Thompson's "From Rolling Thunder to Linebacker: The Air War over

North Vietnam, 1966–1973." This study has now been published as *To Hanoi and Back: The U.S. Air Force and North Vietnam, 1966–1973.* Washington, D.C.: Smithsonian Institution Press, 2000.

U.S. Navy

Two volumes of the Naval Historical Center's series, The United States Navy and the Vietnam Conflict, have been published. The volume bearing on Military Assistance Command, Vietnam is:

Marolda, Edward J. and Fitzgerald, Oscar P. *From Military Assistance to Combat, 1959–1965.* Washington, D.C.: Naval Historical Center, 1986.

The Naval Historical Center also has published an illustrated overview of the Navy's role in Southeast Asia:

Marolda, Edward J. *By Sea, Air, and Land: An Illustrated History of the U.S. Navy and the War in Southeast Asia.* Washington, D.C.: Naval Historical Center, 1994.

U.S. Marine Corps

The Marine Corps History and Museums Division has completed publication of its chronological series on U.S. Marines in Vietnam. The following volumes in this series were of special value:

Cosmas, Graham A. and Murray, Terrence P. *Vietnamization and Redeployment, 1970–1971.* Washington, D.C.: History and Museums Division, Headquarters, U.S. Marine Corps, 1986.
Dunham, George R. and Quinlan, David A. *The Bitter End, 1973–1975.* Washington, D.C.: History and Museums Division, Headquarters, U.S. Marine Corps, 1990.
Melson, Charles D. and Arnold, Curtis G. *The War that Would Not End, 1971–1973.* Washington, D.C.: History and Museums Division, Headquarters, U.S. Marine Corps, 1991.
Shulimson, Jack, Blasiol, Leonard A., Smith, Charles, R., and Dawson, David A. *The Defining Year, 1968.* Washington, D.C.: History and Museums Division, Headquarters, U.S. Marine Corps, 1997.
Smith, Charles R. *High Mobility and Standdown, 1969.* Washington, D.C.: History and Museums Division, Headquarters, U.S. Marine Corps, 1988.

Joint History Office

Cole, Ronald H., Poole, Walter S., Schnabel, James F., Watson, Robert J., and Webb, Willard J. *The History of the Unified Command Plan,*

1946–1993. Washington, D.C.: Joint History Office, Office of the Chairman of the Joint Chiefs of Staff, 1995.

Poole,Walter S., "LAM SON 719: The 'Moment of Truth.' " Draft Paper, Washington, D.C.: Joint History Office, Joint Chiefs of Staff, 2001.

Secondary Works

Books and Articles

Ambrose, Stephen E., ed. *The Haldeman Diaries: Inside the Nixon White House*. New York: G. P. Putnam's Sons, 1994.

_____. *Nixon: The Triumph of a Politician, 1962–1972*. New York: Simon and Schuster, 1989.

Andrade, Dale. *Trial by Fire: The 1972 Easter Offensive, America's Last Vietnam Battle*. New York: Hippocrene Books, 1995.

BDM Corp. *A Study of Strategic Lessons Learned in Vietnam*. vol. 7. *The Soldier*. McLean, Va.: BDM Corp., 1980.

Berman, Larry. *No Peace, No Honor: Nixon, Kissinger, and Betrayal in Vietnam*. New York: Free Press, 2001.

Blaufarb, Douglas S. *The Counterinsurgency Era: U.S. Doctrine and Performance, 1950 to the Present*. New York: Free Press, 1977.

Braestrup, Peter. *Big Story: How the American Press and Television Reported and Interpreted the Crisis of Tet 1968 in Vietnam and Washington*. 2 vols. Boulder, Colo.: Westview Press and Freedom House, 1977.

Clodfelter, Mark. *The Limits of Air Power: The American Bombing of North Vietnam*. New York: Free Press, 1989.

Davidson, Phillip B. *Secrets of the Vietnam War*. Novato, Calif.: Presidio Press, 1990.

_____. *Vietnam at War: The History, 1946–1975*. New York: Oxford University Press, 1988.

DeForest, Orrin and Chanoff, David. *Slow Burn: The Rise and Bitter Fall of American Intelligence in Vietnam*. New York: Simon and Schuster, 1990.

Dillard, Walter S. *Sixty Days to Peace: Implementing the Paris Peace Accords, Vietnam 1973*. Washington, D.C.: National Defense University Press, 1982.

Duiker, William J. *The Communist Road to Power in Vietnam*. Boulder, Colo.: Westview Press, 1981.

Ford, Harold P. *CIA and the Vietnam Policymakers: Three Episodes, 1962–1968*. Washington, D.C.: Center for the Study of Intelligence, Central Intelligence Agency, 1998.

Gatchell, Theodore L., USMC. "Can a Battle Be Lost in the Mind of the Commander?" *Naval War College Review* 23 (January–February 1985): 96.

Gelb, Leslie H. and Betts, Richard K. *The Irony of Vietnam: The System Worked*. Washington, D.C.: Brookings Institution, 1979.

439

Gray, Colin S. "Why Strategy Is Difficult," *Joint Force Quarterly*, 34 (Spring 2003): 80–87.

Hannah, Norman B. *The Key to Failure: Laos and the Vietnam War.* New York: Madison Books, 1987.

Herring, George C. *America's Longest War: The United States and Vietnam, 1950–1975.* New York: Wiley, 1979.

_____. " 'Peoples Quite Apart': Americans, South Vietnamese, and the War in Vietnam." *Diplomatic History* 14 (Winter 1990): 1–23.

Hosmer, Stephen T., Kellen, Konrad, and Jenkins, Brian M. *The Fall of South Vietnam: Statements by Vietnamese Military and Civilian Leaders.* New York: Crane, Russak & Co., 1980.

Hunt, Richard A. *Pacification: The American Struggle for Vietnam's Hearts and Minds.* Boulder, Colo.: Westview Press, 1995.

Johnson, Lyndon B. *The Vantage Point: Perspectives of the Presidency, 1963–1969.* New York: Holt, Rinehart, and Winston, 1971.

Jones, Bruce E. *War Without Windows: A True Account by a Young Army Officer Trapped in an Intelligence Cover-Up in Vietnam.* New York: Vanguard Press, 1987.

Kinnard, Douglas. *The War Managers.* Hanover, N.H.: The University Press of New England, 1977.

Kissinger, Henry. *The White House Years.* Boston: Little, Brown and Co., 1979.

Le Gro, William E. *Vietnam from Cease-Fire to Capitulation.* Washington, D.C.: U.S. Army Center of Military History, 1981.

Mann, Edward C. III, USAF. *Thunder and Lightning: Desert Storm and the Airpower Debates.* Maxwell Air Force Base, Ala.: Air University Press, 1995.

McMaster, H. R. *Dereliction of Duty: Lyndon Johnson, Robert McNamara, the Joint Chiefs of Staff, and the Lies that Led to Vietnam.* New York: HarperCollins, 1997.

McNamara, Francis T. with Hill, Adrian. *Escape with Honor: My Last Hours in Vietnam.* Washington, D.C.: Brassey's, 1997.

Military History Institute of Vietnam. *Victory in Vietnam: The Official History of the People's Army of Vietnam, 1954–1975.* Trans. by Merle L. Pribbenow (Lawrence, Kans.: University Press of Kansas, 2002).

Momyer, William W. *Airpower in Three Wars.* Washington, D.C.: Department of the Air Force, 1978.

Nalty, Bernard C. *Air Power and the Fight for Khe Sanh.* Washington, D.C.: Office of Air Force History, United States Air Force, 1973.

Oberdorfer, Don. *Tet!* Da Capo Edition. New York: Da Capo Press, Inc., 1984.

Palmer, Bruce. *The 25-Year War: America's Military Role in Vietnam.* Lexington: University Press of Kentucky, 1984.

Peers, William R., *The My Lai Inquiry.* New York: W. W. Norton, 1979.

Pike, Douglas. *PAVN: People's Army of Vietnam.* Novato, Calif.: Presidio Press, 1986.

Porter, Gareth, ed. *Vietnam: The Definitive Documentation of Human Decisions.* 2 vols. Stanfordville, N.Y.: Earl M. Coleman Enterprises, 1979.

Schandler, Herbert Y. *The Unmaking of a President: Lyndon Johnson and Vietnam.* Princeton: Princeton University Press, 1977.

Schlight, John, ed. *Second Indochina War Symposium: Papers and Commentary.* Washington, D.C.: U.S. Army Center of Military History, 1986.

Sharp, Ulysses S. G. *Strategy for Defeat: Vietnam in Retrospect.* San Rafael, Calif.: Presidio Press, 1978.

Sheehan, Neil. *A Bright Shining Lie: John Paul Vann and America in Vietnam.* New York: Random House, 1988.

Shore, Moyers S. II, USMC. *The Battle for Khe Sanh.* Washington, D.C.: Historical Branch, G–3 Division, Headquarters, U.S. Marine Corps, 1969.

Sorley, Lewis. *A Better War: The Unexamined Victories and the Final Tragedy of America's Last Years in Vietnam.* New York: Harcourt Brace and Co., 1999.

_____. *Thunderbolt: General Creighton Abrams and the Army of His Times.* New York: Simon and Schuster, 1992.

Stanton, Shelby L. *Vietnam Order of Battle.* New York: Galahad Books, 1986.

Stern, Lewis. "Research Note: North Vietnam's War Dead." *Indochina Chronology,* 18, no. 1 (October 1998–January 1999).

Stevenson, Charles A. *The End of Nowhere: American Policy Toward Laos since 1954.* Boston: Beacon Press, 1972.

Summers, Harry G., Jr. *On Strategy: A Critical Analysis of the Vietnam War.* Novato, Calif.: Presidio Press, 1982.

Swain, Richard M. *"Lucky War": Third Army in Desert Storm.* Fort Leavenworth, Kans.: U.S. Army Command and General Staff College Press, 1994.

Thai, Hoang Van. "A Few Strategic Issues in the Spring 1968 Tet Offensive and Uprising." *Military History Magazine [Tap Chi Lich Su Quan Su],* Issue 2 (26), 1988, published by the Ministry of Defense's Military Institute of Vietnam. Trans. Merle Pribbenow.

Thayer, Thomas C. "How to Analyze a War Without Fronts: Vietnam 1965–1972." *Journal of Defense Research,* Series B, Tactical Warfare Analysis of Vietnam Data, 7B, no. 3, Fall 1975.

Thies, Wallace J. "How We (Almost) Won in Vietnam: Ellsworth Bunker's Reports to the President." *Parameters,* XXI, no. 2 (Summer 1992).

Tilford, Earl H., Jr. *Setup: What the Air Force Did in Vietnam and Why.* Maxwell Air Force Base, Ala.: Air University Press, 1991.

Turley, William S. *The Second Indochina War: A Short Political and Military History, 1954–1975.* New York: New American Library, 1987.

Veith, George J. and Pribbenow, Merle L. II. " 'Fighting Is an Art': The Army of the Republic of Vietnam's Defense of Xuan Loc, 9–21 April 1975." *The Journal of Military History* 68 (January 2004): 163–213.

Westmoreland, William C. *A Soldier Reports*. Garden City, N.Y.: Doubleday and Co., 1976.

Wirtz, James J. *The Tet Offensive: Intelligence Failure in War*. Ithaca, N.Y.: Cornell University Press, 1991.

Zaffiri, Samuel. *Westmoreland: A Biography of General William C. Westmoreland*. New York: William Morrow and Co., 1994.

Zhang, Xiaoming. "The Vietnam War: A Chinese Perspective, 1964–1969," *Journal of Military History* 60 (October 1996): 731–62.

Unpublished Secondary Works

Carland, John M. "The Tet Offensive of 1968: Desperate Gamble or Calculated Risk?" Unpublished paper, U.S. Army Center of Military History, 2001.

Ford, Ronnie E. "Tet 1968: Understanding the Surprise." Master's thesis, Defense Intelligence College, 1993.

Hammond, William M. "Preparations Begin." Unpublished paper, U.S. Army Center of Military History, 2002.

Latimer, Thomas K. "Hanoi's Leaders and their South Vietnam Policies, 1954–1968." Ph.D. diss., Georgetown University, 1972.

Rosson, Gen William B. "Four Periods of American Involvement in Vietnam: Development and Implementation of Policy, Strategy and Programs, Described and Analyzed on the Basis of Service Experience at Progressively Senior Levels." Ph.D. thesis, New College, Oxford, 1979.

Glossary

AAR	After Action Report
ARVN	Army of the Republic of Vietnam (South Vietnam)
CBS	Columbia Broadcasting System
CIA	Central Intelligence Agency
CICV	Combined Intelligence Center, Vietnam
CIDG	Civilian Irregular Defense Group
CIIB	Criminal Investigation and Intelligence Bureau
CINCPAC	Commander in Chief, Pacific
CJCS	Chairman, Joint Chiefs of Staff
CMH	Center of Military History
COC	Combat Operations Center
COMUSMACV	Commander, U.S. Military Assistance Command, Vietnam
CORDS	Civil Operations and Revolutionary Development Support
COSVN	*Central Office for South Vietnam*
CRIMP	Consolidated RVNAF Improvement and Modernization Plan
CTZ	Corps Tactical Zone
DA	Department of the Army
DAO	Defense Attaché Office
DIA	Defense Intelligence Agency
DMZ	Demilitarized Zone
DoD	Department of Defense
FANK	*Forces Armées Nationales Khmères*
FFV	Field Force, Vietnam
FMFPAC	Fleet Marine Force, Pacific
FWMAF	Free World Military Assistance Force
GVN	Government of Vietnam
HQMC	Headquarters, Marine Corps
JCS	Joint Chiefs of Staff (U.S.)

JGS	Joint General Staff (South Vietnam)
JUSPAO	Joint U.S. Public Affairs Office
LBJL	Lyndon Baines Johnson Library
LOI	Letter of Instruction
LRPTG	Long Range Planning Task Group
MACV	Military Assistance Command, Vietnam
MAF	Marine Amphibious Force
MAP	Military Assistance Program
MAW	Marine Aircraft Wing
MCHC	Marine Corps Historical Center
MFR	Memorandum for the Record
MHI	Military History Institute
MiG	Mikoyan & Gurevich (Russian aircraft designers)
MR	Military Region
NARA	National Archives and Records Administration
NATO	North Atlantic Treaty Organization
NAVFORV	(U.S.) Naval Forces, Vietnam
NSC	National Security Council
NSDM	National Security Decision Memorandum
NSSM	National Security Study Memorandum
NVA	North Vietnamese Army
NVN	North Vietnam
OPLAN	Operations Plan
P&D	Pacification and Development
PAVN	*People's Army of Vietnam* (North Vietnam)
PFIAB	President's Foreign Intelligence Advisory Board
PLAF	*People's Liberation Armed Forces* (Viet Cong)
PROVN	Program for the Pacification and Long-Term Development of South Vietnam
PSDF	People's Self-Defense Force
RVN	Republic of Vietnam
RVNAF	Republic of Vietnam Armed Forces (South Vietnam)
SACSA	Special Assistant for Counterinsurgency and Security Activities, JCS
SAM	Surface-to-Air Missile
SEER	System for Evaluating the Effectiveness of RVNAF
SNIE	Special National Intelligence Estimate
SOG	Studies and Observations Group

SVN	South Vietnam
TOW	Tube launched, optically tracked, wire guided
USARPAC	U.S. Army, Pacific
USARV	U.S. Army, Vietnam
USIA	U.S. Information Agency
USSAG/7AF	U.S. Support Activities Group/Seventh Air Force
VAC	Vietnam Assistance Command
VAG	Vietnam Assistance Group
VC	Viet Cong
WIEU	Weekly Intelligence Estimate Update

Index